Practical PHP 7, MySQL 8, and MariaDB Website Databases

A Simplified Approach to Developing Database-Driven Websites

Second Edition

Adrian W. West

Steve Prettyman

Apress®

Practical PHP 7, MySQL 8, and MariaDB Website Databases: A Simplified Approach to Developing Database-Driven Websites

Adrian W. West
Colyton, Devon, United Kingdom

Steve Prettyman
Key West, Florida, USA

ISBN-13 (pbk): 978-1-4842-3842-4
https://doi.org/10.1007/978-1-4842-3843-1

ISBN-13 (electronic): 978-1-4842-3843-1

Library of Congress Control Number: 2018957652

Managing Director, Apress Media LLC: Welmoed Spahr
Acquisitions Editor: Steve Anglin
Development Editor: Matthew Moodie
Coordinating Editor: Mark Powers

Cover designed by eStudioCalamar

Cover image designed by Freepik (www.freepik.com)

Distributed to the book trade worldwide by Springer Science+Business Media New York, 233 Spring Street, 6th Floor, New York, NY 10013. Phone 1-800-SPRINGER, fax (201) 348-4505, e-mail orders-ny@springer-sbm.com, or visit www.springeronline.com. Apress Media, LLC is a California LLC and the sole member (owner) is Springer Science + Business Media Finance Inc (SSBM Finance Inc). SSBM Finance Inc is a **Delaware** corporation.

For information on translations, please e-mail editorial@apress.com; for reprint, paperback, or audio rights, please email bookpermissions@springernature.com.

Apress titles may be purchased in bulk for academic, corporate, or promotional use. eBook versions and licenses are also available for most titles. For more information, reference our Print and eBook Bulk Sales web page at www.apress.com/bulk-sales.

Any source code or other supplementary material referenced by the author in this book is available to readers on GitHub via the book's product page, located at www.apress.com/9781484238424. For more detailed information, please visit www.apress.com/source-code.

Printed on acid-free paper

Contents

About the Authors

Adrian W. West resigned as a chartered design engineer to become the UK director of a correspondence school. He has been teaching in one form or another since 1982. He introduced computers into his workplace in 1987 and taught the staff how to use them. For four years, he taught undergraduates computer skills at a college in Cheshire in the United Kingdom.

Adrian lives in Colyton, a town in Devon, England, and for the last 18 years, he has designed and produced websites for UK businesses and charities.

Adrian is the author of three books published by Apress: *Practical HTML5 Projects*, a book of tips and tricks (now rather out of date); *Practical PHP and MySQL Website Databases* (the first edition of this book); and *Practical Web Design for Absolute Beginners* (published in 2016).

Steve Prettyman earned his Bachelor of Arts degree in secondary education from Oglethorpe University in 1979. He quickly began his teaching career as a high school mathematics instructor while continuing his education by earning a master's degree in business information systems from Georgia State University (1985). Since then, Steve has spent more than 30 years in the IT industry. The last almost 20 of those he has been an instructor and professor at Chattahoochee Technical College, Kennesaw State University, and Southern Polytechnic State University. He is currently the Computer Science Department chairperson for Florida Keys Community College in Key West, Florida. His primary teaching responsibilities include programming, web design, and web application development.

Acknowledgments

I thank my wife, Janice, for her love, support, and encouragement, and for taking over my share of the chores so that I could concentrate on this edition.

My thanks go to the team at Apress and to all the people in Internet forums who helped me and replied to my queries.

My special thanks go to my co-author, Steve Prettyman, who converted the first edition code and instructions to the latest versions of PHP 7 and MySQL/MariaDB for this second edition.

—Adrian W. West

I thank my partner and wife for her love and support for almost 25 years. Her reminders that I needed to get my head out of the book and take a break to enjoy life were vital in this process. My children also stared at me when I ignored them for too long to let me know that I should stop writing and coding to take them outside to swim in the pool. Can we say that Pixee and Buster, our four-legged children, are a little spoiled?

I especially want to thank Adrian W. West and Apress for allowing me to update his successful first edition to provide a modern-day approach to his logical pattern to teaching interactive database programming using PHP.

—Steve Prettyman

Introduction

What's New in This Edition?

The code and instructions in the first edition of this book (written in 2012) were made obsolete by new and very different versions of XAMPP, EasyPHP, phpMyAdmin, PHP, and MySQL/MariaDB. This second edition contains new code and instructions to match the latest versions of the software.

With the massive increase in cybercrime and other cyber threats, this new edition has been fortified with a much stronger emphasis on security. This book takes the approach of sanitizing any data that has been accepted from any outside source and, additionally, sanitizing any data before it is displayed on a web page. Most of the examples use prepared statements that ensure that any externally accepted data cannot be executed and therefore cannot cause security vulnerabilities.

We have chosen Bootstrap to provide responsive web design (RWD) for each of the book's example websites. While Bootstrap provides the CSS and JavaScript to format the examples in this book for any size device, you can easily reformat these examples with your own CSS code if you desire.

This new edition also takes a brief look at Oracle's MySQL 8. A comparison is provided of the tools available in each version. Step-by-step procedures provide you with the ability to upgrade to MySQL 8.

The Teaching Method

This book uses a different way of teaching website database design compared with the majority of manuals. The usual layout starts with several lessons on PHP followed by snippets of code and may eventually conclude with a project or two. This book abandons that approach. The primary focus is on fully worked, practical MySQL/MariaDB database projects built into real-world web pages.

Instead of presenting PHP, SQL, and MySQL/MariaDB as completely separate topics, they are explained in the context of each project. However, you will find a useful quick reference of PHP syntax in Appendix B.

In this book, practical databases and interactive web pages are presented as early as possible; in fact, you will create a database and a table in the first chapter. In the second chapter, you will embed a database into an interactive web page and test it. Each subsequent chapter will introduce you to increasingly sophisticated and useful database-driven website pages.

We assume that you have little or no knowledge of PHP and databases. This book will demonstrate:

- How to create a free environment for testing database-driven web pages.

- How to embed PHP and interactive databases into real-world web pages. This is the primary theme throughout the book.

- How PHP, HTML, and MySQL/MariaDB work together for creating and maintaining a database and its data.

- How to create a user-friendly interface so that an administrator with minimum computer skills can monitor the database.

Because databases need to be viewed and tested on a server, the first part of Chapter 1 has instructions for using a free server that can be downloaded and installed on your computer. This ensures you will have a safe development platform for learning and testing as you explore the book's practical projects.

Starting with a separate study of PHP theory and syntax can deter learners and prolong the time until they get their hands on a practical application. Learners are enthused when they achieve something. This book jumps into the database driving seat right from the beginning. Essential PHP and MySQL/MariaDB techniques are presented in context within each tutorial where they are most relevant.

Who Is This Book For?

The book assumes you are thoroughly familiar with HTML5 and CSS3. However, we assume you have no knowledge of MySQL/MariaDB, PHP, and phpMyAdmin. As the chapters unfold, you will progress from intermediate level to advanced level.

You do not need to acquire an extensive knowledge of PHP to create interactive databases. We introduce all the PHP you will need in the appropriate place within each project. Each piece of PHP code is explained fully in plain English. The step-by-step, fully worked examples will show you what MySQL/MariaDB and PHP can do and how to do it. This book is for web designers who want to begin developing database-driven websites.

With this in mind, this book uses a highly motivational step-by-step approach. We recognize fully that a sense of achievement encourages readers to look forward eagerly to the next step. The book will teach enough PHP and MySQL/MariaDB to complete all the projects in the book. Web developers who have not kept up-to-date with MySQL/MariaDB and PHP will also benefit from this approach. College and university programming instructors will find that this book provides an excellent text, and the projects can form a basis for students to adapt for their course work.

The "Quick and Easy to Learn" Myth

Books frequently state that PHP and MySQL/MariaDB databases are easily and quickly learned, but this discourages beginners, because when they are confronted with the inevitable difficulties (and error messages), they begin to think that they will never grasp even the basic principles.

Beginners should not be discouraged if they remember the following fact: authors claiming that PHP and MySQL/MariaDB are easily and quickly learned have probably been using PHP and MySQL for more than a decade, and they have forgotten the difficulties they encountered when they first began.

If you accept that some time and effort are required to learn PHP and MySQL/MariaDB, then as you work through the book, it will become increasingly apparent that you are learning something very worthwhile. So, have patience and persevere, and you will then begin to enjoy mastering this valuable discipline.

The Origin of This Book

Most of the PHP/MySQL/MariaDB books tend to demonstrate the author's deep and extensive knowledge of PHP and MySQL/MariaDB instead of teaching how to embed MySQL/MariaDB databases into web pages. In contrast, this book uses fully worked examples to demonstrate how to integrate databases into a website.

The boatload of PHP/MySQL/MariaDB database books that this book's authors own (or borrowed) were unnecessarily complicated. The authors of these books had become used to using neat tricks and shortcuts that were second nature, but these cluttered the code and made it difficult for beginners to discern the essential structure.

This book avoids this mistake; a few useful tricks are introduced gradually and are fully explained in plain English. This book is based on a quote from the composer Brahms.

It is easy to compose but wonderfully hard to let the superfluous notes fall under the table.

Almost all the PHP/MySQL/MariaDB books were written backward; they grind away for chapter after chapter with PHP functions and statements (yawn), and then they add the MySQL/MariaDB bit. *Practical PHP and MySQL Website Databases* explains the necessary PHP and MySQL/MariaDB topics in context within each database tutorial.

MySQL/MariaDB books are nearly always written assuming that the web designer will administer the databases. However, small e-commerce websites, clubs, and societies cannot afford to do this and would prefer that their membership secretary be able to administer the database using a user-friendly interface. The majority of the databases created in this book can be administered by both an unskilled membership secretary and the web designer.

Eventually, Adrian W. Wood concluded that he must write his own manual based on what he could learn by concatenating snippets of information from multiple resources. He also based the manual on his own trial-and-error approach as a raw beginner. This automatically ensured that the manual's content was presented in simple, logical, and progressive steps without suddenly introducing unexplained items.

The homegrown manual was so useful that he decided that it should be shared with other website designers; the first edition of this book was the result of that decision.

Computer software and database techniques are constantly improving and updating. Because of this, we have researched the latest versions of the scripts, tools, and the available software. This ensures that, in this second edition, the content and illustrations will remain relevant for as long as possible.

Following the tutorials in this book requires an absolute minimum of software. Some manuals ask readers to download and learn a new piece of software before they can proceed to each new chapter. In fact, Adrian came across one book that required readers to download MySQL, Apache, PHP, phpMyAdmin, Prototype 1.5, Scriptaculous, Zend Framework, Smarty Template Engine, FCK editor, jQuery, and Ajax. In this book, besides a code editor, the software required is limited, as described next.

What Equipment Is Required

The book assumes that, as a web designer, you will already have an HTML editor such as Blue Griffon (free) or Notepad++ (free).

You will need:

- A notebook (real or electronic) for recording the passwords and file names for your databases and table entries. *Don't rely on memory. Write everything down.*

You will need to download:

- The sample code from the book's page, available at www.apress.com

- XAMPP or EasyPHP, which are free, all-in-one packages for testing your work

- The latest browsers (all free): Microsoft Edge, Mozilla Firefox, Safari, Chrome, and Opera

The Conventions Used in This Book

Care has been taken to relate every listing to its screenshot. For instance, Figure 3-6 will be described by Listing 3-6. If two listings are needed, such as the HTML code and the PHP code, both will relate to the screenshot by using *Listing 3-6a* and *Listing 3-6b*. If Figure 4-6 does not need a listing, the next screenshot and listing will use Figure 4-7 and Listing 4-7.

Special tips, notes, and warnings are shown in the following format:

■ **Note**   Security is important when dealing with databases, especially if they contain personal data. The technique for making your work is secure is woven into each step of the instructions.

All code listings use HTML5 and PHP 7; some meta description and meta keywords have been omitted from each <head></head> section to save space.

Code listings are shown as follows:

```
<div id='container'>
<?php include('header.php'); ?><!--include the new header file-->
```

Code lines are sometimes numbered to help with the explanations as follows:

```
if (empty($errors)) { // If no problems occurred, register the user in the database    #1
```

The line numbers are for explanation only and do not need to be included in your own code.

Interactive vs. Dynamic

Most manuals use the term *dynamic* web pages when referring to interactive pages. The words *dynamic* and *interactive* both describe pages that provide a live link between a user and a database. For instance, a user can register for membership and view account details. A membership secretary can view a table of members, but the table is hidden from ordinary members. Because the word *dynamic* can have so many connotations and meanings, we have chosen to use the more precise term *interactive* in this book.

Source Code

You can access the example code used in this book by navigating to www.apress.com/9781484238424 and clicking the Download Source Code button.

CHAPTER 1

■ ■ ■

Create and Test a Database and Table

This chapter introduces the concept of a database and a practical way of testing it. Using the examples, you will create a MariaDB or MySQL database and a table. As you work through the examples, you will become familiar with the database administration interface.

After completing this chapter, the student will be able to

- Define and design a database and table
- Install and use a WAMP package
- Use phpMyAdmin to create a database and table
- Secure phpMyAdmin and databases with a user ID and password
- Delete a database and/or table

Databases can be used to store products, details of customers, records of members of a society or a club, and much more. They can store names, passwords, addresses, e-mail addresses, registration dates, blog entries, and telephone numbers. Databases can be regarded as folders containing tables of data. The table of data has *columns* and *rows*; the rows in database tables are called *records*. Table 1-1 shows a typical database table.

Table 1-1. *A Typical Database*

user_id	first_name	last_name	email	password	phone
1	Kevin	Kettle	kev@kettle.com	K3ttl3fur	305 111 1111
2	Susan	Saucepan	sue@kitchen.org.uk	N@sus5	01111 222 1111
3	Oliver	Oven	oliver@cokker.co.uk	H0tst0v3	03333 111 4444

Defining Developer, Administrator, and User

In this book, the term *developer* (aka *webmaster*) means the person who designs and produces the database; they will integrate the database into a website. Sometimes the term *webmaster* or *web designer* may be used. When it is used, it usually means the same thing as *developer*. The words *administrator* and *membership secretary* have the same meaning in some of the book's tutorials, which are based on building a database for a club. The word *administrator* means the person responsible for monitoring and maintaining the content of the database tables. Clearly, one person can be both a developer and an administrator. However, most developers will maintain the structure of a database but will not want the hassle of amending and deleting records; that should be the role of an administrator (such as a club or society's membership secretary).

The *user* is any member of the general public viewing and possibly interacting with a website database. For security reasons, users have extremely limited access to the database; however, they will be allowed to register for membership, log in to a special section, or change their password.

■ **Caution** The organization commissioning a database must conform to the rules and laws of the country in which the database is developed and resides. In the United Kingdom, the Data Protection Act for the territory in which the database was developed must be followed. This is especially important if that data is going to be used for profit. This may require obtaining a license. In addition, the developer and administrator must normally sign a document confirming that they will never disclose the details of persons recorded in the database. The UK Information Commissioner's Office (ICO) requires an annual license fee based on the revenues of the organization that owns the database. There is no equivalent law in the United States, but privacy laws can differ between states. It is essential that you understand and obey the data-protection laws for your client's territory.

Databases that are accessible to multiple countries will need to meet the requirements for each country. Sometimes this requires the creation of different versions of the database and/or website, when otherwise it would not be required. Many laws and regulations lag behind the overall need to provide the most secure database environment possible. The developer should always err on the side of the "most secure" when designing and using databases. Databases used for educational purposes only (such as the databases shown in this book) do not have to meet the requirements and regulations (such as licensing).

Defining Interactive Websites

Interactive websites are often called *dynamic* websites; however, this book uses the word *interactive* because *dynamic* can signify so many things. For instance, it can mean moving, powerful, eye-catching, flashy, exciting. To a beginner, none of those meanings defines a web page that interacts with a user.

Dynamic is often used to mean exciting, but there is little excitement to be seen in an interactive registration form. *Dynamic* is also a musical term meaning changes or variations in loudness or speed. If *dynamic* can refer to change, why were dynamic templates designed to provide consistency from one web page to another? The term *interactive* has one clear meaning and will be used from now on in this book.

MariaDB and MySQL (with PHP) allow users and administrators to interact with a database using website pages. For instance, users can register as members of an organization via a registration page on a website. Users will be able to supply their personal data for the membership tables. The database management system then enters the users' input into the administrator's tables automatically; this lightens the workload of the administrator. The website's registration page can be programmed to filter users' data input and verify it. From an interactive page, users may even be allowed to update their own records in a database.

Interactivity means that the administrator's workload is greatly reduced, but not completely. For instance, if the database is for a bookshop, the administrator will still have to enter any new titles and prices. On the other hand, an interactive database can be programmed to alert the administrator when the stock of a certain book needs replenishing.

In Chapter 2, you will learn to develop a simple interactive website.

Using MariaDB or MySQL Only for Interactive Database Tables

A noninteractive data table means that only the administrator can enter or amend the table's information. A noninteractive data table would be more easily created and administered using a spreadsheet, such as Microsoft Excel. However, website users cannot interact with such a data table. Employing a MariaDB or MySQL database management system (DBMS) to create a noninteractive (static) version of the data table would be like using a sledgehammer to crack a nut. Website users would have no input and cannot search or update data.

Using MariaDB or MySQL DBMS for a noninteractive version would not reduce the workload of an administrator; they would have to enter all the members' data and verify that the data is genuine.

■ **Note** A few interactive web pages do not need a database to function. For instance, a Contact Us form can be regarded as interactive because it takes a user's input and transmits it to the website's owner via a PHP form handler via an e-mail; this can be achieved easily without a database. In this book, the term *interactive* always means the user can interact with a database.

Methods for Developing and Maintaining Databases

The four methods for managing databases are as follows (with the easiest method first and hardest last):

- phpMyAdmin (or other administrative tool)
- PHP
- SQL scripts
- Command line

In this book, we will be mainly using the first two methods (phpMyAdmin and PHP). We will use SQL scripts and the command line to briefly demonstrate how to create, update, and distribute your database. For interactive databases, you will need some PHP files. You do not need an extensive knowledge of PHP before you can create interactive databases. We will introduce the PHP syntax you require in the appropriate place in each project—that is, in context. The step-by-step, fully worked examples will show you what MariaDB and MySQL can do and how to do it.

Because of their popularity, graphical user interfaces (GUIs) have been developed to facilitate the task of developing and maintaining databases. These administration tools are part of development packages that include web servers (Apache), databases (MariaDB or MySQL), and programming languages (PHP). In this book, we will introduce two of the most popular packages: XAMPP and EasyPHP.

A Brief Look Inside Web Server Communication

Databases need a server, a DBMS, and a PHP processor, as shown in Figure 1-1. These can be downloaded as an all-in-one, already configured package. The testing and development of the projects in this book are based on the free XAMPP and EasyPHP packages.

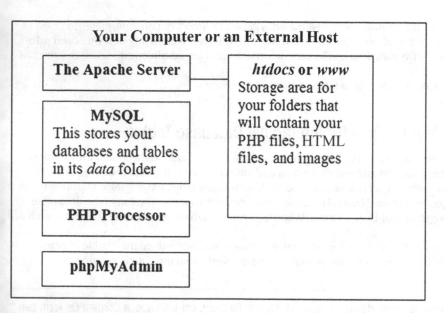

Figure 1-1. Web server communication

Figure 1-1 shows the main components built into the XAMPP and EasyPHP development platforms. They are as follows:

- Apache is the web page server used by the great majority of hosts and for web development on local hosts (user computers). Web servers determine whether web pages contain PHP code by looking at the file ending (*.php*). If PHP code exists, the code is passed to the PHP interpreter for execution. If the PHP interpreter determines database-related code or SQL exists within the PHP program, this information is passed to the MySQL or MariaDB database management system. The database management system executes the SQL statements and returns the results to the PHP interpreter. The PHP interpreter completes executing the PHP code and returns the results to the Apache server. The Apache server gathers the results of the PHP code, along with any HTML, CSS, and/or JavaScript, and sends this information to the web browser on the user's machine. The web browser then executes the HTML, CSS, and/or JavaScript code.

- MySQL and MariaDB are not just databases; they are also database management systems. These packages include tools to create, manage, and secure databases.

- The PHP processor interprets and executes any PHP code. It will throw errors or exceptions if there are syntax (coding errors), logical errors, or system errors (out of memory).

- phpMyAdmin is a GUI-based administration tool for creating and maintaining databases and their tables.

A single all-in-one package such as XAMPP or EasyPHP contains the four programs mentioned in Figure 1-1 and is referred to as a WAMP (Windows, Apache, MySQL/MariaDB, and PHP). In WAMPs, the main components are preconfigured so that they can talk to each other. The equivalent on an Apple OS is MAMP, and on a Linux computer it is LAMP.

The folder *htdocs* (or *eds-www*) is the default storage and executable area for your web pages. Apache, by default, looks in *htdocs* (or *eds-www*) for your web pages. These pages may be designed to allow users to interact with the database. Other pages will operate unseen by the user to transmit information back and forth between the browser and database. The pages are usually HTML and PHP files or a combination of both.

■ **Caution** Everything inside Figure 1-1 may be already installed on a remote host, but you should never use a remote host to create a database while you are learning. For security reasons, do not use a remote host until you have become proficient. We recommend you learn and develop a database using an all-in-one package on your own computer. Note that an all-in-one package installed on your own computer is purely a development tool. The database, when developed and thoroughly tested, can eventually be uploaded to a host to make it available to users.

A Free Development Platform for Testing

You will not be able to test your work in the normal way—that is, by using a browser to view a database and the PHP code located on your hard drive. When a web page containing PHP is requested by the browser, the PHP code is executed in the web server. The results of the executing of the code will display in the browser. If you view the browser code (right-click the web page and select View Source), you will not see the PHP code. You will see the results produced by the execution of the code. This confuses beginning developers who are used to seeing any HTML, CSS, or standard JavaScript code they have created in the browser. Remember, HTML, CSS, and standard JavaScript are executed in the browser. PHP code is executed in the web server, even when that server is on your own PC.

Using an all-in-one package on your computer will allow you to see all the code you create and the results of the execution of this code on your PC. This book assumes that you will use a package on your own computer while you are learning and for developing future database-driven websites.

■ **Note** In the current world of hackers who attempt to corrupt or gather personal, corporate, and government data, all web pages on Internet-hosted websites *must* be secured. The earliest projects in this book are necessarily simple and have some secure features. However, it is not recommended that you upload these pages to an Internet host. When you have gained experience and confidence, and you are sure that you understand how to secure websites and databases, you can adapt the book's later projects for use in your own websites and then upload them to a remote host.

Using XAMPP on Your Own Computer

The XAMPP package is free and is preconfigured so that the components will talk to each other. This eliminates the hassle of the usual practice of downloading several individual components and then configuring them to work together. XAMPP includes packages for Windows (WAMP), Linux (LAMP), and the Apple (Mac) OS (MAMP). The examples in this book are developed using a WAMP environment. However, these examples should also work in a LAMP or MAMP environment.

At the time of writing, the most recent version of XAMPP is version 7.2.4. This version is used throughout the book. It has component versions as follows: Apache 2.4.33, MariaDB 10.1.25, PHP 7.2.4, and phpMyAdmin 4.8.0, along with other tools. The examples in this book are not totally compatible with PHP versions before 7.0.

■ **Note**   If you are installing a version that is newer than demonstrated in this book, the installation steps may be slightly different. You should refer to the XAMPP site (www.apachefriends.org) or search for installation instructions on the Internet (try youtube.com) for any version not demonstrated in this book. If the newer version includes a major upgrade (for example, PHP 8), some code changes may be required. Check the Apress website for code changes related to major version releases.

Before we give you the instructions for downloading XAMPP, we need to settle a question that bothers every beginner concerning the transferring of a developed database from XAMPP or EasyPHP to the remote host. If you use one of these packages on your own computer, a question will arise, as stated in the title of the next section:

Will I Be Able to Transfer the Database from XAMPP or EasyPHP to a Remote Host?

The main thought that haunts a beginner is this: "If I develop a database on a local WAMP, will I be able to move it easily to a remote host?" Beginners have every reason to be worried because most manuals rarely give even a hint on this topic. However, the answer is this: "Yes, you will be able to move the database." You will find full instructions later in this book.

Now we will provide the information for downloading and installing XAMPP.

■ **Caution**   Should you want to install multiple free WAMPs, it is possible to install both EASYPHP and XAMPP on the same computer. However, make sure one of them is shut down before opening the other; otherwise, they will fight for the same ports and cause annoying problems.

Downloading and Installing XAMPP

XAMPP needs minimal configuring. To download the package, go to www.apachefriends.org/.

Click Download from the menu at the top, as shown in Figure 1-2, of the main page. The download page will then display the current versions available. If it's available, select the 7.2.4 version of XAMPP to ensure that all examples you use from this book will be compatible. If there is a minor release of version 7 (such as 7.3.0), it probably will still be compatible. If version 7 is not available, download the latest version. Then check the Apress website to see whether there are any coding changes required to the examples presented in this book. The download page varies from time to time, so you may have to explore the page to find the version shown.

Download

XAMPP is an easy to install Apache distribution containing MariaDB, PHP, and Perl. Just download and start the installer. It's that easy.

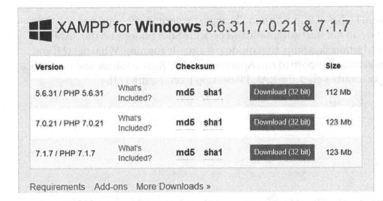

Documentation/FAQs

There is no real manual or handbook for XAMPP. We wrote the documentation in the form of FAQs. Have a burning question that's not answered here? Try the Forums or Stack Overflow.

- Linux FAQs
- Windows FAQs
- OS X FAQs
- OS X XAMPP-VM FAQs

Add-ons and Themes

Figure 1-2. Installing XAMPP

■ **Note** The download page will state that you must have the C++ runtime libraries installed. XAMPP and its related tools are created using C++. If you are using a current version of Windows, you probably already have the correct version of C++. However, if you receive an error indicating that it is missing, follow the link the error provides to download the correct version.

Click the Download button next to the most current version. This will begin the download process. The file will automatically download to the download folder on your PC. Depending on which browser you are using, you could be asked if you want to run or save the program. Some browsers will automatically save the program and require you to click the file to run it. If you are unaware of how to find downloaded files for the browser you are using, search the Internet for directions. Once the file has downloaded, start the setup process by double-clicking the file (or clicking the Run option if prompted).

The environment will prompt you to ask permission to install the program. Click Yes to continue the process. The setup program will determine the security settings on your machine. It may provide a warning that your security might restrict some of the XAMPP options available. You can choose to either continue the installation or stop the current installation and temporarily turn off your security program. If you turn off your security, make sure your PC is no longer connected to the Internet. The setup program will also look at your User Account Control (UAC) settings. These settings limit access to folders and files based on the user ID in which you are signed into the system. If you are using a computer in which you do not have administrative rights, the setup routine will provide a warning message prompting you to install your program in a different location than the default (program files). Do as the prompt suggests and change the default settings when prompted to a different location, such as *c:/XAMPP*.

A Welcome to XAMPP Setup Wizard screen will appear. Just click Next to continue the setup. The next screen will display all the options available for installation. If you are a beginner, just accept the items already checked by clicking the Next button. Intermediate and advanced users might consider removing items that you are sure you will not use. You can always install them later if you need them. The next screen will show the installation location. Use *c:/XAMPP* to avoid any possible security access issues. Click Next.

The next screen will try to convince you to also look at installing CMS programs (such as WordPress). For now, uncheck the Learn More box. You can install it later if you are interested. Click the Next button. The next screen will indicate the setup is ready. Click Next. The installation will begin. By default, the Start Control Panel check box will be checked. Leave it checked. Click the Finish button. You may be prompted with a language selection prompt before the control panel displays.

If you have errors during installation, copy the error message and paste it into a search engine (like Google). Look at the listing of suggested solutions. Go to a trusted website and follow the directions to correct your error.

The items on the XAMPP control panel labeled Running usually appear automatically, and you will then be able to stop the various modules. If they do not start automatically, click the Start buttons on the XAMPP control panel for Apache and MySQL. If a button says Stop, that module is already running. What next? If you are asked about running the modules as services, choose to run Apache and MySQL as services, and then those modules will automatically start when you double-click the XAMPP desktop icon (Figure 1-3).

Figure 1-3. *The XAMPP icon*

Create a shortcut on your Desktop for XAMPP's *htdocs* folder, and place it alongside the XAMPP icon, as shown in Figure 1-4. Use this shortcut for loading your PHP files into the *C:\xampp\htdocs* folder.

Figure 1-4. *Time-saving shortcuts*

If a desktop icon was not created during the installation, we recommend you go to the *C:\xampp* folder and then create a desktop shortcut for the *xampp-control.exe* file.

For maximum convenience, put the two desktop items side by side, as shown in Figure 1-4. One icon starts and stops XAMPP, and the other allows you to create and modify pages directly in the XAMPP *htdocs* folder.

One common problem is that Skype and other applications also use port 80, the default port for Apache. If another application is using this port, Apache won't start. The log (Figure 1-5) will indicate if Apache could not start because the port was in use. If this occurs, go to the XAMPP control panel and click the Netstat button. This window will list all applications running on your PC and what ports they are using. Determine an unused port (such as 8080) and close the Netstat window. Then click the Config button next to Apache. Select *httpd.conf*. The configuration file will open in Notepad (or your default text editor). Click Edit, click Search, and enter **80**. Click Find Next until you discover the following line:

```
Listen 80
```

Change this line to the following:

`Listen 8080`

Or, change it to whatever port you decided to use.

Now go back to search and click Find Next until you find the following line:

`ServerName: localhost: 80`

Change this line to the following:

`ServerName: localhost: 8080`

Or change it to the same port you decided to use.

Save the file, and close Notepad (or your text editor). Go to the XAMPP control panel and click the Config button at the top-right corner of the page. Click the Services and Port Settings button. Click the tab Apache. Enter the new port for Apache (8080 or whatever port you decided to use). Click Save. Close the Config window. Now click the Start button next to Apache in the control panel (Figure 1-5). After a few seconds, Apache should start. This will be indicated by a green background behind Apache. You will also need to start MySQL because it could not start without Apache running first.

Starting XAMPP

From here onward, to test your pages in XAMPP, double-click the desktop icon and check that Apache and MySQL/MariaDB have started. If they have not started, click the Start button for Apache. Once it starts, then click the Start button for MySQL/MariaDB and then minimize the control panel.

Figure 1-5 shows the XAMPP control panel.

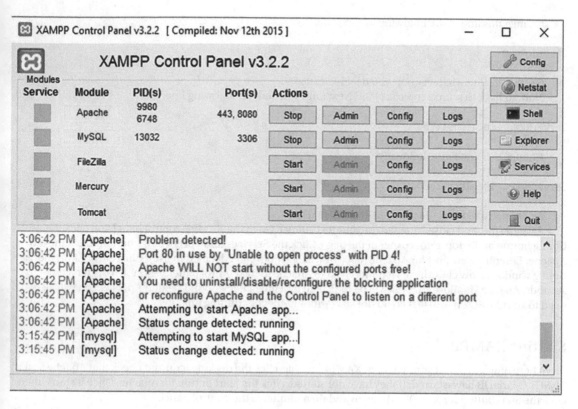

Figure 1-5. *The XAMPP control panel*

We suggest you always minimize the control panel so that you have a clear desktop for starting work on your databases.

After starting Apache and MySQL/MariaDB, you can test your installation and examine all the XAMPP examples and tools; to do this, enter one of the following addresses in your browser:

```
http://localhost/
http://127.0.0.1/
```

If you added a port number, be sure to include the same number in a format like one of the following examples:

```
http://127.0.0.1:8080/
http://localhost:8080/
```

Closing XAMPP

Close XAMPP when you have finished testing your database and PHP files. This will free up memory for tasks other than database development. To close, click the maximize XAMPP control panel on the taskbar and then click the Quit button on the control panel, as shown in Figure 1-6. Alternatively, you can right-click the icon in the Notification area and then click Quit.

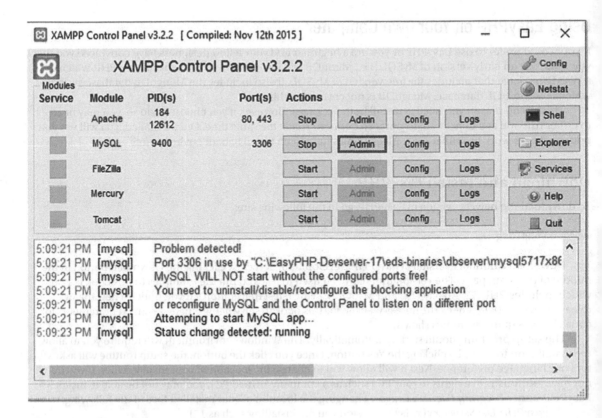

Figure 1-6. *Closing the XAMPP program*

The security of a database and its data is extremely important. XAMPP provides a method for making the database and tables on your computer safe from harmful interference, which is described later in this chapter.

Where Is MariaDB and MySQL 8?

You might be confused at this point about XAMPP and the location of the MariaDB databases. The creators of XAMPP did switch from using MySQL databases to using MariaDB databases; however, everything we just explained seems to indicate that MySQL is still part of XAMPP. However, this is not the case. When the creators decided to switch database systems, they had to make only minor configuration changes to use MariaDB. Since MariaDB does not operate any differently than the free version of MySQL, the creators decided to leave everything with the MySQL title. Since you might be new to this environment, this might be confusing. However, to current users of XAMPP, this allowed an easy transition between database environments. Just remember, wherever you see MySQL in XAMPP, it is MariaDB.

The title of this book includes *MySQL 8*. MySQL 8 is a full, professional version with the latest bells and whistles, including business analytics tools. However, MySQL 8 is not provided with XAMPP or EasyPHP, and the full version is not free. If you are developing sites for corporations or government agencies, you should consider using MySQL 8 (or the latest version). Any version of MySQL can be attached to XAMPP. You do need to read the MySQL documentation to make sure the version you are attaching is compatible with the Apache and PHP versions you have installed. Adding a new version of MySQL is an intermediate skill. We have provided directions in the last chapter to help when you are ready to convert.

Using EasyPHP on Your Own Computer

If you would prefer to use EasyPHP or you are a beginner and your fellow designers have convinced you that you must use an early version of MySQL (i.e., MariaDB will just not do), you can install EasyPHP, which is a WAMP package that includes the free version of MySQL. It also includes the MongoDB database system, which is a non-SQL database. MongoDB is not covered in this book.

There is no reason you need to install both packages. However, if you choose to do so, you may need to either run one at a time or adjust ports so both can run at the same time. Once installed, you will see that both packages work in similar ways. All examples have been tested in both environments.

Download and Install EasyPHP

To download the newest version of EasyPHP, go to the following site:

www.easyphp.org

Download a nonbeta version of easyPHP Development Server by clicking the Download button in the middle of the main page. The version that has been used to test and run the examples in this book is 17.0, which includes PHP 7.2, Apache 2.4, and MySQL 5.7 (the latest free edition). If you notice a new major release (such as 18.0), check the Apress website for this book to see whether there are any requirements for code changes in the examples shown.

The setup program should start up automatically. The Windows environment will require you to allow the installation to occur by clicking the Yes button. Once you click the button, the setup routine will ask for your language preference. Next it will allow you to change the location of your installed files. If you do not have administrative rights to your PC (such as a company-owned PC), you may not be able to install EasyPHP under *Program Files*. We suggest changing the location of your installed files to the following:

C:*EasyPHP-DevServer-xx* (*xx* is the version you are installing such as 17)

Click Next. The installation process will then ask if you want a desktop icon created. We suggest you create one for easy access. Click Next. The current screen will verify the location of your install. Click Install. When the installation is completed, the last screen will ask if you want to launch the development server. Launch it by clicking Finish. If you have errors during install, copy the error into a search engine (like Google) to look for solutions. In the list that is provided, go to a well-known site and attempt to follow the directions to fix your error.

Starting EasyPHP

Go to the EasyPHP icon in the system tray, right-click, and launch the dashboard. If the dashboard fails to launch, close the development server (right-click the icon and select Exit), and try launching it from your desktop shortcut. The dashboard uses port 1111. If you still can't launch the dashboard, right-click the development server icon and select Tools and then Open Port Controller. Verify that another process is not using the same port. If another process is using that port, stop that process and repeat the previous steps.

Within the dashboard (Figure 1-7), click the start button below HTTP SERVER. Clicking this button should start both Apache and MySQL. The start button will change to a stop button if the server starts properly. At this point, both the HTTP SERVER and DATABASE SERVER should be displayed with stop buttons below the titles. If you encounter an error, try stopping the development server (right-click the system tray icon and select Quit) and restart it (click the icon on the desktop). If you still have errors, copy and paste the error in a search engine (such as Google) to see a list of possible solutions. Select a suggested solution from a known site and try to follow the directions.

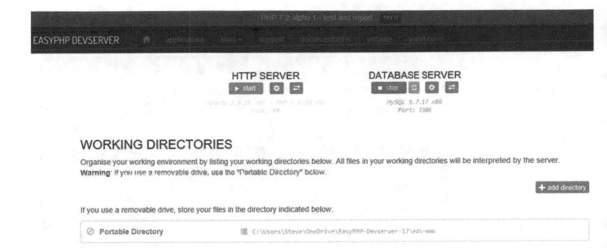

Figure 1-7. *The EasyPHP DevServer*

Closing EasyPHP

Anytime you need to close EasyPHP, just close the development server by going to the system tray, right-clicking the icon, and selecting Quit. This will close all processes related to EasyPHP.

phpMyAdmin Security

The initial installation of phpMyAdmin within XAMPP and EasyPHP has the username *root* and no password. If you use those settings on your own computer, there is a security risk when connected to the Internet. If you are creating databases for more than just personal use or your own education, you should create a phpMyAdmin password. If you work in the same room with other people, the password will provide security if the password is not divulged to the other people. As a best practice, you should password-protect your development environment.

If you are not already in phpMyAdmin, go to the XAMPP control panel or the easyPHP DevServer page. In XAMPP click admin to the right of MySQL. In EasyPHP, click the open button to the right of the version of phpMyAdmin displayed on the page (Figure 1-8).

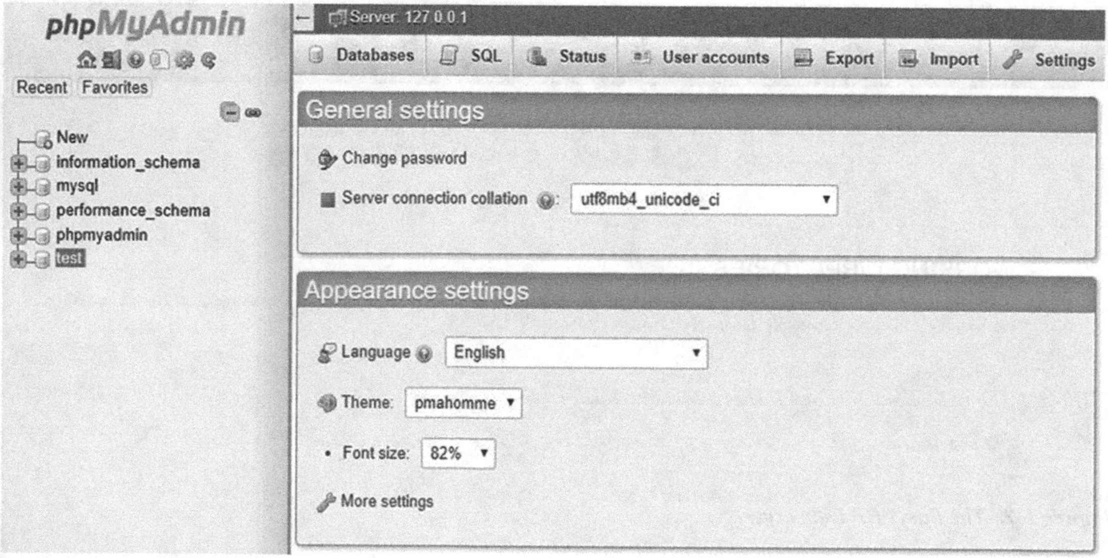

Figure 1-8. *The phpMyAdmin page*

Note that if you have changed the port from the default port, you may need to add the port number when bring up phpMyAdmin. For example, if you changed the port to 8080, the address for phpMyAdmin is now as follows:

```
http://localhost:8080/phpMyAdmin/
```

Click the User accounts tab in phpMyAdmin (Figure 1-9).

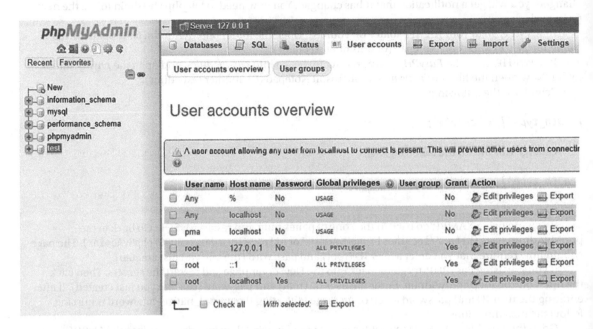

Figure 1-9. *The phpMyAdmin User accounts tab*

Click the Edit privileges link to the right of the last entry, root localhost. An Edit privileges page will display (Figure 1-10). Click the Change password link at the top of the page.

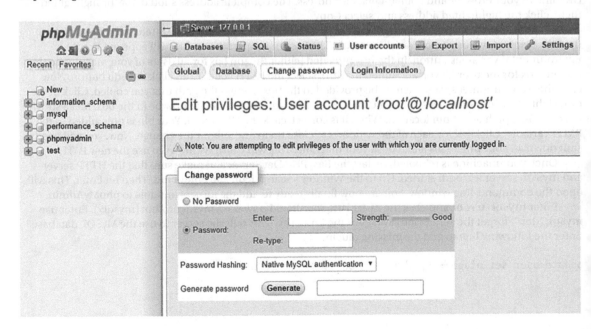

Figure 1-10. *phpMyAdmin Edit privileges page*

15

Enter your password in both boxes. Click the OK button near the bottom of the page. If the password changed, you will get a notification that it has changed. You now need to tell phpMyAdmin to use the new password.

In XAMPP, go to your XAMPP folder on your PC. Open the folder phpMyAdmin. Now open the file *config.inc.php* in Microsoft Notepad (or another text editor).

In easyPHP, go to the *EasyPHP-DevServer-xx* folder, go into *eds-modules*, and open the *phyMyAdmin* folder. Now open the file *config.inc.php* in Microsoft Notepad (or another text editor).

Search for the following:

```
['auth_type'] = 'config';
```

Change this line to the following:

```
['auth_type'] = 'cookie';
```

Save the file.

If you are using XAMPP, go back to the control panel. Stop and restart MySQL. Go back to the phpMyAdmin page (http://localhost/phpMyAdmin/ or http://localhost:8080/phpMyAdmin/). The page should now require that you enter a user ID (root) and password (the one you just created).

If you are using EasyPHP, try going back into the DevServer page and restart the servers. Then click the open button for phpMyAdmin. Enter the user ID (root) and password (the one you just created). If after entering the user ID and password an error message indicating that mysql_native_password is missing, follow the next directions.

Go to the *EasyPHP-DevServer-xx* folder, go into *eds-binaries*, then into *dbserver*, into the *MySQL* folder, and finally into the *bin* folder. This folder contains several applications that can be used to run and administer MySQL and phpMyAdmin. However, these applications only run in the command-line interface. To make finding and using them easier, we are going to place this location in the Path variable for your PC. This allows you to just execute the program you need without entering the complete path name. Go to the URL line in your browser and double-click the address. The complete address should now be highlighted. Right-click the highlighted address and select Copy.

Go to the search icon (bottom right of your system tray), click it, and enter **system variables**. Click the Edit System Environmental Variables result. The System Properties window will appear. Click the Environmental Variables button. In the box provided (either the top box for all users of your machine or the bottom box for the user ID you are signed in with), select the PATH code. Then click the Edit button. Now click the New button. A space will now be provided in the box to enter the path that you copied. Click in the box, right-click, and select Paste (or hit Ctrl+V). The path you copied should now be in the box. Make sure it is a complete path to the bin location. When it is correct, click the OK button. Your bin is now added to the PATH variable. Click OK for each of the windows to close them and submit the change. Now, you will need to shut down all your processes and reboot your machine. This will cause Windows to use the new PATH.

Once your machine is rebooted, restart the EasyPHP DevServer and make sure that the HTTP server and mySQL server are both started. Go to the Window's search icon and enter **cmd**. Then hit Enter. This will open the command-line window. You are now finally ready to add the missing module to phpMyAdmin.

Enter **mysql -u root** and click the Enter key. You should now see a mysql prompt (mysql>). Enter **use mysql**; (don't forget the semicolon) and click the Enter key. This tells the server to use the MySQL database. Enter the following line to add the missing plugin:

```
update user set plugin='mysql_native_password' where user='root';
```

You should see a message "Query OK." Now also change the password in the command line with the following line:

```
update user set Password-PASSWORD('12345') where user-'root';
```

12345 should be replaced with the password you set previously. You should also see a message "Query OK." All your changes should be complete. Close the mysql prompt by entering **exit**. Hit the X to close the command window. Go back into phpMyAdmin and click User accounts. You should now see that the Yes flag has been set indicating that root now has a password. Note EasyPHP still might automatically let you in to phpMyAdmin even with the password set.

This password situation occurs with the current (as of the publish date of this book) version of the free MySQL edition. As you noticed earlier, this does not occur in XAMPP because XAMPP is using MariaDB.

If you have any problems with these steps and want to back out, the easiest way to do so is to uninstall the package using the uninstall program under the main package folder and then reinstall XAMPP or EasyPHP. As said earlier, if you get error messages, copy them into a web search engine (Google) to look for suggested solutions.

Accessing phpMyAdmin Directly

If you have installed XAMPP and the servers have been started, you can access phpMyAdmin directly by entering the following URL in any browser:

```
http://localhost/phpMyAdmin/ or http://127.0.0.1/phpMyAdmin/
```

(Remember to include the final forward slash and the port number if you changed the default port of 80.)

If you have installed easyPHP and the servers have been started, you can access phpMyAdmin directly by entering one of the following URLs in any browser:

```
http://localhost:8080/eds-modules/phpmyadmin470x170718155219/
http://127.0.0.1:8080/eds-modules/phpmyadmin470x170718155219/
```

(Your actual phpmyadmin version/build might be different, which will create a different *phyMyAdmin* folder.)

Be sure to include the http://; otherwise, the browser will look for the location on the Internet instead of your PC.

■ **Note** The sections describing the use of phpMyAdmin apply to any of the development platforms: XAMPP, WAMPServer, or easyPHP.

You might have set the password in XAMPP or EasyPHP earlier, so whenever you access phpMyAdmin, you might need to log in using that password. This prevents Internet robots and human beings from interfering with your database. The latter case is important if you work in an office with others—you could have a spy or mischievous meddler in the place where you work. If you created a password for phpMyAdmin, a dialog box will appear, as shown in Figure 1-11.

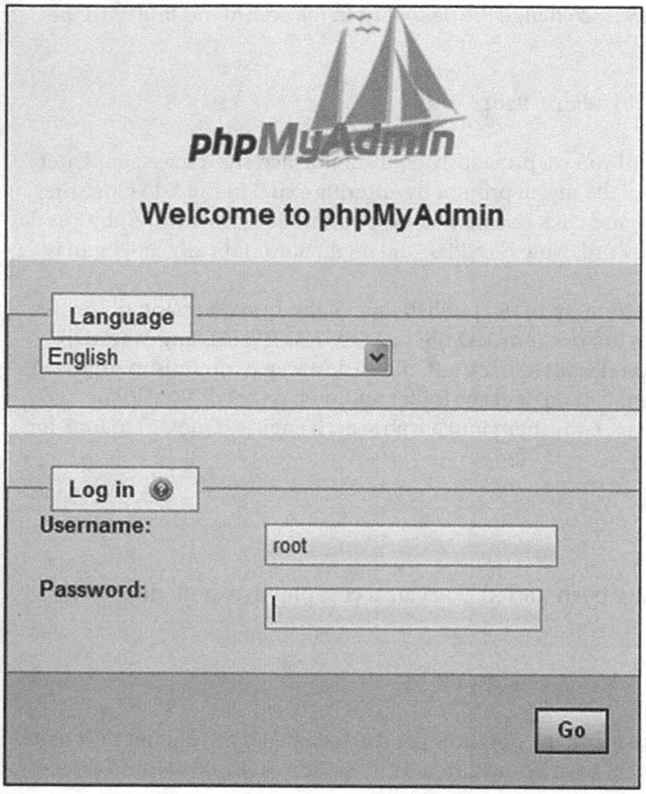

Figure 1-11. *Enter the password in the dialog box to access phpMyAdmin*

Enter your username (root) and password and then click the Go button. phpMyAdmin loads rather slowly, but it will eventually appear.

Note that open source programs are continually being improved and upgraded, and you may find that you have a newer version of phpMyAdmin in your XAMPP or EasyPHP package than that used in this book. You may also see upgrade messages alerting you to a new version in the phpMyAdmin main window. Where personal data is concerned, security is paramount, so these incremental updates are a good thing for you, though they do mean that some of the screenshots in the book might no longer accurately reflect what you see on the screen. Don't worry if an interface looks a little different from the ones shown in this book; the usage will normally be similar.

The phpMyAdmin interface may look a little daunting at first, but we'll cover the relevant parts of it when we need to use them. For the moment, you can close the phpMyAdmin window.

You now know how to install and secure XAMPP and easyPHP, and you also learned how to start and stop the servers. Most of what you have just read will probably be very new, but there are some parts that you will recognize because they follow the normal Microsoft Windows organization of files and folders.

The Familiar Bits

Within the XAMPP package, the structure of the folders and files will be familiar to Windows users, although their names may not be recognizable.

Figure 1-12 shows the XAMPP folders.

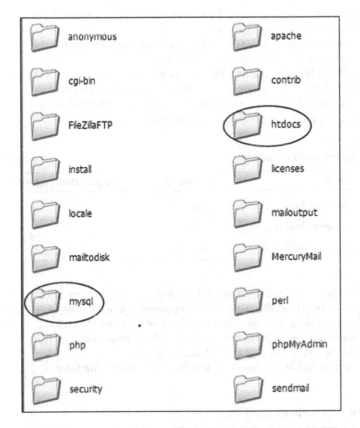

Figure 1-12. *The folders in the XAMPP package; your list might be slightly different*

In Figure 1-12, note the *htdocs* folder. This is where you will place all your PHP files and the HTML pages for your website and databases.

Within the XAMPP folder, you will find a folder called *MySQL*. This folder contains a folder called *data* where the databases and tables will reside. A database must have a unique name. A file within the data folder contains all the information about the database, and it has the file type **.opt*.

Tables are files; when you have created any tables, these will also live inside the folder named *data*, and they will have the file type **.frm*.

In easyPHP once you open the *EasyPHP--Devserver-xx* folder, you will discover an *eds-www* folder. This is where you place all your PHP files and HTML pages. The following file path is the location of the database files:

C:\EasyPHP-Devserver-17\eds-binaries\dbserver\mysql5717x86x170717151041\data

Intermediate or advanced developers should consider creating virtual directories, which are other locations for executable files. While this topic is not covered in this book, you can find additional information on the Internet by searching for *XAMPP Virtual Directory* or *easyPHP Virtual Directory*.

Now that you're familiar with the look and feel of the tools you'll be using, you're ready to move ahead. The next section will take you nearer to creating your first database and table.

Planning a Database: The Essential First Step

The first and most important stage is to plan the database so that you have something practical to use. Let's assume we need to plan a database for the membership of an organization.

First, decide on a name for the database. We will give this database the name *simpledb*. Remember that the database is like an empty folder that will eventually contain one or more tables.

Then, assemble the data items into a table. We have given this table the name *users*.

Next, decide what information you want in the table; your decision is not binding because you can change any part of the database during development. Let's suppose we need five pieces of information about the users. We set out some typical data in Table 1-1 earlier in the chapter and in Table 1-2.

Table 1-2. *Draft Plan for the users Table in the simpledb Database*

user_id	first_name	last_name	email	password	registration_date
	Kevin	Kettle	kev@kettle.co.uk	K3ttl2fur	
	Susan	Saucepan	sue@kitchen.org.uk	n@Sus5	
	Oliver	Oven	oliver@cooker.co.uk	H0tsts0v3	

Each row in a table is called a *record*, and each cell is called a *field*. A database can contain more than one table. We have used some fictitious names to help plan the table. The first column is labeled user_id, and this column is additional to the five columns of data. The column user_id will be explained later; just accept it for the moment and be sure to leave it empty. Also, leave the registration dates empty because this is an automatic entry; it does not need values entered, nor does it need allocated space.

Now we must allocate some space for the data. Table 1-3 shows the number of characters we have allocated for each item.

Table 1-3. *Number of Characters to Allow for Column in the users Table*

user_id	first_name	last_name	email	password	registration_date
6	30	40	50	60	

Write down or print the two tables, and keep them close at hand because you will be referring to them in the next stages.

Now, decide on a username and password for the database, and enter that information in your notebook. Four pieces of information are required: the name of the database, the host, the password, and the username. In this project, these are as follows:

- *Name*: simpledb

- *Host*: localhost

- *Password*: Hmsv1ct0ry1 (this comes from hmsvictory but with an uppercase first letter and by replacing *I* with 1 and *o* with 0 for a strong password)

- *User*: horatio

To generate a more secure password, phpMyAdmin includes a password generator. Next, we will create our first database using phpMyAdmin.

Creating a Database Using phpMyAdmin

Open phpMyAdmin either directly as mentioned at the beginning of this section or through the XAMPP administration page or the easyPHP dashboard. Remember, the database server must be running to use phpMyAdmin.

Click the Databases tab in the top menu. You will then see the interface shown in Figure 1-13.

Figure 1-13. *The phpMyAdmin interface for creating the database*

Type a name for the database. For this example, it will be simpledb, all in lowercase. You should change Collation to utf8-general-ci; the default of latin1_swedish_ci causes confusion.

■ **Note**   Collations determine the type of characters, sorting abilities, performance, and other characteristics of the data. The collation utf8-general-ci is an older standard that meets the needs of the data examples in this book. Your data requirements may require a different collation.

Then click the Create button (set the Collation field to utf8-general-ci). After you click the Create button, the page will switch to the create a table page. However, first we want to change the properties of the database. Check the left arrow at the top of the page (left side). This will return to the main page. Click the Databases tab again. Now the previous page will look similar to Figure 1-14.

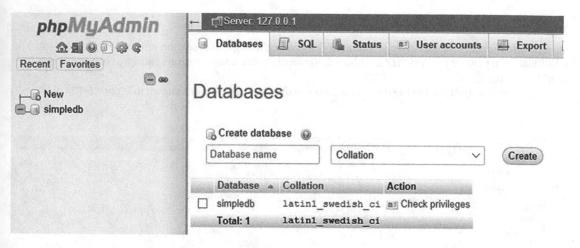

Figure 1-14. *In the lower part of the page, select the box near the name of your database*

When you select the box next to your new database, as shown in Figure 1-14, click Check Privileges, and you will be taken to a screen where you will see a list of users who have access to the database. To make the database secure, you must add a username and password. Click Add user account, as shown in Figure 1-15.

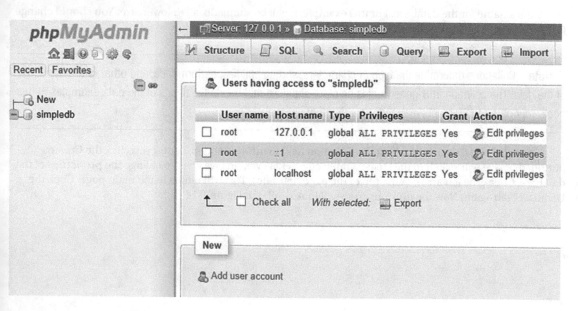

Figure 1-15. *The Add user account icon is at the bottom of this figure*

Clicking Add user account will load the Add user account screen, shown next in Figure 1-16.

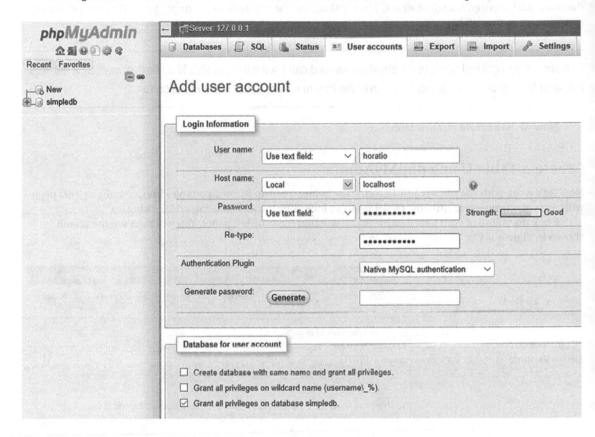

Figure 1-16. *This screen enables you to add a user and a password*

■ **Caution** Adding a username and password is essential; otherwise, your database will be insecure and vulnerable to attack by unscrupulous individuals or their robots. This is the most important habit to cultivate. Be sure to record the user and password details in your notebook. Make sure to create a strong password that includes a combination of lowercase and uppercase, numbers, and special characters. Keeping a detailed record will save you hours of frustration later.

Using the drop-down menus, accept the default Use text field in the first field and enter the username in the field to right of it. In the second field labeled Host, select local. The word *localhost* will appear in the field on the right. Localhost is the default name for the server on your computer. Enter a password in the third field, and confirm your password by retyping it in the lower field. The Generate Password button will create a random strong password if you want something unique and more secure.

Scroll down to Database for user account, and click Grant all privileges on database. Because you are the webmaster, you need to be able to deal with every aspect of the database; therefore, you need all the privileges. If you add other users, you need to restrict their privileges by deselecting boxes such as Drop, Delete, and Shutdown.

Scroll down to the bottom of the form, and click the OK or Go button. You have now created the database and secured it against attack. The database can be regarded as an empty folder that will eventually contain one or more tables.

■ **Note** If you get lost when using phpMyAdmin and can't see what you should do next, always click the little house at the top of the left panel. Hover over the icon to ensure that it is the Home button.

Now we will create our first table.

Create a Table Using phpMyAdmin

Now let's work with the phpMyAdmin web page to insert one or more data tables into a database. This page will give you complete control over your table(s), including troubleshooting and backing up.

Click the name of your new database; you will find it on the left panel. You will then see the screen shown in Figure 1-17.

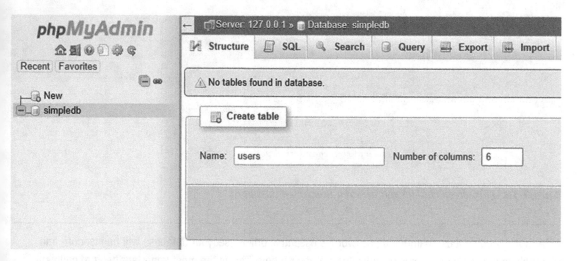

Figure 1-17. *Click the Go button at the bottom of the page to create the table*

Enter a name for the table, and specify the number of columns. Then click the Go button at the bottom of the page. You will be taken to a screen showing the columns flipped 90 degrees so that columns look like rows; this is shown in Figure 1-18. The fields are empty and waiting for you to define the table.

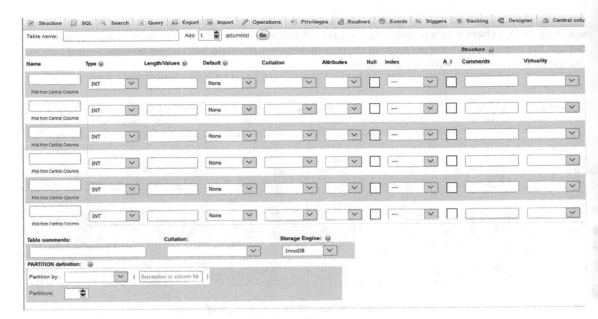

Figure 1-18. *The six rows represent six columns. The column titles will be entered in the fields on the left.*

Use the data from Tables 1-2 and 1-3 that we planned earlier, and enter the column name, data type, and number of characters. The details for creating the users table are given in Table 1-4.

Table 1-4. *The Attributes for the users Table*

Column name	Type	Length/Value	Default	Attributes	Null	Index	A_I
user_id	*MEDIUMINT*	6	None	*Unsigned*	☐	PRIMARY	☑
first_name	VARCHAR	30	None		☐		☐
last_name	VARCHAR	40	None		☐		☐
email	VARCHAR	50	None		☐		☐
password	CHAR	60	None		☐		☐
registration_date	DATETIME				☐		☐

Accept all the default settings for each item except for the user_id. Here, you will need to select UNSIGNED, PRIMARY, and the type; also select the A_I (auto increment) box. If you find entering the values of 6, UNSIGNED, and PRIMARY cause your version of phpMyAdmin to produce errors (or warnings), you can leave the default for those items. As mentioned in the later text, when you click A_I, the system will request you select PRIMARY. MEDIUMINT will default to size 6.

The various categories under the heading Type will be explained later; the heading Length/Value refers to the maximum number of characters. The Length/Value for the registration_date is left blank because the length is predetermined. Do not enter anything under the headings Default and NULL. The attribute UNSIGNED means that the user_id integer cannot be a negative quantity. The Index for the user_id is the primary index, and A_I refers to Automatic Incrementation of the id number; as each user is registered to the database, they are given a unique number. The number is increased by one as each new user is added. When selecting the A_I check box, a pop-up window may ask you to verify that it is the primary index and will request the size again. *Do not* put a size in the pop-up window. If you do, you will get an error. Figure 1-19 shows the screen for specifying the attributes.

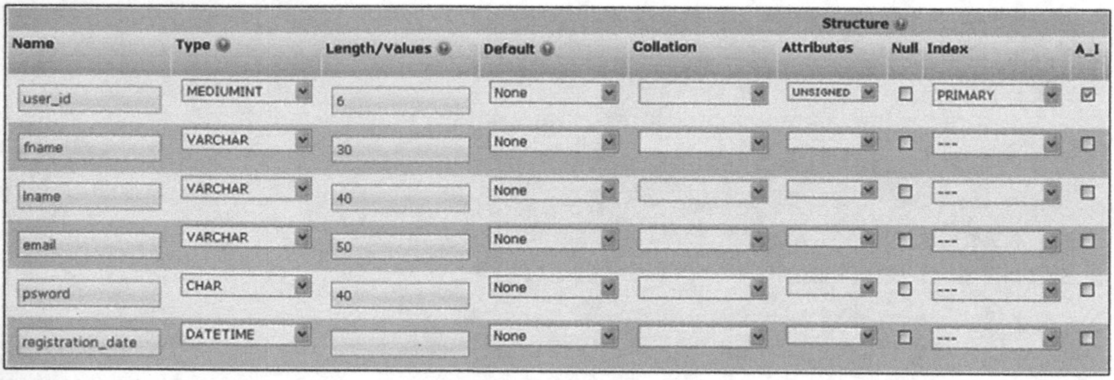

Name	Type ⊕	Length/Values ⊕	Default ⊕	Collation	Attributes	Null	Index	A_I
					Structure ⊎			
user_id	MEDIUMINT	6	None		UNSIGNED	☐	PRIMARY	☑
fname	VARCHAR	30	None			☐	---	☐
lname	VARCHAR	40	None			☐	---	☐
email	VARCHAR	50	None			☐	---	☐
psword	CHAR	40	None			☐	---	☐
registration_date	DATETIME		None			☐	---	☐

Figure 1-19. *This screen allows you to specify column titles and the type of content*

The rows represent columns, and they are very wide; you may have to scroll horizontally to enter some of the information. You will find more options as you scroll right, but we will not need them for this tutorial.

How do you fill out the fields? Enter the six column titles in the fields on the left under the heading Name. Select the type of column in the second column of fields under the heading Type. Select them from the drop-down menus. The types used in this table are as follows:

- MEDIUMINT can store integers ranging from minus 8,388,608 to plus 8,388,607. You could choose the next smallest category SMALLINT if the number of users will never exceed 65,535.

- VARCHAR specifies a variable-length string of characters from 0 to 255 long.

- CHAR is a string of characters traditionally used for passwords. Be sure to size this with 60 characters so that your PHP code can hash the passwords. The current PHP hashing algorithm will convert a password into a hashed string of 60 characters. A user's password can be, say, 6 to 12 characters long, but it will still be stored in the database as a hashed 60-character string. This will be discussed further in Chapter 2.

■ **Note** The length of hashed passwords may increase in newer editions of PHP. Make sure to research the current hashing size before setting the length of this field in the table.

- DATETIME stores the date and time in the format YYYY-MM-DD-HH:MM:SS.

Enter the number of characters in the third column of fields under the heading Length/Values. Refer to Table 1-4 for these numbers.

Under the heading Default, accept the default None. This field allows you to enter a default value if you want.

You might need to scroll to the right to complete filling in the fields. Under the heading Attributes, use the drop-down menu to select UNSIGNED for user_id. This ensures that the integer range becomes zero to 16,777,215. A negative quantity is not applicable for the user_id.

The next two entries concern only the user_id (Figure 1-20).

Figure 1-20. *Two extra entries for the user_id column*

For the user_id, under the heading Index, click the drop-down menu to select PRIMARY. The user_id should always be a primary index.

Under the heading A_I, select the topmost check box so that the user_id number is automatically incremented when each new record is added to the database. As stated earlier, you might see a pop-up window that will ask you to verify that it is primary and size. *Do not* enter a size in the pop-up window. Verify and/or add any missing information and click OK.

Enter the additional information shown in the tables and in Figure 1-20. Once you complete entering the information, scroll to the bottom and click the SAVE button.

■ **Caution**   If you forget to select the A_I box for user_id, you will receive an error message when you later try to enter the second record. The message will say that you are trying to create a duplicate value 0 for user_id.

Some people prefer a blend of a GUI and the command line for programming a table; phpMyAdmin allows you to do this by using the SQL language. However, this book will mainly use the phpMyAdmin GUI. The SQL alternative is described next. You can skip this section if you want, but we recommend that you come back to it at some future date because you will undoubtedly come across SQL in other more advanced books and tutorials.

The SQL Alternative

The next section describes a slightly quicker way of using phpMyAdmin for creating a database and a table. SQL stands for Structured Query Language; it is the official language for MySQL, MariaDB, and many other databases. You will be pleased to see that it uses plain English commands. The only problem is that it is easier to create typographical errors or spelling mistakes in the SQL window than in the phpMyAdmin interface shown earlier in Figure 1-19.

Using SQL, a database can be created complete with a password and username. This saves several steps.

We assume you have created the database simpledb, so we cannot use that name again. Let's assume that an administrator (Adrian) wants to create a database called *members* using the following information:

- *Database name*: members
- *Privileges*: all
- *Username*: adrian
- *Password*: stapler12

Figure 1-21 shows the code to create the database in the SQL window.

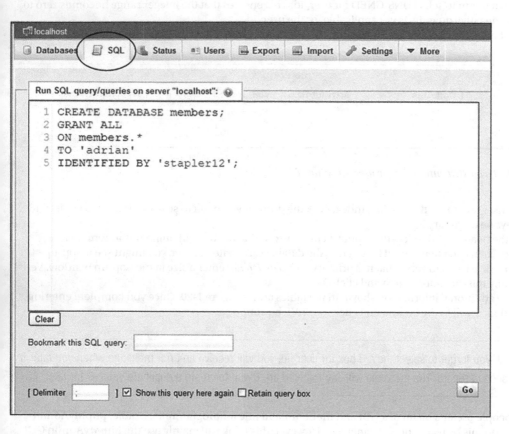

Figure 1-21. *The SQL window*

In phpMyAdmin, click New on the database "tree" on the left panel of the window to notify phpMyAdmin that you are no longer using the simpleDB database. Click the SQL tab (shown circled) to reveal the SQL window.

The details shown in Figure 1-21 must be entered in the following format:

```
CREATE DATABASE members;
GRANT ALL
ON members.*
TO 'adrian'
IDENTIFIED BY 'stapler12';
```

Enter each item is entered on a separate line by pressing Enter at the end of each line. The SQL keywords (like CREATE DATABASE) are traditionally in uppercase. Other items are normally entered in lowercase. Note the semicolons and the single quotes—these are important. When you are satisfied with the entries, click the Go button.

If you entered the code correctly, two query statements will display indicating that the database was created and adrian was attached as the user. They will indicate an empty result set. That is OK because nothing exists in the database.

Now we will create a table named *users* in the members database using the SQL window.

Click the members database in the database "tree" on the left panel of phpMyAdmin. If the members database does not appear, refresh the page so that it does appear. Open the SQL window, and enter this:

```
CREATE TABLE users (
user_id MEDIUMINT (6) UNSIGNED
AUTO_INCREMENT,
first_name VARCHAR(30) NOT NULL,
last_name VARCHAR(40) NOT NULL,
email VARCHAR(50) NOT NULL,
password CHAR(60) NOT NULL,
registration_date DATETIME,
PRIMARY KEY (user_id)
);
```

NOT NULL shown in the previous code will require that data be entered into the field. It is a required field. In this example, all the fields are actually required because registration_date is automatically populated.

Figure 1-22 shows the details in the SQL window.

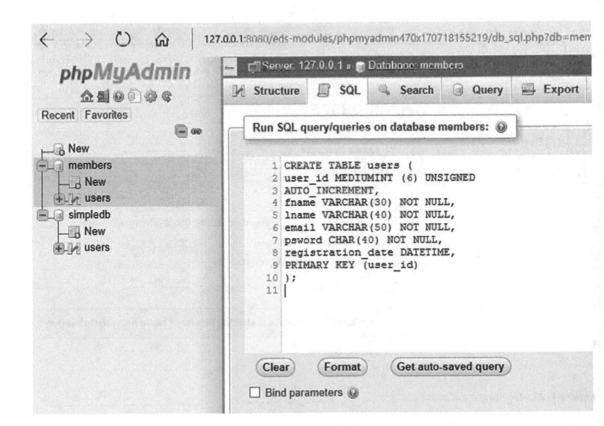

Figure 1-22. *Creating a table in the SQL window of phpMyAdmin*

Note that the brackets are all normal brackets, not curly brackets. Press the Enter key after each line, and remember to put the closing bracket and the semicolon at the end of the last line. Each item is separated by a closing comma (lines 3 through 8); if your table has six columns, you should have six commas. Click the Go button, and the table will be created.

■ **Tip**   We encourage you to explore the SQL topic just described. The ability to work with SQL will be a useful alternative sometime in the future. You can find many free tutorials by searching the Internet.

Deleting Databases and Tables

When learning, beginners often need to start over after creating a database or a table and may want to delete earlier attempts. When you first use phpMyAdmin, you might get carried away and create several databases and tables. Then you might decide to clear up the mess and delete some of them.

Let's look at how to delete a database. If phpMyAdmin is not already open, start it by using one of the methods previously shown. Select the Databases tab (shown in Figure 1-23) and then select the box next to the database to be deleted.

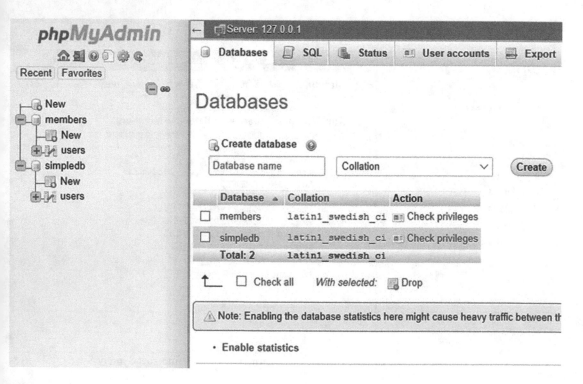

Figure 1-23. *Deleting a database*

When you have selected the database to be deleted, click the Drop icon (at the bottom right). You will be asked if you really want to delete the database; go ahead and complete the deletion. Everything associated with that database will be deleted, including its tables. If successful, a message will tell you that one database has been dropped.

You may want to preserve a database but delete all or one of its tables. In phpMyAdmin, select the database in the "tree" on the left panel. In the next screen, you will see the table(s); select the box next to the table(s) you want to delete. Figure 1-24 shows the users table of the simpledb database.

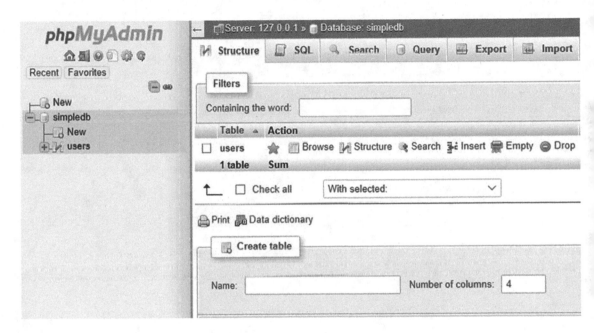

Figure 1-24. *Deleting a table in phpMyAdmin*

After selecting the table to delete, click the Drop icon (to the right of the table name). You will be asked if you really want to delete the table(s). You can choose between Drop and Cancel.

Summary

In this chapter, we defined a database and then looked at two free platforms for developing and testing databases and PHP files. We hope you were successful in downloading and installing XAMPP or easyPHP. We then explored phpMyAdmin and learned how to use it to create a database and a table. SQL was investigated as an alternative method for creating databases and tables. We learned about securing both the phpMyAdmin and databases with a user ID and password. We discovered how to delete databases and tables using phpMyAdmin. In the next chapter, we will create and test simple interactive web pages.

CHAPTER 2

■ ■ ■

Create Web Pages That Interact with Users

This chapter will demonstrate how a simple database can be linked to a web page so that the page can interact with users. The general public will have access to the website but will not have access to the database structure or the data contained in the tables. They will not be permitted to view the protected pages, such as a members-only page, because they have no password until they register. However, the web designer must provide a way for users to interact with the database to register as a member, search the database, and change a password. The PHP language and SQL code will provide the solution.

After completing this chapter, you will be able to

- Create a database and a template for a website

- Understand and use the PHP include function

- Understand how a server processes a PHP page

- Create an interactive template page

- Create mysqli code to connect to the database

- Create a registration page for members of an organization

- Understand and use the PHP echo() statement

- Create sticky forms

- Use simple arrays

- Create forms that display members' records

- Create code that hashes a password

We will use the simpledb database and the users table from the previous projects for our interactive web pages. Be aware that this tutorial is not practical or secure. It is a stepping stone to the more secure and ambitious projects described in subsequent chapters. In practice, you would never allow ordinary members to view a list of members. The interactive elements in this project are as follows:

- Users can register as members by inserting their details into a form displayed on the screen. The registration details would be entered into the database table and could be used by the administrator to send regular newsletters to members.

- Registered users can change their password.

- A user can view the list of members (for this project only). In later chapters, this facility would be available only to the webmaster and (to a limited extent) the membership secretary.

The features that make this example unsuitable for the real-world are as follows:

- No provision is made for registered members to subsequently log in to access a special section or page. This will be dealt with in Chapter 3.

- Users should never be able to access a table of members' details.

- At this early stage, for simplicity, limited filtering of the users' information is provided. The table could therefore contain faulty data and bogus e-mail addresses.

- In this chapter only, any user who knows a member's e-mail address and old password could change the member's password.

All these security issues will be dealt with in subsequent chapters. Despite the drawbacks, the project will provide you with valuable practice in coding and testing the pages. You will also learn more database jargon and some basic PHP code.

Creating the Folder for Holding the Database Pages

Within XAMPP's *htdocs* folder or the easyPHP's *eds-www* folder, create a new subfolder named *simpledb*. All the pages created in this chapter will be placed within the simpledb folder. You have a choice between hand-coding the files from the listings supplied or loading the book's code into the simpledb folder. (You can download the code from Apress.com.) We recommend that you hand-code the programs for this chapter; the files are small and won't take too long to create. You will learn more and learn faster if you type and test the code, especially if you make mistakes and learn to correct them.

Creating the Temporary Template

Obviously, some aspects of an interactive database must be accessible to users. That means incorporating it into a real-world web page. We will name our web page *template.php* (shown in Figure 2-1). As you can see, there is a main header, some body text, a navigation sidebar on the left, an information column on the right, and a footer at the bottom of the page.

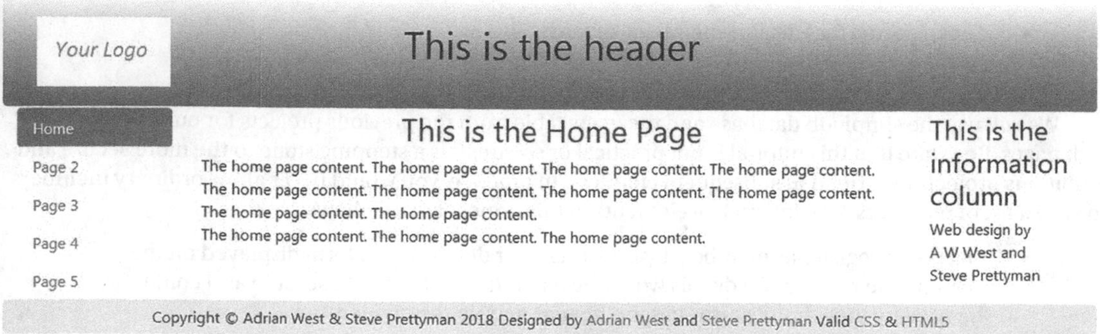

Figure 2-1. The template

In Listing 2-1, the head section contains the DOCTYPE, a page title, and a link to the Bootstrap style sheet. The body of the page contains some PHP code, and this will be explained step-by-step at the end of the listing.

Because the file contains PHP code (no matter how little), the file is saved with the file type *.php*.

Listing 2-1. Creating a Template for the Project (template.php)

```
<!DOCTYPE html>
<html lang="en">
<head>
  <title>Template for an interactive web page</title>
  <meta charset="utf-8">
  <meta name="viewport" content="width=device-width, initial-scale=1, shrink-to-fit=no">
  <!-- Bootstrap CSS File  -->
  <link rel="stylesheet"
  href="https://stackpath.bootstrapcdn.com/bootstrap/4.1.0/css/bootstrap.min.css"
  integrity="sha384-9gVQ4dYFwwWSjIDZnLEWnxCjeSWFphJiwGPXr1jddIhOegiu1FwO5qRGvFXOdJZ4"
  crossorigin="anonymous">
</head>

<body>
<div class="container" style="margin-top:30px">

<!-- Header Section                                                        #1-->
<header class="jumbotron text-center row"
style="margin-bottom:2px; background:linear-gradient(white, #0073e6);padding:20px;">
  <?php include('header-for-template.php'), ?>
</header>

<!-- Body Section                                                          #2-->
  <div class="row" style="padding-left: 0px;">
<!-- Left-side Column Menu Section -->
  <nav class="col-sm-2">
      <ul class="nav nav-pills flex-column">
        <?php include('nav.php'); ?>
      </ul>
  </nav>

<!-- Center Column Content Section -->
  <div class="col-sm-8">
    <h2 class="text-center">This is the Home Page</h2>
      <p>The home page content. The home page content. The home page content. The home
      page content. <br>
      The home page content. The home page content. The home page content. The home page
      content. <br>
      The home page content. The home page content. <br>
      The home page content. The home page content. The home page content. </p>
  </div>
```

```
<!-- Right-side Column Content Section                                    #3-->
    <aside class="col-sm-2">
        <php include('info-col.php'); ?>
    </aside>
  </div>

<!-- Footer Content Section                                               #4-->
<footer class="jumbotron text-center row"
style="padding-bottom:1px; padding-top:8px;">
    <?php include('footer.php'); ?>
</footer>
</div>
</body>
</html>
```

■ **Note** The <?php tag informs the server that PHP code follows. The ?> tag lets the server know where the PHP code ends. The server will pass any code between these tags to the PHP interpreter to be executed. Code outside the tags, HTML and JavaScript code, will eventually be sent to the user's browser without any processing.

The PHP code shown in Listing 2-1 contains the include() function, which will now be explained. (Strictly speaking, the include() function is a PHP language construct, but the difference is so small that we will continue to call it a function for simplicity.)

Introducing the PHP include() Function

You will have noted that there does not seem to be enough code in Listing 2-1 to create the page displayed in Figure 2-1. Here is the reason why.

The four pieces of PHP code shown between the <?php and ?> tags in Listing 2-1 have each pulled an additional file into the page. The page is a combination of five files: a main file plus four external files. The four external files are pulled into the template page using the PHP include() function.

For updating and maintaining a website, the include() function is a wonderful time-saver. Let's suppose you have a client website with 40 pages, and each page needs the same block of menu buttons. If your client asks you to add or delete one menu button, normally you would have to amend 40 pages to add or delete the button on each page. Using the include() function, you would design the website so that each page included this line of PHP code: <?php include('menu.php'); ?>. This would pull the block of menu buttons into each web page. You would design the block of buttons in another file named, say, *menu.php*. To add a new button to all 40 pages, you would have to add the new button only to the one file called *menu.php*.

■ **Note** A PHP function is a tiny program that will perform a particular task. The include() function takes whatever is inside the brackets and pulls it into the page at the place where the include() function is located. PHP has two similar functions: include() and require(). They both pull a file into a page so that the file is included in the displayed page. The difference is in the way they react to a missing or faulty file. If the file to be included is missing or corrupt, include() will not halt the execution of a page. A warning will occur, but the page will continue to load. In contrast, an error will occur if require() can't find the file or the file is faulty. In this case, the page will cease executing. Use include() for anything that is not absolutely necessary for the web page to process properly. In this example, the page could still function without a proper header. But use require() for loading the details of a database because the page will be of little use if the database can't be opened. In addition, PHP also has include_once() and require_once() functions. Both functions will determine whether the file has already been included before. include_once() will not execute if the file has been included before, without complaint. require_once() will not load the file again if it has already been loaded.

The four elements to be pulled into the page are the header, the block of menu buttons, the info panel on the right side, and the footer. Included files can be any type—for instance, a *.txt* file, a *.php* file, or an *.html* file. Note, your choice of file type can affect whether the code from a file can be viewed externally. HTML files can easily be viewed within browsers. However, do not depend on a type of file ending to signal if your file should be secured. Make sure your code is in a secured folder. An include() statement can be placed anywhere within an HTML page as long as it is surrounded by the PHP tags; these start with the tag <?php and close with the tag ?>. The details of the four included external files are explained in the next section.

You might also be wondering why we don't just use a content management system (CMS), such as WordPress, to assemble and display our page. First, this is not a CMS book, and second, you are actually learning about how CMS systems work. They assemble pages in a similar way. Some CMS systems are created using PHP.

The Included Header File

Figure 2-2 shows a display of the included header file.

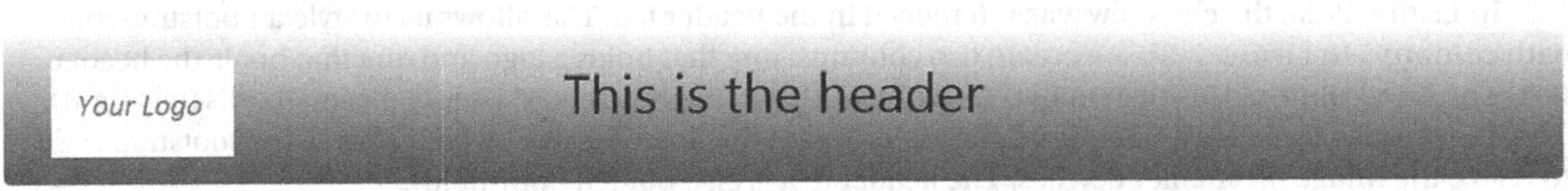

Figure 2-2. The header for the template

This header is temporary. When we create an interactive version of the template, the new header will contain an additional menu so that users can register and thereby insert their details into the simpledb database.

■ **Caution**   Don't be tempted to create the four noninteractive pages yet (*page-2.php*, *page-3.php*, *page-4.php*, and *page-5.php*) because, later in the chapter, these will require a new version of the header.

Listing 2-2a.   Header Section of Template File (template.php)

```
<!-- Header Section                                                       #1-->
<header class="jumbotron text-center row"
    style="margin-bottom:2px; background:linear-gradient(white, #0073e6); padding:20px;">
    <?php include('header-for-template.php'); ?>
</header>
```

The PHP statement in Listing 2-2a imports the contents of the *header-for-template* file into the page (code shown in Listing 2-2b). In addition, Bootstrap CSS code is imported in the head section of the template file (see the top of Listing 2-1). With Bootstrap we can reduce the amount of CSS we develop and automatically create pages that adjust to multiple screen sizes (including smartphones). The Bootstrap jumbotron class produces a large box for displaying important information (such as the header). We have also centered the text (text-center) and declared the header as a row. Bootstrap rows are controlled by grids. Each row is divided into cells to help lay out the page. This is similar to the cells and rows in a spreadsheet. We will determine the amount of cells used for each column of our header in Listing 2-2b. We have made a few adjustments to the default settings of the jumbotron by reducing the bottom margin (2px), changing the background to a gradient (white to blue), and changing the padding (20px). Listing 2-2b includes the code for the temporary header.

Listing 2-2b.   Code for the Temporary Header (header-for-template.php)

```
<div class="col-sm-2">
<img class="img-fluid float-left" src="logo.jpg" alt="Logo">
</div>
<div class="col-sm-8">
 <h1 class="font-bold">Header Goes Here</h1>
</div>
```

In Listing 2-2a, the class row was referenced in the header tag. This allows us to style a Bootstrap row with columns. In Listing 2-2b. we create two columns: one that holds a logo and one that holds the header text. The logo column uses two small cells (col-sm-2), and the header text uses eight small cells (col-sm-8). The img tag also includes an img-fluid class, along with the float-left class, which allows the Bootstrap code to resize the image on smaller devices. The header text is also bolded (font-bold).

This book assumes you have some CSS and Bootstrap programming knowledge. We will provide some links in each chapter and in the appendix to provide additional resources. However, a great method to learn is to adjust existing code to see how it affects the layout. You may want to spend a few minutes adjusting this example and the following examples to see how they will change the layout of the web page.

■ **Note** We have chosen to use Bootstrap to reduce the amount of CSS code that we have to demonstrate. Bootstrap is an open source toolkit that includes HTML, CSS, and JavaScript. This toolkit provides a responsive grid system and prebuilt CSS/JS components. With Bootstrap, the developer can spend less time on HTML, CSS, and JavaScript coding and more time on programming (with PHP).

In this book we will use Bootstrap classes to provide multiplatform formatting of our web pages. The toolkits can be directly linked online (as we have done in our examples) or downloaded from the Bootstrap website. You can adjust the default settings of many of the toolkit components using CSS. If you are not familiar with Bootstrap, we suggest you review and reference the following sites for more information:

www.getboostrap.com

https://www.w3schools.com/bootstrap/bootstrap_get_started.asp

The Included Menu File

Figure 2-3 shows the included block of menu buttons.

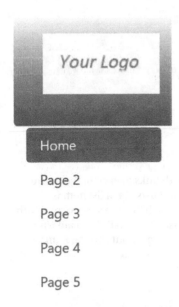

Figure 2-3. *The included menu buttons*

Listing 2-3a gives the HTML code for the menu within the template page.

Listing 2-3a. Navigation Menu of Template File (template.php)

```
<!-- Body Section                                                          #2-->
  <div class="row" style="padding-left: 0px;">
<!-- Left-side Column Menu Section -->
  <nav class="col-sm-2">
      <ul class="nav nav-pills flex-column">
        <?php include('nav.php'); ?>
      </ul>
  </nav>
```

Similar to the header, the body section of the page defines a row. With the row are three columns. The left column (col-sm-2) reserves two cells for the navigation menu. The menu will display in "pill" format (see Figure 2-3) and is flexible for different device sizes. The one PHP statement imports the *nav.php* file, which includes the actual code listing for the links (see Listing 2-3b).

Listing 2-3b. The Navigation Menu (nav.php)

```
<li class="nav-item">
        <a class="nav-link active" href="index.php">Home</a>
</li>
<li class="nav-item">
        <a class="nav-link" href="page-2.php">Page 2</a>
  <li>
  <li class="nav-item">
        <a class="nav-link" href="page-3.php">Page 3</a>
  </li>
  <li class="nav-item">
        <a class="nav-link" href="page-4.php">Page 4</a>
  </li>
  <li class="nav-item">
        <a class="nav-link" href="page-5.php">Page 5</a>
    </li>
```

The code for the navigation section (menu) includes an unordered list with links to each of the future pages of the website. This is a common practice to create menus with unordered lists. Each list item is defined with a class nav-item, which is used by Bootstrap to format the menu. Each link (<a>) is defined with a class nav-link, which formats each button for the menu. The active class is used to visually indicate which page is currently displayed (see Figure 2-3). There is also a deactive class that will gray out a menu item.

The Included Information Column

The included information column sits on the right side of the page, as shown in Figure 2-4.

This is the information column

Web design by A W West and Steve Prettyman

Figure 2-4. Information column for inclusion in the template

Listing 2-4a gives the HTML code for the information column within the template file.

Listing 2-4a. Information Column in Template File (template.php)

```
<!-- Right-side Column Content Section                                    #3-->
    <aside class="col-sm-2">
          <php include('info-col.php'); ?>
    </aside>
```

The information column reserves two small cells for display (col-sm 2). The PHP include statement pulls in the details of the information column from *info-col.php* (see Listing 2-4b).

Listing 2-4b. The Information Column Details (info-col.css)

```
<div>
<h3>This is the information column</h3>
          <p>Web design by <br>A W West and<br>Steve Prettyman</p>
</div>
```

Listing 2-4b includes the HTML code that displays information on the right side of the page. The information moves to the right side because the menu and the main section of the page (discussed soon) are defined with columns and cells first before the information column is defined.

The Included Footer File

Figure 2-5 shows the included footer.

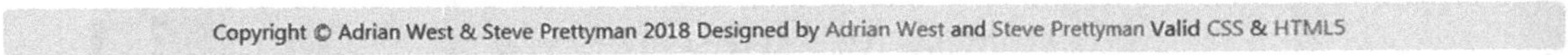

Copyright © Adrian West & Steve Prettyman 2018 Designed by Adrian West and Steve Prettyman **Valid** CSS & HTML5

Figure 2-5. The footer for inclusion in the template

Listing 2-5a gives the HTML code for the footer.

Listing 2-5a. Footer code for Template File (.php)

```
<!-- Footer Content Section                                               #4-->
<footer class="jumbotron text-center row"
style="padding-bottom:1px; padding-top:8px;">
  <?php include('footer.php'); ?>
</footer>
```

The footer is also declared as a jumbotron and a row. The text is centered (text-center). In addition, the default setting for the jumbotron is adjusted to reduce the block size to be more appropriate for a footer. The PHP code pulls in the HTML to be displayed (see Listing 2-5b).

Listing 2-5b. The Footer (footer.php)

```
<p class="h6 col-sm-12">Copyright &copy; Adrian West & Steve Prettyman 2018  Designed by
<a href="http://www.colycomputerhelp.co.uk/">Adrian West </a> and
<a href=http://www.littleoceanwaves.com>Steve Prettyman </a>  Valid
<a href="http://jigsaw.w3.org/css-validator/">CSS</a> &amp;
<a href="http://validator.w3.org/">HTML5</a></p>
```

Listing 2-5b uses the Bootstrap class h6 to determine the attributes of the font used to display the text. The paragraph tag also reserves 12 small columns (the complete width of the page) to display the footer information.

How Does the Server Process the Page?

When an HTML file is saved as a PHP file, the *.php* extension alerts the server to processes the HTML as normal but also looks out for any PHP code. The server is in HTML (copy) mode by default, and any HTML code is sent to the browser as normal. When it finds a <?php tag, the server switches to PHP (interpret) mode. Any PHP code is interpreted. The results of executing the interpreted PHP code are returned to the page, not the actual PHP code itself. It continues in this mode until it encounters the PHP closing tag ?>; it then switches back to HTML (copy) mode. This cyclic behavior continues until the end of the page of code.

The Interactive Version of the Template

In this version of the template, we will introduce interactivity by creating a new header file with an additional menu. This menu will allow users to register and enter their details into the simpledb database. It will also allow users to change their password and view the table of members.

Figure 2-6 shows the new header.

Figure 2-6. *A registration menu is added to the header*

The interactive element will be embedded in the header; therefore, the previous header is now modified to include a menu. The new header will be named *header.php*, and the code is shown in Listing 2-6.

Listing 2-6. Placing a Registration Menu in the New Header (header.php)

```
<div class="col-sm-2">
<img class="img-fluid float-left" src="logo.jpg" alt="Logo">
</div>
<div class="col-sm-8">
 <h1 class="blue-text mb-4 font-bold">Header Goes Here</h1>
 </div>
    <nav class="col-sm-2">
        <div class="btn-group-vertical btn-group-sm" role="group" aria-label="Button Group">
 <button type="button" class="btn btn-secondary" onclick="location.href = 'register-page.php'" >
        Register</button>
 <button type="button" class="btn btn-secondary" onclick="location.href = 'register-view_
users-page.php'">
            View Users</button>
<button type="button" class="btn btn-secondary" onclick="location.href = 'register-password.
php'" >
            New Password</button>
</div>
    </nav>
```

In this example, a Bootstrap vertical button group has been created (btn-group-vertical) with small buttons (btn-group-sm). Each button within the group is defined with the HTML button tag and the Bootstrap btn and btn-secondary classes. The on-click attribute is used to call the page requested by the user. In later chapters, we will also see examples of using the Bootstrap navbar to create a horizontal bar of buttons below a header.

In the template file, we will need to swap the previous included header for the new header. The new template page will be named *index.php*, and it will now have two blocks of menu buttons, as shown in Figure 2-7.

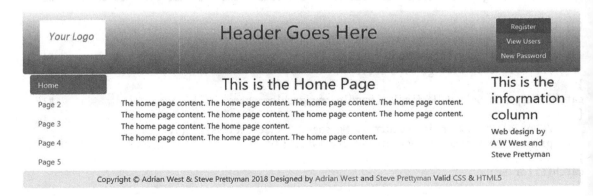

Figure 2-7. *The new home page template with two menus*

The only difference in the code between the old template and the new index file is the new header reference. The changes are shown in the following snippet of code in Listing 2-7. The complete code is contained in the *index.php* file that can be downloaded from the Apress.com website.

Listing 2-7. Including the New Header in the Home Page (index.php)

```
<!-- Header Section -->
<header class="jumbotron text-center row"
    style="margin-bottom:2px; background:linear-gradient(white, #0073e6); padding:20px;">
    <?php include('header-for-template.php'); ?>
</header>
```

Now you can create the four ordinary website pages, using the new template (*index.php*); save four copies of the file, naming the copies *page-2.php*, *page-3.php*, *page-4.php*, and *page-5.php*. Change the content of those pages a little so that they differ from *index.php* and to indicate which page the user is viewing. You might consider changing the active nav-item (button) to the page that is currently being viewed. The code shown previously sets the Home page navigation button to active.

Connecting to the Database

Before we can do anything in the database, we must connect to it. This is achieved by creating a connection file that we will call *mysqli_connect.php*. The code for the connection file is given in the next snippet.

Listing for the Snippet of Code That Connects to the Database (mysqli_connect.php)

```
<?php
// This file provides the information for accessing the database.and connecting to MySQL.
// First, we define the constants:                                            #1
Define ('DB_USER', 'horatio'); // or whatever userid you created
Define ('DB_PASSWORD', 'Hmsv1ct0ry'); // or whatever password you created
Define ('DB_HOST', 'localhost');
Define ('DB_NAME', 'simpledb');

// Next we assign the database connection to a variable that we will call $dbcon:    #2
try
{
    $dbcon = new mysqli(DB_HOST, DB_USER, DB_PASSWORD, DB_NAME);
    mysqli_set_charset($dbcon, 'utf8'); //                                       #4
    // more code will go here later
}
catch(Exception $e) // We finally handle any problems here                       #3
{
    // print "An Exception occurred. Message: " . $e->getMessage();
    print "The system is busy please try later";
}
catch(Error $e)
{
    //print "An Error occurred. Message: " . $e->getMessage();
    print "The system is busy please try again later.";
}
?>
```

Save the file as *mysqli_connect.php*, and place it in the XAMPP *htdocs* or the easyPHP *eds-www* folder.

■ **Note**   When a database is set up on a remote host, this file is placed one level above the root folder for security. Not protecting this file can lead to DOS attacks. Leaving this file located in a public area of the web server will allow anyone to use the code to access the database. Place the file one level above the program code, in an area secured by the web server (or in another secured folder). Use a require statement similar to require('../mysqlconnect.php'); to access your connection information. The examples in this book access the connection file from the same location as the code files. This is done for easy testing but should not be done in a live environment on a publicly accessible web server.

In this book the catch messages used are for debugging. Live sites should not display error messages to the user. A generic message (as shown in the previous listing) should be displayed to the user. Users will be much more willing to come back to a site that is currently "busy" than a site that is displaying error messages. These error messages can also be a security breach by possibility displaying code lines that may cause errors.

Explanation of the Code

The *mysqli_connect.php* file contains some code conventions that you may not be familiar with, so let's briefly run through them here.

Single-line comments begin with a double forward slash or with a hash symbol—for example:

```
// more code will go here later
# more code will go here later
```

Constants are fixed definitions created by using the keyword DEFINE.

```
DEFINE ('DB_USER', 'horatio');
```

Variables like $dbcon are memory storage devices for containing information that can be made to vary; they are preceded by a dollar symbol. Variables are created using the following format: $var = some_information. The equal sign is called an *assignment operator*; it assigns what is on the right side of the equal sign to the variable on the left side. The example assigns some information to the variable $var.

We will now examine the code using the line numbers as references.

```
// First, we define the constants:                                    #1
Define ('DB_USER', 'horatio'); // or whatever userid you created
Define ('DB_PASSWORD', 'Hmsv1ct0ry'); // or whatever password you created
Define ('DB_HOST', 'localhost');
Define ('DB_NAME', 'simpledb');
```

As a convention, not a rule, programmers create constant names with all capital letters. This helps to identify which items are constants (which cannot be changed while the program is running) and which items are variables (can be changed while the program is running). In PHP, we can also tell that an item is a variable if it has the dollar sign as the first character. It is good practice to place your DEFINE code lines near the top of your program code. This makes it easy to find when you must change a value. For example, if you need to change a tax rate.

■ **Note** If you did not create a user ID and password for the simpledb database, the user ID will be root, and the password will be "" (two quotes with no spaces in between them).

```
// Next we assign the database connection to a variable that we will call $dbcon:      #2
try
{
        $dbcon = new mysqli(DB_HOST, DB_USER, DB_PASSWORD, DB_NAME);
        // more code will go here later
}
```

The text following the dollar sign can be anything that is relevant to the information held in the memory. For instance, the variable for connecting to our database in the listing is named $dbcon. This was chosen to signify a connection to a database; it could be $connect_db or any other text that indicates a connection to the database. Some programmers prefer to use camel case ($dbCon), where the first word is lowercase and any words that follow begin with an uppercase letter. Others keep all words lowercase, and some even use an underscore (_) between the words ($db_con). It does not matter what style you use. Just be consistent and name your variables in the same style.

We use the host, username, password, and database name that we defined earlier to connect to the database.

The try block (everything between the { } is considered to be in a block) will "throw" any problems (errors or exceptions) into a catch block for the program to handle.

```
catch(Exception $e) // We finally handle any problems here                            #3
{
        //print "An Exception occurred. Message: " . $e->getMessage();
        print "The system is busy please try later";
}
catch(Error $e)
{
        //print "An Error occurred. Message: " . $e->getMessage();
        print "The system is busy please try again later.";
}
```

For testing purposes, sometimes we will display the error and exception messages that may occur. In production, we would replace the print statements with a generic message to the user, such as "System currently not available, please try later." Allowing users to see error messages gives them a feeling that the design of your website is poor, is vulnerable, and can crash frequently. Users who see error messages on websites usually leave the site and do not return. However, in today's environment, it is not unusual to see a generic "System currently busy or not available" type message. Many sites now limit the number of users to keep from hackers trying to flood and crash the site.

It is also a major security breach to let users see any error messages. These messages may reveal code that provides actual locations of items, such as the database itself. This information, along with a timestamp, should be passed to a log file to assist the system administrator.

You may see example code on the Internet or older books with the PHP database code that uses OR die. This has been a PHP standard since the beginning of time. However, with the release of PHP 7, the designers are encouraging all developers to use the industry-standard try/catch format. Also, when using OR die, you cannot capture all exceptions and errors. With try/catch, you can now do so. In PHP 7, the developer is encouraged to use the mysqli (instead of mysql) method to connect and access databases. It is considered the most secure method of access.

We have changed the HTML-encoded language from the default to utf-8 as suggested in Listing 2-8. The connection to the database must also include code that indicates the correct encoded language. The type of encoded language used on the HTML page must match the encoded language used in the database table. Inconsistent matches can cause problems, including invalid search results.

```
mysqli_set_charset($dbcon, 'utf8');                                                #4
```

(Note that the format is different from the code set in an HTML document because it does not include the hyphen as in utf-8.)

Next, we need some pages for the header's new menu to call. These pages will contain the interactive features. The pages will allow users to register, allow users to view a table of the registered persons, and permit a password to be changed.

The Registration Page

■ **Caution**   When you finally migrate a database to a remote host, be sure to comply with the Data Protection Act for your territory or country, and state clearly on the registration page that the user's personal details will not be shared or sold to other organizations. The rules covering the protection of data vary from country to country, and it is essential that you read them and comply with them. Usually, any person within an organization who can access users' details must sign a document agreeing never to share personal information. An annual registration fee might be required to the government organization that regulates the data protection law. These precautions do not apply to experimental databases using fictitious data such as those described in this book.

The registration page allows users to enter their personal details directly into a table in the database. Figure 2-8 shows the interface.

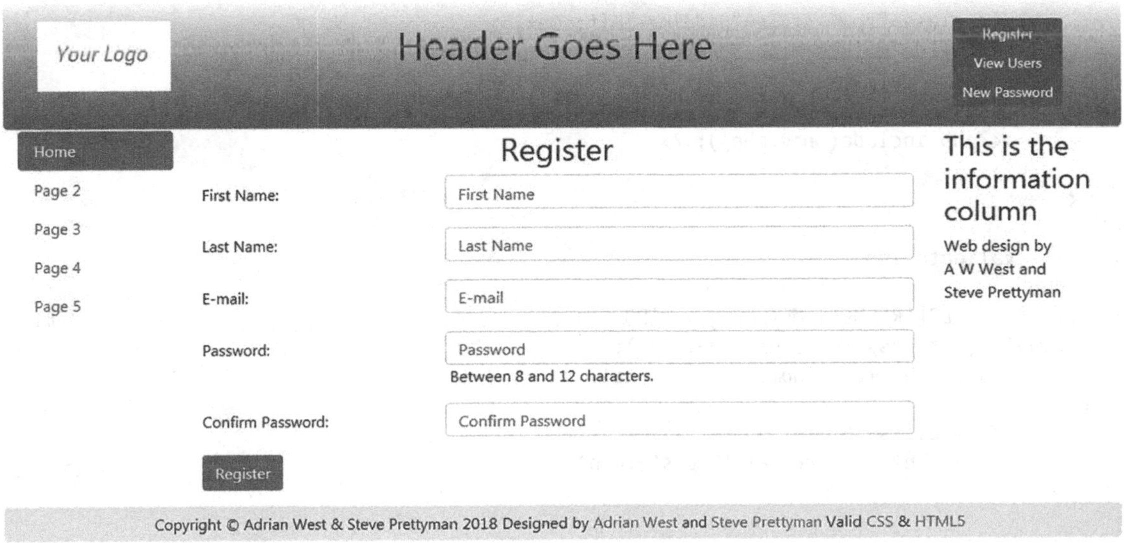

Figure 2-8. The registration page

When the user clicks the Register menu button on the new header, the page shown in Figure 2-8 is displayed. If the user fills out the form correctly and then clicks the Register button (below the entry fields), the user's entries are entered in the users table in the database. A "thank you" page is then displayed.

Note that the Register and New Password buttons on the registration page are now redundant because the user has already accessed the registration page. Obviously, the user does not yet have a password to change. The redundant buttons will be left in place for all the examples in this chapter to avoid complicating the instructions. The redundant buttons will be removed or changed in the next two chapters.

Now we will examine the code for the entire registration page.

Listing 2-8a. Creating the Registration Page (register-page.php)

```
<!DOCTYPE html>
<html lang="en">
<head>
  <title>Template for an interactive web page</title>
  <meta charset="utf-8">
  <meta name="viewport" content="width=device-width, initial-scale=1, shrink-to-fit=no">
  <!-- Bootstrap CSS File -->
  <link rel="stylesheet"
  href="https://stackpath.bootstrapcdn.com/bootstrap/4.1.0/css/bootstrap.min.css"
  integrity="sha384-9gVQ4dYFwwWSjIDZnLEWnxCjeSWFphJiwGPXr1jddIhOegiu1FwO5qRGvFXO4JZ4"
  crossorigin="anonymous">
<script src="verify.js"></script>
</head>
<body>
    <div class="container" style="margin-top:30px">
    <!-- Header Section -->
    <header class="jumbotron text-center row"
        style="margin-bottom:2px; background:linear-gradient(white, #0073e6); padding:20px;">
        <?php include('header.php'); ?>
    </header>
    <!-- Body Section -->
        <div class="row" style="padding-left: 0px;">
    <!-- Left-side Column Menu Section -->
     <nav class="col-sm-2">
      <ul class="nav nav-pills flex-column">
          <?php include('nav.php'); ?>
      </ul>
     </nav>


     <!-- Validate Input -->
     <?php
     if ($_SERVER['REQUEST_METHOD'] == 'POST') {                              //#1
       require('process-register-page.php');
     } // End of the main Submit conditional.
     ?>
     <div class="col-sm-8">
       <h2 class="h2 text-center">Register</h2>
```

48

```
<form action="register-page.php" method="post" onsubmit="return checked(); >        <!-- #2 -->
  <div class="form-group row">

<label for="first_name" class="col-sm-4 col-form-label">First Name:</label>
    <div class="col-sm-8">
      <input type="text" class="form-control" id="first_name" name="first_name"
        placeholder="First Name" maxlength="30" required
        value="<?php if (isset($_POST['first_name'])) echo $_POST['first_name']; ?>" >
    </div>
  </div>

  <div class="form-group row">
    <label for="last_name" class="col-sm-4 col-form-label">Last Name:</label>
    <div class="col-sm-8">
      <input type="text" class="form-control" id="last_name" name="last_name"
        placeholder="Last Name" maxlength="40" required
        value="<?php if (isset($_POST['last_name'])) echo $_POST['last_name']; ?>">
    </div>
  </div>

<div class="form-group row">
    <label for="email" class="col-sm-4 col-form-label">E-mail:</label>
    <div class="col-sm-8">
      <input type="email" class="form-control" id="email" name="email"
        placeholder="E-mail" maxlength="60" required
        value="<?php if (isset($_POST['email'])) echo $_POST['email']; ?>">
    </div>
  </div>

<div class="form-group row">
    <label for="password1" class="col-sm-4 col-form-label">Password:</label>
    <div class="col-sm-8">
      <input type="password" class="form-control" id="password1" name="password1"
        placeholder="Password" minlength="8" maxlength="12"
        required value="<?php if (isset($_POST['password1'])) echo $_POST['password1']; ?>">
      <span id='message'>Between 8 and 12 characters.</span>
    </div>

<div class="form-group row">
    <label for="password2" class="col-sm-4 col-form-label">Confirm Password:</label>
    <div class="col-sm-8">
      <input type="password" class="form-control" id="password2" name="password2"
        placeholder="Confirm Password" minlength="8" maxlength="12" required
        value="<?php if (isset($_POST['password2'])) echo $_POST['password2']; ?>">
    </div>
  </div>
```

```
<div class="form-group row">
    <div class="col-sm-12">
        <input id="submit" class="btn btn-primary" type="submit" name="submit"
        value="Register">
    </div>
 </div>
</form>
</div>


!-- Right-side Column Content Section                                          #3 -->
<?php
if(!isset($errorstring)) {
        echo '<aside class="col-sm-2">';
        include('info-col.php');
        echo '</aside>';
        echo '</div>';
        echo '<footer class="jumbotron text-center row col-sm-14"
                style="padding-bottom:1px; padding-top:8px;">';
 }
 else
 {
        echo '<footer class="jumbotron text-center col-sm-12"
        style="padding-bottom:1px; padding-top:8px;">';
 }
  include('footer.php');
 ?>
</div>
</body>
</html>
```

Explanation of the Code

The basic structure of the code is the same as the index file. The differences occur in the body, specifically in the center column that now contains the form for the user to register.

```
<?php
 if ($_SERVER['REQUEST_METHOD'] == 'POST') {                                    //#1
  require('process-register-page.php');
 } // End of the main Submit conditional.
?>
```

In PHP, forms can be processed either by the form submit attribute passing the information to a separate PHP program or by including PHP code within the same file as the form. In this example, we technically have included the PHP code in the same file, because we are pulling in the code from the process-register-page file. We also know this because the action attribute of the form is calling the file itself (form action="register-page.php") instead of another file (see partial listing next). If the submit button has been clicked, the PHP code in the process register file is executed. If the user has not clicked the submit button (probably the first time the page has been displayed), the form is shown. Let's take a look at the form itself.

```
<form action="register-page.php" method="post" onsubmit="return checked();>        <!-- #2 -->
    <div class="form-group row">

<label for="first_name" class="col-sm-4 col-form-label">First Name:</label>
    <div class="col-sm-8">
        <input type="text" class="form-control" id="first_name" name="first_name"
            placeholder="First Name" maxlength="30" required
            value="<?php if (isset($_POST['first_name'])) echo $_POST['first_name']; ?>" >
    </div>
    </div>
```

The register-page submits to itself when the user clicks the submit button. When submitted, the form calls the JavaScript function checked() to verify the passwords. The code for this function is listed here:

```
function checked() {
    if (document.getElementById('password1').value ==
        document.getElementById('password2').value) {
        document.getElementById('message').style.color = 'green';
        document.getElementById('message').innerHTML = 'Passwords match';
            return true;
    } else {
        document.getElementById('message').style.color = 'red';
        document.getElementById('message').innerHTML = 'Passwords do not match';
            return false;
    }
}
```

This code was imported from the verify.js program along with the Bootstrap CSS code. If the passwords match, the code is submitted. If the passwords do not match, an error message is displayed, allowing the user to correct the problem.

The PHP code, which we will see next, will verify the information the user has provided and insert it into the database. There is a lot that happens within each element (such as the first_name textbox) of the form. The first_name textbox has a label attached that uses four small Boostrap grid cells. The textbox uses eight small grid cells. The form and textboxes are formatted by Boostrap using the form-control class. The maximum length of a first name that can be entered by the user is 30 characters. The required attribute tells HTML that the user must enter information into the textbox before the information will be submitted.

The one line of PHP code, marked as #2, creates a sticky element that saves any entries made by the user. This allows the page to retain any entries when it is reloaded. Every time the user clicks the submit button, the page is reloaded. Normally this would wipe out any entries since HTML pages do not retain information (disconnected data). When the user submits the form, the information is passed to the server via the POST method. We can retrieve any element that has been passed by the form using the $_POST method and the name of the element ($_POST['first_name']). The PHP code uses isset to determine whether there was an entry in the first_name textbox. If there was an entry, the value that was passed is glued back into the textbox. This allows the user to see what they entered originally and to respond to any error messages and correct problems without having to completely retype the entries. The other textboxes work in a similar way.

■ **Note** Displaying information from $_POST directly to a web page can open a risk that hackers can use to manipulate web pages, attempt CSRF/XSS attacks, and manipulate the data in databases. As the chapters progress, the data sanitation and security will increase to reduce the chances of security breaches. The code in this chapter is not meant to be used on a live site.

```php
!-- Right-side Column Content Section                                          #3 -->
<?php
if(!isset($errorstring)) {
        echo '<aside class="col-sm-2">';
        include('info-col.php');
        echo '</aside>';
        echo '</div>';
        echo '<footer class="jumbotron text-center row col-sm-14"
                style="padding-bottom:1px; padding-top:8px;">';
}
 else
 {
        echo '<footer class="jumbotron text-center col-sm-12"
        style="padding-bottom:1px; padding-top:8px;">';
}
  include('footer.php');
```

Error message(s) will be produced if the information entered does not validate. As you will see in the PHP code explained soon, most errors messages are placed in the variable $errorstring. If this variable exists, one or more errors exist. When this occurs, the right column (see #3 in the previous code) is not displayed to provide space for the error message(s). The column size of the footer is also slightly adjusted.

Now let's look at the PHP code that validates the information the user provided.

Listing 2-8b. Validating the Registration Page (process-register-page.php)

```php
<?php
// This script is a query that INSERTs a record in the users table.
// Check that form has been submitted:
        $errors = array(); // Initialize an error array.              #1
        // Check for a first name:                                    #2
        $first_name = trim($_POST['first_name']);
        if (empty($first_name)) {
                $errors[] = 'You forgot to enter your first name.';
        }
                // Check for a last name:
        $last_name = trim($_POST['last_name']);
        if (empty($last_name)) {
                $errors[] = 'You forgot to enter your last name.';
        }
        // Check for an email address:
        $email = trim($_POST['email']);
        if (empty($email)) {
                $errors[] = 'You forgot to enter your email address.';
        }
```

```php
        // Check for a password and match against the confirmed password:              #3
        $password1 - trim($_POST['password1']);
        $password2 = trim($_POST['password2']);
        if (!empty($password1)) {
                if ($password1 !== $password2) {
                        $errors[] = 'Your two passwords did not match.';
                }
        } else {
                $errors[] = 'You forgot to enter your password.';
        }           if (empty($errors)) { // If everything's OK.                       #4
try {

        // Register the user in the database...
        // Hash password current 60 characters but can increase
                $hashed_passcode = password_hash($password1, PASSWORD_DEFAULT);        //#5
                require ('mysqli_connect.php'); // Connect to the db.                  //#6
        // Make the query:                                                            #7
        $query = "INSERT INTO users (userid, first_name, last_name, email, password,
        registration_date) ";
                $query .="VALUES(' ', ?, ?, ?, ?, NOW() )";                           //#8
        $q = mysqli_stmt_init($dbcon);                                                //#9
        mysqli_stmt_prepare($q, $query);
        // use prepared statement to ensure that only text is inserted
        // bind fields to SQL Statement
        mysqli_stmt_bind_param($q, 'ssss', $first_name, $last_name, $email, $hashed_passcode);
        // execute query
        mysqli_stmt_execute($q);
        if (mysqli_stmt_affected_rows($q) == 1) { // One record inserted              #10
                header ("location: register-thanks.php");
                exit();
                } else { // If it did not run OK.
                // Public message:
                        $errorstring = "<p class='text-center col-sm-8'
                                style-'color:red'>";
                        $errorstring .= "System Error<br />You could not be registered due ";
                        $errorstring .= "to a system error. We apologize for any
                        inconvenience.</p>";
                        echo "<p class=' text-center col-sm-2'
                        style='color:red'>$errorstring</p>";
                // Debugging message below do not use in production
                //echo '<p>' . mysqli_error($dbcon) . '<br><br>Query: ' . $query . '</p>';
                        mysqli_close($dbcon); // Close the database connection.
                // include footer then close program to stop execution
                        echo '<footer class="jumbotron text-center col-sm-12"
                                style="padding-bottom:1px; padding-top:8px;">
                                        include("footer.php");
                                </footer>';
                        exit();
        }
}
```

```
catch(Exception $e) // We finally handle any problems here                    #11
{
  // print "An Exception occurred. Message: " . $e->getMessage();
  print "The system is busy please try later";
}
catch(Error $e)
{
  //print "An Error occurred. Message: " . $e->getMessage();
  print "The system is busy please try again later.";
}
    } else { // Report the errors.                                            #12
        $errorstring = "Error! The following error(s) occurred:<br>";
        foreach ($errors as $msg) { // Print each error.
            $errorstring .= " - $msg<br>\n";
        }
        $errorstring .= "Please try again.<br>";
        echo "<p class=' text-center col-sm-2' style='color:red'>$errorstring</p>";
    }// End of if (empty($errors)) IF.
?>
```

■ **Note** At this point, beginners may be mystified because they are more familiar with code that steps through a page from top to bottom. In the preceding example of interactive code, the beginner would expect the form fields to be at the top of the page of code. In fact, they come last in the listing (after the PHP code that has been imported via the require method). There is a main if statement (if ($_SERVER['REQUEST_METHOD'] == 'POST') {) that controls the flow of the program. If the user has already been to the page and clicked the submit button, the if statement is true, and the PHP code is executed (from the included file; process_register_page.php in the previous example). If this is the first time the user has visited the page, the if statement is false. Thus, the HTML code within the else part of the statement is executed. HTML5 code will also do some limited verification of information entered by the user before the form submitted and the PHP code can be executed. In addition, the PHP code will verify that what was received from the web page is "good," verified, and sanitized information.

It may seem that we are duplicating effort by verifying the information twice. However, using HTML5 (and maybe some JavaScript) to do a first attempt to verify information reduces server calls and speeds up the verification process. We still need to verify the information again on the server because it can be manipulated, intentionally or not, before it arrives.

Explanation of the Code

Many of the PHP statements were explained by comments in the listings, but some items need further comment. The PHP code might look horribly complicated, but we will break it apart into smaller pieces to help you understand it. Let's begin now.

```
$errors = array(); // Initialize an error array.                              #1
```

An array is a method to store multiple items of similar information into one storage location. In our example, we are using the array to store any error messages. The previous line initiates the array and gives it the name $errors. Technically, $errors is now pointing to an area in memory that has been reserved for the array. Some additional information on arrays and their use is given at the end of this chapter and in the appendix.

```
// Check for a first name:                                              #2
$first_name = trim($first_name);
if (empty($first_name)) {
        $errors[] = 'You forgot to enter your first name.';
}
```

An element in a global variable such as $_POST['first_name'] is always enclosed in square brackets. This is a feature of super global variables. Technically everything that is passed from our form to the PHP code is passed into a post array (the reason we used square brackets instead of round ones). We then use the POST super global statements to retrieve what we want from the array.

The code beginning with $first_name = trim is an instruction to trim (remove) any spaces or other white spaces from the beginning and end of the user's first_name entry. Spaces at the beginning and end of input data are unwanted characters. The trimmed first_name is then assigned to the variable $first_name. We should do additional removal of invalid characters for strong security. However, for now, let's keep it as simple as possible. The format shown earlier is also used for the last name and e-mail.

■ **Note**   Any variable taking the $_POST[ ] format, such as $_POST['first_name'], is a global variable—it is accessible to that page on the website. Ordinary variables have the format $first_name, and they can be accessed only by loading the page in which they appear. $_POST will pull the information passed from the HTML form via a post array that has been automatically populated when the user clicked the submit button. The variable name contained in the square brackets (first_name) must match the NAME parameter of the HTML input statement exactly.

```
// Check for a password and match against the confirmed password:       #3
$password1 = trim($_POST['password1']);
$password2 = trim($_POST['password2']);
if (!empty($password1)) {
        if ($password1 !== $password2) {
                $errors[] = 'Your two password did not match.';
        }
} else {
        $errors[] = 'You forgot to enter your password.';
}
```

Both of the new passwords are trimmed of unnecessary spaces. If password1 is not empty (!empty), then the comparison of the two new passwords is performed. The !== (one ! and two =) symbols determine whether the passwords entered in the form are the same. This format of the not equals ensures that the uppercase and lowercase are the same. It also ensures that the data types (string compared to integer) are the same. If the passwords are not the same, an error message is placed in the error array to be displayed later.

```
if (empty($errors)) { // If everything's OK.                            #4
```

This block of code is in the successful section. This section starts the registration process when all the fields have been filled out correctly—in which case the $errors array is empty. The line is saying "Because there are no errors, we can connect to the database and insert the user's data."

```
$hashed_passcode = password_hash($password, PASSWORD_DEFAULT);                        //#5
```

We must make sure that any passwords are as secure as possible. The previous code uses the PHP password hashing method to convert the password entered by the user into a secure password. PASSWORD_ DEFAULT will always contain the most current PHP hashing code available. In the database table we have set the password field to hold 60 characters. In the future, new hashing techniques might require you to increase the size of this field.

```
require ('mysqli_connect.php'); // Connect to the db.                                 //#6
```

In this line, the database connection is made with require() instead of include() so that the script will run if the connection is made, but it will not run if no connection is available. This is because there is no point continuing if the database is not accessible because data cannot be inserted into its table. We use require() when something vital is to be included. We could have used require_once here since we want to pull in this code only one time to establish the connection to the database.

```
// Make the query:                                                                    #7
$query = "INSERT INTO users (userid, first_name, last_name, email, password,
registration_date) ";
```

If a successful connection to the database is achieved, this line prepares the data for entry into the table called *users*. The word *query* sometimes means "query," but most often it means "Do something." In this case, it means "Insert a new record using the following data...." The line is saying "Insert into the table named *users*, under the column headings labeled userid, first_name, and so on...." The query is assigned to a variable $query. Line #7 and line #8 are, in fact, SQL prepared queries. This demonstrates how well HTML, PHP, and SQL work together.

```
$query .="VALUES(' ', ?, ?, ?, ?, NOW() )";                                          //#8
```

This piece of SQL code provides a holding place for the data to be entered. We are using a prepared statement because it will never execute data that has been bound to the locations (where the ? marks exist). This keeps hackers from being able to insert additional SQL statements into our SQL string in an attempt to destroy our data. Note that the first value is deliberately empty (quotes with an empty space in between) because it is the field that is automatically incremented and entered by the MySQL or MariaDB database management system, not by the user. The NOW function automatically places the data and time into the registration_date column in the database table.

```
$q = mysqli_stmt_init($dbcon);                                                        //#9
mysqli_stmt_prepare($q, $query);
// use prepared statement to ensure that only text is inserted
// bind fields to SQL Statement
mysqli_stmt_bind_param($q, 'ssss', $first_name, $last_name, $email, $hashed_passcode);
// param must include four variables to match the four s parameters
// execute query
mysqli_stmt_execute($q);
```

The connection string from the previously included file (*mysqli_connect.php*) is attached to mysqli and can be referenced with the $q variable. The $query string is then declared as a prepared statement (which indicates that variables will be inserted into the code) and is associated with the database connection string. The variables ($first_name, $last_name, $email, $hashed_passcode) are attached to the prepared SQL statement. Note the s symbol indicates each individual variable contains a string. To indicate numeric information, you can use i (integer) or d (double). b is also available for BLOB. The statement is then executed against the database table.

```
if (mysqli_stmt_affected_rows($q) == 1) { // One record inserted                          #10
    header ("location: register-thanks.php");
    exit();
```

If the operation was a success, the database will be closed. Then the header method will replace the current registration page with a "thank you" page. The header method produces an HTML Get message to request the page. The exit command will close down the current page since it is no longer in use.

```
catch(Exception $e) // We finally handle any problems here                                 #11
  {
    // print "An Exception occurred. Message: " . $e->getMessage();
    print "The system is busy please try later";
  }
  catch(Error $e)
  {
    //print "An Error occurred. Message: " . $e->getMessage();
    print "The system is busy please try again later.";
  }
```

If there is an error in executing the SQL commands or some other error or exception, the flow of the code will jump into the catch blocks to handle the problem. As mentioned, for testing we can display our errors, but when we switch to production, we will display a generic "System currently not available" message and log the problems in an error log.

```
} else { // Report the errors.                                                            #12

              $errorstring = "Error! The following error(s) occurred:<br>";
              foreach ($errors as $msg) { // Print each error.
                      $errorstring .= " - $msg<br>\n";
              }
              $errorstring .= "Please try again.<br>";
              echo "<p class='text-center col-sm-2' style='color:red'>$errorstring;</p>";
              }// End of if (empty($errors)) IF.
```

If there are user errors (invalid entries), messages will exist in the $error array. The else structure is implemented when there are entries in the array. The foreach loop cycles through the $errors array, and if it finds any error messages, it is then displayed (echoed) on the screen (foreach is one word without a space).

The $errorstring variable is checked in the HTML code to determine whether to display the right column. If there are errors, the right column is not displayed to make room for the error messages.

You might be wondering why we are creating PHP code that does a similar validation to the HTML5 code shown. PHP code is interpreted and executed on the server. HTML code is executed in the browser. Even if the code is validated in the browser, it might get corrupted on its path to the server PHP program. You should validate with HTML (and JavaScript) for quicker validation and response to the user. It also cuts down on server calls.

The PHP Keyword echo

The keyword echo appears in many places in the previous code. It is the PHP way of telling a browser to "Display something on the screen." Some designers use the alternative keyword print, but this book will usually use echo because we have found that beginners confuse this with the command for sending something to an inkjet or laser printer; hard-copy printing is something that PHP cannot do.

■ **Note** Any HTML code that you want can be placed in an echo statement. The echo writes the content into the HTML document (virtually, not literally) so that it can be displayed in a browser.

Beginners can be puzzled by the behavior of echo when a line break is required. For instance, the following code displays no line space:

```
echo "I found that PHP ";
echo "was much easier to learn than Perl";
```

Browsers display this as follows:
I found that PHP was much easier to learn than Perl
To push the second line down, you must insert the line-break tag, <br>, as follows:

```
echo "I found that PHP<br>";
echo "was much easier to learn than Perl";
```

Browsers display this as follows:
I found that PHP was much easier to learn than Perl

The "Thank You" Page

Figure 2-9 shows the "thank you" page.

Figure 2-9. The "thank you" page

The registration page calls up the "thank you" page with the PHP header statement. You will find this in the successful section of the registration page's code. For convenience, we repeat it here:

```
$dbcon->close();
header ("location: register-thanks.php");
exit();
```

Listing 2-9 shows the entire "thank you" page code.

Listing 2-9. Creating the "Thank You" Page (register-thanks.php)

```
<!DOCTYPE html>
<html lang="en">
<head>
    <title>Template for an interactive web page</title>
    <meta charset="utf-8">
    <meta name="viewport" content="width=device-width, initial-scale=1, shrink-to-fit=no">
    <!-- Bootstrap CSS File -->
    <link rel="stylesheet"
    href="https://stackpath.bootstrapcdn.com/bootstrap/4.1.0/css/bootstrap.min.css"
    integrity="sha384-9gVQ4dYFwwWSjIDZnLEWnxCjeSWFphJiwGPXr1jddIhOegiu1FwO5qRGvFXOdJZ4"
    crossorigin="anonymous">
</head>
<body>
<div class="container" style="margin-top:30px">
<!-- Header Section -->
<header class="jumbotron text-center row"
style="margin-bottom:2px; background:linear-gradient(white, #0073e6); padding:20px;">
    <?php include('header.php'); ?>
</header>
<!-- Body Section -->
    <div class="row" style="padding-left: 0px;">
<!-- Left-side Column Menu Section -->
    <nav class="col-sm-2">
        <ul class="nav nav-pills flex-column">
            <?php include('nav.php'); ?>
        </ul>
    </nav>
<!-- Center Column Content Section -->
    <div class="col-sm-8 text-center">
        <h2>Thank you for registering</h2>
        On the Home Page, you will now be able to login and add new quotes to the message board.
<!-- login does not yet work, nut will in the next chapter -->
    </div>
<!-- Right-side Column Content Section -->
        <aside class="col-sm-2">
            <?php include('info-col.php'); ?>
        </aside>
    </div>
<!-- Footer Content Section -->
        <footer class="jumbotron text-center row"
            style="padding-bottom:1px; padding-top:8px;">
```

```
        <?php include('footer.php'); ?>
      </footer>
</div>
</body>
</html>
```

As you can see, the page was created from the template with just a few changes. This keeps the consistency that should occur with a website. We will now look at what happens when invalid information is received at the server. We will use an array to display error messages.

Displaying Error Messages That Are Collected in an Array

If invalid information (empty values) are received in all the fields on the server, multiple errors will be created. The corresponding error messages are inserted into the errors array. These are then displayed so that the user is aware of the situation. It would be annoying if only the first error was shown and then, after clicking the Register button a second time, the second error was displayed, and so on.

Figure 2-10 shows an example of an error that would be displayed if this situation occurs.

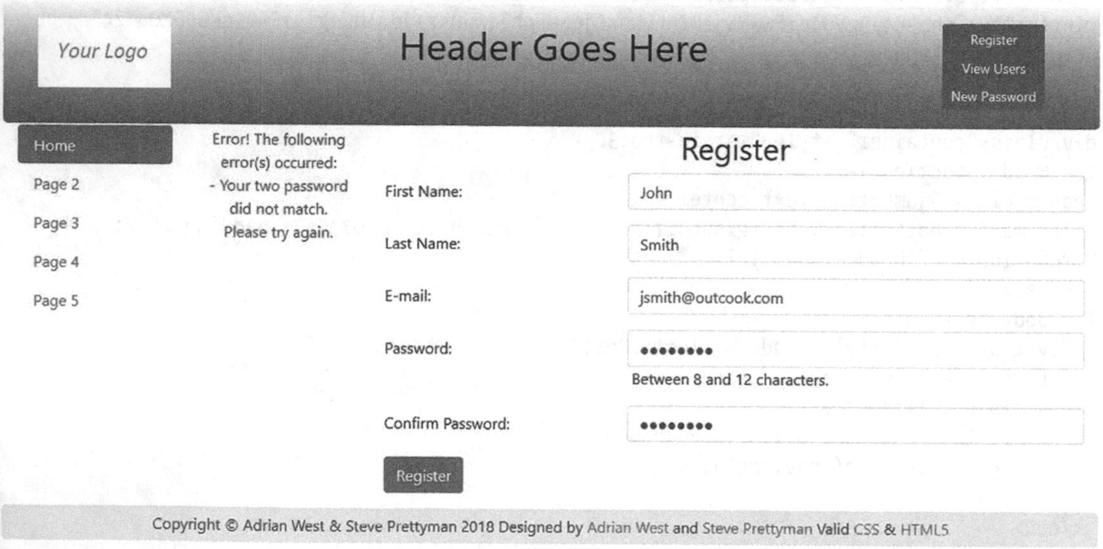

Figure 2-10. *The errors displayed if the user failed to enter any data*

The errors are displayed on the Registration page. As mentioned previously, the right column is removed when user errors occur to provide an area to display the messages. Errors might indicate that somehow the data was corrupted between the browser and the server. If the user enters incorrect information and hits the submit button, the HTML5 and JavaScript code will handle most of the validation situations and display error messages. If you want to test more server error messages, remove the required attributes from each of the HTML textboxes.

Hashing the Password

All passwords must be hashed to keep hackers from discovering them. Starting with PHP 5.5, the developers have created a new password hashing (encoding) method. This method is deemed safe and is one of the best ways to hash passwords. The format is as follows:

```
$hashedPassword = password_hash($password1, PASSWORD_DEFAULT);
```

In this example, $password1 is the unhashed version of the password. PASSWORD_DEFAULT is a PHP constant. As security changes, the PHP developers plan to keep the coding format the same and change the PHP constant to represent any new hashing schemes. The password_hash method will convert the password entered by the user into a secured hashed password that can then be saved in a database table. We will discover later that we must use the password_verify method to determine whether a user entered password will match a hashed password stored in the database.

Viewing Members' Records

When a user has registered, the website administrator can use phpMyAdmin to view the table and its entries. Let's suppose a user registered on April 26, 2018, and they entered the following information:

First name: Steve Last name: Johnson, Email: sjohnson@sjohnson.com, and Password: aaaaaaaa

phpMyAdmin will allow you to view each record in the user table. Access phpMyAdmin, select the simpledb database, click the users table, and then click the Browse tab. Figure 2-11 shows Steve Johnson's entries.

	userId	first_name	last_name	email	password	registration_date
☐ ✐ Edit ⁛⁞ Copy ◎ Delete	1	Steve	Johnson	sjohnson@sjohnson.com	$2y$10$lEmRKPYfu/Nb6ECtbmp7YOuIZeZDYuCnZKRmEBnQ6nR...	2018-04-26 15:11:58

Figure 2-11. Viewing a record in phpMyAdmin

Note that the password aaaaaaaa is hashed as $2y$10$lEmRKPYfu/Nb6ECtbmp7YOuIZeZDYuCn ZKRmEBnQ6nRHDKJIIdEgMK.

Often website designers and database administrators who do not have access to phpMyAdmin may also need to view a table of database entries created by all the registered users. The next example provides the information for doing this.

The View Users Page

When the View Users button is clicked, a table of registered users is displayed, as shown in Figure 2-12.

Figure 2-12. *A table of users is displayed*

The table is displayed when the user clicks the View Users button on the top-right menu. Listing 2-10 shows the code for displaying the table of users.

Listing 2-12. Displaying a Table of Registered Members on the Screen (register-view-users.php)

```
<!DOCTYPE html>
<html lang="en">
<head>
  <title>Template for an interactive web page</title>
  <meta charset="utf-8">
  <meta name="viewport" content="width=device-width, initial-scale=1, shrink-to-fit=no">
  <!-- Bootstrap CSS File -->
  <link rel="stylesheet"
  href="https://stackpath.bootstrapcdn.com/bootstrap/4.1.0/css/bootstrap.min.css"
  integrity="sha384-9gVQ4dYFwwWSjIDZnLEWnxCjeSWFphJiwGPXr1jddIhOegiu1FwO5qRGvFXOdJZ4"
  crossorigin="anonymous">
</head>
<body>
<div class="container" style="margin-top:30px">
<!-- Header Section -->
<header class="jumbotron text-center row"
style="margin-bottom:2px; background:linear-gradient(white, #0073e6); padding:20px;">
  <?php include('header.php'); ?>
</header>
<!-- Body Section -->
  <div class="row" style="padding-left: 0px;">
<!-- Left-side Column Menu Section -->
  <nav class="col-sm-2">
    <ul class="nav nav-pills flex-column">
            <?php include('nav.php'); ?>
```

```
      </ul>
    </nav>
<!-- Center Column Content Section -->
    <div class="col-sm-8">
    <h2 class="text-center">These are the registered users</h2>
<p>
<?php
try {
// This script retrieves all the records from the users table.
require('mysqli_connect.php'); // Connect to the database.
// Make the query:
// Nothing passed from user safe query                                  #1
$query = "SELECT CONCAT(last_name, ', ', first_name) AS name, ";
$query .= "DATE_FORMAT(registration_date, '%M %d, %Y') AS ";
$query .= "regdat FROM users ORDER BY registration_date ASC";
$result = mysqli_query ($dbcon, $query); // Run the query.
if ($result) { // If it ran OK, display the records.
// Table header.                                                        #2
echo '<table class="table table-striped">
<tr><th scope="col">Name</th><th scope="col">Date Registered</th></tr>';
// Fetch and print all the records:                                     #3
while ($row = mysqli_fetch_array($result, MYSQLI_ASSOC)) {
echo '<tr><td>' . $row['name'] . '</td><td>' . $row['regdat'] . '</td></tr>'; }
    echo '</table>'; // Close the table so that it is ready for displaying.
    mysqli_free_result ($result); // Free up the resources.
} else { // If it did not run OK.
// Error message:
echo '<p class="error">The current users could not be retrieved. We apologize';
echo ' for any inconvenience.</p>';
// Debug message:
// echo '<p>' . mysqli_error($dbcon) . '<br><br>Query: ' . $q . '</p>';
exit;
} // End of if ($result)
mysqli_close($dbcon); // Close the database connection.
}
catch(Exception $e) // We finally handle any problems here
   {
     // print "An Exception occurred. Message: " . $e->getMessage();
     print "The system is busy please try later";
   }
   catch(Error $e)
   {
      //print "An Error occurred. Message: " . $e->getMessage();
      print "The system is busy please try again later.";
   }
?>

    </div>
<!-- Right-side Column Content Section -->
        <aside class="col-sm-2">
        <?php include('info-col.php'); ?>
```

```
        </aside>
    </div>
<!-- Footer Content Section -->
<footer class="jumbotron text-center row"
style="padding-bottom:1px; padding-top:8px;">
    <?php include('footer.php'); ?>
</footer>
</div>
</body>
</html>
```

Explanation of the Code

You will have seen most of the code before, but here is an explanation of the new items:

```
// Make the query:
// Nothing passed from user safe query                              #1
$query = "SELECT CONCAT(last_name, ', ', first_name) AS name, ";
$query .= "DATE_FORMAT(registration_date, '%M %d, %Y') AS ";
$query .= "regdat FROM users ORDER BY registration_date ASC";
$result = mysqli_query ($dbcon, $query); // Run the query.
if ($result) { // If it ran OK, display the records.
```

The SQL query selects and strings together (concatenates) the last name, then a comma, then the first name, as well as selecting the registration data. It sets the temporary headings for these as name and regdat. It rearranges the registration dates in the format month-day-year. It uses the select query to extract the information from the users table. Finally, it requests that each row of information be displayed in ascending (ASC) date order (oldest first). To display the records with the latest registrations first (descending order), you use DESC instead of ASC. Since the query is not gathering any information from the user, we do not need to create a prepared statement, passing in variables as shown in the registration page. This query string cannot be hacked.

```
// Table header.                                                    #2
echo '<table class="table table-striped">
<tr><th scope="col">Name</th><th scope="col">Date Registered</th></tr>';
```

This block of code displays (echoes) the table using the Bootstrap classes table and table-stripped to format the display. The column headers, Name and Date Registered, are also declared as the first row of the table displayed.

```
// Fetch and print all the records:                                 #3
while ($row = mysqli_fetch_array($result, MYSQLI_ASSOC)) {
echo '<tr><td>' . $row['name'] . '</td><td>' . $row['regdat'] . '</td></tr>'; }
```

This block of code loops through the rows and displays them while row data from the database table is available. MYSQLI_ASSOC creates an associative array. A PHP associative array uses keys (words) for indexes. For example, $row['name'] contains the concatenated first name and last name pulled from the users table (see #1).

Users sometimes want to change their password. The next section demonstrates how this is done.

The Change Password Page

When the user clicks the New Password button on the menu at the top right of the header, the form shown in Figure 2-13 appears.

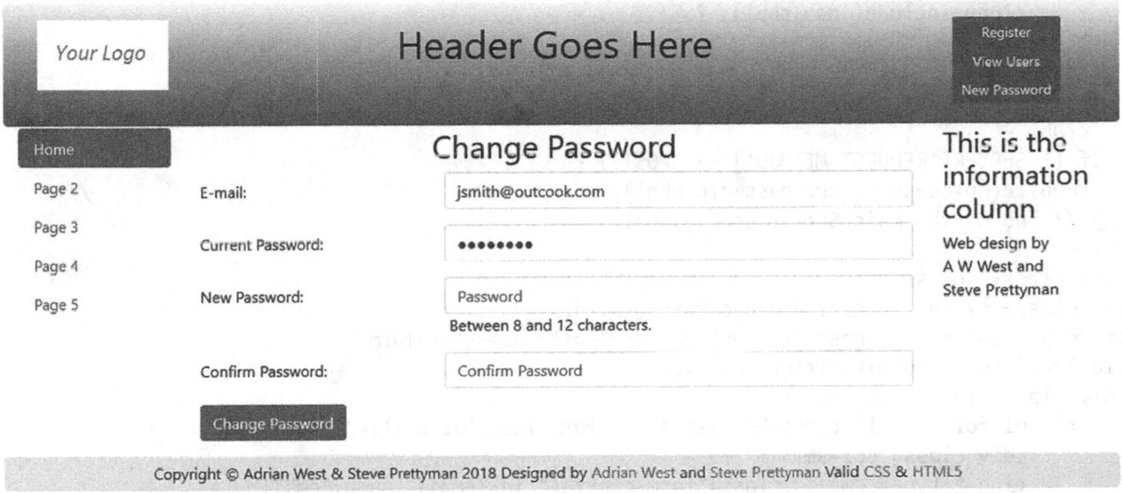

Figure 2-13. *The change password form*

The form is suitable only if the user knows their current password and e-mail address. If they have forgotten their password, a different approach is needed that will be discussed in a later chapter. However, this "new password" page is useful if the user does not like the password they originally chose. Listing 2-13a gives the HTML code for the change password form.

Listing 2-13a. Creating a Page to Allow Users to Change a Password (change-password.php)

```
<!DOCTYPE html>
<html lang="en">
<head>
<title>Template for an interactive web page</title>
<meta charset="utf-8">
<meta name="viewport" content="width=device-width, initial-scale=1, shrink-to-fit=no">
<!-- Bootstrap CSS File -->
<link rel="stylesheet"
href="https://stackpath.bootstrapcdn.com/bootstrap/4.1.0/css/bootstrap.min.css"
integrity="sha384-9gVQ4dYFwwWSjIDZnLEWnxCjeSWFphJiwGPXr1jddIhOegiu1FwO5qRGvFXOdJZ4"
crossorigin="anonymous">
<script src="verify.js"></script>
</head>
<body>
<div class="container" style="margin-top:30px">
<!-- Header Section -->
<header class="jumbotron text-center row col-sm-14"
style="margin-bottom:2px; background:linear-gradient(white, #0073e6); padding:20px;">
 <?php include('header.php'); ?>
```

```php
</header>
<!-- Body Section -->
 <div class="row" style="padding-left: 0px;">
<!-- Left-side Column Menu Section -->
  <nav class="col-sm-2">
     <ul class="nav nav-pills flex-column">
        <?php include('nav.php'); ?>
        </ul>
  </nav>
 <!-- Validate Input -->
   <?php
  if ($_SERVER['REQUEST_METHOD'] == 'POST') {
   require('process-change-password.php');                              //#1
  } // End of the main Submit conditional.
  ?>
<div class="col-sm-8">
<h2 class="h2 text-center">Change Password</h2>
<form action="change-password.php" method="post" name="regform"
 id="regform" onsubmit="return checked();">
<div class="form-group row">
    <label for="email" class="col-sm-4 col-form-label">E-mail:</label>
        <div class="col-sm-8">
        <input type="email" class="form-control" id="email" name="email"
        placeholder="E-mail" maxlength="60" required
        value="<?php if (isset($_POST['email'])) echo $_POST['email']; ?>">
        </div>
 </div>
 <div class="form-group row">
        <label for="password" class="col-sm-4 col-form-label">Current Password:</label>
        <div class="col-sm-8">
        <input type="password" class="form-control" id="password" name="password"
        placeholder="Password" minlength="8" maxlength="12"
        required value="<?php if (isset($_POST['password'])) echo $_POST['password']; ?>">
        </div>
 </div>
<div class="form-group row">
        <label for="password1" class="col-sm-4 col-form-label">New Password:</label>
        <div class="col-sm-8">
         <input type="password" class="form-control" id="password1" name="password1"
         placeholder="Password" minlength="8" maxlength="12"
         required value="<?php if (isset($_POST['password1'])) echo $_POST['password1']; ?>">
         <span id='message'>Between 8 and 12 characters.</span>
</div>
<div class="form-group row">
         <label for="password2" class="col-sm-4 col-form-label">Confirm Password:</label>
         <div class="col-sm-8">
                 <input type="password" class="form-control" id="password2" name="password2"
         placeholder="Confirm Password" minlength="8" maxlength="12" required
         value="<?php if (isset($_POST['password2'])) echo $_POST['password2']; ?>">
         </div>
 </div>
```

```
<div class="form-group row">
        <div class="col-sm-12">
        <input id="submit" class="btn btn-primary" type="submit" name="submit"
        value="Change Password">
        </div>
</div>
</form>
</div>
<!-- Right-side Column Content Section -->
<?php
 if(isset($errorstring)) {
        echo '<footer class="jumbotron text-center col-sm-12"
        style="padding-bottom:1px; padding-top:8px;">';
 }
 else
 {
        echo '<aside class="col-sm-2">';
        include('info-col.php');
        echo '</aside>';
        echo '</div>';
        echo '<footer class="jumbotron text-center row col-sm-14"
        style="padding-bottom:1px; padding-top:8px;">';
 }
  include('footer.php');
  ?>
</footer>
</div>
</body>
</html>
```

Explanation of the Code

This section gives an explanation of the code.

```
if ($_SERVER['REQUEST_METHOD'] == 'POST') {
  require('process-change-password.php');                              //#1
} // End of the main Submit conditional.
```

The HTML for the change password page is similar to the HTML for the register page. The main difference is the PHP code is now imported from the process-change-password file. Let's take a look at the contents of this file in Listing 2-13b.

Listing 2-13b. Processing the Changed Password (process-change-password.php)

```
<?php
// This script is a query that UPDATES the password in the users table.
// Check that form has been submitted:
if ($_SERVER['REQUEST_METHOD'] == 'POST') {
require ('mysqli_connect.php'); // Connect to the db.
$errors = array(); // Initialize an error array.
// Check for an email address:
```

```
$email = trim($_POST['email']);
if (empty($email)) {
        $errors[] = 'You forgot to enter your email address.';
}
// Check for a password and match against the confirmed password:
$password = trim($_POST['password']);
if (empty($password)) {
        $errors[] = 'You forgot to enter your old password.';
}
// Prepare and check new password                                              #1
$new_password = trim($_POST['password1']);
$verify_password = trim($_POST['password2']);
if (!empty($new_password)) {
        if (($new_password != $verify_password) ||
        ( $password == $new_password ))
        {
$errors[] = 'Your new password did not match the confirmed password and/or ';
$errors[] = 'Your old password is the same as your new password.';
        }
} else {
        $errors[] = 'You did not enter a new password.';
}if (empty($errors)) { // If everything's OK.
try {
 // Check that the user has entered the right email address/password combination:    #2
 $query = "SELECT userid, password FROM users WHERE ( email=? )";
$q = mysqli_stmt_init($dbcon);
mysqli_stmt_prepare($q, $query);
 // use prepared statement to ensure that only text is inserted
 // bind fields to SQL Statement
mysqli_stmt_bind_param($q, 's', $email);
 // execute query
 mysqli_stmt_execute($q);
$result = mysqli_stmt_get_result($q);
$row = mysqli_fetch_array($result, MYSQLI_ASSOC);
if ((mysqli_num_rows($result) == 1)                                            //#3
        && (password_verify($password, $row['password'])))
        {    // Found one record
        // Change the password in the database...
        // Hash password current 60 characters but can increase
        $hashed_passcode = password_hash($new_password, PASSWORD_DEFAULT);
        // Make the query:
        $query = "UPDATE users SET password=? WHERE email=?";
        $q = mysqli_stmt_init($dbcon);
        mysqli_stmt_prepare($q, $query);
        // use prepared statement to ensure that only text is inserted
        // bind fields to SQL Statement
        mysqli_stmt_bind_param($q, 'ss', $hashed_passcode, $email);
        // execute query
        mysqli_stmt_execute($q);
        if (mysqli_stmt_affected_rows($q) == 1) {   // one row updated          #4
                  // Thank you
```

```
                header ("location: password-thanks.php");
                        exit();
        } else { // If it did not run OK.                                          #5
                // Public message:
                $errorstring = "System Error! <br /> You could not change password due ";
                $errorstring .= "to a system error. We apologize for any inconvenience.</p>";
                echo "<p class='text-center col-sm-2' style='color:red'>$errorstring</p>";
                // Debugging message below do not use in production
                //echo '<p>' . mysqli_error($dbcon) . '<br><br>Query: ' . $query . '</p>';
                // include footer then close program to stop execution
                echo '<footer class="jumbotron text-center col-sm-12"
                        style="padding-bottom:1px; padding-top:8px;">
                        include("footer.php");
                        </footer>';
                exit();
        }
        } else { // Invalid email address/password combination.
                $errorstring = 'Error! <br /> ';
                        $errorstring .= 'The email address and/or password do not match those
                        on file.';
                $errorstring .= " Please try again.";
                echo "<p class='text-center col-sm-2' style='color:red'>$errorstring</p>";
} }
    catch(Exception $e) // We finally handle any problems here
    {
        // print "An Exception occurred. Message: " . $e->getMessage();
        print "The system is busy please try later";
    }
    catch(Error $e)
    {
        //print "An Error occurred. Message: " . $e->getMessage();
        print "The system is busy please try again later.";
    }
    } else { // Report the errors.                                                 #6
        //header ("location: register-page.php");
        $errorstring = "Error! The following error(s) occurred:<br>";
        foreach ($errors as $msg) { // Print each error.
                $errorstring .= " - $msg<br>\n";
        }
        $errorstring .= "Please try again.<br>";
        echo "<p class=' text-center col-sm-2' style='color:red'>$errorstring</p>";
        }// End of if (empty($errors)) IF.
} // End of the main Submit conditional.
?>
```

Explanation of the Code

This section explains the code.

```
// Prepare and check new password                                                 #1
$new_password = trim($_POST['password1']);
```

```
$verify_password = trim($_POST['password2']);
if (!empty($new_password)) {
        if (($new_password != $verify_password) ||
        ( $password == $new_password ))
        {
$errors[] = 'Your new password did not match the confirmed password and/or ';
$errors[] = 'Your old password is the same as your new password.';
        }
} else {
        $errors[] = 'You did not enter a new password.';
```

The first two lines of code trim any blank spaces from the strings. In later chapters, we will verify that the password is in a proper format. However, for now, we are using prepared statements; thus, any coding the user attempts to insert into the textboxes will not be executed. If the two new passwords match, the new password is placed in $password. If they do not match, an error is sent back to the web page.

```
(
// Check that the user has entered the right email address/password combination:        #2
 $query = "SELECT userid, password FROM users WHERE ( email=? )";
$q = mysqli_stmt_init($dbcon);
mysqli_stmt_prepare($q, $query);
 // use prepared statement to ensure that only text is inserted
 // bind fields to SQL Statement
mysqli_stmt_bind_param($q, 's', $email);
 // execute query
 mysqli_stmt_execute($q);
$result = mysqli_stmt_get_result($q);
$row = mysqli_fetch_array($result, MYSQLI_ASSOC);
```

If all verifications are successful, we must make sure that the user provided an existing e-mail and password. The #2 line in the previous code creates a prepared select statement that pulls the user IS and password from the users table using the e-mail provided. If the SQL statement returns a result, we have verified that the e-mail exists in the database.

```
if ((mysqli_num_rows($result) == 1)                                                   //#3
        && (password_verify($password, $row['password'])))
        {    // Found one record
        // Change the password in the database...
        // Hash password current 60 characters but can increase
        $hashed_passcode = password_hash($new_password, PASSWORD_DEFAULT);
        // Make the query:
        $query = "UPDATE users SET password=? WHERE email=?";
        $q = mysqli_stmt_init($dbcon);
        mysqli_stmt_prepare($q, $query);
        // use prepared statement to ensure that only text is inserted
        // bind fields to SQL Statement
        mysqli_stmt_bind_param($q, 'ss', $hashed_passcode, $email);
        // execute query
        mysqli_stmt_execute($q);
```

If we have gotten a result from the database table, we also need to verify that the password is correct. The if statement uses the function password_verify to compare the old password with the password in the table. This is necessary because the password stored in the table is hashed and the password provided by the user is not hashed. If they match, the new password is hashed. A prepared SQL update query is created to change the password within the users table. This query is then executed.

```
if (mysqli_stmt_affected_rows($q) == 1) {      // one row updated          #4
                        // Thank you
                        header ("location: password-thanks.php");
                                exit();
```

If the SQL update query is successful, the "thank you" page is displayed. The header function calls the password thanks page using an HTML Get command. The current page is closed using the exit method.

```
} else { // If it did not run OK.                                        #5
                // Public message:
                $errorstring = "System Error! <br /> You could not change password due ";
                $errorstring .= "to a system error. We apologize for any inconvenience.</p>";
                echo "<p class='text-center col-sm-2' style='color:red'>$errorstring</p>";
                // Debugging message below do not use in production
                //echo '<p>' . mysqli_error($dbcon) . '<br><br>Query: ' . $query . '</p>';
                // include footer then close program to stop execution
                echo '<footer class="jumbotron text-center col-sm-12"
                        style="padding-bottom:1px; padding-top:8px;">
                        include("footer.php");
                        </footer>';
        exit();
```

If no rows were changed, the query did not execute successfully. The else statement captures this situation and displays a System Error statement. Since this is a serious error, the page is provided with a footer and the code is closed (exit()). This will close any access to the database and will not let any other code execute. Debugging code that will provide more information on the problem is listed in comments. This code should never be activated in live code. The error information provided might display code and database connection information, which would be a major security violation.

```
} else { // Report the errors.                                          #6
        //header ("location: register-page.php");
        $errorstring = "Error! The following error(s) occurred:<br>";
        foreach ($errors as $msg) { // Print each error.
                $errorstring .= " - $msg<br>\n";
        }
        $errorstring .= "Please try again.<br>";
        echo "<p class=' text-center col-sm-2' style='color:red'>$errorstring</p>";
}// End of if (empty($errors)) IF.
```

The last section of code is similar to the registration page. It displays any error messages caused when the user entered invalid information. These errors are provided on the same page as the form to allow the user to make corrections and resubmit the information.

Confirming a Successful Password Change

If the password change is successful, the page shown in Figure 2-14 is displayed.

The page shown in Figure 2-14 is similar to the registration "thank you" page. The code can be viewed from your downloaded files for this chapter.

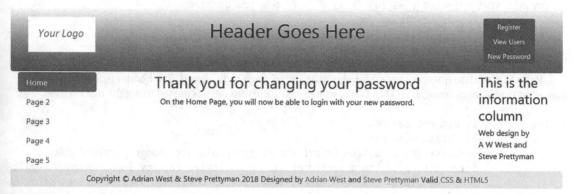

Figure 2-14. *The password has been changed*

Testing the Tutorial's Pages

To see the interactive pages working, double-click the XAMPP or easyPHP icon on your desktop. When the control panel appears, check that Apache and MySQL/MariaDB are running.

Type `http://localhost/simpledb/index.php` into the address field of a browser and then click the Register button so that you can enter some users.

To save you time and the effort of dreaming up fictitious people, use the suggestions provided in Table 2-1.

Table 2-1. *Suggestions for Entering Members' Details*

Name	E-mail	Password
Mike Rosoft	miker@myisp.com	W1llgat3s
Olive Branch	obranch@myisp.com.uk	Ano1ly0n3
Frank Insence	finsence@myisp.net	P3rfum300
Annie Versary	aversary@myisp.com	B1rthd3yg1rl
Terry Fide	tfide@myisp.de	Scar3dst1ff
Rose Bush	rbush@myisp.co.uk	R3dbl00ms

Now that you have some more data in your users table, run XAMPP or EasyPHP and use a browser to click the menu item to display the table of registered users.

■ **Tip** No doubt you will encounter error messages as you create code and test it. For help, refer to the troubleshooting tips in Chapter 12.

Earlier in this chapter, we promised more information on the use of PHP arrays. The next section will help you understand additional aspects of this most useful feature.

More About Arrays

Arrays are used throughout this book, and if you access forums for advice on the use of PHP, you will be confronted with many arrays.

An array is a holding place in memory for multiple similar items (such as cereals shown next). The items are grouped together with the same variable name ($cereals). To refer to an individual element in an array, we must use a key (subscript). In PHP, the subscript can be a number ($cereals[1]) or a string (such as $row['name']). We will be using both formats throughout the book.

Arrays can be populated with elements in several ways. We create an array named $cereals, as follows:

```php
<?php
$cereals = array();
?>
```

A few elements can be inserted into the array as follows (note that the first array element is usually zero):

```php
<?php
$cereals = array[];
$cereals[0] = "oats";
$cereals[1] = "barley";
$cereals[2] = "corn";
$cereals[3] - "wheat";
?>
```

To display the elements of this array, insert the following code just before the closing tag ?>:

```php
echo "$cereals[0] " . "$cereals[1] " . "$cereals[2] " . "$cereals[3]";?>
```

The display will produce the following:
Oats barley corn wheat

The echo statement concatenates the string together using the concatenation symbol (.). However, in PHP we can also place program variables (such as $name) within quotations, as shown here:

```php
$first_name = "Fred";
$middle_name = "Adam";
$last_name = "Smith";

echo "$first_name $middle_name $last_name";
```

PHP will also allow us to insert items into a numeric array without providing the index number.

```php
$error[] = "One error";
$error[] = "Another error";
```

PHP will automatically index the first item with 0 and the second with 1. Thus, we can display the values as follows:

```php
echo "$error[0] $error[1]";
```

There is much more to learn about arrays. However, just this small amount of knowledge should help you understand how we are using arrays when pulling information from a database table and when we are loading and displaying error messages.

■ **Caution** The data entered into the database tables in this chapter are not completely filtered. They have been deliberately stripped of most filters and cleaners so that the essential processes are uncluttered and clearly visible. An increasing number of security and filtering features will be added in later chapters.

Summary

In this chapter, you created your first interactive pages and tested them. You learned a little more about PHP—in particular, you should have grasped the idea of looking for and recognizing logical patterns in the code. You learned how to use several PHP functions: include(), required(), and echo(). You also learned many mysqli functions. You discovered the importance of PHP conditionals for creating interactive database pages. You also learned how to check whether the user has entered information before sending the data to the database table. In the next chapter, we will add some extra security and demonstrate how users and an administrator can log in and log out of private pages on a website. You will also learn how to remove or replace the redundant links in the header menus.

CHAPTER 3

■ ■ ■

Create Login/Logout Functionality for Members and an Administrator

In Chapter 2, we created the first interactive pages using a database and a table. By now, you have probably realized that what we created was not very practical; however, you learned how to embed interactivity into a real-world page. A more practical application is to allow registered users to log in and log out of private pages. When users log in, they should be able to access extra features offered by the website. These could be a page of special offers for members, or it could be the ability to add a comment in a blog, access the minutes of meetings, or view the dates of special events for members only.

After completing this chapter, you should be able to

- Create a new database and table
- Remove or replace menu buttons in headers
- Deal with undesirable characters from HTML textboxes
- Differentiate between two types of membership or user levels
- Create user levels to limit access to private pages
- Create a login and a logout page
- Create a members-only page
- Plan for the administrator's role
- Test the ability to log in and log out

In the previous tutorial, any user could view a table of members, but the members would not be pleased to know that their private details are available to everybody. We must now prevent this and allow only the administrator (such as a membership secretary) and the webmaster to view the table of members.

An administrator is a special category of user: they should be able to view the members' table and to amend or delete records. Computer-savvy administrators can use phpMyAdmin, but many administrators will be membership secretaries with only basic computer skills. They will need a simple interface that enables them to view, alter, and delete records. This chapter will teach you how to create and implement a user-friendly interface for the administrator. Chapters 4, 5, and 6 will progressively improve this interface.

To log in to private pages on a website, registered members and the administrator must enter information known only to them—for instance, the user's e-mail address and password or a username and a password. The login page will automatically check that the login details match the user's information held in the database. If the login details are verified, the user is admitted to the private web pages.

Creating the logindb Database and users Table

The tutorials in this chapter are based on the pages created in Chapter 2. We will clarify the file structure by using a new name for the database and for the folder containing the PHP and HTML pages. This is necessary because we have found that if students pile modification upon modification, they can get into a terrible muddle. Therefore, as a general rule, we will continue to use a separate folder and a new database name for each new chapter in this book. However, a table can have the same name (for example, *users*) as the previous tutorial. This is acceptable if the table is in a different database.

Let's get started. Create a new folder and a new database as follows:

1. In the XAMPP *htdocs* or easyPHP *eds-www* folder, create a new folder called *login*.

2. Download the PHP files for Chapter 3 from the book's page at Apress.com and put them in the new login folder in XAMPP *htdocs* or easyPHP *eds-www*. Alternatively, you can practice creating the PHP and HTML listings by typing each file in your HTML editor as you go through the chapter. Save them in your *login* folder so you can run them.

3. Open phpMyAdmin.

4. Click the Databases tab.

5. Create a new database called *logindb*. Set the encoding, as shown in Chapter 2, to utf8-general-ci.

6. Follow the directions from Chapter 2 to add a user, user ID, and password for the database. Use the following attributes:

   Username: william

   Host: localhost

   Password: CatOnlap

   Database name: logindb

7. In the *login* folder, create the *mysqli_connect.php* file so that it connects to logindb, as shown in the following listing:

Listing for the Snippet of Code Required for Connecting to the New Database (msqli_connect.php)

```php
<?php
// Create a connection to the logindb database.
// Set the encoding and the access details as constants:
Define ('DB_USER', 'william');
Define ('DB_PASSWORD', 'CatOnlap');
Define ('DB_HOST', 'localhost');
Define ('DB_NAME', 'logindb');
// Make the connection:
$dbcon = new mysqli(DB_HOST, DB_USER, DB_PASSWORD, DB_NAME);
mysqli_set_charset($dbcon, 'utf8');
?>
```

In a live environment, this connection file would be saved in a secure folder.

■ **Note** Resist the urge to copy and paste the code from PDF versions of the book. During the editing process some symbol changes can cause the example code not to execute. The best method is to download the code from the Apress.com website. If you do copy the code from the PDF version, drop it in Microsoft Notepad and then save it. This does fix some of the quotation characters that maybe invalid for PHP.

8. In the database logindb, create a new table named *users* with six columns. Its layout and attributes are the same as the users table in Chapter 2. The details are given in Table 3-1. As stated in Chapter 2, some versions of phpMyAdmin do not require entering the length (6) and attributes (UNSIGNED) for the primary index (user_id). The user_id field is an autonum field, in which the database system generates the numbers. Set up this table the same way you set up the previous database in Chapter 2.

Table 3-1. The Attributes for the users Table

Column name	Type	Length/ Value	Default	Attributes	NULL	Index	A_I
user_id	MEDIUMINT	6	None	Unsigned	☐	PRIMARY	☑
first_name	VARCHAR	30	None		☐		☐
last_name	VARCHAR	40	None		☐		☐
email	VARCHAR	50	None		☐		☐
password	CHAR	60	None		☐		☐
registration_date	DATETIME		None		☐		☐

Remember to adjust the size of the password field to fit the latest hashing standards. You can find the current PHP hashing standards here:

```
http://php.net/manual/en/function.password-hash.php
```

Now we will tidy the header menus.

Removing or Replacing Redundant Menu Buttons in the Headers

As mentioned in Chapter 2, some header menu buttons have become redundant, and some new buttons are needed. In this section, the header menus will be amended. We must prevent the public and ordinary members from viewing the membership table. To achieve this, for now, we will remove the link that displays the table of members from all the headers except the header on the administration page. We will also soon require the administrators to log in to access their pages. We also need to remove the login link on the members page, because the member is already logged in. We must add a logout link. The Register link is also redundant because the members and the administrator are already registered; therefore, that menu button will also be removed.

■ **Tip**   Redundant buttons are easily overlooked when you are absorbed in the coding of the database and the website pages. Try to cultivate the habit of checking the header on each new or revised page to ensure that there are no redundant or missing buttons.

In a "real-world" website that uses many pages, we might store the actual menu page links in a database table and use code based on a signed-in user level (such as administrator or user) to determine which links to provide. However, for smaller websites (like this demonstration), it is just as quick (or quicker) to create the few extra header menus needed.

Adding a Login Button to the Home Page Header

We will now add a new button to the header menu on the home page so that members can log in. We will also remove the View Users button because we want to arrange things so that only the administrator is able to view the table of members (we will provide additional restrictions soon). Figure 3-1 shows the revised header.

Figure 3-1. *The revised header for the home page. The New Password button has been removed, and the View Users button is replaced with a Login button.*

The View Users and New Password buttons have been removed, and a Login button is added. The revised header will automatically be included in the nonprivate pages (page-2, page-3, and so on) because the header file name is unchanged.

Listing 3-1 shows the code for the new header.

Listing 3-1.   Revising the Home Page Header Menu (header.php)

```
<div class="col-sm-2">
<img class="img-fluid float-left" src="logo.jpg" alt="Logo">
</div>
<div class="col-sm-8">
 <h1 class="blue-text mb-4 font-bold">Header Goes Here</h1>
 </div>
     <nav class="col-sm-2">
        <div class="btn-group-vertical btn-group-sm" role="group"
        aria-label="Button Group">
  <button type="button" class="btn btn-secondary"
    onclick="location.href = 'login.php'" >Login</button>
  <button type="button" class="btn btn-secondary"
    onclick="location.href = 'register-page.php'">Register</button>
</div>
     </nav>
```

With XAMPP or easyPHP running, enter **http://localhost/login/index.php** into a browser to view the home page with the new login button, as shown in Figure 3-1.

Removing Redundant Buttons from the Registration and New Password Headers

A new header will be required for the registration page and the new password page because the previous headers had redundant menu buttons.

On the registration page, the user has no password and so cannot log in; therefore, the Login and New Password buttons will be removed. The Register button is redundant because the user has already accessed the registration page. We will now remove the redundant buttons from the header for the registration page and replace them with something more useful. Figure 3-2 shows the new header.

Figure 3-2. *The new header for the registration page and the new password page*

The redundant buttons are replaced by two meaningful links, Erase Entries and Cancel. The Erase Entries button reloads the registration page and then displays empty fields. We selected the words E*rase Entries* rather than Clear or Erase All after testing the site with users who were not computer savvy. They were confused by the Clear and Erase All wording, but they immediately understood Erase Entries. The Cancel button returns the user to the home page. Listing 3-2a gives the revised header code for the registration and new password pages.

Listing 3-2a. Replacing Redundant Buttons with Meaningful Buttons (register-header.php)

```
<div class="col-sm-2">
<img class="img-fluid float-left" src="logo.jpg" alt="Logo">
</div>
<div class="col-sm-8">
 <h1 class="blue-text mb-4 font-bold">Header Goes Here</h1>
 </div>
     <nav class="col-sm-2">
         <div class="btn-group-vertical btn-group-sm" role="group"
         aria-label="Button Group">
  <button type="button" class="btn btn-secondary"
    onclick="location.href = 'register-page'" >Erase Entries</button>
  <button type="button" class="btn btn-secondary"
    onclick="location.href = 'index.php'">Cancel</button>
</div>
     </nav>
```

The registration page for this chapter and subsequent chapters will be linked to the new header, as shown in the next snippet of code in Listing 3-2b.

The Revised Registration Page

The rest of the code is the same as the registration page in Chapter 2. The revised code is included in the downloadable files for Chapter 3.

Listing 3-2b. Including the New Header in the Registration Page (register-page.php)

```
<!DOCTYPE html>
<html lang="en">
<head>
  <title>Template for an interactive web page</title>
  <meta charset="utf-8">
  <meta name="viewport"
    content="width=device-width, initial-scale=1, shrink-to-fit=no">
  <!-- Bootstrap CSS File -->
  <link rel="stylesheet"
    href=
"https://stackpath.bootstrapcdn.com/bootstrap/4.1.0/css/bootstrap.min.css"
    integrity=
"sha384-9gVQ4dYFwwWSjIDZnLEWnxCjeSWFphJiwGPXr1jddIhOegiu1FwO5qRGvFXOdJZ4"
    crossorigin="anonymous">
    <script src="verify.js"></script>
</head>
<body>
<div class="container" style="margin-top:30px">
<!-- Header Section -->
<header class="jumbotron text-center row col-sm-14"
style=
  "margin-bottom:2px; background:linear-gradient(white, #0073e6);
  padding:20px;">
  <?php include('register-header.php'); ?>
</header>
<!-- Body Section -->
  <div class="row" style="padding-left: 0px;">
<!-- Left-side Column Menu Section -->
  <nav class="col-sm-2">
      <ul class="nav nav-pills flex-column">
              <?php include('nav.php'); ?>
  </ul>
      </nav>
```

The new header will now be applied to the New Password page.

The New Header for the New Password Page

The same new header will be required for the new password page. (This was shown in Figure 3-2.)

The new password page for this chapter and subsequent chapters will be linked to the new header, as shown in the next snippet of code in Listing 3-2c.

The Erase Entries button reloads the new password page and displays empty fields. The Cancel button returns the user to the home page.

Listing 3-2c. Replacing Redundant Buttons with Meaningful Buttons (password-header.php)

```
<div class="col-sm-2">
<img class="img-fluid float-left" src="logo.jpg" alt="Logo">
</div>
```

```
<div class="col-sm-8">
 <h1 class="blue-text mb-4 font-bold">Header Goes Here</h1>
 </div>
     <nav class="col-sm-2">
       <div class="btn-group-vertical btn-group-sm"
       role="group" aria-label="Button Group">
  <button type="button" class="btn btn-secondary"
       onclick="location.href = 'change-password.php'" >
       Erase Entries</button>
  <button type="button" class="btn btn-secondary"
       onclick="location.href = 'index.php'">Cancel</button>
</div>
     </nav>
```

The included file for the header is amended in the register password file (*change-password.php*), as given in the following code snippet:

```
<!DOCTYPE html>
<html lang="en">
<head>
  <title>Template for an interactive web page</title>
  <meta charset="utf-8">
  <meta name="viewport"
    content="width=device-width, initial-scale=1, shrink-to-fit=no">
  <!-- Bootstrap CSS File -->
  <link rel="stylesheet"
  href=
"https://stackpath.bootstrapcdn.com/bootstrap/4.1.0/css/bootstrap.min.css"
  integrity=
"sha384-9gVQ4dYFwwWSjIDZnLEWnxCjeSWFphJiwGPXr1jddIhOegiu1FwO5qRGvFXOdJZ4"
  crossorigin="anonymous">
  <script src="verify.js"></script>
</head>
<body>
<div class="container" style="margin-top:30px">
<!-- Header Section -->
<header class="jumbotron text-center row col-sm-14"
style="margin-bottom:2px; background:linear-gradient(white, #0073e6);
  padding:20px;">
  <?php include('password-header.php'); ?>
</header>
<!-- Body Section -->
  <div class="row" style="padding-left: 0px;">
<!-- Left-side Column Menu Section -->
  <nav class="col-sm-2">
      <ul class="nav nav-pills flex-column">
              <?php include('nav.php'); ?>
      </ul>
  </nav>
```

The rest of the code goes here and is unchanged from Chapter 2.

A New Header Menu for the Members page

For the members page, the Register button and the View Members button have been removed, and a Logout button has been added, as shown in Figure 3-3.

Figure 3-3. The modified header menu for the members page

Note in Figure 3-3 that when a member is logged into the members page, the Login menu button changes to a Logout button. There are several clever ways of achieving this, but the least complicated way is to load a new header into the members page. This is effective because sometimes the special members page also requires a slightly changed header image or text. Note also that the redundant Register and New Password buttons have been removed from the header menu.

The new file is named *members-header.php*. The new Logout button has a link that sends the user to the page named *logout.php*. This, in turn, sends the user to the home page. Why does the link not go directly to the home page? Because the intermediate page *logout.php* contains some code for closing a session before it accesses the home page. A session is a device that will be explained in the next section. The logout link is shown in the following code snippet for the new header.

Listing 3-3 shows the code for the two links that remain.

Listing 3-3. Creating the New Header for the Members page (members-header.php)

```
<div class="col-sm-2">
<img class="img-fluid float-left" src="logo.jpg" alt="Logo">
</div>
<div class="col-sm-8">
 <h1 class="blue-text mb-4 font-bold">Header Goes Here</h1>
 </div>
     <nav class="col-sm-2">
        <div class="btn-group-vertical btn-group-sm" role="group"
     aria-label="Button Group">
  <button type="button" class="btn btn-secondary"
     onclick="location.href = 'logout.php'" >Logout</button>
  <button type="button" class="btn btn-secondary"
     onclick="location.href = 'change-password.php'" >New Password</button>
</div>
     </nav>
```

If the website has more than one page that is exclusively for members, you could add more buttons with links to the file *members-header.php*; alternatively, you could put links in the body of the members page.

Amend the Header for the "Thank You" Page

When a user reaches the "thank you" page, they have registered and no longer require the Register button, nor do they require any of the other buttons. The "thank you" page header only needs a button that redirects the user to the home page. Figure 3-4 shows the header with the Home Page button.

Figure 3-4. *The revised header for the "thank you" page*

The Home Page menu button in the header redirects the user to the home page (*index.php*), as shown in Listing 3-4a.

Listing 3-4a. Creating the Code for the Revised "Thank You" Header (thanks-header.php)

```
<div class="col-sm-2">
<img class="img-fluid float-left" src="logo.jpg" alt="Logo">
</div>
<div class="col-sm-8">
 <h1 class="blue-text mb-4 font-bold">Header Goes Here</h1>
 </div>
    <nav class="col-sm-2">
       <div class="btn-group-vertical btn-group-sm" role="group"
    aria-label="Button Group">
  <button type="button" class="btn btn-secondary"
      onclick="location.href = 'index.php'" >Home Page</button>
</div>
    </nav>
```

The "thank you" page will now be amended to include the revised header. Listing 3-4b shows the changed *include* statement in the "thank you" page.

Listing 3-4b. Creating the Revised "Thank You" Page (register-thanks.php)

```
<!DOCTYPE html>
<html lang="en">
<head>
  <title>Register Thanks</title>
  <meta charset="utf-8">
  <meta name="viewport"
    content="width=device-width, initial-scale=1, shrink-to-fit=no">
  <!-- Bootstrap CSS File -->
  <link rel="stylesheet"
    href=
"https://stackpath.bootstrapcdn.com/bootstrap/4.1.0/css/bootstrap.min.css"
  integrity=
 "sha384-9gVQ4dYFwwWSjIDZnLEWnxCjeSWFphJiwGPXr1jddIhOegiu1FwO5qRGvFXOdJZ4"
  crossorigin="anonymous">
</head>
<body>
<div class="container" style="margin-top:30px">
<!-- Header Section -->
<header class="jumbotron text-center row"
style="margin-bottom:2px; background:linear-gradient(white, #0073e6);
  padding:20px;">
```

```php
    <?php include('thanks-header.php'); ?>
</header>
<!-- Body Section -->
    <div class="row" style="padding-left: 0px;">
<!-- Left-side Column Menu Section -->
    <nav class="col-sm-2">
        <ul class="nav nav-pills flex-column">
                <?php include('nav.php'); ?>
        </ul>
    </nav>
```

The rest of the code is unchanged from the code in Chapter 2.

The Registration Page and Undesirable Characters

We will now begin to verify that the user provided valid information. Whenever a textbox is used for user input, it can allow the user to enter undesirable characters, which may be an attempt to provide SQL injection (a user trying to gain access to your database) or unintended user entry errors. We will use the PHP input filter function to sanitize the input. An example is shown here:

```php
$first_name = filter_var( $_POST['first_name'], FILTER_SANITIZE_STRING);
```

We'll add that function to our registration page now. While we're at it, let's also add the updated *register-header.php* file that includes only the two buttons Erase Entries and Cancel.

Figure 3-5 shows the registration page with its new header.

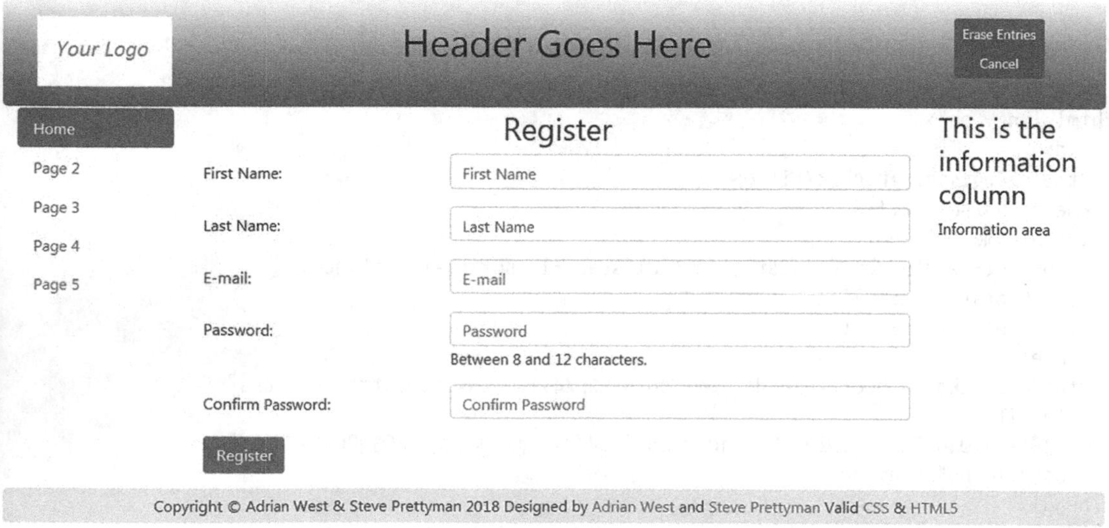

Figure 3-5. The registration page with its new header

Listing 3-5 shows the modified PHP code for filtering entries in *process-register-page.php*.

Listing 3-5. Creating the Amended Registration Page (process-register-page.php)

```php
<?php
// This script is a query that INSERTs a record in the users table.
// Check that form has been submitted:
try {                                                             #1
        $errors = array(); // Initialize an error array.
        // Check for a first name:
    $first_name = filter_var( $_POST['first_name'], FILTER_SANITIZE_STRING);
    if (empty($first_name)) {
            $errors[] = 'You forgot to enter your first name.';
    }
    // Check for a last name:
    $last_name = filter_var( $_POST['last_name'], FILTER_SANITIZE_STRING);
    if (empty($last_name)) {
            $errors[] = 'You forgot to enter your last name.';
    }
    // Check for an email address:                                #2
        $email = filter_var( $_POST['email'], FILTER_SANITIZE_EMAIL);
    if ((empty($email)) || (!filter_var($email, FILTER_VALIDATE_EMAIL))) {
            $errors[] = 'You forgot to enter your email address';
            $errors[] = ' or the e-mail format is incorrect.';
    }
    // Check for a password and match against the confirmed password:
    $password1 = filter_var( $_POST['password1'], FILTER_SANITIZE_STRING);
    $password2 = filter_var( $_POST['password2'], FILTER_SANITIZE_STRING);
    if (!empty($password1)) {
            if ($password1 !== $password2) {
                    $errors[] = 'Your two password did not match.';
            }
    } else {
            $errors[] = 'You forgot to enter your password.';
    }
    if (empty($errors)) { // If everything's OK.
    // Register the user in the database...
    // Hash password current 60 characters but can increase
        $hashed_passcode = password_hash($password1, PASSWORD_DEFAULT);
            require ('mysqli_connect.php'); // Connect to the db.
            // Make the query:
            $query = "INSERT INTO users (userid, first_name, last_name, ";
            $query .= "email, password, registration_date) ";
            $query .="VALUES(' ', ?, ?, ?, ?, NOW() )";
    $q = mysqli_stmt_init($dbcon);
    mysqli_stmt_prepare($q, $query);
    // use prepared statement to ensure that only text is inserted
    // bind fields to SQL Statement
    mysqli_stmt_bind_param($q, 'ssss', $first_name, $last_name, $email, $hashed_passcode);
    // execute query
    mysqli_stmt_execute($q);
    if (mysqli_stmt_affected_rows($q) == 1) {    // One record inserted
            header ("location: register-thanks.php");
            exit();
```

```php
        } else { // If it did not run OK.
              // Public message:
              $errorstring =
              "<p class='text-center col-sm-8' style='color:red'>";
              $errorstring .=
              "System Error<br />You could not be registered due ";
              $errorstring .=
              "to a system error. We apologize for any inconvenience.</p>";
              echo "<p class=' text-center col-sm-2'
              style='color:red'>$errorstring</p>";
              // Debugging message below do not use in production
              //echo '<p>' . mysqli_error($dbcon) . '<br><br>Query: ' .
                  $query . '</p>';
              mysqli_close($dbcon); // Close the database connection.
              // include footer then close program to stop execution
              echo '<footer class="jumbotron text-center col-sm-12"
                  style="padding-bottom:1px; padding-top:8px;">
           include("footer.php");
           </footer>';
              exit();
              }
        } else { // Report the errors.
              $errorstring =
                  "Error! <br /> The following error(s) occurred:<br>";
           foreach ($errors as $msg) { // Print each error.
                  $errorstring .= " - $msg<br>\n";
           }
           $errorstring .= "Please try again.<br>";
           echo "<p class=' text-center col-sm-2'
              style='color:red'>$errorstring</p>";
           }// End of if (empty($errors)) IF.
           }
   catch(Exception $e) // We finally handle any problems here
   {
     // print "An Exception occurred. Message: " . $e->getMessage();
     print "The system is busy please try later";
   }
   catch(Error $e)
   {
      //print "An Error occurred. Message: " . $e->getMessage();
      print "The system is busy please try again later.";
   }
?>
```

Explanation of the Code

This section explains the code.

```php
try {                                                                    #1
        $errors = array(); // Initialize an error array.
        // Check for a first name:
```

```
$first_name = filter_var( $_POST['first_name'], FILTER_SANITIZE_STRING);
if (empty($first_name)) {
        $errors[] = 'You forgot to enter your first name.';
}
```

The filter_var function with the FILTER_SANITIZE_STRING property will trim extra spaces and HTML tags from the values entered by the user. This, in addition to the use of prepared statements, will greatly reduce the ability for the user to use SQL injection to access the database or to enter invalid information in the database. This code will still allow nonalphabetic characters to be entered. We will remove these characters in a later chapter.

```
// Check for an email address:                                        #2
        $email = filter_var( $_POST['email'], FILTER_SANITIZE_EMAIL);
    if ((empty($email)) || (!filter_var($email, FILTER_VALIDATE_EMAIL))) {
        $errors[] = 'You forgot to enter your email address';
        $errors[] = ' or the e-mail format is incorrect.';
    }
```

The filter_var function has a FILTER_SANITIZE_EMAIL property that will remove any invalid e-mail characters. In addition, the property FILTER_VALIDATE_EMAIL will return either true or false if the e-mail entered is in the proper format. In this code, we could have just used this property to validate the e-mail. However, since we wanted to save the e-mail from the form into $email, we also sanitized it. There are additional properties that can be used to sanitize and filter user input. For more information, visit this page:

www.php.net/manual/en/function.filter-input.php

Registering Some Members

At this point, you should register a few fictitious people in the database so that you will have something to play with later in the chapter. To save you time, we have repeated the list of members from Chapter 2, and they are shown in Table 3-2.

Table 3-2. Register Some Members

Name	E-mail	Password
Mike Rosoft	miker@myisp.com	W1llgat3s
Olive Branch	obranch@myisp.com.uk	Ano1ly0n3
Frank Insence	finsence@myisp.net	P3rfum300
Annie Versary	aversary@myisp.com	B1rthd3yg1rl
Terry Fide	tfide@myisp.de	Scar3dst1ff
Rose Bush	rbush@myisp.co.uk	R3dbl00ms

To maintain the security of private pages, we use a device called *sessions*. A session usually includes a complete process (such as a bank transaction). For example, if a person wants to transfer money from a savings account to a checking account, multiple actions occur. First the money is withdrawn from the savings account, and then it is deposited in the checking account. What happens if the action does not deposit the money? If the two actions are not bound together (via a session), the money is lost. However, if a session exists and the action does not complete, it can be rolled back. The worst that happens is the money never is withdrawn and deposited. Thus, the money is not lost.

In web pages, sessions can also be used to relate page content together. This allows the user to sign in once for the whole website. The session can determine that the user already signed in and allocate them the proper access. If a session did not exist, the user might have to sign in for each page. Other data can also be stored within a session to allow multiple pages in the same website to share information.

The session is active in the server until the session is closed or times out. It times out after a period (typically 20 minutes) that is set by the server administrator. The session is also closed if code is provided to close the session (logging out), if the user browses multiple pages away from the original website, or if the user closes the browser. However, the developer should not depend on the user closing the browser or scrolling far enough away from the website. There should always be a way for the session to close.

Differentiating Between Two Types of Membership

The simpledb database in the previous chapter had a security problem; any nonregistered user could view the table of members by simply accessing the website. We will now ensure that the table of members can be viewed only by the developer and the membership secretary (the administrator) and not by the whole world. One solution is to instruct the membership secretary how to install and use phpMyAdmin; however, we will assume that our membership secretary is not very computer literate and does not want to learn phpMyAdmin.

Our solution will be to restrict access to the *view_table.php* page and all other administrator pages so that only the membership secretary can view them. This will be achieved by using sessions and a different user_level number for the administrator. The administrator will be provided with a user-friendly interface so that they can search and amend membership records.

To sum up, our rules for differentiating between types of membership will be as follows:

- Nonmembers will not be able to view private pages because users can't log in until they are registered.

- Registered members will be able to access members pages because they can log in. Doing so initiates a session that allows them to open members pages.

- The administrator is the only person able to access administration pages. When they log in, the act of logging in starts a session that checks the user_level before they can open an administrator's page. The user_level is different from ordinary members' user levels.

Before designing a login page, we must also create a means of differentiating between an ordinary registered member and a member who is also the administrator. The administrator will have extra privileges. In the next tutorial, you will learn how to add a new column with the title *user_level* to an existing database table. This new column will enable us to differentiate between types of membership.

Creating User Levels to Limit Access to Private Pages

To limit access to the view table page, we will add a column to the users table called *user_level*. In this column, we will give the administrator a user level number of 1. Note: If you provide the ability to set this value via a web page, we suggest you use a less obvious value (like 999) to indicate an administrative level. The number relates to the membership secretary's login details and to no other person.

Access phpMyAdmin and click the database logindb. Then click the users table. Click the Structure tab. Look below the records to find the Add symbol, next to the words *Add 1 column*, as illustrated in Figure 3-6.

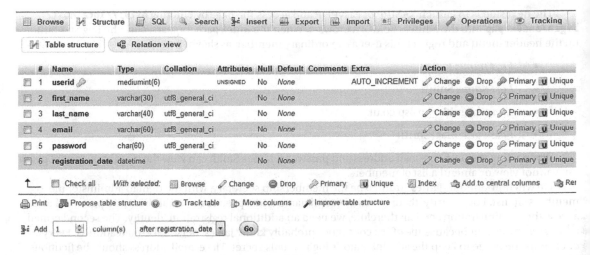

Figure 3-6. *The Add symbol appears at the bottom of this screen*

Next, to the right of the words *Add 1 column*, use the drop-down menu to select registration_date. Alternatively, select the radio button labeled *At end of table* and then click the Go button.

You will be taken to the screen shown in Figure 3-7.

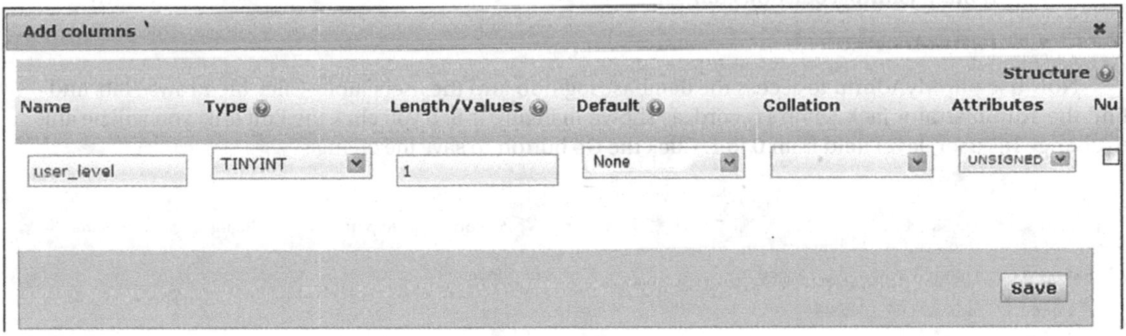

Figure 3-7. *Creating the title and attributes for the new user_level column*

Insert the new column name and its attributes as follows:

- *Name*: user_level

- *Type*: TINYINT

- *Length/Value*: 1

- *Default*: None

- *Attributes*: UNSIGNED

When you are satisfied with the attributes, click the Save button. The new column will be created.

The next step is to launch XAMPP or easyPHP and access the page by entering **http://localhost/login/index.php** into the address field of a browser. When the index page appears, click the Register button on the header menu and register this user as an ordinary member, as shown here:

- *First name*: James

- *Last name*: Smith

- *E-mail*: jsmith@myisp.co.uk

- *Password*: Blacksm1th

When using the proper e-mail address and password, James Smith can view the members' special pages but cannot view or amend a list of members.

We will now appoint James Smith to be the membership secretary, with the right to administer the membership list. For security, there needs a second name and a pseudo e-mail address and password to access the administration section; therefore, we need an additional registration identity. The second e-mail address is important because the office colleagues probably know James' personal e-mail address. Every effort must be made to keep the administrator's login details secret. The e-mail address should be fictitious, but it must conform to the accepted format for e-mails. Now register the membership secretary a second time using the pseudonym ("Jack"), the new e-mail address, and the new password as follows:

- *First name*: Jack

- *Last name*: Smith

- *E-mail*: jsmith@outcook.com

- *Password*: D0gsb0dy

Now use phpMyAdmin to access the database logindb and the users table. Click the Browse tab, and find the administrator Jack Smith's record, as shown in Figure 3-8. If you click the Edit link, you will be able to change his user_level field from 0 to 1. Click the Go button to save the change

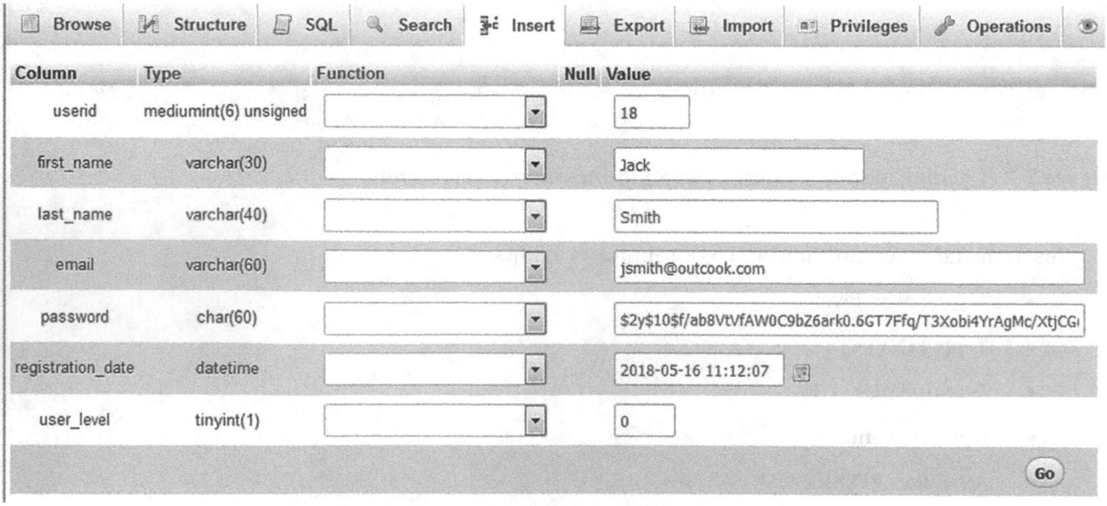

Figure 3-8. Find Jack Smith's record and change user_level to 1

When James Smith logs in with the personal e-mail address and original password, the members page will display just like any other member. This is because the original password has a user_level of zero, the same as all other registered members. However, when James logs in the Jack e-mail address and the administrator's password, the administer page will be displayed because the Jack e-mail address's user_level is 1.

A real-world administrator would ensure that nobody could ever discover the alternative e-mail address and the new password. People contacting the administrator would use the original name and personal e-mail address.

■ **Tip** If James Smith resigns and a new administrator is appointed, the webmaster will delete Jack Smith's record. A new administrator pseudonym and new password will then be assigned to James' replacement. The new membership secretary would be assigned an alternative (fake) e-mail address as the administrator login with a new password. The webmaster would then set the membership secretary's user level to 1.

Now we will create the login page and introduce some new PHP statements.

Log In

From a user's point of view, the ability to log in or log out of a website is pointless unless it leads to some advantage, such as a special page for members or permission to post comments in a blog. In the following sections, we will create new pages that will interact with registered users. These will be a login page, a members-only page, and an administrator's page. The same login page is used for logging into either the members pages or the administrator's pages. You would be forgiven for thinking that the admin and members pages are fully protected by the login process. However, imagine the following scenario.

A member has logged in to a private page and is then called away to take a telephone call. Someone could look at the member's computer and read the URL of the private page in the address field of the browser. If that person then entered the URLs on their own computer, they could access the private page. Clearly, this must be prevented. This is achieved by means of the sessions described later in this chapter.

First, we must create a header for the login page.

The Header for the Login Page

Figure 3-9 shows the login header with three menu buttons.

Figure 3-9. *The login page header*

Listing 3-6 shows the code for the login header.

Listing 3-6. Creating the Header for the Login Page (login-header.php)

```
<div class="col-sm-2">
<img class="img-fluid float-left" src="logo.jpg" alt="Logo">
</div>
```

```
<div class="col-sm-8">
 <h1 class="blue-text mb-4 font-bold">Header Goes Here</h1>
 </div>
    <nav class="col-sm-2">
        <div class="btn-group-vertical btn-group-sm" role="group" aria-label="Button Group">
  <button type="button" class="btn btn-secondary"
    onclick="location.href = 'login.php'" >Erase Entries</button>
  <button type="button" class="btn btn-secondary"
    onclick="location.href = 'register-page.php'">Register</button>
  <button type="button" class="btn btn-secondary"
    onclick="location.href = 'index.php'">Cancel</button>
</div>
    </nav>
```

Now we need to look at a procedure for limiting access to the table of members. We will prevent general users and registered members from viewing the table, but we will allow the administrator to view the table and amend records.

Figure 3-10 shows the appearance of the login page.

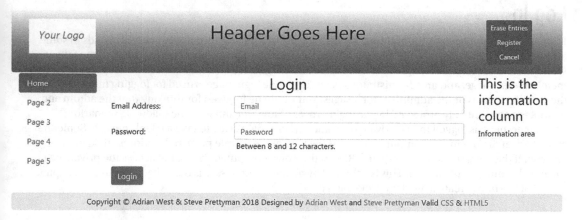

Figure 3-10. *The login page*

Note that the redundant buttons have been removed from the heading on this page.

The Login Page

Now that we have a user_level column, we can create the login page to include two conditionals. The conditionals will recognize the user_level of the administrator (user_level 1) and the ordinary member (user_level 0). When the genuine administrator logs in, they will see the administration page complete with new menu buttons. When registered members log in, they will be redirected to the members page. The HTML code is shown in Listing 3-7a.

Listing 3-7a. Creating the Login Page (login.php)

```
<!DOCTYPE html>
<html lang="en">
<head>
  <title>Template for an interactive web page</title>
```

```html
<meta charset="utf-8">
<meta name="viewport" content=
    "width=device-width, initial-scale=1, shrink-to-fit=no">
<!-- Bootstrap CSS File -->
<link rel="stylesheet"
href=
"https://stackpath.bootstrapcdn.com/bootstrap/4.1.0/css/bootstrap.min.css"
 integrity=
 "sha3849gVQ4dYFwwWSjIDZnLEWnxCjeSWFphJiwGPXr1jddIhOegiu1FwO5qRGvFXOdJZ4"
 crossorigin="anonymous">
  <script src="verify.js"></script>
</head>
<body>
<div class="container" style="margin-top:30px">
<!-- Header Section -->
<header class="jumbotron text-center row col-sm-14"
style="margin-bottom:2px; background:linear-gradient(white, #0073e6);
 padding:20px;">
  <?php include('login-header.php'); ?>
</header>
<!-- Body Section -->
  <div class="row" style="padding-left: 0px;">
<!-- Left-side Column Menu Section -->
  <nav class="col-sm-2">
    <ul class="nav nav-pills flex-column">
            <?php include('nav.php'); ?>
    </ul>
  </nav>
  <!-- Validate Input -->
<?php
if ($_SERVER['REQUEST_METHOD'] == 'POST') {                      //#1
 require('process-login.php');
} // End of the main Submit conditional.
?>
<div class="col-sm-8">
<h2 class="h2 text-center">Login</h2>
<form action="login.php" method="post" name="loginform" id="loginform">
  <div class="form-group row">
    <label for="email" class="col-sm-4 col-form-label">Email Address:</label>
    <div class="col-sm-8">
      <input type="text" class="form-control" id="email" name="email"
          placeholder="Email" maxlength="30" required
          value="<?php if (isset($_POST['email'])) echo $_POST['email']; ?>" >
    </div>
  </div>
  <div class="form-group row">
    <label for="password" class="col-sm-4 col-form-label">Password:</label>
    <div class="col-sm-8">
<input type="password" class="form-control" id="password" name="password"
placeholder="Password" maxlength="40" required
          value=
            "<?php if (isset($_POST['password'])) echo $_POST['password']; ?>">
```

```
            <span>Between 8 and 12 characters.</span></p>
    </div>
  </div>
<div class="form-group row">
    <div class="col-sm-12">
        <input id="submit" class="btn btn-primary" type="submit" name="submit"
        value="Login">
    </div>
        </div>
        </form>
</div>
<!-- Right-side Column Content Section -->
<?php
 if(!isset($errorstring)) {
        echo '<aside class="col-sm-2">';
        include('info-col.php');
        echo '</aside>';
        echo '</div>';
        echo '<footer class="jumbotron text-center row col-sm-14"
               style="padding-bottom:1px; padding-top:8px;">';
 }
 else
 {
        echo '<footer class="jumbotron text-center col-sm-12"
        style="padding-bottom:1px; padding-top:8px;">';
 }
  include('footer.php');
 ?>
</footer>
</div>
</body>
</html>
```

Explanation of the Code

Most of the code will by now be familiar to you. Some code is explained by comments within the listing.

```
if ($_SERVER['REQUEST_METHOD'] == 'POST') {                              //#1
 require('process-login.php');
} // End of the main Submit conditional.
```

One difference is that the login file pulls in the process-login code for verification of the information entered by the user. Listing 3-7b provides the PHP login verification code.

The form is sticky—that is, the user entries are retained and redisplayed by PHP if the user makes a mistake that triggers an error message. With the register page, the entries made by the user are verified before being submitted to the server. If there is a problem, HTML5 requires the user to correct it before the page is submitted. Thus, the data is correct before it is sent to the server. The PHP code on the server will return error messages if the code was corrupted between the browser and server.

When someone logs in, the e-mail and password can be verified as correct only by using PHP code on the server. The PHP server code must first retrieve the e-mail, password, and other information from the database table. Then compare the user-entered e-mail and password with those retrieved. The PHP code on the server (not the HTML5 code) will decide whether it is valid. If it is not valid, the code will return an error message to the browser. Because the error message is sent back by the server, we can also return the user-entered values of the e-mail and password to the form at the same time. This allows a more user-friendly response, without causing any additional server calls. Listing 3-7b shows the e-mail and password verification code.

Listing 3-7b. Verifying the Login (process-login.php)

```php
<?php
// This section processes submissions from the login form
// Check if the form has been submitted:
if ($_SERVER['REQUEST_METHOD'] == 'POST') {
    //connect to database
try {
    require ('mysqli_connect.php');
    // Validate the email address
// Check for an email address:
            $email = filter_var( $_POST['email'], FILTER_SANITIZE_EMAIL);
        if ((empty($email)) || (!filter_var($email, FILTER_VALIDATE_EMAIL))) {
            $errors[] = 'You forgot to enter your email address';
            $errors[] = ' or the e-mail format is incorrect.';
        }
    // Validate the password
        $password =
            filter_var( $_POST['password'], FILTER_SANITIZE_STRING);
        if (empty($password)) {
            $errors[] = 'You forgot to enter your password.';
        }
    if (empty($errors)) { // If everything's OK.                          #1
// Retrieve the user_id, psword, first_name and user_level for that
// email/password combination
 $query =
   "SELECT userid, password, first_name, user_level FROM users WHERE email=?";
    $q = mysqli_stmt_init($dbcon);
    mysqli_stmt_prepare($q, $query);

        // bind $id to SQL Statement
        mysqli_stmt_bind_param($q, "s", $email);
        // execute query
        mysqli_stmt_execute($q);
        $result = mysqli_stmt_get_result($q);
        $row = mysqli_fetch_array($result, MYSQLI_NUM);
        if (mysqli_num_rows($result) == 1) {
        //if one database row (record) matches the input:-
        // Start the session, fetch the record and insert the
        // values in an array
        if (password_verify($password, $row[1])) {                    //#2
            session_start();
            // Ensure that the user level is an integer.
```

```php
                $_SESSION['user_level'] = (int) $row[3];
                // Use a ternary operation to set the URL                    #3
$url = ($_SESSION['user_level'] === 1) ? 'admin-page.php' :
                'members-page.php';
        header('Location: ' . $url);
        // Make the browser load either the members or the admin page
        } else { // No password match was made.                            #4
$errors[] = 'E-mail/Password entered does not match our records. ';
$errors[] = 'Perhaps you need to register, just click the Register ';
$errors[] = 'button on the header menu';
        }
        } else { // No e-mail match was made.
$errors[] = 'E-mail/Password entered does not match our records. ';
$errors[] = 'Perhaps you need to register, just click the Register ';
$errors[] = 'button on the header menu';
}
}
if (!empty($errors)) {
                $errorstring =
                "Error! <br /> The following error(s) occurred:<br>";
                foreach ($errors as $msg) { // Print each error.
                        $errorstring .= " $msg<br>\n";
                }
                $errorstring .= "Please try again.<br>";
echo "<p class=' text-center col-sm-2' style='color:red'>$errorstring</p>";
                }// End of if (!empty($errors)) IF.
                mysqli_stmt_free_result($q);
                mysqli_stmt_close($q);
        }
 catch(Exception $e) // We finally handle any problems here
    {
      // print "An Exception occurred. Message: " . $e->getMessage();
      print "The system is busy please try later";
    }
    catch(Error $e)
    {
       //print "An Error occurred. Message: " . $e->getMessage();
       print "The system is busy please try again later.";
    }
} // no else to allow user to enter values
?>
```

Explanation of the Code

This section explains the code.

```php
if (empty($errors)) { // If everything's OK                                 #1
   // Retrieve the user_id, psword, first_name and user_level for that
  // email/password combination
  $query =
  "SELECT user_id, password, first_name, user_level FROM users WHERE email=?";
```

```
$q = mysqli_stmt_init($dbcon);
mysqli_stmt_prepare($q, $query);
// bind $id to SQL Statement
   mysqli_stmt_bind_param($q, "s", $email);
// execute query
mysqli_stmt_execute($q);
$result = mysqli_stmt_get_result($q);
$row = mysqli_fetch_array($result, MYSQLI_NUM);
if (mysqli_num_rows($result) == 1) {
```

If no problems are encountered (that is, if $email and $password have been entered properly by the user), the e-mail is used to retrieve the record from the database. It is assumed that the e-mail is unique.

```
if (password_verify($password, $row[1])) {                                      //#2
        session_start();
        // Ensure that the user level is an integer.
        $_SESSION['user_level'] = $row[3];
```

The password_verify function must be used to compare passwords since the password stored in the database table has been hashed. If the password from the database matches the password from the user, a session is started. It is used to check the authorization of the person logging in. The user_level is stored in a session variable (which is really a session array) to allow us to access it whenever we need to verify the level of access needed. Sessions will be explained fully at the end of this explanatory section.

```
/ Use a ternary operation to set the URL                                         #3
$url - ($_SESSION['user_level'] --- 1) ? 'admin-page.php' :
 'members-page.php';
        header('Location: ' . $url);
        // Make the browser load either the members' or the admin page
```

At this point, we will break the rule we set for this book: we are introducing a clever piece of shorthand code. It is a common PHP device for choosing between two outcomes and is therefore particularly useful and not too difficult to understand.

The word *ternary* has nothing to do with a reserve for seabirds of the family laridae. It is a mathematical term used by programmers and website developers. It is the third operator in the series "unary, binary, ternary." In other words, *ternary* has three parts. The ternary operator is often called a *ternary conditional* because it is a concise way of setting a conditional (if-then expression). The operator uses the symbols ? and :. The format we are using redirects the user to either the URL for the admin page or the URL for the members page. The code is as follows:

```
$url = ($_SESSION['user_level'] === 1) ? 'admin-page.php' :
 'members-page.php';
```

The first part of the statement on the right (enclosed in brackets) looks at the user_level in the session array and asks if it is identical to 1. The three equal signs mean "identical to." If it is identical to 1, the question mark turns the next two items into a conditional statement. It is saying "If the user_level is identical to 1, then assign the *admin-page.php* to the variable named $url." The colon is the equivalent of *else*; therefore, if the user_level is not identical to 1, the $url is set to *members-page.php*. Remember, registered members have a user_level of 0.

The variable $url, therefore, is set to a page, and the user is redirected to that page using the familiar header statement.

```
header('Location: ' . $url);
```

The longhand equivalent of the ternary statement is as follows:

```
if ($_SESSION['user_level'] === 1) {
header('location: admin-page.php');
}else{
header('location: members-page.php');
}
```

If the user's login data does not match the data in the database table, messages are stored in the error array as shown below.

```
        } else { // No password match was made.                    #4
$errors[] = 'E-mail/Password entered does not match our records. ';
$errors[] = 'Perhaps you need to register, just click the Register ';
$errors[] = 'button on the header menu';
        }
        } else { // No e-mail match was made.
$errors[] = 'E-mail/Password entered does not match our records. ';
$errors[] = 'Perhaps you need to register, just click the Register ';
$errors[] = 'button on the header menu';
}
```

Figure 3-11 shows the error messages that are displayed.

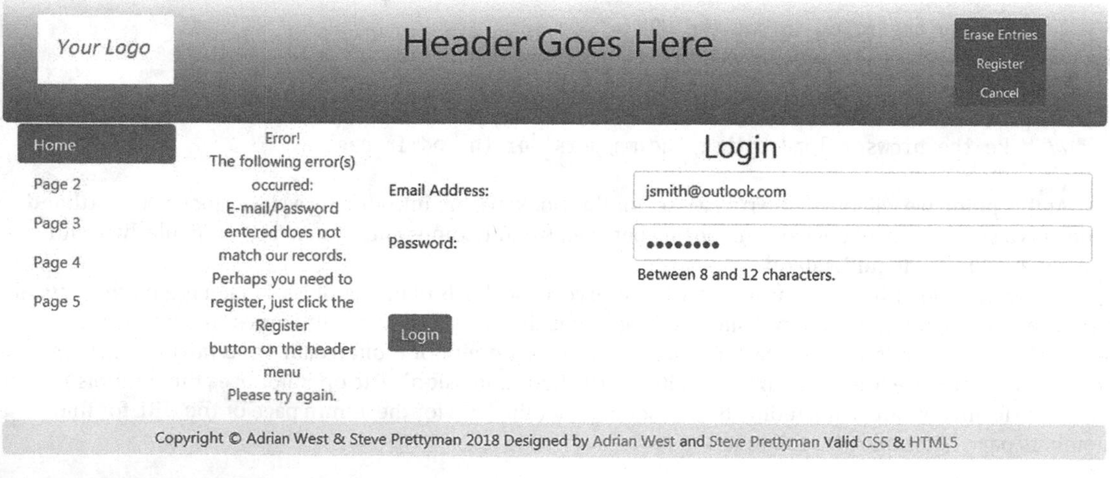

Figure 3-11. *One of the error messages displayed when the login is unsuccessful*

No hint is given as to which of the two entries (e-mail or password) was incorrect; this is a security feature. For instance, if the error message stated that the e-mail address was incorrect but the password was acceptable, a hacker would be able to concentrate on trying possible e-mail addresses. We should also limit the number of invalid attempts to reduce the chance that a hacker can guess the right combination. However, for now, let's just verify the e-mail and password.

The new database logindb will allow registered members to log in and log out of a members page. Nonregistered users will therefore be prevented from accessing the member's page. This is not completely secure because someone could look over the member's shoulder and discover the file name of the member's page in the browser's address field. Using that name, they could then access the member's page, as previously mentioned. This security loophole will be dealt with by using sessions.

Sessions

Pages that need to be kept private will use a feature called *sessions*; therefore, sessions and their application will now be explained. Registered members should be able to log in once per visit to the website. They should not have to log in several times to access several private pages. The login state should persist while the user is logged in. The period between login and logout is called a *session*. Additional information (such as the user_level) can be stored as a session variable. These variables, by default, are actually stored in a session array. These variables will no longer be available after the session is closed. If a session exists, the web page can use these variables to provide extra features for the logged-in user.

■ **Tip** Think of a session as a sort of security pass. When a user has successfully logged in, a security pass (a session and/or session variable) for that person is stored. A security guard is stationed at the door of each private page. When the user tries to open a private page, the security guard on that page checks the security pass (the session and/or session variable). If the pass confirms that the person is authorized to access the page, the private page is opened. When a user logs out, the session and its array (containing the session variables) are destroyed. Sessions carry with them several pieces of useful information about the user that can be accessed and used in the private pages.

The process when using sessions is as follows:

1. If a user is authorized to log in and logs in successfully, a session is created.

2. When a user tries to access a private page, the private page checks to see whether a session for that user exists.

3. If the session exists, the private page is opened.

4. If the session does not exist, the user is directed back to the login page.

5. By using sessions, the server can be made to differentiate between types of users, such as nonmembers, registered members, and administrators.

6. Logged-in users can either move to other private pages or log out. When they log out, the session and its session array are destroyed.

A session is started as follows:

```
// Set the session data:
session_start();
```

A session is closed as follows:

```
}else{ //cancel the session
        $_SESSION = array[]; // Destroy the variables
        $params = session_get_cookie_params();
        // Destroy the cookie
        Setcookie(session_name(), '', time() - 42000,
                $params["path"], $params["domain"],
              · $params["secure"], $params["httponly"]);
        if (session_status() == PHP_SESSION_ACTIVE) { session_destroy(); } // Destroy the
        session itself
        header("location:index.php");
        }
```

Setting $_SESSION to array() will technically point $_SESSION to a new empty array. The old array (containing the session variables) will no longer be associated with the current session. This will cause the system to destroy the original array. More simply, we can say that any session variables that were created during the session are now wiped out. Optionally session information can be stored in a cookie (not recommended). If this option is chosen, the session_get_cookie_params function provides access to the parameters for the active session cookie. The Setcookie function uses the time parameter to set a negative expire time (a time that has already passed). This causes the cookie to immediate expire. The session_destroy function destroys the session, which would also delete the session array. Some developers using PHP 7.1+ have reported that warnings may occur if the session is already inactive. The if statement checks the status of the session before attempting to destroy it.

The act of logging in creates a session that saves variables in an array named $_SESSION. When the user has logged in and tries to open a private page, the PHP code checks that a session has been set up for that user. If it has, the private page will be opened in the user's browser.

In the following statements extracted from the code for *process-login.php*, the data is selected from the database, and then a session is created if the password is correct (the e-mail is also verified because a record would not be returned if the e-mail was not in the table). The user_level is saved into a temporary session variable on the server for use in private pages.

```
$query =
"SELECT userid, password, first_name, user_level FROM users WHERE email=?";
$q = mysqli_stmt_init($dbcon);
mysqli_stmt_prepare($q, $query);
// bind $id to SQL Statement
mysqli_stmt_bind_param($q, "s", $email);
// execute query
mysqli_stmt_execute($q);
$result = mysqli_stmt_get_result($q);
$row = mysqli_fetch_array($result, MYSQLI_NUM);
if (mysqli_num_rows($result) == 1) {
    //if one database row (record) matches the input:-
    // Start the session, fetch the record and insert the
    // values in an array
    if (password_verify($password, $row[1])) {
            session_start();
            // Ensure that the user level is an integer.
            $_SESSION['user_level'] = (int) $row[3];
```

■ **Tip** The session_start() function and the statements checking the session must appear at the top of the page before the HTML tag. Beginners are often puzzled by the session_start() function appearing on every private page: why does it not start a new session to replace the existing session? The answer is that if a session exists, the function does not start another session; instead, it checks the user's credentials, and if they are satisfactory, it allows the private page to load. If a session does not exist, it will start one; however, that session is not effective, and a conditional statement sends the user back to the login page.

Sessions create a unique session ID (SID). The first time the `<?php session_start(); ?>` statement is used, it establishes an SID. It registers the SID on the server and saves the information for use on any private pages. The following is an example of the code at the start of a private page accessible only to the administrator with a user_level number 1):

```php
<?php
session_start();
if (!isset($_SESSION['user_level']) or ($_SESSION['user_level'] != 1))
{ header("Location: login.php");
   exit();
}
?>
<!doctype html>
```

The code must be at the top of the page. The code can be translated as follows: "If the session does not exist or if the user level is not equal to 1, then the user will be sent back to the login page."

Our next step is to create a members-only page protected by this login session.

A Members-Only Page

Download the *members-page.php* file from Apress.com or create the page by hand-coding it using Listing 3-8. Figure 3-12 shows the members page created for this tutorial.

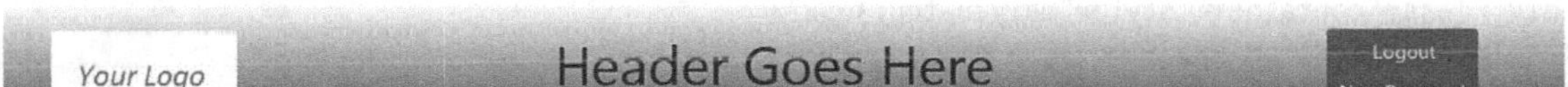

Figure 3-12. The members-only page

Note the revised members' header in Figure 3-12.

Also note the session, the redirection to the login page, and the included file for the new header are shown in Listing 3-8.

Listing 3-8. Creating the Members Page (members-page.php)

```php
<?php
session_start();                                                              //#1
if (!isset($_SESSION['user_level']) or ($_SESSION['user_level'] != 0))
{ header("Location: login.php");
  exit();
}
?>
<!DOCTYPE html>
<html lang="en">
<head>
  <title>Template for an interactive web page</title>
  <meta charset="utf-8">
  <meta name="viewport"
        content="width=device-width, initial-scale=1, shrink-to-fit=no">
  <!-- Bootstrap CSS File -->
  <link rel="stylesheet"
        href=
    "https://stackpath.bootstrapcdn.com/bootstrap/4.1.0/css/bootstrap.min.css"
    integrity=
      "sha384-9gVQ4dYFwwWSjIDZnLEWnxCjeSWFphJiwGPXr1jddIhOegiu1FwO5qRGvFXOdJZ4"
        crossorigin="anonymous">
</head>
<body>
<div class="container" style="margin-top:30px">
<!-- Header Section -->
<header class="jumbotron text-center row"
style="margin-bottom:2px; background:linear-gradient(white, #0073e6);
        padding:20px;">
  <?php include('header-members.php'); ?>
</header>
<!-- Body Section -->
  <div class="row" style="padding-left: 0px;">
<!-- Left-side Column Menu Section -->
  <nav class="col-sm-2">
      <ul class="nav nav-pills flex-column">
                <?php include('nav.php'); ?>
      </ul>
  </nav>
<!-- Center Column Content Section -->
<div class="col-sm-8">
<h2 class="text-center">This is the Member's Page</h2>
<p>The members page content. The members page content. The members page content.
<br>The members page content. The members page content. The members page content.
<br>The members page content. The members page content. The members page content.
<br>The members page content. The members page content. The members page content.
</p>
<p class="h3 text-center">Special offers to members only.</p>
    <p class="text-center"><strong>T-Shirts 10.00</strong></p>
<img class="mx-auto d-block" src="images/polo.png" alt="Polo Shirt"> <!--#2-->
<br>
```

```
</div>
<!-- Right-side Column Content Section -->
        <aside class="col-sm-2">
       <?php include('info-col.php'); ?>
         </aside>
  </div>
<!-- Footer Content Section -->
<footer class="jumbotron text-center row"
style="padding-bottom:1px; padding-top:8px;">
  <?php include('footer.php'); ?>
</footer>
</div>
</body>
</html>
```

Explanation of the Code

This section explains the code.

```php
<?php
session_start();                                                    //#1
if (!isset($_SESSION['user_level']) or ($_SESSION['user_level'] != 0))
{ header("Location: login.php");
  exit();
}
?>
```

The PHP session_start statement must appear immediately at the top of the code (just after the <?php line). There should be no extra spacing (no spaces before the <?php, and the first command after it should be the session_start()) because this can cause errors with the creation of the HTTP header for the page. Don't confuse this discussion of the "header" with the head section and header tag in HTML code as we have already discussed. The header we are referring to here is created to provide information to HTTP about the page itself. This code is generated for us, and in this situation we don't normally have to be concerned with it.

All private pages will begin with the session_start() function. The header redirection statement (header()) ensures that if no session was started or the user_level was not zero, the user would be redirected using the header command to the login page. This command creates an HTTP Get message to retrieve the login page. The exit() function also adds to the security by ending the execution of the page immediately. This ensures that no access is allowed to the rest of the page unless the user is properly signed in.

Optionally we could be more personal and provide a greeting specific to the user on our private pages.

```php
$_SESSION['first_name'] = (int) $row[2];
```

If we add this line of code right after the similar line in the login program, we can also store the user's first name. Remember, we don't want to simply store all the values we retrieved because we returned the password and do not want to store the password to be as secure as possible.

```php
<?php
echo '<h2>Welcome to the Admin Page ';
if (isset($_SESSION['first_name'])){
echo "{$_SESSION['first_name']}";
```

```
}
echo '</h2>';
?>
```

We can modify the welcome code in the members page, as shown previously, to provide a more personal greeting to the members page (or any other private page).

```
<p class="h3 text-center">Special offers to members only.</p>
    <p class="text-center"><strong>T-Shirts 10.00</strong></p>
<img class="mx-auto d-block" src="images/polo.png" alt="Polo Shirt"> <!--#2-->
```

To provide some extra content for members, they are provided with an opportunity to purchase a polo. The display of the h3 header is controlled by the Bootstrap h3 and text-center classes. The display of the image is controlled by the Bootstrap mx-auto and d-block classes. These classes work together to center the image within the column.

The next section demonstrates the importance of planning. Hasty decisions at this stage can cause major headaches later.

Planning the Administrator's Role

We now need to plan very carefully by considering what the membership secretary might want to do with the website and the database.

Let's assume the membership secretary will want to do the following:

- View the members-only page using the original member's password

- View the table of members using the administrator's e-mail and password

- Change the administrator's password occasionally for extra security

To achieve these aims, we need to complete the following tasks:

- Create a new header for the administration page

- Create the administration page

The administrator's requirements will dictate the content of the menu in the header of the administration page.

Later, in Chapters 4 and 5, we will add extra features to incorporate the following requirements:

- Search for and edit members' details using the administrator's password (for example, changing a name due to marriage). The Search button is added to the header; this button will be functional in future chapters.

- Delete records using the administrator's password (necessary when a member has resigned or died).

- The administrator will also need to know the total number of members—someone is bound to ask for them. This will be automatically displayed below the table of members.

We will now create the administrator's header and a private administrator's page.

A New Header for the Administration Page

Based on the first part of the preceding plan, the header for the administration page needs five buttons: Logout, View Members, Search, Search by Address, and New Password. Figure 3-13 shows the new header embedded in the administrator's page.

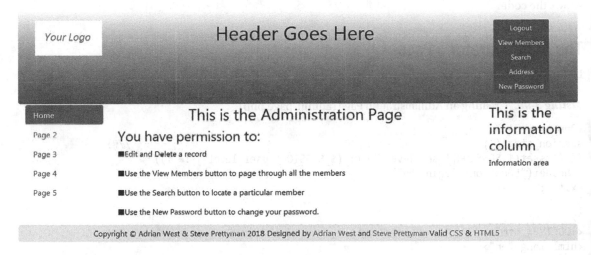

Figure 3-13. *The new header is shown embedded in the administrator's page*

The header now has five buttons. Listing 3-9a shows the new buttons.

Listing 3-9a. Creating the Administration Page Header (admin-header.php)

```
<div class="col-sm-2">
<img class="img-fluid float-left" src="logo.jpg" alt="Logo">
</div>
<div class="col-sm-8">
 <h1 class="blue-text mb-4 font-bold">Header Goes Here</h1>
 </div>
    <nav class="col-sm-2">
        <div class="btn-group-vertical btn-group-sm" role="group"
        aria-label="Button Group">
  <button type="button" class="btn btn-secondary"
        onclick="location.href = 'logout.php'" >Logout</button>
  <button type="button" class="btn btn-secondary"
        onclick="location.href = 'admin_view_users.php'">View Members
        </button>
  <button type="button" class="btn btn-secondary"
        onclick="location.href = '#'">Search</button>
  <button type="button" class="btn btn-secondary"
        onclick="location.href = '#'">Address</button>
  <button type="button" class="btn btn-secondary"
        onclick="location.href = 'register-password.php'">New Password
        </button>
</div>
    </nav>
```

■ **Note**   The search buttons do not work because we have not yet created the search pages. We will create the search pages in Chapter 4.

In the next step, we will add the new header and session details to the administration page. Listing 3-9b shows the code.

The Administrator's Page

Listing 3-9b shows the code for the administration page.

Listing 3-9b.   Creating an Administration Page (admin-page.php)

```php
<?php
session_start();                                                      //#1
if (!isset($_SESSION['user_level']) or ($_SESSION['user_level'] != 1))
{ header("Location: login.php");
exit();
}
?>
<!DOCTYPE html>
<html lang="en">
<head>
  <title>Administration Page/title>
  <meta charset="utf-8">
  <meta name="viewport" content="width=device-width, initial-scale=1,
        shrink-to-fit=no">
  <!-- Bootstrap CSS File -->
  <link rel="stylesheet"
  href=
"https://stackpath.bootstrapcdn.com/bootstrap/4.1.0/css/bootstrap.min.css"
  integrity=
"sha384-9gVQ4dYFwwWSjIDZnLEWnxCjeSWFphJiwGPXr1jddIhOegiu1FwO5qRGvFXOdJZ4"
        crossorigin="anonymous">
</head>
<body>
<div class="container" style="margin-top:30px">
<!-- Header Section -->
<header class="jumbotron text-center row"
style="margin-bottom:2px; background:linear-gradient(white, #0073e6);
        padding:20px;">
  <?php include('header-admin.php'); ?>
</header>
<!-- Body Section -->
  <div class="row" style="padding-left: 0px;">
<!-- Left-side Column Menu Section -->
  <nav class="col-sm-2">
      <ul class="nav nav-pills flex-column">
                <?php include('nav.php'); ?>
      </ul>
  </nav>
```

```
<!-- Center Column Content Section -->
<div class="col-sm-8">
<h2 class="text-center">This is the Administration Page</h2>
<h3>You have permission to:</h3>
<p>Edit and Delete a record</p>
<p>Use the View Members button to page through all the members</p>
<p>Use the Search button to locate a particular member</p>
<p>Use the New Password button to change your password.
</p>
</div>
<!-- Right-side Column Content Section -->
        <aside class="col-sm-2">
      <?php include('info-col.php'); ?>
        </aside>
  </div>
<!-- Footer Content Section -->
<footer class="jumbotron text-center row"
style="padding-bottom:1px; padding-top:8px;">
  <?php include('footer.php'); ?>
</footer>
</div>
</body>
</html>
```

Explanation of the Code

This section explains the code.

```
<?php                                                                        //#1
session_start();
if (!isset($_SESSION['user_level']) or ($_SESSION['user_level'] != 1))
{ header("Location: login.php");
   exit();
}
?>
```

Again, session_start is a security guard and is included at the top of the code to allow only those who are properly signed in with the correct user_level (1) access to the page. If they are not properly signed in or do not have user_level 1 clearance, they will be redirected to the login page. exit() assures that they cannot proceed further in the page.

The Logout Page

The next page enables users to log out. The code destroys the session when it is no longer required.

This is not a page that is visible to users. It acts as an intermediary page between the login page and the home page. Listing 3-9c shows the code.

Listing 3-9c. Creating the Logout Code (logout.php)

```php
<?php
session_start();//access the current session.                                    #1
// if no session variable exists then redirect the user
if (!isset($_SESSION['user_id'])) {                                             //#2
header("location:index.php");
exit();
//cancel the session and redirect the user:
}else{ //cancel the session                                                     //#3
 $_SESSION = array(); // Destroy the variables
      $params = session_get_cookie_params();
      // Destroy the cookie
      Setcookie(session_name(), ", time() - 42000,
      $params["path"], $params["domain"],
      $params["secure"], $params["httponly"]);
if (session_status() == PHP_SESSION_ACTIVE) {
      session_destroy(); } // Destroy the session itself
      header("location:index.php");
      }
```

Explanation of the Code

This section explains the code.

```php
session_start();//access the current session.                                    #1
```

The code allows the logged-in user to access the information in the memory of the session that was initiated in the login page. Line #1 links the new page to the information stored in that session.

```php
//if no session variable then redirect the user
if (!isset($_SESSION['user_id'])) {                                             //#2
header("location:index.php");
exit();
```

If the session variable user_id does not exist, the user is redirected to the home page. This would be an indication that they never signed in.

```php
}else{ //cancel the session                                                      #3
 $_SESSION = array(); // Destroy the variables
      $params = session_get_cookie_params();
      // Destroy the cookie
      Setcookie(session_name(), ", time() - 42000,
      $params["path"], $params["domain"],
      $params["secure"], $params["httponly"]);
if (session_status() == PHP_SESSION_ACTIVE) {
session_destroy(); } // Destroy the session itself
header("location:index.php");
      }
```

If the session exists and if a cookie was created, the user logs out by expiring the cookie (setting the time to a negative value). The session is destroyed, and the user is redirected to the home page.

Testing the Login/Logout Function

The web designer or a database administrator can access a table of members using phpMyAdmin. Normally an administrator/membership secretary will view a table of members through a web page. The administrator/membership secretary should only be able to view, edit, or delete a record. This is covered in the next section.

Start XAMPP or easyPHP, and use a browser to test the login facility. Enter the following URL into the browser's address field:

```
http://localhost/login/login.php
```

You should now be able to load the members page for ordinary members. You will also be able to load the administrator's page when the administrator logs in. The only buttons that do not yet function are the search buttons. These will be dealt with in Chapter 4. Concerning the administrator's page, the table view is not very helpful yet because the administrator cannot delete or amend a record. This will be achieved in Chapter 4 by the addition of delete and edit links.

Amending and deleting individual records is easy in phpMyAdmin, but the term *delete* is used instead of the term *drop*. Drop is used to delete whole tables and databases.

Amending and Deleting Individual Records

The webmaster/developer can amend and delete records as follows:

1. Access phpMyAdmin by entering the following into the address field of a browser:

    ```
    http://localhost/phpmyadmin/
    ```

2. Access the logindb database and then the users table.

3. Select the Browse tab, which displays a list of registered members. This is shown in Figure 3-14.

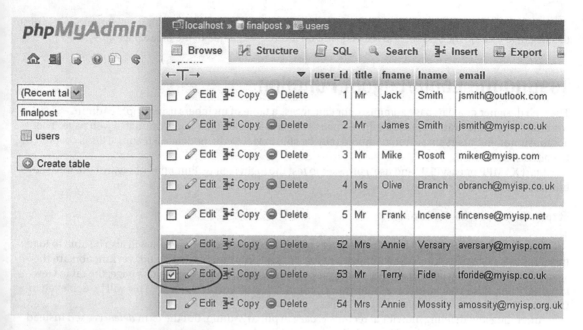

Figure 3-14. *Edit or delete an individual record*

Find the member's record to be amended or deleted and select its check box (shown circled in Figure 3-14). Then click Edit; you will be presented with a screen that will enable you to change the information about the user. You can also click Delete to remove the member. You will be asked if you really mean it. You can then decline or accept.

■ **Note**   We have increased security in this chapter. However, we will be adding additional security in future chapters. The code in this chapter is more secure than in Chapter 2. However, it's not yet ready for the "real world."

Summary

In this chapter, we amended various headers to give them more meaningful menu buttons, and we also removed redundant buttons. We discovered how to log in to private pages and how to log out of those special pages. We discovered a way of differentiating between different types of members by using sessions. We created a members-only page and learned how to use sessions to protect private pages. We also learned how to use a session so that only the administrator could access the administrator's page.

In each tutorial, explanations were provided for the PHP and SQL code. We added a little more security by removing the ability of ordinary members to view the table of members. We prevented unauthorized people from using a browser to enter the URLs of private pages. We also discovered how a developer could amend or delete individual records.

In the next chapter, we will learn how the membership secretary/administrator can search, amend, and delete records.

◼◼◼

Create an Administration Interface

In this chapter, we will present a user-friendly set of pages for an administrator who has moderate computer skills. We assume the administrator is not capable of using phpMyAdmin but that they know enough to be able to log in, access easy-to-use displays, and use simple editing facilities. We will make the table of members interactive so that the administrator can search, edit, delete, and re-order records. Only the administrator is permitted to access these facilities for deleting and amending records.

After completing this chapter, you will be able to create web pages that do the following:

- Administer a database

- Delete and edit records

- Paginate the displaying of records

- Search for an individual record

◼ **Caution**   When we talk about tables in this book, try not to confuse tables displayed on the screen with the database tables. These types of tables are two distinct entities. For instance, Table 4-1 is a database table and is not visible to the user. Figure 4-2 is a table displayed on the user's screen.

The Administration Database

The tutorials in this chapter are based on the templates used in previous chapters. We will keep things separate from previous tutorials by using new names for the database and its folder. However, a table can have the same name as earlier tutorials if the table lives in a different database. The table will therefore continue to be called *users*.

Let's begin by creating the database and the ability to access it.

Create a new folder and a new database as follows:

1. In the XAMPP *htdocs* folder or the easyPHP *eds-www* folder, create a new folder called *admintable*.

2. Either download the PHP files from the book's web page at www.apress.com (recommended) or type in the code as shown in this chapter and the previous chapter and place it in the new *admintable* folder.

■ **Note** If you copy paste code from the e-book, some of the quotes may not copy correctly. You can easily avoid problems by first copying the code into a basic text editor (like Microsoft Notepad). The editor will convert any incorrect quotes to standard quotes automatically. Then save the file and open it in a PHP editor (such as Notepad++).

If you are creating your own files, copy all the files from Chapter 3 and paste them into your new folder *admintable*. In the new folder, modify the file *mysqli_connect.php* as listed on the next page. Rename the file *admin-header.php* as *header-admin*.

3. Now open phpMyAdmin.

4. Create a new database called *admintable*.

5. Select the check box next to *admintable* and click Check Privileges.

6. Click the Add User button.

7. Enter a new user and password as follows:

   User: webmaster

   Password: C0ffeep0t

   Host: localhost

8. Be sure to record the new user and password details in your notebook.

9. Scroll down to Global privileges (Check All/Uncheck All), and click Check All.

10. Scroll down to the bottom of the form and click the Add User button (or the Go button on some versions).

To connect to the administration database, you use the code shown in Listing 4-1.

Listing 4-1. Creating the Code for Connecting to the admintable Database (mysqli_connect.php)

```php
<?php
// Create a connection to the admintable database and set the encoding
Define ('DB_USER', 'webmaster');
Define ('DB_PASSWORD', 'C0ffeep0t');
Define ('DB_HOST', 'localhost');
Define ('DB_NAME', 'admintable');
// Make the connection:
$dbcon = new mysqli(DB_HOST, DB_USER, DB_PASSWORD, DB_NAME);
mysqli_set_charset($dbcon, 'utf8'); // Set the encoding...
```

Make sure to test your access to the database before attempting to run any other programs. Once you are sure that your user ID and password does access the database correctly, then continue with the procedures shown in the following sections. To test the connection, type **http://localhost/admintable/mysqi_connect.php** in your browser. If you get no errors and see a blank page, the test was successful.

The Users Table

In phpMyAdmin, make sure you click the new database admintable and then create this users table with seven columns. Set the encoding to utf8-general-ci. Give the columns the titles and attributes shown in Table 4-1.

Remember, when selecting the A_I check box in phpMyAdmin, a pop-up window may ask you to verify that *userid* is the primary index and will request the size again. *Do not* put a size in the pop-up window. If you do, you will get an error.

Table 4-1. *The Attributes for the users Table*

Column name	Type	Length/Values	Default	Attributes	NULL	Index	A_I
userid	MEDIUMINT	6	None	UNSIGNED	☐	PRIMARY	☑
first_name	VARCHAR	30	None		☐		☐
last_name	VARCHAR	40	None		☐		☐
email	VARCHAR	50	None		☐		☐
password	CHAR	60	None		☐		☐
registration_date	DATETIME		None		☐		☐
user_level	TINYINT	1	None	UNSIGNED	☐		☐

The password column size will be determined by the latest hashing standards for PHP. Please visit www.php.net and adjust the size as required.

Use the *register-page.php* file (included in the downloadable files for Chapter 4 from Apress.com) to register the administrator as an ordinary member using the following data:

- *First name*: James
- *Last name*: Smith
- *E-mail*: jsmith@myisp.co.uk
- *Password*: Blacksm1th

The registered member James Smith will be appointed as the membership secretary using the pseudonym *Jack Smith*. We can safely assume that James Smith (alias Jack Smith) would like to view the members page occasionally as well as viewing the administration page. He will use his membership e-mail and password to view the members page, but he needs a different e-mail and password to access the administration section. Now register the membership secretary a second time with his pseudonym and a new password as follows:

- *First name*: Jack
- *Last name*: Smith
- *E-mail*: jsmith@outcook.com
- *Password*: D0gsb0dy

■ **Important**   Use phpMyAdmin to change Jack Smith's user level to 1.

■ **Note** To change the user_level, in phpMyAdmin click the database name (in the column listing) and then click the users table listed below the database name. Click the edit icon to the left of Jack Smith. Change the level to 1 and click Go (or Save).

Now register these members so that we have something to play with. Use the details in Table 4-2.

Table 4-2. *Suggested Details for Members*

First Name	Last Name	Email	Password
Mike	Rosoft	miker@myisp.com	W1llg@t3s
Olive	Branch	obranch@myisp.co.uk	An01yon@
Frank	Incense	fincense@myisp.net	P@rfum3
Terry	Fide	tfide@myisp.de	Scar@dst1ff
Rose	Bush	rbush@myisp.co.uk	R@dbl00ms
Annie	Versary	aversary@myisp.com	H8ppy#d8y

You will now have a total of eight records.

■ **Note** Now that we are using sessions together with the member's user_level, you will not be able to access any of the administration pages without first logging in as the administrator (user_level = 1). If you attempt to access the pages directly, they will redirect you to the login page.

We will be using the administrator's page from Chapter 3 (Figure 4-1) to access the new features in this chapter. The following section will explain these changes.

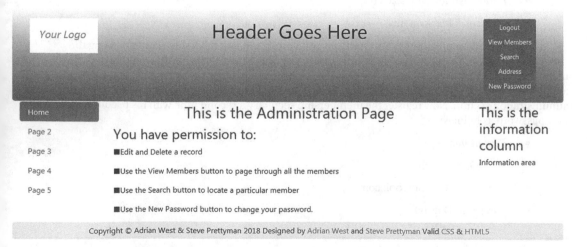

Figure 4-1. The admin page

We will display an extended table of data using a revised page named *view_users.php*. The next section demonstrates this concept.

Revising the View Users Page to Include Editing and Deleting

The display table needs two extra columns for links that will enable the administrator to edit and delete records. In Chapter 3, we concatenated (joined) the first and last names so that they appeared in one column. To be able to re-order the records, the first and last names are displayed in separate columns. Passwords must always be secured and never displayed within a table. Administrators usually have abilities to reset passwords but not the ability to see current passwords. The revised display for the administrator will have six columns, as shown in Table 4-3. Remember that this is not the *user's* database table but the table that will be displayed on the screen for the administrator; the two tables are quite different.

Table 4-3. *The Format of the New Table As It Will Be Displayed for the Administrator Only*

Edit	Delete	Last Name	First Name	Email	Date Registered
Edit	Delete	Rosoft	Mike	miker@myisp.com	October 30, 2018

Two of the new columns now have links to enable the administrator to interact with the records. Most importantly, this page is only for the administrator; therefore, it needs a security guard, in other words, a *session*. Figure 4-2 shows the appearance of this interactive table

Figure 4-2. *The interactive table for an administrator*

115

■ **Note** You can view the table using XAMPP or easyPHP and a browser, but the Edit and Delete links will not work until we create the pages for deleting and editing a record. These pages are described later in the chapter.

Listing 4-2 shows the amendments to create the new View Users page. The administrator's page begins with session code for security.

Listing 4-2. Amending the Table View to Include Two Links (admin-view-users.php)

```
<?php                                                                //#1
session_start();
if (!isset($_SESSION['user_level']) || ($_SESSION['user_level'] != 1))
{
 header("Location: login.php");
exit();
}
?>
 <!DOCTYPE html>
<html lang="en">
<head>
 <title>Template for an interactive web page</title>
 <meta charset="utf-8">
 <meta name="viewport"
content="width=device-width, initial-scale=1, shrink-to-fit=no">
  <!-- Bootstrap CSS File -->
  <link rel="stylesheet"
        href=
"https://stackpath.bootstrapcdn.com/bootstrap/4.1.0/css/bootstrap.min.css"
        integrity=
"sha384-9gVQ4dYFwwWSjIDZnLEWnxCjeSWFphJiwGPXr1jddIhOegiu1FwO5qRGvFXOdJZ4"
        crossorigin="anonymous">
</head>
<body>
<div class="container" style="margin-top:30px">
<!-- Header Section -->
<header class="jumbotron text-center row"
style="margin-bottom:2px; background: linear-gradient(white, #0073e6); padding:20px;">
                <?php include('header.php'); ?>
</header>
<!-- Body Section -->
<div class="row" style="padding-left: 0px;">
<!-- Left-side Column Menu Section -->
 <nav class="col-sm-2">
        <ul class="nav nav-pills flex-column">
<?php include('nav.php'); ?>
        </ul>
  </nav>
<!-- Center Column Content Section -->
<div class="col-sm-8">
<h2 class="text-center">These are the registered users</h2>
<p>
```

```php
<?php
try {
// This script retrieves all the records from the users table.          #2
require('mysqli_connect.php'); // Connect to the database.
// Make the query:
// Nothing passed from user safe query
$query = "SELECT last_name, first_name, email, ";
$query .= "DATE_FORMAT(registration_date, '%M %d, %Y')";
$query .=
        " AS regdat, userid FROM users ORDER BY registration_date ASC";
// Prepared statement not needed since hardcoded
$result = mysqli_query ($dbcon, $query); // Run the query.
if ($result) { // If it ran OK, display the records.
// Table header.                                                        #3
echo '<table class="table table-striped">
<tr>
<th scope="col">Edit</th>
<th scope="col">Delete</th>
<th scope="col">Last Name</th>
<th scope="col">First Name</th>
<th scope="col">Email</th>
<th scope="col">Date Registered</th>
</tr>';
// Fetch and print all the records:                                     #4
while ($row = mysqli_fetch_array($result, MYSQLI_ASSOC)) {
            // Remove special characters that might already be in table to   #5
            // reduce the chance of XSS exploits
            $user_id = htmlspecialchars($row['userid'], ENT_QUOTES);
            $last_name = htmlspecialchars($row['last_name'], ENT_QUOTES);
            $first_name = htmlspecialchars($row['first_name'], ENT_QUOTES);
            $email = htmlspecialchars($row['email'], ENT_QUOTES);
            $registration_date =
htmlspecialchars($row['regdat'], ENT_QUOTES);                           //#6
            echo '<tr>
                    <td><a href="edit_user.php?id=' . $user_id .
'">Edit</a></td>
                    <td><a href="delete_user.php?id=' . $user_id .
                        '">Delete</a></td>';                            //#7
            echo '<td>' . $last_name . '</td>
                    <td>' . $first_name . '</td>
                    <td>' . $email . '</td>
                    <td>' . $registration_date . '</td>
            </tr>';
    }
    echo '</table>'; // Close the table.                                #8
    mysqli_free_result ($result); // Free up the resources.
}
else { // If it did not run OK.
// Error message:
echo
'<p class="text-center">The current users could not be retrieved. ';
echo 'We apologize for any inconvenience.</p>';
```

```php
// Debug message:
// echo '<p>' . mysqli_error($dbcon) . '<br><br>Query: ' . $q . '</p>';
exit;
} // End of if ($result)
mysqli_close($dbcon); // Close the database connection.
}
catch(Exception $e) // We finally handle any problems here
{
    // print "An Exception occurred. Message: " . $e->getMessage();
    print "The system is busy please try later";
}
catch(Error $e)
{
    //print "An Error occurred. Message: " . $e->getMessage();
    print "The system is busy please try again later.";
    }
?>
</div>
<!-- Right-side Column Content Section -->
<aside class="col-sm-2">
    <?php include('info-col.php'); ?>
</aside>
</div>
<!-- Footer Content Section -->
<footer class="jumbotron text-center row"
style="padding-bottom:1px; padding-top:8px;">
  <?php include('footer.php'); ?>
</footer>
</div>
</body>
</html>
```

Explanation of the Code

This section explains the code.

```php
<?php
session_start();
//                                                                    #1
if (!isset($_SESSION['user_level']) or ($_SESSION['user_level'] != 1))
{
    header("Location: login.php");
    exit();
}
?>
```

This session code secures the page and returns any unauthorized users to the login page. No one can access the page unless they are an administrator (user_level = 1).

```php
<?php
try {
// This script retrieves all the records from the users table.          #2
```

```php
require('mysqli_connect.php'); // Connect to the database.

// Make the query:
// Nothing passed from user safe query

$query =
"SELECT last_name, first_name, email, DATE_FORMAT(registration_date, '%M %d, %Y')";

$query .=
        " AS regdat, userid FROM users ORDER BY registration_date ASC";

// Prepared statement not needed since hardcoded
$result = mysqli_query ($dbcon, $query); // Run the query.

if ($result) { // If it ran OK, display the records.
```

The previous code selects the items from the users table that will populate the columns in the displayed table. The DATE_FORMAT function will format the registration_date retrieved from the table in month, day, year format. The AS statement will allow us to retrieve this formatted date using the regdat name. If we retrieved the date using the registration_date name, it would still be in whatever format exists in the table. The table records are displayed in ascending order (ASC) by registration date. To display the records in descending order, use DESC.

```php
// Table header.                                                          #3
echo '<table class="table table-striped">
<tr>
<th scope="col">Edit</th>
<th scope="col">Delete</th>
<th scope="col">Last Name</th>
<th scope="col">First Name</th>
<th scope="col">Email</th>
<th scope="col">Date Registered</th>
</tr>';
```

This code displays an HTML table with six headings in the title row. Each row will have alternating colors.

```php
// Fetch and print all the records:                                      #4
while ($row = mysqli_fetch_array($result, MYSQLI_ASSOC)) {
```

The code loops through the user's table's data (contained in $result) until all the data has been displayed. This is achieved by the while() function. The data is placed into an associative array named $row. An associative array uses a key (such as user_id) instead of an index (number) to determine what column to use. For example, in the following code, the associate array $row includes a column with a key of *userid*. The keys are automatically created using the column names from the table in the database.

```php
        // Remove special characters that might already be in table to    #5
            // reduce the chance of XSS exploits
            $user_id = htmlspecialchars($row['userid'], ENT_QUOTES);
            $last_name = htmlspecialchars($row['last_name'], ENT_QUOTES);
            $first_name = htmlspecialchars($row['first_name'], ENT_QUOTES);
            $email = htmlspecialchars($row['email'], ENT_QUOTES);
            $registration_date =
htmlspecialchars($row['regdat'], ENT_QUOTES);
```

We are making every effort to insert good valid data in the database table. So, can't we assume we just pulled good data from the database? No! There are two reasons why; the first is that the data in the table could contain harmful code that can be executed, and the second is that our program could get tricked into believing that data came from the table, when it actually came from someplace else. So, we must make sure that what we have code that can't be executable. The easiest way to do this is to convert all executable characters (like quotes, commas, brackets) into escaped characters (" -> /"). This will not clean the data, but it will keep it from being executable. The ENT_QUOTES parameter insists that both single and double quotes are escaped. All code in this chapter and the remaining chapters will use this format to ensure any data displayed is not executable.

```
//                                                                          #6
            echo '<tr>
<td><a href="edit_user.php?id=' . $user_id . '">Edit</a></td>
<td><a href="delete_user.php?id=' . $user_id . '">Delete</a></td>';
```

The previous code creates a link in the first two cells in each row. The links connect to the pages *edit_user.php* and *delete_user.php*. The URL link created includes an id parameter, which is given the value in the $user_id variable (which came from the table). As the code loops through the data in the users table, it stores the corresponding user_id for each row.

The user_id for the row is "passed" to the page that will handle the deletion or editing through the URL address of the PHP program. Here's an example:

```
<td><a href="delete_user.php?id=1">Delete</a></td>
```

The ID (user_id) is the actual row number in the database table. The PHP program will use this number to determine which row to edit or delete. The whole line of code is a link that, when clicked, will edit or delete the identified row. For clarification, Figure 4-3 shows a fragment of the interactive table and the two links.

These are the registered users

Edit	Delete	Last Name	First Name	Email	Date Registered
Edit	Delete	Smith	James	jsmith@myisp.co.uk	November 28, 2017

Figure 4-3. *Showing one record and the two links in the first two cells*

```
//                                                                          #7
            echo '<td>' . $last_name . '</td>
            <td>' . $first_name . '</td>
            <td>' . $email . '</td>
            <td>' . $registration_date . '</td>
            </tr>';
```

In the previous block of code, the values contained in $last_name, $first_name, $email, and $registration_date are displayed in the related columns of the table.

```
echo '</table>'; // Close the table.                                        #8
mysqli_free_result ($result); // Free up the resources.
```

The table's closing tag completes the display of the table, and memory resources are freed up. The program itself will free up resources when it stops, but we can also do so when the statement shown. The rest of the code deals with error messages and adds the footer to the displayed page. Before we create the pages for searching, editing, and deleting, we need to pause for a useful diversion.

The next section describes a method of displaying tables one page at a time.

Displaying Pages of Records (Pagination)

The table display created by the file *view_users.php* is fine for up to 30 records. A greater number of records will cause the table to extend beyond the viewing size of most monitors. This will force the administrator to scroll down the page to view additional records. Imagine what would happen if the database contained 1,000 records or more. Creating the ability to view the table data one screen at a time would provide a solution; however, even this would be inconvenient for a large database. Later in this chapter, we will examine a slicker way of selecting and viewing one particular record in a large database; meanwhile, we will learn how to display a table so that the administrator can see one page at a time. The process is called *pagination*.

A page length of 20 to 25 rows would be a sensible choice; however, for the purposes of this tutorial, let's test this ability without having to enter lots of records in the database. We will set the number of rows per displayed page to four, so we need to enter only a few more members for the demonstration. This will give us four pages to display.

Table 4-4 suggests another ten members to register.

Table 4-4. *Details for Registering Members*

First Name	Last Name	E-mail	Password
Percy	Veer	pveer@myisp.com	K@@pg0ing
Stan	Dard	sdard@myisp.net	B@ttl3fl@g
Nora	Bone	nbone@myisp.com	L1k@t@rr1@r
Barry	Cade	bcade@myisp.co.uk	Bl0ckth@m
Dee	Jected	djected@myisp.ork.uk	Gl00mnd00m#
Lynn	Steed	lseed@mylsp.com	Pa1nt@rs01
Barry	Tone	btone@myisp.net	N1c@v01c3
Helen	Back	hback@myisp.net	Agr1ms0rt1@
Justin	Case	jcase@myisp.co.uk	Caut10u@
Jerry	Attrik	jattrik@myisp.com	Eld@rlyman

The database will now have 18 records. When we divide this by four (rows per page), we will have four-and-a-half pages. Following this explanation, in Listing 4-3a for *admin_view_users.php*, you will see that the number of rows per page is set by the variable $pagerows as follows:

```
$pagerows = 4;
```

Experiment with this value by giving the variable a value of, say, 9 or 15 to see the effect of the display in the web page.

Figure 4-4 shows the display of four records per page and the links for displaying the contents of the table by moving back and forward. The page also displays the total number of members.

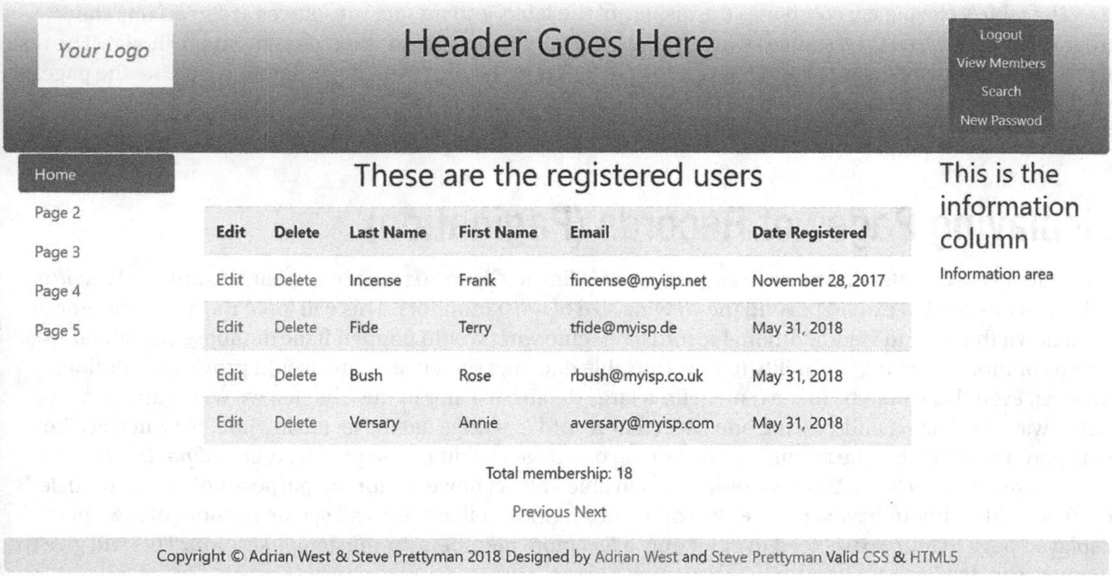

Figure 4-4. *The display now shows four records per page and indicates the total membership*

The page named process_*admin_view_users.php* contains the pagination code.

In Figure 4-4, the links Previous and Next, displayed below the table, enable movement through the table. Instead of those links, we could have used clickable page numbers or buttons. However, if you do not know what is on each page, a page number is not much use. The ability to browse through the pages and have the total membership displayed will be useful to the administrator. The pagination will also enable the administrator to print each page. This will be described in Chapter 7. For displaying a particular member's record, we will use the new Search menu button shown later in this chapter.

Listing 4-3a incorporates the code to enable pagination. A required statement has been placed in the file *admin_view_users.php* to separate the PHP code from the other code. The *admin_view_users.php* file is not listed since it is similar to other files already shown. You can view it in the downloaded files for this chapter.

Listing 4-3a. Creating a Table Display That Will Paginate (process_admin_view_users.php)

```php
<?php
try {
        // This script retrieves all the records from the users table.
        require('mysqli_connect.php'); // Connect to the database.
        //set the number of rows per display page
        $pagerows = 4; //                                                    #1
        // Has the total number of pages already been calculated?
        if ((isset($_GET['p']) && is_numeric($_GET['p']))) {
        //already been calculated
                $pages = htmlspecialchars($_GET['p'], ENT_QUOTES);
                // make sure it is not executable XSS
        }else{//use the next block of code to calculate the number of pages   #2
                //First, check for the total number of records
                $q = "SELECT COUNT(userid) FROM users";
                $result = mysqli_query ($dbcon, $q);
                $row = mysqli_fetch_array ($result, MYSQLI_NUM);
```

```
        $records = htmlspecialchars($row[0], ENT_QUOTES);
        // make sure it is not executable XSS
        //Now calculate the number of pages
        if ($records > $pagerows){ //                                    #3
          //if the number of records will fill more than one page
          //Calculate the number of pages and round the result up to the
          //  nearest integer
                  $pages = ceil ($records/$pagerows); //
        }else{
                  $pages = 1;
        }
}//page check finished
//Declare which record to start with                                      #4
if ((isset($_GET['s'])) &&( is_numeric($_GET['s'])))
{
        $start = htmlspecialchars($_GET['s'], ENT_QUOTES);
        // make sure it is not executable XSS
}else{
        $start = 0;
}
$query = "SELECT last_name, first_name, email, "; //                      #5
$query .= "DATE_FORMAT(registration_date, '%M %d, %Y')";
$query .=
" AS regdat, userid FROM users ORDER BY registration_date ASC";
$query .=" LIMIT ?, ?";
$q = mysqli_stmt_init($dbcon);
mysqli_stmt_prepare($q, $query);
// bind start and pagerows to SQL Statement
mysqli_stmt_bind_param($q, "ii", $start, $pagerows);
// execute query
mysqli_stmt_execute($q);
$result = mysqli_stmt_get_result($q);
if ($result) {
// If it ran OK (records were returned), display the records.
        // Table header.
        echo '<table class="table table-striped">
        <tr>
        <th scope="col">Edit</th>
        <th scope="col">Delete</th>
        <th scope="col">Last Name</th>
        <th scope="col">First Name</th>
        <th scope="col">Email</th>
        <th scope="col">Date Registered</th>
        </tr>';
                // Fetch and print all the records:
        while ($row = mysqli_fetch_array($result, MYSQLI_ASSOC)) {
        // Remove special characters that might already be in table to
                // reduce the chance of XSS exploits
                $user_id = htmlspecialchars($row['userid'], ENT_QUOTES);
                $last_name =
                        htmlspecialchars($row['last_name'], ENT_QUOTES);
                $first_name =
```

```
                                htmlspecialchars($row['first_name'], ENT_QUOTES);
                $email = htmlspecialchars($row['email'], ENT_QUOTES);
                $registration_date =
                        htmlspecialchars($row['regdat'], ENT_QUOTES);
                echo '<tr>
                <td><a href="edit_user.php?id=' . $user_id .
                        '">Edit</a></td>
                <td><a href="delete_user.php?id=' . $user_id .
                        '">Delete</a></td>
                <td>' . $last_name . '</td>
                <td>' . $first_name . '</td>
                <td>' . $email . '</td>
                <td>' . $registration_date . '</td>
                </tr>';
        }
        echo '</table>'; // Close the table.
        mysqli_free_result ($result); // Free up the resources.
}
else { // If it did not run OK.
        // Error message:
echo '<p class="text-center">The current users could not be ';
echo 'retrieved. We apologize for any inconvenience.</p>';
        // Debug message:
// echo '<p>' . mysqli_error($dbcon) . '<br><br>Query: ' . $q . '</p>';
        exit;
} // End of else ($result)
// Now display the total number of records/members.                          #6
$q = "SELECT COUNT(userid) FROM users";
$result = mysqli_query ($dbcon, $q);
$row = mysqli_fetch_array ($result, MYSQLI_NUM);
$members = htmlspecialchars($row[0], ENT_QUOTES);
mysqli_close($dbcon); // Close the database connection.
$echostring = "<p class='text-center'>Total membership: $members </p>";
$echostring .= "<p class='text-center'>";
if ($pages > 1) {    //                                                      #7
        //What number is the current page?
        $current_page = ($start/$pagerows) + 1;
        //If the page is not the first page then create a Previous link
        if ($current_page != 1) {
                $echostring .=
        '<a href="admin_view_users.php?s=' . ($start - $pagerows) .
                        '&p=' . $pages . '">Previous</a> ';
        }
        //Create a Next link                                                 #8
        if ($current_page != $pages) {
                $echostring .=
        ' <a href="admin_view_users.php?s=' . ($start + $pagerows) .
                        '&p=' . $pages . '">Next</a> ';
        }
        $echostring .= '</p>';
echo $echostring;
}
```

```
} //end of try
catch(Exception $e) // We finally handle any problems here
{
        // print "An Exception occurred. Message: " . $e->getMessage();
        print "The system is busy please try later";
}
catch(Error $e)
{
        //print "An Error occurred. Message: " . $e->getMessage();
        print "The system is busy please try again later.";
}
?>
```

Explanation of the Code

This section explains the code.

```
$pagerows = 4;                                                           // #1
```

$pagerows controls the amount of lines to display per page. The display is set to four records per page. (You would set this to about 20 in a real-world page.)

```
}else{//use the next block of code to calculate the number of pages           #2
        //First, check for the total number of records
        $q = "SELECT COUNT(userid) FROM users";
        $result = mysqli_query ($dbcon, $q);
        $row = mysqli_fetch_array ($result, MYSQLI_NUM);
        $records = htmlspecialchars($row[0], ENT_QUOTES);
        // make sure it is not executable XSS
        //Now calculate the number of pages
```

The previous code will count the number of records (COUNT(user_id)) in the users table of the database. A numerical array (indicated by the user of MYSQLI_NUM) $row is created, and the number of rows is placed into it. The only contents of this array are the number of records. This value is copied from the zero position of array, sanitized, and placed into the variable $records.

The following code checks to see whether the number of records is greater than the number of records displayed per page ($pagerows).

```
           if ($records > $pagerows){ //                                 #3
                   //if the number of records will fill more than one page
//Calculate the number of pages and round the result up to the nearest integer
                   $pages = ceil ($records/$pagerows); //
           }else{
                   $pages = 1;
           }
```

If the number of records is greater than the number of records displayed per page, the PHP function ceil() will round up the number of pages needed (as determined by dividing the number of records by the number of records per page). In the tutorial, we have 18 records, resulting in four-and-a-half pages (18 divided by 4). This is rounded up to five pages. The fifth page will display only two records. If the number of records is not greater than the number of rows per display, there will be only one page. The function ceil() means *set the ceiling* or *set to an integer above the actual count*; in this case, 4.5 becomes 5.

125

```
//Declare which record to start with                                          #4
if ((isset($_GET['s'])) &&( is_numeric($_GET['s'])))
{
        $start = htmlspecialchars($_GET['s'], ENT_QUOTES);
        // make sure it is not executable XSS
}else{
        $start = 0;
}
```

The value in s is passed when the user clicks the Previous or Next link on the web page (that code will be explained soon). If the user does click one of these links, it will contain a start point (such as record number 5) for the records to be displayed, and the value will be placed in $start. If no value has been passed (s is not set), it is assumed that the first set of the records is to be displayed, and the value of $start is set to 0. If somehow a non-numerical value exists in s, $start will also be set to 0.

```
$query = "SELECT last_name, first_name, email, "; //                          #5
$query .= "DATE_FORMAT(registration_date, '%M %d, %Y')";
$query .=
" AS regdat, userid FROM users ORDER BY registration_date ASC";
$query .=" LIMIT ?, ?";
$q = mysqli_stmt_init($dbcon);
mysqli_stmt_prepare($q, $query);
// bind start abd pagerows to SQL Statement
mysqli_stmt_bind_param($q, "ii", $start, $pagerows);
// execute query
mysqli_stmt_execute($q);
$result = mysqli_stmt_get_result($q);
```

The query selects the columns to be displayed (last_name, first_name, email, reg_dat) from the users table. The information retrieved from the table is limited to only the records required to be displayed on the current page. For example, on the first page, $start will be set to 0, and $pagerows will be set to 4. Only the rows from 0 to 4 will be retrieved. The records retrieved will also be sorted in ascending order. Even though we sanitized $start and $pagerows before, we will use a prepared statement just to be extra secure.

Some programmers may choose to retrieve all records from the database at one time and place them into an array. This is a common practice. However, because we must send a request to the server every time we want to display another page, we can just pull the next set of records directly from the database. This is efficient for smaller tables of information.

```
// Now display the total number of records/members.                           #6
$q = "SELECT COUNT(userid) FROM users";
$result = mysqli_query ($dbcon, $q);
$row = mysqli_fetch_array ($result, MYSQLI_NUM);
$members = htmlspecialchars($row[0], ENT_QUOTES);
mysqli_close($dbcon); // Close the database connection.
$echostring = "<p class='text-center'>Total membership: $members </p>";
$echostring .= "<p class='text-center'>";
```

As explained earlier, this code counts the total number of rows in the table. The value returned will be placed into $row[0]. The value is sanitized and placed into $members, which will be displayed on the page.

```
if ($pages > 1) {   //                                                         #7
        //What number is the current page?
        $current_page = ($start/$pagerows) + 1;
```

```
        //If the page is not the first page then create a Previous link
        if ($current_page != 1) {
                $echostring .= '<a href="admin_view_users.php?s=' .
                        ($start - $pagerows) .
                        '&p=' . $pages . '">Previous</a> ';
        }
```

The link named Previous is created that calls the admin_view_users.php program. As previously mentioned, s (start position) will contain the first record (such as record 0 or record 4) to be displayed on the page. This is calculated by subtracting the total number of rows to display in a page ($pagerow) from the previous start position ($start). For example, if the current start position is 20 and we subtract 4 from this position, the new start position (placed in s) is now 16. $pages contains the required number of pages as previously calculated. If the $current_page is 1, no previous link will be displayed.

```
        //Create a Next link                                              #8
        if ($current_page != $pages) {
                $echostring .=
        ' <a href="admin_view_users.php?s=' . ($start + $pagerows) .
                        '&p=' . $pages . '">Next</a> ';
        }
        $echostring .= '</p>';
echo $echostring;
}
```

The Next link is created in a similar way as the Previous link. The only difference is the calculation. The start position ($start) is added to the number of rows to display on the page ($pagerow) to determine the value of s (the start position). If the current start position is zero and the number of rows to display on a page is 4, the next start position (s) is 4. When the link is clicked, the page will display records 4–7. If the current page is the last page ($current_page == $pages), the Next link will not be displayed. The completed string is now displayed on the page.

Fire up XAMPP or easyPHP and then log in as the administrator to view the pagination. Adjust the value of $pagerows to see how it changes the behavior of the pages.

While this was a good exercise, it is more common that we just want to search for one record and not display all records (especially if there are hundreds of them). Let's determine how to search for one particular record and then display it.

You may have noticed that the header for the *admin_view_users.php* page is changed so that the View Members button is a link to the *admin_view_users.php* page. Also, a new button links to the search page *search.php*. Listing 4-3b shows the changes.

Listing 4-3b. Creating the Revised Administration Header (header-admin.php)

```
<div class="col-sm-2">
        <img class="img-fluid float-left" src="logo.jpg" alt="Logo">
</div>
<div class="col-sm-8">
        <h1 class="blue-text mb-4 font-bold">Header Goes Here</h1>
 </div>
<nav class="col-sm-2">
<div class="btn-group-vertical btn-group-sm" role="group"
        aria-label="Button Group">
        <button type="button" class="btn btn-secondary"
                onclick="location.href = 'logout.php'" >Logout</button>
```

```
        <button type="button" class="btn btn-secondary"
            onclick="location.href = 'admin_view_users.php'">View Members</button>
        <button type="button" class="btn btn-secondary"
            onclick="location.href = 'search.php'">Search</button>
        <button type="button" class="btn btn-secondary"
            onclick="location.href = 'register-password.php'">New Password</button>
</div>
</nav>
```

Planning the Search Criteria

The administrator needs a search facility that does not require scrolling through scores of records to edit or delete one. The importance of forward planning cannot be over-emphasized; deciding how to organize the search facility requires careful thought.

The administrator can edit and delete records. So, what events would require them to use these facilities? For editing, the event would typically be caused by members requesting the administrator to change an e-mail address or a name. Deletions would occur if a member resigns or dies.

Some names are common—for instance, we may have five people named James Smith. In our example, we would need to display all five and then use their e-mail addresses to distinguish them so that we don't delete the wrong James Smith.

■ **Note**   It is also common to create a unique key to identify which record is affected. In our example, e-mail can be used to accomplish this. More commonly, a unique member ID would be created. Some organizations in the United States use the Social Security number. However, this is not a good choice because this number is tied to many personal financial records (such as retirement, medical, and checking accounts).

The next tutorial describes the creation of a page that displays the results of a search. For this, you will need to register four more members named James Smith. Table 4-5 offers some suggestions.

Table 4-5. *Some Identical Common Names*

First Name	Last Name	E-mail	Password
James	Smith	jimsmith@myisp.org.uk	Ch@vr0n1
James	Smith	James.smith@myisp.com	Incl1n3d
James	Smith	Jimmy.smith@myisp.co.uk	P@d@stal
James	Smith	jims@myisp.net	Tungst@n

When you have registered them, there will be a total of five members named James Smith, and the total number of records in our database will be 22.

A Temporary Search Page for Displaying Specified Members

We will eventually create a search facility, but first we must create a page that will produce a table of members named James Smith. The target or end result of a search for *James Smith* will be a table, as shown in Figure 4-5.

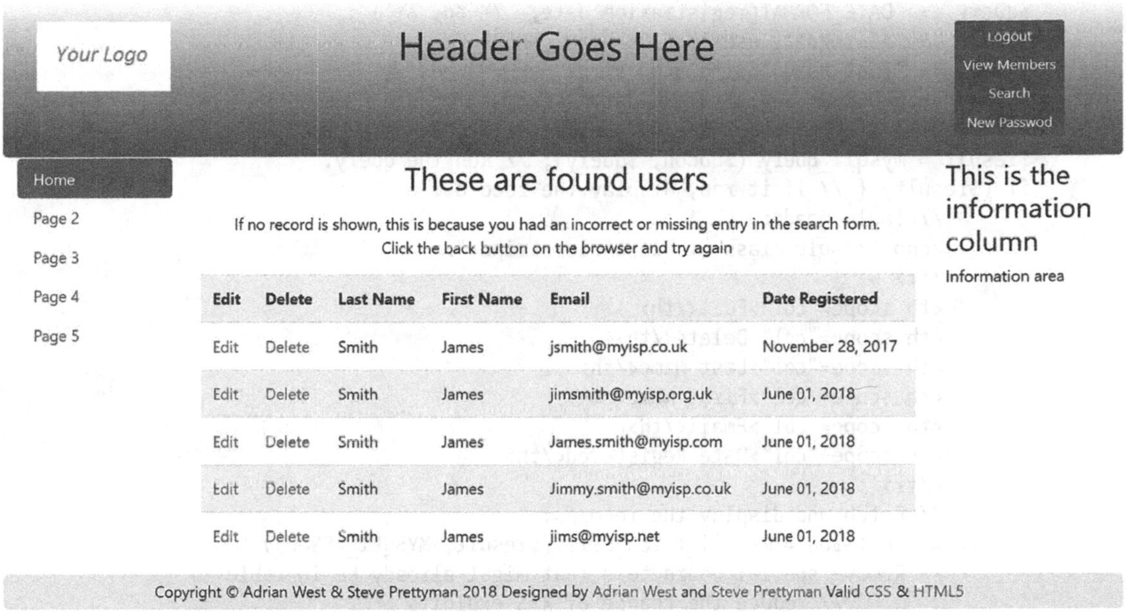

Your Logo		Header Goes Here		Logout
				View Members
				Search
				New Passwod

Home		These are found users		This is the
Page 2				information
Page 3		If no record is shown, this is because you had an incorrect or missing entry in the search form. Click the back button on the browser and try again		column
Page 4				Information area
Page 5				

Edit	Delete	Last Name	First Name	Email	Date Registered
Edit	Delete	Smith	James	jsmith@myisp.co.uk	November 28, 2017
Edit	Delete	Smith	James	jimsmith@myisp.org.uk	June 01, 2018
Edit	Delete	Smith	James	James.smith@myisp.com	June 01, 2018
Edit	Delete	Smith	James	Jimmy.smith@myisp.co.uk	June 01, 2018
Edit	Delete	Smith	James	jims@myisp.net	June 01, 2018

Copyright © Adrian West & Steve Prettyman 2018 Designed by Adrian West and Steve Prettyman Valid CSS & HTML5

Figure 4-5. *The five James Smiths have been located and are now displayed*

To ensure that we can display the table shown in Figure 4-5, we need to create a page that we will call *temp_view_found_record.php*. Because we have not created a search page, we will enter the names **James** and **Smith** directly into SQL query in the code as a temporary expedient. The PHP code is in the file *process_ temp_view_found_record.php* and is shown in Listing 4-4.

■ **Note** These are temporary versions of the page. It is a helpful stage before producing the final version. It demonstrates an important principle and is a useful exercise for proving that a table will be displayed. The temporary versions are included in the downloadable files for this chapter as *temp_view_found_record.php* and *process_temp_view_found_record.php*.

Listing 4-4. Creating a Temporary Page for Displaying the Results of a Search (process_temp_view_found_ record.php)

```php
<?php
try
{

        // This script retrieves records from the users table.              #1
        require ('mysqli_connect.php'); // Connect to the db.
        echo '<p class="text-center">If no record is shown, ';
        echo 'this is because you had an incorrect ';
        echo ' or missing entry in the search form.';
        echo '<br>Click the back button on the browser and try again</p>';
        $query = "SELECT last_name, first_name, email, ";
```

```php
$query .= "DATE_FORMAT(registration_date, '%M %d, %Y')";
$query .=" AS regdat, userid FROM users WHERE ";
$query .= "last_name='Smith' AND first_name='James' ";
$query .="ORDER BY registration_date ASC ";
// Prepared statement not needed because string is hard coded
$result = mysqli_query ($dbcon, $query); // Run the query.
if ($result) { // If it ran, display the records.
        // Table header.
        echo '<table class="table table-striped">
        <tr>
        <th scope="col">Edit</th>
        <th scope="col">Delete</th>
        <th scope="col">Last Name</th>
        <th scope="col">First Name</th>
        <th scope="col">Email</th>
        <th scope="col">Date Registered</th>
        </tr>';
        // Fetch and display the records:
        while ($row = mysqli_fetch_array($result, MYSQLI_ASSOC)) {
        // Remove special characters that might already be in table to
                // reduce the chance of XSS exploits
                $user_id = htmlspecialchars($row['userid'], ENT_QUOTES);
                $last_name =
                        htmlspecialchars($row['last_name'], ENT_QUOTES);
                $first_name =
                        htmlspecialchars($row['first_name'], ENT_QUOTES);
                $email = htmlspecialchars($row['email'], ENT_QUOTES);
                $registration_date =
                        htmlspecialchars($row['regdat'], ENT_QUOTES);
                echo '<tr>
                        <td><a href="edit_user.php?id=' . $user_id .
                         '">Edit</a></td>
                        <td><a href="delete_user.php?id=' . $user_id .
                         '">Delete</a></td>
                        <td>' . $last_name . '</td>
                        <td>' . $first_name . '</td>
                        <td>' . $email . '</td>
                        <td>' . $registration_date . '</td>
                        </tr>';
        }
        echo '</table>'; // Close the table.
        mysqli_free_result ($result); // Free up the resources.
} else { // If it did not run OK.
        // Public message:
echo '<p class="error">The current users could not be retrieved.';
        echo 'We apologize for any inconvenience.</p>';
        // Debugging message:
//echo '<p>' . mysqli_error($dbcon) . '<br><br>Query: ' . $q . '</p>';
        //Show $q is debug mode only
}
```

```
// End of if ($result). Now display the total number of records/members.
        mysqli_close($dbcon); // Close the database connection.
}
catch(Exception $e)
{
        print "The system is currently busy. Please try later.";
        //print "An Exception occurred.Message: " . $e->getMessage();
}
catch(Error $e)
{
        print "The system us busy. Please try later.";
        //print "An Error occurred. Message: " . $e->getMessage();
}
?>
```

Explanation of the Code

This section explains the code.

```
// This script retrieves records from the users table.                    #1
require ('mysqli_connect.php'); // Connect to the db.
echo '<p class="text-center">If no record is shown, ';
echo 'this is because you had an incorrect ';
echo ' or missing entry in the search form.';
echo '<br>Click the back button on the browser and try again</p>';
$query = "SELECT last_name, first_name, email, ";
$query .= "DATE_FORMAT(registration_date, '%M %d, %Y')";
$query .=" AS regdat, userid FROM users WHERE ";
$query .= "last_name='Smith' AND first_name='James' ";
$query .="ORDER BY registration_date ASC ";
```

This select statement will pull all James Smith records from the users table and place them in ascending order by registration date.

This SQL query is almost the same as the one in *process_admin_view_users.php* except that the LIMIT on the number of rows has been removed and a new keyword, WHERE, has been introduced. Removing the limit on the number of rows ensures that all the James Smith records will be displayed no matter how many there are. The WHERE clause specifies exactly which records to display. We entered names as a temporary expedient so that we can test the page and ensure that it works as expected. This is a common technique and is known as *hard-coding*. The resulting table display was shown in Figure 4-5.

Remember, this is a temporary version of the search page. We would not code the actual first and last names in our select statement in a regular search.

To view this table, fire up your server and log in as administrator. In the address field of your browser, enter **http://localhost/admintable/temp_view_found_record.php**.

■ **Note** Now that we are using sessions, you will not be able to access any of the administration pages without logging in as the administrator.

We now have a page that will display a table of specified records. With that working correctly, the next step is to provide a search form so that the administrator can request a table showing any specified members rather than only James Smith.

This example was fine for testing but not very practical. Let's adjust our logic to make this more useful.

The Search Form

When the administrator clicks the Search button on the header menu, the *search.php* page will appear. This page has a form containing two fields where search criteria can be entered. Planning is needed to decide what the search criteria should be. While the e-mail address would provide the administrator with a unique identifier for finding a member, it might not be known. The member's registration date is a poor choice for locating the member because members will inevitably forget the exact date they registered. The administrator needs to know some unique but obvious information to display the member's record. The obvious criteria are the member's first and last names; therefore, that is what we will use. The first and last names might not be unique, but as we did with James Smith, we can display all users with the same first and last names and then decide which is the correct member information to be modified.

Note: It is beneficial to provide more than one way to search for a member record. You could enhance this example to allow the administrator to search either on the e-mail address or on the first and last names. By providing both, you allow the ability to pull up the unique record only, if the e-mail is known. Otherwise, all members with the same first and last names can be searched for the correct record.

Figure 4-6 shows the search form.

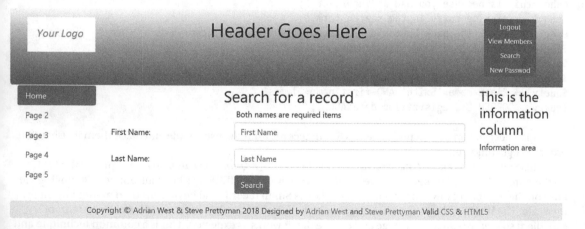

Figure 4-6. *The search form*

The search form enables the administrator to search for a particular record. If the search is successful, the form will call the *view_found_record.php* page. This page will display the user (or users). If several people have the same first and last names, the table will display all of them.

Don't try entering a search just yet. We will need to adjust our view found page, which currently always show James Smith's records. This temporary page will be changed to accept values from the search form described in Listing 4-5a.

Listing 4-5a. Creating the Search Form (search.php)

```php
<?php
        session_start();                                                    // #1
        if (!isset($_SESSION['user_level']) or ($_SESSION['user_level'] != 1))
        {
                header("Location: login.php");
                exit();
        }
?>
<!DOCTYPE html>
<html lang="en">
<head>
<title>Search Page</title>
<meta charset="utf-8">
<meta name="viewport" content=
        "width=device-width, initial-scale=1, shrink-to-fit=no">
 <!-- Bootstrap CSS File -->
 <link rel="stylesheet"
        href=
"https://stackpath.bootstrapcdn.com/bootstrap/4.1.0/css/bootstrap.min.css"
        integrity=
"sha384-9gVQ4dYFwwWSjIDZnLEWnxCjeSWFphJiwGPXr1jddIhOegiu1FwO5qRGvFXOdJZ4"
        crossorigin="anonymous">
</head>
<body>
<div class="container" style="margin-top:30px">
<!-- Header Section -->
<header class="jumbotron text-center row col-sm-14"
        style=
"margin-bottom:2px; background:linear-gradient(white, #0073e6);padding:20px;">
        <?php include('header-admin.php'); ?>
</header>
<!-- Body Section -->
 <div class="row" style="padding-left: 0px;">
<!-- Left-side Column Menu Section -->
<nav class="col-sm-2">
     <ul class="nav nav-pills flex-column">
                <?php include('nav.php'); ?>
     </ul>
 </nav>
<div class="col-sm-8">
<h2 class="h2 text-center">Search for a record</h2>
<h6 class="text-center">Both names are required items</h6>
<form action="view_found_record.php" method="post">
<div class="form-group row">                                            <!-- #2 -->
    <label for="first_name" class="col-sm-4 col-form-label">First Name:</label>
    <div class="col-sm-8">
    <input type="text" class="form-control" id="first_name" name="first_name"
        placeholder="First Name" maxlength="30" required
        value=
            "<?php if (isset($_POST['first_name']))
```

```
                      echo htmlspecialchars($_POST['first_name'], ENT_QUOTES); ?>" >
  </div>
  </div>
  <div class="form-group row">
  <label for="last_name" class="col-sm-4 col-form-label">Last Name:</label>
  <div class="col-sm-8">
  <input type="text" class="form-control" id="last_name" name="last_name"
          placeholder="Last Name" maxlength="40" required
          value=
                "<?php if (isset($_POST['last_name']))
                echo htmlspecialchars($_POST['last_name'], ENT_QUOTES); ?>">
  </div>
  </div>
<div class="form-group row">
<label for="" class="col-sm-4 col-form-label"></label>
<div class="col-sm-8">
        <input id="submit" class="btn btn-primary" type="submit"
                name="submit" value="Search">
</div>
</div>
</form>
</div>
<!-- Right-side Column Content Section -->
<?php
 if(!isset($errorstring)) {
        echo '<aside class="col-sm-2">';
        include('info-col.php');
        echo '</aside>';
        echo '</div>';
        echo '<footer class="jumbotron text-center row col-sm-14"
                style="padding-bottom:1px; padding-top:8px;">';
 }
else
 {
        echo '<footer class="jumbotron text-center col-sm-12"
        style="padding-bottom:1px; padding-top:8px;">';
 }
  include('footer.php');
 ?>
</footer>
</div>
</body>
</html>
```

Explanation of the Code

This section explains the code.

```
<?php
        session_start();                                              // #1
        if (!isset($_SESSION['user_level']) or ($_SESSION['user_level'] != 1))
        {
```

```
                header("Location: login.php");
                exit();
        }
?>
```

All of our admin HTML pages include this code. The session is our security guard; unauthorized people (anyone who is not an administrator) will be redirected to the login page.

```
<div class="form-group row">                                              <!-- #2 -->
    <label for="first_name" class="col-sm-4 col-form-label">First Name:</label>
    <div class="col-sm-8">
    <input type="text" class="form-control" id="first_name" name="first_name"
            placeholder="First Name" maxlength="30" required
            value=
                    "<?php if (isset($_POST['first_name']))
                    echo htmlspecialchars($_POST['first_name'], ENT_QUOTES); ?>" >
    </div>
    </div>
```

The code supplies a *sticky form*. A sticky form is one that retains the user's entries when an error is flagged. Users can become annoyed if they have to fill out the entire form each time they need to correct an error such as failing to fill out one field. The sticky component is the PHP code following the value, for example:

```
value=
        "<?php if (isset($_POST['first_name']))
        echo htmlspecialchars($_POST['first_name'], ENT_QUOTES); ?>" >
```

The form will use POST to submit all form data. We would hope that our form data does not get modified by some outside force. However, it is possible that the data could be modified to attack our system, database, or network. Therefore, we are using the htmlspecialchars function to sanitize the data. As mentioned, all symbols that could be included in executable code are now escaped (" -> \"). This ensures that the information is not executable. It does not clean the data, but at least it is less likely to be harmful.

We will add some human detection ability later, which will reduce the ability for a program to use our forms.

We will now make the form handler *temp_view_found_record.php* more versatile.

The Final Form Handler for Receiving Search Form Input

The following code (process_*view_found_record.php*) shows what has been added or modified in the PHP code. These items enable the file to receive the first name and the last name sent from the *search.php* page. The first and last names are assigned to variables, and these variables are used to search the database so that they can be verified. The variables are then used to display the record(s).

Listing 4-5b shows the code to eliminate the hard-coding and allow searches for any registered member's record.

Listing 4-5b. The Code for Displaying the Search Results (process_view_found_record.php)

```
<?php
try
{
    // This script retrieves records from the users table.
```

```php
require ('./mysqli_connect.php'); // Connect to the db.
echo '<p class="text-center">If no record is shown, ';
echo 'this is because you had an incorrect ';
echo ' or missing entry in the search form.';
echo '<br>Click the back button on the browser and try again</p>';
//                                                                      #1
$first_name = htmlspecialchars($_POST['first_name'], ENT_QUOTES);
$last_name = htmlspecialchars($_POST['last_name'], ENT_QUOTES);
// Since it's a prepared statement below this sanitizing is not needed
// However, to consistently retrieve than sanitize is a good habit
//                                                                      #2
$query = "SELECT last_name, first_name, email, ";
$query .= "DATE_FORMAT(registration_date, '%M %d, %Y')";
$query .=" AS regdat, userid FROM users WHERE ";
$query .= "last_name=? AND first_name=? ";
$query .="ORDER BY registration_date ASC ";
$q = mysqli_stmt_init($dbcon);
mysqli_stmt_prepare($q, $query);

// bind values to SQL Statement
mysqli_stmt_bind_param($q, 'ss', $last_name, $first_name);

// execute query
mysqli_stmt_execute($q);

$result = mysqli_stmt_get_result($q);

if ($result) { // If it ran, display the records.
// Table header.
        echo '<table class="table table-striped">
        <tr>
        <th scope="col">Edit</th>
        <th scope="col">Delete</th>
        <th scope="col">Last Name</th>
        <th scope="col">First Name</th>
        <th scope="col">Email</th>
        <th scope="col">Date Registered</th>
        </tr>';
        // Fetch and display the records:
        while ($row = mysqli_fetch_array($result, MYSQLI_ASSOC)) {
        // Remove special characters that might already be in table to
                // reduce the chance of XSS exploits
                $user_id = htmlspecialchars($row['userid'], ENT_QUOTES);
                $last_name =
                        htmlspecialchars($row['last_name'], ENT_QUOTES);
                $first_name =
                        htmlspecialchars($row['first_name'], ENT_QUOTES);
                $email =
                        htmlspecialchars($row['email'], ENT_QUOTES);
                $registration_date =
                        htmlspecialchars($row['regdat'], ENT_QUOTES);
                echo '<tr>
```

```
                <td><a href="edit_user.php?id=' . $user_id .
                '">Edit</a></td>
                <td><a href="delete_user.php?id=' . $user_id .
                    '">Delete</a></td>
                <td>' . $last_name . '</td>
                <td>' . $first_name . '</td>
                <td>' . $email . '</td>
                <td>' . $registration_date . '</td>
                </tr>';
            }
            echo '</table>'; // Close the table.
            //
            mysqli_free_result ($result); // Free up the resources.
    } else { // If it did not run OK.
            // Public message:
echo '<p class="text-center">The current users could not be retrieved.';
            echo 'We apologize for any inconvenience.</p>';
            // Debugging message:
        //echo '<p>' . mysqli_error($dbcon) . '<br><br>Query: ' . $q . '</p>';
            //Show $q is debug mode only
    }
// End of if ($result). Now display the total number of records/members.
        mysqli_close($dbcon); // Close the database connection.
    }
    catch(Exception $e)
    {
        print "The system is currently busy. Please try later.";
        //print "An Exception occurred. Message: " . $e->getMessage();
    }
    catch(Error $e)
    {
        print "The system us busy. Please try later.";
        //print "An Error occurred. Message: " . $e->getMessage();
    }
?>
```

Explanation of the Code

This section explains the code.

```
//                                                                          #1
$first_name = htmlspecialchars($_POST['first_name'], ENT_QUOTES);
$last_name = htmlspecialchars($_POST['last_name'], ENT_QUOTES);
// Since it's a prepared statement below this sanitizing is not needed
// However, to consistently retrieve than sanitize is a good habit
```

We should stay in a flow of always sanitizing data received from outside the current program. The previous two statements could be removed, and the data would still not execute because of the prepared statement. But if we always remember "input then sanitize," we are creating a more secure program.

```
//                                                                              #2
$query = "SELECT last_name, first_name, email, ";
$query .= "DATE_FORMAT(registration_date, '%M %d, %Y')";
$query .=" AS regdat, userid FROM users WHERE ";
$query .= "last_name=? AND first_name=? ";
$query .="ORDER BY registration_date ASC ";
$q = mysqli_stmt_init($dbcon);
mysqli_stmt_prepare($q, $query);

// bind values to SQL Statement
mysqli_stmt_bind_param($q, 'ss', $last_name, $first_name);

// execute query
mysqli_stmt_execute($q);

$result = mysqli_stmt_get_result($q);
if ($result) { // If it ran, display the records.
```

The query has been adjusted to accept the last name and first name to search for matching records. Since this information is received from the user, a *prepared statement* has been created. Using this format, any values entered by the user cannot be executed. The user cannot attempt to use *SQL injection* to access information that should not be accessible.

The SQL statement includes two question marks. The first question mark is bound to the value in $last_name. The second question mark is bound to $first_name. The statement expects each to be a string (ss). The query is then executed, and the results are placed in $result.

At last, you can test the search facility. Run XAMPP or easyPHP, and type the following into the address field of a browser:

http://localhost/admintable/login.php

Use the administrator's e-mail address and password to log in. The e-mail is jsmith@outlook.com, and the password is d0gsb0dy. Then click the search button on the header menu. In the search form, try entering **Jack Smith** to see a single record displayed.

The result should be the record shown in Figure 4-7.

Figure 4-7. Showing a single record selected by using the search page

Try entering **James Smith** to see a group of records that have the same first and last names.

Now we have reached the stage where we can demonstrate how the administrator deletes and edits the records.

Editing Records

When the administrator clicks the Edit link on the record displayed, the *edit_user.php* page is displayed. The page displays the fields and the data currently held in the database table. This is illustrated in Figure 4-8.

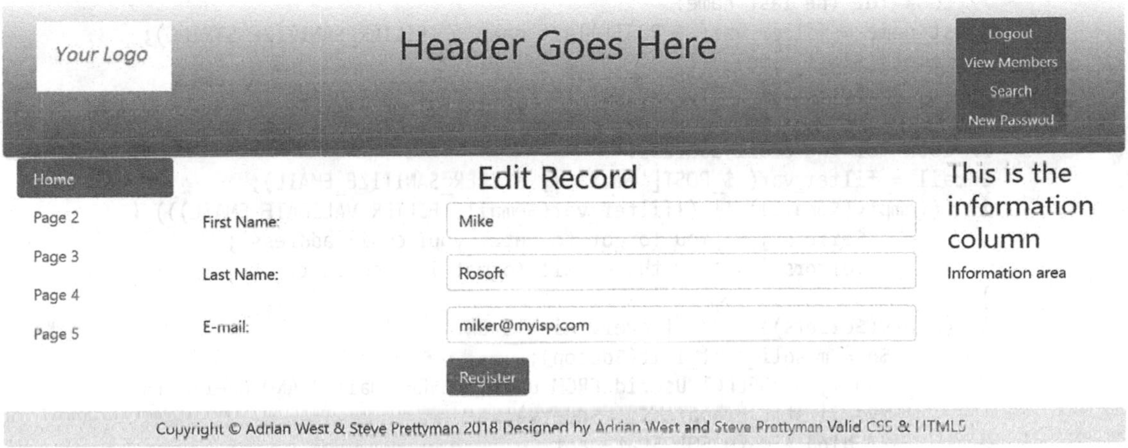

Figure 4-8. *The Edit a User screen showing the existing data*

The administrator can amend the details and then click the Edit button to complete the editing process.

Listing 4-6 shows the PHP code for *process_edit_record.php*. The *edit_user.php* file contains the same HTML format as previously shown. You can view this code from the downloaded files.

Listing 4-6. Creating the Editing Interface (process_edit_record.php)

```php
<?php
    try
    {
        // After clicking the Edit link in the found_record.php page.
        // This code is executed                                          #1
        // The code looks for a valid user ID, either through GET or POST:
        if ( (isset($_GET['id'])) && (is_numeric($_GET['id'])) ) {
        // From view_users.php
                $id = htmlspecialchars($_GET['id'], ENT_QUOTES);
        } elseif ( (isset($_POST['id'])) && (is_numeric($_POST['id'])) ) {
        // Form submission.
                $id = htmlspecialchars($_POST['id'], ENT_QUOTES);
        } else { // No valid ID, kill the script.
      echo '<p class="text-center">This page has been accessed in error.</p>';
                include ('footer.php');
                exit();
        }
```

```
    require ('./mysqli_connect.php');
    // Has the form been submitted?
    if ($_SERVER['REQUEST_METHOD'] == 'POST') {
        $errors = array();
        // Look for the first name:                                        #2
        $first_name =
                filter_var( $_POST['first_name'], FILTER_SANITIZE_STRING);
        if (empty($first_name)) {
                $errors[] = 'You forgot to enter your first name.';
        }
        // Look for the last name:
        $last_name = filter_var( $_POST['last_name'], FILTER_SANITIZE_STRING);
        if (empty($last_name)) {
                $errors[] = 'You forgot to enter your last name.';
        }
        // Look for the email address:
        $email = filter_var( $_POST['email'], FILTER_SANITIZE_EMAIL);
        if  ((empty($email)) || (!filter_var($email, FILTER_VALIDATE_EMAIL))) {
                $errors[] = 'You forgot to enter your email address';
                $errors[] = ' or the e-mail format is incorrect.';
        }
        if (empty($errors)) { // If everything's OK.                        #3
                $q = mysqli_stmt_init($dbcon);
                $query = 'SELECT userid FROM users WHERE email=? AND userid !=?';
                mysqli_stmt_prepare($q, $query);
                // bind $id to SQL Statement
                mysqli_stmt_bind_param($q, 'si', $email, $id);
                // execute query
                mysqli_stmt_execute($q);
                $result = mysqli_stmt_get_result($q);

                if (mysqli_num_rows($result) == 0) {
                // e-mail does not exist in another record                  #4
                $query = 'UPDATE users SET first_name=?, last_name=?, email=?';
                        $query .= ' WHERE userid=? LIMIT 1';
                        $q = mysqli_stmt_init($dbcon);
                        mysqli_stmt_prepare($q, $query);
                        // bind values to SQL Statement
mysqli_stmt_bind_param($q, 'sssi', $first_name, $last_name, $email, $id);
                        // execute query
                        mysqli_stmt_execute($q);
                        if (mysqli_stmt_affected_rows($q) == 1) { // Update OK
                                // Echo a message if the edit was satisfactory:
                    echo '<h3 class="text-center">The user has been edited.</h3>';
                        } else { // Echo a message if the query failed.
            echo '<p class="text-center">The user could not be edited due ';
            echo 'to a system error.';
            echo ' We apologize for any inconvenience.</p>'; // Public message.
            //echo '<p>' . mysqli_error($dbcon) . '<br />Query: ' . $q . '</p>';
            // Debugging message.
            // Message above is only for debug and should not display SQL in live //mode
                        }
```

```
                  } else { // Already registered.
                  echo '<p class="text-center">The email address has ';
                  echo 'already been registered.</p>';
                  }
            } else { // Display the errors.
            echo '<p class="text-center">The following error(s) occurred:<br />';
                  foreach ($errors as $msg) { // Echo each error.
                        echo " - $msg<br />\n";
                  }
                  echo '</p><p>Please try again.</p>';
            } // End of if (empty($errors))section.
      } // End of the conditionals
      // Select the user's information to display in textboxes:                    #5
      $q = mysqli_stmt_init($dbcon);
      $query = "SELECT first_name, last_name, email FROM users WHERE userid=?";
      mysqli_stmt_prepare($q, $query);
      // bind $id to SQL Statement
      mysqli_stmt_bind_param($q, 'i', $id);
      // execute query
      mysqli_stmt_execute($q);
      $result = mysqli_stmt_get_result($q);
      $row = mysqli_fetch_array($result, MYSQLI_NUM);

      if (mysqli_num_rows($result) == 1) { // Valid user ID, display the form.
            // Get the user's information:
            // Create the form:
?>
<h2 class="h2 text-center">Edit Record</h2>
<form action="edit_record.php" method="post"
      name="editform" id="editform">
<div class="form-group row">
      <label for="first_name" class="col-sm-4 col-form-label">
            First Name:</label>
<div class="col-sm-8">
    <input type="text" class="form-control" id="first_name" name="first_name"
       placeholder="First Name" maxlength="30" required
       value="<?php echo htmlspecialchars($row[0], ENT_QUOTES); ?>" >
</div>
</div>
<div class="form-group row">
      <label for="last_name" class="col-sm-4 col-form-label">
            Last Name:</label>
<div class="col-sm-8">
    <input type="text" class="form-control" id="last_name" name="last_name"
       placeholder="Last Name" maxlength="40" required
       value="<?php echo htmlspecialchars($row[1], ENT_QUOTES); ?>">
</div>
</div>
<div class="form-group row">
      <label for="email" class="col-sm-4 col-form-label">E-mail:</label>
<div class="col-sm-8">
    <input type="email" class="form-control" id="email" name="email"
```

```
            placeholder="E-mail" maxlength="60" required
            value="<?php echo htmlspecialchars($row[2], ENT_QUOTES); ?>">
</div>
</div>
    <input type="hidden" name="id" value=" <?php echo $id  ?>" />                    <!-- #6 -->
<div class="form-group row">
            <label for="" class="col-sm-4 col-form-label"></label>
<div class="col-sm-8">
            <input id="submit" class="btn btn-primary" type="submit" name="submit"
value="Register">
</div>
</div>
</form>
<?php
    } else { // The user could not be validated
echo '<p class="text-center">This page has been accessed in error.</p>';
    }
    mysqli_stmt_free_result($q);
    mysqli_close($dbcon);
    }
    catch(Exception $e)
    {
      print "The system is busy. Please try later";
        //print "An Exception occurred. Message: " . $e->getMessage();
    }
    catch(Error $e)
    {
        print "The system is currently buys. Please try later";
        //print "An Error occurred. Message: " . $e->getMessage();
    }
?>
```

Explanation of the Code

Most of the code has been explained already, but we will now examine some code that is new to this chapter.

```
// After clicking the Edit link in the found_record.php page.
//This code is executed                                                    #1
// The code looks for a valid user ID, either through GET or POST:

if ( (isset($_GET['id'])) && (is_numeric($_GET['id'])) ) {
// From view_users.php

        $id = htmlspecialchars($_GET['id'], ENT_QUOTES);

} elseif ( (isset($_POST['id'])) && (is_numeric($_POST['id'])) ) {
// Form submission.

        $id = htmlspecialchars($_POST['id'], ENT_QUOTES);

} else { // No valid ID, kill the script.
```

```
echo '<p class="text-center">This page has been accessed in error.</p>';
        include ('footer.php');
        exit();


}
```

We must be sure we are editing the right record, and this is achieved by checking the ID of the selected user. If the user's details were entered incorrectly or the user did not exist in the database table, an error message is shown. Note the is_numeric() function that ensures that the ID is a number and not a string. If the ID is numeric, it is sanitized and assigned to the variable $id ready for the next step. The sanitizing is not required because we will be using a prepared statement. However, we want to be consistent and sanitize all input.

Note: The number received might still not be valid; for example, someone could try to skip the search form and pass the program a number. However, once the search is complete, if the number is not found, an error message will display.

```
// Look for the first name:                                               #2
    $first_name - filter_var( $_POST['first_name'], FILTER_SANITIZE_STRING);
    if (empty($first_name)) {
            $errors[] = 'You forgot to enter your first name.';
    }
```

Each entry in the form is sanitized. If the user did not enter a value for the first name, an error message is stored in the error array. This is the same code we used in the register program.

```
if (empty($errors)) { // If everything's OK.                              #3
            $q = mysqli_stmt_init($dbcon);
            $query = 'SELECT userid FROM users WHERE email=? AND userid !=?';
            mysqli_stmt_prepare($q, $query);
            // bind $id to SQL Statement
            mysqli_stmt_bind_param($q, 'si', $email, $id);
            // execute query
             mysqli_stmt_execute($q);
            $result = mysqli_stmt_get_result($q);

            if (mysqli_num_rows($result) == 0) {
// e-mail does not exist in another record
```

If there are no verification errors, determine whether the new e-mail is in the database and is related to a different user ID. If it is not related to a different ID, we can then update the record.

```
// e-mail does not exist in another record                               #4
      $query = 'UPDATE users SET first_name=?, last_name=?, email=?';
            $query .= ' WHERE userid=? LIMIT 1';

            $q = mysqli_stmt_init($dbcon);
            mysqli_stmt_prepare($q, $query);

            // bind values to SQL Statement
mysqli_stmt_bind_param($q, 'sssi', $first_name, $last_name, $email, $id);

            // execute query
            mysqli_stmt_execute($q);
```

```
            if (mysqli_stmt_affected_rows($q) == 1) { // Update OK
            // Echo a message if the edit was satisfactory:
            echo '<h3 class="text-center">The user has been edited.</h3>';
```

If the error array contains no error messages and the e-mail is not associated with another record, the query will run. Using the keyword UPDATE, the query updates the record in the users table for the record that has the correct user ID. Using the keyword LIMIT with 1 ensures that only one record is updated. Once completed successfully, a message is displayed to the user.

```
// Select the user's information to display in textboxes:                    #5

$q = mysqli_stmt_init($dbcon);

$query = "SELECT first_name, last_name, email FROM users WHERE userid=?";

mysqli_stmt_prepare($q, $query);

// bind $id to SQL Statement
mysqli_stmt_bind_param($q, 'i', $id);

// execute query
mysqli_stmt_execute($q);
$result = mysqli_stmt_get_result($q);
$row = mysqli_fetch_array($result, MYSQLI_NUM);

if (mysqli_num_rows($result) == 1) { // Valid user ID, display the form.
        // Get the user's information:
        // Create the form:
?>
<h2 class="h2 text-center">Edit Record</h2>
<form action="edit_record.php" method="post"
        name="editform" id="editform">
<div class="form-group row">
        <label for="first_name" class="col-sm-4 col-form-label">First Name:</label>
<div class="col-sm-8">
    <input type="text" class="form-control" id="first_name" name="first_name"
        placeholder="First Name" maxlength="30" required
        value="<?php echo htmlspecialchars($row[0], ENT_QUOTES); ?>" >
</div>
</div>
```

The user ID passed from the *admin_view_users.php* page is used to pull the user information from the users table to display in the form. The form containing the selected user's data is displayed. The user can then edit any information displayed on the form and click the submit button to return the changes to the table in the database.

```
<input type="hidden" name="id" value=" <?php echo $id  ?>" />                <!-- #6 -->
```

The hidden input value (id) ensures that no field for the user ID is displayed in the form unless an ID has been passed either from the *admin_view_users.php* page (via GET) or from the *edit_user.php* (via POST).

Deleting Records

If the administrator deletes the wrong record, the delete cannot be undone; therefore, the program will verify with the administrator that the record should be deleted. When the administrator clicks the Delete link on a displayed record, the *delete_user.php* page is displayed. The Delete a Record screen displays the name of the person the administrator is about to delete. The administrator can then click either the Yes button or the No button, as shown in Figure 4-9.

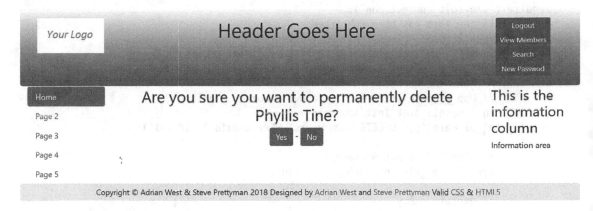

Figure 4-9. *The screen for deleting a record*

The page displays the name of the member to be deleted and gives the administrator the chance to verify the correct record is being removed. Before we describe the listing for the delete page, a few more names are suggested in Table 4-6. Register them so that you can try deleting them.

Table 4-6. *Some Names You Can Register and Then Try Deleting*

First Name	Last Name	E-mail	Password
Phyllis	Tine	ptine@myisp.co.uk	Vulg@r1@n
Des	Cant	dcant@myisp.com	P0lyph0n1c#
Bill	Board	bboard@myisp.net	H0ard1ng#
Eva	Nescent	enescent@myisp.de	Fl@@t1ng

In the next step, we will create a page for the administrator so records can safely be deleted. The HTML code is similar to previous code. You can view it from the downloaded files. Listing 4-7 shows the PHP code.

Listing 4-7. Creating a Page for Deleting Records (process_delete_record.php)

```php
<?php
try {
// Check for a valid user ID, through GET or POST:          #1
if ( (isset($_GET['id'])) && (is_numeric($_GET['id'])) ) {
// From view_users.php
    $id = htmlspecialchars($_GET['id'], ENT_QUOTES);
} else
```

```php
    if ( (isset($_POST['id'])) && (is_numeric($_POST['id'])) ) {
    // Form submission.
            $id = htmlspecialchars($_POST['id'], ENT_QUOTES);
    } else { // No valid ID, kill the script.
            // return to login page
            header("Location: login.php");
            exit();
            }
    require ('./mysqli_connect.php');
    // Check if the form has been submitted:                               #2
    if ($_SERVER['REQUEST_METHOD'] == 'POST') {
            $sure = htmlspecialchars($_POST['sure'], ENT_QUOTES);
            if ($sure == 'Yes') { // Delete the record.
            // Make the query:
            // Use prepare statement to remove security problems
            $q = mysqli_stmt_init($dbcon);
    mysqli_stmt_prepare($q, 'DELETE FROM users WHERE userid=? LIMIT 1');

            // bind $id to SQL Statement
            mysqli_stmt_bind_param($q, "s", $id);

            // execute query
            mysqli_stmt_execute($q);

            if (mysqli_stmt_affected_rows($q) == 1) { // It ran OK
            // Print a message:
            echo '<h3 class="text-center">The record has been deleted.</h3>';
            } else { // If the query did not run OK display public message

            echo '<p class="text-center">The record could not be deleted.';
        echo '<br>Either it does not exist or due to a system error.</p>';
        // echo '<p>' . mysqli_error($dbcon ) . '<br />Query: ' . $q . '</p>';
        // Debugging message. When live comment out because this displays SQL


            }
        } else { // User did not confirm deletion.
        echo '<h3 class="text-center">The user has NOT been deleted as ';
        echo 'you requested</h3>';
            }
    } else { // Show the form.                                             #3
        $q = mysqli_stmt_init($dbcon);
        $query = "SELECT CONCAT(first_name, ' ', last_name) FROM ";
        $query .= "users WHERE userid=?";
        mysqli_stmt_prepare($q, $query);

        // bind $id to SQL Statement
        mysqli_stmt_bind_param($q, "s", $id);

        // execute query
        mysqli_stmt_execute($q);
```

```php
        $result = mysqli_stmt_get_result($q);

        $row = mysqli_fetch_array($result, MYSQLI_NUM); // get user info

        if (mysqli_num_rows($result) == 1) {
        // Valid user ID, display the form.

        // Display the record being deleted:                                    #4
                $user = htmlspecialchars($row[0], ENT_QUOTES);
?>
<h2 class="h2 text-center">
Are you sure you want to permanently delete <?php echo $user; ?>?</h2>
<form action="delete_user.php" method="post"
        name="deleteform" id="deleteform">
<div class="form-group row">
        <label for="" class="col-sm-4 col-form-label"></label>
<div class="col-sm-8" style="padding-left: 70px;">
        <input type="hidden" name="id" value="<?php echo $id; ?>">
        <input id="submit-yes" class="btn btn-primary" type="submit" name="sure"
        value="Yes"> -
        <input id="submit-no" class="btn btn-primary" type="submit" name="sure" value="No">
</div>
</div>
</form>
<?php
    } else { // Not a valid user ID.
    echo '<p class="text-center">This page has been accessed in error.</p>';
      }
    } // End of the main submission conditional.
        mysqli_stmt_close($q);
        mysqli_close($dbcon );
    }
    catch(Exception $e)
    {
        print "The system is busy. Please try again.";
        //print "An Exception occurred. Message: " . $e->getMessage();
    }
    catch(Error $e)
    {
        print "The system is currently busy. Please try again soon.";
        //print "An Error occurred. Message: " . $e->getMessage();
    }
?>
```

Explanation of the Code

This section explains the code.

```
// Check for a valid user ID, through GET or POST:                              #1
if ( (isset($_GET['id'])) && (is_numeric($_GET['id'])) ) {
// From view_users.php

    $id = htmlspecialchars($_GET['id'], ENT_QUOTES);

} else
    if ( (isset($_POST['id'])) && (is_numeric($_POST['id'])) ) {
    // Form submission.

            $id = htmlspecialchars($_POST['id'], ENT_QUOTES);

    } else { // No valid ID, kill the script.
            // return to login page

            header("Location: login.php");
            exit();

            }
```

If the ID has not been passed, do not continue; go to login page.

```
// Check if the form has been submitted:                                        #2

if ($_SERVER['REQUEST_METHOD'] == 'POST') {

        $sure = htmlspecialchars($_POST['sure'], ENT_QUOTES);

        if ($sure == 'Yes') { // Delete the record.
        // Make the query:
        // Use prepare statement to remove security problems

        $q = mysqli_stmt_init($dbcon);
mysqli_stmt_prepare($q, 'DELETE FROM users WHERE userid=? LIMIT 1');

// bind $id to SQL Statement
mysqli_stmt_bind_param($q, "s", $id);

// execute query
        mysqli_stmt_execute($q);

        if (mysqli_stmt_affected_rows($q) == 1) { // It ran OK
        // Print a message:

        echo '<h3 class="text-center">The record has been deleted.</h3>';
```

A check is made to see whether the Yes button has been clicked. If it has, the SQL code for deleting a record is run; if it is successful, a message is displayed.

```
} else { // Show the form.                                          #3
        $q = mysqli_stmt_init($dbcon);
        $query =
"SELECT CONCAT(first_name, ' ', last_name) FROM users WHERE userid=?";

    mysqli_stmt_prepare($q, $query);

    // bind $id to SQL Statement
    mysqli_stmt_bind_param($q, "s", $id);

    // execute query
    mysqli_stmt_execute($q);

    $result = mysqli_stmt_get_result($q);

    $row = mysqli_fetch_array($result, MYSQLI_NUM); // get user info

    if (mysqli_num_rows($result) == 1) {
    // Valid user ID, display the form.
```

This code formats the name selected to be displayed:

```
// Display the record being deleted:                                #4
            $user = htmlspecialchars($row[0], ENT_QUOTES);
?>
<h2 class="h2 text-center">
Are you sure you want to permanently delete <?php echo $user; ?>?</h2>
<form action="delete_user.php" method="post"
        name="deleteform" id="deleteform">
<div class="form-group row">
        <label for="" class="col-sm-4 col-form-label"></label>
<div class="col-sm-8" style="padding-left: 70px;">

        <input type="hidden" name="id" value="<?php echo $id; ?>">

        <input id="submit-yes" class="btn btn-primary" type="submit" name="sure"
        value="Yes">

        <input id="submit-no" class="btn btn-primary" type="submit" name="sure" value="No">
</div>
</div>
</form>';
```

The user's name and the Yes and No buttons are displayed. The result of clicking one of these buttons is to send the value Yes or No to the preceding block of code numbered #2.

■ **Note**   Only files that needed modifying have been described to save space. Many PHP files for this chapter have not been mentioned because they are the same as the files in Chapter 3. If you have not already done so, download the complete set of Chapter 4 files from the Apress.com website. Use XAMPP or easyPHP to work though the examples from this chapter to understand the logic used to display, edit, and delete members.

Summary

In this chapter, you discovered how to create a user-friendly method of allowing an administrator to amend the contents of a database. This included the ability to paginate the whole table of members. A search form was described, and this can be used for selecting specific members so that their record can be amended or deleted. Code was provided that allowed the administrator to edit and delete records. Security was increased by sanitizing all input (no matter the source) to make sure that the values do not contain executable code. We will continue to add more security features in the next several chapters.

In the next chapter, we will explore a database with a few extra features. For instance, we will include the user's title and the user's postal address and telephone number. Additional validation and security devices will also be introduced.

CHAPTER 5

■ ■ ■

Expand and Enrich Your Website

The tutorials in this chapter assume that website users are applying for membership in an organization that requires a membership fee—for instance, a political party or a conservation society.

Website databases for such organizations require addresses and possibly the telephone numbers of their members. These forms can also use pull-down menus to allow the user to choose a class of membership.

As you may have experienced yourself, registration forms contain many fields; some are required, and some are optional. This chapter deals with a larger registration form than the previous chapters, with two of the fields as optional.

After completing this chapter, you will be able to

- Create a database that includes two tables

- Understand the importance of documentation

- Create an extended registration form with a drop-down menu

- Add PayPal and debit/credit card information

- Create variable pricing displays

- Apply pagination to the display of records

- Create code that edits records

The first step is to create a new database.

Creating a New Database, a Table with 15 Columns, and a Price Table

Follow these steps to create a new database and two tables:

1. Open the XAMPP *htdocs* or easyPHP *eds-www* folder, and create a new folder named *postal*.

2. Download the files for Chapter 5 from the book's website at www.apress.com and place the files in *htdocs* or *eds-www* under the new *postal* folder. If you want to hand-code your files, copy the files from Chapter 4 and paste them into your new *postal* folder. Then alter the code to match the revised code listed in this chapter. Also change the database in *mysqli_connect.php* to postaldb.

■ **Note** As mentioned in previous chapters, if you copy the code from the e-book, paste the code into a basic editor (such as Notepad) to ensure that all quotes are standard quotes. Save the code and then reopen the code in a PHP editor (such as Notepad++).

---

3. Use a browser to access phpMyAdmin, click the Databases tab, and create a new database called *postaldb*. Pick utf8-general-ci from the encoding selections.

4. In the next screen, create a table named *users*, enter **15** for the number of columns, and click Go (click Submit in some versions of phpMyAdmin). Enter the information shown in Table 5-1. After you have created the users table, click the New listing below the database name *postaldb* on the left column. This will display the new table page. Create another table named *prices*, enter **10** for the number of columns ,and click Go. Enter the information shown in Table 5-2. Also enter the values shown in Table 5-2.

5. Click Check Privileges and then scroll down and click the Add User Account. Now add a new user and password as follows:

   - *Username*: jenner

   - *Host*: LocalHost

   - *Password*: Vacc1nat10n

   Scroll down and click Check All, which is next to Global Privileges.

6. Scroll to the bottom and click Go.

Creating the File for Connecting to the Database

Name the following file *mysqli_connect.php* (or download it from www.apress.com), and add it to the *postal* folder in the *htdocs* folder:

```
<?php
// Create a connection to the postaldb database
// Set the encoding to utf-8
// Set the database access details as constants
Define ('DB_USER', 'jenner');
Define ('DB_PASSWORD', 'Vacc1nat10n');
Define ('DB_HOST', 'localhost');
Define ('DB_NAME', 'postaldb');
// Make the connection
$dbcon = new mysqli(DB_HOST, DB_USER, DB_PASSWORD, DB_NAME);
mysqli_set_charset($dbcon, 'utf8'); // Set the encoding...
```

Test your connection (*http://localhost/postal/mysqli_connect.php*). Remember, if you do not see anything on the screen, your connection was successful.

Next, if you have not already done so, create the table with columns and attributes as described in the next section. When you have successfully entered the information from Table 5-1, scroll down to the bottom of the phpMyAdmin page and click Go (or Submit).

Creating the Tables

We will now create a table suitable for a membership database that requires addresses and telephone numbers. The database table will also include extra items for the benefit of the administrator. These are classes of membership and a field to indicate whether members have paid their subscription fee. The table will have columns with the titles and attributes shown in Table 5-1.

Table 5-1. *The Titles and Attributes for the users Table*

Column name	Type	Length/Values	Default	Attributes	NULL	Index	A_I
userid	MEDIUMINT	6	None	UNSIGNED	☐	PRIMARY	☑
first_name	VARCHAR	30	None		☐		☐
last_name	VARCHAR	40	None		☐		☐
email	VARCHAR	50	None		☐		☐
password	CHAR	60	None		☐		☐
registration_date	DATETIME		None		☐		☐
user_level	TINYINT	1	None	UNSIGNED	☐		☐
class	CHAR	20	None		☐		☐
address1	VARCHAR	50	None		☐		☐
address2	VARCHAR	50	None		☑		☐
city	VARCHAR	50	None		☐		☐
state_country	CHAR	25	None		☐		☐
zocde_pcode	CHAR	10	None		☐		☐
phone	CHAR	15	None		☑		☐
paid	ENUM	"yes", "no"	None		☐		☐

Note that the address2 (the second address) and phone columns have their NULL INDEX boxes selected. They are optional fields. NULL simply means that a field can be left empty by the user. Many users might not have an additional address (such as a district in a large town or an apartment number). Some users do not want to disclose their telephone numbers to reduce the nuisance created by cold-callers.

While the postal or ZIP code will directly relate to the city in which the person lives, it is still a good idea to include the city and state or country information for verification that the correct code has been entered.

People who want to register for membership are required to pay a fee. However, fees change over time. To avoid requiring the developer to make changes every time there is a price adjustment, we will store the prices in a table and retrieve them when needed. This will allow the webmaster to make price changes in the database, and the prices will instantly appear on the pages. We could also create a price changes page for the administrator, but we will leave that to you to develop.

Table 5-2 shows the details for the prices table

Table 5-2. *The Titles and Attributes for the prices Table*

Column Name	Type	Length/Values	Default	Attributes	NULL	Index	A_I
oneyeargb	DECIMAL	6	None	UNSIGNED	☐		☐
oneyearus	DECIMAL	6	None	UNSIGNED	☐		☐
fiveyeargb	DECIMAL	6	None	UNSIGNED	☐		☐
fiveyearus	DECIMAL	6	None	UNISGNED	☐		☐
militarugb	DECIMAL	6	None	UNISGNED	☐		☐
militaryus	DECIMAL	6	None	UNSIGNED	☐		☐
u21gb	DECIMAL	6	None	UNSIGNED	☐		☐
u21us	DECIMAL	6	None	UNSIGNED	☐		☐
minpricegb	DECIMAL	6	None	UNSIGNED	☐		☐
minpriceus	DECIMAL	6	None	UNSIGNED	☐		☐

After creating the prices table, click the Insert tab in phpMyAdmin and enter numbers in the Value textboxes for each cell as shown here. Then click the Go button to save the values into the table.

oneyeargb 30.00   **oneyearus** 40.00   **fiveyeargb** 125.00

fiveyeargb 140.00   **militarygb** 5.00   **militaryus** 8.00

u21gb 2.00   **u21us** 3.00   **minpricegb** 15.00

minpriceus 20.00

Using ENUM

ENUM (enumeration) provides the ability to list the valid choices to be entered into the database. It ensures that only those values that you specify can be stored in that cell in the table. In our tutorial, only No or Yes can be entered. The choices must be separated by commas, and each must be surrounded by single or double quotes. You can type the values in the box or click the link below the box. If you click the Edit ENUM/Set Values link, you can type in a list of values, and the system will add the quotes and commas for you. If you choose NOT NULL for the paid column, the first value (No) will be the default. If you select the NULL box for an ENUM column, an empty field will be a valid value.

The Importance of Documentation

Because the database is becoming increasingly complex, it is imperative that you continue to record everything that you do. If you don't, you will spend many unhappy hours wondering what you did and why certain changes won't work. This is especially true with many pages, as in the current project. Remember, a database administrator is responsible for many databases. It may be months or years before a database or table is adjusted. Even if the webmaster created the original database, it is unlikely that they will remember the original design. By creating documentation of the design, it will help the webmaster to quickly remember or understand the logic and make any necessary changes.

We suggest keeping careful records in a notebook (physical or electronic). Create a flowchart that shows the logical relationships between the database and programs; in fact, it can be difficult to work without a flowchart. Charts often extend over several pages. You might want to print your charts and paste them together. It is not unusual to place charts on the wall of a conference room when teams are redesigning the logic of an application and its database(s). Many also place the charts in a shareable system like Microsoft SharePoint. By using this type of system, the design team can easily keep track of different versions.

The example charts that follow show all the pages, page titles, headers, and links between the pages. As the work progresses, flowcharts are amended by correcting faults, adding pages, and adding any new features required by the client. Amending the chart as you develop a database-driven website is vital. As an exercise, you could amend this example to include the prices table.

Figure 5-1 shows a small section of an example flowchart.

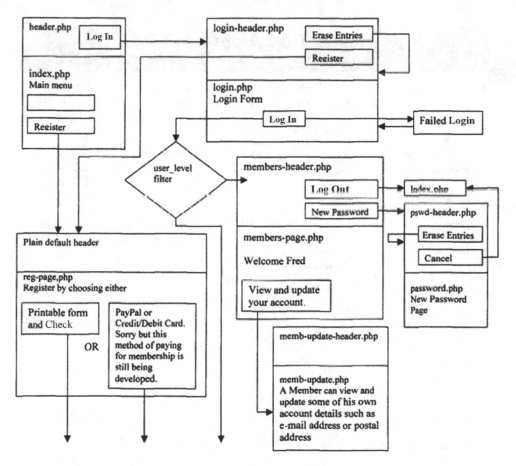

Figure 5-1. *A small section of a flow chart*

Commercial programs are available for creating flow charts, but you can use the drawing toolbar and textboxes in Microsoft Word. The diamond-shaped textbox denotes a decision structure (switch). This structure in the flowchart shown in Figure 5-1 determines a member's user_level and switches the logic of the code to either the members or administrator's page. There are many free tutorials and videos on the Internet that can demonstrate how to create flowcharts. Visio is a paid alternative with many additional features; for an excellent free program, try Diagram Designer from the following website:

http://meesoft.logicnet.dk/

Additional free flowchart programs can be found at `www.download.com`.

Now let's create a registration page based on the code used in the previous tutorials. We will adjust the code to include the extra fields in our new table. The code will also provide a pull-down selection menu. The registration page will display 12 fields; other fields will be hidden from the user.

Extending the Registration Form and Adding a Pull-Down Menu

Figure 5-2 shows the extended registration page.

Figure 5-2. *The extended registration page*

The required fields are denoted by the asterisk. When the fields are filled out correctly and the Register button is clicked, the user is taken to a "thank you" page containing a PayPal payment button and logo. The user will then pay the appropriate registration fee by PayPal or debit/credit card.

Always Announce Prices and Fee Payments Up-Front

Always declare up-front the full cost and the available payment methods. This is now a legal requirement in the United Kingdom. In other parts of the world, this might not be a legal requirement, but you should always declare all costs in advance. Users become irritated if extra costs are suddenly announced at the end of a transaction. They will usually close your website without paying. As well as stating the cost, we will add an image supplied by PayPal showing the various acceptable credit cards. However, users will not be able to pay until they submit the registration form and the "thank you" page appears.

■ **Note**   As previously stated, websites must conform to the required regulations of the country in which they are used. This might require different websites for different countries.

The registration page now contains 12 visible fields and hidden fields. The hidden fields are registration_date and paid. Hidden fields are not visible on the page that is displayed on the user's screen because they are relevant only to the administrator. Listing 5-1a shows the new fields.

Listing 5-1a. Creating the New Registration Page with 12 Visible Fields (register-page.php)

```
<!DOCTYPE html>
<html lang="en">
<head>
  <title>Register Page</title>
  <meta charset="utf-8">
  <meta name="viewport"
        content="width=device-width, initial-scale=1, shrink-to-fit=no">
  <!-- Bootstrap CSS File -->
  <link rel="stylesheet"
  href=
"https://stackpath.bootstrapcdn.com/bootstrap/4.1.0/css/bootstrap.min.css"
  integrity=
"sha384-9gVQ4dYFwwWSjIDZnLEWnxCjeSWFphJiwGPXr1jddIhOegiu1FwO5qRGvFXOdJZ4"
  crossorigin="anonymous">
    <script src="verify.js"></script>
</head>
<body>
<div class="container" style="margin-top:30px">
<!-- Header Section -->
<header class="jumbotron text-center row col-sm-14"
style="margin-bottom:2px; background:linear-gradient(white, #0073e6);
       padding:20px;">
        <?php include('register-header.php'); ?>
</header>
<!-- Body Section -->
  <div class="row" style="padding-left: 0px;">
<!-- Left-side Column Menu Section -->
```

```
  <nav class="col-sm-2">
      <ul class="nav nav-pills flex-column">
              <?php include('nav.php'); ?>
      </ul>
  </nav>
<!-- Validate Input -->
<?php
if ($_SERVER['REQUEST_METHOD'] == 'POST') {
 require('process-register-page.php');
} // End of the main Submit conditional.
?>
<div class="col-sm-8">
<h2 class="h2 text-center">Register</h2>
<h3 class="text-center">Items marked with an asterisk * are required</h3>
<?php
try {
        require_once ("mysqli_connect.php");$query = "SELECT * FROM prices";          //#1
        $result = mysqli_query ($dbcon, $query); // Run the query.
        if ($result) { // If it ran OK, display the records.
                $row = mysqli_fetch_array($result, MYSQLI_NUM);
                $yearsarray = array(
                "Standard one year:", "Standard five year:",
                "Military one year:", "Under 21 one year:",
                "Other - Give what you can. Maybe:" );
echo '<h6 class="text-center text-danger">Membership classes:</h6>' ;
echo '<h6 class="text-center text-danger small"> ';
for ($j = 0, $i = 0; $j < 5; $j++, $i = $i + 2) {
        echo $yearsarray[$j] . " &pound; " .
                htmlspecialchars($row[$i], ENT_QUOTES)  .
                " GB, &dollar; " .
                htmlspecialchars($row[$i + 1], ENT_QUOTES) .
                " US";
        if ($j != 4) {
        if ($j % 2 == 0) {
                echo "</h6><h6 class='text-center text-danger small'>"; }
        else {
                echo " , "; }
        }
}
echo "</h6>";
}
?>
<form action="register-page.php" method="post" onsubmit="return checked();"
        name="regform" id="regform">
<div class="form-group row">
    <label for="first_name" class="col-sm-4 col-form-label">
        *First Name:</label>
<div class="col-sm-8">
        <input type="text" class="form-control" id="first_name"
        name="first_name"
        placeholder="First Name" maxlength="30" required
        value=
```

158

```
                    "<?php if (isset($_POST['first_name']))
                    echo htmlspccialchars($_POST['first_name'], ENT_QUOTES); ?>" >
</div>
  </div>
  <div class="form-group row">
  <label for="last_name" class="col-sm-4 col-form-label">*Last Name:</label>
  <div class="col-sm-8">
      <input type="text" class="form-control" id="last_name" name="last_name"
              placeholder="Last Name" maxlength="40" required
              value=
                            "<?php if (isset($_POST['last_name']))
              echo htmlspecialchars($_POST['last_name'], ENT_QUOTES); ?>" >
  </div>
  </div>
  <div class="form-group row">
      <label for="email" class="col-sm-4 col-form-label">*E-mail:</label>
  <div class="col-sm-8">
      <input type="email" class="form-control" id="email" name="email"
              placeholder="E-mail" maxlength="60" required
              value=
                      "<?php if (isset($_POST['email']))
              echo htmlspecialchars($_POST['email'], ENT_QUOTES); ?>" >
  </div>
  </div>
  <div class="form-group row">
      <label for="password1"
                  class="col-sm-4 col-form-label">*Password:</label>
  <div class="col-sm-8">
      <input type="password" class="form-control" id="password1"
          name="password1"
          placeholder="Password" minlength="8" maxlength="12" required
              value=
                      "<?php if (isset($_POST['password1']))
              echo htmlspecialchars($_POST['password1'], ENT_QUOTES); ?>" >
      <span id='message'>Between 8 and 12 characters.</span>
  </div>
  </div>
  <div class="form-group row">
      <label for="password2" class="col-sm-4 col-form-label">
              *Confirm Password:</label>
  <div class="col-sm-8">
      <input type="password" class="form-control" id="password2"
          name="password2"
          placeholder="Confirm Password" minlength="8" maxlength="12" required
              value=
                      "<?php if (isset($_POST['password2']))
              echo htmlspecialchars($_POST['password2'], ENT_QUOTES); ?>" >
  </div>
  </div>
  <div class="form-group row">
      <label for="level" class="col-sm-4 col-form-label">
              *Membership Class</label>
```

```
    <div class="col-sm-8">                                                  <!--#2-->
            <select id="level" name="level" class="form-control" required>
            <option value="0" >-Select-</option>
<?php
    for ($j = 0, $i = 0; $j < 5; $j++, $i = $i + 2) {
            echo '<option value="' .
            htmlspecialchars($row[$i], ENT_QUOTES) . '" ';
    if ((isset($_POST['level'])) && ( $_POST['level'] == $row[$i]))
            {
    ?>
            selected
    <?php }
    echo ">" . $yearsarray[$j] . " " .
        htmlspecialchars($row[$i], ENT_QUOTES) .
            " &pound; GB, " .
            htmlspecialchars($row[$i + 1], ENT_QUOTES) .
            "&dollar; US</option>";
}
?>
</select>
</div>
</div>
<div class="form-group row">                                                <!--#3-->
    <label for="address1" class="col-sm-4 col-form-label">*Address:</label>
<div class="col-sm-8">
    <input type="text" class="form-control" id="address1" name="address1"
        placeholder="Address" maxlength="30" required
            value=
                    "<?php if (isset($_POST['address1']))
            echo htmlspecialchars($_POST['address1'], ENT_QUOTES); ?>" >
</div>
</div>
<div class="form-group row">
    <label for="address2" class="col-sm-4 col-form-label">Address:</label>
<div class="col-sm-8">
    <input type="text" class="form-control" id="address2" name="address2"
        placeholder="Address" maxlength="30"
            value=
                    "<?php if (isset($_POST['address2']))
            echo htmlspecialchars($_POST['address2'], ENT_QUOTES); ?>" >
</div>
</div>
<div class="form-group row">
    <label for="city" class="col-sm-4 col-form-label">*City:</label>
<div class="col-sm-8">
    <input type="text" class="form-control" id="city" name="city"
        placeholder="City" maxlength="30" required
            value=
                    "<?php if (isset($_POST['city']))
            echo htmlspecialchars($_POST['city'], ENT_QUOTES); ?>" >
    </div>
    </div>
```

```
    <div class="form-group row">
      <label for="state_country"
          class="col-sm-4 col-form-label">*State/Country:</label>
    <div class="col-sm-8">
        <input type="text" class="form-control"
                id="state_country" name="state_country"
                placeholder="State or Country" maxlength="30" required
                value=
                        "<?php if (isset($_POST['state_country']))
                echo htmlspecialchars($_POST['state_country'], ENT_QUOTES); ?>" >
    </div>
    </div>
    <div class="form-group row">
      <label for="zcode_pcode" class="col-sm-4 col-form-label">
                *Zip Code/Post Code:</label>
      <div class="col-sm-8">
                <input type="text" class="form-control" id="zcode_pcode"
                        name="zcode_pcode"
                placeholder="Zip Code or Postal Code" maxlength="15" required
                value=
                        "<?php if (isset($_POST['zcode_pcode']))
                echo htmlspecialchars($_POST['zcode_pcode'], ENT_QUOTES); ?>" >
    </div>
    </div>
    <div class="form-group row">
        <label for="phone" class="col-sm-4 col-form-label">
                Phone Number:</label>
    <div class="col-sm-8">
        <input type="tel" class="form-control" id="phone" name="phone"
                placeholder="Phone Number" maxlength="30"
                value=
                        "<?php if (isset($_POST['phone']))
                echo htmlspecialchars($_POST['phone'], ENT_QUOTES); ?>" >
    </div>
    </div>
    <div class="form-group row">
        <label for="" class="col-sm-4 col-form-label"></label>
    <div class="col-sm-8">
        <input id="submit" class="btn btn-primary" type="submit"
                name="submit" value="Register">
    </div>
    </div>
</form>
</div>
<!-- Right-side Column Content Section -->
<?php

 if(!isset($errorstring)) {
        echo '<aside class="col-sm-2">';
        include('info-col-cards.php');
        echo '</aside>';
        echo '</div>';
```

```php
        echo '<footer class="jumbotron text-center row col-sm-14"
                style="padding-bottom:1px; padding-top:8px;">';
}
else
{
        echo '<footer class="jumbotron text-center col-sm-12"
        style="padding-bottom:1px; padding-top:8px;">';
}

        include('footer.php');
        echo "</footer>";
        echo "</div>";
}
catch(Exception $e) // We finally handle any problems here
    {
      // print "An Exception occurred. Message: " . $e->getMessage();
      print "The system is busy please try later";
    }
catch(Error $e)
    {
      //print "An Error occurred. Message: " . $e->getMessage();
      print "The system is busy please try again later.";
    }
 ?>
</body>
</html>
```

Explanation of the Code

This section explains the code.

```php
$query = "SELECT * FROM prices";                                        //#1
$result = mysqli_query ($dbcon, $query); // Run the query.
if ($result) { // If it ran OK, display the records.
        $row = mysqli_fetch_array($result, MYSQLI_NUM);
```

All the prices are pulled from the prices table, creating a numerically indexed array called *$row*.

```php
$yearsarray = array(
"Standard one year:", "Standard five year:",
"Military one year:", "Under 21 one year:",
"Other - Give what you can. Maybe:" );
```

An array, $yearsarray, is created to hold the text of the different classes. In most programming languages, you cannot change the contents of an array created with this format. However, in PHP you can.

```php
echo '<h6 class="text-center text-danger">Membership classes:</h6>' ;
echo '<h6 class="text-center text-danger small"> ';
for ($j = 0, $i = 0; $j < 5; $j++, $i = $i + 2) {
```

In PHP a for loop can have more than one index, and each index can be incremented or decremented individually. In this example, $j is increased by one each time, while $i is increased by two each time. There are two values (GB and US) for each single description (Standard one year). Thus, as the descriptions change one at a time, the prices jump two positions.

```
        echo $yearsarray[$j] . " &pound; " .
                htmlspecialchars($row[$i], ENT_QUOTES) .
                " GB, &dollar; " .
                htmlspecialchars($row[$i + 1], ENT_QUOTES) .
                " US";
$j is controlling the description. $i is controlling the two prices to be displayed.
        if ($j != 4) {
        if ($j % 2 == 0) {
                echo "</h6><h6 class='text-center text-danger small'>"; }
        else {
                echo " , "; }
        }
```

For every two jumps of $J (so we can have two descriptions on one line), we close the line (</h6>) and open a new line for the next description, except when $j is 4. This would indicate there is not another description, so we don't need to start a new line.

```
}
echo "</h6>";
}
At the end we close the line of the last description.
<div class="col-sm-8">                                                      <!--#2-->
                <select id="level" name="level" class="form-control" required>
                <option value="0" >-Select-</option>
<?php
        for ($j = 0, $i = 0; $j < 5; $j++, $i = $i + 2) {
                echo '<option value="' .
                htmlspecialchars($row[$i], ENT_QUOTES) . '" ';
        if ((isset($_POST['level'])) && ( $_POST['level'] == $row[$i]))
                {
        ?>
                selected
        <?php }
        echo ">" . $yearsarray[$j] . " " .
           htmlspecialchars($row[$i], ENT_QUOTES) .
                " &pound; GB, " .
                htmlspecialchars($row[$i + 1], ENT_QUOTES) .
                "&dollar; US</option>";
}
?>
</select>
```

The looping and controlling of information for this example is similar to the previous example. However, we are creating a select statement for the form. Note that the code checks to see if the user previously selected a level. If they did, it places "selected" in the option statement being created for that level (such as Standard one year). Notice for selected to work correctly on the form, it must not be within an echo statement inside of PHP code.

```
<div class="form-group row">                                              <!--#3-->
    <label for="address1" class="col-sm-4 col-form-label">*Address:</label>
<div class="col-sm-8">
        <input type="text" class="form-control" id="address1" name="address1"
          placeholder="Address" maxlength="30" required
                value=
                        "<?php if (isset($_POST['address1']))
                echo htmlspecialchars($_POST['address1'], ENT_QUOTES); ?>" >
</div>
</div>
```

The HTML code for the additional fields within the form are in the same format as we have seen before. The input tags will stick any input the user entered back into the form, after sanitizing them using PHP.

Listing 5-2b. Code for the New Registration Page with 12 Visible Fields (process-register-page.php)

```
<?php
// This script is a query that INSERTs a record in the users table.
// Check that form has been submitted:
try {
        $errors = array(); // Initialize an error array.
        // Check for a first name:
        $first_name =
        filter_var( $_POST['first_name'], FILTER_SANITIZE_STRING);
        if (empty($first_name)) {
                $errors[] = 'You forgot to enter your first name.';
        }
        // Check for a last name:
           $last_name =
        filter_var( $_POST['last_name'], FILTER_SANITIZE_STRING);
        if (empty($last_name)) {
                $errors[] = 'You forgot to enter your last name.';
        }
        // Check for an email address:
           $email = filter_var( $_POST['email'], FILTER_SANITIZE_EMAIL);
        if  ((empty($email)) || (!filter_var($email, FILTER_VALIDATE_EMAIL))) {
                $errors[] = 'You forgot to enter your email address';
                $errors[] = ' or the e-mail format is incorrect.';
        }
        // Check for a password and match against the confirmed password:
                        $password1 =
        filter_var( $_POST['password1'], FILTER_SANITIZE_STRING);
                        $password2 = f
        ilter_var( $_POST['password2'], FILTER_SANITIZE_STRING);
        if (!empty($password1)) {
                if ($password1 !== $password2) {
                        $errors[] = 'Your two password did not match.';
                }
        } else {
                $errors[] = 'You forgot to enter your password(s).';
        }
```

```php
        // Check for an membership class
        if(isset($_POST['level'])) {
                $class =
                filter_var( $_POST['level'], FILTER_SANITIZE_STRING); }
        if (empty($class)) {
                $errors[] = 'Please choose your membership class.';
        }
        // Check for address:
                $address1 =
                        filter_var( $_POST['address1'], FILTER_SANITIZE_STRING);
        if (empty($address1)) {
                $errors[] = 'You forgot to enter your address.';
        }
        // Check for address2:                                              #1
                $address2 =
                filter_var( $_POST['address2'], FILTER_SANITIZE_STRING);
        if (empty($address2)) {
                $address2 = NULL;
        }
        // Check for city:
                $city =
                        filter_var( $_POST['city'], FILTER_SANITIZE_STRING);
        if (empty($city)) {
                $errors[] = 'You forgot to enter your City.';
        }
// Check for the county:
                $state_country =
                filter_var( $_POST['state_country'], FILTER_SANITIZE_STRING);
        if (empty($state_country)) {
                $errors[] = 'You forgot to enter your country.';
        }
        // Check for the post code:
                $zcode_pcode =
                filter_var( $_POST['zcode_pcode'], FILTER_SANITIZE_STRING);
        if (empty($zcode_pcode)) {
                $errors[] = 'You forgot to enter your post code.';
        }
        // Check for the phone number:
                $phone =
                filter_var( $_POST['phone'], FILTER_SANITIZE_STRING);
                if (empty($phone)) {
                        $phone = NULL;
        }
        if (empty($errors)) { // If everything's OK.
        //Determine whether the email address has already been registered    #2
                require ('mysqli_connect.php'); // Connect to the db.
                $query = "SELECT userid FROM users WHERE email = ? ";
                $q = mysqli_stmt_init($dbcon);
                mysqli_stmt_prepare($q, $query);
                mysqli_stmt_bind_param($q, 's', $email);
                mysqli_stmt_execute($q);
                $result = mysqli_stmt_get_result($q);
```

```php
            if (mysqli_num_rows($result) == 0){
            //The email address has not been registered
    // Register the user in the database...
    // Hash password current 60 characters but can increase
        $hashed_passcode = password_hash($password1, PASSWORD_DEFAULT);
            require ('mysqli_connect.php'); // Connect to the db.
            // Make the query:
            $query =
"INSERT INTO users (userid, first_name, last_name, email, password, ";
            $query .=
"class, address1, address2, city, state_country, zcode_pcode, phone, ";
            $query .= "registration_date ) ";
            $query .=
        "VALUES(' ', ?, ?, ?, ?, ?, ?, ?, ?, ?, ?, ?, NOW() )";
    $q = mysqli_stmt_init($dbcon);
    mysqli_stmt_prepare($q, $query);
    // use prepared statement to ensure that only text is inserted
    // bind fields to SQL Statement
    mysqli_stmt_bind_param($q, 'ssssssssss',
                    $first_name, $last_name, $email, $hashed_passcode,
                    $class, $address1, $address2, $city, $state_country,
                    $zcode_pcode, $phone);
// execute query
mysqli_stmt_execute($q);
if (mysqli_stmt_affected_rows($q) == 1) { // One record inserted
        header ("location: register-thanks.php?class=" . $class);
        exit();
        } else { // If it did not run OK.
        // Public message:
            $errorstring =
        "<p class='text-center col-sm-8' style='color:red'>";
        $errorstring .=
                "System Error<br />You could not be registered due ";
        $errorstring .=
        "to a system error. We apologize for any inconvenience.</p>";
        echo "<p class=' text-center col-sm-2'
                style='color:red'>$errorstring</p>";
        // Debugging message below do not use in production
        //echo '<p>' . mysqli_error($dbcon) . '<br><br>Query: ' . $query . '</p>';
        mysqli_close($dbcon); // Close the database connection.
        // include footer then close program to stop execution
        echo '<footer class="jumbotron text-center col-sm-12"
                style="padding-bottom:1px; padding-top:8px;">
    include("footer.php");
    </footer>';
exit();
        }else{//The email address is already registered          #3
        $errorstring = 'The email address is already registered.';
                echo "<p class=' text-center col-sm-2'
                style='color:red'>$errorstring</p>";
}
```

```
        } else { // Report the errors.
                $errorstring =
                "Error! <br /> The following error(s) occurred:<br>";
                foreach ($errors as $msg) { // Print each error.
                        $errorstring .= " - $msg<br>\n";
                }
                $errorstring .= "Please try again.<br>";
                echo "<p class=' text-center col-sm-2'
                        style='color:red'>$errorstring</p>";
                }// End of if (empty($errors)) IF.
        }
    catch(Exception $e) // We finally handle any problems here
    {
       // print "An Exception occurred. Message: " . $e->getMessage();
       print "The system is busy please try later";
    }
    catch(Error $e)
    {
        //print "An Error occurred. Message: " . $e->getMessage();
        print "The system is busy please try again later.";
    }
?>
```

Explanation of the Code

This section explains the code.

```
// Check for address2:                                                    #1
                $address2 =
                filter_var( $_POST['address2'], FILTER_SANITIZE_STRING);
        if (empty($address2)) {
                $address2 = NULL;
        }
```

The second address field (address2) is not a required field. This field has no required attribute because it can be deliberately left empty by the user. If the field is empty, the else statement will execute. There is no error message. Instead, the key word NULL is assigned to the variable $adress2. NULL indicates no value. If the registration form field for address2 is empty, the address2 cell in the database table will also be set to NULL. Examine the rest of the code and see whether you can find the same pattern being used for another optional field.

```
//Determine whether the email address has already been registered        #2
        require ('mysqli_connect.php'); // Connect to the db.
        $query = "SELECT userid FROM users WHERE email = ? ";
        $q = mysqli_stmt_init($dbcon);
        mysqli_stmt_prepare($q, $query);
        mysqli_stmt_bind_param($q, 's', $email);
        mysqli_stmt_execute($q);
        $result = mysqli_stmt_get_result($q);

        if (mysqli_num_rows($result) == 0){
```

Now a check is done to determine whether the e-mail is already in the database. If it is not, the information is inserted.

```
}else{//The email address is already registered                            #3
            $errorstring = 'The email address is already registered.';
                echo "<p class=' text-center col-sm-2'
                style='color:red'>$errorstring</p>";
        }
If the email already exists, display an error message.
```

The extended registration page informs the user that membership fees can be paid using PayPal or a debit/credit card. This is achieved pictorially using a PayPal image in the information column on the right side, as shown in the next section.

Adding PayPal Debit/Credit Card Images

The image is downloaded from the PayPal website and added to a new version of the info column. The result is shown in Figure 5-3.

Figure 5-3. *The revised info column*

The new *info-col-cards.php* file is included only in the registration page and the "thank you" page. All the other pages have no need for this information; therefore, they will include the original *info-col.php*.

Including PayPal on the "Thank You" Page

A payment method will now be added to the "thank you" page. This is shown in Figure 5-4.

Figure 5-4. *A PayPal link added to the "thank you" page*

The "thank you" page from the previous chapter forms the basis of the new page. The user's membership application will be recorded in the database, but the Paid cell will contain the default value No. This is because the Paid item is an ENUM hidden from the user. The administrator is the only person allowed to enter data in that field. The administrator will change the Paid cell to Yes when they receive an e-mail from PayPal confirming the payment (or when a card payment has arrived). The PayPal e-mail also provides the new member's address and e-mail. If the administrator is satisfied that the details match the information that the user entered in the database, the member's paid field in the database will be set to Yes. The administrator will need to compare the membership class selected originally by the user and the class the user paid to make sure they match. If there is a difference, the administrator will also need to adjust the class paid for in the database.

We are using PayPal in the "thank you" page because it is a popular payment system. A website owner can sign up at the paypal.com page (or paypal.co.uk page). They will be given a merchant ID and the option to generate and copy a snippet of code to embed the payment link in any page. If the owner already has a PayPal account, they can log in and go to My Profile and My Business Info, where they can find the merchant account ID. That ID will enable them to access the appropriate generated code to embed in the page.

NOTE: The PayPal code in *register-thanks.php* is for demonstration only. The code provided will not work because you must have a merchant account ID. PayPal does provide the ability to test payment transactions without processing PayPal or debit/credit card accounts. Once you have an account, PayPal will provide code that you can copy and paste to replace the example code in this demonstration. You can find more information on setting up a test environment here:

https://developer.paypal.com/docs/classic/paypal-payments-standard/ht_test-pps-buttons/

Listing 5-4 presents the code for the "thank you" page.

Listing 5-4. Creating a Combined "Thank You" and PayPal Payment Page (register-thanks.php)

```
<!DOCTYPE html>
<html lang="en">
<head>
  <title>Register Thanks</title>
```

```html
<meta charset="utf-8">
<meta name="viewport"
      content="width=device-width, initial-scale=1, shrink-to-fit=no">
<!-- Bootstrap CSS File -->
<link rel="stylesheet"
  href=
"https://stackpath.bootstrapcdn.com/bootstrap/4.1.0/css/bootstrap.min.css"
  integrity=
"sha384-9gVQ4dYFwwWSjIDZnLEWnxCjeSWFphJiwGPXr1jddIhOegiu1FwO5qRGvFXOdJZ4"
  crossorigin="anonymous">
</head>
<body>
<div class="container" style="margin-top:30px">
<!-- Header Section -->
<header class="jumbotron text-center row"
style="margin-bottom:2px;
background:linear-gradient(white, #0073e6); padding:20px;">
  <?php include('thanks-header.php'); ?>
</header>
<!-- Body Section -->
  <div class="row" style="padding-left: 0px;">
<!-- Left-side Column Menu Section -->
  <nav class="col-sm-2">
      <ul class="nav nav-pills flex-column">
              <?php include('nav.php'); ?>
      </ul>
  </nav>
<!-- Center Column Content Section -->
<div class="col-sm-8">
<h3 class="h2 text-center" >Thank you for registering</h2>
<h6 class="text-center">
To confirm your registration please verify membership class and pay the membership fee
now.</h6>
<h6 class="text-center">
You can use PayPal or a credit/debit card.</h6>
<p class="text-center" >
When you have completed your registration you will be able to login
to the member's only pages.</p>
<?php
try {
        require ("mysqli_connect.php");
        $query = "SELECT * FROM prices";
        $result = mysqli_query ($dbcon, $query); // Run the query.
        if ($result) { // If it ran OK, display the records.
        $row = mysqli_fetch_array($result, MYSQLI_NUM);
        $yearsarray = array(
"Standard one year:", "Standard five year:", "Military one year:",
"Under 21 one year:", "Other - Give what you can. Maybe:" );
echo '<h6 class="text-center text-danger">Membership classes:</h6>' ;
echo '<h6 class="text-center text-danger small"> ';
for ($j = 0, $i = 0; $j < 5; $j++, $i = $i + 2) {
```

```php
            echo $yearsarray[$j] . " &pound; " .
                    htmlspecialchars($row[$i], ENT_QUOTES)  .
                    " GB, &dollar; " .
                    htmlspecialchars($row[$i + 1], ENT_QUOTES) .
                    " US";

            if ($j != 4) {
            if ($j % 2 == 0) { echo "</h6><h6 class='text-center text-danger small'>"; }
            else { echo " , "; }
            }
    }
echo "</h6>";
}
?>
<p></p>
<form action="https://www.paypal.com/cgi-bin/webscr" method="post">
<input type="hidden" name="cmd" value="_s-xclick">
<input type="hidden" name="hosted_button_id" value="XXXXXXXXXXXXX">
<div class="form-group row">
    <label for="level" class="col-sm-4 col-form-label">
        *Membership Class</label>
<div class="col-sm-8">
        <select id="level" name="level" class="form-control" required>
        <option value="0" >-Select-</option>
<?php                                                                         //#1
$class = htmlspecialchars($_GET['class'], ENT_QUOTES);
for ($j = 0, $i = 0; $j < 5; $j++, $i = $i + 2) {

        echo '<option value="' .
                htmlspecialchars($row[$i], ENT_QUOTES) . '" ';
        if ((isset($class)) && ( $class == $row[$i]))
                {
                        echo ' selected ';
        }
        echo '>" . $yearsarray[$j] . " " .
            htmlspecialchars($row[$i], ENT_QUOTES) .
                " &pound; GB, " .
                htmlspecialchars($row[$i + 1], ENT_QUOTES) .
                "&dollar; US</option>";
}
?>
</select>
</div>
</div>
<div class="form-group row">
    <label for="" class="col-sm-4 col-form-label"></label>
    <div class="col-sm-8">
<!--                                                                          #2-->
<!-- Replace the code below with code provided by PayPal once you obtain a Merchant ID -->
<input type="hidden" name="currency_code" value="GBP">
<input style="margin:10px 0 0 40px" type="image"
src="https://www.paypalobjects.com/en_US/GB/i/btn/btn_buynowCC_LG.gif" name="submit"
alt="PayPal  The safer, easier way to pay online.">
```

```
<img alt="" src="https://www.paypalobjects.com/en_GB/i/scr/pixel.gif" width="1" height="1">
<!-- Replace code above with PayPal provided code -->
</div>
</div>
</form>
</div>
<!-- Right-side Column Content Section -->
        <aside class="col-sm-2">
                <?php include('info-col-cards.php'); ?>
        </aside>
  </div>
<!-- Footer Content Section -->
<footer class="jumbotron text-center row"
style="padding-bottom:1px; padding-top:8px;">
        <?php include('footer.php'); ?>
</footer>
<?php
} // end try
catch(Exception $e) // We finally handle any problems here
 {
        // print "An Exception occurred. Message: " . $e->getMessage();
        print "The system is busy please try later";
 }
catch(Error $e)
{
        //print "An Error occurred. Message: " . $e->getMessage();
        print "The system is busy please try again later.";
}
?>
</body>
</html>
```

Explanation of the Code

This section describes the code.

```
<?php                                                                         //#1
$class = htmlspecialchars($_GET['class'], ENT_QUOTES);
for ($j = 0, $i = 0; $j < 5; $j++, $i = $i + 2) {

        echo '<option value="' .
                htmlspecialchars($row[$i], ENT_QUOTES) . '" ';
        if ((isset($class)) && ( $class == $row[$i]))
                {
                        echo ' selected ';
         }
        echo ">" . $yearsarray[$j] . " " .
            htmlspecialchars($row[$i], ENT_QUOTES) .
                " &pound; GB, " .
                htmlspecialchars($row[$i + 1], ENT_QUOTES) .
                "&dollar; US</option>";

}
```

The code to create the drop-down list for the classes is similar to the code in the *register_page.php* file. However, the determination of which class to set as selected is decided by the value in $class, which was passed into the page from the register page.

```
<!--                                                                    #2-->
<!-- Replace the code below with code provided by PayPal once you obtain a Merchant ID -->
<input type="hidden" name="currency_code" value="GBP">
<input style="margin:10px 0 0 40px" type="image"
src="https://www.paypalobjects.com/en_US/GB/i/btn/btn_buynowCC_LG.gif" name="submit"
alt="PayPal  The safer, easier way to pay online.">
<img alt="" src="https://www.paypalobjects.com/en_GB/i/scr/pixel.gif" width="1" height="1">
<!-- Replace code above with PayPal provided code -->
```

This is a small portion of the code generated by PayPal. For security we have used a dummy value for the PayPal ID for this tutorial. PayPal provides a 13-character ID code. The header now has no menu buttons; until the registrant's payment is received, the registrant can only access the home page. The home page is accessible from the main menu.

Before we go any further, you need to register some extra members.

Registering Some Members

■ **Tip**   Entering the data can be tedious. To reduce the tedium in this tutorial, the addresses and telephone numbers can be identical for each entry. A set of suitable data is suggested next.

When experimenting, the following data was used for every record. This is acceptable because no searches are made using addresses and telephone numbers.

- *Membership class*: For each entry's membership class, choose any of the drop-down selections.

- *Address 1*: 2 The Street.

- *Address 2*: The Village (to demonstrate the effect of the NULL setting in the database, leave some of these fields empty and populate a few with The Village).

- *City*: Townsville.

- *Country or State*: UK (or CA, for example, if a U.S. state).

- *Post or Zip code* : EX7 9PP (or a U.S. ZIP code, 33040).

- *Phone*: 01234 777 888 (or a U.S. phone number, 3055551111. This field is optional, and you should omit the phone in some records.

Register the members listed in Table 5-3.

Table 5-3. *Some Member Names*

First Name	Last Name	E-mail	Password
James	Smith	jsmith@myisp.com	Bl3cksmith
Jack	Smith	jsmith@outcook.com	D0gsb0dy
Mike	Rosoft	miker@myisp.com	Willgat3s
Olive	Branch	obranch@myisp.co.uk	An0lly0ne
Frank	Incense	fincense@myisp.net	P3rfum3s
Annie	Versary	aversary@myisp.com	h@ppyd@y
Terry	Fide	tfide@myisp.de	sc@r3dst1ff
Rose	Bush	rbush@myisp.co.uk	R3db100ms
Annie	Mossity	amositty@myisp.org.uk	Y0ur3n3my
Percey	Veer	pveer@myisp.com	K33pg01ng
Darrel	Doo	ddoo@myisp.co.uk	Sat1sf1ed
Stan	Dard	sdard@myisp.net	b@ttl3fl@g
Nora	Bone	nbone@myisp.com	L1k3t3rr13r
Barry	Cade	bcade@myisp.co.uk	Bl0ckth3m

If you later require more data to play with, some suggestions are given in Table 5-4.

Table 5-4. *Some Additional Suggestions for Registrations*

First Name	Last Name	E-mail	Password
Dee	Jected	djected@myisp.org.uk	Gl00mnd00m
Lynn	Seed	lseed@myisp.com	Pa1nt3rs01l
Barry	Tone	btone@myisp.net	Nic3v01c3
Helen	Back	hback@myisp.net	Agr1ms0rt1e
Patrick	O'Hara	pohara@myisp.org.uk	Shamr0ck
Dawn	Chorus	dchorus@myisp.com	Tr1ll1ng
Connie	Firs	cfirst@myisp.com	P1n3tr33s
Eva	Nessant	enessant@outlook.com	Trans13nt
Al	Fresco	sfresco@myisp.net	Fr3sha1rf00d

■ **Important**   Jack Smith will once again act as the administrator. Go into phpMyAdmin and change Jack Smith's user_level from 0 to 1. Also, be sure to use phpMyAdmin to change the administrator's paid column to Yes. Change some other members' paid columns to Yes.

To change the paid field to Yes, after entering all the members, open phpMyAdmin, and in the left panel click the + sign next to postaldb and then click the underlined word *users*. The user's records will be displayed in horizontal format. To change a member's paid field, click the Edit item on the left of each member's record. The record will then be displayed in a more convenient vertical format. Scroll down to the paid ENUM radio buttons and click the Yes button. Then click Go.

■ **Note**   Remember that if you can't log in to a member's account, it is probably because his paid column is not set to Yes. This is as it should be.

A Small Amendment to the Login Page

The login page (included in the downloaded files) is almost the same as the one in the previous chapter, except that we must prevent an applicant from accessing the members-only pages before the administrator has received the membership fee. The following snippet of code shows the amendment to the query:

```
// Retrieve the user_id, psword, first_name and user_level for that
// email/password combination
 $query = "SELECT user_id, psword, fname, user_level FROM users ";
 $query .= "WHERE paid='Yes' AND email=?";
```

The error message is also modified as follows:

```
echo '<p class="error">our E-mail/Password does not match our records.';
echo ' Perhaps your fee has not yet been processed from PayPal or the credit card.';
echo '<br>Perhaps you need to register, just click the Register' ;
echo 'button on the header menu</p>';
```

We must now alter the administrator's pages to match the extra columns. For instance, the membership secretary (administrator) will want to update which members have paid their fees or requested other changes. For example, Eva Nessant might move or change her name. In Chapter 6, we will also add the ability to include a title (Mr. Mrs. Miss, Mx., Dr.) to each member. In Chapter 7, we will lighten the administrator's workload and allow the members to update these fields in their own records.

We will now make a change to the administration page's header to incorporate a new button.

Amending the Administrator's Header

To avoid having a mile-wide table display, the large number of columns will be split into two separate displays: one displaying membership details and the other displaying members' addresses and telephone numbers. A new search facility is required so that the members' addresses can be displayed in the table. This will be launched by means of a new button on the header menu labeled *Addresses*.

We have modified the header to include the Addresses button, as shown in Figure 5-5. Because the header is the launch pad, we will begin by listing the new header.

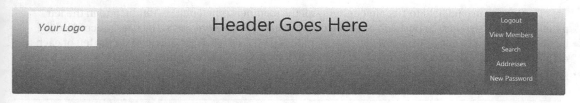

Figure 5-5. *The new header containing the new Addresses button*

The new addresses button is shown in Listing 5-5.

Listing 5-5. Installing a New Addresses Button in the Header (header-admin.php)

```
<div class="col-sm-2">
<img class="img-fluid float-left" src="logo.jpg" alt="Logo">
</div>
<div class="col-sm-8">
        <h1 class="blue-text mb-4 font-bold">Header Goes Here</h1>
</div>
        <nav class="col-sm-2">
        <div class="btn-group-vertical btn-group-sm" role="group"
                aria-label="Button Group">
                <button type="button" class="btn btn-secondary"
                        onclick="location.href = 'logout.php'" >
                        Logout</button>
                <button type="button" class="btn btn-secondary"
                        onclick="location.href = 'admin_view_users.php'">
                        View Members</button>
                <button type="button" class="btn btn-secondary"
                        onclick="location.href = 'search.php'">
                        Search</button>
                <button type="button" class="btn btn-secondary"
                        onclick="location.href = '#'">
                        Addresses</button>
                <button type="button" class="btn btn-secondary"
                        onclick="location.href = 'register-password.php'">
                        New Password</button>
        </div>
</nav>
```

■ **Note**   The link search addresses will not work until we have produced the *search_address.php* page. We will do this in the next chapter.

The table displayed by the *admin_view_users.php* file needs two extra columns, called *class* and *paid*.

Adding Class and Paid to the admin_view_users Table

From the administrator's point of view, the admin_view_users table needs to be revised to show some of the new columns. The paginated table needs to display the columns shown in Figure 5-6.

Figure 5-6. *The new table display. Note the new Class and Paid columns*

To save you the tedious task of entering a huge number of registrations, each table has again been limited to four records. In a real-world situation, you would display about 20 to 25 rows per page. Figure 5-6 shows the table display with two extra columns.

Listing 5-6 shows the amendments to the code. Note that the right info column has been removed to allow more space for the table. In the next section, we will show the code changes to accomplish this.

Listing 5-6. Code for Creating the Paginated Table to Display Two Extra Columns (process_admin_view_users.php)

```php
<?php
try {
        // This script retrieves all the records from the users table.
        require('mysqli_connect.php'); // Connect to the database.
        //set the number of rows per display page
        $pagerows = 4;
        // Has the total number of pages already been calculated?
        if ((isset($_GET['p']) && is_numeric($_GET['p']))) {
                //already been calculated
                $pages = htmlspecialchars($_GET['p'], ENT_QUOTES);
                // make sure it is not executable XSS
        }else{//use the next block of code to calculate the number of pages
                //First, check for the total number of records
```

```php
        $query = "SELECT COUNT(userid) FROM users";
        $result = mysqli_query ($dbcon, $query);
        $row = mysqli_fetch_array ($result, MYSQLI_NUM);
        $records = htmlspecialchars($row[0], ENT_QUOTES);
        // make sure it is not executable XSS
        //Now calculate the number of pages
        if ($records > $pagerows){
                //if the number of records will fill more than one page
                //Calculate the number of pages and round the result up
                // to the nearest integer
                $pages = ceil ($records/$pagerows);
        }else{
                $pages = 1;
        }
}//page check finished
//Declare which record to start with
if ((isset($_GET['s'])) &&( is_numeric($_GET['s'])))
{
        $start = htmlspecialchars($_GET['s'], ENT_QUOTES);
        // make sure it is not executable XSS
}else{
        $start = 0;
}
        $query = "SELECT last_name, first_name, email, ";                    //#1
        $query .= "DATE_FORMAT(registration_date, '%M %d, %Y')";
        $query .=" AS regdat, class, paid, userid FROM users ORDER BY ";
        $query .="registration_date DESC";
        $query .=" LIMIT ?, ?";

        $q = mysqli_stmt_init($dbcon);
        mysqli_stmt_prepare($q, $query);

        // bind $id to SQL Statement
        mysqli_stmt_bind_param($q, "ii", $start, $pagerows);

        // execute query
        mysqli_stmt_execute($q);
        $result = mysqli_stmt_get_result($q);

        if ($result) { //                                                    #2
        // If it ran OK (records were returned), display the records.
        // Table header
        echo '<table class="table table-striped">
        <tr>
        <th scope="col">Edit</th>
        <th scope="col">Delete</th>
        <th scope="col">Last Name</th>
        <th scope="col">First Name</th>
        <th scope="col">Email</th>
        <th scope="col">Date Registered</th>
        <th scope="col">Class</th>
        <th scope="col">Paid</th>
```

```php
            </tr>';
            // Fetch and print all the records:
            while ($row = mysqli_fetch_array($result, MYSQLI_ASSOC)) {
        // Remove special characters that might already be in table to
            // reduce the chance of XSS exploits                              #3
            $user_id = htmlspecialchars($row['userid'], ENT_QUOTES);
            $last_name = htmlspecialchars($row['last_name'], ENT_QUOTES);
            $first_name = htmlspecialchars($row['first_name'], ENT_QUOTES);
            $email = htmlspecialchars($row['email'], ENT_QUOTES);
            $registration_date =
            htmlspecialchars($row['regdat'], ENT_QUOTES);
            $class = htmlspecialchars($row['class'], ENT_QUOTES);
            $paid = htmlspecialchars($row['paid'], ENT_QUOTES);
            echo '<tr>
            <td><a href="edit_user.php?id=' . $user_id . '">Edit</a></td>
            <td><a href="delete_user.php?id=' . $user_id . '">Delete</a></td>
            <td>' . $last_name . '</td>
            <td>' . $first_name . '</td>
            <td>' . $email . '</td>
            <td>' . $registration_date . '</td>
            <td>' . $class . '</td>
            <td>' . $paid . '</td>
            </tr>';
        }
            echo '</table>'; // Close the table.
            mysqli_free_result ($result); // Free up the resources.
}
else { // If it did not run OK.
// Error message:
        echo '<p class="text-center">The current users could not be ';
        echo 'retrieved We apologize for any inconvenience.</p>';
// Debug message:
// echo '<p>' . mysqli_error($dbcon) . '<br><br>Query: ' . $q . '</p>';
// exit;
} // End of else ($result)
// Now display the total number of records/members.
$q = "SELECT COUNT(userid) FROM users";
$result = mysqli_query ($dbcon, $q);
$row = mysqli_fetch_array ($result, MYSQLI_NUM);
$members = htmlspecialchars($row[0], ENT_QUOTES);
mysqli_close($dbcon); // Close the database connection.
$echostring = "<p class='text-center'>Total membership: $members </p>";
$echostring .= "<p class='text-center'>";
if ($pages > 1) {//
        //What number is the current page?
        $current_page = ($start/$pagerows) + 1;
        //If the page is not the first page then create a Previous link
        if ($current_page != 1) {
        $echostring .= '<a href="admin_view_users.php?s=' .
            ($start - $pagerows) . '&p=' . $pages . '">
            Previous</a> ';
}
```

```php
//Create a Next link
if ($current_page != $pages) {
        $echostring .= ' <a href="admin_view_users.php?s=' .
        ($start + $pagerows) . '&p=' . $pages . '">Next</a> ';
}
$echostring .= '</p>';
echo $echostring;
}
} //end of try
catch(Exception $e) // We finally handle any problems here
{
    // print "An Exception occurred. Message: " . $e->getMessage();
    print "The system is busy please try later";
}
catch(Error $e)
{
    //print "An Error occurred. Message: " . $e->getMessage();
    print "The system is busy please try again later.";
}
?>
```

Explanation of the Code

This section explains the code.

```php
$query = "SELECT last_name, first_name, email, ";                               //#1
$query .= "DATE_FORMAT(registration_date, '%M %d, %Y')";
$query .=" AS regdat, class, paid, userid FROM users ORDER BY ";
$query .="registration_date DESC";
$query .=" LIMIT ?, ?";

$q = mysqli_stmt_init($dbcon);
mysqli_stmt_prepare($q, $query);

// bind $id to SQL Statement
mysqli_stmt_bind_param($q, "ii", $start, $pagerows);

// execute query
mysqli_stmt_execute($q);
$result = mysqli_stmt_get_result($q);

if ($result) {
```

The two columns called *class* and *paid* are added to the SELECT query. The rows are again ordered by registration date, but now they will be in descending order (DESC) because our imaginary administrator prefers to view the latest registrations at the top of the table.

```php
if ($result) { //                                                               #2
// If it ran OK (records were returned), display the records.
// Table header
echo '<table class="table table-striped">
<tr>
```

```
<th scope="col">Edit</th>
<th scope="col">Delete</th>
<th scope="col">Last Name</th>
<th scope="col">First Name</th>
<th scope="col">Email</th>
<th scope="col">Date Registered</th>
<th scope="col">Class</th>
<th scope="col">Paid</th>
</tr>';
```

If no problem was encountered, then display the table titles including the extra two items.

```
// reduce the chance of XSS exploits                                          #3
            $user_id = htmlspecialchars($row['userid'], ENT_QUOTES);
            $last_name = htmlspecialchars($row['last_name'], ENT_QUOTES);
            $first_name = htmlspecialchars($row['first_name'], ENT_QUOTES);
            $email = htmlspecialchars($row['email'], ENT_QUOTES);
            $registration_date =
                    htmlspecialchars($row['regdat'], ENT_QUOTES);
            $class = htmlspecialchars($row['class'], ENT_QUOTES);
            $paid = htmlspecialchars($row['paid'], ENT_QUOTES);
            echo '<tr>
            <td><a href="edit_user.php?id=' . $user_id . '">Edit</a></td>
            <td><a href="delete_user.php?id=' . $user_id . '">Delete</a></td>
            <td>' . $last_name . '</td>
            <td>' . $first_name . '</td>
            <td>' . $email . '</td>
            <td>' . $registration_date . '</td>
            <td>' . $class . '</td>
            <td>' . $paid . '</td>
            </tr>';
    }
            echo '</table>'; // Close the table.
```

We sanitized the two new columns and placed the results into the last two columns of the table. Now let's update our ability to search and edit the records.

Searching and Editing Records

The search form and its code are the same as those in Chapter 4; therefore, they will not be repeated here. We do, however, need to add the Class and Paid columns to the table displayed on the screen when a record is displayed using the Search button on the header menu.

Figure 5-7 shows the search result with the two new columns.

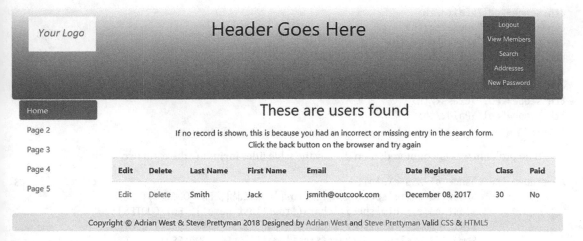

Figure 5-7. *The search result now displays a record with the two extra columns, Class and Paid*

To make room for long e-mail addresses, last names, and the two new columns, we have removed the information column in the display. The partial listing from the last few lines of the *view_found_record.php* file is shown here:

```
<div class="col-sm-10">
  <h2 class="text-center">These are users found</h2>
<p>
<?php
    require ("process_view_found_record.php");
?>
</div>
</div>
<!-- Footer Content Section -->
<footer class="jumbotron text-center row"
    style="padding-bottom:1px; padding-top:8px;">
  <?php include('footer.php'); ?>
</footer>
</div>
</body>
</html>
```

The number of Bootstrap columns to display the table has been increased from 8 to 10 (col-sm-10). The information column code has been removed.

Listing 5-7 shows the changes to the PHP code for adding the two extra columns to the table.

Listing 5-7. Creating Two Extra Columns in the Table Display (process_view_found_record.php)

```
<?php
try
{
        // This script retrieves records from the users table.
        require ('./mysqli_connect.php'); // Connect to the db.
        echo '<p class="text-center">If no record is shown, ';
        echo 'this is because you had an incorrect ';
```

```php
echo ' or missing entry in the search form.';
echo '<br>Click the back button on the browser and try again</p>';
$first_name = htmlspecialchars($_POST['first_name'], ENT_QUOTES);
$last_name = htmlspecialchars($_POST['last_name'], ENT_QUOTES);
// Since it's a prepared statement below this sanitizing is not needed
// However, to consistently retrieve than sanitize is a good habit

$query = "SELECT last_name, first_name, email, ";
$query .= "DATE_FORMAT(registration_date, '%M %d, %Y')";
$query .=" AS regdat, class, paid, userid FROM users WHERE ";
$query .= "last_name=? AND first_name=? ";
$query .="ORDER BY registration_date ASC ";

$q = mysqli_stmt_init($dbcon);
mysqli_stmt_prepare($q, $query);

// bind values to SQL Statement
mysqli_stmt_bind_param($q, 'ss', $last_name, $first_name);

// execute query
mysqli_stmt_execute($q);

$result = mysqli_stmt_get_result($q);

if ($result) { // It it ran, display the records.
// Table header.
echo '<table class="table table-striped">
<tr>
<th scope="col">Edit</th>
<th scope="col">Delete</th>
<th scope="col">Last Name</th>
<th scope="col">First Name</th>
<th scope="col">Email</th>
<th scope="col">Date Registered</th>
<th scope="col">Class</th>
<th scope="col">Paid</th>
</tr>';
// Fetch and display the records:
while ($row = mysqli_fetch_array($result, MYSQLI_ASSOC)) {
// Remove special characters that might already be in table to
// reduce the chance of XSS exploits
        $user_id = htmlspecialchars($row['userid'], ENT_QUOTES);
        $last_name = htmlspecialchars($row['last_name'], ENT_QUOTES);
        $first_name = htmlspecialchars($row['first_name'], ENT_QUOTES);
        $email = htmlspecialchars($row['email'], ENT_QUOTES);
        $registration_date =
                htmlspecialchars($row['regdat'], ENT_QUOTES);
        $class = htmlspecialchars($row['class'], ENT_QUOTES);
        $paid = htmlspecialchars($row['paid'], ENT_QUOTES);
        echo '<tr>
        <td><a href="edit_user.php?id=' . $user_id . '">Edit</a></td>
        <td><a href="delete_user.php?id=' . $user_id . '">Delete</a></td>
```

```
                <td>' . $last_name . '</td>
                <td>' . $first_name . '</td>
                <td>' . $email . '</td>
                <td>' . $registration_date . '</td>
                <td>' . $class . '</td>
                <td>' . $paid . '</td>
                </tr>';
        }
        echo '</table>'; // Close the table.
        //
        mysqli_free_result ($result); // Free up the resources.
} else { // If it did not run OK.
        // Public message:
        echo '<p class="center-text">The current users could not ';
        echo 'be retrieved.';
        echo 'We apologize for any inconvenience.</p>';
        // Debugging message:
        //echo '<p>' . mysqli_error($dbcon) . '<br><br>Query: ' . $q . '</p>';
        //Show $q is debug mode only
} // End of if ($result). Now display the total number of records/members.
mysqli_close($dbcon); // Close the database connection.
}
catch(Exception $e)
{
        print "The system is currently busy. Please try later.";
        //print "An Exception occurred.Message: " . $e->getMessage();
}catch(Error $e)
{
        print "The system us busy. Please try later.";
        //print "An Error occurred. Message: " . $e->getMessage();
}
?>
</html>
```

Explanation of the Code

The changes to the code are the same as we discussed related to a previous listing, so we will not explain them again here.

Modifying the Form for Editing Records

The form for editing a record will now contain two more fields, Membership Class and Paid. This enables the membership secretary to view a member's chosen class of membership. They can also enter Yes in the Paid field when the member's PayPal payment is processed. These fields are shown in Figure 5-8.

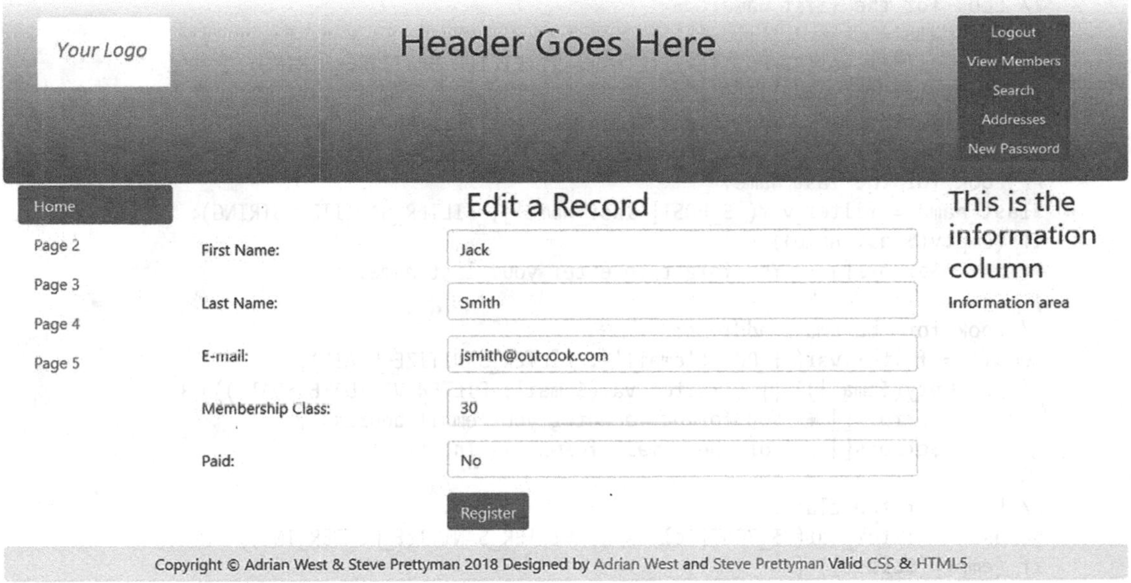

Figure 5-8. *The screen for editing a record*

All five fields can be edited. When the Edit button is clicked, the revised data is shown, together with a message saying that the record was edited successfully. Editing an address or telephone number will be covered in Chapter 6. Listing 5-8 shows the code for editing a record.

Listing 5-8. The Code for Creating an Editing Screen to Include the Two Additional Fields (process_edit_record.php)

```php
<?php
try
{
// After clicking the Edit link in the found_record.php page. This code is executed
// The code looks for a valid user ID, either through GET or POST:
if ( (isset($_GET['id'])) && (is_numeric($_GET['id'])) ) {
// From view_users.php
    $id = htmlspecialchars($_GET['id'], ENT_QUOTES);
} elseif ( (isset($_POST['id'])) && (is_numeric($_POST['id'])) ) {
// Form submission.
    $id = htmlspecialchars($_POST['id'], ENT_QUOTES);
} else { // No valid ID, kill the script.
    echo '<p class="text-center">
            This page has been accessed in error.</p>';
    include ('footer.php');
    exit();
}

require ('./mysqli_connect.php');
// Has the form been submitted?
if ($_SERVER['REQUEST_METHOD'] == 'POST') {
    $errors = array();
```

```php
// Look for the first name:
$first_name =
        filter_var( $_POST['first_name'], FILTER_SANITIZE_STRING);
if (empty($first_name)) {
        $errors[] = 'You forgot to enter your first name.';
}
// Look for the last name:
$last_name = filter_var( $_POST['last_name'], FILTER_SANITIZE_STRING);
if (empty($last_name)) {
        $errors[] = 'You forgot to enter your last name.';
}
// Look for the email address:
$email = filter_var( $_POST['email'], FILTER_SANITIZE_EMAIL);
if  ((empty($email)) || (!filter_var($email, FILTER_VALIDATE_EMAIL))) {
        $errors[] = 'You forgot to enter your email address';
        $errors[] = ' or the e-mail format is incorrect.';
}
// Look for the class:                                                       #1
$class = filter_var( $_POST['class'], FILTER_SANITIZE_NUMBER_INT);
if (empty($class)) {
        $errors[] = 'You forgot to the class or it is not numeric.';
}
// Look for the Paid Status:                                                 #2
$paid = filter_var( $_POST['paid'], FILTER_SANITIZE_STRING);
if (empty($paid)) {
        $errors[] = 'You forgot to enter the paid status.';
}
if (!(($paid == "No") || ($paid == "Yes"))) {
        $errors[] = "Paid must be No or Yes.";
}
if (empty($errors)) { // If everything's OK.
        $q = mysqli_stmt_init($dbcon);
        $query = 'SELECT userid FROM users WHERE email=? AND userid !=?';
        mysqli_stmt_prepare($q, $query);

        // bind $id to SQL Statement
        mysqli_stmt_bind_param($q, 'si', $email, $id);

// execute query
mysqli_stmt_execute($q);
        $result = mysqli_stmt_get_result($q);

        if (mysqli_num_rows($result) == 0) {
        // e-mail does not exist in another record
        $query = 'UPDATE users SET first_name=?, last_name=?, email=?,';
        $query .= ' class=?, paid=?';
        $query .= ' WHERE userid=? LIMIT 1';
        $q = mysqli_stmt_init($dbcon);
        mysqli_stmt_prepare($q, $query);
```

```php
                // bind values to SQL Statement
mysqli_stmt_bind_param($q, 'ssssssi', $first_name, $last_name, $email, $class, $paid, $id);
        // execute query
        mysqli_stmt_execute($q);

                        if (mysqli_stmt_affected_rows($q) == 1) { // Update OK
                        // Echo a message if the edit was satisfactory:
                                echo '<h3 class="text-center">
                                        The user has been edited.</h3>';
                        } else { // Echo a message if the query failed.
                                echo '<p class="text-center">
                                The user could not be edited due to a system error.';
                                echo ' We apologize for any inconvenience.</p>';
                                // Public message.
                //echo '<p>' . mysqli_error($dbcon) . '<br />Query: ' . $q . '</p>';
                // Debugging message.
                // Message above is only for debug and should not in live mode
                        }
        } else { // Already registered.
                echo '<p class="text-center">
                        The email address has already been registered.</p>';
                }
        } else { // Display the errors.
                echo '<p class="text-center">
                        The following error(s) occurred:<br />';
                foreach ($errors as $msg) { // Echo each error.
                        echo " - $msg<br />\n";
                }
                echo '</p><p>Please try again.</p>';
} // End of if (empty($errors))section.
} // End of the conditionals
// Select the user's information to display in textboxes:

        $q = mysqli_stmt_init($dbcon);
        $query =
"SELECT first_name, last_name, email, class, paid FROM users WHERE userid=?";
        mysqli_stmt_prepare($q, $query);
        // bind $id to SQL Statement
        mysqli_stmt_bind_param($q, 'i', $id);
        // execute query
        mysqli_stmt_execute($q);
        $result = mysqli_stmt_get_result($q);
        $row = mysqli_fetch_array($result, MYSQLI_NUM);
        if (mysqli_num_rows($result) == 1) {
        // Valid user ID, display the form.
        // Get the user's information:
        // Create the form:
?>
<h2 class="h2 text-center">Edit a Record</h2>
<form action="edit_user.php" method="post"
        name="editform" id="editform">
```

```html
<div class="form-group row">
        <label for="first_name" class="col-sm-4 col-form-label">
                First Name:</label>
<div class="col-sm-8">
        <input type="text" class="form-control" id="first_name"
        name="first_name" placeholder="First Name" maxlength="30" required
        value="<?php echo htmlspecialchars($row[0], ENT_QUOTES); ?>" >
</div>
</div>
<div class="form-group row">
        <label for="last_name" class="col-sm-4 col-form-label">
                Last Name:</label>
<div class="col-sm-8">
        <input type="text" class="form-control" id="last_name"
        name="last_name" placeholder="Last Name" maxlength="40" required
        value="<?php echo htmlspecialchars($row[1], ENT_QUOTES); ?>">
</div>
</div>
<div class="form-group row">
        <label for="email" class="col-sm-4 col-form-label">
        E-mail:</label>
<div class="col-sm-8">
        <input type="email" class="form-control" id="email"
        name="email" placeholder="E-mail" maxlength="60" required
        value="<?php echo htmlspecialchars($row[2], ENT_QUOTES); ?>">
</div>
</div>
<div class="form-group row">
    <label for="class" class="col-sm-4 col-form-label">
        Membership Class:</label>
<div class="col-sm-8">
        <input type="text" class="form-control" id="class"
        name="class" placeholder="Membership Class" maxlength="60" required
        value="<?php echo htmlspecialchars($row[3], ENT_QUOTES); ?>">
</div>
</div>
<div class="form-group row">
        <label for="paid" class="col-sm-4 col-form-label">Paid:</label>
<div class="col-sm-8">
        <input type="text" class="form-control" id="paid"
        name="paid" placeholder="Paid" maxlength="60" required
        value="<?php echo htmlspecialchars($row[4], ENT_QUOTES); ?>">
</div>
</div>
<input type="hidden" name="id" value="<?php echo $id ?>" />
<div class="form-group row">
        <label for="" class="col-sm-4 col-form-label"></label>
<div class="col-sm-8">
        <input id="submit" class="btn btn-primary" type="submit"
        name="submit" value="Register">
</div>
</div>
```

```php
</form>
<?php
} else { // The user could not be validated
        echo '<p class="text-center">
                This page has been accessed in error.</p>';
}
mysqli_stmt_free_result($q);
mysqli_close($dbcon);
}
catch(Exception $e)
{
        print "The system is busy. Please try later";
        //print "An Exception occurred.Message: " . $e->getMessage();
}catch(Error $e)
{
        print "The system is currently busy. Please try again later";
        //print "An Error occurred. Message: " . $e->getMessage();
}
?>
```

```php
// Look for the class:                                                  #1
        $class = filter_var( $_POST['class'], FILTER_SANITIZE_NUMBER_INT);
        if (empty($class)) {
                $errors[] = 'You forgot to the class or it is not numeric.';
        }
```

The integer parameter of the filter_var method is used to make sure the class is numeric.

```php
        // Look for the Paid
Status:                                                                 #2
        $paid = filter_var( $_POST['paid'], FILTER_SANITIZE_STRING);
        if (empty($paid)) {
                $errors[] = 'You forgot to enter the paid status.';
        }
        if (!(($paid == "No") || ($paid == "Yes"))){
                $errors[] = "Paid must be No or Yes.";
        }
```

An additional check is used to make sure that paid is No or Yes. Other values would cause errors because we set the column in the database to only accept these two values.

All the remaining code has been seen and explained before; therefore, further explanation is unnecessary. Where anything new has been inserted, the comments within the listing give a full explanation.

Note the screen for deleting a record is the same as in Chapter 4 and will not be repeated here to save space. However, the file *delete_record.php* is included in the downloads for Chapter 5.

We need to limit the amount of information shown to the administrator. An extremely wide and confusing table would be required to display a member's full details. Therefore, a member's details will be split and displayed using two separate pages. The administrator will be able to view the address separately from the rest of the member's information by means of the *search-address.php* page. The new Address button was added to the menu to access this page. However, we will create the code for this page in the next chapter.

■ **Note** The downloaded files for Chapter 5 include all files required for these demonstrations, including unchanged files from Chapter 4.

Summary

In this chapter, we created a database containing many more fields than the ones in prior chapters. We added sessions to all the administration pages for security. We added a new Addresses button to the administrator's page header. We learned how to add PayPal logos and buttons to the pages. We discussed how to obtain the necessary code to link to the PayPal system to accept payments. Pagination was demonstrated in a tabular display of members. The form for editing records was modified to include extra data. A second table was created to hold the current pricing information for membership. This information was displayed both in the class pricing and in the drop-down list provided for the user to select a class.

In the next chapter, you will learn how the administrator can view and edit addresses and telephone numbers. Also, in the next chapter, we will add the finishing touches to the database. The filing system will be tidied up by placing the included files in an includes folder. For increased security, extra user input filters will be introduced. A title column will be added to the table display for editing and deleting a record, and the title column will also be added to the table display for editing addresses and phone numbers.

■ ■ ■

CHAPTER 6

Add the Finishing Touches: Security and Validation

In the previous chapter, we created the beginnings of a useful database and several interactive website pages. However, the administrator was not able to edit all the member information. In this chapter, we will provide the ability to edit the address and telephone number information. This will be achieved by using the Addresses menu button. In addition, we will add an additional Title field to the database. This field will also be editable through the Addresses menu button. The folder and filing system for the PHP pages will be tidied up to reduce the clutter. More information will be placed in folders for easier discovery and retrieval. The previous interactive pages had a minimum of user input validation and sanitation. This chapter will introduce a more secure system.

After completing this chapter, you will be able to

- Generate a SQL script from an existing database and its associated tables

- Import a SQL script into phpMyAdmin to generate a new database and associated tables

- Add an additional field to an existing database table

- Create an organized folder structure to store related files and web pages

- Provide more security for access to and storage of database information

- Validate and sanitize user input before entry into a database

- Provide additional searching capabilities for titles, addresses, and phone numbers

- Provide additional capabilities to view and edit titles, addresses, and phone numbers

Creating the Database

First, we will create a new version of the postaldb database and rename it *finalpost*.

1. Open the XAMPP *htdocs* or easyPHP *eds-www* folder, and create a new folder named *finalpost*.

2. Download the files for Chapter 6 from the book's website at www.apress.com and place the files in the new folder called *finalpost*.

3. Then use a browser to access phpMyAdmin, click the Database tab, and create a new database called *finalpost*.

4. Scroll down and find the newly created database. Then select the check box alongside it.

5. Click Check Privileges, click Add User, and then add a new user and password as follows:

    - *Username*: cabbage

    - *Password*: in4aPin4aL

    - *Host*: localhost

    Scroll down; next to Global Privileges, click Check All.

6. Accept the default for Resource limits.

7. Scroll to the bottom and click Go to save the user's details.

Creating the File for Connecting to the Database

Create a new connection file named *mysqli_connect.php*. (If you don't need to practice creating the file from scratch, it is already included in the downloaded files for Chapter 6.)

Listing 6-1. The Database Connection File (mysqli_connect.php)

```php
<?php
// Create a connection to the postaldb database
// Set the database access details as constants and set the encoding to utf-8

Define ('DB_USER', 'cabbage');
Define ('DB_PASSWORD', 'in4aPin4aL');
Define ('DB_HOST', 'localhost');
Define ('DB_NAME', 'finalpost');
// Make the connection
$dbcon = new mysqli(DB_HOST, DB_USER, DB_PASSWORD, DB_NAME);
mysqli_set_charset($dbcon, 'utf8'); // Set the encoding...
```

Test your connection in a browser (http://localhost/finalpost/mysqli_connect.php). Remember, if you do not see anything on the screen, your connection was successful.

■ **Tip** When composing a password for use in the real world, you should make it as complex as possible. Ensure that it is not related in any way to the name of the database. A complex password can be easily remembered by means of a mnemonic. The mnemonic can then be written down and placed under lock and key. The mnemonic chosen for the password (in4aPin4aL) in this tutorial is the old British saying, "In for a penny, in for a pound." One of the meanings of this maxim is, "If we start this, we must make sure we finish it; there is no turning back." In the password itself, the uppercase *P* stands for Penny, and the uppercase *L* is the archaic symbol for a British pound (100 pennies).

Creating the users Table by Importing a SQL Dump File

We now need to create a table named *users* with 17 columns.

We can hear you groaning, "Oh, no! Not another table!" Don't worry, we are about to show you a shortcut using the Import/Export facility in phpMyAdmin.

The generated code is already created for you and exported into a file called *users.sql*. This file actually contains code to create both the users and prices tables. You will find this among the downloaded files that you installed in the folder *finalpost*.

However, you can also create the *users.sql* file from your current postaldb database from Chapter 5. *You can ignore the following directions and skip to the import directions if you want to start with a database and table not affected by anything you did in Chapter 5.*

To create a file to import, follow these steps:

1. Open up phpMyAdmin. Select the postaldb database from the listing on the left of the screen.

2. Then select the export tab at the top of the page. Create a name for the template, such as *users*, and enter it in the new template textbox.

3. Click the create button to the right of the textbox. The new template name, users, should now appear in the existing templates drop-down box to the right. Leave the quick export method selected. Also make sure that SQL is displayed in the Format dropbox list.

4. If everything looks correct, click the Go button. The system will download a file containing SQL code that will not only create your tables for you but will also copy your existing data from the Chapter 5 database into the new database for Chapter 6.

5. Open the downloaded file into Notepad++ or a similar editor that displays the code line by line. Examine the code and see whether you can determine which lines are creating the tables and which lines are adding the data into the tables.

6. Select Save As from the File menu and save the file as *users.sql*.

To import the *users.sql* file from the textbook files for Chapter 6 or to import the file you created from exporting the tables from Chapter 5, complete the following directions:

1. In the home page of phpMyAdmin, click the database finalpost.

2. Click the Import tab.

3. Click the Browse button on the Import screen, as shown in Figure 6-1.

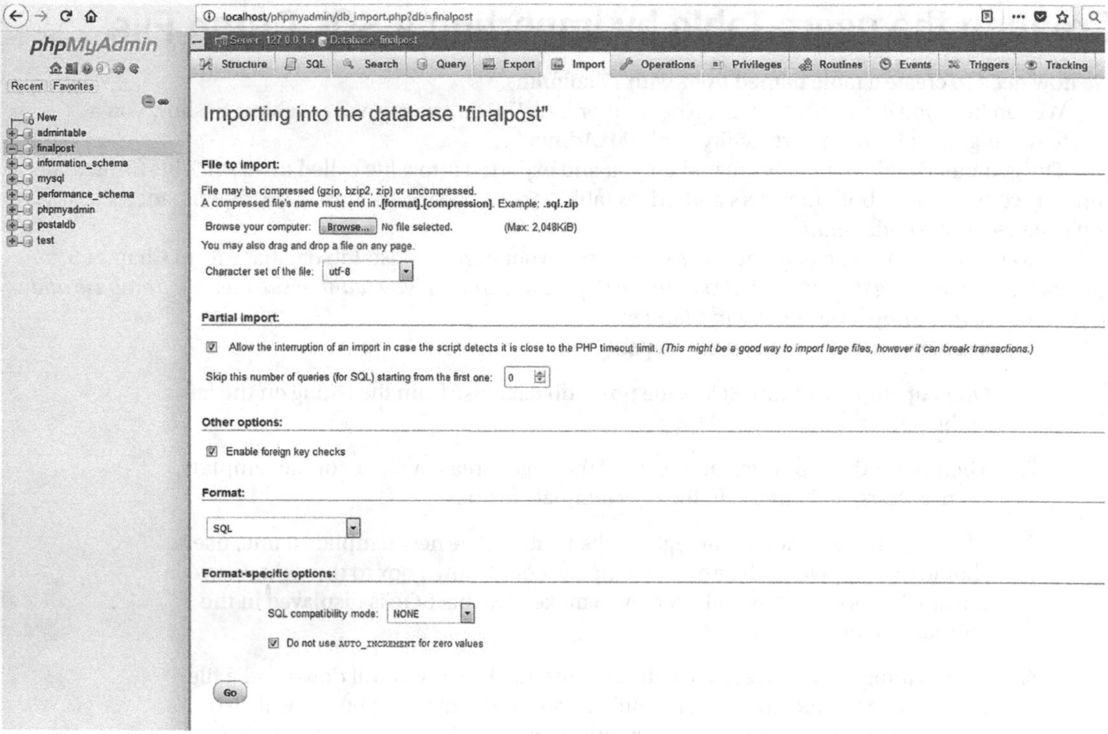

Figure 6-1. *The Import screen in phpMyAdmin*

The Browse button allows you to navigate to the file *users.sql*. Open the *users.sql* file.

4.   Then click Go, and the file will be imported.

5.   Now open the users table in phpMyAdmin (click the browse tab), you will be able to view the table and its data.

You can alternatively use the Operations tab, after selecting the database, to copy a table from one database to another. Table 6-1 shows the structure of the imported users table.

Table 6-1. *The Titles and Attributes of the Chapter 6 Imported users Table*

Column Name	Type	Length/Values	Default	Attributes	NULL	Index	A_I
userid	MEDIUMINT	6	None	UNSIGNED	☐	PRIMARY	☑
title	VARCHAR	10	None		☑		☐
first_name	VARCHAR	30	None		☐		☐
last_name	VARCHAR	40	None		☐		☐
email	VARCHAR	50	None		☐		☐
password	CHAR	60	None		☐		☐
registration_date	DATETIME		None		☐		☐
user_level	TINYINT	1	None	UNSIGNED	☐		☐
class	CHAR	20	None		☐		☐
address1	VARCHAR	50	None		☐		☐
city	VARCHAR	50	None		☐		☐
state_country	CHAR	25	None		☐		☐
zcode_pcode	CHAR	10	None		☐		☐
phone	CHAR	15	None		☑		☐
secret	VARCHAR	30	None		☐		☐
paid	ENUM	"yes", "no"	None		☐		☐

If you imported the *users.sql* file from the textbook files, the structure will also include a title and a secret field. These fields did not exist in the database in Chapter 5. We will soon explain how you can add these columns if you imported your own data from the previous chapter. Also, note that the columns for the title, the second address and the phone number, have their NULL boxes checked. This is because they will be optional fields that can be ignored by the user. Many users may not have an additional address, such as an apartment number. Some users are ex-directory and do not want to disclose their telephone numbers.

Registering Some Members Manually

If you did not import the existing data (users) from the users table, you will need to manually enter them. To register the members, run XAMPP or EasyPHP and use a browser to enter this URL:

http://localhost/finalpost/safer-register-page.php

The file *safer-register-page.php* is a more secure version of the *register-page.php* file from Chapter 5. The file is included in the downloadable files for Chapter 6. The enhancements for the safer file are described later in this chapter.

As in Chapter 5, James Smith is registered first as a member and then also as the membership secretary (administrator) with the alias Jack Smith. As a reminder, their details are given next:

- *First name*: James

- *Last name*: Smith

- *E-mail*: jsmith@myisp.co.uk

- *Password*: Bl@cksm1th

- *First name*: Jack

- *Last name*: Smith

- E-mail: jsmith@outcook.com

- *Password*: D@gsb0dy

Set Jack Smith's user level to 1. By using phpMyAdmin, both Smiths should have their paid column set to Yes. You may optionally add titles and a secret answer for both users.

■ **Tip**   When adding new members, use phpMyAdmin to put Yes in a member's Paid column. To do this, click the box next to finalpost in the left panel to expand it and then click the users item. You will see the registered members. In the user's record, click Edit. In the next screen, scroll down and click the Yes radio button at the bottom right. Then click Go.

Members are unable to log in unless their Paid column has been marked Yes by the membership secretary (administrator).

So that you can access the members' data, the downloadable members' details are shown in Table 6-2. This is the same data from Chapter 5. The data is already placed in the table from the imported *users.sql* file. This chapter assumes the data is as shown. If you imported your own data, you may want to make some manual adjustments to reflect this information. You do not need to manually enter the information again.

Table 6-2. *Details of the Downloadable Registered Members*

Title	First Name	Last Name	E-mail	Password
Mr	Mike	Rosoft	miker@myisp.com	Willg@t3s
Ms	Olive	Branch	obranch@myisp.co.uk	An@lly0ne
Mr	Frank	Incense	fincense@myisp.net	P@rfum3s
Ms	Annie	Versary	aversary@myisp.com	H@ppyd8y
Mr	Terry	Fide	tfide@myisp.de	sc@r3Dst1ff
Mrs	Rose	Bush	rbush@myisp.co.uk	R@db100ms
Mrs	Annie	Mossity	amositty@myisp.org.uk	Y0ur@n3my
Mr	Percey	Veer	pveer@myisp.com	K33pg0!ng
Mr	Darrel	Doo	ddoo@myisp.co.uk	Sat!sf1ed
Mr	Stan	Dard	sdard@myisp.net	b@TTl3fl@g
Mrs	Nora	Bone	nbone@myisp.com	L1k@t@rr13r
Mr	Barry	Cade	bcade@myisp.co.uk	Bl0ckth@m

■ **Tip**   Remember as stated in the previous chapter, entering the data can be tedious using the manual method. To reduce the tedium, you can enter some identical addresses, telephone numbers, and secret answers for different users. A set of suitable data is suggested next.

In Chapter 5, we entered the following information in every record to save time and effort. Here are some suggested default entries:

Address 1	2 The Street
Address 2	The Village (this is optional and should be omitted when registering some of the members' addresses)
City	Townsville
State or Country	UK (or US)
Postal or Zip code	EX7 9PP (or in the United States, 33040)
Phone	01234 777 888 (or in the United States, 999 888 4444; this is optional and should be omitted when registering some of the members' telephone numbers)

Remember, in phpMyAdmin, change the paid column to Yes for several of the members. Only those members with a paid column set to Yes will be able to sign into the system.

Adding a Title Column to the users Table

If you imported your own data from Chapter 5, the table does not include a title and a secret column. *If you did use the users.sql file from the Chapter 6 textbook files, these columns were created already, and you can skip this section.*

Let's add a title column to allow members to optionally provide a preferred title (such as Mr., Mrs., Ms., Mx., or Dr.).

1.   In phpMyAdmin, select the finalpost database on the listing to the left of the screen.

2.   Then select the users table in the database.

3.   Select the Structure tab at the top of the page. The screen shown in Figure 6-2 will now appear.

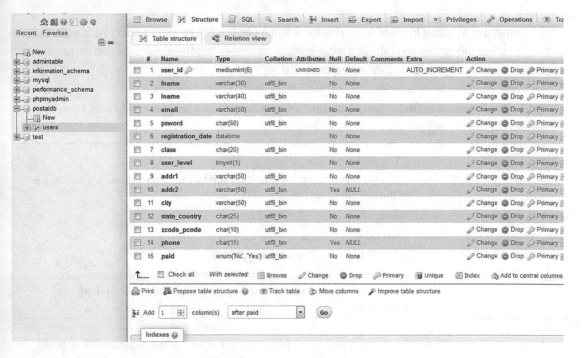

Figure 6-2. *The Structure screen in phpMyAdmin*

4. Locate the Add Columns information below the listing of the current columns.

5. Change the settings to indicate that 1 column will be added after the user_id column and click the Go button.

6. Enter the following settings for the new title column.

Column name	Type	Length/Values	Default	Attributes	NULL	Index	A_I
title	VARCHAR	10	None		☑		☐

Notice that the new column will allow null values. This will make the entering of a title optional.

7. Once you have entered the new settings, click the Save button. The new column will now appear in the structure of the table between the userid and first_name columns.

8. Now click the browse tab to view the current data in the table. Randomly select some users by clicking the Edit link to the left side of the data, enter a title, and save the changes. You need some titles in the table to display when search results for members are displayed.

9. Repeat these steps to add the secret column using the following settings.

Column name	Type	Length/Values	Default	Attributes	NULL	Index	A_I
secret	VARCHAR	30	None		☐		☐

Creating the Prices Table by Importing a SQL Dump File

If you imported the users.sql file from the Chapter 6 textbook files, it already imported the prices table, so you can skip this section. We now need to repeat the import procedure to copy the prices table from Chapter 5 into the finalpost database.

1. In the home page of phpMyAdmin, click the database finalpost.

2. Click the Import tab.

3. Click the Browse button on the Import screen (see Figure 6-1). The browse button allows you to navigate to the file *prices.sql.*

4. Open the *prices.sql* file and then click Go. The file will be imported.

You can alternatively use the Operations tab, after selecting the database, to copy a table from one database to another. If you now open the prices table in phpMyAdmin (click the browse tab), you will be able to view the table and its data.

Table 6-3 shows the structure of the prices table.

Table 6-3. *The Titles and Attributes for the prices Table*

Column Name	Type	Length/Values	Default	Attributes	NULL	Index	A_I
oneyeargb	DECIMAL	6	None	UNSIGNED	☐		☐
oneyearus	DECIMAL	6	None	UNSIGNED	☐		☐
fiveyeargb	DECIMAL	6	None	UNSIGNED	☐		☐
fiveyearus	DECIMAL	6	None	UNISGNED	☐		☑
militarugb	DECIMAL	6	None	UNISGNED	☐		☐
militaryus	DECIMAL	6	None	UNSIGNED	☐		☐
u21gb	DECIMAL	6	None	UNSIGNED	☐		☐
u21us	DECIMAL	6	None	UNSIGNED	☐		☐
minpricegb	DECIMAL	6	None	UNSIGNED	☐		☐
minpriceus	DECIMAL	6	None	UNSIGNED	☐		☐

The table should now also include the data that was entered in Chapter 5. You can also export and import your own data from the Chapter 5 database.

Let's now take a diversion to do some housekeeping before we continue. The ever-increasing number of PHP and HTML files can become a problem if we don't provide better organization.

Tidying Up the Folders and Filing System

The number of files in the postal folder has increased as each chapter has added more features. The clutter can be confusing. To tidy the new *finalpost* folder, we will place all the included files in their own *include* folder. This has already been accomplished in the downloadable files for this chapter. Note that all files that are inserted into the PHP programs using the include statement are now in the new includes folder. In the main files, all the PHP includes now have the prefix includes/, as shown in the following snippet:

```php
<?php
        include("includes/header-admin.php");
        include("includes/nav.php");
        include("includes/info-col.php");
?>
```

We will now provide some additional validation and sanitation for the data. Security is the most important aspect of the development process and perhaps the most tedious. Inappropriate input from a user can insert faulty or corrupt data into a database table. More seriously, it can cause a leakage of private information or allow nefarious people to trash a table. It can also allow people to take control of the server and any data residing on the server. Unacceptable input or control can be the work of criminals, or it could simply be caused by users' mistakes. Therefore, all user input must be filtered to ensure that it is fit for your database.

Degrees of Security

A database can be insecure or partially secure; it can never be 100 percent secure. However, this statement must be qualified because the risk depends on several other factors besides the built-in security of the database. Postal addresses, e-mail addresses, credit card information, and users' preferences can be harvested from an insecure database and sold for substantial amounts of money.

Databases for small firms, clubs, or societies must still provide a layer of security. The administrator has a legal responsibility to keep data as secure as possible. Even if hackers do not attack the database, users could inadvertently enter invalid information. Remember, it is much easier to filter out any potential problems before the data is entered into the database. Once bad data exists in a database, it is more difficult to remove it.

Adding a Layer of Security

The database must have a unique name (up to 16 characters long), a password (as complex as possible), a host name (such as localhost), a designated user, and a set of permissions.

Multiple users are permissible, and their permissions should be limited. The number of user IDs for a database must be restricted for maximum security. Users should be provided only with the permissions needed to complete their job (task). There have been many recent examples in the news of employees who were granted more permissions than necessary and thus exposed users' personal information to either criminals or other websites. Most users should not have permissions such as GRANT, SHUTDOWN, or DROP.

The PHP code that we have demonstrated in previous chapters hashes the password before storing it on the server. Additionally, the webmaster should choose a password that is difficult to deduce. Never use a word that can be found in a dictionary or a word that is an anagram of the webmaster's name. You could take a popular saying such as "Raining again, good weather for ducks" and create a password something like RaGw4dux.

Always assume that everything a user enters will be a danger to the database. In addition, the data should be as accurate as possible. The age of a person is not a good entry for a database. The person's age changes over time. The data would soon be invalid. A better entry is the person's date of birth. That does not change. The age of the person can then be calculated from their birthdate and will always be accurate.

Additionally, e-mail addresses with incorrect formats are of no use to the user or to the owner of the database. Code should be provided to ensure the e-mail is in the proper format. Some systems even sent a verification to the e-mail entered to ensure that not only is the format correct, but it is an actual live e-mail.

We are using prepared SQL statements in our example code. This ensures that no user data can be executed and cause harm to the database. However, we currently are not eliminating any invalid or unnecessary characters from the user entries. We want to avoid, as much as possible, allowing invalid or corrupt data into the database.

We should always sanitize any input strings to eliminate the possibility of executable code being entered into the database. Prepared statements will also prevent the execution of data.

Validate e-mail addresses, phone numbers, and all numerical items and any other items that have a standard format (such as ZIP/postal codes). Anything that is too general to be validated should, at least, be sanitized. The two techniques *validation* and *sanitization* will be explained later in this chapter.

Sanitize all user input before it is displayed to the page or inserted into the database. Scripts can infiltrate the database using HTML tags, such as the <script> tag, in conjunction with JavaScript.

In a live website, when possible, store the file that accesses the database in a folder located one level above the root folder. (The root folder is *htdocs* or eds-*www*.) You may need to contact your remote host provider to see whether this is possible. Moving this file to a folder outside of *htdocs* or eds-*www* will make it harder to access. Leaving this file in the root folder can allow a person or program to access the database. The connection code we have been using is as follows:

```
require ('mysqli_connect.php');
```

When using a file in a folder one level above the root level, the connection code is as follows:

```
require ('../mysqli_connect.php');
```

■ **Note** The downloadable PHP files for this tutorial will retain the code require ('mysqli_connect.php'); because the database will be located on your computer and not on a remote host. You should move the location of this file (and change all similar statements) to a more secure folder when uploading your files to a production server. You are leaving a large security risk if you do not secure this file.

Where possible, prevent browsers from displaying error messages that reveal the structure of the database. In the example code, the catch blocks of code capture and display error messages. In the real world, the catch blocks will store error messages in an error log that is not accessible by a user. E-mails can also be sent to the web administrator to inform them that an error has occurred. The log can then be viewed to determine the problem. The user will be provided with a generic message asking them to return to the site at a later time. Chapter 7 will provide an example of logging error messages.

As we have shown in previous chapters, always use sessions to restrict access to vulnerable pages, such as an administration page and members' special pages. You might also consider providing different levels of access, such as a user level, a membership chairperson level, and a web administrator level. This can be accomplished by setting the user_level to different values (such as 1, 2, 3) and then checking for one (or more) of these values within the session code at the top of each secured page.

You can safely accept payments through a website by using PayPal, Stripe, or a similar secure payment system. But *never* store members' bank/debit/credit card details. Also, do not store government-identifying numbers (such as a Social Security number). Remember that access to this type of information can provide the ability for a hacker to destroy a person's credit, steal tax refunds, and steal retirement checks. If you need a unique identifier, generate a user ID using autonum as we have previously shown.

An Increased Layer of Protection

If your clients want to use an internal payment system rather than using PayPal or a similar third-party company, they will need a more expensive security budget. For sites where security is important or when users' financial details are stored, the site will require specialist staff or a third party to supervise and continually monitor the website. This can be costly and time-consuming.

A Secure Sockets Layer (SSL) is necessary whenever secure information must travel from the client to the server. SSL will provide an encrypted channel for the information to flow. Sites that include SSL use the HTTPS protocol instead of the HTTP protocol. Many browsers also provide a lock icon to indicate that the communication channel is encrypted by SSL. Some hosts, such as Facebook, now require SSL for all hosted applications. The client may have to pay a higher annual fee to use a Secure Sockets Layer.

Validation and Sanitization

Let's demonstrate the difference between validation and sanitization.

- *Validating*: The validator checks the format of the users' input. If the format is incorrect, the form is not submitted, and an error message asks the user to correct the input. For example, validation ensures that e-mail addresses are in the correct format (i.e., a username followed by an @ symbol followed by an ISP address). This prevents incorrect data from being entered into a database table.

- *Sanitizing*: This can be achieved by two methods: using standard PHP cleaners or using the filter_var() function with a SANITIZE attribute. Sanitizing removes undesirable characters automatically before the data is sent to the database table or displayed on the page. When you are using the SANITIZE attribute, no error message is displayed. Users are not alerted to the fact that they have made a mistake or that their input contains dangerous characters or scripts. This may not be desirable, as it does not provide the user with the opportunity to correct what they have entered. Sanitization will remove or inactivate HTML tags and JavaScript commands that could harm a database.

Validation and sanitization can be applied by means of the function filter_var().

The filter_var() Function

The function filter_var() is included with PHP version 5.2 and later. Its purpose is to simplify the validation and sanitization of user input. The function is used in conjunction with either a FILTER_VALIDATE or FILTER_SANITIZE attribute. For more detailed information on this function, see http://php.net/manual/en/function.filter-var.php.

Validation

In Chapter 5, some validation was provided in the registration page using HTML 5. However, users could still enter information that was invalid. In addition, even if the information has been validated on the client machine using HTML 5 or JavaScript, it still can be corrupted while traveling from the client to the server. Data could be received on the server side that would either damage the web page or the server or interfere with the database. The user could have also entered items that were in the wrong format. As an example of a wrong format, a user could make a mistake when entering an e-mail address. The incorrect address could contain spaces or unacceptable characters as follows:

```
rbush 'myisp.com
```

This faulty e-mail address contains no @ symbol, and it has two spaces and an apostrophe. These are unacceptable e-mail characters. The VALIDATION process will recognize the problems and provide an error message asking the user to correct the e-mail address.

In Chapter 5, in the file *register-page.php*, the code for the e-mail was as follows:

```php
// Check for an email address:
            $email = filter_var( $_POST['email'], FILTER_SANITIZE_EMAIL);
        if ((empty($email)) || (!filter_var($email, FILTER_VALIDATE_EMAIL))) {
            $errors[] = 'You forgot to enter your email address';
            $errors[] = ' or the e-mail format is incorrect.';
        }
```

This code sanitizes the input, checks that the field contained some characters, and validates the format of the e-mail. This keeps the e-mail format from being complete nonsense; that nonsense would have been entered into the database table. Some programmers use regex (*regex* is an abbreviation of "regular expressions") to validate the format of the e-mail address, but with the advent of PHP 5.2 and later versions, the filter_var() function became available and is easier to use. Validation by means of regex is rather complicated and prone to typing errors, as you will see from the following example:

```php
$email = "name@usersisp.com";
if (preg_match('/^[^0-9][a-zA-Z0-9_]+([.][a-zA-Z0-9_]+)*[@][a-zA-Z0-9_]+([.]↩

[a-zA-Z0-9_]+)*[.][a-zA-Z]{2,4}$/',$email)) {
echo "Your email is in the acceptable format";
} else {
echo "Your email address does not have an acceptable format";
}
```

Validating by means of the filter_var() function is a great improvement. This code is used in the safer registration code (*process_register_page.php*).

Some text input does not follow a standard format. Let's look at first_name. In Chapter 5, we checked the contents of first_name using the following code:

```php
// Check for a first name:
$first_name = filter_var( $_POST['first_name'],
        FILTER_SANITIZE_STRING);
if (empty($first_name)) {
        $errors[] = 'You forgot to enter your first name.';
}
```

In this example, the string first_name was sanitized; however, no validation was provided to attempt to gather good data before it is entered into the database.

In this chapter, we provide some additional validation.

```php
// Trim the first name
    $first_name = filter_var( $_POST['first_name'], FILTER_SANITIZE_STRING);
if ((!empty($first_name)) && (preg_match('/[a-z\s]/i',$first_name)) &&
                (strlen($first_name) <= 30)) {
            //Sanitize the trimmed first name
        $first_nametrim = $first_name;
            }else{
            $errors[] =
            'First name missing or not alphabetic and space characters. Max 30';
            }
```

In addition to checking whether $first_name is empty, we now are checking the string for a limited set of characters and that the string is less than or equal to 30 characters. The character length matches the length of the column in the database table and the length set in the HTML file (*safer-register-page.php*).

Since a filter_var function parameter does not exist for verifying first names, we must develop our own.

```
preg_match('/[a-z\s]/i',$first_name)
```

The preg_match function will compare a string ($first_name) with a regular expression ('/[a-z\s]/i') and return True if the string meets the requirements or False if it does not.

In this example, a-z allows all alphabetic characters. The \s also indicates that spaces will be allowed. The [] symbols are used to contain the values to be compared. The i character (along with the //, which holds the other characters) indicates that we are ignoring the case. The following example provides the same ability without the use of i:

```
preg_match('[a-zA-z\s]', $first_name)
```

We will look at some additional regular expressions soon. However, as you can see, it is easy to make mistakes creating expressions. It is safer to use an existing function when they meet your needs.

■ **Tip** Some text input might not have a valid format because it does not conform to a set pattern—for instance, a text area for comments or a person's title. In the United Kingdom, some titles are a holdover from medieval feudalism, such as quaint things like Baroness, Lord, Lady, or Sir. Some retired military members use their armed forces titles like Major or Colonel. College instructors might use Professor or Prof. Text that does not conform to a set pattern can be validated using a regular expression with a regex function.

Sanitization

In our safer registration page, we will use the filter_var function with a sanitization parameter to remove any harmful characters.

```
//Is the last name present? If it is, sanitize it
$last_name = filter_var( $_POST['last_name'], FILTER_SANITIZE_STRING);
if ((!empty($last_name)) && (preg_match('/[a-z\-\s\'']/i',$last_name)) &&
            (strlen($last_name) <= 40)) {
        //Sanitize the trimmed last name
        $last_nametrim = $last_name;
        }else{
        $errors[] =
'Last name missing or not alphabetic, dash, quote or space. Max 30.';
        }
```

As we have seen in Chapter 5, the FILTER_SANITIZE_STRING parameter is used to sanitize any string that does not have a common format. There are sanitizing filters (such as FILTER_SANITIZE_EMAIL) that should be used for specific formats. The e-mail sanitize filter is much easier than attempting to create a regular expression for all e-mail formats.

Validating Telephone Numbers

Telephone numbers do not conform to a common format. Users will enter any combination of numbers, spaces, hyphens, and brackets. Also there are international differences. To complicate matters, some users will write the numbers in groups as follows:

0111 222 333 or (0111) 222 333 or 0111-222-333

Some programmers will attempt to use several regex statements to validate multiple formats of phone numbers. This book offers a simplified approach. The neatest solution is to strip out every character that is not a number. We will use a filter_var() function as shown next:

```
//Is the phone number present? If it is, sanitize it
$phone = filter_var( $_POST['phone'], FILTER_SANITIZE_STRING);
if ((!empty($phone)) && (strlen($phone) <= 30)) {
        //Sanitize the trimmed phone number
        $phonetrim = (filter_var($phone, FILTER_SANITIZE_NUMBER_INT));
    $phonetrim = preg_replace('/[^0-9]/', ", $phonetrim);
        }else{
        $phonetrim = NULL;
        }
```

If a user enters (01234) 777 888, then after sanitization it will enter the database as 01234777888. The preg_replace function will replace any characters in the regular expression with the character(s) in the second parameter. In this example, the ∧ symbol indicates a NOT (like the ! symbol in PHP). Thus, the expression is telling us to replace any character that is NOT a number with " (nothing). This cleans out all characters that are not numbers. We can place characters back into our telephone number when we display them to the user, using the format of the countries in which our pages are used.

■ **Tip**   See Appendix B for a list of the available validation and sanitation types.

A Safer Registration Page

To make the registration page more secure, several techniques are employed. The revised registration page has the similar appearance as the registration page in Chapter 5 (with the addition of the title entry, a security question, and Captcha), as shown in Figure 6-3.

Figure 6-3. *The registration page*

Additional security and cleaning have been included, and this will be explained at the end of Listing 6-3a and Listing 6-3b.

Listing 6-3a. Creating a More Secure Registration Page (safer-register-page.php)

```php
<?php
if ($_SERVER['REQUEST_METHOD'] == 'POST') {
        require("cap.php"); // recaptcha check
}
?>
<!DOCTYPE html>
<html lang="en">
<head>
  <title>Register Page</title>
  <meta charset="utf-8">
  <meta name="viewport" content=
        "width=device-width, initial-scale=1, shrink-to-fit=no">
<!-- Bootstrap CSS File -->
<link rel="stylesheet"
        href=
"https://stackpath.bootstrapcdn.com/bootstrap/4.1.0/css/bootstrap.min.css"
        integrity=
"sha384-9gVQ4dYFwwWSjIDZnLEWnxCjeSWFphJiwGPXr1jddIhOegiu1FwO5qRGvFXOdJZ4"
```

```
        crossorigin="anonymous">
<script src="verify.js"></script>
<script src='https://www.google.com/recaptcha/api.js'></script>
// Required for Captcha Verification
</head>
<body>
<div class="container" style="margin-top:30px">
<!-- Header Section -->
<header class="jumbotron text-center row col-sm-14"
        style="margin-bottom:2px; background:linear-gradient(white, #0073e6);
                padding:20px;">
        <?php include('includes/register-header.php'); ?>
</header>
<!-- Body Section -->
<div class="row" style="padding-left: 0px;">
<!-- Left-side Column Menu Section -->
<nav class="col-sm-2">
    <ul class="nav nav-pills flex-column">
                <?php include('includes/nav.php'); ?>
    </ul>
</nav>
<!-- Validate Input -->
<?php
if ($_SERVER['REQUEST_METHOD'] == 'POST') {
        require('process-register-page.php');
} // End of the main Submit conditional.
?>
<div class="col-sm-8">
        <h2 class="h2 text-center">Register</h2>
        <h3 class="text-center">
                Items marked with an asterisk * are required</h3>
        <?php
        try {
        require_once("mysqli_connect.php");
        $query = "SELECT * FROM prices";
        $result = mysqli_query ($dbcon, $query); // Run the query.
        if ($result) { // If it ran OK, display the records.
                $row = mysqli_fetch_array($result, MYSQLI_NUM);
                $yearsarray = array(
                        "Standard one year:", "Standard five year:",
                        "Military one year:", "Under 21 one year:",
                        "Other - Give what you can. Maybe:" );
                echo '<h6 class="text-center text-danger">
                        Membership classes:</h6>' ;
                echo '<h6 class="text-center text-danger small"> ';
                for ($j = 0, $i = 0; $j < 5; $j++, $i = $i + 2) {

                        echo $yearsarray[$j] . " &pound; " .
                                htmlspecialchars($row[$i], ENT_QUOTES) .
                                " GB, &dollar; " .
                                htmlspecialchars($row[$i + 1], ENT_QUOTES) .
                                " US";
```

```
                                    if ($j != 4) {
                                    if ($j % 2 == 0) {
                                                echo "</h6><h6 class=
                                                        'text-center text-danger small'>"; }
                                    else { echo " , "; }
                                    }
                        }
                    echo "</h6>";
            }
?>
<form action="safer-register-page1.php" method="post"
        onsubmit="return checked();" name="regform" id="regform">
<div class="form-group row">
        <label for="title" class="col-sm-4 col-form-label
                text-right">Title:</label>
<div class="col-sm-8">
        <input type="text" class="form-control" id="title" name="title"
                placeholder="Title" maxlength="12"
                pattern='[a-zA-Z][a-zA-Z\s\.]*'
                title="Alphabetic, period and space max 12 characters"
                value=
                        "<?php if (isset($_POST['title']))
                        echo htmlspecialchars($_POST['title'], ENT_QUOTES); ?>" >
</div>
</div>
<div class="form-group row">                                          <!--#1-->
        <label for="first_name" class="col-sm-4 col-form-label
                text-right">First Name*:</label>
<div class="col-sm-8">
        <input type="text" class="form-control" id="first_name"
                name="first_name" pattern="[a-zA-Z][a-zA-Z\s]*"
                title="Alphabetic and space only max of 30 characters"
                placeholder="First Name" maxlength="30" required
                value=
                        "<?php if (isset($_POST['first_name']))
                        echo htmlspecialchars($_POST['first_name'], ENT_QUOTES); ?>" >
</div>
</div>
<div class="form-group row">
        <label for="last_name" class="col-sm-4 col-form-label text-right">
                Last Name*:</label>
<div class="col-sm-8">
        <input type="text" class="form-control" id="last_name" name="last_name"
                pattern="[a-zA-Z][a-zA-Z\s\-\']*"
                title="Alphabetic, dash, quote and space only max of 40 characters"
                placeholder="Last Name" maxlength="40" required
                value=
                        "<?php if (isset($_POST['last_name']))
                        echo htmlspecialchars($_POST['last_name'], ENT_QUOTES); ?>" >
</div>
</div>
```

```
<div class="form-group row">
        <label for-"email" class="col-sm-4 col-form-label text-right">
                E-mail*:</label>
<div class="col-sm-8">
        <input type="email" class="form-control" id="email" name="email"
                placeholder="E-mail" maxlength="60" required
                value=
                        "<?php if (isset($_POST['email']))
                echo htmlspecialchars($_POST['email'], ENT_QUOTES); ?>" >
</div>
</div>
<div class="form-group row">                                                    <!--#2-->
        <label for="password1" class="col-sm-4 col-form-label
                text-right">Password*:</label>
<div class="col-sm-8">
        <input type="password" class="form-control" id="password1"
                name="password1"
                pattern="(?=.*\d)(?=.*[a-z])(?=.*[A-Z]).{8,12}"
                title="One number, one upper, one lower, one special, with 8 to 12
                characters"
                placeholder="Password" minlength="8" maxlength="12" required
                value=
                        "<?php if (isset($_POST['password1']))
                echo htmlspecialchars($_POST['password1'], ENT_QUOTES); ?>" >
<span id='message'>Between 8 and 12 characters.</span>
</div>
</div>
<div class="form-group row">
        <label for="password2" class="col-sm-4 col-form-label
                text-right">Confirm Password*:</label>
<div class="col-sm-8">
        <input type="password" class="form-control" id="password2"
                name="password2"
                pattern="(?=.*\d)(?=.*[a-z])(?=.*[A-Z]).{8,12}"
                title="One number, one uppercase, one lowercase letter, with 8 to 12
                characters"
                placeholder="Confirm Password" minlength="8"
                maxlength="12" required
                value=
                        "<?php if (isset($_POST['password2']))
                echo htmlspecialchars($_POST['password2'], ENT_QUOTES); ?>" >
</div>
</div>
<div class="form-group row">
        <label for="level" class="col-sm-4 col-form-label
                text-right">Membership Class*</label>
<div class="col-sm-8">
                <select id="level" name="level" class="form-control" required>
                <option value="0" >-Select-</option>
<?php
for ($j = 0, $i = 0; $j < 5; $j++, $i = $i + 2) {
```

```
            echo '<option value="' .
                    htmlspecialchars($row[$i], ENT_QUOTES) . '" ';
            if ((isset($_POST['level'])) && ( $_POST['level'] == $row[$i]))
                    {
            ?>
                            selected
            <?php }
            echo ">" . $yearsarray[$j] . " " .
            htmlspecialchars($row[$i], ENT_QUOTES) .
                " &pound; GB, " .
                htmlspecialchars($row[$i + 1], ENT_QUOTES) .
                "&dollar; US</option>";
    }
    echo "here";
    ?>
    </select>
    </div>
    </div>
    <div class="form-group row">
            <label for="address1" class="col-sm-4 col-form-label
                    text-right">Address*:</label>
    <div class="col-sm-8">
            <input type="text" class="form-control" id="address1" name="address1"
                    pattern="[a-zA-Z0-9][a-zA-Z0-9\s\.\,\-]*"
                    title="Alphabetic, numbers, period, comma, dash and space only max of 30
                    characters"
                    placeholder="Address" maxlength="30" required
                    value=
                            "<?php if (isset($_POST['adress1']))
                            echo htmlspecialchars($_POST['address1'], ENT_QUOTES); ?>" >
    </div>
    </div>
    <div class="form-group row">
            <label for="address2" class="col-sm-4 col-form-label
                    text-right">Address:</label>
    <div class="col-sm-8">
            <input type="text" class="form-control" id="address2" name="address2"
                    pattern="[a-zA-Z0-9][a-zA-Z0-9\s\.\,\-]*"
                    title="Alphabetic, numbers, period, comma, dash and space only max of 30
                    characters"
                    placeholder="Address" maxlength="30"
                    value=
                            "<?php if (isset($_POST['address2']))
                            echo htmlspecialchars($_POST['address2'], ENT_QUOTES); ?>" >
    </div>
    </div>
    <div class="form-group row">
            <label for="city" class="col-sm-4 col-form-label
                    text-right">City*:</label>
    <div class="col-sm-8">
            <input type="text" class="form-control" id="city" name="city"
                    pattern="[a-zA-Z][a-zA-Z\s\.]*"
```

```
                    title="Alphabetic, period and space only max of 30 characters"
                    placeholder="City" maxlength="30" required
                    value=
                            "<?php if (isset($_POST['city']))
                    echo htmlspecialchars($_POST['city'], ENT_QUOTES); ?>" >
</div>
</div>
<div class="form-group row">
            <label for="state_country" class="col-sm-4 col-form-label text-right">
                    Country/state*:</label>
<div class="col-sm-8">
            <input type="text" class="form-control" id="state_country"
                    name="state_country"
                    pattern="[a-zA-Z][a-zA-Z\s\.]*"
                    title="Alphabetic, period and space only max of 30 characters"
                    placeholder="State or Country" maxlength="30" required
                    value=
                            "<?php if (isset($_POST['state_country']))
                    echo htmlspecialchars($_POST['state_country'], ENT_QUOTES); ?>" >
</div>
</div>
<div class="form-group row">
            <label for="zcode_pcode" class="col-sm-4 col-form-label text-right">
                    Zip/Postal Code*:</label>
<div class="col-sm-8">
            <input type="text" class="form-control" id="zcode_pcode"
                    name="zcode_pcode"
                    pattern="[a-zA-Z0-9][a-zA-Z0-9\s]*"
                    title="Alphabetic, period and space only max of 30 characters"
                    placeholder="Zip or Postal Code" minlength="5" maxlength="30"
                    required
                    value=
                            "<?php if (isset($_POST['zcode_pcode']))
                    echo htmlspecialchars($_POST['zcode_pcode'], ENT_QUOTES); ?>" >
</div>
</div>
<div class="form-group row">
            <label for="phone" class="col-sm-4 col-form-label
                    text-right">Telephone:</label>
<div class="col-sm-8">
            <input type="tel" class="form-control" id="phone" name="phone"
                    placeholder="Phone Number" maxlength="30"
            value=
                            "<?php if (isset($_POST['phone']))
            echo htmlspecialchars($_POST['phone'], ENT_QUOTES); ?>" >
</div>
</div>
<div class="form-group row">
            <label for="question" class="col-sm-4 col-form-label text-right">
                    Secret Question*:</label>
<div class="col-sm-8">
```

```
        <select id="question" class="form-control">
                <option selected value="">- Select -</option>
                <option value="Maiden">Mother's Maiden Name</option>
                <option value="Pet">Pet's Name</option>
                <option value="School">High School</option>
                <option value="Vacation">Favorite Vacation Spot</option>
        </select>
</div>
</div>
<div class="form-group row">                                          <!--#3-->
        <label for="secret" class="col-sm-4 col-form-label
                text-right">Answer*:</label>
<div class="col-sm-8">
        <input type="text" class="form-control" id="secret" name="secret"
                pattern="[a-zA-Z][a-zA-Z\s\.\,\-]*"
                title="Alphabetic, period, comma, dash and space only max of 30
                characters"
                placeholder="Secret Answer" maxlength="30" required
                value=
                        "<?php if (isset($_POST['secret']))
                echo htmlspecialchars($_POST['secret'], ENT_QUOTES); ?>" >
</div>
</div>
<div class="form-group row">                                          <!--#4-->
        <label class="col-sm-4 col-form-label"></label>
<div class="col-sm-8">
<div class="float-left g-recaptcha"
        data-sitekey="yourdatasitekeyhere"></div>
</div>
</div>
<div class="form-group row">
        <label for="" class="col-sm-4 col-form-label"></label>
<div class="col-sm-8 text-center">
        <input id="submit" class="btn btn-primary" type="submit"
                name="submit" value="Register">
</div>
</div>
</form>
</div>
<!-- Right-side Column Content Section -->
<?php

if(!isset($errorstring)) {
        echo '<aside class="col-sm-2">';
        include('includes/info-col-cards.php');
        echo '</aside>';
        echo '</div>';
        echo '<footer class="jumbotron text-center row col-sm-14"
                style="padding-bottom:1px; padding-top:8px;">';
 }
```

```
else
{
        echo '<footer class="jumbotron text-center col-sm-12"
        style="padding-bottom:1px; padding-top:8px;">';
}
  include('includes/footer.php');
  echo "</footer>";
  echo "</div>";
  }
catch(Exception $e) // We finally handle any problems here
  {
        // print "An Exception occurred. Message: " . $e->getMessage();
        print "The system is busy please try later";
  }
catch(Error $e)
  {
        //print "An Error occurred. Message: " . $e->getMessage();
        print "The system is busy please try again later.";
  }
?>
</body>
</html>
```

Explanation of the Code

This section explains the code.

```
<div class="form-group row">                                            <!--#1-->
        <label for="first_name" class="col-sm-4 col-form-label
                text-right">First Name*:</label>
<div class="col-sm-8">
        <input type="text" class="form-control" id="first_name"
                name="first_name" pattern="[a-zA-Z][a-zA-Z\s]*"
                title="Alphabetic and space only max of 30 characters"
                placeholder="First Name" maxlength="30" required
                value=
                        "<?php if (isset($_POST['first_name']))
                echo htmlspecialchars($_POST['first_name'], ENT_QUOTES); ?>" >
</div>
</div>
```

The pattern attribute of the input HTML tag allows us to use regular expressions to validate information in relation to the validation we provide in the PHP code. The pattern shown in this example allows uppercase and lowercase alphabetic characters and spaces. The title attribute is the message displayed when the pattern is not matched. This information is required and has a maximum length of 30 characters. The same validation is also achieved on the server side with the PHP code shown previously.

```
<div class="form-group row">                                            <!--#2-->
        <label for="password1" class="col-sm-4 col-form-label
                text-right">Password*:</label>
<div class="col-sm-8">
        <input type="password" class="form-control" id="password1"
```

213

```
                    name="password1"
                    pattern="(?=.*\d)(?=.*[a-z])(?=.*[A-Z]).{8,12}"
                    title="One number, one upper, one lower, one special, with 8 to 12
                    characters"
                    placeholder="Password" minlength="8" maxlength="12" required
                    value=
                            "<?php if (isset($_POST['password1']))
                    echo htmlspecialchars($_POST['password1'], ENT_QUOTES); ?>" >
<span id='message'>Between 8 and 12 characters.</span>
</div>
</div>
```

The password restrictions have increased. The previous pattern restricts the input to require one uppercase letter, one lowercase letter, one number, and one special character. The special character is actually not validated here but is validated in the PHP code. We have left this challenge for you to discover the pattern for special characters. Both the pattern and the attributes of the input statement require that the user enter eight to twelve characters. In the "real world," we would increase these numbers to provide even more security. The other values accepted from the user are validated in a similar manner.

```
<div class="form-group row">                                              <!--#3-->
        <label for="secret" class="col-sm-4 col-form-label
                text-right">Answer*:</label> ·
<div class="col-sm-8">
        <input type="text" class="form-control" id="secret" name="secret"
                pattern="[a-zA-Z][a-zA-Z\s\.\,\-]*"
                title="Alphabetic, period, comma, dash and space only max of 30
                characters"
                placeholder="Secret Answer" maxlength="30" required
                value=
                        "<?php if (isset($_POST['secret']))
                echo htmlspecialchars($_POST['secret'], ENT_QUOTES); ?>" >
</div>
</div>
```

A new secret question is now requested from the user. This information would be used to allow the user to reset their password when they forget the password. In Chapter 11 we will create a form for the user to request a new password.

```
<div class="form-group row">                                              <!--#4-->
        <label class="col-sm-4 col-form-label"></label>
<div class="col-sm-8">
<div class="float-left g-recaptcha"
        data-sitekey="yourdatasitekeyhere"></div>
</div>
</div>
```

Currently we still have a security weakness that we can easily fix. We don't have the ability to detect if a human is really using our program. This can be a major problem as programs can just flood our site with bogus registrations until the database and server crash. Also, as we have mentioned, they can attempt to insert executable code that will cause harm to the site, database, and server.

Banks and other high-security organizations will use multiple methods to validate human input, including verification of the IP address used. We will take a common approach and use Google's Recaptcha system to request that the user verify they are human. Using Recaptcha only requires the importing of the required JavaScript code and the display of the Recaptcha application. The code for displaying the application is shown in #4 in the previous code. The code for importing the required JavaScript code is as follows:

```
<script src='https://www.google.com/recaptcha/api.js'></script>
// Required for Captcha Verification
```
We will also need to verify that a human did actually check the box on the server side.
```php
<?php
if ($_SERVER['REQUEST_METHOD'] == 'POST') {
        require("cap.php"); // recaptcha check
}
?>
```

The previous code is at the top of safer-register-page to insert the verification that the check box has been checked.

```php
<?php
        if(isset($_POST['g-recaptcha-response'])){
                        $captcha=$_POST['g-recaptcha-response'];
                        $secretKey = "Put your secret key here";
                        $ip_address = $_SERVER['REMOTE_ADDR'];
                        $response=
file_get_contents("https://www.google.com/recaptcha/api/siteverify?secret-".
$secretKey."&response=".$captcha."&remoteip=".$ip_address);
                $keys = json_decode($response,true);
                if(intval($keys["success"]) !== 1) {
        echo "<h4 class='text-center'>Are you human? Click recaptcha</h4>";
                        header( "refresh:1;" );
                }
        }
        else {
echo "<h4 class='text-center'>Are you human? Click recaptcha!</h4>";
                        header( "refresh:1;" );
        }
?>
```

Recaptcha will create a g-recaptcha-response POST value if an attempt has been made to be verified as a human. If it exists, the secret key and current IP address are placed in variables, which are then used to retrieve the contents of the response by using the function file_get_contents. The response is in the format of a JSON data structure. The function json_decode converts the structure to a PHP array ($keys). The intval function is used to determine whether the contents of the success column of the array is the number 1 (equivalent to checking if it is true). If it is not, a message is displayed, and the page is reset (after one second). If the response does not exist, a similar message is displayed, and the page is reset. If the human did check the box, all is well, and the program continues. The require statement to link the file with this code (*cap.php*) is commented out in the example files since it requires a secret key to work successfully.

To sign up for a site and secret keys and to read more information, visit this site:

```
https://www.google.com/recaptcha
```

Now let's look at some of the PHP code.

Listing 6-3b. Code for a More Secure Registration Page (process-register-page.php)

```php
<?php
// Has the form been submitted?
try {
        require ('mysqli_connect.php'); // Connect to the database
        $errors = array(); // Initialize an error array.
        // --------------------check the entries------------
        //Is the title present? If it is, sanitize it                              #1
        $title = filter_var( $_POST['title'], FILTER_SANITIZE_STRING);
        if ((!empty($title)) && (preg_match('/[a-z\.\s]/i',$title)) &&
                (strlen($title) <= 12)) {
                //Sanitize the trimmed title
                $titletrim = $title;
        }else{
                $titletrim = NULL; // Title is optional
        }
        // Trim the first name
        $first_name =
                filter_var( $_POST['first_name'], FILTER_SANITIZE_STRING);
                if ((!empty($first_name)) && (preg_match('/[a-z\s]/i',$first_name)) &&
                (strlen($first_name) <= 30)) {
                //Sanitize the trimmed first name
                $first_nametrim = $first_name;
        }else{
                $errors[] =
        'First name missing or not alphabetic and space characters. Max 30';
        }
        //Is the last name present? If it is, sanitize it
        $last_name = filter_var( $_POST['last_name'], FILTER_SANITIZE_STRING);
        if ((!empty($last_name)) &&
                (preg_match('/[a-z\-\s\']/i',$last_name)) &&
                        (strlen($last_name) <= 40)) {
                //Sanitize the trimmed last name
                $last_nametrim = $last_name;
        }else{
                $errors[] =
        'Last name missing or not alphabetic, dash, quote or space. Max 30.';
        }
        // Check that an email address has been entered
        $emailtrim = filter_var( $_POST['email'], FILTER_SANITIZE_EMAIL);
        if ((empty($emailtrim)) ||
                (!filter_var($emailtrim, FILTER_VALIDATE_EMAIL))
                        || (strlen($emailtrim > 60))) {
                $errors[] = 'You forgot to enter your email address';
                $errors[] = ' or the e-mail format is incorrect.';
        }
        // Check for a password and match against the confirmed password:      #2
        $password1trim =
                filter_var( $_POST['password1'], FILTER_SANITIZE_STRING);
                $string_length = strlen($password1trim);
```

216

```
        if (empty($password1trim)){
                $errors[] ='Please enter a valid password';
        }
        else {
        if(!preg_match(
'/^(?=.*[a-z])(?=.*[A-Z])(?=.*\d)(?=.*[#$@!%&*?])[A-Za-z\d#$@!%&*?]{8,12}$/',
$password1trim)) {
        $errors[] =
'Invalid password, 8 to 12 chars, 1 upper, 1 lower, 1 number, 1 special.';
        } else
        {
                $password2trim =
                filter_var( $_POST['password2'], FILTER_SANITIZE_STRING);
        if($password1trim === $password2trim) {
                $password = $password1trim;
        }else{
                $errors[] = 'Your two passwords do not match.';
                $errors[] = 'Please try again';
                }
        }
        }
        //Is the 1st address present? If it is, sanitize it
        $address1 = filter_var( $_POST['address1'], FILTER_SANITIZE_STRING);
        if ((!empty($address1)) &&
                (preg_match('/[a-z0-9\.\s\,\-]/i', $address1)) &&
                        (strlen($address1) <= 30)) {
                //Sanitize the trimmed 1st address
                $address1trim = $address1;
        }else{
        $errors[] =
'Missing address. Numeric, alphabetic, period, comma, dash and space.Max 30.';
        }
        //If the 2nd address is present? If it is, sanitize it
        $address2 = filter_var( $_POST['address2'], FILTER_SANITIZE_STRING);
        if ((!empty($address2)) &&
                (preg_match('/[a-z0-9\.\s\,\-]/i', $address2)) &&
                        (strlen($address2) <= 30)) {
                //Sanitize the trimmed 2nd address
                $address2trim = $address2;
        }else{
                $address2trim = NULL;
        }
        //Is the city present? If it is, sanitize it
        $city = filter_var( $_POST['city'], FILTER_SANITIZE_STRING);
        if ((!empty($city)) && (preg_match('/[a-z\.\s]/i', $city)) &&
                (strlen($city) <= 30)) {
                //Sanitize the trimmed city
                $citytrim = $city;
        }else{
                $errors[] =
                'Missing city. Only alphabetic, period and space. Max 30.';
        }
```

```php
//Is the state or country present? If it is, sanitize it
$state_country =
        filter_var( $_POST['state_country'], FILTER_SANITIZE_STRING);
if ((!empty($state_country)) &&
        (preg_match('/[a-z\.\s]/i', $state_country)) &&
                (strlen($state_country) <= 30)) {
        //Sanitize the trimmed state or country
        $state_countrytrim = $state_country;
}else{
        $errors[] =
'Missing state/country. Only alphabetic, period and space. Max 30.';}
//Is the zip code or post code present? If it is, sanitize it
$zcode_pcode =
        filter_var( $_POST['zcode_pcode'], FILTER_SANITIZE_STRING);
$string_length = strlen($zcode_pcode);
if ((!empty($zcode_pcode)) &&
        (preg_match('/[a-z0-9\s]/i', $zcode_pcode)  &&
                ($string_length <= 30) && ($string_length >= 5)) {
//Sanitize the trimmed zcode_pcode
        $zcode_pcodetrim = $zcode_pcode;
}else{
        $errors[] =
'Missing zip code or post code. Alpha, numeric, space only max 30 characters';
}
        //Is the secret present? If it is, sanitize it
        $secret = filter_var( $_POST['secret'], FILTER_SANITIZE_STRING);
        if ((!empty($secret)) && (preg_match('/[a-z\.\s\,\-]/i', $secret)) &&
                (strlen($secret) <= 30)) {
                //Sanitize the trimmed city
                $secrettrim = $secret;
        }else{
                $errors[] =
'Missing city. Only alphabetic, period, comma, dash and space. Max 30.';
        }
        //Is the phone number present? If it is, sanitize it
        $phone = filter_var( $_POST['phone'], FILTER_SANITIZE_STRING);
        if ((!empty($phone)) && (strlen($phone) <= 30)) {
                //Sanitize the trimmed phone number
                $phonetrim = (filter_var($phone, FILTER_SANITIZE_NUMBER_INT));
                $phonetrim = preg_replace('/[^0-9]/', ", $phonetrim);
        }else{
                $phonetrim = NULL;
        }
        //Is the class present? If it is, sanitize it
        $class = filter_var( $_POST['level'], FILTER_SANITIZE_STRING);
        if ((!empty($class)) && (strlen($class) <= 3)) {
                //Sanitize the trimmed phone number
                $classtrim = (filter_var($class, FILTER_SANITIZE_NUMBER_INT));
        }else{
                $errors[] = 'Missing Level Selection.';
        }
```

```
        if (empty($errors)) { // If everything's OK.
                // If no problems encountered, register user in the database
                //Determine whether the email address has already been registered
                $query = "SELECT userid FROM users WHERE email = ? ";
                $q = mysqli_stmt_init($dbcon);
                mysqli_stmt_prepare($q, $query);
                mysqli_stmt_bind_param($q,'s', $emailtrim);
                mysqli_stmt_execute($q);
                $result = mysqli_stmt_get_result($q);

        if (mysqli_num_rows($result) == 0){
        //The email address has not been registered
        //already therefore register the user in the users table
        //-------------Valid Entries - Save to database -----
        //Start of the SUCCESSFUL SECTION.
        // i.e., all the required fields were filled out
                $hashed_password = password_hash($password, PASSWORD_DEFAULT);
                // Register the user in the database...
                $query = "INSERT INTO users (userid, title, first_name, ";
                $query .= "last_name, email, password, class, ";
                $query .= "address1, address2, city, state_country, ";
                $query .= "zcode_pcode, phone, secret, registration_date) ";
                $query .= "VALUES ";
                $query .= "(' ',?,?,?,?,?,?,?,?,?,?,?,?,?,NOW())";
                $q = mysqli_stmt_init($dbcon);
                mysqli_stmt_prepare($q, $query);
// use prepared statement to ensure that only text is inserted
// bind fields to SQL Statement
                mysqli_stmt_bind_param($q, 'sssssssssssss',
                        $titletrim, $first_nametrim, $last_nametrim, $emailtrim,
                        $hashed_password, $classtrim, $address1trim,
                        $address2trim, $citytrim, $state_countrytrim,
                        $zcode_pcodetrim, $phonetrim, $secrettrim);
                // execute query
                mysqli_stmt_execute($q);
                if (mysqli_stmt_affected_rows($q) == 1) {
                header ("location: register-thanks.php?class=" . $classtrim);
        } else {
        // echo 'Invalid query:' . $dbcon->error;
                $errorstring = "System is busy, please try later";
                echo "<p class=' text-center col-sm-2'
                        style='color:red'>$errorstring</p>";
        }
        }else{//The email address is already registered
                $errorstring = 'The email address is already registered.';
                echo "<p class=' text-center col-sm-2'
                        style='color:red'>$errorstring</p>";
        }
} else {//End of SUCCESSFUL SECTION
        // ---------------Process User Errors---------------
        // Display the users entry errors
```

```
        $errorstring = 'Error! The following error(s) occurred: ';
        foreach ($errors as $msg) { // Print each error.
                $errorstring .= " - $msg<br>\n";
        }
        $errorstring .= 'Please try again.';
        echo "<p class=' text-center col-sm-2' style=
                'color:red'>$errorstring</p>";
}// End of if (empty($errors)) IF.
}
catch(Exception $e)
{
        print "The system is busy, please try later";
        //print "An Exception occurred. Message: " . $e->getMessage();
}
catch(Error $e)
{
        print "The system is busy, please come back later";
        //print "An Error occurred. Message: " . $e->getMessage();
}
?>
```

Explanation of the Code

This section explains the code.

```
//Is the title present? If it is, sanitize it                           #1
        $title = filter_var( $_POST['title'], FILTER_SANITIZE_STRING);
        if ((!empty($title)) && (preg_match('/[a-z\.\s]/i',$title)) &&
                (strlen($title) <= 12)) {
                //Sanitize the trimmed title
                $titletrim = $title;
        }else{
                $titletrim = NULL; // Title is optional
        }
```

The title is sanitized. If the sanitized input is not empty, it is compared to the required format, which allows alphabetic characters, spaces, and periods. If it fails the verification checks, $title is set to NULL. Since title is optional, no error message is produced if it is missing or invalid. For variables that are not optional, an error message is placed in the error array.

```
// Check for a password and match against the confirmed password:      #2
$password1trim =
        filter_var( $_POST['password1'], FILTER_SANITIZE_STRING);
        $string_length = strlen($password1trim);
if (empty($password1trim)){
        $errors[] ='Please enter a valid password';
}
else {
if(!preg_match(
'/^(?=.*[a-z])(?=.*[A-Z])(?=.*\d)(?=.*[#$@!%&*?])[A-Za-z\d#$@!%&*?]{8,12}$/',
$password1trim)) {
$errors[] = 'Invalid password, 8 to 12 chars, 1 upper, 1 lower, 1 number, 1 special.';
```

Note the exclamation mark in front of preg_match. This means "If the password does NOT match, put an error message into the $errors array." The regex function preg_match() checks the first password for the correct combination of characters. There must be one uppercase letter, one lowercase letter, one number, and one special character (#$@!%&*?). In addition, there must be at least eight characters and no more than twelve. Since the second password must match the first password, this check is not necessary for the second password. For more information on preg_match, see this page:

```
http://php.net/manual/en/function.preg-match.php
```

If the two passwords do not match or the format is incorrect, an error message is placed in the $errors array. Both checks are completed to provide the user with all error feedback at once. For example, if the format is incorrect and the passwords do not match, the user will see both errors displayed.

■ **Note**　The downloadable files from www.apress.com for this chapter now include the safer registration page link in the Register menu button for the headers. All other files from Chapter 5 has also been updated using the sanitation and validation techniques shown in this chapter. The verification techniques used in this file are for demonstration.

In a real-world situation, you would allow additional characters in many of the user inputs and require a longer password. Always think about the users and the requirements that they need. It is a balance between security and convenience of the user.

Run XAMPP or easyPHP and enter **http://localhost/finalpost/safer-register-page.php** in the address field of a browser. Then register some members, but make deliberate errors to see the results.

In the previous chapter, we created and listed a screen for searching addresses. We will now make use of that screen so that we can search and edit titles, addresses, and phone numbers.

Searching for a Title, an Address, or a Telephone Number

In the file *header-admin.php*, the dead link in the Addresses menu button has been replaced with a link to the page *search_addresses.php*. Figure 6-4 shows the screen for searching a title, an address, and a phone number.

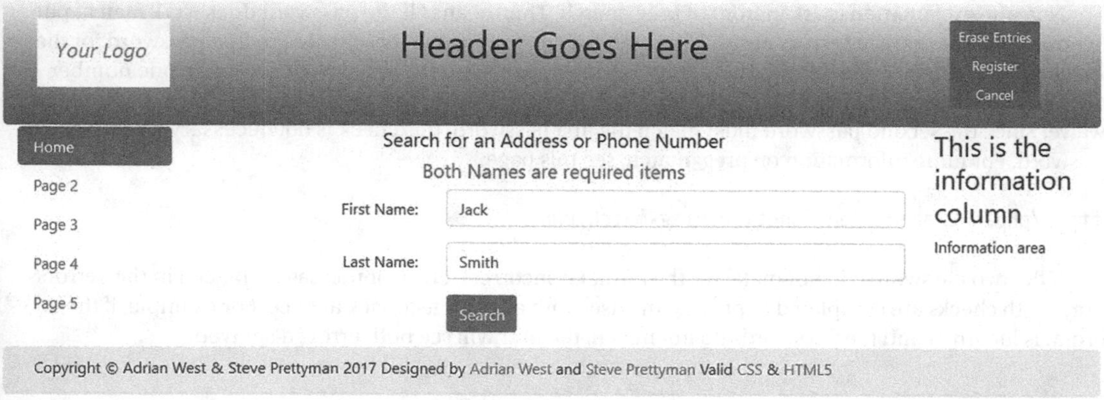

Figure 6-4. Searching for a title, address, or phone number

The code begins with a session to ensure that only the administrator can view and amend the member's record. In this case, we have assumed that the administrator's session is sufficient protection. Only the administrator can search for users' records. The HTML code is shown in Listing 6-4.

Listing 6-4. Creating the Search Address Page (search_address.php)

```php
<?php
session_start();
if (!isset($_SESSION['user_level']) or ($_SESSION['user_level'] != 1)) //#1
{ header("Location: login.php");
exit();
}
?>
<!DOCTYPE html>
<html lang="en">
<head>
  <title>Search Address Page</title>
  <meta charset="utf-8">
  <meta name="viewport" content=
        "width=device-width, initial-scale=1, shrink-to-fit=no">
  <!-- Bootstrap CSS File -->
  <link rel="stylesheet"
        href=
"https://stackpath.bootstrapcdn.com/bootstrap/4.1.0/css/bootstrap.min.css"
        integrity=
"sha384-9gVQ4dYFwwWSjIDZnLEWnxCjeSWFphJiwGPXr1jddIhOegiu1FwO5qRGvFXOdJZ4"
        crossorigin="anonymous">
<script src="verify.js"></script>
</head>
<body>
<div class="container" style="margin-top:30px">
<!-- Header Section -->
<header class="jumbotron text-center row col-sm-14"
style="margin-bottom:2px; background:linear-gradient(white, #0073e6);
        padding:20px;">
```

```
        <?php include('includes/login-header.php'); ?>
</header>
<!-- Body Section -->
<div class="row" style="padding-left: 0px;">
<!-- Left-side Column Menu Section -->
<nav class="col-sm-2">
        <ul class="nav nav-pills flex-column">
                <?php include('includes/nav.php'); ?>
        </ul>
</nav>
<!-- Validate Input -->
<?php
if ($_SERVER['REQUEST_METHOD'] == 'POST') {
        require('process-view_found_addresses.php');
} // End of the main Submit conditional.
?>
<div class="col-sm-8">
<div class="h2 text-center">
<h5>Search for an Address or Phone Number</h5>
<h5 style="color: red;">Both Names are required items</h5>
</div>
<form action="view_found_address.php" method="post" name="searchform"
        id="searchform">
<div class="form-group row">
        <label for="first_name" class=
                "col-sm-4 col-form-label text-right">First Name:</label>
<div class="col-sm-8">
        <input type="text" class="form-control" id="first_name"
                name="first_name"
                placeholder="First Name" maxlength="30" required
                value=
                "<?php if (isset($_POST['first_name']))
                echo htmlspecialchars($_POST['first_name'], ENT_QUOTES); ?>" >
</div>
</div>
<div class="form-group row">
        <label for="last_name" class="col-sm-4 col-form-label text-right">
                Last Name:</label>
<div class="col-sm-8">
        <input type="text" class="form-control" id="last_name"
                name="last_name"
                placeholder="Last Name" maxlength="40" required
                value=
                "<?php if (isset($_POST['last_name']))
                echo htmlspecialchars($_POST['last_name'], ENT_QUOTES); ?>" >
</div>
</div>
<div class="form-group row">
        <label for="l" class="col-sm-4 col-form-label"></label>
<div class="col-sm-8">
        <input id="submit" class="btn btn-primary" type="submit" name="submit"
                value="Search">
```

```
</div>
</div>
</form>
</div>
<!-- Right-side Column Content Section -->
<?php
 if(!isset($errorstring)) {
        echo '<aside class="col-sm-2">';
        include('includes/info-col.php');
        echo '</aside>';
        echo '</div>';
        echo '<footer class="jumbotron text-center row col-sm-14"
                style="padding-bottom:1px; padding-top:8px;">';
 }
 else
 {
        echo '<footer class="jumbotron text-center col-sm-12"
        style="padding-bottom:1px; padding-top:8px;">';
 }
   include('includes/footer.php');
 ?>
</footer>
</div>
</body>
</html>
```

Explanation of the Code

This section explains the code.

```
<?php
session_start();
if (!isset($_SESSION['user_level']) or ($_SESSION['user_level'] != 1))
{
header("Location: login.php");
exit();
}
?>
```

Only the administrator can access the page as shown previously.

```
<form action="view_found_address.php" method="post" name="searchform"
        id="searchform">
```

The <form> section of the file has been amended in the downloadable file so that it connects to the file *view_found_address.php* as follows.

We will now examine the screen for the retrieved title, addresses, and phone numbers.

Note that the Delete column is absent from the table displayed in Figure 6-5 because the act of deleting is rather final; it must be done using the *delete_record.php* page, where the administrator is given a second chance to decide whether to delete the record.

Viewing the Retrieved Title, Address, and Phone Number

Figure 6-5 shows titles, addresses and phone numbers.

Figure 6-5. *The new table displays the title, address, and telephone number of the selected member*

Listing 6-5 shows the code that displays the two new columns. Note that because there is no room to include an e-mail column, the e-mail address can be edited in the *admin_view_users.php* page.

Listing 6-5. Code for Displaying a Table with Title, Address, and Phone Number (process_view_found_address.php)

```php
<?php
try
{
        // This script retrieves records from the users table.
        require ('./mysqli_connect.php'); // Connect to the db.
        echo '<p class="text-center">If no record is shown, ';
        echo 'this is because you had an incorrect ';
        ' or missing entry in the search form.';
        echo '<br>Click the back button on the browser and try again</p>';
        $first_name = htmlspecialchars($_POST['first_name'], ENT_QUOTES);
        last_name = htmlspecialchars($_POST['last_name'], ENT_QUOTES);
// Since it's a prepared statement below this sanitizing is not needed
        // However, to consistently retrieve than sanitize is a good habit

        $query = "SELECT userid, title, last_name, first_name, ";
$query .= "address1, address2, city, state_country, zcode_pcode, phone ";
        $query .= "FROM users WHERE ";
        $query .= "last_name=? AND first_name=?";

        $q = mysqli_stmt_init($dbcon);
        mysqli_stmt_prepare($q, $query);

        // bind values to SQL Statement
```

```
        mysqli_stmt_bind_param($q, 'ss', $last_name, $first_name);

        // execute query
        mysqli_stmt_execute($q);

        $result = mysqli_stmt_get_result($q);

        if ($result) { // If it ran, display the records.
                // Table header.                                                   #1
                echo '<table class="table table-striped table-sm">
                <tr>
                <th scope="col">Edit</th>
                <th scope="col">Title</th>
                <th scope="col">Last Name</th>
                <th scope="col">First Name</th>
                <th scope="col">Address1</th>
                <th scope="col">Address2</th>
                <th scope="col">City</th>
                <th scope="col">State or Country</th>
                <th scope="col">Zip or Postal Code</th>
                <th scope="col">Phone</th>
                </tr>';

// Fetch and display the records:
while ($row = mysqli_fetch_array($result, MYSQLI_ASSOC)) {
        // Remove special characters that might already be in table to
        // reduce the chance of XSS exploits
        $user_id = htmlspecialchars($row['title'], ENT_QUOTES);
        $title = htmlspecialchars($row['state_country'], ENT_QUOTES);
        $last_name = htmlspecialchars($row['last_name'], ENT_QUOTES);
        $first_name = htmlspecialchars($row['first_name'], ENT_QUOTES);
        $address1 = htmlspecialchars($row['address1'], ENT_QUOTES);
        $address2 = htmlspecialchars($row['address2'], ENT_QUOTES);
        $city = htmlspecialchars($row['city'], ENT_QUOTES);
        $state_country = htmlspecialchars($row['state_country'], ENT_QUOTES);
        $zcode_pcode = htmlspecialchars($row['zcode_pcode'], ENT_QUOTES);
        $phone = htmlspecialchars($row['phone'], ENT_QUOTES);
        //                                                                         #2
        echo '<tr>
        <td scope="row"><a href="edit_address.php?id=' . $user_id .
        '">Edit</a></td>
        <td scope="row">' . $title . '</td>
        <td scope="row">' . $first_name . '</td>
        <td scope="row">' . $last_name . '</td>
        <td scope="row">' . $address1 . '</td>
        <td scope="row">' . $address2 . '</td>
        <td scope="row">' . $city . '</td>
        <td scope="row">' . $state_country . '</td>
        <td scope="row">' . $zcode_pcode . '</td>
        <td scope="row">' . $phone . '</td>
        </tr>';
}
```

```
echo '</table>'; // Close the table.
//
mysqli_free_result ($result); // Free up the resources.
} else { // If it did not run OK.
        // Public message:
        echo
        '<p class="center-text">The current users could not be retrieved.';
        echo 'We apologize for any inconvenience.</p>';
        // Debugging message:
        //echo '<p>' . mysqli_error($dbcon) . '<br><br>Query: ' . $q . '</p>';
        //Show $q is debug mode only
} // End of if ($result). Now display the total number of records/members.
mysqli_close($dbcon); // Close the database connection.
}
catch(Exception $e)
{
        print "The system is currently busy. Please try later.";
        //print "An Exception occurred.Message: " . $e->getMessage();
}
catch(Error $e)
{
        print "The system us busy. Please try later.";
        //print "An Error occurred. Message: " . $e->getMessage();
}
?>
```

Explanation of the Code

This section explains the code.

```
// Table header.                                                          #1
echo '<table class="table table-striped table-sm">
<tr>
<th scope="col">Edit</th>
<th scope="col">Title</th>
<th scope="col">Last Name</th>
<th scope="col">First Name</th>
<th scope="col">Address1</th>
<th scope="col">Address2</th>
<th scope="col">City</th>
<th scope="col">State or Country</th>
<th scope="col">Zip or Postal Code</th>
<th scope="col">Phone</th>
</tr>';
```

The column headings now include the member's title, address, and telephone number.

```
//                                                                        #2
        echo '<tr>
        <td scope="row"><a href="edit_address.php?id=' . $user_id .
        '">Edit</a></td>
        <td scope="row">' . $title . '</td>
        <td scope="row">' . $first_name . '</td>
```

227

```
<td scope="row">' . $last_name . '</td>
<td scope="row">' . $address1 . '</td>
<td scope="row">' . $address2 . '</td>
<td scope="row">' . $city . '</td>
<td scope="row">' . $state_country . '</td>
<td scope="row">' . $zcode_pcode . '</td>
<td scope="row">' . $phone . '</td>
</tr>';
```

The table is displayed and populated with the member's title, address, and telephone number. Note the link for editing the title/address/phone table is now *edit_address.php*. We will be creating this file next.

Editing the Title, Addresses, and Telephone Numbers

When the record is found and the Edit link is clicked, the screen shown in Figure 6-6 appears. This allows the administrator to edit any field in the display. Note that the administrator cannot delete a record from the title/address/phone search because this must be done using the record displayed by the *delete.php* page. Deleting a record from the *delete.php* page automatically removes the title, address, and phone details because they are part of the record.

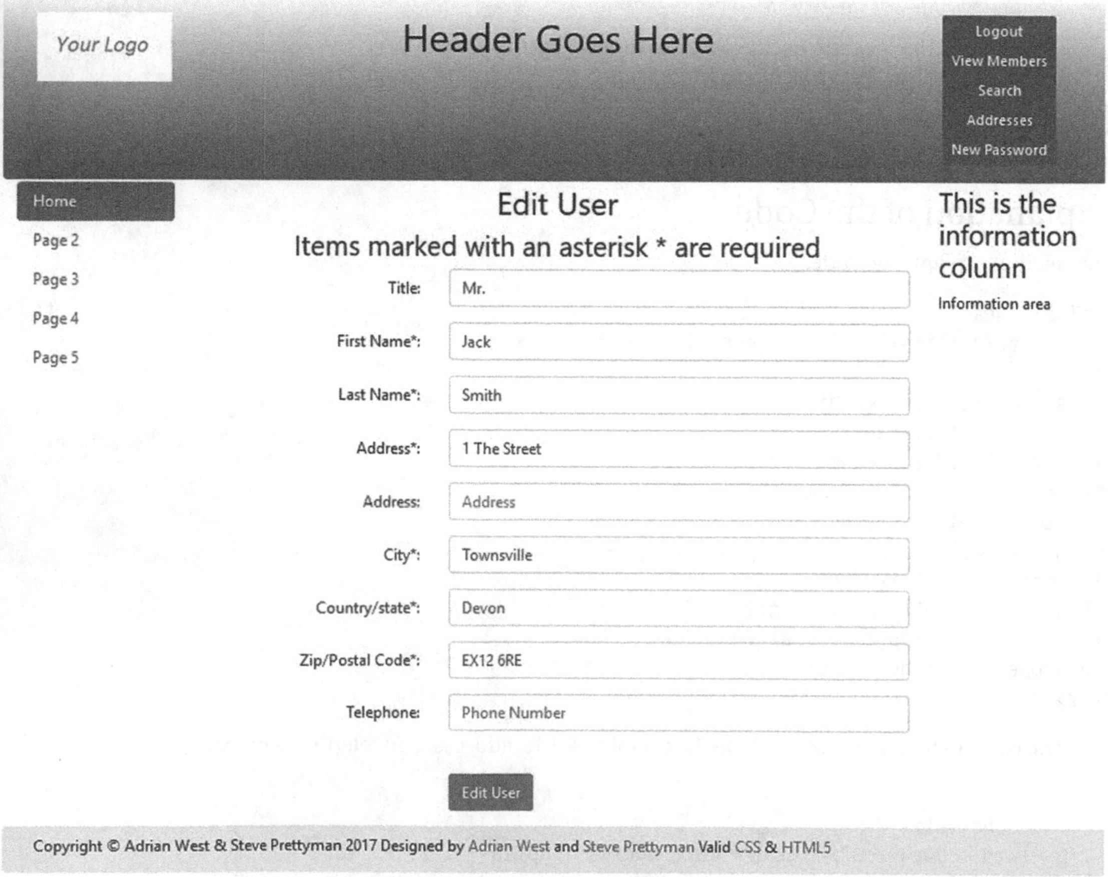

Figure 6-6. *The screen for editing fields in the title/address/phone display*

In this screen, all the fields can be edited. The title, second address, and phone fields are optional—that is, they can remain empty if necessary. Listing 6-6 shows the code for the screen.

■ **Note**   Validation and sanitation have been used in Listing 6-6 and also in the file *edit_record.php*. The file *edit_record.php* is not listed here, but you can examine it by viewing the downloaded file in your text editor.

Listing 6-6. Creating a Screen for Editing the Title, Address, and Phone Number (process_edit_address.php)

```php
<?php
try
{
// After clicking the Edit link in the found_record.php page. This code is executed
// The code looks for a valid user ID, either through GET or POST:
if ( (isset($_GET['id'])) && (is_numeric($_GET['id'])) ) {
    $id = htmlspecialchars($_GET['id'], ENT_QUOTES);
} elseif ( (isset($_POST['id'])) && (is_numeric($_POST['id'])) ) {
// Form submission.
        $id = htmlspecialchars($_POST['id'], ENT_QUOTES);
} else { // No valid ID, kill the script.
        echo
        '<p class="text-center">This page has been accessed in error.</p>';
        include ('footer.php');
        exit();
}
require ('mysqli_connect.php');
// Has the form been submitted?
if ($_SERVER['REQUEST_METHOD'] == 'POST') {
        $errors = array();
        // Look for the first name:
        //Is the title present? If it is, sanitize it
        $title = filter_var( $_POST['title'], FILTER_SANITIZE_STRING);
        if ((!empty($title)) && (preg_match('/[a-z\.\s]/i',$title)) &&
                (strlen($title) <= 12)) {
                //Sanitize the trimmed title
                $titletrim = $title;
        }else{
                $titletrim = NULL; // Title is optional
        }
        // Sanitize the first name
        $first_name =
        filter_var( $_POST['first_name'], FILTER_SANITIZE_STRING);
        if ((!empty($first_name)) && (preg_match('/[a-z\s]/i',$first_name)) &&
                (strlen($first_name) <= 30)) {
                //Sanitize the trimmed first name
                $first_nametrim = $first_name;
        }else{
                $errors[] =
        'First name missing or not alphabetic and space characters. Max 30';
        }
```

```php
        //Is the last name present? If it is, sanitize it
        $last_name = filter_var( $_POST['last_name'], FILTER_SANITIZE_STRING);
if ((!empty($last_name)) && (preg_match('/[a-z\-\s\']/i',$last_name)) &&
                (strlen($last_name) <= 40)) {
        //Sanitize the trimmed last name
    $last_nametrim = $last_name;
        }else{
        $errors[] = 'Last name missing or not alphabetic, dash, quote or space. Max 30.';
        }
        //Is the 1st address present? If it is, sanitize it
$address1 = filter_var( $_POST['address1'], FILTER_SANITIZE_STRING);
if ((!empty($address1)) && (preg_match('/[a-z0-9\.\s\,\-]/i', $address1)) &&
  (strlen($address1) <= 30)) {
        //Sanitize the trimmed 1st address
        $address1trim = $address1;
}else{
        $errors[] =
'Missing address. Numeric, alphabetic, period, comma, dash, space. Max 30.';
        }
        //If the 2nd address is present? If it is, sanitize it
        $address2 = filter_var( $_POST['address2'], FILTER_SANITIZE_STRING);
        if ((!empty($address2)) &&
                (preg_match('/[a-z0-9\.\s\,\-]/i', $address2)) &&
                (strlen($address2) <= 30)) {
                //Sanitize the trimmed 2nd address
                $address2trim = $address2;
        }else{
                $address2trim = NULL;
        }
        //Is the city present? If it is, sanitize it
        $city = filter_var( $_POST['city'], FILTER_SANITIZE_STRING);
        if ((!empty($city)) && (preg_match('/[a-z\.\s]/i', $city)) &&
                (strlen($city) <= 30)) {
                //Sanitize the trimmed city
                $citytrim = $city;
        }else{
                $errors[] =
                'Missing city. Only alphabetic, period and space. Max 30.';
        }
        //Is the state or country present? If it is, sanitize it
        $state_country =
                filter_var( $_POST['state_country'], FILTER_SANITIZE_STRING);
        if ((!empty($state_country)) &&
                (preg_match('/[a-z\.\s]/i', $state_country)) &&
                        (strlen($state_country) <= 30)) {
                //Sanitize the trimmed state or country
                $state_countrytrim = $state_country;
        }else{
                $errors[] =
        'Missing state/country. Only alphabetic, period and space. Max 30.';
        }
```

```php
        //Is the zip code or post code present? If it is, sanitize it
        $zcode_pcode =
                filter_var( $_POST['zcode_pcode'], FILTER_SANITIZE_STRING);
        $string_length = strlen($zcode_pcode);
        if ((!empty($zcode_pcode)) &&
                (preg_match('/[a-z0-9\s]/i', $zcode_pcode))  &&
                        ($string_length <= 30) && ($string_length >= 5)) {
                //Sanitize the trimmed zcode_pcode
        $zcode_pcodetrim = $zcode_pcode;
        }else{
                $errors[] =
        'Missing zip-post code. Alphabetic, numeric, space. Max 30 characters';
        }
        //Is the phone number present? If it is, sanitize it
        $phone = filter_var( $_POST['phone'], FILTER_SANITIZE_STRING);
        if ((!empty($phone)) && (strlen($phone) <= 30)) {
                //Sanitize the trimmed phone number
                $phonetrim = (filter_var($phone, FILTER_SANITIZE_NUMBER_INT));
                $phonetrim = preg_replace('/[^0-9]/', ", $phonetrim);
        }else{
                $phonetrim = NULL;
        }
        if (empty($errors)) { // If everything's OK.
                $query =
        'UPDATE users SET title=?, first_name=?, last_name=?, address1=?,';
                $query .=
                        ' address2=?, city=?, state_country=?, zcode_pcode=?,';
                $query .= ' phone=?';
                $query .= ' WHERE userid=? LIMIT 1';
                $q = mysqli_stmt_init($dbcon);
                mysqli_stmt_prepare($q, $query);

                // bind values to SQL Statement

mysqli_stmt_bind_param($q, 'ssssssssss', $titletrim, $first_nametrim,
        $last_nametrim, $address1trim, $address2trim, $citytrim,
        $state_countrytrim, $zcode_pcodetrim, $phonetrim, $id);
        // execute query

        mysqli_stmt_execute($q);

        if (mysqli_stmt_affected_rows($q) == 1) { // Update OK

        // Echo a message if the edit was satisfactory:
                echo '<h3 class="text-center">The user has been edited.</h3>';
        } else { // Echo a message if the query failed.
                echo
'<p class="text-center">The user could not be edited due to a system error.';
                echo
        ' We apologize for any inconvenience.</p>'; // Public message.
//echo '<p>' . mysqli_error($dbcon) . '<br />Query: ' . $q . '</p>';
```

```php
// Debugging message.
// Message above is only for debug and should not display sql in live mode
                }
        } else { // Display the errors.
        echo '<p class="text-center">The following error(s) occurred:<br />';
                foreach ($errors as $msg) { // Echo each error.
                        echo " - $msg<br />\n";
                }
                echo '</p><p>Please try again.</p>';
        } // End of if (empty($errors))section.
} // End of the conditionals
// Select the user's information to display in textboxes:

        $q = mysqli_stmt_init($dbcon);
        $query = "SELECT * FROM users WHERE userid=?";
        mysqli_stmt_prepare($q, $query);
        // bind $id to SQL Statement
        mysqli_stmt_bind_param($q, 'i', $id);
        // execute query
        mysqli_stmt_execute($q);
        $result = mysqli_stmt_get_result($q);
        $row = mysqli_fetch_array($result, MYSQLI_ASSOC);
        if (mysqli_num_rows($result) == 1) {
        // Valid user ID, display the form.
        // Get the user's information:
        // Create the form:
?>
<h2 class="h2 text-center">Edit User</h2>
<h3 class="text-center">Items marked with an asterisk * are required</h3>
<form action="edit_address.php" method="post"
        name="editform" id="editform">
<div class="form-group row">
        <label for="title" class="col-sm-4 col-form-label
                text-right">Title:</label>
<div class="col-sm-8">
        <input type="text" class="form-control" id="title" name="title"
                placeholder="Title" maxlength="12"
                pattern='[a-zA-Z][a-zA-Z\s\.]*'
                title="Alphabetic, period and space max 12 characters"
                value=
                "<?php if (isset($row['title']))
                echo htmlspecialchars($row['title'], ENT_QUOTES); ?>" >
</div>
</div>
<div class="form-group row">
        <label for="first_name" class="col-sm-4 col-form-label
                text-right">First Name*:</label>
<div class="col-sm-8">
        <input type="text" class="form-control" id="first_name"
                name="first_name"
                pattern="[a-zA-Z][a-zA-Z\s]*"
                title="Alphabetic and space only max of 30 characters"
```

```
                placeholder="First Name" maxlength="30" required
                value=
                "<?php if (isset($row['first_name']))
                echo htmlspecialchars($row['first_name'], ENT_QUOTES); ?>" >
</div>
</div>
<div class="form-group row">
        <label for="last_name" class="col-sm-4 col-form-label text-right">
                Last Name*:</label>
<div class="col-sm-8">
        <input type="text" class="form-control" id="last_name" name="last_name"
                pattern="[a-zA-Z][a-zA-Z\s\-\']*"
                title="Alphabetic, dash, quote and space only max of 40 characters"
                placeholder="Last Name" maxlength="40" required
                value=
                        "<?php if (isset($row['last_name']))
                echo htmlspecialchars($row['last_name'], ENT_QUOTES); ?>" >
</div>
</div>
<div class="form-group row">
        <label for="address1" class="col-sm-4 col-form-label
                text-right">Address*:</label>
<div class="col-sm-8">
        <input type="text" class="form-control" id="address1" name="address1"
                pattern="[a-zA-Z0-9][a-zA-Z0-9\s\.\,\-]*"
                title="Alphabetic, numbers, period, comma, dash and space only max of 30
                characters"
                placeholder="Address" maxlength="30" required
                value=
                        "<?php if (isset($row['address1']))
                echo htmlspecialchars($row['address1'], ENT_QUOTES); ?>" >
</div>
</div>
<div class="form-group row">
        <label for="address2" class="col-sm-4 col-form-label
                text-right">Address:</label>
<div class="col-sm-8">
        <input type="text" class="form-control" id="address2" name="address2"
                pattern="[a-zA-Z0-9][a-zA-Z0-9\s\.\,\-]*"
                title="Alphabetic, numbers, period, comma, dash and space only max of 30
                characters"
                placeholder="Address" maxlength="30"
                value=
                        "<?php if (isset($row['address2']))
                echo htmlspecialchars($row['address2'], ENT_QUOTES); ?>" >
</div>
</div>
<div class="form-group row">
        <label for="city" class="col-sm-4 col-form-label
                text-right">City*:</label>
<div class="col-sm-8">
```

```
        <input type="text" class="form-control" id="city" name="city"
                pattern="[a-zA-Z][a-zA-Z\s\.]*"
                title="Alphabetic, period and space only max of 30 characters"
                placeholder="City" maxlength="30" required
                value=
                        "<?php if (isset($row['city']))
                echo htmlspecialchars($row['city'], ENT_QUOTES); ?>" >
</div>
</div>
<div class="form-group row">
        <label for="state_country" class="col-sm-4 col-form-label text-right">
                Country/state*:</label>
<div class="col-sm-8">
        <input type="text" class="form-control" id="state_country"
                name="state_country"
                pattern="[a-zA-Z][a-zA-Z\s\.]*"
                title="Alphabetic, period and space only max of 30 characters"
                placeholder="State or Country" maxlength="30" required
                value=
                        "<?php if (isset($row['state_country']))
                echo htmlspecialchars($row['state_country'], ENT_QUOTES); ?>" >
</div>
</div>
<div class="form-group row">
        <label for="zcode_pcode" class="col-sm-4 col-form-label text-right">
                Zip/Postal Code*:</label>
<div class="col-sm-8">
        <input type="text" class="form-control" id="zcode_pcode"
                name="zcode_pcode"
                pattern="[a-zA-Z0-9][a-zA-Z0-9\s]*"
                title="Alphabetic, period and space only max of 30 characters"
                placeholder="Zip or Postal Code" minlength="5" maxlength="30"
                required
                value=
                        "<?php if (isset($row['zcode_pcode']))
                echo htmlspecialchars($row['zcode_pcode'], ENT_QUOTES); ?>" >
</div>
</div>
<div class="form-group row">
        <label for="phone" class="col-sm-4 col-form-label
                text-right">Telephone:</label>
<div class="col-sm-8">
        <input type="tel" class="form-control" id="phone" name="phone"
                placeholder="Phone Number" maxlength="30"
                value=
                        "<?php if (isset($row['phone']))
                echo htmlspecialchars($row['phone'], ENT_QUOTES); ?>" >
</div>
</div>
        <input type="hidden" name="id" value="<?php echo $id ?>" />
<div class="form-group row">
        <label class="col-sm-4 col-form-label"></label>
```

```
<div class="col-sm-8">
<div class="float-left g-recaptcha"
        data-sitekey="Yourdatakeygoeshere"></div>
</div>
</div>
<div class="form-group row">
        <label for="" class="col-sm-4 col-form-label"></label>
<div class="col-sm-8">
        <input id="submit" class="btn btn-primary" type="submit" name="submit"
        value="Edit User">
</div>
</div>
</form>
<?php
} else { // The user could not be validated
        echo '<p class="text-center">
                This page has been accessed in error.</p>';
}
mysqli_stmt_free_result($q);
mysqli_close($dbcon);
}
catch(Exception $e)
{
        print "The system is busy. Please try later";
        //print "An Exception occurred.Message: " . $e->getMessage();
}catch(Error $e)
{
        print "The system is currently busy. Please try again later";
        //print "An Error occurred. Message: " . $e->getMessage();
}
?>
```

Explanation of the Code

The majority of the code you will have seen before. The administrator is not allowed to view users' passwords. The password has been hashed before being placed into the database. Thus, the password pulled from the database would not be in a readable format. The administrator would derive no benefit from viewing the hashed password.

■ **Note** The listings for some files are not included in this chapter because some of them are the same as those in Chapter 5. To examine the code, view the downloadable files for Chapter 6 in your text editor.

Summary

In this chapter, we created a copy of the database from Chapter 5. We created a new name and password for the database. We then created two tables. The process for importing a SQL file was described, and the chapter provided a quick method for creating tables. We also discovered how to insert an additional column (title) in a table. As an alternative to using the SQL file, sufficient information was provided to enable you to create the populated database tables from scratch.

Next, we tidied up the filing system by putting all the included files into a folder named *includes*. We discussed security, briefly mentioned sanitization, and investigated validation. We then created a new safer registration page. We learned how to create pages for searching and editing titles, addresses, and telephone numbers.

In the next chapter, you will learn how to make those inevitable last-minute changes and also how to migrate a database to a remote host. Advice will be given on how to back up tables. We will also provide an e-mail and logging ability in the catch routines.

■ ■ ■

Migrate to a Host and Back Up Your Website Database

You might think that the database-driven website created in Chapter 6 is finished and ready for migrating to the host. However, in a real-world situation, a client probably will ask for some last-minute changes. To reduce the number of last-minute changes, the client should always be involved in the development process. As each phase of the site is completed, the client should "sign off" on the changes to indicate they accept the current version of the site. Keeping the client involved is essential. A web designer/developer cannot anticipate everything that a client might expect to achieve with a website. Even if the client does not have last-minute changes, there still might be necessary changes when new laws are implemented that require additional website or database adjustments. In this chapter, we will make some last-minute changes, which might be suggested by a client, before our site is finished. We will also upload our database and website to a remote host and back up all information.

After completing this chapter, you will be able to

- Create a site that allows users to change their own personal information

- Create a secure user feedback form

- Migrate a database to a remote host

- Back up a database

Making Last-Minute Changes

In our example, we will assume that the client has asked for some last-minute changes as follows:

- To reduce the workload of the membership secretary, we have been asked to allow registered members to update their own details. For instance, telephone numbers, addresses, and e-mail addresses can change. Also, someone might need to change their title or name. We agreed to allow registered members to update their titles, names, addresses, telephone numbers, and e-mail addresses.

- The client asked for an inquiry form so that users can ask for more information about the organization before registering as members. We have agreed to create a secure inquiry form.

Let's begin by creating a new database and table.

Creating a New Database

The last-minute changes were requested for the database that we created in the previous chapter, but to avoid confusion we will implement the changes in a new version of the database called *migrate*. Download the files for Chapter 7 from the book's page at www.apress.com, and load them into the new *migrate* folder, using the following steps:

1. In XAMPP *htdocs* or EasyPHP *eds-www* folder, create a new folder called *migrate*.

2. From the book's page at Apress.com, download and unzip the files for Chapter 7 into your new folder.

3. In the address field of a browser, enter **http://localhost/phpmyadmin/** to access phpMyAdmin.

4. Click the databases tab, create a database named *migrate*, choose utf8_general_ci from the pull-down collation list, and then click Go.

5. In the left panel, click the box next to the database *migrate*.

6. Do not enter anything on the next screen, but click the Import tab.

7. Click the Browse button (see Figure 7-1) and navigate to where your SQL dump file *users.sql* is located.

8. Click the *users.sql* file and then click the Open button; the field will fill with the URL of the dump file. Notice that the dump file contains both the users and prices tables.

9. Ensure that the character set in the pull-down menu is utf-8 and that the format is shown as SQL.

10. Click Go.

11. In the left panel, click the database migrate, and on the next screen click the Privileges tab.

12. Scroll down and click Add user account. Then enter the following details:

    - *Username*: trevithick

    - *Host Select*: Local

    - *Password*: l0c0m0t1v3

13. Scroll down to the Global privileges and click the box next to Check all.

14. Scroll down and on the right click Go.

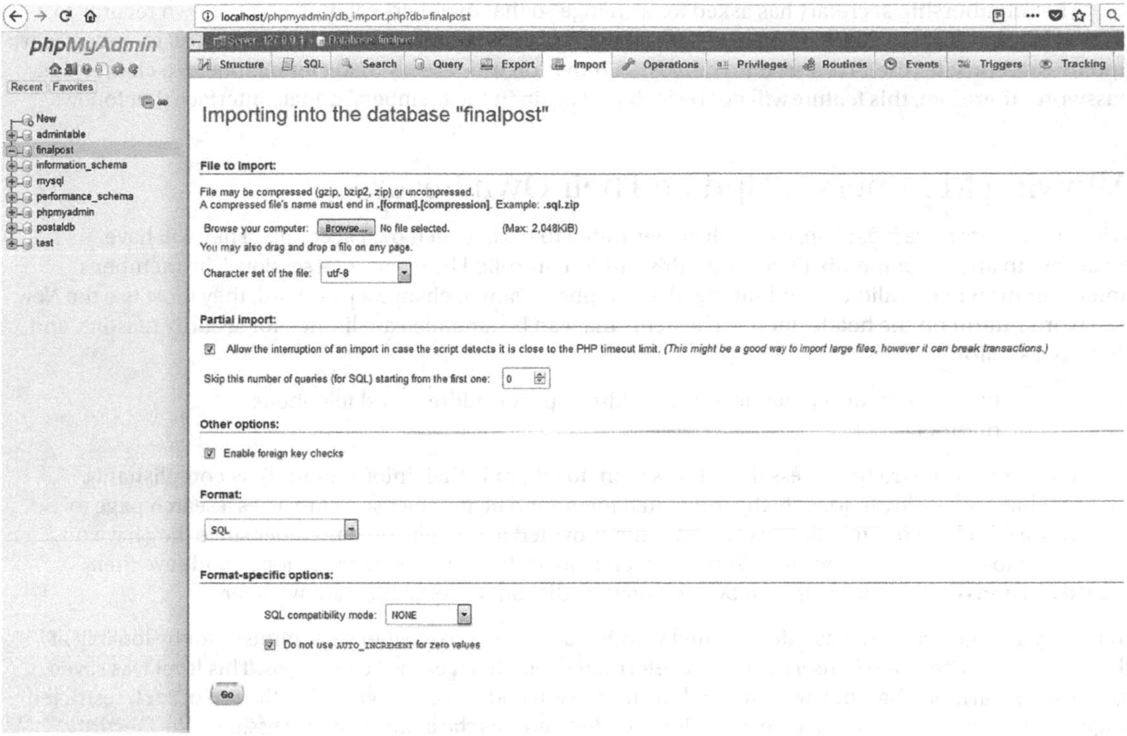

Figure 7-1. The import interface in phpMyAdmin

Details of the Downloaded File for Connecting to the Database

The file *mysqli_connect.php* is already created for you in the download files for this chapter. The contents are shown here:

```php
<?php
// This creates a connection to the migrate database and to MySQL,
// It also sets the encoding.
// Set the access details as constants:
Define ('DB_USER', 'trevithick');
Define ('DB_PASSWORD', 'l0c0m0t1v3');
Define ('DB_HOST', 'localhost');
Define ('DB_NAME', 'migrate');
// Make the connection:
$dbcon = new mysqli(DB_HOST, DB_USER, DB_PASSWORD, DB_NAME);
// Set the encoding...optional but recommended
mysqli_set_charset($dbcon, 'utf8');
```

■ **Caution**   Remember to log in as administrator to view the table of members. The login e-mail is jsmith@outcook.com, and the password is d0g3b0dy.

The membership secretary has asked for a change so that members can update their own records to a limited extent. This is a common feature in database-driven websites. For instance, in PayPal, members can update their profile (their own account details). A provision was already made for members to change their password; therefore, this feature will not be included again in the members' update interface that follows.

Allowing Members to Update Their Own Records

When members have logged in, they will be permitted to update their own accounts. They will have no access to any other member's account; this can be controlled by means of a session. The member's amendments will be validated and sanitized. If members want to change a password, they must use the New Password button on the header menu. The items that can be amended are limited for security reasons, and they are as follows:

> title, first name, last name, e-mail address, postal address, and telephone number

The user has restricted access that allows them to edit only their information. To accomplish this, we must have an ability to identify the individual member. The member secretary uses a search page to determine which record to edit. This screen is not provided to an individual member since they have no choice but to edit their own record. Thus, we need to identify the user when they log in and save their identity in a session variable that can be used on the edit your account page shown later.

In the login page, we previously determined whether a user was a member or administrator by looking at the user_level. The value in user_level also determined which pages they can access. This level was saved in a session variable that then was checked by the session code (security guard) at the top of each restricted page. We can make a minor change to the login code to give us the ability use the session code (security guard) at the top of the edit your account page to determine the user information that can be edited.

```
if (password_verify($p, $row[1])) {
session_start();
// Ensure that the user level is an integer.
$_SESSION['user_level'] = (int) $row[3];
$_SESSION['user_id'] = (int) $row[0]; // Determine individual user
```

The only change needed is the addition of the last line in the previous code snippet. The user_id, which is the record row number in the database, is saved in a session variable with the same name. This uniquely identifies the user. This identification is secure because session variables are accessible only during active sessions. The user must be logged in, as indicated by the if statement in this code segment, for the session user ID and user level to be created. We can now use this information in the edit the account page.

However, before we do that, let's change the header for the members-only page so that registered members can view and amend their records. The header shown in Figure 7-2 is modified to allow this.

Figure 7-2. *The new Your Account button in the header for the members page*

Listing 7-2 shows the code for the revised header. This is in the *includes* folder in the download code.

Listing 7-2. Adding a New Menu Button to the Header of the Members Page

```
<div class="col-sm-2">
    <img class="img-fluid float-left" src="logo.jpg" alt="Logo">
</div>
<div class="col-sm-8">
    <h1 class="blue-text mb-4 font-bold">Header Goes Here</h1>
 </div>
    <nav class="col-sm-2">
        <div class="btn-group-vertical btn-group-sm" role="group"
                aria-label="Button Group">
                    <button type="button" class="btn btn-secondary"
                onclick="location.href = 'logout.php'" >Logout</button>
                    <button type="button" class="btn btn-secondary"
                onclick="location.href = 'edit_your_account.php'">
                    Your Account</button>
                    <button type="button" class="btn btn-secondary"
                onclick="location.href =
                'safer-register-password.php'">New Password</button>
</div>
    </nav>
```

When the Your Account button is clicked, a new page is displayed, as shown in Figure 7-3.

Figure 7-3. *The new Edit Your Account Details page*

The importance of logging out is stressed on the members page and on the update screens. When fields are edited and the Edit Your Record button is clicked, the confirmation message appears, as shown in Figure 7-4. By displaying the details again, the user has another chance to change any information that is incorrect before logging out.

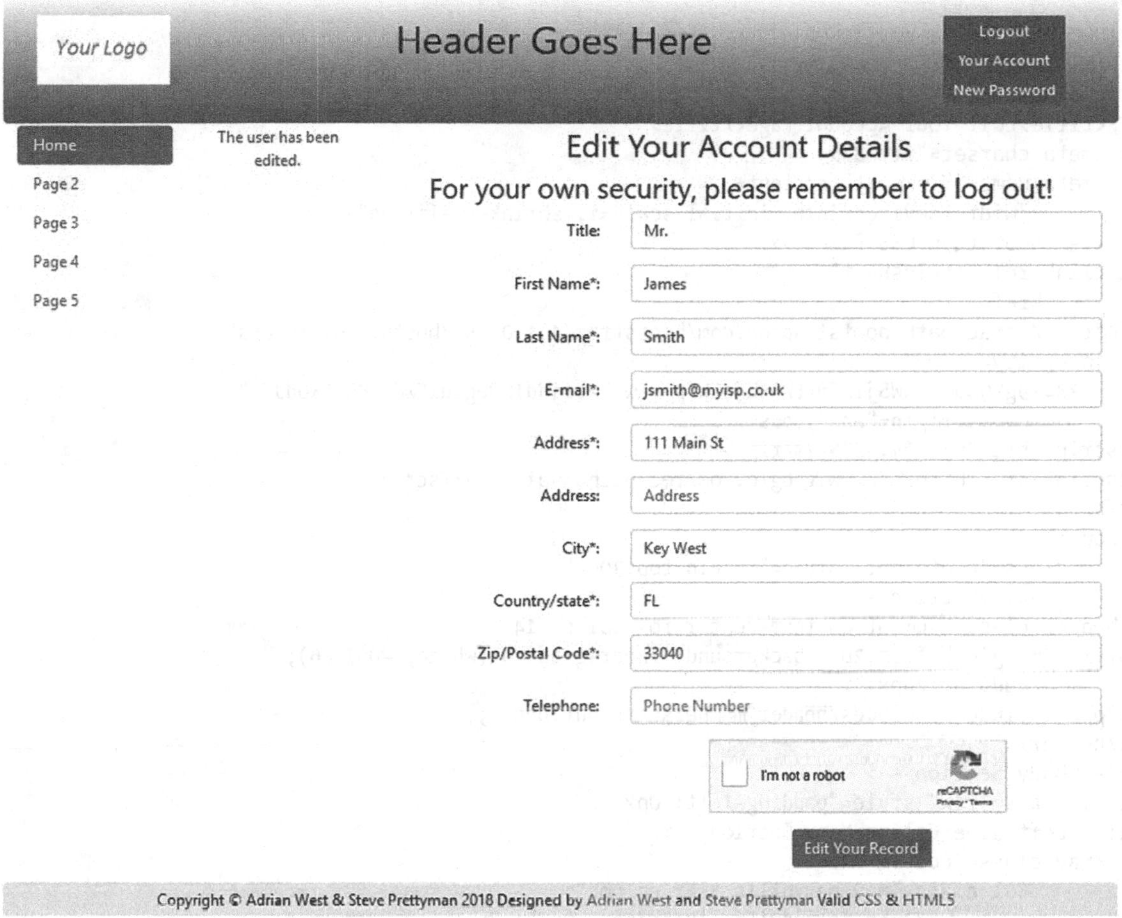

Figure 7-4. *The update is confirmed*

Listing 7-4a shows the code for the screens shown in Figures 7-3 and 7-4.

Listing 7-4a. Creating an Interface for Members to Edit Their Accounts (edit_your_account.php)

```php
<?php
if ($_SERVER['REQUEST_METHOD'] == 'POST') {
        require("cap.php");
}
session_start();
//                                                                                      #1
if (isset($_SESSION['user_id']) && ($_SESSION['user_level'] == 0)){
$id = filter_var( $_SESSION['user_id'], FILTER_SANITIZE_STRING);
        define('ERROR_LOG',"errors.log");
} else {
        header("Location: login.php");
        exit();
}
```

```
?>
<!DOCTYPE html>
<html lang="en">
<head>
  <title>Edit Your Account Page</title>
  <meta charset="utf-8">
  <meta name="viewport" content=
      "width=device-width, initial-scale=1, shrink-to-fit=no">
  <!-- Bootstrap CSS File -->
  <link rel="stylesheet"
      href=
"https://stackpath.bootstrapcdn.com/bootstrap/4.1.0/css/bootstrap.min.css"
  integrity=
"sha384-9gVQ4dYFwwWSjIDZnLEWnxCjeSWFphJiwGPXr1jddIhOegiu1FwO5qRGvFXOdJZ4"
      crossorigin="anonymous">
<script src="verify.js"></script>
<script src='https://www.google.com/recaptcha/api.js'></script>
</head>
<body>
<div class="container" style="margin-top:30px">
<!-- Header Section -->
<header class="jumbotron text-center row col-sm-14"
style="margin-bottom:2px; background:linear-gradient(white, #0073e6);
      padding:20px;">
<?php include('includes/header_members_account.php'); ?>
</header>
<!-- Body Section -->
<div class="row" style="padding-left: 0px;">
<!-- Left-side Column Menu Section -->
  <nav class="col-sm-2">
      <ul class="nav nav-pills flex-column">
              <?php include('includes/nav.php'); ?>
      </ul>
  </nav>
<?php
try {
require ('mysqli_connect.php');
// Has the form been submitted?
if ($_SERVER['REQUEST_METHOD'] == 'POST') {
      $errors = array();
//Is the title present? If it is, sanitize it
    $title = filter_var( $_POST['title'], FILTER_SANITIZE_STRING);
      if ((!empty($title)) && (preg_match('/[a-z\.\s]/i',$title)) &&
              (strlen($title) <= 12)) {
              //Sanitize the trimmed title
              $titletrim = $title;
      }else{
              $titletrim = NULL; // Title is optional
      }
```

```php
// Trim the first name
    $first_name = filter_var( $_POST['first_name'], FILTER_SANITIZE_STRING);
if ((!empty($first_name)) && (preg_match('/[a-z\s]/i',$first_name)) &&
                (strlen($first_name) <= 30)) {
                //Sanitize the trimmed first name
                $first_nametrim = $first_name;
                }else{
        $errors[] =
'First name missing or not alphabetic and space characters. Max 30';
        }
//Is the last name present? If it is, sanitize it
$last_name = filter_var( $_POST['last_name'], FILTER_SANITIZE_STRING);
if ((!empty($last_name)) && (preg_match('/[a-z\-\s\']/i',$last_name)) &&
                (strlen($last_name) <= 40)) {
        //Sanitize the trimmed last name
        $last_nametrim = $last_name;
}else{
        $errors[] =
'Last name missing or not alphabetic, dash, quote or space. Max 30.';
        }
// Check that an email address has been entered
$emailtrim = filter_var( $_POST['email'], FILTER_SANITIZE_EMAIL);
if ((empty($emailtrim)) || (!filter_var($emailtrim, FILTER_VALIDATE_EMAIL))
                || (strlen($emailtrim > 60))) {
                $errors[] = 'You forgot to enter your email address';
                $errors[] = ' or the e-mail format is incorrect.';
        }
//Is the 1st address present? If it is, sanitize it
$address1 = filter_var( $_POST['address1'], FILTER_SANITIZE_STRING);
if ((!empty($address1)) && (preg_match('/[a-z0-9\.\s\,\-]/i', $address1)) &&
   (strlen($address1) <= 30)) {
        //Sanitize the trimmed 1st address
        $address1trim = $address1;
}else{
        $errors[] =
'Missing address. Numeric, alphabetic, period, comma, dash, space. Max 30.';
}
//If the 2nd address is present? If it is, sanitize it
$address2 = filter_var( $_POST['address2'], FILTER_SANITIZE_STRING);
if ((!empty($address2)) && (preg_match('/[a-z0-9\.\s\,\-]/i', $address2)) &&
   (strlen($address2) <= 30)) {
        //Sanitize the trimmed 2nd address
        $address2trim = $address2;
}else{
        $address2trim = NULL;
}
//Is the city present? If it is, sanitize it
$city = filter_var( $_POST['city'], FILTER_SANITIZE_STRING);
if ((!empty($city)) && (preg_match('/[a-z\.\s]/i', $city)) &&
   (strlen($city) <= 30)) {
```

```php
        //Sanitize the trimmed city
        $citytrim = $city;
}else{
        $errors[] =
'Missing city. Only alphabetic, period and space. Max 30.';
        }
//Is the state or country present? If it is, sanitize it
$state_country = filter_var( $_POST['state_country'], FILTER_SANITIZE_STRING);
if ((!empty($state_country)) && (preg_match('/[a-z\.\s]/i', $state_country))
        && (strlen($state_country) <= 30))        {
        //Sanitize the trimmed state or country
        $state_countrytrim = $state_country;
}else{
        $errors[] =
        'Missing state/country. Only alphabetic, period and space. Max 30.';
//Is the zip code or post code present? If it is, sanitize it
$zcode_pcode = filter_var( $_POST['zcode_pcode'], FILTER_SANITIZE_STRING);
$string_length = strlen($zcode_pcode);
if ((!empty($zcode_pcode)) && (preg_match('/[a-z0-9\s]/i', $zcode_pcode))  &&
    ($string_length <= 30) && ($string_length >= 5)) {
        //Sanitize the trimmed zcode_pcode
     $zcode_pcodetrim = $zcode_pcode;
}else{
        $errors[] =
'Missing zip code or post code. Alphabetic, numeric, space only max 30 chars';
}
//Is the phone number present? If it is, sanitize it
$phone = filter_var( $_POST['phone'], FILTER_SANITIZE_STRING);
if ((!empty($phone)) && (strlen($phone) <= 30)) {
        //Sanitize the trimmed phone number
        $phonetrim = (filter_var($phone, FILTER_SANITIZE_NUMBER_INT));
        $phonetrim = preg_replace('/[^0-9]/', ", $phonetrim);
}else{
        $phonetrim = NULL;
}
if (empty($errors)) { // If everything's OK.
        //   make the query
        $q = mysqli_stmt_init($dbcon);
        $query =
                'SELECT userid FROM users WHERE email=? AND userid !=?';
      mysqli_stmt_prepare($q, $query);
        // bind $id to SQL Statement
        mysqli_stmt_bind_param($q, 'si', $emailtrim, $id);
        // execute query
        mysqli_stmt_execute($q);
        $result = mysqli_stmt_get_result($q);
        if (mysqli_num_rows($result) == 0) {
        // e-mail does not exist in another record
                // Make the update query:
                $query =
```

```
'UPDATE users SET title=?, first_name=?, last_name=?, email=?, ';
                $query .=
'address1=?, address2=?, city=?, state_country=?, zcode_pcode=?, ';
                $query .=
'phone=?';
        $query .= ' WHERE userid=?';
        $q = mysqli_stmt_init($dbcon);
         mysqli_stmt_prepare($q, $query);
        // bind values to SQL Statement
              mysqli_stmt_bind_param($q, 'sssssssssssi', $titletrim,
        $first_nametrim, $last_nametrim,
        $emailtrim, $address1trim, $address2trim, $citytrim,
        $state_countrytrim,
        $zcode_pcodetrim, $phonetrim, $id);
        // execute query
        mysqli_stmt_execute($q);
                if (mysqli_stmt_affected_rows($q) == 1) { // Update OK
                        // Echo a message if the edit was satisfactory:
                        $errorstring = 'The user has been edited.';
                        echo "<p class=' text-center col-sm-2'
                        style='color:green'>$errorstring</p>";
                } else { // Echo a message if the query failed.
                        $errorstring =
        'The user could not be edited. Did you change anything?';
        $errorstring .=
        ' We apologize for any inconvenience.'; // Public message.
                        echo "<p class=' text-center col-sm-2'
                        style='color:red'>$errorstring</p>";
        //echo '<p>' . mysqli_error($dbcon) . '<br />Query: ' . $q . '</p>';
        // Debugging message.
        // Message above is only for debug and should not display sql
        }
}
} else { // Display the errors.
        // ---------------Process User Errors---------------
        // Display the users entry errors
        $errorstring = 'Error! The following error(s) occurred: ';
        foreach ($errors as $msg) { // Print each error.
                $errorstring .= " - $msg<br>\n";
                }
        $errorstring .= 'Please try again.';
        echo "<p class=' text-center col-sm-2' style='color:red'>$errorstring</p>";
        }// End of if (empty($errors)) IF.
} // End of the conditionals
// Select the user's information:
$query = "SELECT title, first_name, last_name, email, address1,
        address2, city, state_country, zcode_pcode, phone ";
$query .=" FROM users WHERE userid=?";
// id was retrieved from database prepared not needed
$q = mysqli_stmt_init($dbcon);
 mysqli_stmt_prepare($q, $query);
```

```php
// bind $id to SQL Statement
mysqli_stmt_bind_param($q, 'i', $id);
// execute query
mysqli_stmt_execute($q);
$result = mysqli_stmt_get_result($q);
if (mysqli_num_rows($result) == 1) { // Valid user ID, display the form.
        // Get the user's information:
        $row = mysqli_fetch_array ($result, MYSQLI_ASSOC);
        // Create the form:
?>
  <!-- Validate Input -->
<div class="col-sm-8">
<h2 class="h2 text-center">Edit Your Account Details</h2>
<h3 class="text-center">
For your own security, please remember to log out!</h3>
<form action="edit_your_account.php" method="post"                  <!-- #2 -->
name="editform" id="editform">
 <div class="form-group row">
    <label for="title" class="col-sm-4 col-form-label
        text-right">Title:</label>
 <div class="col-sm-8">
      <input type="text" class="form-control" id="title" name="title"
        placeholder="Title" maxlength="12"
        pattern='[a-zA-Z][a-zA-Z\s\.]*'
        title="Alphabetic, period and space max 12 characters"
        value=
            "<?php if (isset($row['title']))
            echo htmlspecialchars($row['title'], ENT_QUOTES); ?>" >
 </div>
 </div>
<div class="form-group row">
    <label for="first_name" class="col-sm-4 col-form-label text-right">
                First Name*:</label>
    <div class="col-sm-8">
      <input type="text" class="form-control" id="first_name"
                name="first_name"
                pattern="[a-zA-Z][a-zA-Z\s]*"
                title="Alphabetic and space only max of 30 characters"
                placeholder="First Name" maxlength="30" required
                value=
                "<?php if (isset($row['first_name']))
                echo htmlspecialchars($row['first_name'], ENT_QUOTES); ?>" >
 </div>
 </div>
 <div class="form-group row">
    <label for="last_name" class="col-sm-4 col-form-label text-right">
                Last Name*:</label>
 <div class="col-sm-8">
      <input type="text" class="form-control" id="last_name" name="last_name"
        pattern="[a-zA-Z][a-zA-Z\s\-\']*"
        title="Alphabetic, dash, quote and space only max of 40 characters"
```

```
            placeholder="Last Name" maxlength="40" required
            value=
                "<?php if (isset($row['last_name']))
                echo htmlspecialchars($row['last_name'], ENT_QUOTES); ?>" >
</div>
</div>
<div class="form-group row">
    <label for="email" class="col-sm-4 col-form-label text-right">
                E-mail*:</label>
    <div class="col-sm-8">
      <input type="email" class="form-control" id="email" name="email"
        placeholder="E-mail" maxlength="60" required
        value=
                "<?php if (isset($row['email']))
                echo htmlspecialchars($row['email'], ENT_QUOTES); ?>" >
</div>
</div>
<div class="form-group row">
    <label for="address1" class="col-sm-4 col-form-label
        text-right">Address*:</label>
    <div class="col-sm-8">
      <input type="text" class="form-control" id="address1" name="address1"
        pattern="[a-zA-Z0-9][a-zA-Z0-9\s\.\,\-]*"
        title="Alphabetic, numbers, period, comma, dash and space only max of 30 characters"
          placeholder="Address" maxlength="30" required
          value=
                "<?php if (isset($row['address1']))
                echo htmlspecialchars($row['address1'], ENT_QUOTES); ?>" >
 </div>
</div>
<div class="form-group row">
    <label for="address2" class="col-sm-4 col-form-label text-right">Address:</label>
    <div class="col-sm-8">
      <input type="text" class="form-control" id="address2" name="address2"
        pattern="[a-zA-Z0-9][a-zA-Z0-9\s\.\,\-]*"
        title="Alphabetic, numbers, period, comma, dash and space only max of 30 characters"
        placeholder="Address" maxlength="30"
        value=
            "<?php if (isset($row['address2']))
            echo htmlspecialchars($row['address2'], ENT_QUOTES); ?>" >
</div>
</div>
<div class="form-group row">
    <label for="city" class="col-sm-4 col-form-label
        text-right">City*:</label>
    <div class="col-sm-8">
      <input type="text" class="form-control" id="city" name="city"
        pattern="[a-zA-Z][a-zA-Z\s\.]*"
        title="Alphabetic, period and space only max of 30 characters"
```

```
            placeholder="City" maxlength="30" required
            value=
                "<?php if (isset($row['city']))
                echo htmlspecialchars($row['city'], ENT_QUOTES); ?>" >
</div>
</div>
<div class="form-group row">
    <label for="state_country" class="col-sm-4 col-form-label text-right">
                Country/state*:</label>
    <div class="col-sm-8">
      <input type="text" class="form-control" id="state_country"
                name="state_country"
      pattern="[a-zA-Z][a-zA-Z\s\.]*"
          title="Alphabetic, period and space only max of 30 characters"
          placeholder="State or Country" maxlength="30" required
          value=
                "<?php if (isset($row['state_country']))
                echo htmlspecialchars($row['state_country'], ENT_QUOTES); ?>" >
</div>
</div>
<div class="form-group row">
    <label for="zcode_pcode" class="col-sm-4 col-form-label text-right">
                Zip/Postal Code*:</label>
    <div class="col-sm-8">
      <input type="text" class="form-control" id="zcode_pcode"
                name="zcode_pcode"
      pattern="[a-zA-Z0-9][a-zA-Z0-9\s]*"
      title="Alphabetic, period and space only max of 30 characters"
      placeholder="Zip or Postal Code" minlength="5"
                maxlength="30" required
      value=
                "<?php if (isset($row['zcode_pcode']))
                echo htmlspecialchars($row['zcode_pcode'], ENT_QUOTES); ?>" >
</div>
</div>
<div class="form-group row">
    <label for="phone" class="col-sm-4 col-form-label
                text-right">Telephone:</label>
    <div class="col-sm-8">
      <input type="tel" class="form-control" id="phone" name="phone"
      placeholder="Phone Number" maxlength="30"
      value=
          "<?php if (isset($row['phone']))
          echo htmlspecialchars($row['phone'], ENT_QUOTES); ?>" >
</div>
</div>
      <input type="hidden" name="id" value="' . $id . '">
<div class="form-group row">
  <label class="col-sm-4 col-form-label"></label>
  <div class="col-sm-8">
  <div class=
```

```
"float-left g-recaptcha" style="padding-left: 80px;"
data-sitekey="6LcrQ1wUAAAAAPxlrAkLuPdpY5qwS9rXF1j46fhq"></div>
</div>
</div>
<div class="form-group row">
        <label for="" class="col-sm-4 col-form-label"></label>
    <div class="col-sm-8 text-center">
        <input id="submit" class="btn btn-primary" type="submit"
                name="submit" value="Edit Your Record">
</div>
</div>
</form>
</div>
<?php
    }
 if(!isset($errorstring)) {
        echo '<aside class="col-sm-2">';
        include('includes/info-col.php');
        echo '</aside>';
        echo '</div>';
        echo '<footer class="jumbotron text-center row col-sm-14"
                style="padding-bottom:1px; padding-top:8px;">';
 }
 else
 {
        echo '<footer class="jumbotron text-center col-sm-12"
        style="padding-bottom:1px; padding-top:8px;">';
 }
  include('includes/footer.php');
  echo "</footer>";
  echo "</div>";


}
catch(Exception $e) // We finally handle any problems here
   {
       // print "An Exception occurred. Message: " . $e->getMessage();
       print "The system is busy please try later";
       // $date = date('m.d.y h:i:s');
       // $errormessage = $e->getMessage();
       // $eMessage = $date . " | Exception Error | " , $errormessage . |\n";
       // error_log($eMessage,3,ERROR_LOG);
       // e-mail support person to alert there is a problem
       // error_log("Date/Time: $date - Exception Error, Check error log for
//details", 1, noone@helpme.com, "Subject: Exception Error \nFrom: Error Log <errorlog
@helpme.com>" . "\r\n");
   }
   catch(Error $e)
   {
       // print "An Error occurred. Message: " . $e->getMessage();
       print "The system is busy please try later";
```

```
        // $date = date('m.d.y h:i:s');
        // $errormessage = $e->getMessage();
        // $eMessage = $date . " | Error | " , $errormessage . |\n";
        // error_log($eMessage,3,ERROR_LOG);
        // e-mail support person to alert there is a problem
   //   error_log("Date/Time: $date - Error, Check error log for
//details", 1, noone@helpme.com, "Subject: Error \nFrom: Error Log <errorlog@helpme.com>"."\r\n");
    }
?>
</body>
</html>
```

Explanation of the Code

This section explains the code.

```
<?php
session_start();
//                                                                      #1
if (isset($_SESSION['user_id']) && ($_SESSION['user_level'] == 0)){
$id = filter_var( $_SESSION['user_id'], FILTER_SANITIZE_STRING);
} else {
header("Location: login.php");
exit();
}
?>
```

The access to the page is allowed only if there is a value in the session variable user_id and the user level is 0. The user_id was set as a session variable when the user signed in using the login page. Thus, this value is valid as long as the session is still active. The user_id is then saved in the $id variable because it will be used to display and update the user's record.

```
form action="edit_your_account.php" method="post"                    <!--#2-->
        onsubmit="return checked();"
        name="regform" id="regform">
 <div class="form-group row">
        <label for="title" class="col-sm-4 col-form-label text-right">
                Title:</label>
 <div class="col-sm-8">
        <input type="text" class="form-control" id="title" name="title"
                placeholder="Title" maxlength="12"
                pattern='[a-zA-Z][a-zA-Z\s\.]*'
                title="Alphabetic, period and space max 12 characters"
                value=
                        "<?php if (isset($row['title']))
                echo htmlspecialchars($row['title'], ENT_QUOTES); ?>" >
    </div>
    </div>
```

This segment of code shows part of the sticky form for editing the member's account. The $row array was created by pulling the user's record from the database table using a SELECT statement. The code is similar to what we have seen before, except that we are pulling the data from $row and not from $_POST.

All sanitation and validation in the file *process_edit_your_account* is the same as shown in Chapter 6. Therefore, we will not discuss it here. You can view the contents of this file, with a text editor, from the downloaded Chapter 7 files.

Let's diverge for a quick second. In the previous chapters, we have not taken a moment to point out that, in most cases, our web pages are already mobile (small screen) enabled. Figure 7-5 shows the mobile size version of the safer-register-page.

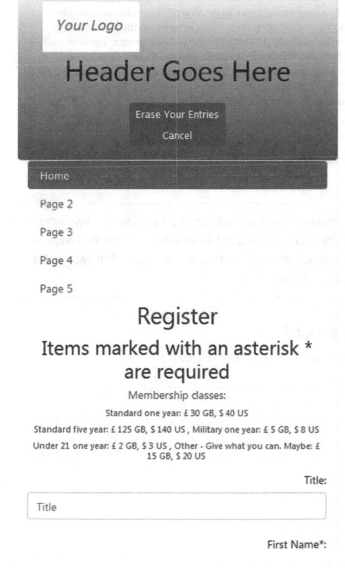

Figure 7-5. *Mobile size registration page*

The Bootstrap classes we have been using throughout the previous chapters have given our pages this capability. In the remaining chapters, we will make slight adjustments to the Bootstrap code to personalize our buttons and to hide some menus when viewed from a mobile device.

This concludes the tutorial on the membership website and the database migrate. However, we can add some useful additions and changes to this website (or any website), as we will see next.

A Secure Feedback Form

A Contact Us form is not strictly related to databases; however, it is an interactive element and provides an excellent application of PHP code.

E-mails and feedback forms are the most popular contact methods for allowing users to communicate easily with website owners. Unfortunately, both contact methods can be abused. E-mail addresses are harvested and sold to spammers. Both actions cause distress and an influx of spam to the site owner. Hackers can hijack a form and use it to send frequent spam messages to the website owner. These usually contain malware that can be activated via a link in the text area. As stated, no one should click a link embedded within an e-mail, unless absolutely sure that the link is valid. This section describes some options to reduce these risks.

When designing feedback forms, we need to consider the following points:

- Blind and severely visually impaired users will use screen readers to read and reply to forms. Accessibility rules must be observed.

- Filters must be built into the form handler to prevent the form from being hijacked for nefarious purposes.

■ **Note** Many government agencies require companies to comply with accessibility guidelines in websites. Many countries will not provide government contracts to companies that do not follow accessibility guidelines. The guidelines are usually not difficult to implement and increase the goodwill of an organization by providing visually impaired users access to the information on the site.

What Does a Feedback Reply Look Like?

The following is a genuine e-mail received from a secure form and its handler:

```
--------------------------------------------------------------
Name of sender: Andrew Eastman
Email of sender: aeastman@myisp.co.uk
Telephone No: 01111 222333
XP?: No
Vista?: No
Windows7?: No
Windows 8: Yes
Laptop?: Yes
Desktop?; No
------------------------ MESSAGE ----------------------------
How can I change back to Windows 7?
--------------------------------------------------------------
```

The Feedback Form

Figure 7-6 shows a typical feedback form.

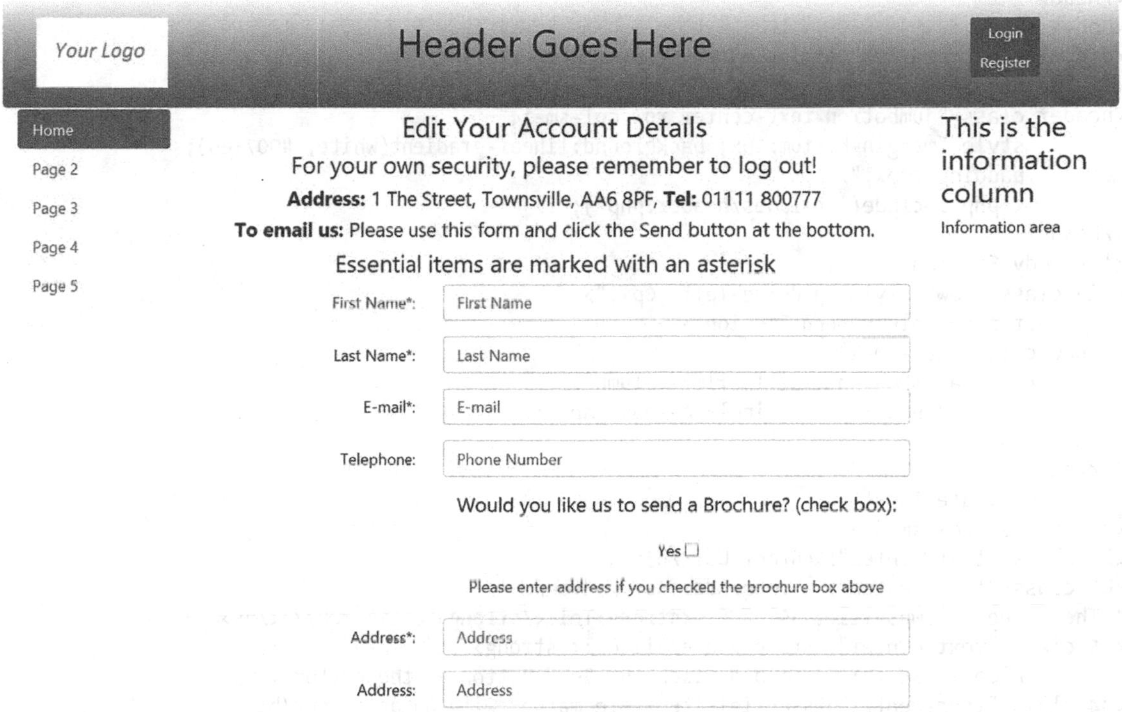

Figure 7-6. *The feedback form*

The code for the feedback page concentrates on preventing URLs from being entered because these are the main concern with forms filled in by robots.

Listing 7-6a provides a look at the code to display the form.

Listing 7-6a. Creating the Contact Us Form (feedback-form.php)

```php
<?php
if ($_SERVER['REQUEST_METHOD'] == 'POST') {
        require("cap.php");
}
?>
<!DOCTYPE html>
<html lang="en">
<head>
  <title>Feedback Form</title>
  <meta charset="utf-8">
  <meta name="viewport"
        content="width=device-width, initial-scale=1, shrink-to-fit=no">
  <!-- Bootstrap CSS File -->
  <link rel="stylesheet"
```

```
        href="https://stackpath.bootstrapcdn.com/bootstrap/4.1.0/css/bootstrap.min.css"
  integrity="sha384-9gVQ4dYFwwWSjIDZnLEWnxCjeSWFphJiwGPXr1jddIhOegiu1FwO5qRGvFXOdJZ4"
        crossorigin="anonymous">
<script src='https://www.google.com/recaptcha/api.js'></script>
</head>
<body>
<div class="container" style="margin-top:30px">
<!-- Header Section -->
<header class="jumbotron text-center row col-sm-14"
        style="margin-bottom:2px; background:linear-gradient(white, #0073e6);
        padding:20px;">
        <?php include('includes/header.php'); ?>
</header>
<!-- Body Section -->
<div class="row" style="padding-left: 0px;">
<!-- Left-side Column Menu Section -->
  <nav class="col-sm-2">
      <ul class="nav nav-pills flex-column">
              <?php include('includes/nav.php'); ?>
      </ul>
  </nav>
  <!-- Validate Input -->
<div class="col-sm-8">
<h3 class="text-center">Contact Us!</h3>
<h5 class="text-center"><strong>Address:</strong>
1 The Street, Townsville, AA6 8PF, <strong>Tel:</strong> 01111 800777</h5>
<h5 class="text-center"><strong>To email us:</strong>
        Please use this form and click the Send button at the bottom.</h5>
<h4 class="text-center">Essential items are marked with an asterisk</h4>
<!--                                                                              #1-->
<form action="feedback-handler.php" method="post" name="feedbackform"
        id="feedbackform">
<!--START OF TEXT FIELDS-->
<div class="form-group row">
        <label for="first_name" class="col-sm-4 col-form-label text-right">
              First Name*:</label>
<div class="col-sm-8">
        <input type="text" class="form-control" id="first_name"
              name="first_name"
              pattern="[a-zA-Z][a-zA-Z\s]*"
              title="Alphabetic and space only max of 30 characters"
              placeholder="First Name" maxlength="30" required
              value=
                    "<?php if (isset($row['first_name']))
              echo htmlspecialchars($row['first_name'], ENT_QUOTES); ?>" >
</div>
</div>
<div class="form-group row">
        <label for="last_name" class="col-sm-4 col-form-label text-right">
              Last Name*:</label>
<div class="col-sm-8">
        <input type="text" class="form-control" id="last_name" name="last_name"
```

```
                pattern="[a-zA-Z][a-zA-Z\s\-\']*"
                title="Alphabetic, dash, quote and space only max of 40 characters"
                placeholder="Last Name" maxlength="40" required
                value=
                        "<?php if (isset($row['last_name']))
                echo htmlspecialchars($row['last_name'], ENT_QUOTES); ?>" >
</div>
</div>
<div class="form-group row">
        <label for="email" class="col-sm-4 col-form-label text-right">
                E-mail*:</label>
<div class="col-sm-8">
        <input type="email" class="form-control" id="email" name="email"
                placeholder="E-mail" maxlength="60" required
                value=
                        "<?php if (isset($row['email']))
                echo htmlspecialchars($row['email'], ENT_QUOTES); ?>" >
</div>
</div>
<div class="form-group row">
        <label for="phone" class="col-sm-4 col-form-label
                text-right">Telephone:</label>
<div class="col-sm-8">
        <input type="tel" class="form-control" id="phone" name="phone"
                placeholder="Phone Number" maxlength="30"
                value=
                        "<?php if (isset($row['phone']))
                echo htmlspecialchars($row['phone'], ENT_QUOTES); ?>" >
</div>
</div>
<div class="form-group row">
    <label for="" class="col-sm-4 col-form-label text-right"></label>
<h5 class="col-sm-8 text-center">Would you like us to send a Brochure?
        (check box):</h5>
</div>
<div class="form-group row">
    <label for="" class="col-sm-4 col-form-label text-right"></label>
<div class="checkbox col-sm-8 text-center">Yes
        <input class="" type="checkbox" name="brochure" id="brochure" value="yes">
</div>
</div>
<div class="form-group row">
    <label for="" class="col-sm-4 col-form-label text-right"></label>
<h6 class="col-sm-8 text-center">
        Please enter address if you checked the brochure box above</h6>
</div>
<div class="form-group row">
        <label for="address1" class="col-sm-4 col-form-label
            text-right">Address*:</label>
<div class="col-sm-8">
        <input type="text" class="form-control" id="address1" name="address1"
                pattern="[a-zA-Z0-9][a-zA-Z0-9\s\.\,\-]*"
```

```
                title="Alphabetic, numbers, period, comma, dash and space only max of 30
                characters"
                placeholder="Address" maxlength="30" required
                value=
                        "<?php if (isset($row['address1']))
                echo htmlspecialchars($row['address1'], ENT_QUOTES); ?>" >
</div>
</div>
<div class="form-group row">
        <label for="address2" class="col-sm-4 col-form-label
                text-right">Address:</label>
<div class="col-sm-8">
        <input type="text" class="form-control" id="address2" name="address2"
                pattern="[a-zA-Z0-9][a-zA-Z0-9\s\.\,\-]*"
                title="Alphabetic, numbers, period, comma, dash and space only max of 30
                characters"
                placeholder="Address" maxlength="30"
                value=
                        "<?php if (isset($row['address2']))
                echo htmlspecialchars($row['address2'], ENT_QUOTES); ?>" >
</div>
</div>
<div class="form-group row">
        <label for="city" class="col-sm-4 col-form-label
                text-right">City*:</label>
<div class="col-sm-8">
      <input type="text" class="form-control" id="city" name="city"
                pattern="[a-zA-Z][a-zA-Z\s\.]*"
                title="Alphabetic, period and space only max of 30 characters"
                placeholder="City" maxlength="30" required
                value=
                        "<?php if (isset($_POST['city']))
                echo htmlspecialchars($_POST['city'], ENT_QUOTES); ?>" >
</div>
</div>
<div class="form-group row">
        <label for="state_country" class="col-sm-4 col-form-label text-right">
                Country/state*:</label>
<div class="col-sm-8">
        <input type="text" class="form-control" id="state_country"
                name="state_country"
                pattern="[a-zA-Z][a-zA-Z\s\.]*"
                title="Alphabetic, period and space only max of 30 characters"
                placeholder="State or Country" maxlength="30" required
                value=
                        "<?php if (isset($_POST['state_country']))
                echo htmlspecialchars($_POST['state_country'], ENT_QUOTES); ?>" >
 </div>
 </div>
 <div class="form-group row">
        <label for="zcode_pcode" class="col-sm-4 col-form-label text-right">
                Zip/Postal Code*:</label>
```

```
<div class="col-sm-8">
        <input type="text" class="form-control" id="zcode_pcode"
                name="zcode_pcode"
                pattern="[a-zA-Z0-9][a-zA-Z0-9\s]*"
                title="Alphabetic, period and space only max of 30 characters"
                placeholder="Zip or Postal Code" minlength="5" maxlength="30"
                required
                value=
                        "<?php if (isset($_POST['zcode_pcode']))
                echo htmlspecialchars($_POST['zcode_pcode'], ENT_QUOTES); ?>" >
</div>
</div>
<div class="form-group row">
        <label for="" class="col-sm-4 col-form-label text-right"></label>
<h5 class="col-sm-8 text-center">
        Would you like to receive emailed newsletters?</h5>
</div>
<fieldset class="form-group row">
                <label for="" class="col-sm-4 col-form-label text-right"></label>
<div class="col-sm-8 text-center">                                          <!--#2 -->
<div class="form-check form-check-inline">
        <input class="form-check-input" type="radio" name="letter"
                id="letter" value="yes" checked>
        <label class="form-check-label" for="letter">
            Yes
        </label>
</div>
<div class="form-check form-check-inline">
        <input class="form-check-input" type="radio" name="noletter"
                id="noletter" value="no">
        <label class="form-check-label" for="noletter">
            No
        </label>
</div>
</div>
</fieldset>
<div class="form-group row">                                              <!--#3-->
        <label for="" class="col-sm-4 col-form-label text-right"></label>
<div class="col-sm-8 text-center">
        <label for="comment">Please enter your message below</label>
        <textarea class="form-control" id="comment" name="comment" rows="12"
                cols="40"
                value=
                        "<?php if (isset($_POST['comment']))
                echo htmlspecialchars($_POST['comment'], ENT_QUOTES); ?>" >
        </textarea>
</div>
</div>
<div class="form-group row">
        <label class="col-sm-4 col-form-label"></label>
<div class="col-sm-8">
```

```
<div class="g-recaptcha" style="margin-left: 80px;"
        data-sitekey="placeyoursitekeyhere"></div>
  </div>
</div>
<div class="form-group row">
        <label for="" class="col-sm-4 col-form-label"></label>
<div class="col-sm-8 text-center">
        <input id="submit" class="btn btn-primary" type="submit" name="submit"
                value="Send">
</div>
</div>
</form>
</div>
<!-- Right-side Column Content Section -->
        <aside class="col-sm-2">
                <?php include('includes/info-col.php'); ?>
        </aside>
<!-- Footer Content Section -->
</div>
<footer class="jumbotron text-center row"
        style="padding-bottom:1px; padding-top:8px;">
        <?php include('includes/footer.php'); ?>
</footer>
</body>
</html>
```

Explanation of the Code

This section explains the code.

```
<!--                                                                    #1-->
<form action="feedback-handler.php" method="post" name="feedbackform"
      id="feedbackform">
```

Bogus feedback from the feedback form will be stopped by means of a PHP handler file that is called by the form. If a URL has been entered in any text field, the form handler will display an error message after the submit button is clicked. This will stop bogus replies. Listing 7-3b shows the PHP code for the handler.

```
<div class="col-sm-8 text-center">                                      <!--#2 -->
<div class="form-check form-check-inline">
        <input class="form-check-input" type="radio" name="letter"
            id="letter" value="yes" checked>
      <label class="form-check-label" for="letter">
          Yes
      </label>
</div>
<div class="form-check form-check-inline">
        <input class="form-check-input" type="radio" name="noletter"
                id="noletter" value="no">
```

```
            <label class="form-check-label" for="noletter">
                No
            </label>
</div>
Radio buttons are used to determine if the user wants to join the e-mail newsletter.
<div class="form-group row">                                                    <!--#3-->
            <label for="" class="col-sm-4 col-form-label text-right"></label>
<div class="col-sm-8 text-center">
            <label for="comment">Please enter your message below</label>
            <textarea class="form-control" id="comment" name="comment" rows="12"
                cols="40"
                value=
                      "<?php if (isset($_POST['comment']))
                echo htmlspecialchars($_POST['comment'], ENT_QUOTES); ?>" >
            </textarea>
  </div>
  </div>
```

Textarea is used to gather the message to be sent. This message will be sanitized on the server side. All other code is similar to the code in safer-register-page shown in Chapter 6. Let's look at the PHP code in Listing 7-6b.

Listing 7-6b. Creating the Feedback Form Handler (feedback-handler.php)

Note that dummy e-mail addresses and URLs have been used. Replace them with your client's details.

```php
<?php

// Feedback form handler
// set the error and thank you pages                                              #1
$formurl = "feedback_form.php" ;
$errorurl = "feedback/error.php" ;
$thankyouurl = "feedback/thankyou.php" ;
$emailerrurl = "feedback/emailerr.php" ;
$errorcommenturl =  "feedback/commenterror.php" ;
// set to the email address of the recipient
$mailto = "none@noone.com" ;
// Is first name present? If it is, sanitize it                                    #2
    $first_name = filter_var( $_POST['first_name'], FILTER_SANITIZE_STRING);
if ((!empty($first_name)) && (preg_match('/[a-z\s]/i',$first_name)) &&
                (strlen($first_name) <= 30)) {
        //Save first name
        $first_nametrim = $first_name;
}else{
        $errors = 'yes';
}
//Is the last name present? If it is, sanitize it
$last_name = filter_var( $_POST['last_name'], FILTER_SANITIZE_STRING);
if ((!empty($last_name)) && (preg_match('/[a-z\-\s\']/i',$last_name)) &&
                (strlen($last_name) <= 40)) {
```

```
        //Save last name
        $last_nametrim = $last_name;
}else{
        $errors = 'yes';
}
// Check that an email address has been entered correctly                     #3
$emailtrim = filter_var( $_POST['email'], FILTER_SANITIZE_EMAIL);
if ((empty($emailtrim)) || (!filter_var($emailtrim, FILTER_VALIDATE_EMAIL))
        || (strlen($emailtrim > 60))) {
        // if email is bad display error page
        header( "Location: $emailerrurl" );
    exit ;
}
// Is the phone number present? if so, sanitize it
$phone = filter_var( $_POST['phone'], FILTER_SANITIZE_STRING);
if ((!empty($phone)) && (strlen($phone) <= 30)) {
        //Sanitize and validate phone number
        $phonetrim = (filter_var($phone, FILTER_SANITIZE_NUMBER_INT));
        $phonetrim = preg_replace('/[^0-9]/', ", $phonetrim);
}else{
        $phonetrim = NULL; // if not valid or missing do not save
}
//Is the 1st address present? If it is, sanitize it
$address1 = filter_var( $_POST['address1'], FILTER_SANITIZE_STRING);
if ((!empty($address1)) && (preg_match('/[a-z0-9\.\s\,\-]/i', $address1) &&
        (strlen($address1) <= 30)) {
        //Save the 1st address
        $address1trim = $address1;
}else{
        $errors = 'yes';
}
//If the 2nd address is present? If it is, sanitize it
$address2 = filter_var( $_POST['address2'], FILTER_SANITIZE_STRING);
if ((!empty($address2)) && (preg_match('/[a-z0-9\.\s\,\-]/i', $address2) &&
        (strlen($address2) <= 30)) {
        //Save the 2nd address
        $address2trim = $address2;
}else{
        $address2trim = NULL; // If missing or not valid do not save
}
//Is the city present? If it is, sanitize it
$city = filter_var( $_POST['city'], FILTER_SANITIZE_STRING);
if ((!empty($city)) && (preg_match('/[a-z\.\s]/i', $city) &&
        (strlen($city) <= 30)) {
        //Save the city
        $citytrim = $city;
}else{
        $errors = 'yes';
}
//Is the state or country present? If it is, sanitize it
$state_country = filter_var( $_POST['state_country'], FILTER_SANITIZE_STRING
```

```
if ((!empty($state_country)) && (preg_match('/[a-z\.\s]/i', $state_country))
        && (strlen($state_country) <= 30))      {
        //Save the state or country
        $state_countrytrim = $state_country;
}else{
        $errors = 'yes';
}
//Is the zip code or post code present? If it is, sanitize it
$zcode_pcode = filter_var( $_POST['zcode_pcode'], FILTER_SANITIZE_STRING);
$string_length = strlen($zcode_pcode);
if ((!empty($zcode_pcode)) && (preg_match('/[a-z0-9\s]/i', $zcode_pcode))  &&
        ($string_length <= 30) && ($string_length >= 5)) {
        //Save the zcode_pcode
        $zcode_pcodetrim = $zcode_pcode;
}else{
        $errors = 'yes';
        }

$brochure = filter_var( $_POST['brochure'], FILTER_SANITIZE_STRING);              //#4
if($brochure != "yes") {$brochure = "no";} // if not yes, then no
$letter = filter_var( $_POST['letter'], FILTER_SANITIZE_STRING);
if($letter != "yes") {$letter = "no"; } // if not yes, then no

$comment = filter_var( $_POST['comment'], FILTER_SANITIZE_STRING);                //#5
if ((!empty($comment)) && (strlen($comment) <= 480)) {
        // remove ability to create link in email
        $patterns = array("/http/", "/https/", "/\:/","/\/\//","/www./");
        $commenttrim = preg_replace($patterns," ", $comment);
}else{    // if comment not valid display error page
        header( "Location: $errorcommenturl" );
        exit;
}

if (!empty($errors)) { // if errors display error page
        header( "Location: $errorurl" );
        exit ; }
// everything OK send e-mail                                                      #6
$subject = "Message from customer " . $first_nametrim . " " . $last_nametrim;
$messageproper =
"------------------------------------------------------------\n" .
"Name of sender: $first_nametrim $last_nametrim\n" .
"Email of sender: $emailtrim\n" .
"Telephone: $phonetrim\n" .
"brochure?: $brochure\n" .
"Address: $address1trim\n" .
"Address: $address2trim\n" .
"City: $citytrim\n" .
"Postcode: $zcode_pcodetrim\n" .
"Newsletter?:$letter\n" .
"----------------------- MESSAGE ------------------------\n\n" .
$commenttrim .
```

```
"\n\n------------------------------------------------------------\n" ;
mail($mailto, $subject, $messageproper, "From: \"$first_nametrim $last_nametrim\"
<$emailtrim>" );
header( "Location: $thankyouurl" );
exit ;
?>
```

> ■ **Caution**   The form handler requires an e-mail server to reside on the machine in which the code executes. Unless you installed your own e-mail server, this code will not execute on your computer. However, most web hosting companies provide access to e-mail servers. You can upload this code to a hosting site. Then verify the code to access the e-mail server with the hosting company. Sometimes there are minor but important changes required to complete the process.

Explanation of the Code

This section explains the code.

```
// set the error and thank you pages                                    #1
$formurl = "feedback_form.php" ;
$errorurl = "feedback/error.php" ;
$thankyouurl = "feedback/thankyou.php" ;
$emailerrurl = "feedback/emailerr.php" ;
$errorcommenturl =  "feedback/commenterror.php" ;
// set to the email address of the recipient
$mailto = "none@noone.com" ;
```

The dummy e-mail addresses and URLs will need to be replaced by real-world addresses and URLs. Five files are assigned to variables. Four lines refer to pages containing error messages.

```
// Is first name present? If it is, sanitize it                         #2
    $first_name = filter_var( $_POST['first_name'], FILTER_SANITIZE_STRING);
if ((!empty($first_name)) && (preg_match('/[a-z\s]/i',$first_name)) &&
                (strlen($first_name) <= 30)) {
        //Save first name
        $first_nametrim = $first_name;
}else{
        $errors = 'yes';
}
```

Sanitation and validation of most variables are similar to the process-register-page code discussed in Chapter 6. However, instead of creating an error array, an errors variable is set to yes to indicate there is a problem. The e-mail and comment are the most vital information that needs to be gathered. Thus, we will treat these variables differently.

```
// Check that an email address has been entered correctly              #3
$emailtrim = filter_var( $_POST['email'], FILTER_SANITIZE_EMAIL);
if ((empty($emailtrim)) || (!filter_var($emailtrim, FILTER_VALIDATE_EMAIL))
        || (strlen($emailtrim > 60))) {
```

```
        // if email is bad display error page
        header( "Location: $emailerrurl" );
    exit ;
}
```

If the e-mail is not valid, there is no reason to continue to attempt to send the message. Thus, the e-mail error page is displayed to the user.

```
$brochure = filter_var( $_POST['brochure'], FILTER_SANITIZE_STRING);        //#4
if($brochure != "yes") {$brochure = "no";} // if not yes, then no
$letter = filter_var( $_POST['letter'], FILTER_SANITIZE_STRING);
if($letter != "yes") {$letter = "no"; } // if not yes, then no
```

If the user did not click the yes box for the brochure, we assume they did not want it and set the variable to no. This also eliminates any other possible invalid values. We also do the same with the e-mail letter variable.

```
$comment = filter_var( $_POST['comment'], FILTER_SANITIZE_STRING);        //#5
if ((!empty($comment)) && (strlen($comment) <= 480)) {
        // remove ability to create link in email
        $patterns = array("/http/", "/https/", "/\:/","/\/\//","/www./");
        $commenttrim = preg_replace($patterns," ", $comment);
}else{  // if comment not valid display error page
        header( "Location: $errorcommenturl" );
        exit;
}
```

If the comment is not properly formatted, again there is no reason to try to send the message. Thus, we call an error page related to the comment. If the comment is formatted correctly, however, an attempt might be made to include a URL link, and we will deactivate the URL link by removing the protocol header (http, https). The preg_replace function will replace any of the formats shown in the patterns array with a blank space, thus removing possible harmful entries. We are assuming the customer may have sent a link to provide information. However, we don't want it clickable for security reasons.

```
// everything OK send e-mail                                              #6
$subject = "Message from customer " . $first_nametrim . " " . $last_nametrim;
$messageproper =
"------------------------------------------------------------\n" .
"Name of sender: $first_nametrim $last_nametrim\n" .
"Email of sender: $emailtrim\n" .
"Telephone: $phonetrim\n" .
"brochure?: $brochure\n" .
"Address: $address1trim\n" .
"Address: $address2trim\n" .
"City: $citytrim\n" .
"Postcode: $zcode_pcodetrim\n" .
"Newsletter?:$letter\n" .
"----------------------- MESSAGE ------------------------\n\n" .
$commenttrim .
"\n\n------------------------------------------------------------\n" ;
```

```
mail($mailto, $subject, $messageproper, "From: \"$first_nametrim $last_nametrim\"
<$emailtrim>" );
header( "Location: $thankyouurl" );
exit ;
```

This block of code constructs the e-mail using the variables that have been sanitized and validated. Note the full stops after each item; these are important. The code \n inserts a line break (or Enter) between each item. This format is required when sending an e-mail. The last two lines send the e-mail using the PHP function mail(). After the e-mail has been sent, the user is redirected to the "thank you" page.

The "Thank You" Page and the Error Messages

The "thank you" page confirms that the e-mail was sent successfully. We have provided a return button to allow the user to keep using the site if they so choose. Figure 7-7 shows the "thank you" page, and Listing 7-7a shows the code. You could choose to replace the Return to Home Page button with your main navigation menu.

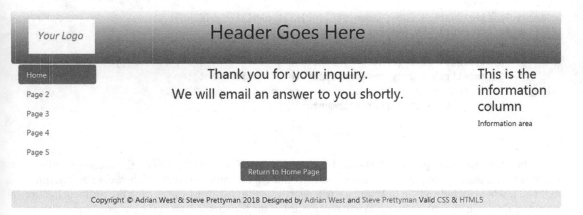

Figure 7-7. *The "thank you" page message*

Listing 7-7a. Creating the "Thank You" Page (thankyou.php)

```
<!DOCTYPE html>
<html lang="en">
<head>
  <title>Thank you for your inquiry</title>
  <meta charset="utf-8">
  <meta name="viewport" content=
      "width=device-width, initial-scale=1, shrink-to-fit=no">
  <!-- Bootstrap CSS File -->
  <link rel="stylesheet"
      href=
"https://stackpath.bootstrapcdn.com/bootstrap/4.1.0/css/bootstrap.min.css"
      integrity=
"sha384-9gVQ4dYFwwWSjIDZnLEWnxCjeSWFphJiwGPXr1jddIhOegiu1FwO5qRGvFXOdJZ4"
      crossorigin="anonymous">
</head>
<body>
```

```
<div class="container" style="margin-top:30px">
<!-- Header Section -->
<header class="jumbotron text-center row"
      style=
"margin-bottom:2px; background:linear-gradient(white, #0073e6);
      padding:20px;">
          <?php include('../includes/thankyou-header.php'); ?>
</header>
<!-- Body Section -->
<div class="row" style="padding-left: 0px;">
<!-- Left-side Column Menu Section -->
  <nav class="col-sm-2">
      <ul class="nav nav-pills flex-column">
                <?php include('../includes/nav.php'); ?>
      </ul>
  </nav>
<!-- Center Column Content Section -->
<div class="col-sm-8">
<h3 class="text-center" >Thank you for your inquiry.</h3>
<h3 class="text-center" >We will email an answer to you shortly.</h3>
</div>
<!-- Right-side Column Content Section -->
        <aside class="col-sm-2">
                <?php include('../includes/info-col.php'); ?>
        </aside>
  </div>
<div class="row col-sm-12" style="padding-left: 0px;  padding-bottom: 20px;">
<div class="col-sm-5"></div>
<nav class="col-sm-4 text-center">
<ul class="nav nav-pills">
<li class="nav-item">
        <a class="nav-link active" href="index.php">Return to Home Page</a>
</li>
</ul>
</nav>
</div>
<!-- Footer Content Section -->
<footer class="jumbotron text-center row"
style="padding-bottom:1px; padding-top:8px;">
  <?php include('../includes/footer.php'); ?>
</footer>
</div>
</body>
</html>
```

If the e-mail message was not sent successfully, an explanatory error message will appear.

Why use error pages instead of echoing a piece of text to the screen? We found that many of our clients prefer the distinct message, and the help that a page provides, rather than the usual small error messages in red that can be overlooked or that are so often too brief. If you prefer to echo messages to the page, create an $error array to hold the messages as we did in the registration page.

Listing 7-7b provides the code for the error message for empty or invalid fields.

Listing 7-7b. Creating the Page for Empty Field Errors (error.php)

```
<!DOCTYPE html>
<html lang="en">
<head>
  <title>Error Message</title>
  <meta charset="utf-8">
  <meta name="viewport" content=
      "width=device-width, initial-scale=1, shrink-to-fit=no">
  <!-- Bootstrap CSS File -->
  <link rel="stylesheet"
  href=
"https://stackpath.bootstrapcdn.com/bootstrap/4.1.0/css/bootstrap.min.css"
  integrity=
"sha384-9gVQ4dYFwwWSjIDZnLEWnxCjeSWFphJiwGPXr1jddIhOegiu1FwO5qRGvFXOdJZ4"
  crossorigin="anonymous">
</head>
<body>
<div class="container" style="margin-top:30px">
<!-- Header Section -->
<header class="jumbotron text-center row"
        style=
"margin-bottom:2px; background:linear-gradient(white, #0073e6);
        padding:20px;">
        <?php include('../includes/thankyou-header.php'); ?>
</header>
<!-- Body Section -->
<div class="row" style="padding-left: 0px;">
<!-- Left-side Column Menu Section -->
  <nav class="col-sm-2">
      <ul class="nav nav-pills flex-column">
              <?php include('../includes/nav.php'); ?>
      </ul>
  </nav>
<!-- Center Column Content Section -->
<div class="col-sm-8">
<h4 class="text-center">
One or more of the essential items in the form has not been filled in.</h4>
<h4 class="text-center">
Essential items have an asterisk like this <span>*</span></h4>
<h4 class="text-center">
Return to the form by clicking the back button on your browser<br>
        and then fill in the missing items.</h4>
</div>
<!-- Right-side Column Content Section -->
      <aside class="col-sm-2">
        <?php include('../includes/info-col.php'); ?>
      </aside>
</div>
```

```
<!-- Footer Content Section -->
<footer class="jumbotron text-center row"
style="padding-bottom:1px; padding-top:8px;">
  <?php include('../includes/footer.php'); ?>
</footer>
</div>
</body>
</html>
```

The other error pages include a similar format to this example and are not listed here. You can view them from the downloaded files for this chapter.

■ **Note**   You will need to add one more button to the main side menu (*includes/nav.php*). Label the button with the words *Contact Us* and link it to the file *feedback_form.php*.

A Common Header

You probably have noticed that we have developed a lot of headers for our individual files. We can optionally choose to handle all of our determination of buttons to display in one header by creating a universal header that includes a case statement. Let's take a look at the code in Listing 7-8.

Listing 7-8. Creating a Universal Header (header1.php)

```
<div class="col-sm-2">
<img class="img-fluid float-left" src="logo.jpg" alt="Logo">
</div>
<div class="col-sm-8">
        <h1 class="blue-text mb-4 font-bold">Header Goes Here</h1>
 </div>
    <nav class="col-sm-2">
        <div class="btn-group-vertical btn-group-sm" role="group"
                aria-label="Button Group">
        <div class="btn-group-vertical btn-group-sm" role="group"
                aria-label="Button Group">
 // Case statement to determine which buttons to display                          #1
        <?php
        switch ($menu) {
        case 1: //header.php
        ?>
                <button type="button" class="btn btn-secondary"
                onclick="location.href = 'login.php'" >Login</button>
                <button type="button" class="btn btn-secondary"
                onclick="location.href =
                        'safer-register-page.php'">Register</button>

        <?php
        break;
```

```php
        case 2: //header_members_account.php
        ?>
                <button type="button" class="btn btn-secondary"
                        onclick="location.href = 'logout.php'" >Logout</button>
                <button type="button" class="btn btn-secondary"
                        onclick="location.href = 'edit_your_account.php'">
                                Your Account</button>
        <button type="button" class="btn btn-secondary"
                        onclick="location.href =
                        'safer-register-password.php'">New Password</button>
  <?php
    break;

 case 3: // header-thanks.php
    ?>
                <button type="button" class="btn btn-secondary"
                        onclick="location.href = 'index.php'" >Cancel</button>
  <?php
    break;

case 4: // login-header.php
        ?>
                <button type="button" class="btn btn-secondary"
                        onclick="location.href = 'login.php'" >
                                Erase Entries</button>
                <button type="button" class="btn btn-secondary"
                        onclick="location.href =
                        'safer-register-page.php'">Register</button>
        <button type="button" class="btn btn-secondary"
                onclick="location.href = 'index.php'">Cancel</button>
<?php
   break;

case 5: //; members-header.php
        ?>
                <button type="button" class="btn btn-secondary"
                        onclick="location.href = 'logout.php'" >Logout</button>
          <button type="button" class="btn btn-secondary"
                onclick="location.href = 'change-password.php'" >
                        New Password</button>
<?php
    break;

case 6: //password-header.php
        ?>
                <button type="button" class="btn btn-secondary"
                        onclick="location.href = 'register-password.php'" >
                        Erase Entries</button>
        <button type="button" class="btn btn-secondary"
                        onclick="location.href = 'index.php'">Cancel</button>
<?php
    break;
```

```
case 7: //password-header.php
      ?>
                <button type="button" class="btn btn-secondary"
                onclick="location.href = 'index.php'" >Home Page</button>
<?php
   break;

case 8: //thankyou-header.php
      ?>
                <!-- <button type="button" class="btn btn-secondary"
                onclick="location.href = 'index.php'" >Home Page</button>-->
<?php
   break;
case 9: //register-header.php
      ?>
                <button type="button" class="btn btn-secondary"
                          onclick="location.href = 'register-page'" >
                       Erase Your Entries</button>
                <button type="button" class="btn btn-secondary"
                          onclick="location.href = 'index.php'">Cancel
                          </button>
<?php
    break;
}
?>
</div>
</nav>
```

Explanation of the Code

This section explains the code.

```
// Case statement to determine which buttons to display                    #1
      <?php
      switch ($menu) {
      case 1: //header.php
        ?>
                <button type="button" class="btn btn-secondary"
                onclick="location.href = 'login.php'" >Login</button>
                <button type="button" class="btn btn-secondary"
                onclick="location.href =
                        'safer-register-page.php'">Register</button>

      <?php
       break;
```

The variable $menu is checked to determine which combination of buttons to display in the header. To use this common header, two changes must occur in each of the files.

1. A variable must be created in the file holding the number corresponding to the set of buttons to be displayed. For example, in the file *index.php*, the following code can be added to the top of the file:

```php
<?php
        $menu = 1;
?>
```

2. The include statement that pulls in the header must also be updated to include the new header. For example, in the *index.php* file (and all the files to be updated), the update code would be as shown here:

```php
include("include/header1.php");
```

The files in this chapter have not be updated to include the universal header. However, the user can update them using the previous steps. For an example of the use of a common header, view the downloaded files from Chapter 11.

Logging Exceptions and Error

For several chapters we have included the ability to handle exceptions and errors using catch blocks. However, we have done nothing more than display a generic message. To complete our application, we should provide the ability to be notified when problems occur. The easiest way to provide this ability is to place error messages in a log file. PHP applications can log messages into the default PHP error file or in an application-specific file. It is common for an application to have separate files for informational logs, authentication (login) logs, error logs, and security logs. You can create a constant at the top of your program code to indicate the location of your log file(s). This allows anyone who supports your code to quickly determine the location of the file(s) and allows them to easily change the location when required.

```php
define(ERROR_LOG,"errors.log");
```

Using this constant we can then send error information to the log file using the error_log function.

```php
error_log("A general error",3,ERROR_LOG);
```

This would send the message shown directly to the *errors.log* file. However, this does not give us enough meaningful information. For example, we probably want to include the time and date of the occurrence and a title indicating the type of message.

```php
$date = date('m.d.y h:i:s');
$errormessage = "This is the error";
$eMessage = $date . " | User Error | " . $errormessage . "\n";
error_log($eMessage,3,ERROR_LOG);
```

The code would produce the following:

```
07.04.2018 03:00:55 | User Error | This is the error
```

A standard text editor (Notepad++) or a log-monitoring software program can be used to view the contents of a log file.

PHP also makes it easy to send an e-mail alert when something has been written to the log file. Of course, your file must exist on a server that includes an e-mail server. We can add the e-mail information into another error_log statement as follows:

```
error_log("Date/Time: $date - Serious Problem. Check error log for details", 1 ,
noone@helpme.com, "Subject: User Errors \nFrom: Error Log <errorlog@helpme.com>" . "\r\n");
```

The first parameter specifies the message of the e-mail. The second parameter informs the error_log to e-mail this information. The third parameter provides the "To" e-mail address. The fourth parameter is an extra header field. This field is commonly used to include the subject of the e-mail and the e-mail address that sent the message. The "From" address must be included or the message will not be sent.

In the downloaded code for this chapter, we have included the error_log code to send errors to an error_log and to send an e-mail when there are problems. The snippet of this code is shown here:

```
catch(Exception $e) // We finally handle any problems here
    {
        // print "An Exception occurred. Message: " . $e->getMessage();
        print "The system is busy please try later";
        $date = date('m.d.y h:i:s');
        $errormessage = $e->getMessage();
        $eMessage = $date . " | Exception Error | " , $errormessage . |\n";
        error_log($eMessage,3,ERROR_LOG);
        // e-mail support person to alert there is a problem
        error_log("Date/Time: $date - Exception Error, Check error log for
            details", 1, noone@helpme.com, "Subject: Exception Error \nFrom: Error Log
            <errorlog@helpme.com>" . "\r\n");
    }
```

The format of the Error catch block would be similar, with the difference of changing the titles to indicate that it is an error and not an exception. We could also change it to save the errors in a different log file. This code is commented out in the download files until you are ready to use it.

Now that you have built-in exception handling and error handling, before upgrading your programs to production, you need to edit the *php.ini* file to turn off error reporting to the user.

When you are ready, you will need to locate the *php.ini* configuration file. In XAMPP you can easily find the file by going into the Control Panel and clicking the config button to the right of the Apache server, as shown in Figure 7-8.

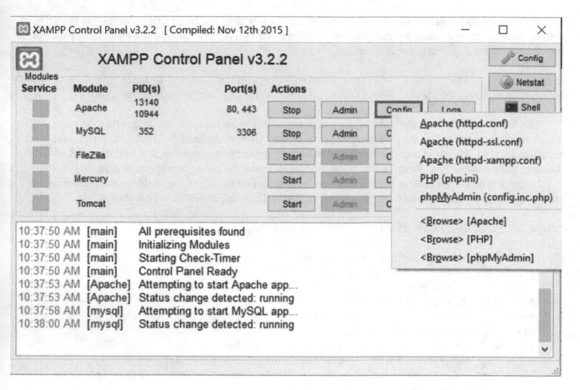

Figure 7-8. *Finding the php.ini configuration file*

Click the *php.ini* menu selection to open it. For easyPHP you will have to dig down into the development server folder to find the *php.ini* file. It should be in a location similar to the link shown here:

```
C:\Users\yourcomputername\EasyPHP-Devserver-17\EasyPHP-Devserver-17\eds-binaries\php\
php713vc14x86x170718155219
```

Of course, your version name and the build numbers will be different than shown. Once you find the file, open it with Notepad++ or another text editor.

Immediately save the current version of the config file with another name (and remember where you saved it) just in case you make a mistake and need to revert to the original settings.

Locate this line: display_errors = On. Change the setting to the following: display_errors = Off. Save the file. Then turn the Apache server off and on. Your error messages should now be directed to the error log instead of the web page. This, of course, does not include any error messages that were created for the user with echo statements (such as your e-mail is missing).

Now we might be ready to move our files to a remote production server. Let's look at the process to accomplish this.

Migrating the Database and Tables to a Remote Host

Having created a database and table(s) using phpMyAdmin, how can we transfer them to a hosting company? The process for migrating a database from XAMPP or easyPHP to a remote host worries beginners more than any other aspect of database development. This is because MySQL/MariaDB manuals and Internet tutorials rarely provide proper explanations for the procedure.

For this tutorial, we chose to use the finalpostal database, which is included in the *users.sql* file included with this chapter.

■ **Caution**   You will need to determine which operating system is used in your chosen hosting package. Linux and Windows require a slightly different migration procedure.

A Puzzling Error Message

You may experience an occasional problem when trying to transfer a database to another computer. An error message sometimes appears saying that the table already exists. This is weird because there is definitely not a table in that empty database. The solution is to access the *XAMPP* or *easyPHP* folder on the first computer and then drill down to the *MySQL/MariaDB* folder and then the *Data* folder. Save a copy of the *somefilename.frm* file on a flash drive (memory stick) or in the cloud. Now copy that file into the same data folder on the destination computer, and the problem will be solved. You should regularly save copies of the *.frm* files as well as the SQL dumps in case you need to recover data after the database has been corrupted. For other error messages, copy and paste the message into a search engine (like Google) to discover suggested solutions.

Creating and Exporting the SQL File

The first stage for migrating a database consists of creating a SQL export file. You will be able to export two types of dumps: for the tables only or for the database and tables. We will be using the tables-only file. If your database is large, you should import tables individually. We will use phpMyAdmin to export the file. The exported SQL file is a simple text file with the name format of *filename.sql*, although other file types can be chosen for the exported file. The content of the file and the process will be explained next.

To Create a Dump File of a Table or Tables

Open a browser and in the address bar type **http://localhost/phpmyadmin/**.

In the left panel of phpMyAdmin, click the database containing the tables to be exported. Then click the Export tab to display the page shown in Figure 7-9.

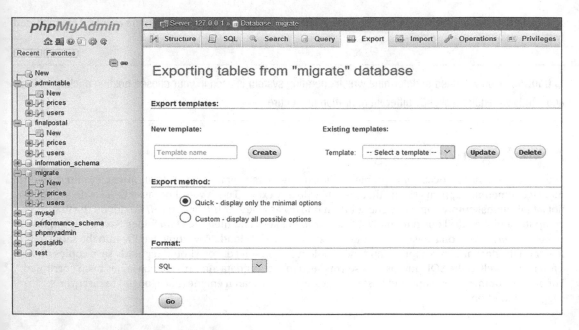

Figure 7-9. The screen for dumping the database table

Select the Quick option and ensure that the format is SQL. Then click the Go button. Depending on your browser and settings, you will be asked whether to open or save the file, as shown in Figure 7-10.

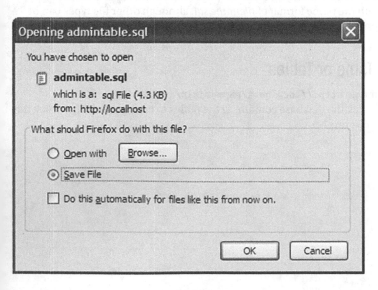

Figure 7-10. Choose to save the SQL file

Choose to save the file and click OK. Save the file in a folder where you can access it to upload it to the host later. The default location, in Windows, of all downloaded files is the *Downloads* folder.

What Does a SQL Dump Look Like?

Examine the *users.sql* file in your text editor (such as Notepad++).
You will see many commented-out lines. SQL supports three comment styles as follows:

- A line beginning with a hash symbol like this: *#some text*

- A line beginning with a double dash followed by a space like this: *-- some text*

- A block of text between tags like this:

  ```
  /*some text
  some text
  some text*/
  ```

An example of the dump for the tables in the finalpostal database is shown next (your dump might be slightly different). This is the code in the *users.sql* file provided with the chapter files.

```
-- phpMyAdmin SQL Dump
-- version 4.8.0
-- https://www.phpmyadmin.net/
--
-- Host: 127.0.0.1
-- Generation Time: Dec 31, 2017 at 06:40 PM
-- Server version: 10.1.22-MariaDB
-- PHP Version: 7.1.4
```

This code specifies the versions of applications on the original computer. This is for information only and is in comments.

```
SET SQL_MODE = "NO_AUTO_VALUE_ON_ZERO";
SET AUTOCOMMIT = 0;
START TRANSACTION;
SET time_zone = "+00:00";

/*!40101 SET @OLD_CHARACTER_SET_CLIENT=@@CHARACTER_SET_CLIENT */;
/*!40101 SET @OLD_CHARACTER_SET_RESULTS=@@CHARACTER_SET_RESULTS */;
/*!40101 SET @OLD_COLLATION_CONNECTION=@@COLLATION_CONNECTION */;
/*!40101 SET NAMES utf8mb4 */;
```

Notice that the utf8 version is included in these comments:

```
--
-- Database: `finalpost`
--


-- --------------------------------------------------------


--
-- Table structure for table `prices`
--
```

```
CREATE TABLE `prices` (
  `oneyeargb` decimal(6,0) UNSIGNED NOT NULL,
  `oneyearus` decimal(6,0) UNSIGNED NOT NULL,
  `fiveyeargb` decimal(6,0) UNSIGNED NOT NULL,
  `fiveyearus` decimal(6,0) UNSIGNED NOT NULL,
  `militarygb` decimal(6,0) UNSIGNED NOT NULL,
  `militaryus` decimal(6,0) UNSIGNED NOT NULL,
  `u21gb` decimal(6,0) UNSIGNED NOT NULL,
  `u21us` decimal(6,0) UNSIGNED NOT NULL,
  `minpricegb` decimal(6,0) UNSIGNED NOT NULL,
  `minpriceus` decimal(6,0) UNSIGNED NOT NULL
) ENGINE=InnoDB DEFAULT CHARSET=utf8;
```

This is the actual SQL code that creates the prices table:

```
--
-- Dumping data for table `prices`
--

INSERT INTO `prices` (`oneyeargb`, `oneyearus`, `fiveyeargb`, `fiveyearus`, `militarygb`,
`militaryus`, `u21gb`, `u21us`, `minpricegb`, `minpriceus`) VALUES
('30', '40', '125', '140', '5', '8', '2', '3', '15', '20');
```

This is the SQL code that loads the data into the prices table:

```
-- --------------------------------------------------------

--
-- Table structure for table `users`
--

CREATE TABLE `users` (
  `userid` mediumint(6) UNSIGNED NOT NULL,
  `title` tinytext NOT NULL,
  `first_name` varchar(30) NOT NULL,
  `last_name` varchar(40) NOT NULL,
  `email` varchar(50) NOT NULL,
  `password` char(60) NOT NULL,
  `registration_date` datetime NOT NULL,
  `class` char(20) NOT NULL,
  `user_level` tinyint(2) UNSIGNED NOT NULL,
  `address1` varchar(50) NOT NULL,
  `address2` varchar(50) DEFAULT NULL,
  `city` varchar(50) NOT NULL,
  `state_country` char(25) NOT NULL,
  `zcode_pcode` char(10) NOT NULL,
  `phone` char(15) DEFAULT NULL,
  `paid` enum('No','Yes') NOT NULL,
  `secret` varchar(30) DEFAULT NULL
) ENGINE=InnoDB DEFAULT CHARSET=utf8;
```

This is the code that creates the users table:

```
--
-- Dumping data for table `users`
--

INSERT INTO `users` (`user_id`, `title`, `first_name`, `last_name`, `email`, `password`,
`registration_date`, `class`, `user_level`, `address1`, `address2`, `city`, `state_country`,
`zcode_pcode`, `phone`, `paid`) VALUES
(1, 'Mr', 'Mike', 'Rosoft', 'miker@myisp.com', '$2y$10$UiiBhmXca.0/bwopveFq8uInuX.
EVrecinUQYQG546WjAWwZLJNoe', '2017-12-06 08:43:41', '30', 0, '4 The Street', 'The Village',
'Townsville', 'USA', 'WA', '0123777888', 'Yes'),
 (32, 'Mr', 'James', 'Smith', 'jsmith@myisp.co.uk', '$2y$10$Yu.c/cw/TSFa9vcMBGAfAe5vzyOwp3
SZarBVc/9vEksfp.F8BzSiW', '2017-12-29 11:58:51', '30', 0, '2 The Street', '', 'Townsville',
'UK', 'EX24 6PS', '01234777888', 'Yes');
```

The previous code loads data into the users table. Only the first and last records are shown to save space.

```
--
-- Indexes for dumped tables
--


--
-- Indexes for table `users`
--
ALTER TABLE `users`
  ADD PRIMARY KEY (`userid`);
```

This code defines user_id as the primary key:

```
--
-- AUTO_INCREMENT for dumped tables
--


--
-- AUTO_INCREMENT for table `users`
--
ALTER TABLE `users`
  MODIFY `user_id` mediumint(6) UNSIGNED NOT NULL AUTO_INCREMENT, AUTO_INCREMENT=35;COMMIT;
```

This code refines the primary key to the settings requested in the original design:

```
/*!40101 SET CHARACTER_SET_CLIENT=@OLD_CHARACTER_SET_CLIENT */;
/*!40101 SET CHARACTER_SET_RESULTS=@OLD_CHARACTER_SET_RESULTS */;
/*!40101 SET COLLATION_CONNECTION=@OLD_COLLATION_CONNECTION */;
```

The next steps accomplish the following:

- Examining the destination server (the host) and preparing it to receive the SQL file and the contents of the *htdocs* or *eds-www* folder

- Uploading the SQL file (or use the import feature on the remote host) and website files to the host

- Importing the SQL file using phpMyAdmin in the host

Investigate the Remote Host's Server

We will assume that you have purchased space for your website and registered a domain name either with your host provider or with another party. Many providers allow you to choose a hosting package that uses Linux/Unix or a Microsoft web server. While many websites are hosted on Unix servers, this is a common preference; it not a requirement.

Before choosing your host provider, make sure that packages they provide include PHP, phpMyAdmin, and MySQL (or MariaDB). Also, especially if you are selecting a Unix operating system, make sure that Apache is provided. PHP and MySQL can now also interface with Microsoft's web server. However, the host provider can choose to use Apache with a Microsoft server, as you may have implemented on your computer. If you are not sure whether PHP and MySQL (or MariaDB) are installed at the host, type the following in a text editor and save it as *phpinfo.php*:

```
<?php
phpinfo();
?>
```

Your will want to either save this phpinfo file in a secure location or remove it after testing to prevent anyone from seeing what is installed on your server.

Use your FTP client, or the host provided process to upload files, to load this file and then open it in a browser (enter a URL like **http://yourwebsitename.com/phpinfo.php**). You will see a table like the one in Figure 7-11. Scroll down the table, and you should see details of the MySQLi installation on the host's server. If you see a version of MySQLi installed and this program ran, then you should be able to upload and run the programs from this book.

System	Windows NT ADRIAN-3CBBE1C0 5.1 build 2600 (Windows XP Home Edition Service Pack 3) i586
Build Date	Jan 10 2012 16:15:55
Compiler	MSVC9 (Visual C++ 2008)
Architecture	x86
Configure Command	cscript /nologo configure.js "--enable-snapshot-build" "--disable-isapi" "--enable-debug-pack" "--disable-isapi" "--without-mssql" "--without-pdo-mssql" "--without-pi3web" "--with-pdo-oci=D:\php-sdk\oracle\instantclient10\sdk,shared" "--with-oci8=D:\php-sdk\oracle\instantclient10\sdk,shared" "--with-oci8-11g=D:\php-sdk\oracle\instantclient11\sdk,shared" "--enable-object-out-dir=../obj/" "--enable-com-dotnet" "--with-mcrypt=static" "--disable-static-analyze"
Server API	Apache 2.0 Handler
Virtual Directory Support	enabled
Configuration File (php.ini) Path	C:\WINDOWS
Loaded Configuration File	C:\Program Files\EasyPHP-5.3.9\apache\php.ini
Scan this dir for additional .ini files	(none)
Additional .ini files parsed	(none)
PHP API	20090626
PHP Extension	20090626
Zend Extension	220090626
Zend Extension Build	API220090626,TS,VC9
PHP Extension Build	API20090626,TS,VC9
Debug Build	no

Figure 7-11. *The result of opening phpinfo.php in a server*

■ **Caution** Some basic hosting packages do not accept databases. In this case, you will have to upgrade to a more expensive package. Check the product range on your intended host before proceeding.

Using the GUIs on a Remote Host's Server

Read the documentation or contact a service representative for your host provider to determine how to access phpMyAdmin or a similar type of program to create, upload, and modify MySQL/MariaDB databases. Your host provider may include a control panel, like Figure 7-12, or may provide another way to access phpMyAdmin.

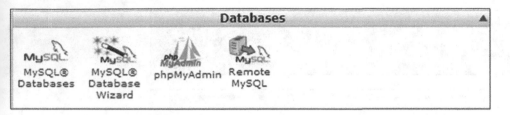

Figure 7-12. *The database section of the control panel*

To install the database, follow these steps:

- Open phpMyAdmin and create an empty database. In this example, we will create the finalpostal database.

When creating the finalpostal database, either the resulting database will have the name finalpostal or the host will add a prefix to the database name. Hosts that add a prefix nearly always append the website owner's user ID for accessing the control panel. Let's assume the owner's user ID is mywebsite; the host might create the database name as *mywebsite_finalpostal*. In this example, we will assume that the database name has the prefix *myusername*.

- Now you must immediately protect the newly created database by creating a user ID and a password. Do this by using phpMyAdmin as described in previous chapters. (Some hosts will automatically provide the user ID—if that's the case, use that one.)

Create a user with the following details:

- *User*: webmaster (or a name provided by the host)
- *Password*: c0ff33p0t
- *Host*: (the name of your website URL)

The password in a real-world database must be much more complex than *c0ff33p0t*. Make a careful note of the database name, password, and user.

Connecting to the Database on the Remote Host

Now that we know the name of the empty database (in this example, it is myusername_finalpostal), we can amend the connection file to suit the remote host. Do not create this in XAMPP's *htdocs* or easyPHP's *eds-www* folder on your computer. If you do, you will no longer be able to access the finalpostal database from your database-driven pages on your computer's server. Use a text editor such as Notepad++ to create the file and store the new *mysqli_connect.php* file anywhere except in the *htdocs* or *eds-www* folder. The amended file is not included in the downloadable files because it would be unique for your database. The code might be as shown in the next snippet of code.

The Snippet of Code for Connecting to the New Database (mysqli_connection.php)

```php
<?php
// Create a connection to the admintable database and set the encoding
// The user name might be provided by the host.
// If not, use the name from your XAMPP version
Define ('DB_USER', 'webmaster');
Define ('DB_PASSWORD', 'c0ff33p0t');
```

```
Define ('DB_HOST', 'www.yourwebsite.com');
Define ('DB_NAME', 'myusername_admintable');
// Make the connection
$dbcon = new mysqli(DB_HOST, DB_USER, DB_PASSWORD, DB_NAME);
// Set the encoding...optional but recommended
mysqli_set_charset($dbcon, 'utf8');
```

You now have all the following items necessary for migrating the database-driven website to the remote host:

- An account and a domain name registered with the remote host
- A newly created empty database located on the host's server
- The SQL dump files for the tables
- The folder containing the includes and the folder containing the images
- The modified *mysqli_connect.php* file

The main PHP and HTML files need an amendment before they can be uploaded, and this amendment is described in the next section.

Securely Uploading the *mysqli_connection.php* File

For maximum security, the database connection file should be located outside the root folder. The file is then not directly accessible via the website. Make sure the folder in which it resides is secured from outside access.

Most hosting companies provide the ability to use an FTP program to upload and change files on their servers. There are many free FTP programs available, including FileZilla (https://filezilla-project.org/). The FTP program settings that will work for your site will depend on the security settings provided by the hosting company. You will also need a user ID, password (which may or may not be different from your normal user ID and password to access your host account), and your URL or TCP/IP address. You will be restricted to access only your folders and files. Figure 7-13 shows an example FTP window that includes a typical folder structure for a Linux/Unix remote host.

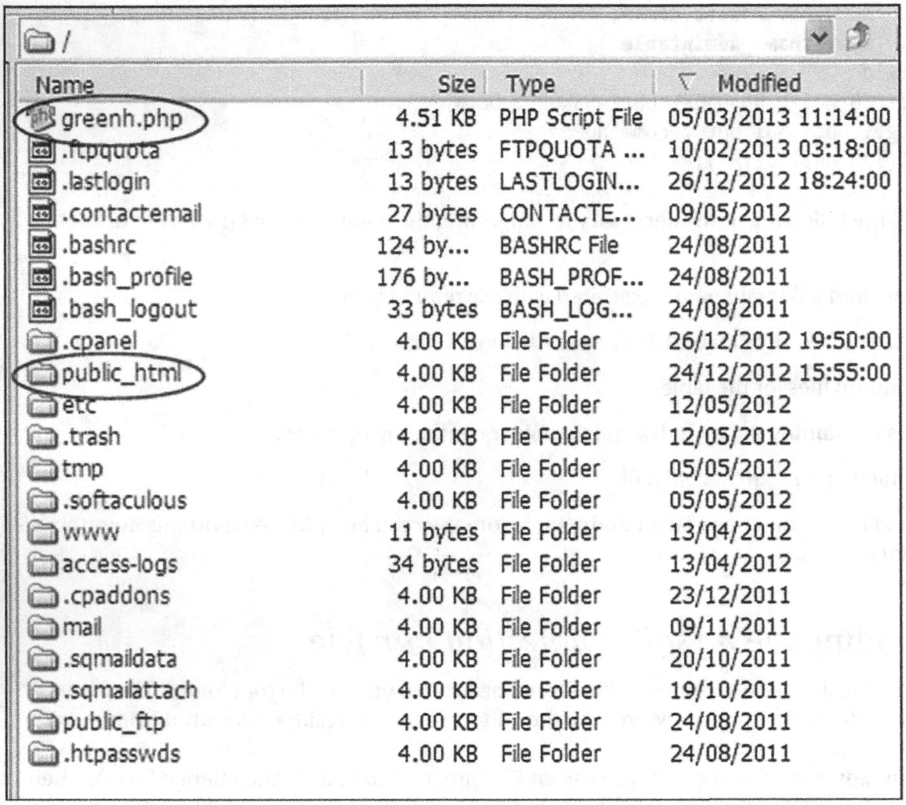

Figure 7-13. *Typical files and folders for a Linux/Unix environment as shown in an FTP program's window*

In Figure 7-13, the database connection file (circled) has been renamed as *greenh.php* and uploaded outside the *public_html* root folder (circled). This folder exists within Linux/Unix operations systems to house any websites displayed to the public. On a Microsoft web server, this folder may be named *www*, *htdocs*, or similar. The user of your website will not have access to any files that do not reside in a public folder (*public_html*). Your host might also only allow you access to this public folder and not access to the root level, as shown in Figure 7-13.

If you can locate the connection file (*greenh.php*) outside the public folder (*public_html*) on the host, none of your current interactive pages will be able to find it. To solve this, use your code editor to open every file that contains a *mysqli_connect.php* link and run a Find and Replace All operation to amend its location as follows.

Find *mysqli_connect.php* and replace it with *../greenh.php*. The symbols *../* tell the pages that the file is located one level above the current folder. For connecting to the database on your own computer/server, you may have used require ('mysqli_connect.php'); as provided in the example files for this book. Remember, that the user will not normally see the link to the connection file, because any PHP code is executed on the server and only the results, such as information pulled from the database, are displayed to the user. However, we do want to be as secure as possible just in case the unexpected happens.

Now that the connection file is safer and the interactive pages have been modified to match, you can upload the HTML, CSS, and PHP pages to the remote host.

Uploading the Interactive Pages to the Host

The final steps are as follows:

- The public folder that will hold your web pages does not include an *htdocs* or *eds-www* folder. These folder names are specific to the development package (XAMPP or EasyPHP) that was used to create the pages. The actual folder names are not necessary in a live environment. The web server knows that all publicly available web pages reside in the public folder (*public_html*, *www*, or *htdocs*). Therefore, you need to use your FTP client (FileZilla) to upload the HTML, CSS, and PHP pages from your finalpostal's *htdocs* or *eds-www* folder into the public folder in the host's server. Because you already uploaded an amended and renamed *mysqli_connect.php* file, take great care not to upload the unmodified version. Now use your FTP client to create a subfolder (such as SQL) in your public folder. Upload the SQL files that will be used to install the tables into the database.

- Open and sign into phpMyAdmin (or the similar host-provided program) on the remote server.

- In phpMyAdmin, on the left panel, click the name of the newly created empty database, and click the Import tab.

- You will be asked to select the SQL file to be imported. Browse to the *public_html* folder, then to the subfolder (*SQL*), and find each uploaded SQL file. Open it (or them) and then click Go.

- Your public folder might have a default *index.html* file. Your new *index.php* file must replace the HTML file; otherwise, *index.html* will load instead of your *index.php* file. Rename the *index.html* file at the host as *old-index.html* or delete it. The web server will search for all index files with different extensions. If it finds an index file with an *.html* extension, it will attempt to display that file as the main page for the website. If that file does not exist, it will look for other index files, such as *index.php*.

Now view your uploaded interactive website online by typing your website's URL into the address field of a browser. Note, if you decided to load your files under a subfolder instead of directly in the public folder, include that folder name in your URL, such as http://yourwebsite.com/finalpostal/. You should see your home page, and from there you can test the website. Make sure to test all of your pages that interact with the database to ensure that your database connections are correct.

Be aware that you might have to wait a little while for some hosts to update their server cache (memory) to display your web page changes. Web pages are displayed using Domain Name System (DNS) servers. These servers convert the website name to an actual TCP/IP numerical address that uniquely identifies the location of your website. If you made changes to your URL address or the index page, the DNS servers will also gradually update this information.

As with any computer work, backups are an essential precaution against hardware or software failure. These backup files also will provide the ability to roll back to an earlier version of your files, if you discover some major coding issues.

Backing Up Your Database

While you are learning to create and use databases and websites that use databases, these four steps are essential:

1. Continue writing in your notebook or a software note-keeping system.

2. Be sure to update your flowchart.

3. Use the Export tab in phpMyAdmin to back up your tables.

4. Back up your *htdocs* or *eds-www* folder.

Recording important steps and details such as usernames and passwords can save a lot of grief. While creating many experimental databases and variations of those databases, you cannot possibly remember the details of each one. Also, you will not remember all changes you have made from day to day (or week to week). Record the details of each stage of changes you have completed and what you intended to do next. This will especially be important if you must stop for an extended period of time (maybe to update some other clients' websites). Clients never seem to request updates singly; they come in bunches, with four or five clients clamoring for updates at the same time.

Also record useful website URLs. If you come across a helpful tip in a book or blog, make a note of it. This can save you from having to crawl through your shelf of books or many blogs to find the item again. A ring-back notebook is ideal because you can insert dividers to help you find where you wrote that vital bit of information. But if you are not old-school, an electronic notebook will also be a good choice.

For backups, use phpMyAdmin (or the database management system provided by your host) to export SQL dumps for the tables from each database. Then save them to a USB flash drive or other cloud location so that you can recover your tables from a known good timeframe in case they become corrupted.

Make a copy of the *htdocs* or *eds-www* folder on a flash drive or on a cloud drive so that you have the most recent versions of successful and tested web pages. Store them (and your SQL files) in multiple locations so you do not suffer when a hard disk or OS failure occurs. Also, consider creating a XAMPP or easyPHP environment on another computer. Extra work is entailed in keeping each copy of the website up-to-date, but if a computer dies, you can continue working on another computer. Peace of mind is a wonderful thing.

You should also set up the automatic backup system that every website host provides to ensure that your data is automatically backed up and can be automatically recovered if something happens.

Summary

In this chapter, we added some last-minute improvements suggested by the client and the membership secretary. These included allowing registered members to update their own details. The client also asked for an inquiry form for the website. All these additions to the website were described and listed. The chapter provided some extra features you can add to your website, including the ability to log errors. The chapter concluded with a full description of the procedures for migrating a database to a host and backing up database tables.

In the next chapter, we will learn how to create a product catalog for a real estate agent.

■ ■ ■

Create a Product Catalog

In the previous chapters, you have learned the basics of PHP and MySQL/MariaDB. These concepts have provided a foundation that can be used to create a full database-driven website. In this chapter, we will use these skills and an example product catalog to create a fully functional database-driven site. Most e-commerce websites incorporate a catalog to display products and services. Some websites use catalogs to display items that cannot be purchased over the Internet, such as tourist attractions or houses. The tutorials in this chapter assume a real estate agency is offering various types of houses in a limited region. Real estate is an excellent example of a website that has a catalog for the user to browse but not actually purchase anything. Buying a house (for most people) over the Internet is impractical. Sensible buyers will view a property and its location before even considering the purchase.

Because so many people are involved in the purchase and sale of a house, their actions must all be carefully coordinated. The parties involved include the seller, the buyer, the real estate agent, separate lawyers for the buyer and seller, the buyer's and seller's banks or mortgage companies, and the buyer's surveyor. In addition, there will probably be a chain of events involved—for example, the sellers cannot proceed with the transaction until they have found and agreed to buy another house. Similarly, buyers cannot proceed until they have a firm offer on their current house. These dependencies highlight the reasons why providing just a house catalog on a real estate website is logical. Attempting to provide all the different transactions that must occur for the sale to be complete would be complicated and impractical.

After completing this chapter, you will be able to

- Design and prepare a database and administration plan

- Create a real estate database and table

- Create a searchable home page where users can find a suitable house

- Create a page for the administrator to view the entire stock of houses or search for and view a specific house

- Create code that display pages that provide the full specification of each property listed

- Create an inquiry form for users interested in viewing a house

Preparing the Database and Administration Plan

As with any project, we must involve the user (owner) in the development process. A user who has been engaged in the complete life cycle of the development process is much more likely to be happy with the final product. To begin the process, we must first gather any important information that will determine the design and limitations of the completed site.

After our meeting with the real estate agency owner, we have agreed on the following priorities:

- The most important page is the search page. This must engage the user by enabling them to quickly find any houses in which they are interested.

- The following are the top priorities when searching for a house:

  - Location

  - Price

  - Number of bedrooms

  - Type of house

Therefore, the search page will contain fields for these four items:

- The approximate location of a house will be disclosed, but the street name and house number must not be disclosed. This prevents users from bypassing the real estate agent and going directly to the house owner. In addition, this provides security to the home owner, and the agent, as no one will have access to the house location unless escorted by an agent. Any potential clients will already be screened by the real estate office before being shown a house for security and financial reasons.

- The term *Vacant Possession* will not be used. A house that is empty is a magnet for miscreants. Vacant houses can be vandalized, be illegally occupied, or provide a security risk for the selling agent and their clients.

- The real estate agent's photographer will provide a thumbnail image (*.jpg*, *.gif*, or *.png* file) for each house. Thumbnail images will be 150 pixels wide with a maximum height of 120 pixels. The photographer also will provide enlarged versions of the photographs for the full specification pages; these will be standardized at 350 pixels wide. The photographer will take extra caution to ensure that no latitude, longitude, or other directional indications are embedded in the image itself.

■ **Caution** A catalog always contains images, but the real estate's administrator might not be able to handle them. The real estate company administrator would need to place new images in the appropriate folders on the remote host via an FTP client. The administrator would also need basic HTML and CSS skills to format text for house descriptions. We will assume that the administrator does not have these skills. Thus, the solution we will adopt is to ask the webmaster to administer the contents of the site.

First, we need to create the new database.

Creating a New Database

To create a new database, follow these steps:

1. In the *htdocs* folder within *xampp* or in the EasyPHP folder *eds_www*, create a new folder named *estate*.

2. Download the files for Chapter 8 from the book's link at Apress.com and unzip them in your new *estate* folder.

3. In the address field of a browser, enter `localhost/phpmyadmin/` to access phpMyAdmin.

4. Click the Databases tab and create a database named *estatedb*. Choose utf8_general_ci from the pull-down collation list and then click Create.

5. Click the Privileges tab and then scroll down and click Add new user.

6. Enter these details:

   - *Username*: smeeton

   - *Password*: L1ghth0us3

   - *Host*: Localhost

7. In the left panel, click the box next to the database estatedb.

8. Do not enter anything on the next screen, but click the Import tab.

9. Click the Browse button and navigate to the *estate* folder and the SQL dump file *houses.sql*.

10. Click the *houses.sql* file and then click the Open button. The field will fill with the URL of the dump file.

11. Ensure that the Character set in the pull-down menu is utf-8 and that the Format is shown as SQL.

12. Click Go.

Creating the File for Connecting to the Database

Name the file *mysqli_connect.php*. If you are using the download files, this file is already created for you and can be found in the folder named *estate*.

```php
<?php
// Create a connection to the migrate database and to MySQL
// Set the encoding to utf-8
// Set the database access details as constants
Define ('DB_USER', 'smeeton');
Define ('DB_PASSWORD', 'L1ghth0us3');
Define ('DB_HOST', 'localhost');
Define ('DB_NAME', 'estatedb');
// Make the connection:
$dbcon = new mysqli(DB_HOST, DB_USER, DB_PASSWORD, DB_NAME);
// Set the encoding...optional but recommended
mysqli_set_charset($dbcon, 'utf8');
?>
```

The houses table and its content (along with a users table) were created when you imported and ran the *houses.sql* file previously. Verify the houses table created has the columns shown in Table 8-1.

Table 8-1. *The Attributes for the houses Database Table*

Column Name	Type	Length/Value	Default	Attributes	NULL	Index	A_I
ref_number	MEDIUMINT	6	None	UNSIGNED	☐	Primary	☑
location	TINYINT	60	None		☐		☐
price	DECIMAL	9,2	None		☐		☐
type	TINYTEXT	50	None		☐		☐
mini_description	VARCHAR	100	None		☐		☐
bedrooms	TINYINT	2	None		☐		☐
thumb	VARCHAR	45	None		☐		☐
full_description	VARCHAR	600	None		☐		☐
full_picture	VARCHAR	45	None		☐		☐
status	TINYTEXT	30	None		☐		☐

The house reference number will be used by viewers when they inquire about a property. This value will also be used to display details about the house when the user clicks the Details link.

The column type MEDIUMINT (when unsigned) allows integers from 0 to 8,388,606. This size will provide the real estate company with a lot of space for potential inquires.

TINYTEXT allows up to 255 characters. This provides plenty of flexibility to describe the bedrooms.

DECIMAL allows prices up to the limit set by the first number shown in the table. The second number indicates the number of decimal places. The size 9,2 means that when entering nine figures, such as 123456789, the recorded result will be 1234567.89. This allows inquires for up to almost 410 million! The column thumb holds the URL of an image—for example, *images/thumbs/house_01.jpg*. We have allowed 45 characters in the thumbnail image column because the file names for thumbnails are often long—for instance, *images/thumbs/bungalow_South_Devon_150px.png*.

The full_description column will contain the detailed description of the house. The administrator can enter HTML and CSS to control the format of the text in this field. The full_picture column hosts the URL link for each house's enlarged image.

The status column will indicate whether the house is available, under offer, withdrawn from the market, or sold.

Security

As previously described, an unskilled administrator would not be able to cope with the preparation of images and might not be capable of using an FTP program to place new images inside the appropriate folder at the remote host. Because these tasks must be performed by the webmaster, the webmaster will be the administrator. The skilled webmaster can use phpMyAdmin for any changes.

Any administration pages that are created also need to be secured with a user ID and password. These pages would include session code (security guard) similar to examples we have seen in previous chapters. The downloadable files for this chapter include a users table, a register page, and a login page.

No login menu button is provided in the website. Only the administrator knows that this exists, and they will enter localhost/estate/login.php to access the login page.

The users table includes our administrator Jack Smith from the previous chapter whose information can be used to access any administration page. Jack's sign-in information is as follows:

- *E-mail*: jsmith@outcook.com

- *Password*: D0g3b@dy

Based on the agreed specifications, the required pages will be as follows:

- The home page, which includes a house search ability for the user (*index.php*).

- The search results page, which displays the houses selected by the user's search criteria.

- A full-specification page, which displays the details of each individual house. The user accesses this information by clicking a link on the search results page.

- The Contact Us page, which will be used for user inquiries.

- An administration page, which will be provided so that the webmaster can conveniently view the whole stock of houses.

- Another administration page, which will allow the webmaster to search for and view a specific house.

- The administrator can also add new houses. Only the webmaster knows the URL for this page, and it is not accessible from the website. As an additional precaution, the admin page will not include the word *admin* in the page title; it has the less obvious name *advert.php*.

None of the preceding pages allows the list of houses to be edited or deleted. The administrator will use phpMyAdmin to edit and delete houses. We can now create a home page for the real estate website.

Creating a Home Page with Search Capability

Figure 8-1 shows the home page.

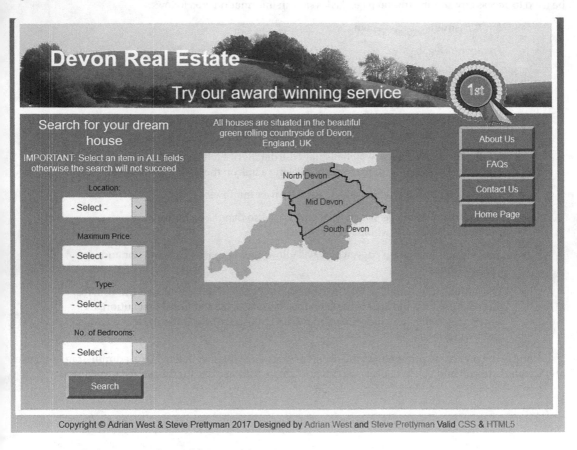

Figure 8-1. *The home page for a real estate website*

The green background for the pages in this tutorial is a CSS3 gradient. The area within the white borders has a transparent background so that the gradient can be seen.

The home page has four pull-down menus to eliminate user-input errors and ensure that only acceptable data is entered into the database table. To save space and provide better security, the database in this tutorial is simplified by restricting the choices in these pull-down menus. British prices and terminology are used in the menus. In the United States, different terminology is used; for instance, the term *semi-detached* might be replaced by side-by-side duplex. In the United Kingdom, a bungalow is a single-story building, whereas a house has two or more stories. For an American real estate agent, you would also replace the currency entity £ with the dollar entity $.

Although we limited the drop-down choices severely to save space and code and increase security, a real-world house catalog would adopt the same principle but use a more extensive choice of location, price, and type of house.

In the body of the home page, the code for the main menu (*menu.php*) is given in the following snippet:

```
<div style="padding-top: 10px; padding-bottom: 10px; padding-right: 15px;">
  <nav class="float-right navbar navbar-expand-md navbar-dark">
        <button class="navbar-toggler" type="button" data-toggle="collapse"
            data-target="#collapsibleMenu1">
            <span class="navbar-toggler-icon"></span>
        </button>
        <div class="btn-group-vertical btn-group-sm collapse navbar-collapse"
        id="collapsibleMenu1"
            role="group" aria-label="Button Group">
            <ul class="navbar-nav flex-column" style="width: 140px;">
                <li class="nav-item">
                <a class="btn btn-primary"
                style="background:#559a55; border: 5px outset #559a55;" href="#"
                role="button">About Us</a>
                </li>
            <li class="nav-item">
                <a class="btn btn-primary" style="background:#559a55; border: 5px
                outset #559a55;"
                href="#" role="button">FAQs</a>
            </li>
            <li class="nav-item">
                <a class="btn btn-primary" style="background:#559a55; border: 5px
                outset #559a55;"
                href="contact.php" role="button">Contact Us</a>
            </li>
            <li class="nav-item">
                <a class="btn btn-primary" style="background:#559a55; border: 5px
                outset #559a55;"
                href="index.php" role="button">Home Page</a>
            </li>
            </ul>
        </div>
  </nav>
</div>
```

In the downloadable menu file, the About Us and FAQs links are dead because no target pages have been made available for those two links in this tutorial.

We will now examine the header for the home page and the majority of the web pages.

The Header for the Majority of the Pages

The header code is changed to include the header file as follows:

```
<header>
<?php include('includes/header.php'); ?>
</header>
```

The main style sheet formats the header and provides the background image.

The Home Page Code

Let's now examine the home page, which also doubles as a search page (Listing 8-1).

Listing 8-1. Creating the Home Page (index.php)

```
<!DOCTYPE html>
<html lang="en">
<head>
<title>Estate Home Page</title>
        <meta charset="utf-8">
        <meta name="viewport" s
content="width=device-width, initial-scale=1, shrink-to-fit=no">
        <!-- Bootstrap CSS File -->
        <link rel="stylesheet"
href=
"https://stackpath.bootstrapcdn.com/bootstrap/4.1.0/css/bootstrap.min.css"
             integrity=
"sha384-9gVQ4dYFwwWSjIDZnLEWnxCjeSWFphJiwGPXr1jddIhOegiu1FwO5qRGvFXOdJZ4"
             crossorigin="anonymous">
<link rel="stylesheet" type="text/css" href="transparent.css">
</head>
<body>
<div class="container" style="margin-top:10px">
<!-- Header Section -->
<header>
<?php include('includes/header.php'); ?>
</header>
<!-- Body Section -->
<div class="content mx-auto" id="contents">
        <div class="row mx-auto" style="padding-left: 0px; height: auto;">
<!-- Center Column Content Section -->
        <div class="col-sm-12 text-center"
style="padding:0px; margin-top: 5px;">
        <!--Start of admin add paintings content-->
<div class="row">
                <div class="col-sm-4">
                        <h4>Search for your dream house</h4>
                        <h6>IMPORTANT: Select an item in
                        ALL fields otherwise the search will not succeed</h6>
<form action="found_houses.php" method="post"
name="searchform" id="searchform">
<div class="form-group row form-control-sm no-gutters"
        style="padding: 0px;">
<div class="col-sm-3"></div>
<div class="col-sm-6" style="padding: 0px;">
                        <label for="location" class="col-form-label text-right">
                            Location:</label>
                        <select id="location" name="location" class="form-control"
                            required>
                            <option selected value="">- Select -</option>
                            <option value="South_Devon">South Devon</option>
```

```
                  <option value="Mid_Devon">Mid Devon</option>
                  <option value="North_Devon">North Devon</option>
            </select>
      </div>
      </div>
<div class="form-group row form-control-sm no-gutters"
      style="padding: 0px;" >
<div class="col-sm-3"></div>
<div class="col-sm-6" style="padding: 0px;">
                  <label for="price" class=" col-form-label text-right">
                  Maximum Price:</label>
                  <select id="price" name="price" class="form-control"
                        required>
                        <option selected value="">- Select -</option>
                        <option value="200000">&pound;200,000</option>
                        <option value="300000">&pound;300,000</option>
                        <option value="400000">&pound;400,000</option>
                  </select>
            </div>
            </div>
<div class="form-group row form-control-sm no-gutters"
      style="padding: 0px;" >
<div class="col-sm-3"></div>
<div class="col-sm-6" style="padding: 0px;" >
                  <label for="type" class="col-form-label text-right">
                  Type:</label>
                  <select id="type" name="type" class="form-control"
                        required>
                        <option selected value="">- Select -</option>
                        <option value="Det-bung">Detached Bungalow</option>
                        <option value="Semi-det-bung">
Semi-detached Bungalow</option>
                        <option value="Det-house">Detached House</option>
                        <option value="Semi-det-house">
Semi-detached House</option>
                  </select>
            </div>
            </div>
<div class="form-group row form-control-sm no-gutters"
      style="padding: 0px;">
<div class="col-sm-3"></div>
<div class="col-sm-6" style="padding: 0px;">
                  <label for="bedrooms" class="col-form-label text-right">
                  No. of Bedrooms:</label>
<select id="bedrooms" name="bedrooms" class="form-control"
style="margin: 0px;" required>
                              <option selected value="">- Select -</option>
                              <option value="1">1</option>
                              <option value="2">2</option>
```

```
                        <option value="3">3</option>
                        <option value="4">4</option>
                </select>
            </div>
            </div>
<div class="form-group row form-control-sm ">
                <label for="" class="col-sm-3 col-form-label"></label>
            <div class="col-sm-6 text-center "style="padding: 0px;" >
                <input id="submit" class="btn btn-primary" type="submit"
                    name="submit" value="Search">
            </div>
        </div>
    </div>
</div>
<div class="col-sm-4">
<h6>All houses are situated in the beautiful green rolling countryside
        of Devon, England, UK</h6>
        <img alt="SW England"  src="images/devon-map-crop.jpg" >
</div>
<div class="col-sm-4">
<?php include ('includes/menu.php'); ?>
</div>
</div>
</div>
</div>
</div>
<div class="row mx-auto" style="padding-left: 0px; height: auto;">
<div class="col-sm-12 text-center" style="padding:0px; margin-top: 5px;">
<footer>
<?php include ('includes/footer.php'); ?>
</footer>
</div>
</div>
</div>
</body>
</html>
```

The code for the index page is similar to code we have seen in other chapters. No additional explanation is needed.

Displaying the Catalog

After the user enters the search criteria into the home page fields (*index.php* as shown in Figure 8-1), clicking the Search button will reveal the selected houses, as shown in Figure 8-2.

Enter the following details into the home page to see the selected houses as displayed in Figure 8-2:

- *Location*: South Devon

- *Max Price*: £400,000

- *Type*: Detached house

- *Bedrooms*: 4

Note that all thumbnail images will be stored in a subfolder under the *images* folder named *thumbs*. All full-size pictures, used in the full description pages (explained later), will be stored in the subfolder *pictures* under the *images* folder. When the user clicks the Details link, a full description of the house selected is displayed.

Figure 8-2. *The houses selected by the search criteria are displayed*

The search criteria resulting in the display shown in Figure 8-2 were as follows:

- *Location*: South Devon
- *Max Price*: £400,000
- *Type*: Detached house
- *Bedrooms*: 4

■ **Note**   if you click the Details link for house 1003, you will see the full details for that house. If you click the
Details link for house 1007, you will see an example of the full details with the default picture.

Listing 8-2 gives the code for displaying the found houses.

The main menu is removed so that the table can span the width of the page. To enable the user to return
to the home page, a Home Page button has been added to the header.

Listing 8-2. Creating the Results Page (found_houses.php)

```php
<?php
session_start();
// Data from valid source?                                                    #1
if ((empty($_SESSION['user_level'])) && (!isset($_SESSION['previous_url']) or
($_SESSION['previous_url'] != "index")))
{ header("Location: index.php");
exit();
}
else
{
if (!empty($_SESSION['user_level'])) {
      $user_level = $_SESSION['user_level'];

if(($user_level == 1) && (!empty($_POST['ref_number'])))
{
      $ref_number = htmlspecialchars($_POST['ref_number'], ENT_QUOTES);
}
} else { $user_level = 0; }
}
define('ERROR_LOG',"errors.log");
?>
 <!DOCTYPE html>
<html lang="en">
<head>
<title>Found Houses Page</title>
      <meta charset="utf-8">
      <meta name="viewport" content=
"width=device-width, initial-scale=1, shrink-to-fit=no">
      <!-- Bootstrap CSS File -->
      <link rel="stylesheet"
href=
"https://stackpath.bootstrapcdn.com/bootstrap/4.1.0/css/bootstrap.min.css"
            integrity=
"sha384-9gVQ4dYFwwWSjIDZnLEWnxCjeSWFphJiwGPXr1jddIhOegiu1FwO5qRGvFXOdJZ4"
            crossorigin="anonymous">
<link rel="stylesheet" type="text/css" href="transparent.css">
</head>
<body>
<div class="container" style="margin-top:10px">
<!-- Header Section -->
<header>
```

```php
<?php
if ($user_level == 0)
{
include("includes/header_found_houses.php");
}
else if($user_level==1)
{
include('includes/header_4btn.php');
}
?>
</header>
<!-- Body Section -->
<div class="content mx-auto" id="contents">
<div class="row mx-auto" style="padding-left: 0px; height: auto;">
<!-- Center Column Content Section -->
<div class="col-sm-12 text-center"
style="padding:20px; margin-top: 5px;">
<!--Start of admin add paintings content-->
<div class="row">
<h3>To arrange a viewing please use the Contact Us button
on the menu and quote the reference number.</h3>
<?php
// This script retrieves all the records from the houses table
try {
require ('mysqli_connect.php'); // Connect to the database.
// Make the query:
$query = "SELECT ref_number, location, thumb, price, ";
$query .= "mini_description, type, bedrooms, ";
$query .= "status FROM houses ";
if(($user_level == 1) && (!empty($_POST['ref_number']))) {
$query .= "WHERE ref_number=? ";
} else {
$query .= "WHERE location= ? AND ";
$query .= "(price <= ?) AND (price >= (? - 100000)) AND ";
$query .= "type= ? AND bedrooms= ?  ORDER BY ref_number ASC ";
}
$q = mysqli_stmt_init($dbcon);
mysqli_stmt_prepare($q, $query);
// bind values to SQL Statement
if(($user_level == 1) && (!empty($_POST['ref_number']))) {
            mysqli_stmt_bind_param($q, 's', $ref_number);
} else {
$location = htmlspecialchars($_POST['location'], ENT_QUOTES);
$price = htmlspecialchars($_POST['price'], ENT_QUOTES);
$type = htmlspecialchars($_POST['type'], ENT_QUOTES);
$bedrooms = htmlspecialchars($_POST['bedrooms'], ENT_QUOTES);
mysqli_stmt_bind_param($q, 'sssss', $location, $price, $price,
$type, $bedrooms);
}
```

#2

```php
// execute query
mysqli_stmt_execute($q);
$result = mysqli_stmt_get_result($q);
// SELECT is safe execution - read only
if ($result) { // If it ran OK, display the records.
// Table header.
?>
<table class="table table-responsive table-striped"
style="background: white;color:black;">
<tr>
<th scope="col">Ref.</th>
<th scope="col">Location</th>
<th scope="col">Thumb</th>
<th scope="col">Price</th>
<th scope="col">Features</th>
<th scope="col">Bedrooms</th>
<th scope="col">Details</th>
<th scope="col">Status</th>
</tr>
<?php
while ($row = mysqli_fetch_array($result, MYSQLI_ASSOC)) {
    // Remove special characters that might already be in table to
    // reduce the chance of XSS exploits
    $ref_number = htmlspecialchars($row['ref_number'], ENT_QUOTES);
    $thumb = htmlspecialchars($row['thumb'], ENT_QUOTES);
    $price = htmlspecialchars($row['price'], ENT_QUOTES);
    $mini_description =
htmlspecialchars($row['mini_description'], ENT_QUOTES);
    $bedrooms = htmlspecialchars($row['bedrooms'], ENT_QUOTES);
    $status = htmlspecialchars($row['status'], ENT_QUOTES);

    echo '<tr>
    <td scope="row">' . $row['ref_number'] . '</td>
    <td scope="row">' . $row['location'] . '</td>';
    if ($row['thumb'] == "")                                      //#3
        {
echo '<td scope="row"><img src="images/thumbs/default.jpg">';
}
    else {
echo'<td scope="row">  <img src='.$row['thumb'] . '></td>';
}
    echo'<td scope="row">' . $row['price'] . '</td>
    <td scope="row">' . $row['mini_description'] . '</td>
    <td scope="row">' . $row['bedrooms'] . '</td>
    <td scope="row">
<a href="house_details.php?ref_number=' . $row['ref_number'] .
                '">Details</a></td>
    <td scope="row"> ' . $row['status'] . '</td>
    </tr>';
    }
```

```
        echo '</table>'; // Close the table.
        mysqli_free_result ($result); // Free up the resources.
        } else { // If it did not run OK.
// Public message:
        echo '<p class="center-text">
The current users could not be retrieved.';
        echo 'We apologize for any inconvenience.</p>';
        // Debugging message:
        //echo '<p>' . mysqli_error($dbcon) . '<br><br>Query: ' . $q . '</p>';
        //Show $q is debug mode only
} // End of if ($result). Now display the total number of records/members.
mysqli_close($dbcon); // Close the database connection.
}
catch(Exception $e) // We finally handle any problems here
    {
// print "An Exception occurred. Message: " . $e->getMessage();
        print "The system is busy please try later";
        // $date = date('m.d.y h:i:s');
        // $errormessage = $e->getMessage();
        // $eMessage = $date . " | Exception Error | " , $errormessage . |\n";
        //   error_log($eMessage,3,ERROR_LOG);
// e-mail support person to alert there is a problem
        //   error_log("Date/Time: $date - Exception Error, Check error log for
//details", 1, noone@helpme.com, "Subject: Exception Error \nFrom:
// Error Log <errorlog@helpme.com>" . "\r\n");
    }
    catch(Error $e)
    {
        // print "An Error occurred. Message: " . $e->getMessage();
        print "The system is busy please try later";
        // $date = date('m.d.y h:i:s');
        // $errormessage = $e->getMessage();
        // $eMessage = $date . " | Error | " , $errormessage . |\n";
        // error_log($eMessage,3,ERROR_LOG);
        // e-mail support person to alert there is a problem
        //   error_log("Date/Time: $date - Error, Check error log for
//details", 1, noone@helpme.com, "Subject: Error \nFrom: Error Log
// <errorlog@helpme.com>" . "\r\n");
    }
?>
<div class="row mx-auto" style="padding-left: 0px; height: auto;">
<div class="col-sm-12 text-center" style="padding:0px; margin-top: 5px;">
<h5 class="text-center">No houses displayed? Sorry we have nothing
that matches your requirements at the moment</h5>
</div>
</div>
</div><!-- End of table display content -->
</div>
</div>
</div>
```

```
<div class="row mx-auto" style="padding-left: 0px; height: auto;">
<div class="col-sm-12 text-center" style="padding:0px; margin-top: 5px;">
<footer>
<?php include ('includes/footer.php'); ?>
</footer>
</div>
</div>
</body>
</html>
```

Explanation of the Code

This section explains the code.

```
<?php
session_start();
// Data from valid source?                                             #1
if ((empty($_SESSION['user_level'])) && (!isset($_SESSION['previous_url']) or
($_SESSION['previous_url'] != "index")))
{ header("Location: index.php");
exit();
}
else
{
if (!empty($_SESSION['user_level'])) {
      $user_level = $_SESSION['user_level'];

if(($user_level == 1) && (!empty($_POST['ref_number'])))
{
      $ref_number = htmlspecialchars($_POST['ref_number'], ENT_QUOTES);
}
} else { $user_level = 0; }
}
define('ERROR_LOG',"errors.log");
?>
```

This security guard checks for the existence of the previous_url session variable and the value of index. This check allows only the index file to call this page and pass content to it. The index page requires a selection for all drop-down boxes. It also restricts what values are passed to this page by using these drop-down lists.

```
// Make the query:                                                     #2
$query = "SELECT ref_number, location, thumb, price, ";
$query .= "mini_description, type, bedrooms, ";
$query .= "status FROM houses ";
if(($user_level == 1) && (!empty($_POST['ref_number']))) {
$query .= "WHERE ref_number=? ";
} else {
$query .= "WHERE location= ? AND ";
$query .= "(price <= ?) AND (price >= (? - 100000)) AND ";
$query .= "type= ? AND bedrooms= ?  ORDER BY ref_number ASC ";
}
```

302

If the user is not an administrator, the entries provided by the drop-down menus are assigned to the SQL query. If the user is an administrator, the WHERE clause will contain the house reference number, which is provided on an administration form that we will explore soon.

The price needs some explanation. The statement is as follows:

```
(price <= ?) AND (price >= (?'-100000)
```

If the price was simply <= ?, a search using a maximum price of £400,000 would display every house valued at £400,000 or less. People looking for a house with maximum price of £400,000 would not be interested in houses at, say, £280,000 or £120,000. Therefore, the following statement is used to give a minimum price that is £100,000 below the searcher's maximum:

```
AND (price >= (?-100000)
```

The display is ordered by ascending reference numbers; however, you could change this to order it by price in descending order.

```
if ($row['thumb'] == "")                                                    //#3
        {
echo '<td scope="row"><img src="images/thumbs/default.jpg">';
}
     else {
echo'<td scope="row">  <img src='.$row['thumb'] . '></td>';
}
```

If there is no link to a thumbnail picture in the database, a default picture is used. This may occur if the agent decides to post the house for sale before the photographer has had a chance to take pictures.

The Header for the Page of Search Results

Figure 8-3 shows the header.

Figure 8-3. *One of the two buttons is a Contact Us button so that the user can request an appointment to view the house*

Listing 8-3 gives the code for the header.

Listing 8-3. Creating the Search Result Header (header_found_houses.php)

```
<div class="jumbotron text-center row mx-auto" id="includeheader">
<div class="col-sm-10">
        <h1 class="text-left"><strong>Devon Real Estate</strong></h1>
        <h2 class="text-center">Try our award winning service</h2>
</div>
  <nav class="col-sm-2">
        <div class="btn-group-vertical btn-group-sm" role="group"
            style="width: 140px;" aria-label="Button Group">
                    <button type="button" class="btn btn-secondary" id="buttons"
                        onclick="location.href = 'contact.php'" >Contact Us</button>
                    <button type="button" class="btn btn-secondary" id="buttons"
                        onclick="location.href = 'index.php'">Home Page</button>
        </div>
  </nav>
</div>
<img id="rosette1" alt="Rosette" title="Rosette" height="127"
    src="images/rosette-128.png" width="128">
```

Now, let's create the details page. This page is accessed by clicking the link provided for an individual house in the *found_houses.php* page.

Creating the House Details Page

The house details page provides a more comprehensive description of the house. The page pulls this additional information from the database when the user clicks the Details link. This page is called either by the index page or by the administrators search page, which will be explained soon. Figure 8-4 shows the page.

Figure 8-4. House details for house 1003 (house_details.php)

The found_houses page passes the house reference number (via GET) to the house_details page. This value is then used to retrieve the detailed description of the house.

If there is no link to a picture in the database, a default picture is used. This may occur if the agent decides to post the house for sale before the photographer has had a chance to take pictures.

Listing 8-4 shows the code for the house details page.

Listing 8-4. House Details Page (house_details.php)

```php
<?php
session_start();
// Data from valid source?                                            #1
if ((!empty($SESSION['user_level'])) &&
(!isset($_SESSION['previous_url'])
     or ($_SESSION['previous_url'] != "index")))
{ header("Location: index.php");
exit();
}
define('ERROR_LOG','errors.log');
?>
```

```
<!DOCTYPE html>
<html lang="en">
<head>
  <title>House Details Page</title>
  <meta charset="utf-8">
  <meta name="viewport" content="width=device-width,
initial-scale=1, shrink-to-fit=no">
  <!-- Bootstrap CSS File -->
  <link rel="stylesheet"
href=
"https://stackpath.bootstrapcdn.com/bootstrap/4.1.0/css/bootstrap.min.css"
      integrity=
"sha384-9gVQ4dYFwwWSjIDZnLEWnxCjeSWFphJiwGPXr1jddIhOegiu1FwO5qRGvFXOdJZ4"
  crossorigin="anonymous">
  <link rel="stylesheet" type="text/css" href="transparent.css">
</head>
<body>
<div class="container" style="margin-top:10px">
<!-- Header Section -->
<header>
<?php include('includes/header.php'); ?>
</header>
<!-- Body Section -->
<div class="content mx-auto" id="contents">
<div class="row mx-auto" style="padding-left: 10px; height: auto;">
<!-- Center Column Content Section -->
<div class="col-sm-12 text-center" style="padding:20px; margin-top: 5px;">
<!--Start of admin add paintings content-->
<div class="row">
<div class="col-sm-5" style="background-color: white; padding-top: 10px;">
<?php
try {
$ref_number = htmlspecialchars($_GET['ref_number'], ENT_QUOTES);
require ('mysqli_connect.php'); // Connect to the database.
// Make the query:                                                    #2
$query = "SELECT price, full_description, full_picture ";
$query .= "FROM houses WHERE ref_number=?";
$q = mysqli_stmt_init($dbcon);
mysqli_stmt_prepare($q, $query);
// bind values to SQL Statement
mysqli_stmt_bind_param($q, 's', $ref_number);
// execute query
mysqli_stmt_execute($q);
$result = mysqli_stmt_get_result($q);
if ($result) { // If it ran OK, display the records.
$row = mysqli_fetch_array($result, MYSQLI_ASSOC);
?>
<h5 style="color:green"><strong>
Details for House Reference No
<?php echo $ref_number; ?>
</strong></h5>
```

```php
<?php
echo '<img class-"img-fluid float-left" alt="house reference ' .
        $ref_number;
echo '" src="';                                                     //#3
if ($row['full_picture']=="")
{echo 'images/pictures/default.jpg"/>';}
else { echo $row['full_picture'];
echo '">';
}
?>
</div>
<div class="col-sm-4"
style=" background-color: white; color:black; padding-top: 10px;">
<h4 style="color:green;">
To arrange a viewing please click the Contact Us button
        and quote the reference number
<?php echo $ref_number . '</h4>';
echo '<p>&pound;';
echo $row['price'] . '</p>';
echo $row['full_description'];
?>
</div>
<?php
mysqli_free_result ($result); // Free up the resources.
}
else { // If it did not run OK.
// Message:
        echo '<p class="error">The record could not be retrieved. ';
        echo 'We apologize for any inconvenience.</p>';
        // Debugging error message:
//echo '<p>' . mysqli_error($dbcon) . '<br><br>Query: ' . $q . '</p>';
}
mysqli_close($dbcon); // Close the database connection.
}
catch(Exception $e) // We finally handle any problems here
    {
// print "An Exception occurred. Message: " . $e->getMessage();
        print "The system is busy please try later";
        // $date = date('m.d.y h:i:s');
        // $errormessage = $e->getMessage();
        // $eMessage = $date . " | Exception Error | " , $errormessage . |\n";
        // error_log($eMessage,3,ERROR_LOG);
        // e-mail support person to alert there is a problem
        // error_log("Date/Time: $date - Exception Error, Check error log for
//details", 1, noone@helpme.com, "Subject: Exception Error \n
//From: Error Log <errorlog@helpme.com>" . "\r\n");
    }
    catch(Error $e)
    {
        // print "An Error occurred. Message: " . $e->getMessage();
        print "The system is busy please try later";
```

```
        // $date = date('m.d.y h:i:s');
        // $errormessage = $e->getMessage();
        // $eMessage = $date . " | Error | " , $errormessage . |\n";
        // error_log($eMessage,3,ERROR_LOG);
        // e-mail support person to alert there is a problem
        // error_log("Date/Time: $date - Error, Check error log for
//details", 1, noone@helpme.com, "Subject: Error \nFrom:
// Error Log <errorlog@helpme.com>" . "\r\n");
    }
?>
<div class="col-sm-3">
<?php include ('includes/menu.php'); ?>
</div>
</div>
</div>
</div>
</div>
</div>
</body>
</html>
```

Explanation of Code

This section explains the code.

```
<?php
session_start();
// Data from valid source?                                            #1
if ((!empty($SESSION['user_level'])) && (!isset($_SESSION['previous_url'])
        or ($_SESSION['previous_url'] != "index")))
{ header("Location: index.php");
exit();
}
define('ERROR_LOG','errors.log');
?>
```

The security guard again requires that the data selected was from the index page, which in turn was also passed to the found houses page. A regular user can get here only if they started with the index page and clicked the details link in the found_houses page. Once an administrator signs in to the login page, it redirects them to the advert page. The session is not closed by the code to allow the user to return to the found houses page and click another link if available.

```
// Make the query:                                                    #2
$query = "SELECT price, full_description, full_picture ";
$query .= "FROM houses WHERE ref_number=?";
$q = mysqli_stmt_init($dbcon);
mysqli_stmt_prepare($q, $query);
```

```
// bind values to SQL Statement
mysqli_stmt_bind_param($q, 's', $ref_number);
```

The house reference number was passed via the link in the found_houses page. The house_details page uses this reference number to pull a full description of the house from the database.

■ **Note** The administrator is responsible for controlling the format of the data. The administrator would use HTML and/or CSS to ensure that data is properly displayed. Since these skills might not be known by a real estate employee, this duty has been assigned to the web administrator.

```
echo '" src="';                                                              //#3
if ($row['full_picture']=="")
{echo 'images/pictures/default.jpg"/>';}
else { echo $row['full_picture'];
echo '">';
```

If the link to the full size picture does not exist in the database, a default picture is provided.
Now let's add some pages to help our administrator add and view a house.

Creating the Admin/Adding a House Page

Figure 8-5a shows the administrator's page.

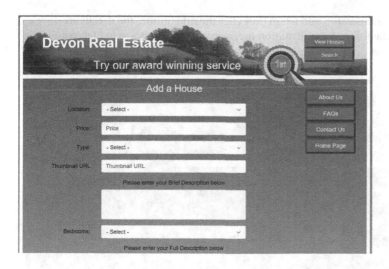

Figure 8-5a. *The admin and add-a-house page*

Figure 8-5a shows the administrator's page (*advert.php*). This is a page for adding new houses to the houses table in the database.

Let's examine the elements on the administrator's page. The page contains four pull-down menus, three of which are replicas of the pull-downs in the index page; these are location, type, and number of bedrooms. The status menu is the fourth pull-down menu and is used to inform the user whether the house is available, under offer, or already sold. The price field is not a pull-down because house values are rarely set at precisely £400,000 or £300,000 or £200,000.

Concerning the status, you might wonder why we would enter Sold. Why not delete the house from the database if it is sold? Real estate agents do this for two reasons.

- Prospective buyers might have used the site at some earlier date and were attracted by a particular house. Later, when they see that the house is sold, they would have no need to contact the agent to see if it still on the market.

- If prospective visitors see several sold houses listed on the website, they will be confident that the agent is actively selling houses.

The administrator will use phpMyAdmin to delete sold houses after a suitable time interval.

Assuming that the thumbnail images are in the subfolder *thumbs* under the folder *images*, the URL for the image must be entered by the administrator in the following format:

```
c://estate/images/thumbs/house06.gif
```

The price must be entered (without currency symbols) in this format: 300000.

The full-size images are in the subfolder *pictures* under the folder *images*, and the URL must be entered in the following format:

```
c://estate/images/pictures/fullhouse06.gif
```

The fields are filled out by the administrator, and when they click the Add button, the details are inserted into the houses table in the database. A confirmation message is given, as shown in Figure 8-5b.

Figure 8-5b. *Showing the confirmation message*

Listing 8-5 gives the code for the administrator's page.

Listing 8-5. Creating the Administrator's Page (advert.php)

```php
<?php
session_start();
if (!isset($_SESSION['user_level']) || ($_SESSION['user_level'] != 1))
{
      header("Location: login.php");
      exit();
}
define('ERROR_LOG','errors.log');
if ($_SERVER['REQUEST_METHOD'] == 'POST') {
      //require("cap.php");
}
?>
<!DOCTYPE html>
<html lang="en">
<head>
  <title>Add Home Page</title>
  <meta charset="utf-8">
  <meta name="viewport" content="width=device-width, initial-scale=1, shrink-to-fit=no">
  <!-- Bootstrap CSS File -->
  <link rel="stylesheet"
      href="https://stackpath.bootstrapcdn.com/bootstrap/4.1.0/css/bootstrap.min.css"
      integrity=
      "sha384-9gVQ4dYFwwWSjIDZnLEWnxCjeSWFphJiwGPXr1jddIhOegiu1Fw05qRGvFXOdJZ4"
      crossorigin="anonymous">
<link rel="stylesheet" type="text/css" href="transparent.css">
<script src='https://www.google.com/recaptcha/api.js'></script>
</head>
<body>
<div class="container" style="margin-top:10px">
<!-- Header Section -->
<header>
        <?php include('includes/header_advert.php'); ?>
</header>
<?php
// This script is a query that INSERTs a record in the houses table.
// Check that form has been submitted:
if ( ($_POST['submit'] == 'Add')) {
      // only accept values from same site via post
try {
      $errors = array(); // Initialize an error array.
      require('mysqli_connect.php'); // Connect to the db.
      // Check for a location
      $location = filter_var($_POST['location'], FILTER_SANITIZE_STRING);
      if ((empty($location)) || ($location == '- Select -')) {
            $errors[] = 'You forgot to enter the location.';
      } else {
```

```php
            if (($location == "South_Devon") ||
                    ($location == "Mid_Devon") ||
                    ($location == "North_Devon"))
            {
                    // OK
            } else {
                    $errors[] = "Invalid location";
            }
    }
// Has a price been entered?
$price = filter_var( $_POST['price'], FILTER_SANITIZE_NUMBER_INT);
if ((empty($price)) || (strlen($price) > 15)) {
    $errors[] ='You forgot to enter the price.' ;
}
// check type
$type = (filter_var($_POST['type'], FILTER_SANITIZE_STRING));
    if ((empty($_POST['type'])) || ($_POST['type'] == '- Select -')) {
            // user could choose - Select - by mistake
            $errors[] = 'You forgot to enter the type of house.';
    } else {
            if (($type == "Det-bung") ||
                    ($type == "Sem-det-bung") ||
                    ($type == "Det-house") ||
                    ($type == "Semi-det-house"))
            {
                    //OK
            } else {
                    $errors[] = "Invalid type";
            }
    }
// Check for brief description
$mini_descriptiontrim = filter_var( $_POST['mini_description'], FILTER_SANITIZE_STRING);
if ((!empty($mini_descriptiontrim)) && (preg_match('/[a-z0-9\.\!\?\s\,\-]/i', $mini_
descriptiontrim)) &&
        (strlen($mini_descriptiontrim) <= 120)) {
        $mini_description = $mini_descriptiontrim;
}else{
        $errors[] = 'Missing description. Only numeric, alphabetic, period, comma, dash and
        space. Max 120.';
}
        // Check for number of bedrooms
        $bedrooms = filter_var( $_POST['bedrooms'], FILTER_SANITIZE_NUMBER_INT);
        if ((empty($bedrooms)) || ($bedrooms == '- Select -')) {
            $errors[] = 'You forgot to enter the number of bedrooms';
        } else {
            if (($bedrooms == "1") ||
                    ($bedrooms == "2") ||
                    ($bedrooms == "3") ||
                    ($bedrooms == "4"))
            {
                    // OK
```

```php
            } else {
                    $errors[] = "Invalid number of bedrooms";
            }
    }
// Check if a thumbnail url has been entered
$thumb = filter_var( $_POST['thumb'], FILTER_SANITIZE_URL);
if ((empty($thumb)) || (strlen($thumb > 45))) {
        // thumbnail link is optional
        $thumb = NULL;
}
// Check if full description has been entered
$full_descriptiontrim =
        filter_var( $_POST['full_description'], FILTER_SANITIZE_STRING);
if ((!empty($full_descriptiontrim)) &&
        (preg_match('/[a-z0-9\.\!\?\s\,\-]/i', $full_descriptiontrim)) &&
        (strlen($full_descriptiontrim) <= 400)) {
        $full_description = $full_descriptiontrim;
}else{
        $errors[] =
        'Missing description. Only numeric, alphabetic, period, comma, dash and space. Max 30.';
        }
        // full picture
        $full_picture = filter_var( $_POST['full_picture'], FILTER_SANITIZE_URL);
                if ((empty($full_picture)) || (strlen($full_picture) > 45)){
                // optional
                        $full_picture = NULL;
                }
        // Check for status of the house
        $status = filter_var( $_POST['status'], FILTER_SANITIZE_STRING);
                if ((empty($status)) || ($status == '- Select -')) {
                        $errors[] = 'You forgot to select a status';
                } else {
                if (($status == "Available") ||
                        ($status == "Under offer") ||
                        ($status == "Withdrawn") ||
                        ($status == "Sold"))
                {
                        // OK
                } else {
                        $errors[] = "Invalid status";
                }
        }
if (empty($errors)) { // If everything's OK.
    // Register the house in the database
    // Make the query:
    $query = "INSERT INTO houses (ref_number, location, price, type, mini_description,
            bedrooms, ";
    $query .= "thumb, status, full_description, full_picture) ";
    $query .= " VALUES ";
    $query .= "(' ', ?, ?,?,?,?,?,?,?,? )";
```

```
$q = mysqli_stmt_init($dbcon);
mysqli_stmt_prepare($q, $query);
// use prepared statement to ensure that only text is inserted
// bind fields to SQL Statement
mysqli_stmt_bind_param($q, 'ssssssss', $location, $price, $type, $mini_description,
$bedrooms,
        $thumb, $status, $full_description, $full_picture);
// execute query
mysqli_stmt_execute($q);
if (mysqli_stmt_affected_rows($q) == 1) {
        // Good
        header ("location: another.php");
} else { // If it did not run OK.
        // Message:
        $errorstring = 'System Error ';
        $errorstring .= 'The house could not be added due to a system error. ';
        $errorstring .= 'We apologize for any inconvenience.';
        // Debugging message:
        // echo '<p>' . mysqli_error($dbcon) . '<br><br>Query: ' . $q . '</p>';
        } // End of if ($r) IF.
mysqli_close($dbcon); // Close the database connection.
exit();
} else { // Report the errors.
        $errorstring = 'Error!';
        $errorstring .= ' The following error(s) occurred:<br>';
        foreach ($errors as $msg) { // Print each error.
                $errorstring .= " - $msg<br>\n";
        }
                $errorstring .= 'Please try again.';
}// End of if (empty($errors)) IF.
} // try
catch(Exception $e) // We finally handle any problems here
    {
        // print "An Exception occurred. Message: " . $e->getMessage();
        print "The system is busy please try later";
        //    $date = date('m.d.y h:i:s');
        //    $errormessage = $e->getMessage();
        //    $eMessage = $date . " | Exception Error | " , $errormessage . |\n";
        //    error_log($eMessage,3,ERROR_LOG);
        // e-mail support person to alert there is a problem
        //    error_log("Date/Time: $date - Exception Error, Check error log for
        //details", 1, noone@helpme.com, "Subject: Exception Error \nFrom: Error Log
        //<errorlog@helpme.com>" . "\r\n");
    }
    catch(Error $e)
    {
        // print "An Error occurred. Message: " . $e->getMessage();
        print "The system is busy please try later";
        // $date = date('m.d.y h:i:s');
        // $errormessage = $e->getMessage();
        // $eMessage = $date . " | Error | " , $errormessage . |\n";
```

```
        // error_log($eMessage,3,ERROR_LOG);
        // e-mail support person to alert there is a problem
        //  error_log("Date/Time: $date - Error, Check error log for
        // details", 1, noone@helpme.com, "Subject: Error \nFrom:
        // Error Log <errorlog@helpme.com>" . "\r\n");
    }
} // End of the main Submit conditional.
?>
<div class="content mx-auto" id="contents" style="padding-top:10px">
<!-- Body Section -->
  <div class="row" style="padding-left: 0px;">
<div class="col-sm-8">
<form action="advert.php" method="post" name="advert" id="advert">
<!--START OF TEXT FIELDS-->
<div class='form-group row'>
    <label for="" class="col-sm-4 col-form-label text-right"></label>
<div class="col-sm-8 text-center">
    <h3>Add a House</h3>
    <h5>
    <?php
    If (!empty($errorstring)) {
        echo $errorstring;
    }
    ?></h5>
</div>
</div>
<div class="form-group row">
    <label for="location" class="col-sm-4 col-form-label text-right">
      Location:</label>
      <div class="col-sm-8">
    <select id="location" name="location" class="form-control" required>
        <option value="">- Select -</option>
        <option value="South_Devon">South Devon</option>
        <option value="Mid_Devon">Mid Devon</option>
        <option value="North_Devon">North Devon</option>
    </select>
</div>
</div>
<div class="form-group row">
    <label for="price" class="col-sm-4 col-form-label text-right">Price:</label>
<div class="col-sm-8">
    <input type="num" class="form-control" id="price" name="price"
        placeholder="Price" maxlength="15"
        pattern="[0-9\.]*"
        title="Numbers only max of 120 characters"
        value=
            "<?php if (isset($_POST['price']))
        echo htmlspecialchars($_POST['price'], ENT_QUOTES); ?>" >
    </div>
</div>
```

```
<div class="form-group row">
      <label for="type" class="col-sm-4 col-form-label text-right">
        Type:</label>
        <div class="col-sm-8">
    <select id="type" name="type" class="form-control" required>
    <option value="">- Select -</option>
    <option value="Det-bung">Detached Bungalow</option>
    <option value="Sem-det-bung">Semi-detached Bungalow</option>
    <option value="Det-house">Detached House</option>
    <option value="Semi-det-house">Semi-detached House</option>
    </select>
</div>
</div>
<div class="form-group row">
    <label for="thumb" class="col-sm-4 col-form-label text-right">Thumbnail URL</label>
    <div class="col-sm-8">
      <input type="url" class="form-control" id="thumb" name="thumb"
        placeholder="Thumbnail URL" maxlength="45"
         value=
            "<?php if (isset($_POST['thumb']))
            echo htmlspecialchars($_POST['thumb'], ENT_QUOTES); ?>" >
    </div>
  </div>
 <div class="form-group row">
      <label for="" class="col-sm-4 col-form-label text-right"></label>
<div class="col-sm-8 text-center">
      <label for="comment">Please enter your Brief Description below</label>
      <textarea class="form-control" id="mini_description"
            name="mini_description" rows="3" cols="40"
            pattern="[a-zA-Z0-9][a-zA-Z0-9\s\.\,\-\?\!]*"
            title="Alphabetic, numbers, comma, ., -, ?, !, space only max of 120 characters"
            value=
            " <?php if (isset($_POST['mini_description']))
            echo htmlspecialchars($_POST['mini_description'], ENT_QUOTES); ?>" >
      </textarea>
 </div>
 </div>
<div class="form-group row">
      <label for="bedrooms" class="col-sm-4 col-form-label text-right">
            Bedrooms:</label>
<div class="col-sm-8">
      <select id="bedrooms" name="bedrooms" class="form-control" required>
            <option value="">- Select -</option>
            <option value="1">1</option>
            <option value="2">2</option>
            <option value="3">3</option>
            <option value="4">4</option>
      </select>
</div>
</div>
```

```
<div class="form-group row">
      <label for="" class="col-sm-4 col-form-label text-right"></label>
<div class="col-sm-8 text-center">
      <label for="comment">Please enter your Full Description below</label>
      <textarea class="form-control" id="full_description" name="full_description"
            rows="10" cols="40"
            pattern="[a-zA-Z0-9][a-zA-Z0-9\s\.\,\-\?\!]*"
            title="Alphabetic, numbers, comma, ., -, ?, !, space only max of 400
            characters"
            value=
                  "<?php if (isset($_POST['full_description']))
            echo htmlspecialchars($_POST['full_description'], ENT_QUOTES); ?>" >
      </textarea>
</div>
</div>
<div class="form-group row">
      <label for="full_picture" class="col-sm-4 col-form-label text-right">Full Picture URL</label>
      <div class="col-sm-8">
      <input type="url" class="form-control" id="full_picture" name="full_picture"
            placeholder="Full Picture URL" maxlength="45"
            value=
                  "<?php if (isset($_POST['full_picture']))
            echo htmlspecialchars($_POST['full_picture'], ENT_QUOTES); ?>" >
 </div>
 </div>
<div class="form-group row">
      <label for="status" class="col-sm-4 col-form-label text-right">
            Status:</label>
<div class="col-sm-8">
      <select id="status" name="status" class="form-control" required>
            <option value="">- Select -</option>
            <option value="Available">Available</option>
            <option value="Under offer">Under offer</option>
            <option value="Withdrawn">Withdrawn</option>
            <option value="Sold">Sold</option>
      </select>
</div>
</div>
<div class="form-group row">
      <label class="col-sm-4 col-form-label"></label>
  <div class="col-sm-8">
  <div class="float-left g-recaptcha" style="padding-left: 50px;"
      data-sitekey="6LcrQ1wUAAAAAPxlrAkLuPdpY5qwS9rXF1j46fhq"></div>
  </div>
  </div>
<div class="form-group row">
      <label for="" class="col-sm-4 col-form-label"></label>
<div class="col-sm-8 text-center">
      <input id="submit" class="btn btn-primary" type="submit" name="submit" value="Add">
</div>
</div>
```

```
</form><!-- End of the add house content. -->
</div>
<!-- Left-side Column Menu Section -->
        <nav class="col-sm-4">
                <?php include('includes/menu.php'); ?>
        </nav>
</div>
</div>
<div>
<div class="row mx-auto" style="padding-left: 0px; height: auto;">
<div class="col-sm-12 text-center" style="padding:0px; margin-top: 5px;">
    <footer>
            <?php include ('includes/footer.php'); ?>
    </footer>
</div>
</div>
</div>
</div>
</body>
</html>
```

The HTML5 code uses the required attribute to make sure the user enters information in the required fields. The drop-down boxes allow the user to select only from a list of items. This provides good validation because invalid entries cannot be entered. Once the user has entered information in the form, the information received from textboxes is validated. The coding used is similar to code used in a previous chapter. Thus, we won't repeat the explanation here.

You will have noticed that the header for the administrator's page differs from the general header. We will examine this next.

The Header for the Administrator's Page

Three of the admin pages need two extra buttons because the wide table display fills the content area, leaving no room for the main menu.

Figure 8-6 shows the two extra buttons.

Figure 8-6. *Showing the two extra menu buttons*

Listing 8-6 gives the code for the administrator's header.

Listing 8-6. Creating the Header with One Extra Button (header_3btn.php)

```
<div class="jumbotron text-center row mx-auto" id="includeheader">
<div class="col-sm-10">
<h1 class="text-left"><strong>Devon Real Estate</strong></h1>
<h2 class="text-center">Try our award winning service</h2>
</div>
  <nav class="col-sm-2">
      <div class="btn-group-vertical btn-group-sm" role="group"
                style="width: 140px; margin-top:-25px;"
                aria-label="Button Group">
                <button type="button" class="btn btn-secondary" id="buttons"
                onclick="location.href = 'advert_houses.php'" >
                    View Houses</button>
                <button type="button" class="btn btn-secondary" id="buttons"
                     onclick="location.href = 'advert_search.php'">
                            Search</button>
                <button type="button" class="btn btn-secondary" id="buttons"
                     onclick="location.href = 'index.php'">Home Page</button>
</div>
</nav>
</div>
<img id="rosette1" alt="Rosette" title="Rosette" height="127"
        src="images/rosette-128.png" width="128">
```

The administrator can view the entire stock using a paginated display. This is discussed next.

Administrator's View of the Entire Stock of Houses for Sale

Figure 8-7 shows the first page of the full-stock view.

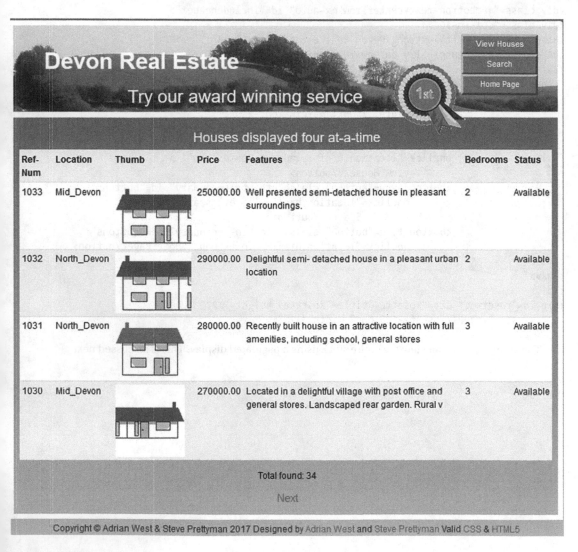

Figure 8-7. One of the pages in a full-stock display

Listing 8-7a shows the code for displaying the stock of houses.

The code for the full-stock display uses a table and pagination similar to those described in previous chapters. Therefore, no explanation of the code will be given.

Listing 8-7a. Creating a Paginated Table of the Entire Stock of Houses (advert_houses.php)

```php
<?php
session_start();
if (!isset($_SESSION['user_level']) || ($_SESSION['user_level'] != 1))
{
     header("Location: login.php");
     exit();
}
define('ERROR_LOG', 'errors.log');
?>
<!DOCTYPE html>
<html lang="en">
<head>
     <title>Admin View All Houses</title>
     <meta charset="utf-8">
     <meta name="viewport" content="width-device-width, initial-scale=1, shrink-to-fit=no">
      <!-- Bootstrap CSS File -->
      <link rel="stylesheet"
href="https://stackpath.bootstrapcdn.com/bootstrap/4.1.0/css/bootstrap.min.css"
           integrity=
"sha384-9gVQ4dYFwwWSjIDZnLEWnxCjeSWFphJiwGPXr1jddIhOegiu1FwO5qRGvFXOdJZ4"
           crossorigin="anonymous">
     <link rel="stylesheet" type="text/css" href="transparent.css">
     <script src='https://www.google.com/recaptcha/api.js'></script>
</head>
<body>
<div class="container" style="margin-top:10px">
<!-- Header Section -->
<header>
     <?php include('includes/header_3btn.php'); ?>
</header>
<div class="content mx-auto" id="contents" style="padding-top:10px">
<!-- Body Section -->
 <div class="row" style="padding: 10px;">
<div class="col-sm-12">
     <h4 class="text-center">Houses displayed four at-a-time</h4>
     <h5>
          <?php
          If (!empty($errorstring)) {
               echo $errorstring;
          }
          ?>
     </h5>
<?php
     try {
     // This script retrieves all the records from the users table.
     require ('mysqli_connect.php'); // Connect to the database.
     //set the number of rows per display page
     $pagerows = 4;
     // Has the total number of pages already been calculated?
```

```php
        if (isset($_GET['pages'])) {
                $pages = (filter_var($_GET['pages'], FILTER_SANITIZE_NUMBER_INT));
        } else {
                //use the next block of code to calculate the number of pages
                //First, check for the total number of records
                $query = "SELECT COUNT(ref_number) FROM houses";
                $result = mysqli_query ($dbcon, $query);
                $row = mysqli_fetch_array ($result, MYSQLI_NUM);
                $records = $row[0];
                //Now calculate the number of pages
                if ($records > $pagerows){ //if the number of records will fill more than one
                page
                        //Calculate the number of pages and round the result up to the nearest
                        integer
                        $pages = ceil ($records/$pagerows);
                }else{
                        $pages = 1;
                }
        }//page check finished. Declare which record to start with
        If (isset($_GET['start'])) {
                $start = (filter_var($_GET['start'], FILTER_SANITIZE_NUMBER_INT));
        } else {
                $start = 0;
        }
// Make the query:
$query = "SELECT ref_number, location, thumb, price, mini_description, bedrooms, status ";
$query .= "FROM houses ORDER BY ref_number DESC LIMIT ?, ?";
 $q = mysqli_stmt_init($dbcon);
 mysqli_stmt_prepare($q, $query);
 // use prepared statement to ensure that only text is inserted
 // bind fields to SQL Statement
 mysqli_stmt_bind_param($q, 'ii', $start, $pagerows );
 // execute query
 mysqli_stmt_execute($q);
$result = mysqli_stmt_get_result($q);
if ($result) { // If it ran OK, display the records.
        // Table header.
        echo '<table class="table table-striped table-sm" style="color: black; background-
        color:white;">
        <tr>
                <th scope="col">Ref-Num</th>
                <th scope="col">Location</th>
                <th scope="col">Thumb</th>
                <th scope="col">Price</th>
                <th scope="col">Features</th>
                <th scope="col">Bedrooms</th>
                <th scope="col">Status</th>
        </tr>';
```

```php
        // Fetch and print all the records:
        while ($row = mysqli_fetch_array($result, MYSQLI_ASSOC)) {
                // Remove special characters that might already be in table to
                // reduce the chance of XSS exploits
                $ref_number = htmlspecialchars($row['ref_number'], ENT_QUOTES);
                $location = htmlspecialchars($row['location'], ENT_QUOTES);
                $thumb = htmlspecialchars($row['thumb'], FILTER_FLAG_NO_ENCODE_QUOTES);
                $price = htmlspecialchars($row['price'], ENT_QUOTES);
                $mini_description = htmlspecialchars($row['mini_description'], ENT_QUOTES);
                $bedrooms = htmlspecialchars($row['bedrooms'], ENT_QUOTES);
                $status = htmlspecialchars($row['status'], ENT_QUOTES);
                echo '<tr>
                        <td scope="row">' . $ref_number . '</td>
                        <td scope="row">' . $location . '</td>
                        <td scope="row"><img src='. $thumb . '></td>
                        <td scope="row">' . $price . '</td>
                        <td scope="row">' . $mini_description . '</td>
                        <td scope="row">' . $bedrooms . '</td>
                        <td scope="row">' . $status . '</td>
                </tr>';
        }
        echo '</table>'; // Close the table.
        mysqli_free_result ($result); // Free up the resources.
} else { // If it did not run OK.
        // Message:
        $errorstring = '<p class="text-center">The record could not be retrieved. ';
        $errorstring .= 'We apologize for any inconvenience.</p>';
        // Debugging message:
        //echo '<p>' . mysqli_error($dbcon) . '<br><br>Query: ' . $q . '</p>';
} // End of if ($result). Now display the total number of records/houses
$q = "SELECT COUNT(ref_number) FROM houses";
$result = mysqli_query ($dbcon, $q);
$row = mysqli_fetch_array ($result, MYSQLI_NUM);
$houses = (filter_var($row[0], FILTER_SANITIZE_NUMBER_INT));
mysqli_close($dbcon); // Close the database connection.
echo "<p class='text-center' style='color:black'>Total found: $houses</p>";
if ($pages > 1) {
        echo '<h5 class="text-center">';
        //What number is the current page?
        $current_page = ($start/$pagerows) + 1;
        //If the page is not the first page then create a Previous link
        if ($current_page != 1) {
                echo '<a href="advert_houses.php?start=' . ($start - $pagerows) . '&pages=' .
                        $pages . '">Previous</a> ';
        }
        //Create a Next link
        if ($current_page != $pages) {
                echo '<a href="advert_houses.php?start=' . ($start + $pagerows) . '&pages=' .
                        $pages . '">Next</a> ';
        }
```

```php
echo '</h5>';
}
}
catch(Exception $e) // We finally handle any problems here
    {
        // print "An Exception occurred. Message: " . $e->getMessage();
        print "The system is busy please try later";
        //   $date = date('m.d.y h:i:s');
        //   $errormessage = $e->getMessage();
        //   $eMessage = $date . " | Exception Error | " , $errormessage . |\n";
        //    error_log($eMessage,3,ERROR_LOG);
        // e-mail support person to alert there is a problem
        //   error_log("Date/Time: $date - Exception Error, Check error log for
        // details", 1, noone@helpme.com, "Subject: Exception Error \nFrom: Error Log
        // <errorlog@helpme.com" . "\r\n");
    }
    catch(Error $e)
    {
        // print "An Error occurred. Message: " . $e->getMessage();
        print "The system is busy please try later";
        // $date = date('m.d.y h:i:s');
        // $errormessage = $e->getMessage();
        // $eMessage = $date . " | Error | " , $errormessage . |\n";
        // error_log($eMessage,3,ERROR_LOG);
        // e-mail support person to alert there is a problem
        //   error_log("Date/Time: $date - Error, Check error log for
        // details", 1, noone@helpme.com, "Subject: Error \nFrom: Error Log <errorlog@helpme.
            com>" . "\r\n");
    }
?>
</div><!-- End of table display content -->
</div>
</div>
<div class="row mx-auto" style="padding-left: 0px; height: auto;">
<div class="col-sm-12 text-center" style="padding:0px; margin-top: 5px;">
    <footer>
            <?php include ('includes/footer.php'); ?>
    </footer>
</div>
</div>
</div>
</body>
</html>
```

The administrator can also search for individual records by using the house reference number, as described in the next section.

The Administrator's Search Page

Figure 8-8 shows the administrator's search page.

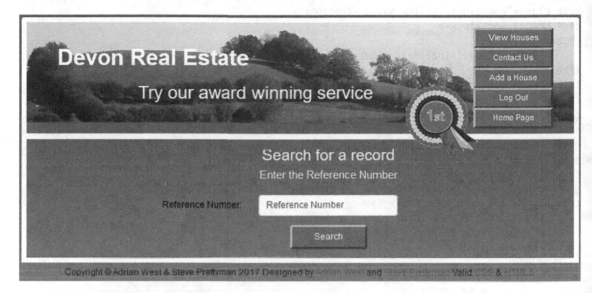

Figure 8-8. *The administrator can search for a specific house*

Notice that an additional menu selection has been added to the header for the search page. You can view the code for the new header by opening the *header_4btn.php* file in your editor. Listing 8-8 gives the code for the administrator's search page.

Listing 8-8. The Administrator's Search Page (advert_search.php)

```php
<?php
session_start();
if (!isset($_SESSION['user_level']) || ($_SESSION['user_level'] != 1))
{
    header("Location: login.php");
    exit();
}
?>
<!DOCTYPE html>
<html lang="en">
<head>
    <title>Admin Search Page</title>
    <meta charset="utf-8">
    <meta name="viewport" content="width=device-width, initial-scale=1, shrink-to-fit=no">
    <!-- Bootstrap CSS File -->
    <link rel="stylesheet"
    href="https://stackpath.bootstrapcdn.com/bootstrap/4.1.0/css/bootstrap.min.css"
    integrity="sha384-9gVQ4dYFwwWSjIDZnLEWnxCjeSWFphJiwGPXr1jddIhOegiu1FwO5qRGvFXOdJZ4"
    Crossorigin="anonymous">
```

```
        <link rel="stylesheet" type="text/css" href="transparent.css">
        <script src='https://www.google.com/recaptcha/api.js'></script>
</head>
<body>
<div class="container" style="margin-top:10px">
<!-- Header Section -->
<header>
        <?php include('includes/header_4btn.php'); ?>
</header>
<div class="content mx-auto" id="contents" style="padding-top:10px">
<!-- Body Section -->
<div class="row" style="padding-left: 0px;">
<div class="col-sm-10">
<form action="found_houses.php" method="post" name="find" id="find">
<!--START OF TEXT FIELDS-->
<div class='form-group row'>
        <label for="" class="col-sm-4 col-form-label text-right"></label>
<div class="col-sm-8 text-center">
        <h3>Search for a record</h3>
        <h5>Enter the Reference Number</h5>
        <h5>
        <?php
        If (!empty($errorstring)) {
                echo $errorstring;
        }
        ?>
        </h5>
</div>
</div>
<div class="form-group row">
<div class="col-sm-2"></div>
        <label for="ref_number" class="col-sm-4 col-form-label text-right">Reference Number:
        </label>
        <div class="col-sm-4">
        <input type="num" class="form-control" id="ref_number" name="ref_number"
                placeholder="Reference Number" maxlength="30"
                        pattern="[0-9]*"
                title="Numbers only max of 30 characters"
                value=
                        "<?php if (isset($_POST['ref_number']))
                echo htmlspecialchars($_POST['ref_number'], ENT_QUOTES); ?>" >
  </div>
   </div>
<div class="form-group row">
        <label for="" class="col-sm-4 col-form-label"></label>
<div class="col-sm-8 text-center">
        <input id="submit" class="btn btn-primary" type="submit" name="submit" value="Search">
</div>
</div>
```

```
</form><!-- End of the add house content. -->
</div>
</div>
</div>
<div class="row mx-auto" style="padding-left: 0px; height: auto;">
<div class="col-sm-12 text-center" style="padding:0px; margin-top: 5px;">
<footer>
        <?php include ('includes/footer.php'); ?>
</footer>
</div>
</div>
</body>
</html>
```

When the Search button is clicked, the record relating to the house reference number is displayed.

The Result of a Search

Figure 8-9 shows that any specified house can be displayed by the administrator.

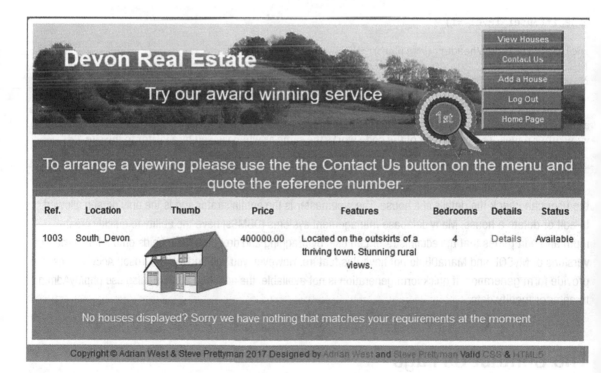

Figure 8-9. *The record is selected and displayed*

The *found_houses.php* page, previously explained, is called to display the individual house by reference number.

```
$query = "SELECT ref_number, location, thumb, price, mini_description, type, bedrooms, ";
$query .= "status FROM houses ";
if(($user_level == 1) && (!empty($_POST['ref_number']))) {
$query .= "WHERE ref_number=? ";
} else {
$query .= "WHERE location= ? AND ";
$query .= "(price <= ?) AND (price >= (? - 100000)) AND ";
$query .= "type= ? AND bedrooms= ?  ORDER BY ref_number ASC ";
}
```

This snippet of code from the found houses page will use the reference number, instead of multiple fields, to pull the specific record specified by the administrator.

```
<?php
if ($user_level == 0)
{
include("includes/header_found_houses.php");
}
else if($user_level==1)
{
include('includes/header_4btn.php');
}
?>
```

This block of code at the top of the found houses page will individualize the page displayed to include the administrator header instead of the general header for all users. This will provide the administrator buttons to view other pages. The remainder of the code works the same as when viewed by a visitor to the site.

■ **Note**   The found houses page contains no way of editing or deleting a house. The page exists purely so that the user can check the details of a house. The webmaster is the administrator and is the only person allowed to edit or delete a house. Many database management systems (DBMSs) have the ability to quickly create input and edit pages that the administrator can use, by dragging and dropping table fields onto a form. The free versions of MySQL and MariaDB do not have this feature. However, you will find that Microsoft Access does provide form generation. If quick form generation is not available, the administrator can also use phpMyAdmin to enter or modify data.

The Contact Us Page

Figure 8-10 shows an example of a suitable Contact Us page. This is a cut-down version of the Contact Us page from Chapter 7.

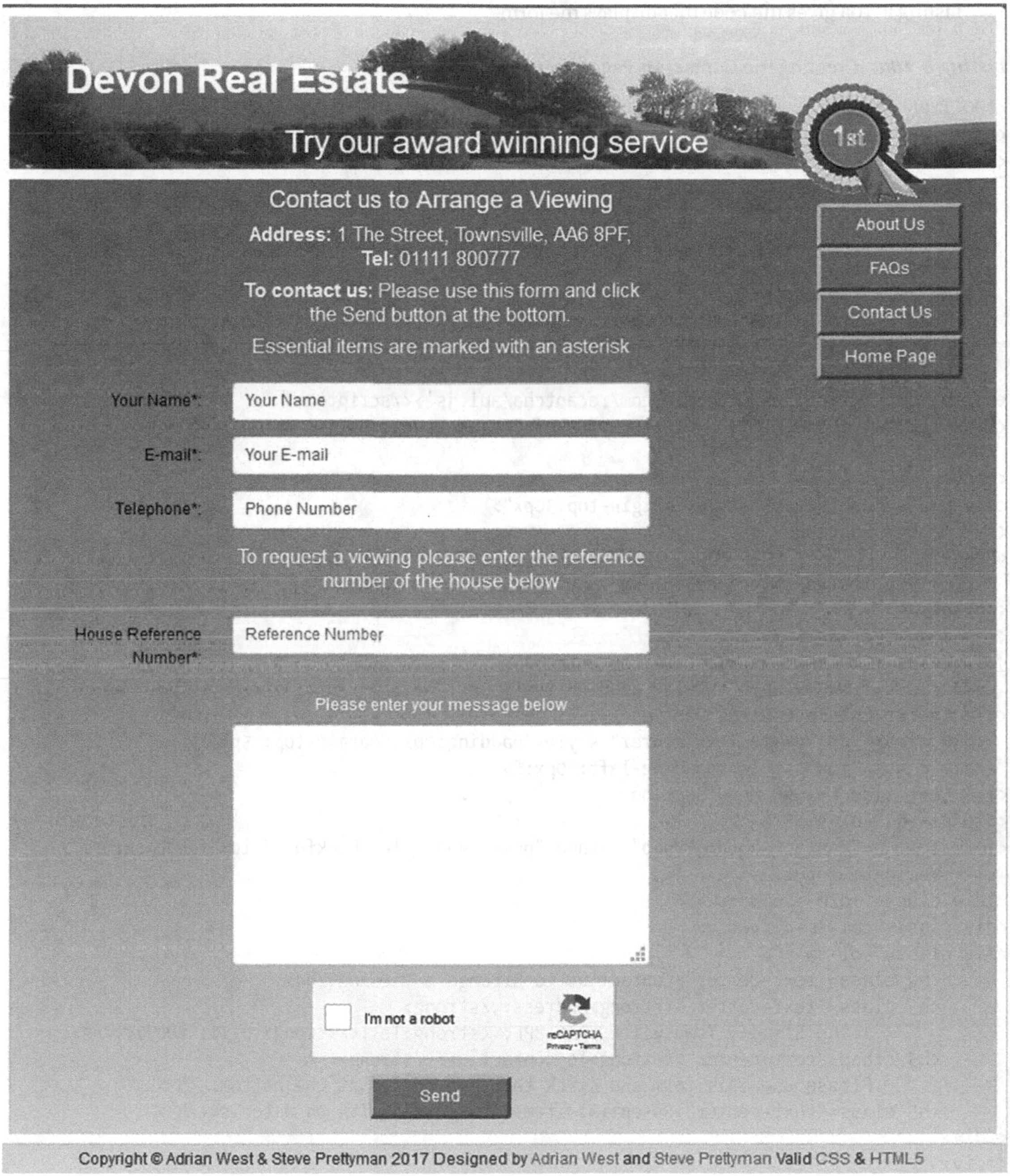

Figure 8-10. *The Contact Us page*

Listing 8-10a gives the code that displays the form.

Listing 8-10a. Creating the Contact Us Page (contact.php)

```
<!DOCTYPE html>
<html lang="en">
<head>
  <title>Contact Us Form</title>
  <meta charset="utf-8">
  <meta name="viewport" content="width=device-width, initial-scale=1, shrink-to-fit=no">
  <!-- Bootstrap CSS File -->
  <link rel="stylesheet"
      href="https://stackpath.bootstrapcdn.com/bootstrap/4.1.0/css/bootstrap.min.css"
      integrity="sha384-9gVQ4dYFwwWSjIDZnLEWnxCjeSWFphJiwGPXr1jddIhOegiu1FwO5qRGvFXOdJZ4"
      crossorigin="anonymous">
<script src='https://www.google.com/recaptcha/api.js'></script>
<link rel="stylesheet" type="text/css" href="transparent.css">
</head>
<body>
<div class="container" style="margin-top:30px">
<!-- Header Section -->
<header>
      <?php include('includes/header.php'); ?>
</header>
<!-- Body Section -->
<div class="content mx-auto" id="contents">
 <div class="row mx-auto" style="padding-left: 0px; height: auto;">
<!-- Center Column Content Section -->
  <div class="col-sm-12 text-center" style="padding:0px; margin-top: 5px;">
  <div class="row" style="padding-left: 0px;">
<!-- Left-side Column Menu Section -->
<div class="col-sm-8">
<form action="contact-handler.php" method="post" name="feedbackform" id="feedbackform">
 <!-- Validate Input -->
 <div class="form-group row">
<div class="col-sm-4"></div>
<div class="col-sm-8">
      <h4 class="text-center">Contact us to Arrange a Viewing</h4>
      <h5 class="text-center"><strong>Address:</strong>
            1 The Street, Townsville, AA6 8PF, <strong>Tel:</strong> 01111 800777</h5>
      <h5 class="text-center"><strong>To contact us:</strong>
            Please use this form and click the Send button at the bottom.</h5>
      <h5 class="text-center">Essential items are marked with an asterisk</h5>
</div>
</div>
<!--START OF TEXT FIELDS-->
<div class="form-group row">
      <label for="username" class="col-sm-4 col-form-label text-right">Your Name*:</label>
<div class="col-sm-8">
```

```
            <input type="text" class="form-control" id="username" name="username"
                pattern="[a-zA-Z][a-zA-Z\s]*" title="Alphabetic and space only max of
                30 characters"
                placeholder="Your Name" maxlength="30" required
                value=
                        "<?php if (isset($_POST['username']))
                echo htmlspecialchars($_POST['username'], ENT_QUOTES); ?>" >
    </div>
    </div>
<div class="form-group row">
        <label for="useremail" class="col-sm-4 col-form-label text-right">E-mail*:</label>
<div class="col-sm-8">
        <input type="email" class="form-control" id="useremail" name="useremail"
            placeholder="Your E-mail" maxlength="60" required
            value=
                    "<?php if (isset($_POST['useremail']))
            echo htmlspecialchars($_POST['useremail'], ENT_QUOTES); ?>" >
    </div>
    </div>
    <div class="form-group row">
        <label for="phone" class="col-sm-4 col-form-label text-right">Telephone*:</label>
    <div class="col-sm-8">
        <input type="tel" class="form-control" id="phone" name="phone"
            placeholder="Phone Number" maxlength="30"
            value-
                    "<?php if (isset($_POST['phone']))
            echo htmlspecialchars($_POST['phone'], ENT_QUOTES); ?>" >
    </div>
    </div>
    <div class="form-group row">
        <label for="" class="col-sm-4 col-form-label text-right"></label>
        <h5 class="col-sm-8 text-center">To request a viewing please enter the reference
    number of the house below</h5>
    </div>
    <div class="form-group row">
        <label for="address1" class="col-sm-4 col-form-label text-right">
            House Reference Number*:</label>
<div class="col-sm-8">
        <input type="num" class="form-control" id="ref_number" name="ref_number"
            pattern="[0-9]*"
            title="Numbers only max of 30 characters"
            placeholder="Reference Number" maxlength="30" required
            value=
                    "<?php if (isset($_POST['ref_number']))
            echo htmlspecialchars($_POST['ref_number'], ENT_QUOTES); ?>" >
    </div>
    </div>
<div class="form-group row">
        <label for="" class="col-sm-4 col-form-label text-right"></label>
```

```
<div class="col-sm-8 text-center">
      <label for="comment" style="color:white;">Please enter your message below</label>
      <textarea class="form-control" id="comment" name="comment" rows="8" cols="40"
            value="<?php if (isset($_POST['comment']))
            echo htmlspecialchars($_POST['comment'], ENT_QUOTES); ?>" >
      </textarea>
 </div>
 </div>
 <div class="form-group row">
      <label class="col-sm-4 col-form-label"></label>
 <div class="col-sm-8">
 <div class="g-recaptcha" style="margin-left: 80px;"
      data-sitekey="6LcrQ1wUAAAAAPxlrAkLuPdpY5qwS9rXF1j46fhq"></div>
 </div>
 </div>
<div class="form-group row">
      <label for="" class="col-sm-4 col-form-label"></label>
<div class="col-sm-8 text-center">
      <input id="submit" class="btn btn-primary" type="submit" name="submit" value="Send">
</div>
</div>
</form>
</div>
<div class="col-sm-4">
      <?php include ('includes/menu.php'); ?>
</div>
</div>
</div>
</div>
</div>
<div class="row mx-auto" style="padding-left: 0px; height: auto;">
<div class="col-sm-12 text-center" style="padding:0px; margin-top: 5px;">
      <footer>
            <?php include ('includes/footer.php'); ?>
      </footer>
</div>
</div>
</div>
</body>
</html>
```

The format of the form and the verification of the information is similar to the code explained in Chapter 7. Therefore, we will not repeat the explanation in this chapter.

We will now examine the contact form handler in Listing 8-10b.

Listing 8-10b. Creating the Contact Form Handler (contact_handler.php)

```
<?php
// Feedback form handler
// set the error and thank you pages
$formurl = "feedback/feedback_form.html" ;
$errorurl = "feedback/error.html" ;
```

```php
$thankyouurl = "feedback/thankyou.html" ;
$emailerrurl = "feedback/emailerr.html" ;
$errorcommenturl =  "feedback/commenterror.html" ;
// set to the email address of the recipient
$mailto = "none@noone.com" ;
// Is first name present? If it is, sanitize it
$username = filter_var( $_POST['username'], FILTER_SANITIZE_STRING);
if ((!empty($username)) && (preg_match('/[a-z\s]/i',$username)) &&
            (strlen($username) <= 30)) {
              //Save user name
              $usernametrim = $username;
}else{
      $errors = 'yes';
}
// Check that an email address has been entered correctly
$useremailtrim = filter_var( $_POST['useremail'], FILTER_SANITIZE_EMAIL);
if  ((empty($useremailtrim)) || (!filter_var($useremailtrim, FILTER_VALIDATE_EMAIL))
                || (strlen($useremailtrim > 60))) {
              // if email is bad display error page
              header( "Location: $emailerrurl" );
              exit ;
}
// Is the phone number present? if so, sanitize it
$phone = filter_var( $_POST['phone'], FILTER_SANITIZE_STRING);
if ((!empty($phone)) && (strlen($phone) <= 30)) {
      //Sanitize and validate phone number
      $phonetrim = (filter_var($phone, FILTER_SANITIZE_NUMBER_INT));
      $phonetrim = preg_replace('/[^0-9]/', ", $phonetrim);
}else{
      $phonetrim = NULL; // if not valid or missing do not save
}
      /
$ref_number = filter_var( $_POST['ref_number'], FILTER_SANITIZE_STRING);
if ((!empty($ref_number)) && (preg_match('/[0-9]/', $ref_number)) &&
  (strlen($ref_number) <= 30)) {
      //Save the 1st address
      $ref_numbertrim = $ref_number;
}else{
      $errors = 'yes';
}
$comment = filter_var( $_POST['comment'], FILTER_SANITIZE_STRING);
if ((!empty($comment)) && (strlen($comment) <= 320)) {
      // remove ability to create link in email
      $patterns = array("/http/", "/https/", "/\:/","/\/\//","/www./");
      $commenttrim = preg_replace($patterns," ", $comment);
      }else{ // if comment not valid display error page
      header( "Location: $errorcommenturl" );
      exit;
}
```

```
if (!empty($errors)) { // if errors display error page
      header( "Location: $errorurl" );
      exit ; }
// everything OK send e-mail
$subject = "Message from customer " . $usernametrim;
$messageproper =
      "----------------------------------------------------------\n" .
      "Name of sender: $usernametrim\n" .
      "Email of sender: $useremailtrim\n" .
      "Telephone: $phonetrim\n" .
      "Ref Number: $ref_numbertrim\n" .
      "----------------------- MESSAGE ------------------------\n\n" .
      $commenttrim .
      "\n\n----------------------------------------------------------\n" ;
      mail($mailto, $subject, $messageproper, "From: \"$usernametrim\" <$useremailtrim>" );
      header( "Location: $thankyouurl" );
      exit ;
?>
```

When the message is sent, a "thank you" page appears. If information was entered incorrectly or required information is missing, an error message will be displayed. Since this code is like the code in Chapter 7, please review the explanation there. Remember that this code will not execute unless it resides on a server that includes the ability to send e-mails via program code.

■ **Note** The "thank you" page and the error message pages are included in the downloadable files, and they are like those in Chapter 7.

Summary

In this chapter, you learned how to plan a database for a real estate catalog. We created a home page in which users could search for a suitable house. We produced a house details page to provide the user with more specifics from the database. We provided the administrator with a page so that they could add new houses. We produced a page that allowed the administrator to view the entire stock of houses or to search for and view a specific house. We created an inquiry form for users who want to personally inspect a house.

In the next chapter, you will learn how to extract data from multiple tables by joining them, how to create a form to allow payments by check, and how to implement an economical method for printing online forms.

■ ■ ■

CHAPTER 9

Join Multiple Tables and Other Enhancements

Database-driven websites can benefit from the three practical enhancements described in this chapter. For instance, multiple tables can give more specific search results and are essential for the administration of forums and e-commerce sites, membership fees can be paid by check as well as by using PayPal and credit/debit cards, and check payments can be accompanied by printable application forms.

After completing this chapter, you will be able to

- Create multiple tables using phpMyAdmin

- Understand the difference between inner and outer joins

- Join multiple tables using phpMyAdmin

- Join multiple tables using program code

- Provide printable online forms

Introduction to Multiple Tables

The previous chapters displayed information from one table at a time. Sometimes databases use several tables that can be related to each other. These databases are called *relational* databases. Data from each table can be joined (combined) to form virtual tables that can be displayed in a browser. In this tutorial, we will concentrate entirely on the process of joining tables. For simplicity and clarity, the website for these tutorials will be stripped of several features, such as logging in and administration. The buttons for these functions will appear on the headers, but they will be dead links.

You may wonder why we need more than one table. Why not put all the data in one table? We could use one huge table, but it would lead to no end of trouble. A great deal of information would be entered many times, causing the database to be inefficient, and the administration would be time-consuming and tedious.

As an example, suppose we had an e-commerce website selling telephones and intercoms. We could have a set of records as shown in Table 9-1.

Table 9-1. *A Table with Many Duplicate Entries*

Order_id	Customer Name	Address	Product	Stock
1006	Charlie Smith	3 Park Road Townsville TV77 99JP	Phone 123	1
1007	Charlie Smith	3 Park Road Townsville TV77 99JP	Intercom 456	4
1008	Robert Bruce	4 Linden Street Urbania UT88 66XY	Intercom 456	5
1009	Nellie Dean	7 Elm Avenue Milltown MT 78 88WZ	Phone 456	6
1010	Robert Bruce	4 Linden Street Urbania UT88 66XY	Phone 678	1
1011	Nellie Dean	7 Elm Avenue Milltown MT78 88WZ	Intercom 396	3
1012	Charlie Smith	3 Park Road Townsville TV77 99JP	Phone Dock A2	4

This single table containing the latest orders has many problems.

On different dates, Charlie Smith has ordered three items, and his address is repeated three times. If he changed his address, we would need to amend three rows in the table. Charlie's name and address should be kept in a separate table; this would allow us the ability to change his address only once. Stock levels usually change. We currently would have to scroll through the records to determine the lowest stock level for a particular item. The stock level and the product description should be kept in another table so only one table would need updating when the stock level changes. The user and the administrator can then easily see an accurate figure for the stock level when the product is displayed.

Normalization

The process of eliminating duplicates and other maintenance problems is called *normalization*. Table 9-1 contains items that illustrate very bad practices. The first name and last name should be in separate columns. The address should be split into separate columns for street, town, and ZIP code or postal code. This process is known by the rather clumsy name of *atomicity* because, like atoms, the data is separated into minimal components. It is then *atomic* or *indivisible*.

Normalization is achieved by applying rigorous *atomicity* and splitting the data into several tables, instead of using just one table, so that each table has a specific and singular purpose. Also, the information in each table must have closely related data, such as first name, last name, and e-mail address; if the customer changes his or her e-mail address, you have to amend only one record. Normalization allows a database to be easily extended so that it can hold more types of information. For instance, a table could be added to hold the colors of the phones, or you could have a table for dispatch dates.

Normalization can be difficult to understand at first, but you will be automatically normalizing your tables if you apply atomicity and then group closely related data into separate tables. By breaking data down to the lowest level, you allow for future growth and better data control, and you leave yourself more options in the future to modify and manipulate the data. Being able to have a one-to-many relationship on multiple tables ensures less data redundancy.

■ **Note** In most cases, properly designed database tables are in (at least) third normal form (3NF).

A table is considered to be in first normal form (1NF) when it has a relationship as defined by the following requirements.

- Each cell holds a single value.

- All column values are of the same type.

- Each column is uniquely identified (column name).

- The columns can be in any order.

- The rows can be in any order.

- Each row contains unique data.

A table is in second normal form (2NF) if the table is in 1NF and includes a primary key that uniquely identifies each row. A table is in third normal form if it is in 2NF and there are no columns that are defined (dependent) on other column. The data is *atomic* or *indivisible*. Additionally, tables can be classified as fourth normal form (4NF) and fifth normal form (5NF). However, these classifications go beyond the scope of this book.

There are situations in which a database administrator may reduce normalization and duplicate data across tables. This can increase efficiently of data retrieval in heavily used databases, such as inventory databases for major department stores.

Let's now create a database with two tables.

Creating the Database and Tables

For the first part of this tutorial, we will create a database to contain two small tables. In phpMyAdmin, create a database called *birdsdb* and then set up a user and a password as follows:

1. In the *htdocs* folder within XAMPP or in the EasyPHP folder *eds_www*, create a new folder named *birds*.

2. Download the files for Chapter 9 from the book's page at Apress.com and unzip them in your new *birds* folder.

3. Start XAMPP or EasyPHP, and in the address field of a browser enter **localhost/phpmyadmin/** to access phpMyAdmin.

4. Click the Databases tab and create a database named *birdsdb*. From the pull-down Collation list, choose utf8_general_ci and then click Create.

5. Click the Privileges tab and then scroll down and click Add new user.

6. Enter these details:

   - *Username*: faraday

   - *Password*: Dynam01831

   - *Host*: Localhost

   - *Database* name: birdsdb

7. Click Go.

Viewing the Connection File

The file *mysqli_connect.php* has the following code:

```php
<?php
// Create a connection to the migrate database and to MySQL
// Set the encoding to utf-8
// Set the database access details as constants
define ('DB_USER', 'faraday');
define ('DB_PASSWORD', 'Dynamo1831');
define ('DB_HOST', 'localhost');
define ('DB_NAME', 'birdsdb');
// Make the connection:
$dbcon = new mysqli(DB_HOST, DB_USER, DB_PASSWORD, DB_NAME);
// Set the encoding...optional but recommended
mysqli_set_charset($dbcon, 'utf8');
```

We have not provided dump files for the birds, location, and rsvinfo tables; therefore, you must create and populate the tables manually. This will not be tedious because the tables are very small.

Click the database birdsdb in the left panel of phpMyAdmin to manually create a table named *birds* with four columns and the attributes shown in Table 9-2.

Table 9-2. The birds Table

Column Name	Type	Length/Value	Default	Attributes	NULL	Index	A_I
bird_id	MEDIUMINT	4	None	UNSIGNED	☐	PRIMARY	☑
bird_name	TINYTEXT	60	None		☐		☐
rarity	TINYTEXT	60`	None		☐		☐
best_time	TINYTEXT	60	None		☐		☐

The birds table contains a column named *bird_id*. This column is configured as the PRIMARY KEY.

You will see a pop-up dialog as shown in Figure 9-1; remember to not enter a size as you have already defined it in the column description.

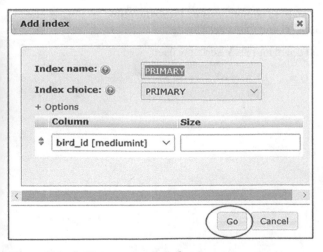

Figure 9-1. Setting a primary index

We now need to create the additional table named *location*.

Creating a Second Table

Click the database birdsdb in the left panel of phpMyAdmin to manually create a table named *location* with four columns and the attributes shown in Table 9-3. A pop-up window (like Figure 9-1) will display to allow you to confirm that location_id is the PRIMARY KEY. Just click Go to confirm the information.

Table 9-3. *The Attributes for the location Table*

Column Name	Type	Length/Value	Default	Attributes	NULL	Index	A_I
location_id	MEDIUMINT	4	None	UNSIGNED	☐	PRIMARY	☑
location	TINYTEXT	60	None		☐		☐
location_type	TINYTEXT	60`	None		☐		☐
bird_id	MEDIUMINT	4	None	UNSIGNED	☐		☐

■ **Important**   In the location table, make sure item bird_id has the same name, length, and type as bird_id in the birds table. In our example, they both have the same name (bird_id), the same length (4), and the same type (MEDIUMINT). This is vital for joining and displaying data from multiple tables.

Foreign Keys

Under normal circumstances, you would not expect to see an item named *bird_id* in a table for location details. The bird_id item in the location table is called a *foreign key*. By including the column bird_id in both tables, we will be able to combine and display selected data from the two tables; we achieve this with a JOIN statement, which we will explain shortly.

■ **Caution**   Do not enter data in the tables. We will do this later when the tables have been prepared for joining.

Meanwhile, we must begin with some preparation.

Preparing the Tables for Joining

Now the indexes need to be set for the location table. The column location_id is already indexed because it is a primary key. The foreign key named bird_id in the location table will be indexed. In phpMyAdmin, click the location table in the left panel. Select the Structure tab, and in the right panel check the box next to the bird_id column. Scroll down to the Indexes button, and you will see the message indicating the primary index is defined but no foreign key is defined.

Scroll back up and then click Index at the bottom right of Figure 9-2 (shown circled). If you checked the box to the left of bird_id, then the index will be automatically created for you. Scroll down to the Indexes area. You should now see both the primary key and the bird_id indexes.

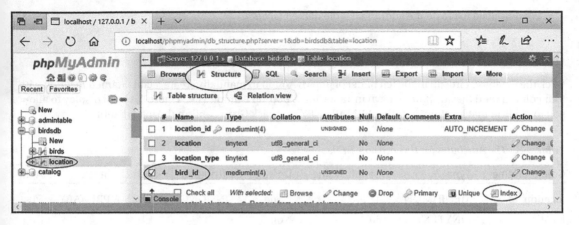

Figure 9-2. *Creating an index for the foreign key*

Populating the Two Tables

As previously stated, because we do not have a page for registering birds or locations, we need to populate them manually using phpMyAdmin. This will not be tedious because the tables contain very few items. Also, for your own adaptations of the book's websites, you will not be provided with SQL dump files for the birds and locations tables. Therefore, learning how to use phpMyAdmin to populate tables is essential.

To populate the birds table, in phpMyAdmin click the database birdsdb (circled in Figure 9-3) in the left column and then click the Structure tab. You will see the two tables in the right pane.

Figure 9-3. *Using phpMyAdmin to populate the birds table*

Check the box next to the birds table (circled in Figure 9-3) and then in the birds record (row) click the Insert icon (circled in Figure 9-3). The Insert page will now appear, as shown in Figure 9-4.

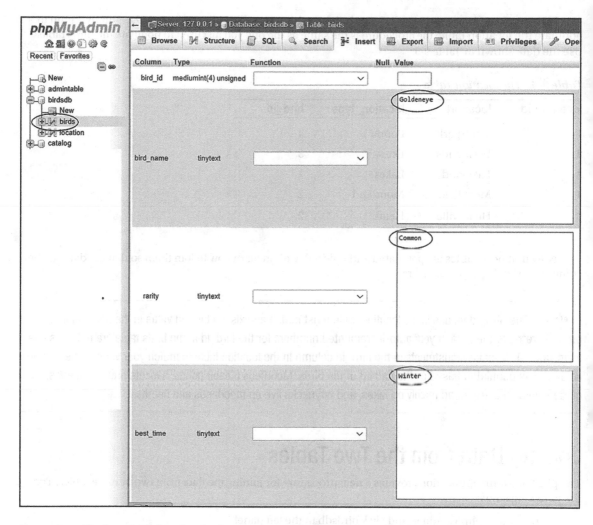

Figure 9-4. *The Insert tab showing the details inserted for the Goldeneye duck*

On the left you will see the table columns listed: bird_name, rarity, and best_time. In the text fields on the right you will be able to populate those items. As an example, you will see in Figure 9-3 that we have entered Goldeneye, Common, and Winter.

Use the data in Table 9-4 to repeat this procedure for the other birds.

Table 9-4. *The birds Table*

bird_id	bird_name	rarity	best_time
1	Goldeneye	Common	Winter
2	Wryneck	Rare	Summer
3	Avocet	Common	Winter
4	Moorhen	Common	Any time

Now continue to use phpMyAdmin and click the location table in the left panel. Use phpMyAdmin to populate the location table; the procedure is the same as the one you just used to populate the birds table. Use the data shown in Table 9-5.

Table 9-5. *The location Table*

location_id	location	location_type	bird_id
1	southpark	Ponds	4
2	Westlands	Estuary	3
3	Lakeland	Lakes	1
4	Moorfield	Moorland	2
5	Heathville	Heath	2

Now that both tables are populated and indexed, we can learn how to join them so that the data can be combined and displayed on a screen.

■ **Note**   The bird_id values in the location table must match an existing bird_id value in the birds table to properly retrieve the data. If your auto-incremented numbers for the bird_id in the birds table are not the same as in Table 9-4, make adjustments in the bird_id column in the location table to match your values. The bird_id column was populated based on the habitat of the birds. Moorhens inhabit ponds, avocets prefer estuaries, goldeneye ducks are found mainly on lakes, and wrynecks live on moorlands and heaths.

Joining Data from the Two Tables

The phpMyAdmin application provides a neat procedure for joining the data from two or more tables. Try the following steps:

1. Open phpMyAdmin and click birdsdb in the left panel.

2. Click the Designer tab; if you don't see the Designer tab, click the More pull-down tab and click Designer.

3. You should see the two tables; drag them around using your mouse so that they are roughly in the positions shown in Figure 9-5.

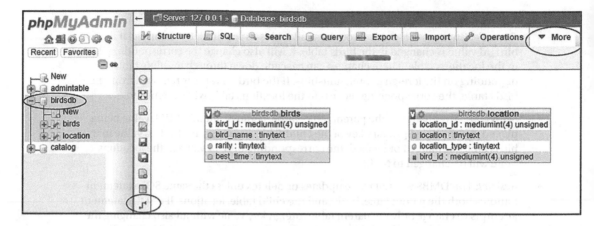

Figure 9-5. Positioning the tables ready for joining

4. On the vertical tool bar, click the Create relationship icon, which is shown circled in Figure 9-5.

5. Click bird_id in the birds table and then click bird_id in the location table. If you do this in the wrong order (i.e., click location first), you will see an error message.

6. You will see a pop-up panel, as shown in Figure 9-6.

Figure 9-6. The pop-up dialog for specifying the type of relationship

From the pull-down menus, select RESTRICT in both field and then click OK.

■ **Note** MySQL and MariaDB allow several options when creating relationships between tables. These options are based on what to do when an update or delete occurs to the parent table (birds) and how this will affect the child table (locations). When reading data (SELECT), the actual relationship does not matter. The actual determination of how the information is pulled from the tables is determined by the SQL statement itself.

The following options are available:

- *Cascade*: Changes will occur throughout all tables as required. For example, if the bird_id value is changed in the birds table, it will also change the corresponding IDs in the locations table. These changes can cascade down through multiple tables depending on the foreign key relationships. If the bird_id value is removed from the birds table, the corresponding records in the locations table will be removed.

- *Set NULL*: Any change to the parent table, birds, could result in a NULL value being placed in the related primary key of the child table, locations. If a bird_id value in the birds table is changed or deleted, the corresponding bird_id value in the locations table will be changed to NULL.

- *Restrict*: The DMBS will not make updates or deletes unless the same SQL statement handles both the parent table, birds, and the child table, locations. If a SQL statement attempts to change only the parent table foreign key value without also changing the related primary key in the child table, the statement will be rejected. Also, if a SQL statement tries to remove a parent table record or foreign key without removing (or changing) the related record (or primary key) from the child table, the statement will be rejected.

Our example sets both the delete and update values to restrict, which would provide the administrator with feedback if somehow the birds table was changed without corresponding changes occurring in the locations table. While this chapter covers how to read data from multiple tables, you can test how these relations affect the tables by changing them and attempting to update or delete records within phpMyAdmin.

7.   You will see the tables linked (related), as shown in Figure 9-7.

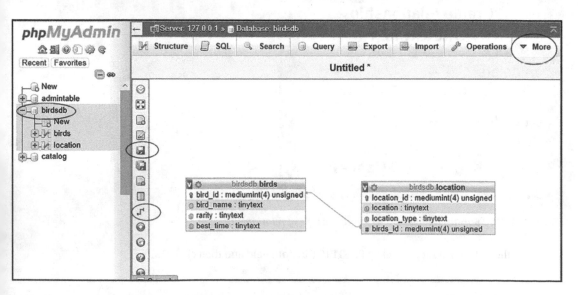

Figure 9-7. *The tables are now related*

8.   Save the link by clicking the Save icon circled in Figure 9-7.

We will now use phpMyAdmin to create a third table named reserves_info; this table will contain information about the reserves such as access to bird hides (shelters) and the entrance fee, if any.

Creating the Third Table

Click the database birdsdb in the left panel of phpMyAdmin to manually create a table named *reserves_info* with five columns and the attributes in Table 9-6. Verify the primary key as shown previously.

Table 9-6. *The Structure and Attributes for the reserves_info Table*

Column Name	Type	Length/Value	Default	Attributes	NULL	Index	A_I
reserses_id	MEDIUMINT	4	None	UNSIGNED	☐	PRIMARY	☑
bird_hides	ENUM	'yes', 'no'	None		☐		☐
entrance_member	TINYTEXT	60`	None		☐		☐
entr_non_member	TINYTEXT	60	None		☐		☐
location_id	MEDIUMINT	4	None	UNSIGNED	☐	INDEX	☐

■ **Important**   Follow the same procedure as previously shown for bird_id in the location table and make location_id an index.

Using the Insert tab in phpMyAdmin, populate the reserves_info table with the data given in Table 9-7.

Table 9-7. *The Data for the reserves_info Table (Entrance Refers to the Entrance Fee)*

reserves_id	bird_hides	entrance_member	entr_non_member	location_id
1	yes	free	£1	1
2	yes	£1	£2	2
3	yes	free	£1	3
4	no	free	free	4
5	no	free	free	5

■ **Note**   The location_id value in the reserves_info table must match a location_id value in the location table. If your values are different than shown in Table 9-5 and Table 9-7, make the needed adjustments so the values match.

When you have created and populated the reserves_info table, in phpMyAdmin click the birdsdb database name on the left side of the page. Then click the Designer tab to display the current relationships between the tables. You will see the first two tables with their connecting link, but you may not see the third table.

In this case, click the topmost icon on the vertical toolbar (circled in Figure 9-8), and a list of tables will appear in a new panel on the right. The third table will be listed, but its box will not be checked. Check the third table's box to make the table appear. Slide the third table around so that it is roughly positioned above and to the left of the other two tables, as shown in Figure 9-8.

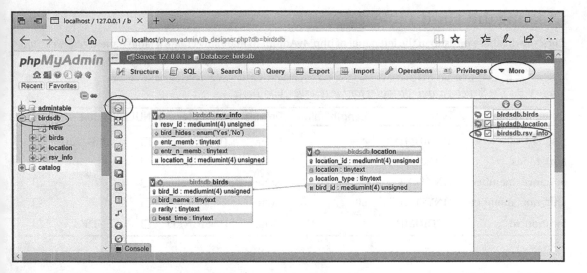

Figure 9-8. *Displaying and positioning the third table in Designer view*

The third table will not be linked, as shown in Figure 9-8.

We now need to create a relationship between the location table and the reserves_info table.

1. In the vertical toolbar, click the Create a relationship icon (shown circled in Figure 9-9).

2. Click location_id in the location table and then click the location_id in the reserves_info table. If you do this in the wrong order (i.e., if you click location_id in the reserves_info table first), you will see an error message.

3. When the Foreign key pop-up appears, select RESTRICT in both fields and click Go.

You should now see the tables linked, as shown in Figure 9-9.

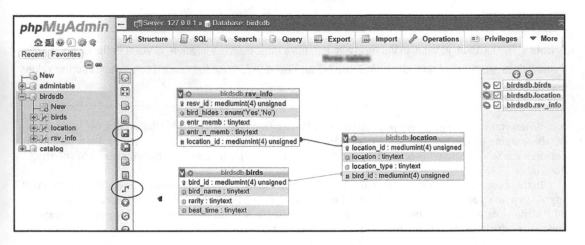

Figure 9-9. *Creating and saving the relationship between the second and third tables*

Creating Pages to Display the Data from Your Joined Tables

The joined tables are virtual tables in the database management system (DBMS) and cannot be seen by the public.

We will now create some pages so that your tables can be displayed in public browsers. In addition to a home page, we will create pages to display the table of birds, the location of the reserves, two joined tables, and three joined tables. These pages are included in the downloadable files for Chapter 9.

The Home Page

Figure 9-10 shows the home page for our website.

Figure 9-10. *The home page*

Listing 9-10 shows the code for the home page.

Listing 9-10. The Code for the Home Page (index.php)

```
<!DOCTYPE html>
<html lang="en">
<head>
<title>Birds Home Page</title>
<meta charset="utf-8">
<meta name="viewport" content="width=device-width, initial-scale=1,
      shrink-to-fit=no">
<!-- Bootstrap CSS File -->
<link rel="stylesheet"
  href=
"https://stackpath.bootstrapcdn.com/bootstrap/4.1.0/css/bootstrap.min.css"
```

```
  integrity=
"sha384-9gVQ4dYFwwWSjIDZnLEWnxCjeSWFphJiwGPXr1jddIhOegiu1FwO5qRGvFXOdJZ4"
  crossorigin="anonymous">
<link rel="stylesheet" type="text/css" href="birds.css">
</head>
<body>
<div class="container" style="margin-top:30px;border: 3px black solid;">
<!-- Header Section -->
<header class="jumbotron text-center row" id="includeheader"
        style="margin-bottom:2px; padding:20px;background-color:#CCFF99;">
                <?php include('includes/header.php'); ?>
</header>
<!-- Body Section -->
<div class="content mx-auto" id="contents">
<div class="row mx-auto" style="padding-left: 0px; height: auto;">
<!-- Left-side Column Menu Section -->
  <nav class="col-sm-2">
      <ul class="nav nav-pills flex-column">
                <?php include('includes/nav.php'); ?>
      </ul>
  </nav>
<!-- Center Column Content Section -->
<div class="col-sm-8 row" style="padding-left: 30px;">
<h2 style="padding-left: 50px; padding-top: 20px;">
        Help Save Our Devon Birds From Extinction</h2>
<div class="col-sm-8 text-left">
<p>The Devon bird reserves were established in an effort to combat the massive decline in
the bird population. Farmers (the self proclaimed Guardians of the Countryside!) spray
insecticides, weed killers and pesticides that kill the birds' main source of food. They
also rip out the hedges that provide the birds with nesting sites and their means of
travelling safely from field to field. Any birds that survive will probably be shot to
satisfy a blood lust for living targets</p>
</div>
<div class="col-sm-4">
<h4 class="text-center"><strong>
        Become a member and support our cause</strong></h4>
<p class="text-left">
        The annual membership fee includes free or reduced entrance fees to the reserves,
        a free quarterly magazine, news updates and more.
</p>
</div>
</div>
<!-- Right-side Column Content Section -->
        <aside class="col-sm-2" style="padding-top: 20px;
                padding-right: 0px;">
                <?php include('includes/info-col.php'); ?>
        </aside>
</div>
```

```
<!-- Footer Content Section -->
<footer class="jumbotron text-center row"
style="padding-bottom:1px; padding-top:8px;
        background-color:#CCFF99;">
        <?php include('includes/footer.php'); ?>
</footer>
</div>
</body>
</html>
```

This code is like other index pages we have discussed. Thus, we have provided no additional explanation here.

Listing 9-10a shows the CSS style sheet for the website.

Listing 9-10a. The Code for the Style Sheet (birds.css)

```
body {text-align:center; background-color:#CCFF99; color:green;
font-family: "times new roman";
font-size: 120%; margin: auto; }
#container {margin:auto; border:5px black solid; }

header {color:white; background-color:#CCFF99;}
}
label { color: black; }
#submit {margin: 0px; background:#559a55; border: 5px
    outset #559a55; width: 140px;}
#includemenu {padding-top: 10px; padding-bottom: 10px;
    padding-right: 0px;}
#includefooter {background:#68CE53; padding-top: 5px;
    padding-bottom: 5px; margin: 0px;}
#includeheader { height:auto; background:#95b522;
    margin-bottom: 0px; padding:0px;
    background:url('images/header3.jpg');
    background-repeat:no-repeat;}
#contents {background-color:transparent ;margin-top: -7px;
    color: black; margin: 0px; padding: 0px;}
  #buttons {background:#559a55; border: 5px outset #559a55;}
```

The Main Menu for the Pages

The buttons on the main menu will enable the general public to view the individual tables and the joined tables. Figure 9-10 shows this menu. The menu is stored in the *includes* folder, and Listing 9-10b gives the code.

Listing 9-10b. The Main Menu (nav.php)

```
<div style="padding-top: 10px; padding-bottom: 10px; padding-right: 15px;">
        <nav class="float-left navbar navbar-expand-md navbar-dark">
        <button class="navbar-toggler" type="button"
                data-toggle="collapse" data-target="#collapsibleMenu1">
                <span class="navbar-toggler-icon"></span>
        </button>
```

349

```
<div class="btn-group-vertical btn-group-sm collapse navbar-collapse"
        id="collapsibleMenu1"  role="group" aria-label="Button Group">
        <ul class="navbar-nav flex-column" style="width: 140px;">
                <li class="nav-item">
                        <a class="btn btn-primary" id="buttons"
                        title="Page Two" href="#" role="button">
                        About Us</a>
                </li>
                <li class="nav-item">
                        <a class="btn btn-primary" id="buttons"
                        title="The Birds" href="birds.php"
                        role="button">The Birds</a>
                </li>
                <li class="nav-item">
                        <a class="btn btn-primary" id="buttons"
                        title="The Reserves" href="reserves.php"
                        role="button">The Reserves</a>
                </li>
                <li class="nav-item">
                        <a class="btn btn-primary" id="buttons"
                        title="Page Five" href="join-2.php"
                        role="button">Join 2 Tables</a>
                </li>
                <li class="nav-item">
                        <a class="btn btn-primary" id="buttons"
                        title="Page Six" href="join-3.php"
                        role="button">Join 3 Tables</a>
                </li>
                <li class="nav-item">
                        <a class="btn btn-primary" id="buttons"
                        title="Return to Home Page" href="index.php"
                        role="button">Home Page</a>
                </li>
        </div>
    </nav>
</div>
```

The Header for All the Pages

The header for all the pages contains two menu buttons. You can see this header in Figure 9-10.
Listing 9-10c gives the code for the header.

Listing 9-10c. The Code for the Header (includes/header.php)

```
<meta name="viewport" content="width=device-width, initial-scale=1">
    <script src=
    "https://ajax.googleapis.com/ajax/libs/jquery/3.3.1/jquery.min.js">
    </script>
```

```
        <script src=
"https://cdnjs.cloudflare.com/ajax/libs/popper.js/1.14.0/umd/popper.min.js">
        </script>
        <script src=
"https://maxcdn.bootstrapcdn.com/bootstrap/4.1.0/js/bootstrap.min.js">
        </script>
<div class="col-sm-8" style="color: white; padding-top: 5%;">
 <div class="h1 display-4 text-left" >The Devon Bird Reserves</div>
</div>
<div class="col-sm-4" style="padding-top: 10px; padding-bottom: 10px;">
    <nav class="float-right navbar navbar-expand-md navbar-dark">
            <button class="navbar-toggler" type="button"
            data-toggle="collapse" data-target="#collapsibleMenu">
                <span class="navbar-toggler-icon"></span>
            </button>
<div class="btn-group-vertical btn-group-sm collapse navbar-collapse"
        id="collapsibleMenu" role="group" aria-label="Button Group">
        <ul class="navbar-nav flex-column" style="width: 140px;">
            <li class="nav-item">
        <a class="btn btn-primary" id="buttons" href="#"
                        role="button">Login</a>
        </li>
        <li class="nav item">
            <a class="btn btn-primary" id="buttons"
                        href="member_reg.php" role="button">Register</a>
        </li>
</ul>
</div>
</nav>
</div>
```

Now let's look at some birds.

The Page for Viewing the Birds

Figure 9-11 shows the display for viewing the birds table.

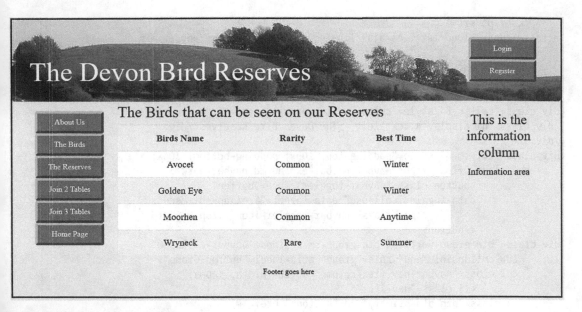

Figure 9-11. *The table of birds*

Listing 9-11 gives the code for the bird table display.

Listing 9-11. Creating a Display for the Bird's Table (birds.php)

```php
<?php
        define('ERROR_LOG','errorlog.log');
?>
<!DOCTYPE html>
<html lang="en">
<head>
        <title>Birds Home Page</title>
        <meta charset="utf-8">
        <meta name="viewport" content=
                "width=device-width, initial-scale=1, shrink-to-fit=no">
        <!-- Bootstrap CSS File -->
        <link rel="stylesheet"
                href="https://stackpath.bootstrapcdn.com/bootstrap/4.1.0/css/bootstrap.
                min.css"
                integrity="sha384-9gVQ4dYFwwWSjIDZnLEWnxCjeSWFphJiwGPXr1jddIhOegiu1FwO5qR
                GvFXOdJZ4"
                crossorigin="anonymous">
        <link rel="stylesheet" type="text/css" href="birds1.css">
</head>
<body>
<div class="container" style="margin-top:30px;border: 3px black solid;">
<!-- Header Section -->
<header class="jumbotron text-center row" id="includeheader"
style="margin-bottom:2px; padding:20px;background-color:#CCFF99;">
        <?php include('includes/header.php'); ?>
```

```
</header>
<!-- Body Section -->
<div class="content mx-auto" id="contents">
<div class="row mx-auto" style="padding-left: 0px; height: auto;">
<!-- Left-side Column Menu Section -->
  <nav class="col-sm-2">
      <ul class="nav nav-pills flex-column">
                  <?php include('includes/nav.php'); ?>
      </ul>
  </nav>
<!-- Center Column Content Section -->
<div class="col-sm-8 row" style="padding-left: 30px;">
          <h2>The Birds that can be seen on our Reserves</h2>
          <?php
          try
          {
          // This script retrieves all the records from the birds table
          require ('mysqli_connect.php'); // Connect to the database
          // Make the query:
          $q = "SELECT bird_name, rarity, best_time FROM birds ORDER BY bird_name ASC";
          $result = mysqli_query ($dbcon, $q); // Run the query
          if ($result) { // If it ran OK, display the records
                      // Table header
                      ?>
                      <table class="table table-striped" style=
                              "background: white;color:black;">
                      <tr>
                              <th scope="col">Birds Name</th>
                              <th scope="col">Rarity</th>
                              <th scope="col">Best Time</th>
                      </tr>
<?php
          // Fetch and print all the records
          while ($row = mysqli_fetch_array($result, MYSQLI_ASSOC)) {
                  $bird_name = htmlspecialchars($row['bird_name'], ENT_QUOTES);
                  $rarity = htmlspecialchars($row['rarity'], ENT_QUOTES);
                  $best_time = htmlspecialchars($row['best_time'], ENT_QUOTES);
                  echo '<tr>
                          <td scope="row">' . $bird_name . '</td>
                          <td scope="row">' . $rarity . '</td>
                          <td scope="row">' . $best_time . '</td>
                  </tr>';
          }
          echo '</table>'; // Close the table
          mysqli_free_result ($result); // Free up the resources
          } else { // If it did not run OK
                  // Message
                  echo '<p class="text-center">
                  The current birds could not be retrieved. ';
                  echo 'We apologize for any inconvenience.</p>';
                  // Debugging message
```

```
                    //echo '<p>' . mysqli_error($dbcon) . '<br><br />Query: ' .
                            $q . '</p>';
            } // End of if ($result)
            mysqli_close($dbcon); // Close the database connection.
}
catch(Exception $e) // We finally handle any problems here
{
            // print "An Exception occurred. Message: " . $e->getMessage();
            print "The system is busy please try later";
            // $date = date('m.d.y h:i:s');
            // $errormessage = $e->getMessage();
            // $eMessage = $date . " | Exception Error | " , $errormessage . |\n";
            //   error_log($eMessage,3,ERROR_LOG);
            // e-mail support person to alert there is a problem
            //   error_log("Date/Time: $date - Exception Error,
            // Check error log for details", 1, noone@helpme.com,
            // "Subject: Exception Error \nFrom: Error Log
            // <errorlog@helpme.com>" . "\r\n");
    }
    catch(Error $e)
    {
            // print "An Error occurred. Message: " . $e->getMessage();
            print "The system is busy please try later";
            // $date = date('m.d.y h:i:s');
            // $errormessage = $e->getMessage();
            // $eMessage = $date . " | Error | " , $errormessage . |\n";
            // error_log($eMessage,3,ERROR_LOG);
            // e-mail support person to alert there is a problem
            //   error_log("Date/Time: $date - Error, Check error log for
            //details", 1, noone@helpme.com, "Subject: Error \nFrom:
            // Error Log <errorlog@helpme.com>" . "\r\n");
    }
?>
</div><!-- End of the view birds page content. -->
<!-- Right-side Column Content Section -->
            <aside class="col-sm-2" style=
                    "padding-top: 20px; padding-right: 0px;">
                    <?php include('includes/info-col.php'); ?>
            </aside>
</div>
<!-- Footer Content Section -->
<footer class="jumbotron text-center row"
            style="padding-bottom:1px;
            padding-top:8px;background-color:#CCFF99;">
            <?php include('includes/footer.php'); ?>
</footer>
</div>
</div>
</body>
</html>
```

This page can be viewed by clicking the Birds menu button on the home page.

Explanation of the Code

You have seen all this code in earlier chapters. Therefore, we are not providing any additional explanation here.

We will now examine the locations table, which is the second table for this tutorial. It can be viewed by clicking the menu button The Reserves.

The Page for Viewing the Locations and Habitats of the Reserves

Figure 9-12 shows the display for viewing the reserve's location table.

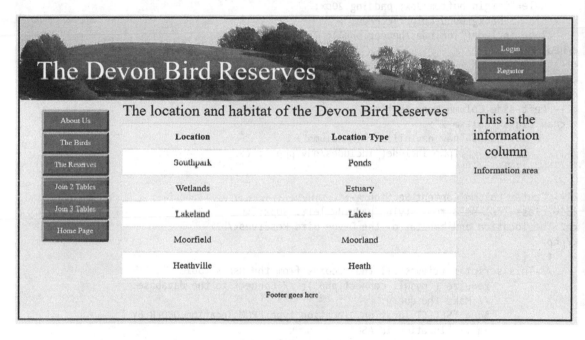

Figure 9-12. *Showing the location and type of reserve*

Listing 9-12 gives the code for displaying the location and habitat of the reserves.

Listing 9-12. Creating the Page for Displaying the Locations and Habitats of the Reserves (reserves.php)

```php
<?php
    define('ERROR_LOG','errorlog.log');
?>
<!DOCTYPE html>
<html lang="en">
<head>
  <title>Reserves Page</title>
  <meta charset="utf-8">
  <meta name="viewport" content=
          "width=device-width, initial-scale=1, shrink-to-fit=no">
```

```
<!-- Bootstrap CSS File -->
<link rel="stylesheet"
href="https://stackpath.bootstrapcdn.com/bootstrap/4.1.0/css/bootstrap.min.css"
            integrity="sha384-9gVQ4dYFwwWSjIDZnLEWnxCjeSWFphJiwGPXr1jddIhOegiu1FwO5qRGvFXOdJZ4"
            crossorigin="anonymous">
    <link rel="stylesheet" type="text/css" href="birds1.css">
</head>
<body>
<div class="container" style="margin-top:30px;border: 3px black solid;">
<!-- Header Section -->
<header class="jumbotron text-center row" id="includeheader"
    style="margin-bottom:2px; padding:20px;
            background-color:#CCFF99;">
    <?php include('includes/header.php'); ?>
</header>
<!-- Body Section -->
<div class="content mx-auto" id="contents">
<div class="row mx-auto" style="padding-left: 0px; height: auto;">
<!-- Left-side Column Menu Section -->
  <nav class="col-sm-2">
        <ul class="nav nav-pills flex-column">
                  <?php include('includes/nav.php'); ?>
        </ul>
  </nav>
<!-- Center Column Content Section -->
<div class="col-sm-8 row" style="padding-left: 30px;">
<h2>The location and habitat of the Devon Bird Reserves</h2>
<?php
    try {
    // This script retrieves all the records from the users table
            require ('mysqli_connect.php'); // Connect to the database
            // Make the query:
            $q = "SELECT location, location_type FROM location ORDER BY ";
            $q .= "location_id ASC";
            $result = mysqli_query ($dbcon, $q); // Run the query
            if ($result) { // If it ran OK, display the records
            // Table header
    ?>
        <table class="table table-striped"
            style="background: white;color:black;">
            <tr>
                    <th scope="col">Location</th>
                    <th scope="col">Location Type</th>
            </tr>
    <?php
    // Fetch and print all the records
            while ($row = mysqli_fetch_array($result, MYSQLI_ASSOC)) {
                    $location = htmlspecialchars($row['location'], ENT_QUOTES);
                    $location_type = htmlspecialchars($row['location_type'], ENT_QUOTES);
                    echo '<tr>
                    <td scope="row">' . $location . '</td>
```

```php
                    <td scope="row">' . $location_type . '</td>
                    </tr>';
            }
            echo '</table>'; // Close the table
            mysqli_free_result ($result); // Free up the resources
        } else { // If it did not run OK
            // Message
            echo '<p class="text-center">
                    The current locations could not be retrieved. ';
            echo 'We apologize for any inconvenience.</p>';
            // Debugging message
            //echo '<p>' . mysqli_error($dbcon) . '<br><br />Query: ' .
                    // $q . '</p>';
        } // End of if ($result)
    mysqli_close($dbcon); // Close the database connection.
}
catch(Exception $e) // We finally handle any problems here
{
    // print "An Exception occurred. Message: " . $e->getMessage();
    print "The system is busy please try later";
    // $date = date('m.d.y h:i:s');
    // $errormessage = $e->getMessage();
    // $eMessage - $date . " | Exception Error | " , $errormessage .
//|\n";
    // error_log($eMessage,3,ERROR_LOG);
    // e mail support person to alert there is a problem
    // error_log("Date/Time: $date - Exception Error, Check error log for
    //details", 1, noone@helpme.com, "Subject: Exception Error
    //\nFrom: Error Log <errorlog@helpme.com>" . "\r\n");

}
catch(Error $e)
{
    // print "An Error occurred. Message: " . $e->getMessage();
    print "The system is busy please try later";
    // $date = date('m.d.y h:i:s');
    // $errormessage = $e->getMessage();
    // $eMessage = $date . " | Error | " , $errormessage . |\n";
    // error_log($eMessage,3,ERROR_LOG);
    // // e-mail support person to alert there is a problem
    //   error_log("Date/Time: $date - Error, Check error log for
    //details", 1, noone@helpme.com, "Subject: Error \nFrom:
    // Error Log <errorlog@helpme.com>" . "\r\n");
}
?>
</div><!-- End of the view birds page content. -->
<!-- Right-side Column Content Section -->
    <aside class="col-sm-2" style="padding-top: 20px;
            padding-right: 0px;">
    <?php include('includes/info-col.php'); ?>
    </aside>
</div>
```

```
<!-- Footer Content Section -->
<footer class="jumbotron text-center row"
    style="padding-bottom:1px; padding-top:8px;
           background-color:#CCFF99;">
           <?php include('includes/footer.php'); ?>
</footer>
</div>
</div>
</body>
</html>
```

We will now show the display for two joined tables. Later in the chapter we will provide a more in-depth discussion on how to join tables.

Displaying Data from the Joined Tables

When the two tables are joined, some data from each of the tables birds and location will be displayed, as shown in Figure 9-13.

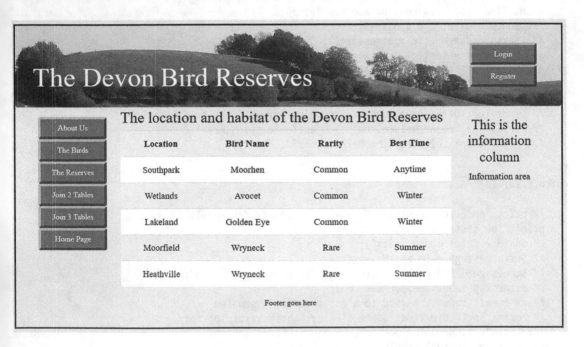

Figure 9-13. *Displaying two joined tables*

Listing 9-13 shows the code for displaying selected data from the two joined tables.

Listing 9-13. Creating the Page for Displaying Selected Data from Two Joined Tables (join-2.php)

```php
<?php
        define('ERROR_LOG','errorlog.log');
?>
 <!DOCTYPE html>
<html lang="en">
<head>
        <title>Two Tables Page</title>
        <meta charset="utf-8">
        <meta name="viewport" content="width=device-width, initial-scale=1, shrink-to-fit=no">
        <!-- Bootstrap CSS File -->
        <link rel="stylesheet"
ref="https://stackpath.bootstrapcdn.com/bootstrap/4.1.0/css/bootstrap.min.css"
                integrity="sha384-9gVQ4dYFwwWSjIDZnLEWnxCjeSWFphJ1wGPXr1jddIhOegiu1FwO5qRGvFX
                OdJZ4"
                crossorigin="anonymous">
        <link rel="stylesheet" type="text/css" href="birds1.css">
</head>
<body>
        <div class="container" style="margin-top:30px;border: 3px black solid;">
        <!-- Header Section -->
        <header class="jumbotron text-center row" id="includeheader"
                style="margin-bottom:2px; padding:20px;background-color:#CCFF99;">
                        <?php include('includes/header.php'); ?>
        </header>
        <!-- Body Section -->
        <div class="content mx-auto" id="contents">
        <div class="row mx-auto" style="padding-left: 0px; height: auto;">
        <!-- Left-side Column Menu Section -->
        <nav class="col-sm-2">
                <ul class="nav nav-pills flex-column">
                        <?php include('includes/nav.php'); ?>
                </ul>
        </nav>
        <!-- Center Column Content Section -->
        <div class="col-sm-8 row" style="padding-left: 30px;">
                <h2>The location and habitat of the Devon Bird Reserves</h2>
        <?php
        try {
        // This script retrieves all the records from the birds table
                require ('mysqli_connect.php'); // Connect to the database
                // Make the query:
                $q = "SELECT location.location, birds.bird_name, birds.rarity, birds.best_time
                        FROM location INNER JOIN birds ON location.bird_id=birds.bird_id";
                $result = mysqli_query ($dbcon, $q); // Run the query
                if ($result) { // If it ran OK, display the records
                        // Table header
                        ?>
```

```
                <table class="table table-striped" style="background:
                white;color:black;">
                <tr>
                        <th scope="col">Location</th>
                        <th scope="col">Bird Name</th>
                        <th scope="col">Rarity</th>
                        <th scope="col">Best Time</th>
                </tr>
        <?php
        // Fetch and print all the records
        while ($row = mysqli_fetch_array($result, MYSQLI_ASSOC)) {
                $location = htmlspecialchars($row['location'], ENT_QUOTES);
                $bird_name = htmlspecialchars($row['bird_name'], ENT_QUOTES);
                $rarity = htmlspecialchars($row['rarity'], ENT_QUOTES);
                $best_time = htmlspecialchars($row['best_time'], ENT_QUOTES);
                echo '<tr>
                        <td scope="row">' . $location . '</td>
                        <td scope="row">' . $bird_name . '</td>
                        <td scope="row">' . $rarity . '</td>
                        <td scope="row">' . $best_time . '</td>
                </tr>';
        }
        echo '</table>'; // Close the table
        mysqli_free_result ($result); // Free up the resources
} else { // If it did not run OK
        // Message
        echo '<p class="text-center">The current birds or locations could not be
        retrieved. ';
        echo 'We apologize for any inconvenience.</p>';
        // Debugging message
//echo '<p>' . mysqli_error($dbcon) . '<br><br />Query: ' . $q . '</p>';
} // End of if ($result)
mysqli_close($dbcon); // Close the database connection
}
catch(Exception $e) // We finally handle any problems here
{
        // print "An Exception occurred. Message: " . $e->getMessage();
        print "The system is busy please try later";
        // $date = date('m.d.y h:i:s');
        // $errormessage = $e->getMessage();
        // $eMessage = $date . " | Exception Error | " , $errormessage . |\n";
        //    error_log($eMessage,3,ERROR_LOG);
        // e-mail support person to alert there is a problem
        //    error_log("Date/Time: $date - Exception Error, Check error log for
        //details", 1, noone@helpme.com, "Subject: Exception Error \nFrom: Error Log
        // <errorlog@helpme.com>" . "\r\n");
}
catch(Error $e)
{
        // print "An Error occurred. Message: " . $e->getMessage();
        print "The system is busy please try later";
```

```
        // $date = date('m.d.y h:i:s');
        // $errormessage = $e->getMessage();
        // $eMessage = $date . " | Error | " , $errormessage . |\n";
        // error_log($eMessage,3,ERROR_LOG);
        // e-mail support person to alert there is a problem
        //  error_log("Date/Time: $date - Error, Check error log for
        //details", 1, noone@helpme.com, "Subject: Error \nFrom:
        // Error Log <errorlog@helpme.com>" . "\r\n");
    }
?>
</div><!-- End of the view birds page content. -->
<!-- Right-side Column Content Section -->
        <aside class="col-sm-2" style="padding-top: 20px; padding-right: 0px;">
                <?php include('includes/info-col.php'); ?>
        </aside>
</div>
<!-- Footer Content Section -->
<footer class="jumbotron text-center row"
        style="padding-bottom:1px; padding-top:8px;background-color:#CCFF99;">
                <?php include('includes/footer.php'); ?>
</footer>
</div>
</div>
</body>
</html>
```

Note that the order of the items following the ON word can be reversed, and you will get the same result. For example, the following:

```
ON location.bird_id=birds.bird_id)" ;
```

can be written as follows:

```
ON birds.bird_id=location.bird_id";
```

You can view the two joined tables by clicking the Join 2 Tables menu button. You will be able to see that the table contains data from both tables, as shown in Figure 9-13.

The SQL ON keyword joined the two tables by linking the related bird_id fields together. Let's take some time to discuss how and why we join tables together.

We will now create an environment for displaying three virtual joined tables. These pages will be accessible by menu buttons in the home page.

■ **Note**   As previously mentioned, joined tables are virtual tables. They cannot be seen until they are displayed in a browser. The pages in this tutorial are designed specifically to demonstrate the results of joining tables. The table displays are selected by clicking buttons on the menu. A real-world website would not have buttons labeled Join 2 Tables and Join 3 Tables. These labels are for your convenience only.

Creating a Page to Display the Three Joined Tables

Previously we created the joined relationship of the three tables in our database using myPhpAdmin, as shown in Figure 9-14.

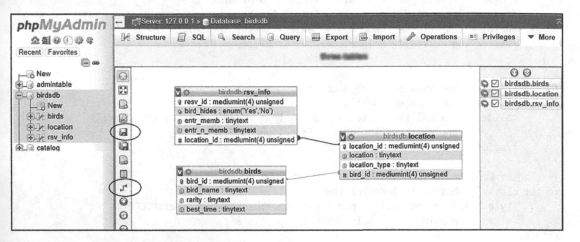

Figure 9-14. *Creating and saving the relationship between the second and third tables*

We will now create a page to select and display data from the three tables. The principle is quite logical: first join two tables to produce a virtual table and then join that to the third table. The syntax for a query for joining and selecting data from three tables is as follows:

```
$q= "SELECT some column, some other column, another column ↵
      FROM table1 ↵
            INNER JOIN table2 USING (the key that links table1 and table2) ↵
            INNER JOIN table3 USING (the key that links table2 and table3) ";
```

Let's select some data from our three joined tables to display on the web page.

```
$q = "SELECT bird_name, best_time, location, bird_hides, entrance_member, ↵
      entr_non_member FROM birds ↵
            INNER JOIN location USING (bird_id) ↵
            INNER JOIN reserves_info USING (location_id) ";
```

The results from executing this SQL statement are displayed in Figure 9-15.

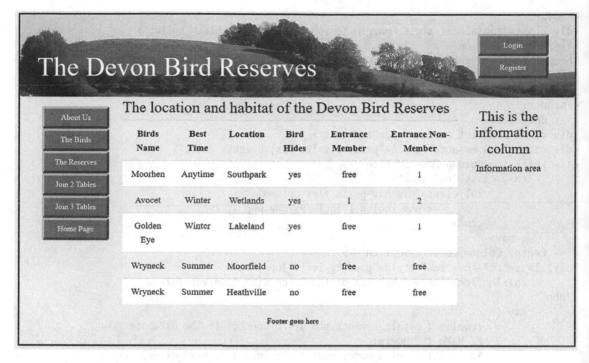

Figure 9-15. Three tables joined and displayed in a browser

The page displaying this table can be viewed by clicking the Join 3 Tables menu button from the index page.

Listing 9-15 shows the code for this page.

Listing 9-15. Creating the Page for Displaying Three Joined Tables (join-3.php).

```php
<?php
        define('ERROR_LOG','errorlog.log');
?>
<!DOCTYPE html>
<html lang="en">
<head>
        <title>Three Tables Page</title>
        <meta charset="utf-8">
        <meta name="viewport" content="width=device-width, initial-scale=1, shrink-to-fit=no">
        <!-- Bootstrap CSS File -->
        <link rel="stylesheet"
        href="https://stackpath.bootstrapcdn.com/bootstrap/4.1.0/css/bootstrap.min.css"
                integrity="sha384-9gVQ4dYFwwWSjIDZnLEWnxCjeSWFphJiwGPXr1jddIhOegiu1FwO5qRGv
                FXOdJZ4"
                crossorigin="anonymous">
        <link rel="stylesheet" type="text/css" href="birds1.css">
</head>
```

```
<body>
<div class="container" style="margin-top:30px;border: 3px black solid;">
<!-- Header Section -->
<header class="jumbotron text-center row" id="includeheader"
        style="margin-bottom:2px; padding:20px;background-color:#CCFF99;">
        <?php include('includes/header.php'); ?>
</header>
<!-- Body Section -->
<div class="content mx-auto" id="contents">
<div class="row mx-auto" style="padding-left: 0px; height: auto;">
<!-- Left-side Column Menu Section -->
        <nav class="col-sm-2">
                <ul class="nav nav-pills flex-column">
                        <?php include('includes/nav.php'); ?>
                </ul>
        </nav>
<!-- Center Column Content Section -->
<div class="col-sm-8 row" style="padding-left: 30px;">
        <h2>The location and habitat of the Devon Bird Reserves</h2>
<?php
        try {
                require ('mysqli_connect.php'); // Connect to the database
                // Make the query:
                $q = "SELECT bird_name, best_time, location, bird_hides,
                        entrance_member, entr_non_member FROM birds
                        INNER JOIN location USING (bird_id)
                        INNER JOIN reserves_info USING (location_id)";
                $result = mysqli_query ($dbcon, $q); // Run the query
                if ($result) { // If it ran OK, display the records
                // Table header
                        ?>
                        <table class="table table-responsive table-striped"
                                style="background: white;color:black;">
                                <tr>
                                        <th scope="col">Birds Name</th>
                                        <th scope="col">Best Time</th>
                                        <th scope="col">Location</th>
                                        <th scope="col">Bird Hides</th>
                                        <th scope="col">Entrance Member</th>
                                        <th scope="col">Entrance Non-Member</th>
                                </tr>
                        <?php
                        // Fetch and print all the records
                        while ($row = mysqli_fetch_array($result, MYSQLI_ASSOC)) {
                                $bird_name = htmlspecialchars($row['bird_name'], ENT_QUOTES);
                                $best_time = htmlspecialchars($row['best_time'], ENT_QUOTES);
                                $location = htmlspecialchars($row['location'], ENT_QUOTES);
                                $bird_hides = htmlspecialchars($row['bird_hides'], ENT_QUOTES);
                                $entrance_member = htmlspecialchars($row['entrance_member'],
                                ENT_QUOTES);
```

```
                            $entrance_non_member = htmlspecialchars($row['entr_non_
                            member'], ENT_QUOTES);
                            echo '<tr>
                            <td scope="row">' . $bird_name . '</td>
                            <td scope="row">' . $best_time . '</td>
                            <td scope="row">' . $location . '</td>
                            <td scope="row">' . $bird_hides . '</td>
                            <td scope="row">' . $entrance_member . '</td>
                            <td scope="row">' . $entrance_non_member . '</td>
                        </tr>';
                        }
                echo '</table>'; // Close the table
                mysqli_free_result ($result); // Free up the resources
        } else { // If it did not run OK
                // Message
                echo '<p class="error">The current data could not be retrieved. ';
                echo 'We apologize for any inconvenience.</p>';
                // Debugging message
                echo '<p>' . mysqli_error($dbcon) . '<br><br />Query: ' . $q . '</p>';
        } // End of if ($result)
        mysqli_close($dbcon); // Close the database connection
}
catch(Error $e)
{
        // print "An Error occurred. Message: " . $e->getMessage();
        print "The system is busy please try later";
        // $date = date('m.d.y h:i:s');
        // $errormessage = $e->getMessage();
        // $eMessage = $date . " | Error | " , $errormessage . |\n";
        // error_log($eMessage,3,ERROR_LOG);
        // e-mail support person to alert there is a problem
        //  error_log("Date/Time: $date - Error, Check error log for
        //details", 1, noone@helpme.com, "Subject: Error \nFrom: Error Log
        <errorlog@helpme.com>" .
        //"\r\n");
    }
?>
</div><!-- End of the view birds page content. -->
<!-- Right-side Column Content Section -->
        <aside class="col-sm-2" style="padding-top: 20px; padding-right: 0px;">
                <?php include('includes/info-col.php'); ?>
        </aside>
    </div>
<!-- Footer Content Section -->
<footer class="jumbotron text-center row"
style="padding-bottom:1px; padding-top:8px;background-color:#CCFF99;">
    <?php include('includes/footer.php'); ?>
</footer>
</div>
</div>
</body>
</html>
```

Explanation of the Code

This section explains the code.

```
$q = "SELECT bird_name, best_time, location, bird_hides,
        entrance_member,
        entr_non_member FROM birds
                INNER JOIN location USING (bird_id)
                INNER JOIN reserve_info USING (location_id)";
```

The code is similar to the code for two tables except for an additional INNER JOIN statement.

We selected some data (but not all) from the three joined tables. Six items were selected from three tables using the SELECT query.

We will now learn how to add an alternative method of paying for goods or membership fees using a check instead of PayPal or debit/credit cards.

Payments by Check

There are still customers who prefer to pay by check because either they do not have a PayPal account or they prefer not to disclose their debit/credit card details over the Internet. Check payments usually need to be accompanied by a printed form, which contains information explaining why the payment has been sent. This form usually contains the customer's name, address, e-mail address, telephone number, and other related information such as a payment number.

This tutorial uses a simplified printable form for an organization that requires online registration; the form requires the user's full details, together with a choice of payment methods. This is ideal for websites that require membership registrations.

Let's assume that Devon Bird Reserves requires an online registration form, as shown in Figure 9-16.

Figure 9-16. *The registration page*

You can view the registration page by clicking the Register button on the home page header.

■ **Note** The SQL file membership has been included with the chapter files. This file contains the code to create the required tables for the registration pages. This code must be imported using phpMyAdmin before attempting to run any of the following code.

The registration page and related tables are essentially the same as used in Chapter 7. The majority of the code is from Chapter 7 and is embedded into the birds template and saved as *member_reg.php*. Since the code is similar, it is not included here but is included with the chapter files.

When users register successfully, the Register button redirects them to a "thank you" page that contains the alternative methods of paying the membership fee.

A Choice of Payment Method

When the membership registration form has been filled out, clicking the Register button sends the user to a page and gives the user a choice of the three payment methods, as shown in Figure 9-17.

Figure 9-17. Giving the user a choice of payment method

The display of PayPal logos has been deliberately duplicated on the page to show that you have a choice of either a vertical or horizontal logo. To avoid cluttering the page, you would choose one only. Listing 9-17 gives the code for creating the page shown in Figure 9-17.

Listing 9-17. Creating a Page for Alternative Methods of Payment (register-thanks.php)

```php
<?php
        define("ERROR_LOG","errorlog.log");
?>
<!DOCTYPE html>
<html lang="en">
<head>
        <title>Register Page</title>
        <meta charset="utf-8">
        <meta name="viewport" content="width=device-width, initial-scale=1,
        shrink-to-fit=no">
        <!-- Bootstrap CSS File -->
        <link rel="stylesheet"
        href="https://stackpath.bootstrapcdn.com/bootstrap/4.1.0/css/bootstrap.min.css"
        integrity=
"sha384-9gVQ4dYFwwWSjIDZnLEWnxCjeSWFphJiwGPXr1jddIhOegiu1FwO5qRGvFXOdJZ4"
        crossorigin="anonymous">
        <script src="verify.js"></script>
        <script src='https://www.google.com/recaptcha/api.js'></script>
        <link rel="stylesheet" type="text/css" href="birds1.css">
</head>
<body>
        <div class="container" style="margin-top:30px;border: 3px black solid;">
        <!-- Header Section -->
        <header class="jumbotron text-center row" id="includeheader"
                style="margin-bottom:2px; padding:20px;background-color:#CCFF99;">
                <?php include('includes/header.php'); ?>
        </header>
        <!-- Body Section -->
        <div class="content mx-auto" id="contents">
        <div class="row mx-auto" style="padding-left: 0px; height: auto;">
        <!-- Left-side Column Menu Section -->
                <nav class="col-sm-2">
                        <ul class="nav nav-pills flex-column">
                                <?php include('includes/nav.php'); ?>
                        </ul>
                </nav>
        <!-- Center Column Content Section -->
        <div class="col-sm-8">
        <h3 class="h2 text-center" >Thank you for registering</h2>
        <h6 class="text-center">
        To confirm your registration please verify membership class and
        pay the membership fee now.</h6>
```

```
                <h6 class="text-center">You can use PayPal, a check or a credit/debit card.</h6>
                <p class="text-center" >When you have completed your registration you will be
                able to login to the member's only pages.</p>
<?php
try {

                require ("mysqli_connect.php");
                $query = "SELECT * FROM prices";
                $result = mysqli_query ($dbcon, $query); // Run the query.
                if ($result) { // If it ran OK, display the records.
                        $row = mysqli_fetch_array($result, MYSQLI_NUM);
                        $yearsarray = array(
                "Standard one year:", "Standard five year:", "Military one year:", "Under 21 one year:",
                "Other - Give what you can. Maybe:" );
                        echo '<h6 class="text-center text-danger">Membership classes:</h6>' ;
                        echo '<h6 class="text-center text-danger small"> ';
                        for ($j = 0, $i = 0; $j < 5; $j++, $i = $i + 2) {
                                echo $yearsarray[$j] . " &pound; " .
                                htmlspecialchars($row[$i], ENT_QUOTES)   .
                                " GB, &dollar; " .
                                htmlspecialchars($row[$i + 1], ENT_QUOTES) .
                                " US";
                        if ($j != 4) {
                                if ($j % 2 == 0) { echo "</h6><h6 class='text-center text-danger
                                small'>"; }
                                else { echo " , "; }
                        }
                }
                echo "</h6>";
}
?>
<form action="https://www.paypal.com/cgi-bin/webscr" method="post">
        <input type="hidden" name="cmd" value="_s-xclick">
        <input type="hidden" name="hosted_button_id" value="XXXXXXXXXXXXX">
        <div class="form-group row">
        <label for="level" class="col-sm-4 col-form-label text-right">*Membership Class</label>
        <div class="col-sm-8">
                <select id="level" name="level" class="form-control" required>
                <option value="0" >-Select-</option>
        <?php
                $class = htmlspecialchars($_GET['class'], ENT_QUOTES);
                for ($j = 0, $i = 0; $j < 5; $j++, $i = $i + 2) {
                        echo '<option value="' .
                        htmlspecialchars($row[$i], ENT_QUOTES) . '" ';
                        if ((isset($class)) && ( $class == $row[$i]))
                        {
                                echo ' selected ';
                        }
```

```
                echo ">" . $yearsarray[$j] . " " .
                htmlspecialchars($row[$i], ENT_QUOTES) .
                " &pound; GB, " .
                htmlspecialchars($row[$i + 1], ENT_QUOTES) .
                "&dollar; US</option>";
                }
        ?>
        </select>
</div>
</div>
<div class="form-group row">
<div class="col-sm-6 col-form-label">
        <nav class="float-right navbar navbar-expand-md navbar-dark">
                <button class="navbar-toggler" type="button" data-toggle="collapse"
                        data-target="#collapsibleMenu">
                        <span class="navbar-toggler-icon"></span>
                </button>
<div class="btn-group-vertical btn-group-sm collapse navbar-collapse" id="collapsibleMenu"
        role="group" aria-label="Button Group">
                <ul class="navbar-nav flex-column" style="width: 140px;">
                        <li class="nav-item">
                                <a class="btn btn-primary" id="buttons"
                                href="pay-with-check.php" role="button">Pay By Check</a>
                        </li>
                </ul>
</div>
</nav>
</div>
<div class="col-sm-6">
<!-- Replace the code below with code provided by PayPal once you obtain a Merchant ID -->
        <input type="hidden" name="currency_code" value="GBP">
                <input style="margin:10px 0 0 40px" type="image"
                src="https://www.paypalobjects.com/en_US/GB/i/btn/btn_buynowCC_LG.gif"
                name="submit" alt="PayPal  The safer, easier way to pay online.">
        <img alt="" src=
                "https://www.paypalobjects.com/en_GB/i/scr/pixel.gif" width="1" height="1">
<!-- Replace code above with PayPal provided code -->
</div>
</div>
</form>
</div>
<!-- Right-side Column Content Section -->
        <aside class="col-sm-2">
                <?php include('includes/info-col-cards.php'); ?>
        </aside>
</div>
<!-- Footer Content Section -->
<footer class="jumbotron text-center row"
        style="padding-bottom:1px; padding-top:8px;background-color:#CCFF99;">
        <?php include('includes/footer.php'); ?>
</footer>
```

```php
<?php
} // end try
catch(Exception $e) // We finally handle any problems here
{
        // print "An Exception occurred. Message: " . $e->getMessage();
        print "The system is busy please try later";
        //   $date = date('m.d.y h:i:s');
        //   $errormessage = $e->getMessage();
        //   $eMessage = $date . " | Exception Error | " , $errormessage . |\n";
        //    error_log($eMessage,3,ERROR_LOG);
        // e-mail support person to alert there is a problem
        //   error_log("Date/Time: $date - Exception Error, Check error log for
        //details", 1, noone@helpme.com, "Subject: Exception Error \nFrom: Error Log
                <errorlog@helpme.com>" . "\r\n");
}
catch(Error $e)
{
        // print "An Error occurred. Message: " . $e->getMessage();
        print "The system is busy please try later";
        //   $date = date('m.d.y h:i:s');
        //   $errormessage = $e->getMessage();
        //   $eMessage = $date . " | Error | " , $errormessage . |\n";
        //   error_log($eMessage,3,ERROR_LOG);
        // e-mail support person to alert there is a problem
        //   error_log("Date/Time: $date - Error, Check error log for
        //details", 1, noone@helpme.com, "Subject: Error \nFrom: Error Log
        //   <errorlog@helpme.com>" . "\r\n");
    }
?>
</body>
</html>
```

When the PayPal Pay Now button is clicked, the user is taken to the usual PayPal page for processing the payment. Alternatively, the user can now click the Pay By Check button to fill out and print a form to send with their check. This code is similar to the register_thanks program from Chapter 7.

The Check Payment

When users click the Pay By Check button, they will be taken to a page containing a printable form, as shown in Figure 9-18.

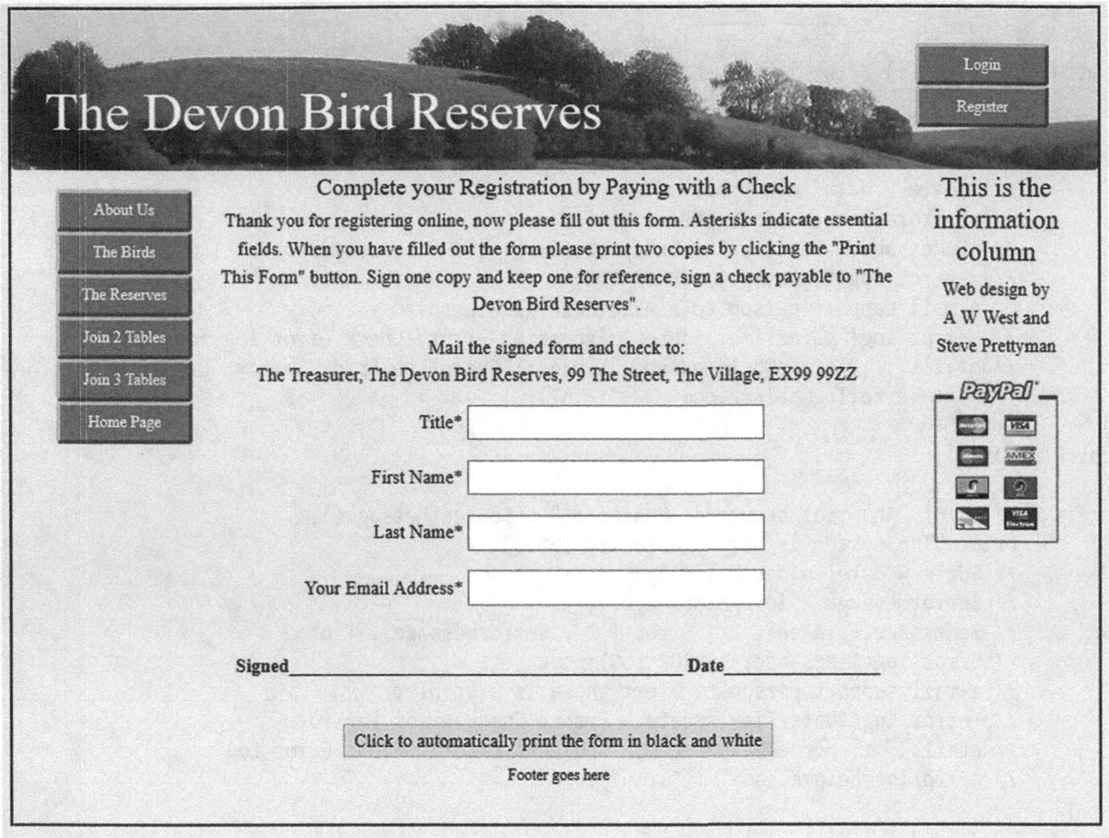

Figure 9-18. *The printable form can be filled out on the screen except for the signature and date (pay-with-check.php)*

Listing 9-18 gives the code for creating the printable form.
The form is designed to be filled out on the screen and then printed.

Listing 9-18. Creating the Printable Form (pay-with-check.php)

```
<!DOCTYPE html>
<html lang="en">
<head>
  <title>Register Page</title>
  <meta charset="utf-8">
  <meta name="viewport" content=
           "width=device-width, initial-scale=1, shrink-to-fit=no">
  <!-- Bootstrap CSS File -->
  <link rel="stylesheet"
  href=
"https://stackpath.bootstrapcdn.com/bootstrap/4.1.0/css/bootstrap.min.css"
  integrity=
"sha384-9gVQ4dYFwwWSjIDZnLEWnxCjeSWFphJiwGPXr1jddIh0egiu1Fw05qRGvFX0dJZ4"
  crossorigin="anonymous">
```

```
<script src="verify.js"></script>
<script src='https://www.google.com/recaptcha/api.js'></script>

<link rel="stylesheet" type="text/css" href="birds1.css" media="screen">
<link rel="stylesheet" type="text/css" href="print.css" media="print">

<style type="text/css">
    label { margin-bottom:5px; }
    label { width:570px; float:left; text-align:right; }
    .sign { font-weight:bold;}
</style>
</head>
<body>
<div class="container" style="margin-top:30px;border: 3px black solid;">
<!-- Header Section -->
<header class="jumbotron text-center row" id="includeheader"
    style="margin-bottom:2px; padding:20px;background-color:#CCFF99;">
            <?php include('includes/header.php'); ?>
</header>
<!-- Body Section -->
<div class="content mx-auto" id="contents">
<div class="row mx-auto" style="padding-left: 0px; height: auto;">
<!-- Left-side Column Menu Section -->
    <nav class="col-sm-2">
    <ul class="nav nav-pills flex-column">
                    <?php include('includes/nav.php'); ?>
    </ul>
    </nav>
<!-- Center Column Content Section -->
<div class="col-sm-8">
    <h4>Complete your Registration by Paying with a Check</h4>
    <p>Thank you for registering online, now please fill out this
    form. Asterisks indicate essential fields. When you
    have filled out the form please print two copies by clicking
    the "Print This Form" button. Sign one copy and keep one for
    reference sign a check payable to &quot;The Devon Bird
    Reserves&quot;. </p><p>Mail the signed form and check to:
    <br>The Treasurer, The Devon Bird Reserves, 99 The Street,
    The Village, EX99 99ZZ </p>
<form>
<div id="fields">
    <label class="label" for="title">Title<span
            class="large-red">*</span>
    <input id="title" name="title" size="35" type="text" required>
    </label>
    <br><br><label class="label" for="firstname">First Name
<span>*</span>
    <input id="firstname" name="firstname" size="35" type="text"
            required></label><br>
<br><label class="label" for="lastname">Last Name
<span>*</span>
```

```
<input id="lastname" name="lastname" size="35" type="text"
        required></label><br>
<br><label class="label" for="useremail">Your Email Address
<span>*</span>
<input id="useremail" name="useremail" type="email" size="35"
        required></label><br>
</div>
</form>
<br><br>
<p class="sign">
 Signed_____ Date_____
</p>
<br>
<div id="button">
    <input type="button" value=
    "Click to automatically print the form in black and white"
            onclick="window.print()" title="Print this Form"><br>
</div>
<!--End of content.-->
</div>
<!-- Right-side Column Content Section -->
    <aside class="col-sm-2">
    <?php include('includes/info-col-cards.php'); ?>
    </aside>
</div>
<!-- Footer Content Section -->
<footer class="jumbotron text-center row"
    style="padding-bottom:1px; padding-top:8px;
            background-color:#CCFF99;">
            <?php include('includes/footer.php'); ?>
</footer>
</div>
</div>
</body>
</html>
```

Explanation of the Code

This section explains the code.

```
<link rel="stylesheet" type="text/css" href="birds.css" media="screen">
<link rel="stylesheet" type="text/css" href="print.css" media="print">
```

It is impossible to print the form using PHP because PHP is a server-side script. However, the form is displayed by a browser, and we can print from a screen displayed by a browser. We achieve this by means of a link to a separate conditional style sheet with the media attribute media="print".

The first line links to the main style sheet *birds.css* that displays the page on the screen using the media attribute media="screen". The second line links the page to the print version of the page. This is automatically invoked when the display is sent to a printer or print preview. The printed form does not need the header, menu, or footer. Also, using the CSS style sheet, we can cause it to print using only black ink so that the user does not have to use the more expensive color cartridge.

```
<div id="button">
        <input type="button" value=
                "Click to automatically print the form in black and white"
                onclick="window.print()" title="Print this Form"><br>
</div>
```

This is the code for the button on the page that sets the browser display to the printer.

Printing Online Forms

Figure 9-19 shows the printed page.

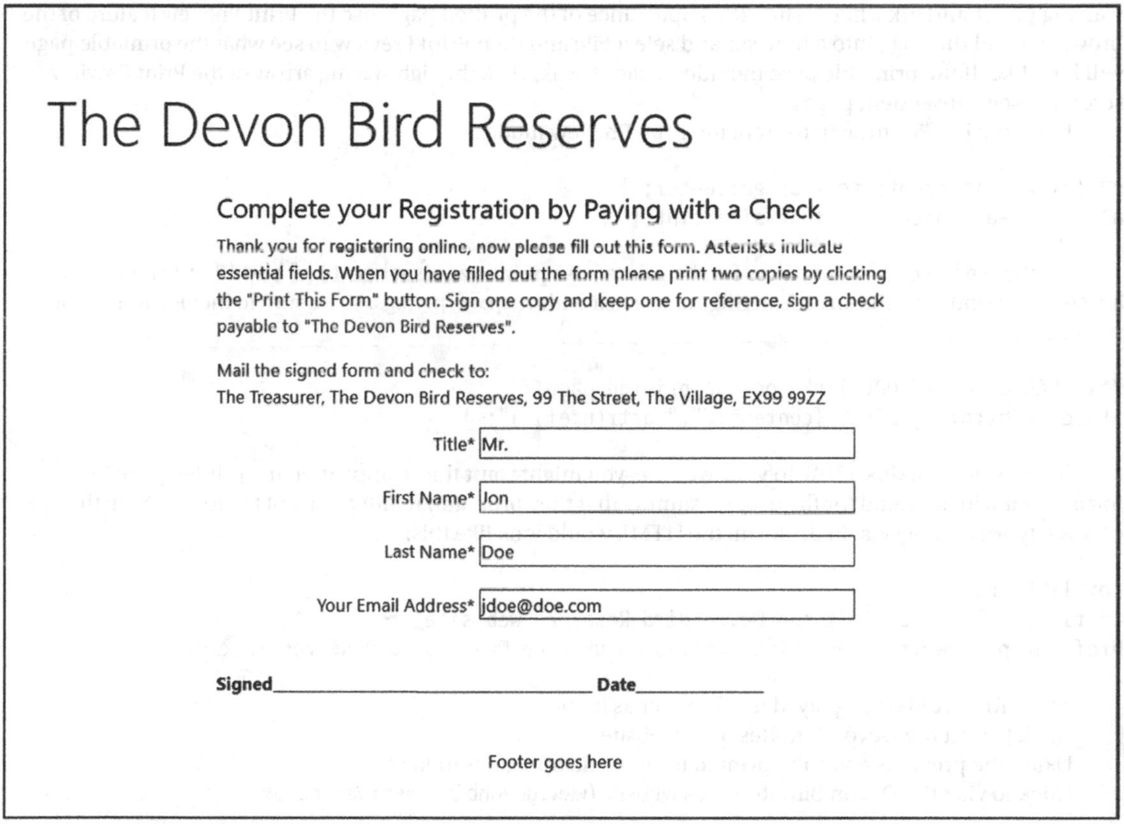
The Devon Bird Reserves

Complete your Registration by Paying with a Check

Thank you for registering online, now please fill out this form. Asterisks indicate essential fields. When you have filled out the form please print two copies by clicking the "Print This Form" button. Sign one copy and keep one for reference, sign a check payable to "The Devon Bird Reserves".

Mail the signed form and check to:
The Treasurer, The Devon Bird Reserves, 99 The Street, The Village, EX99 99ZZ

Title* Mr.

First Name* Jon

Last Name* Doe

Your Email Address* jdoe@doe.com

Signed____________________ **Date**__________

Footer goes here

Figure 9-19. *The top half of the printed page in black ink contains all the essential information*

To produce the printout shown in Figure 9-19, the form was filled out on the user's screen, and then the Print button was clicked. The result used minimal ink and no colored ink; however, it contained all that is necessary to become a member of the Devon Bird Reserves. The user signs the form and mails it with the check. The user's address is entered into the database when they fill out the registration page; therefore, this does not need be repeated in the printed form.

The style sheet *print.css* is the key to producing the printable form. Listing 9-19 shows the code for this style sheet.

Listing 9-19. Creating the Style Sheet for Printing Forms (print.css)

```
/*PRINT.CSS: style amendments for printing only*/
/*SELECT ITEMS THAT YOU DO NOT WANT TO PRINT, e.g.,
header, menu, print-this-page button, and footer*/
#header, #nav, #leftcol, #button, #rightcol, #footer,
#info-col, ul { display:none; }
input { border:1px black solid; }
h2 { font-size:16pt; color:black; text-align:center; }
h3 { text-align:center; font-size:11pt;}
/*REVEAL OUTGOING URL links on printed page*/
a[href^="http://":after {content: "(" attr(href)")"; }
```

The CSS statement { display:none; } tells the printer which items should not be printed. To avoid wasting paper and ink when testing the appearance of the printed page, use the Print Preview feature of the browser. Load the page into a browser and select File and then Print Preview to see what the printable page will look like. If the printable page includes a page break, click the right-facing arrow of the Print Preview screen to see subsequent pages.

Press the Esc key to switch out of the Print Preview mode.

```
h2 { font-size:16pt; text-align:center; }
h3 { text-align:center; font-size:11pt;}
```

To choose the correct font sizes for the printer, use point sizes (such as 16 pt. and 12 pt.) and use trial and error to optimize the sizes. You might have text within <p> </p> tags, so be sure to include a style for the paragraph font size.

```
/*REVEAL OUTGOING URL links on the printed page*/
a[href^="http://]:after {content: "(" attr(href)")"; }
```

If the page contains a URL to your website, you might want this to appear on the printed page in a format that will be useful for the user (assuming that they print and retain a copy of the form). Note the use of three types of brackets. In the form, the HTML would look like this:

```
<p>Click for
<a title="Click to visit the Devon Bird Reserves web site" ↵
href="http://www.the devonbirdreserves.co.uk">The Devon Bird Reserves</a></p>
```

The URL would be displayed in a browser as follows:
Click to visit the Devon Bird Reserves website.
Using the previous code, the printed form would appear as follows:
Click to visit the Devon Bird Reserves website (`www.devonbirdreserves.co.uk`).

Summary

In this chapter, we introduced the theory and practice of using multiple tables. You learned that such tables are virtual tables that are present only in the volatile memory of the server and that they can be viewed in a DBMS such as MySQL or MariaDB. The difference between various join methods was described. We then demonstrated that the virtual tables could be made visible in a web page by using SQL queries and PHP. A tutorial showed you how to implement membership payments by check. This was augmented by a demonstration of economical form printing so that an application form and a check could be sent to the organization. In the next chapter, we will introduce you to an online message board.

CHAPTER 10

Create a Message Board

A message board can be a stand-alone feature or an important component in a forum. A basic forum has at least four tables, one each for messages, membership registrations, threads, and replies. However, to save space and to defer to what's in the subtitle of this book, *A Simplified Approach*, this chapter describes a simple message board with a table for messages and a table for members. Our hope is that a grasp of the principles of this message board will inspire you to expand its features and explore more complex solutions. For your interest, at the end of this chapter we have added a chart showing how you could enhance the message board to create a forum.

Message boards have fewer features than a forum; generally, they lack the ability to accept replies in a manner that allows them to be collected as threads. In a forum, the replies are connected to the original posting ID and displayed in ascending date order. Our message board is designed to collect wise and comical quotations and then insert them into a searchable database.

After completing this chapter, you will be able to

- Create a message board with a database and tables
- Create a registration page
- Create login and logout pages
- Create a gateway to the message board categories
- Create pages to display the quotations
- Create search facilities

■ **Caution** To prevent the display of unpleasant content, message boards require constant monitoring (moderating). Your potential clients should be warned about this before they commit themselves to a design contract with you. In 2018, the United States implemented laws that place the responsibility of the content of public message boards and other public forums on the forum provider. This is a reversal of previous enforcement, which relieved forum providers from responsibility for public content.

The Plan

To simplify the message board in this chapter, users will not be able to view messages until they are registered and logged in. However, some of the messages will be shown on the home page to tempt users to register. In our example, the messages are quotations, and the aim is to build up a useful database of quotations. The Login button on the home page will redirect registered users to a page where they will be able choose which of the types of quotation to view, either comical quotes or wise quotes.

When the message board is accessed, the registered member will be able to contribute a quote. Because the member is contributing quotations, we refer to threads as *quotations* in the tutorial. For further simplification, the number of columns in the tables is reduced to a practical minimum.

The username for logging in will be a unique pseudonym chosen by the user because message boards and forums should protect a user's personal information. When members post a new quote, their pseudonym is the only name shown on the message board. However, when registering, they might also be asked to provide additional information, such as their e-mail address, so that the site administrator can contact them if necessary. Their e-mail address is never disclosed on the message board.

We will now create the database and tables for the message board.

Creating the Database

Download the files for this chapter from the book's page at Apress.com and place them in a new folder named *msgboard* within the *htdocs* or *eds-www* folder.

Start XAMPP or EasyPHP, and create the database named *msgboarddb* in phpMyAdmin. Set the encoding to utf8_general_ci. Scroll down and click Add new user. Then select the Databases tab, select the box next to msgboarddb, and click privileges. Add a new user with the following details:

- *Username*: brunel

- *Host*: localhost

- *Password*: tra1lblaz3r

Scroll down to Global privileges and check the check all box. Click Save (or Go in some versions).

The database connection file *mysqli_connect.php* is included in the downloadable files. Be sure to add it to your *htdocs* or *eds-www* folder. If you want to create the file manually, use the following code:

```
<?php
// Create a connection to the msgboarddb database and to MySQL
// Set the encoding to utf-8
// Set the database access details as constants
define ('DB_USER', 'brunel');
define ('DB_PASSWORD', 'tra1lblaz3r');
define ('DB_HOST', 'localhost');
define ('DB_NAME', 'msgboarddb');
// Make the connection:
$dbcon = new mysqli(DB_HOST, DB_USER, DB_PASSWORD, DB_NAME);
// Set the encoding...optional but recommended
mysqli_set_charset($dbcon, 'utf8');
```

Creating the Tables

Either import the tables using the downloadable *.sql* files or create them manually.

If you want to create the tables from scratch, within phpMyAdmin, in the left panel, click the word *msgboarddb*. Then create the first table with six columns and name the table members.

Use the attributes in Table 10-1 and select the collation utf8_general_ci for the columns that will accept a collation (reg_date and member_level do not have a collation). As you create the columns, pop-up dialog boxes will appear for the member_id and user_name indexes. For the member_id pop-up, both fields will be PRIMARY. In the user_name index pop-up, enter **user_name** in the first field and **UNIQUE** in the second field.

Table 10-1. *The members Table*

Column Name	Type	Length/Value	Default	Attributes	NULL	Index	A_I
member_id	INT	8	None	UNSIGNED	☐	PRIMARY	☑
user_name	VARCHAR	12	None		☐	UNIQUE	☐
email	VARCHAR	60	None		☐		☐
passcode	CHAR	60	None		☐		☐
reg_date	DATETIME		None		☐		☐
member_level	TINYINT	2	None		☐		☐

The member_id column is the PRIMARY key, and the user_name column has a UNIQUE index to prevent duplicate entries. Scroll down and click Save.

Creating the Second Table

You can import the forum table from the downloadable SQL file or manually create the forum table with five columns. It contains a column named post_id, and this is configured as the PRIMARY KEY. Our project will enable users to search for a phrase or word from a quotation; therefore, a full text search is provided. Give the message column a FULL TEXT index.

Table 10-2 shows the table details.

Table 10-2. *The Attributes for the forum Table*

Column Name	Type	Length/Value	Default	Attributes	NULL	Index	A_I
post_id	INT	8	None	UNSIGNED	☐	PRIMARY	☑
user_name	VARCHAR	12	None		☐		☐
subject	VARCHAR	60	None		☐		☐
message	TEXT		None		☐	FULL TEXT	☐
post_date	DATETIME		None		☐		☐

When you create the post_id column in the forum table, you will see a pop-up dialog. For the column post_id, both fields should contain the word *PRIMARY*. Click Go. When you create the message column in the forum table, you will see the pop-up dialog shown in Figure 10-1.

Add index   ✖

    Index name: ⓘ   PRIMARY

    Index choice: ⓘ   INDEX   ∨

    + Options

⇕	**Column**	**Size**
	message [text] ∨	

    ‹   ›

                                        Go   Cancel

***Figure 10-1.** Add index dialog*

Next we will examine some of the pages for the website.

Creating the Home Page for the Message Board

The home page displays some sample quotes to encourage people to register. After they register and log in, they will be able to view more quotes and also contribute quotes to the collection. If you prefer to create the tables from scratch, no quotes (messages) will be displayed on the home page until the messages table is populated.

Figure 10-2 shows the home page when the tables are populated.

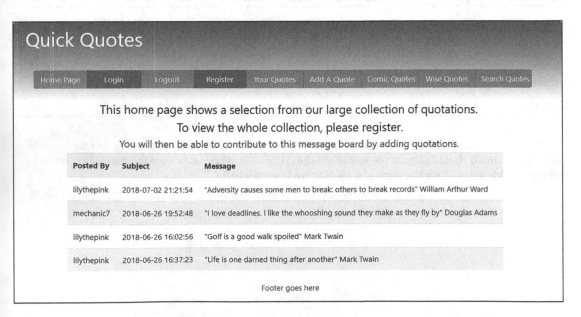

Figure 10-2. The tables are populated, so the home page displays four quotes

Listing 10-2a shows the code for producing the home page.

Listing 10-2a. Creating the Home Page for the Forum's Website (index.php)

```php
<?php // Start the session.
session_start() ;
    if ( isset( $_SESSION[ 'member_id' ] ) )
                { $menu = 1;}
    else { $menu = 5; }
?>
<!DOCTYPE html>
<html lang="en">
<head>
    <title>Message Board Home Page</title>
    <meta charset="utf-8">
    <meta name="viewport" content=
                "width=device width, initial-scale=1, shrink-to-fit=no">
    <!-- Bootstrap CSS File -->
    <link rel="stylesheet"
                href="https://stackpath.bootstrapcdn.com/bootstrap/4.1.0/css/
                bootstrap.min.css"
                integrity="sha384-9gVQ4dYFwwWSjIDZnLEWnxCjeSWFphJiwGPXr1jddIhOegiu1FwO5q
                RGvFXOdJZ4"
                crossorigin="anonymous">
    <link rel="stylesheet" type="text/css" href="msgboard.css">
</head>
<body>
    <div class="container"
                style="margin-top:30px;border: 2px black solid;">
    <!-- Header Section -->
    <header class="jumbotron text-center row" id="includeheader"
        style="margin-bottom:2px;
        background:linear-gradient(#0073e6, white); padding:10px;">
                <?php include('includes/header.php'); ?>
    </header>
<!-- Body Section -->
<div class="content mx-auto" id="contents">
<div class="row mx-auto" style="padding-left: 0px; height: auto;">
<div class="col-sm-12">
    <h4 class="text-center">
        This home page shows a selection from our large collection
            of quotations.</h4>
        <h4 class="text-center">To view the whole collection,
            please register. </h4>
        <h5 class="text-center">You will then be able to contribute to
            this message board by adding quotations.</h5>
    <?php
    // Connect to the database
    require ( 'mysqli_connect.php' ) ;
    // Make the query
    $query =
    "SELECT user_name,post_date, subject, message FROM forum LIMIT 4" ;
```

```php
    $result = mysqli_query( $dbcon, $query ) ;
    if ( mysqli_num_rows( $result ) > 0 )
    {
        ?>
        <table class="table table-responsive table-striped col-sm-12"
        style="background: white;color:black; padding-left: 80px;">
            <tr>
                        <th scope="col">Posted By</th>
                        <th scope="col">Subject</th>
                        <th scope="col">Message</th>
            </tr>
        <?php
        while ( $row = mysqli_fetch_array( $result, MYSQLI_ASSOC ))
        {
            $user_name =
            htmlspecialchars($row['user_name'], ENT_QUOTES);
            $post_date =
            htmlspecialchars($row['post_date'], ENT_QUOTES);
            $message =
            htmlspecialchars($row['message'], ENT_QUOTES);
            echo '<tr>
                        <td scope="row">' . $user_name . '</td>
                        <td scope="row">' . $post_date . '</td>
                        <td scope="row">' . $message . '</td>
            </tr>';
        }
        echo '</table>' ;
    }
    else { echo '<p class="text-center">
            There are currently no messages.</p>' ; }
    mysqli_close( $dbcon ) ;
?>
</div>
</div>
<footer class="jumbotron row mx-auto" id="includefooter"
    style="padding-bottom:1px; margin: 0px; padding-top:8px;
            background-color:white;">
    <div class="col-sm-12 text-center">
            <?php include('includes/footer.php'); ?>
    </div>
</footer>
</div>
</div>
</body>
</html>
```

The header uses a case statement that contains every horizontal menu button required by this chapter, but various buttons will be disabled to suit each page.

Listing 10-2b gives the code for the home page header code segment for the index page.

Listing 10-2b. Creating the Header for the Home Page (includes/header.php)

```php
<meta name="viewport" content="width=device-width, initial-scale=1">
<script src=
"https://ajax.googleapis.com/ajax/libs/jquery/3.3.1/jquery.min.js">
</script>
<script src=
"https://cdnjs.cloudflare.com/ajax/libs/popper.js/1.14.0/umd/popper.min.js">
    </script>
<script src="https://maxcdn.bootstrapcdn.com/bootstrap/4.1.0/js/bootstrap.min.js">
    </script>
<div class="col-sm-8">
    <h1 class="mb-4 font-bold float-left" style="color:white">
            <?php
            if (!empty($_GET['name'])) {
                    $name =
                    filter_var( $_GET['name'], FILTER_SANITIZE_STRING);
                    echo $name;
            }
            else { echo "Quick Quotes"; }
            ?>
    </h1>
</div>
    <nav class="float-left navbar navbar-expand-xl navbar-trans navbar-light">
        <button class="navbar-toggler" type="button" data-toggle="collapse"
        data-target="#collapsibleMenu">
    <span class="navbar-toggler-icon"></span>
  </button>
      <div class="btn-group btn-group-md collapse navbar-collapse navbar"
      id="collapsibleMenu"  role="group" aria-label="Button Group">    <?php
            switch ($menu) {
                    case 1: //index.php
                    ?>
                            <button type="button" style="width: 110px;"
                            class="btn btn-secondary bg-primary disabled"
                            onclick="location.href = "">Home Page
                            </button>

                            <button type="button" style="width: 110px;"
                            class="btn btn-secondary bg-primary disabled"
                            onclick="location.href = "" >Login
                            </button>

                            <button type="button" style="width: 110px;"
                            class="btn btn-secondary bg-primary"
                            onclick="location.href =
                            'logout.php?name=Logout'">Logout
                            </button>

                            <button type="button" style="width: 110px;"
                            class="btn btn-secondary bg-primary disabled"
                            onclick="location.href = "" >Register
                            </button>
```

```
                    <button type="button" style="width: 120px;"
                    class="btn btn-secondary bg-primary"
                    onclick="location.href =
                    'view_posts.php?name=Your Quotes'" >
                    Your Quotes
                    </button>

                    <button type="button" style="width: 120px;"
                    class="btn btn-secondary bg-primary"
                    onclick="location.href =
                    'post.php?name=Add A Quote'">Add A Quote
                    </button>

                    <button type="button" style="width: 120px;"
                    class="btn btn-secondary bg-primary"
                    onclick="location.href =
                    'forum_c.php?name=Comic Quotes'" >
                    Comic Quotes
                    </button>

                    <button type="button" style="width: 120px;"
                    class="btn btn-secondary bg-primary"
                    onclick="location.href =
                    'forum_w.php?name=Wise Quotes'">
                    Wise Quotes
                    </button>

                    <button type="button" style="width: 120px;" class=
                    "btn btn-secondary bg-primary"
                    onclick="location.href =
                    'search.php?name=Search Quotes'" >
                    Search Quotes
                    </button>
        <?php
        break;
```

The header uses a horizontal menu to provide the maximum amount of room on the page for members' postings and replies. The code segment shown in Listing 10-2b includes Bootstrap code to change the menu to a "pancake menu" in smaller devices (cell phones). The first segment (case 1) of the case statement demonstrates the status of the index page menu when the user is logged in. All buttons are enabled except for the Login and Register buttons. If the user is not logged in, a different block of buttons (case 5, not shown) will display only the login and register buttons as active (as shown in Figure 10-2).

```
<?php // Start the session.
session_start() ;
    if ( isset( $_SESSION[ 'member_id' ] ) )
                { $menu = 1;}
    else { $menu = 5; }
?>
```

The top of the code for the index page (Listing 10-2a) includes the previous segment. This segment determines which menu to display by searching for the member_id value. If it is present, the user has signed in. The variable $menu is set to 1, which activates all buttons, except Login and Register. If the member_id value does not exist, the user has not signed in. The variable $menu is set to 5. The menu block for case 5 (in the *header.php* file) activates only the Login and Register buttons.

■ **Note** At the moment, very few of the buttons work because we have not yet created the other pages. This will be rectified later after we create some data.

The next step will be to create the registration page so that we can register some member data.

Creating the Registration Form

The registration form is a cut-down version of the form in Chapter 7. The form is shown in Figure 10-3.

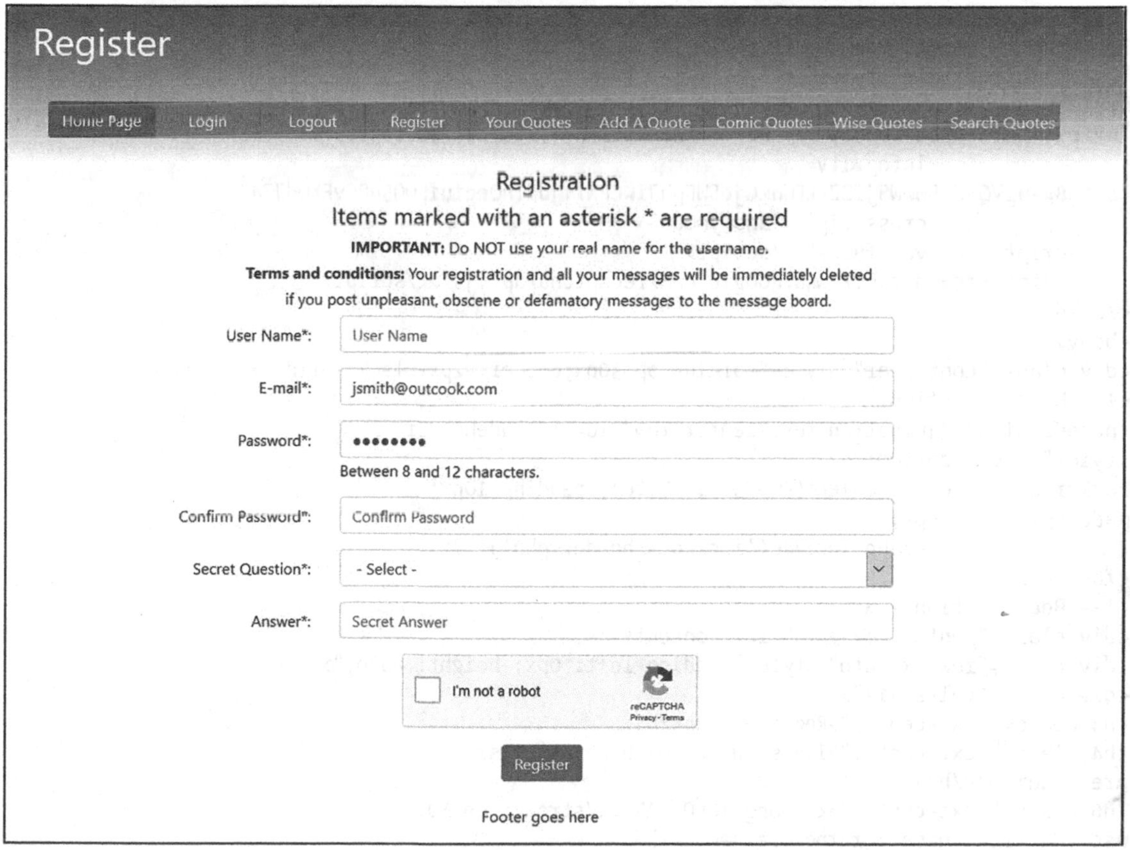

Figure 10-3. *The registration page*

As previously mentioned, the username is not the actual name of the member but a pseudonym for the purpose of logging in to the website anonymously.

Listing 10-3a shows the code for the registration form and inserts a record into the members table, and Listing 10-3b gives the PHP code.

Listing 10-3a. Creating the Registration Page (safer-register-page.php)

```php
<?php
$menu = 2;
if ($_SERVER['REQUEST_METHOD'] == 'POST') {
//require("cap.php");
}
?>
<!DOCTYPE html>
<html lang="en">
<head>
        <title>Register Page</title>
        <meta charset="utf-8">
        <meta name="viewport" content=
"width=device-width, initial-scale=1, shrink-to-fit=no">
        <!-- Bootstrap CSS File -->
        <link rel="stylesheet"
href=
"https://stackpath.bootstrapcdn.com/bootstrap/4.1.0/css/bootstrap.min.css"
                integrity=
"sha384-9gVQ4dYFwwWSjIDZnLEWnxCjeSWFphJiwGPXr1jddIhOegiu1FwO5qRGvFXOdJZ4"
                crossorigin="anonymous">
   <script src="verify.js"></script>
   <script src='https://www.google.com/recaptcha/api.js'></script>
</head>
<body>
<div class="container" style="margin-top:30px;border: 2px black solid;">
<!-- Header Section -->
<header class="jumbotron text-center row" id="includeheader"
style="margin-bottom:2px;
background:linear-gradient(#0073e6, white); padding:10px;
padding-right: 5px;">
                <?php include('includes/header.php'); ?>
</header>
<!-- Body Section -->
<div class="content mx-auto" id="contents">
<div class="row mx-auto" style="padding-left: 0px; height: auto;">
<div class="col-sm-12">
<h4 class="text-center">Registration</h4>
<h4 class="text-center">Items marked with an asterisk *
are required</h4>
<h6 class="text-center"><strong>IMPORTANT:</strong> Do NOT
use your real name for the username.</h6>
<h6 class="text-center"><strong>Terms and conditions:</strong>
Your registration and all your messages
will be immediately deleted </h6>
```

```html
<h6 class="text-center">if you post unpleasant, obscene or
defamatory messages to the message board.</h6>
<?php
try {
if ($_SERVER['REQUEST_METHOD'] == 'POST') {
                require('process-register-page.php');
} // End of the main Submit conditional.
?>
<div class="col-sm-10">
<form action="safer-register-page.php" method="post"
onsubmit="return checked();" name="regform" id="regform">
<div class="form-group row">
    <label for="user_name" class="col-sm-4 col-form-label text-right">
User Name*:</label>
    <div class="col-sm-8">
<input type="text" class="form-control" id="user_name"
        name="user_name"
                        pattern="[a-zA-Z][a-zA-Z0-9\s]*" title=
"Alphabetic, numeric and space only max of 30 characters"
                        placeholder="User Name" maxlength="30" required
                        value=
                        "<?php if (isset($_POST['user_name']))
                        echo htmlspecialchars($_POST['user_name'], ENT_QUOTES);
                        ?>" >
    </div>
</div>
<div class="form-group row">
<label for="email" class="col-sm-4 col-form-label text-right">
E-mail*:</label>
<div class="col-sm-8">
        <input type="email" class="form-control" id="email"
name="email" placeholder="E-mail" maxlength="60"
required
                        value=
                        "<?php if (isset($_POST['email']))
                        echo htmlspecialchars($_POST['email'], ENT_QUOTES);
?>" >
    </div>
</div>
<div class="form-group row">
<label for="password1" class="col-sm-4 col-form-label
text-right">Password*:</label>
<div class="col-sm-8">
        <input type="password" class="form-control" id="password1"
                        name="password1"
                        pattern="(?=.*\d)(?=.*[a-z])(?=.*[A-Z]).{8,12}"
                        title=
"One number, one upper, one lower, one special, with 8 to 12 characters"
                placeholder="Password" minlength="8" maxlength="12" required
                        value=
                        "<?php if (isset($_POST['password1']))
```

```
                    echo htmlspecialchars($_POST['password1'], ENT_QUOTES); ?>" >
                            <span id='message'>Between 8 and 12 characters.</span>
    </div>
</div>
<div class="form-group row">
<label for="password2" class="col-sm-4 col-form-label text-right">
Confirm Password*:</label>
<div class="col-sm-8">
        <input type="password" class="form-control" id="password2"
          name="password2"
                  pattern="(?=.*\d)(?=.*[a-z])(?=.*[A-Z]).{8,12}"
                        title=
"One number, one uppercase, one lowercase letter, with 8 to 12 characters"
                        placeholder=
"Confirm Password" minlength="8" maxlength="12" required
                        value=
                                "<?php if (isset($_POST['password2']))
                    echo htmlspecialchars($_POST['password2'], ENT_QUOTES); ?>" >
    </div>
</div>
<div class="form-group row">
<label for="question" class="col-sm-4 col-form-label text-right">
          Secret Question*:</label>
<div class="col-sm-8">
          <select id="question" class="form-control">
                        <option selected value="">- Select -</option>
<option value="Maiden">Mother's Maiden Name</option>
                        <option value="Pet">Pet's Name</option>
                        <option value="School">High School</option>
                        <option value="Vacation">Favorite Vacation Spot</option>
                </select>
        </div>
</div>
<div class="form-group row">
<label for="secret" class="col-sm-4 col-form-label
text-right">Answer*:</label>
<div class="col-sm-8">
      <input type="text" class="form-control" id="secret" name="secret"
                pattern="[a-zA-Z][a-zA-Z\s\.\,\-]*"
                title="Alphabetic, period, comma, dash and space only max of 30
                        characters"
                placeholder="Secret Answer" maxlength="30" required
                value=
                        "<?php if (isset($_POST['secret']))
                        echo htmlspecialchars($_POST['secret'], ENT_QUOTES); ?>" >
    </div>
</div>
<div class="form-group row">
<label class="col-sm-4 col-form-label"></label>
<div class="col-sm-8" style="padding-left: 80px;">
<div class="float-left g-recaptcha"
```

```
data-sitekey=
"6LcrQ1wUAAAAAPxlrAkLuPdpY5qwS9rXF1j46fhq"></div>
</div>
</div>
<div class="form-group row">
<label for="" class="col-sm-3 col-form-label"></label>
<div class="col-sm-8 text-center">
        <input id="submit" class="btn btn-primary" type="submit" name="submit"
        value="Register">
</div>
</div>
</form>
</div>
</div>
</div>
<!-- Footer Section -->
<footer class="jumbotron row mx-auto" id="includefooter"
style="padding-bottom:1px; margin: 0px; padding-top:8px;
padding-left: 0px; background-color:white;">
<div class="col-sm-12 text-center">
                <?php include('includes/footer.php'); ?>
  </div>
</footer>
</div>
</div>
<?php
}
catch(Exception $e) // We finally handle any problems here
 {
// print "An Exception occurred. Message: " . $e->getMessage();
        print "The system is busy please try later";
        //  $date = date('m.d.y h:i:s');
        //  $errormessage = $e->getMessage();
        //  $eMessage = $date . " | Exception Error | " , $errormessage . |\n";
        //   error_log($eMessage,3,ERROR_LOG);
// e-mail support person to alert there is a problem
        //   error_log("Date/Time: $date - Exception Error, Check error log for
//details", 1, noone@helpme.com, "Subject: Exception Error \nFrom:
// Error Log <errorlog@helpme.com>" . "\r\n");
 }
catch(Error $e)
 {
   // print "An Error occurred. Message: " . $e->getMessage();
   print "The system is busy please try later";
   // $date = date('m.d.y h:i:s');
   // $errormessage = $e->getMessage();
   // $eMessage = $date . " | Error | " , $errormessage . |\n";
   // error_log($eMessage,3,ERROR_LOG);
   // e-mail support person to alert there is a problem
        //   error_log("Date/Time: $date - Error, Check error log for
```

```
//details", 1, noone@helpme.com, "Subject: Error \nFrom: Error Log
// <errorlog@helpme.com>" . "\r\n");
 }
 ?>
</body>
</html>
```

Listing 10-3b. Checking the Registration Page (process-register-page.php)

```php
<?php
define("ERROR_LOG","errors.log");
// Has the form been submitted?
try {
require ('mysqli_connect.php'); // Connect to the database
$errors = array(); // Initialize an error array.
// -------------------check the entries-------------
// Trim the first name
        $user_name = filter_var( $_POST['user_name'], FILTER_SANITIZE_STRING);
if ((!empty($user_name)) && (preg_match('/[a-z0-9\s]/i',$user_name)) &&
                (strlen($user_name) <= 30)) {
                //Save the trimmed first name
        $user_nametrim = $user_name;
        }else{
                $errors[] =
'First name missing or not alphabetic, numeric and space characters.
        Max 30';
        }
// Check that an email address has been entered
        $emailtrim = filter_var( $_POST['email'], FILTER_SANITIZE_EMAIL);
        if  ((empty($emailtrim)) ||
(!filter_var($emailtrim, FILTER_VALIDATE_EMAIL))
                        || (strlen($emailtrim > 60))) {
                $errors[] = 'You forgot to enter your email address';
                $errors[] = ' or the e-mail format is incorrect.';
        }
// Check for a password and match against the confirmed password:
$password1trim = filter_var( $_POST['password1'], FILTER_SANITIZE_STRING);
if (empty($password1trim)){   //
$errors[] ='Please enter a valid password';
}
else {
if(!preg_match(
'/^(?=.*[a-z])(?=.*[A-Z])(?=.*\d)(?=.*[#$@!%&*?])
[A-Za-z\d#$@!%&*?]{8,12}$/',
$password1trim)) {   //
$errors[] =
'Invalid password, 8 to 12 chars, one upper, one lower,
one number, one special.';
} else
```

```
{
$password2trim =
filter_var( $_POST['password2'], FILTER_SANITIZE_STRING);
if($password1trim === $password2trim) { //
$password = $password1trim;
}else{
$errors[] = 'Your two passwords do not match.';
$errors[] = 'Please try again';
}
}
}
//Is the secret present? If it is, sanitize it
$secret = filter_var( $_POST['secret'], FILTER_SANITIZE_STRING);
if ((!empty($secret)) && (preg_match('/[a-z\.\s\,\-]/i', $secret)) &&
        (strlen($secret) <= 30)) {
        //Sanitize the trimmed city
        $secrettrim = $secret;
}else{
        $errors[] =
'Missing city. Only alphabetic, period, comma, dash and space. Max 30.';
}
if (empty($errors)) { // If everything's OK.
// If no problems encountered, register user in the database
//Determine whether the email address has already been registered
$query = "SELECT user_name FROM members WHERE email = ? ";
$q = mysqli_stmt_init($dbcon);
mysqli_stmt_prepare($q, $query);
mysqli_stmt_bind_param($q,'s', $emailtrim);
mysqli_stmt_execute($q);
$result = mysqli_stmt_get_result($q);

if (mysqli_num_rows($result) == 0){
//The email address has not been registered
//already therefore register the user in the users table
                        //-------------Valid Entries - Save to database -----
                //Start of the SUCCESSFUL SECTION. i.e.
//all the required fields were filled out
                $hashed_password = password_hash($password, PASSWORD_DEFAULT);
                // Register the user in the database...
                // Register the user in the database...
                $query =
"INSERT INTO members (member_id, user_name, email,
        passcode, secret, reg_date) ";
        $query .= "VALUES(' ', ?, ?, ?, ?, NOW() )";
$q = mysqli_stmt_init($dbcon);
mysqli_stmt_prepare($q, $query);
// use prepared statement to ensure that only text is inserted
// bind fields to SQL Statement
mysqli_stmt_bind_param($q, 'ssss', $user_nametrim, $emailtrim,
        $hashed_password, $secrettrim);
// execute query
mysqli_stmt_execute($q);
```

```
if (mysqli_stmt_affected_rows($q) == 1) {
                        header ("location: register-thanks.php");
                } else {
                        // echo 'Invalid query:' . $dbcon->error;
                $errorstring = "System is busy, please try later";
echo "<p class=' text-center col-sm-2' style='color:red'>$errorstring</p>";
                }
        }else{//The email address is already registered
        $errorstring = 'The email address is already registered.';
echo "<p class=' text-center col-sm-2'
style='color:red'>$errorstring</p>";
}
} else {//End of SUCCESSFUL SECTION
// ---------------Process User Errors----------------
// Display the users entry errors
$errorstring = 'Error! The following error(s) occurred: ';
foreach ($errors as $msg) { // Print each error.
$errorstring .= " - $msg<br>\n";
    }
$errorstring .= 'Please try again.';
echo "<p class=' text-center col-sm-2'
        style='color:red'>$errorstring</p>";
}// End of if (empty($errors)) IF.
}
catch(Exception $e) // We finally handle any problems here
{
// print "An Exception occurred. Message: " . $e->getMessage();
print "The system is busy please try later";
//  $date = date('m.d.y h:i:s');
//  $errormessage = $e->getMessage();
//  $eMessage = $date . " | Exception Error | " , $errormessage . |\n";
//    error_log($eMessage,3,ERROR_LOG);
// e-mail support person to alert there is a problem
//   error_log("Date/Time: $date - Exception Error, Check error log for
//details", 1, noone@helpme.com, "Subject: Exception Error \nFrom:
//Error Log <errorlog@helpme.com>" . "\r\n");
}
catch(Error $e)
{
// print "An Error occurred. Message: " . $e->getMessage();
print "The system is busy please try later";
//  $date = date('m.d.y h:i:s');
//  $errormessage = $e->getMessage();
//  $eMessage = $date . " | Error | " , $errormessage . |\n";
//  error_log($eMessage,3,ERROR_LOG);
// e-mail support person to alert there is a problem
//   error_log("Date/Time: $date - Error, Check error log for
//details", 1, noone@helpme.com, "Subject: Error \nFrom:
//Error Log <errorlog@helpme.com>" . "\r\n");
}
?>
```

No explanation of the code is required because it is similar to the registration form in Chapter 7.

■ **Note** Most menu items are deactivated, leaving only the Home Page button active. The Register button on the home page's header will now work because it can link to our newly created registration page.

The "Thank You" Page

If the registration is successful, the "thank you" is displayed, as shown in Figure 10-4.

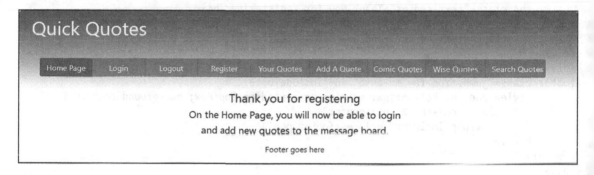

Figure 10-4. The "thank you" page

■ **Note** The same block of buttons (case 2) is used in the "thank you" file as was used in *safer-register-page. php*. Only the home page is active.

Listing 10-4 shows the code for the "thank you" page.

Listing 10-4. Creating the "Thank You" Page (register-thanks.php)

```php
<?php
        $menu = 2;
?>
<!DOCTYPE html>
<html lang="en">
<head>
        <title>Thank You Page</title>
        <meta charset="utf-8">
        <meta name="viewport" content="width=device-width, initial-scale=1,
        shrink-to-fit=no">
        <!-- Bootstrap CSS File -->
        <link rel="stylesheet"
                href="https://stackpath.bootstrapcdn.com/bootstrap/4.1.0/css/bootstrap.min.css"
                integrity=
        "sha384-9gVQ4dYFwwWSjIDZnLEWnxCjeSWFphJiwGPXr1jddIhOegiu1FwO5qRGvFXOdJZ4"
                crossorigin="anonymous">
```

```
          <link rel="stylesheet" type="text/css" href="msgboard.css">
</head>
<body>
<div class="container" style="margin-top:30px;border: 2px black solid;">
<!-- Header Section -->
<header class="jumbotron text-center row" id="includeheader"
        style="margin-bottom:2px; background:linear-gradient(#0073e6, white); padding:10px;">
        <?php include('includes/header.php'); ?>
</header>
<!-- Body Section -->
<div class="content mx-auto" id="contents">
<div class="row mx-auto" style="padding-left: 0px; height: auto;">
<div class="col-sm-12">
        <h4 class="text-center">Thank you for registering</h4>
        <h5 class="text-center">On the Home Page, you will now be able to login</h5>
        <h5 class="text-center">and add new quotes to the message board.</h5>
</div>
</div>
<footer class="jumbotron row mx-auto" id="includefooter"
        style="padding-bottom:1px; margin: 0px; padding-top:8px; background-color:white;">
        <div class="col-sm-12 text-center">
                <?php include('includes/footer.php'); ?>
        </div>
</footer>
</div>
</div>
</body>
```

Populating the Members Table

Now that you have a registration form, you can use the Register button in the header to register the members given in Table 10-3, or you can import the downloadable SQL file.

Table 10-3. *The Attributes for the members Table*

User Name	E-mail Address	Password
lilythepink	jsmith@myisp.co.uk	BumB!3b33
giantstep12	ndean@myisp.co.uk	C3rtr1dg@
mechanic7	jdoe@myisp.co.uk	B@tt3ry4c3r
skivvy	jsmith@outcook.com	D0gs0dy!2
mythking	arthur@myisp.net	Cam@10t4

The members will automatically have the default member_level value of zero. To save space, in this tutorial we have not included administration facilities. If you want to add this feature, register a member as an administrator with a member_level value of 1. Then provide them with admin pages as described in earlier chapters. Without this feature, the webmaster will need to monitor the latest posts and remove any offensive ones using phpMyAdmin.

Now that we have some registered members, they can log in.

The Login Page

Figure 10-5 shows the login page.

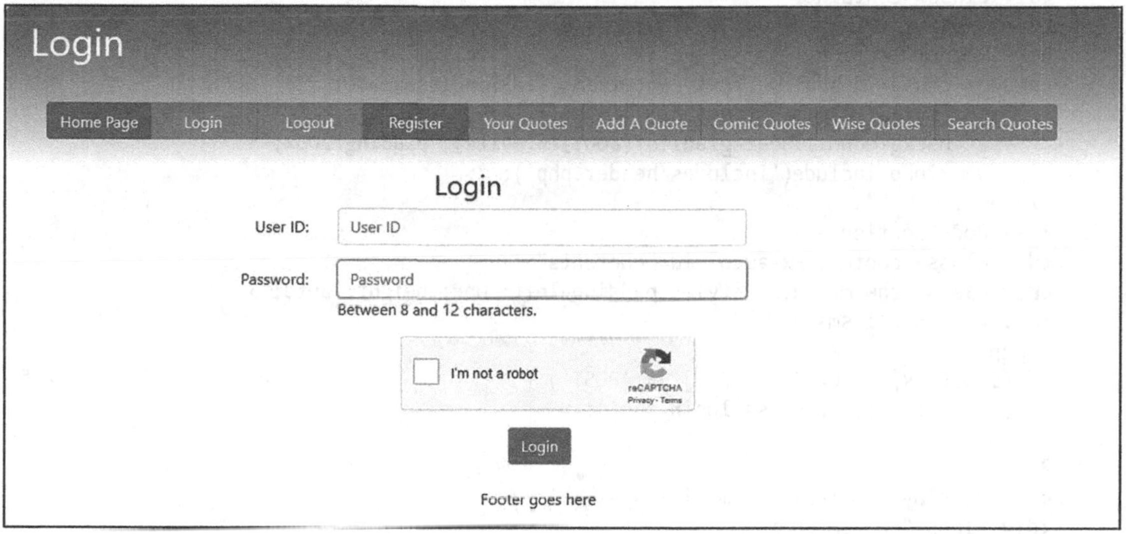

Figure 10-5. *The login page*

Listing 10-5a gives the code for the login page.

The header block (case 3) deactivates all buttons except for Register and Home Page. This code processes the submissions from the login form.

Listing 10-5a. Creating the Login Page (login.php)

```php
<?php
if ($_SERVER['REQUEST_METHOD'] == 'POST') {
      //require("cap.php");
}
$menu = 3;
?>
<!DOCTYPE html>
<html lang="en">
<head>
      <title>Login Page</title>
      <meta charset="utf-8">
      <meta name="viewport"
              content="width=device-width, initial-scale=1, shrink-to-fit=no">
      <!-- Bootstrap CSS File -->
      <link rel="stylesheet"
              href=
"https://stackpath.bootstrapcdn.com/bootstrap/4.1.0/css/bootstrap.min.css"
              integrity="sha384-9gVQ4dYFwwWSjIDZnLEWnxCjeSWFphJiwGPXr1jddIhOegiu1FwO5qRGvFXOdJZ4"
              crossorigin="anonymous">
```

```
        <script src='https://www.google.com/recaptcha/api.js'></script>
        <link rel="stylesheet" type="text/css" href="msgboard.css">
</head>
<body>
        <div class="container"
                style="margin-top:30px;border: 2px black solid;">
        <!-- Header Section -->
        <header class="jumbotron text-center row" id="includeheader"
                style="margin-bottom:2px;
                background:linear-gradient(#0073e6,whit1); padding:20px;">
                <?php include('includes/header.php'); ?>
        </header>
        <!-- Body Section -->
        <div class="content mx-auto" id="contents">
        <div class="row mx-auto" style="padding-left: 0px; height: auto;">
        <div class="col-sm-12">
        <?php
        if ($_SERVER['REQUEST_METHOD'] == 'POST') {                            //#1
                require('process-login.php');
        }
        ?>
        <!-- Display the login form fields -->
        <div class="col-sm-10">
                <h3 class="h3 text-center">
                        <?php if(empty($errorstring)) { echo "Login"; }
                                else { echo $errorstring; }
                        ?>
                </h3>
        <form action="login.php" method="post" name="loginform" id="loginform">
                <div class="form-group row">
        <label for="user_name" class="col-sm-4 col-form-label text-right">
                User ID:</label>
        <div class="col-sm-6">
          <input type="user_name" class="form-control" id="user_name"
                        name="user_name"
                        placeholder="User ID" maxlength="30" size="30" required
                        value=
                        "<?php if (isset($_POST['user_name']))
                echo htmlspecialchars($_POST['user_name'], ENT_QUOTES); ?>" >
    </div>
</div>
<div class="form-group row">
    <label for="passcode" class="col-sm-4 col-form-label
                text-right">Password:</label>
    <div class="col-sm-6">
                <input type="password" class="form-control" id="passcode"
                        name="passcode"
                        pattern="(?=.*\d)(?=.*[a-z])(?=.*[A-Z]).{8,12}"
                        title="One number, one upper, one lower, one special,
                                with 8 to 12 characters"
                        placeholder="Password" minlength="8" maxlength="12"
```

396

```
                        required
                        value=
                        "<?php if (isset($_POST['passcode']))
                  echo htmlspecialchars($_POST['passcode'], ENT_QUOTES); ?>" >
                        <span id='message'>Between 8 and 12 characters.</span>
        </div>
</div>
<div class="form-group row">
        <label class="col-sm-4 col-form-label"></label>
<div class="col-sm-8" style="padding-left: 80px;">
<div class="float-left g-recaptcha" data-sitekey=
                "6LcrQ1wUAAAAAPxlrAkLuPdpY5qwS9rXF1j46fhq"></div>
</div>
</div>
<div class="form-group row">
        <label for="" class="col-sm-3 col-form-label"></label>
<div class="col-sm-8 text-center">
        <input id="submit" class="btn btn-primary" type="submit" name="submit"
                value="Login">
        </div>
    </div>
</form>
</div>
</div>
</div>
<footer class="jumbotron row mx-auto" id="includefooter"
        style="padding-bottom:1px; margin: 0px; padding-left: 0px;
        padding-top:8px; background-color:white;">
        <div class="col-sm-12 text-center">
            <?php include('includes/footer.php'); ?>
        </div>
</footer>
</div>
</div>
</body>
</html>
```

Explanation of the Code

You have seen all the code before, but the line numbered #1 refers to a file that needs explaining.

```
if ($_SERVER['REQUEST_METHOD'] == 'POST') {                                    //#1
        require('process-login.php');
}
```

The file named *process-login.php* launches the login process. The code for this is given in Listing 10-5b.

Listing 10-5b. Creating the Code for Processing the Login (process_login.php)

```php
<?php
        define('ERROR_LOG',"errors.log");
        // This section processes submissions from the login form
        // Check if the form has been submitted:
        if ($_SERVER['REQUEST_METHOD'] == 'POST') {
        //connect to database
        try {
                require ('mysqli_connect.php');
                // Check that user name has been entered
                $user_name = filter_var( $_POST['user_name'], FILTER_SANITIZE_STRING);
                if  ((empty($user_name))
                        || (strlen($user_name > 30))) {
                        $errors[] = 'You forgot to enter your User ID';
                        $errors[] = ' or the User ID format is incorrect.';
                }
        // Check for a password and match against the confirmed password:
        $password = filter_var( $_POST['passcode'], FILTER_SANITIZE_STRING);
        //$string_length = strlen($password);
        if (empty($password)){
                $errors[] ='Please enter a valid password';
        }
        else {
                if(!preg_match(
                '/^(?=.*[a-z])(?=.*[A-Z])(?=.*\d)(?=.*[#$@!%&*?])[A-Za-z\d#$@!%&*?]{8,12}$/',
                        $password)) {
                $errors[] = 'Invalid password, 8 to 12 chars, one upper, one lower, one
                number, one special.';
        }
}
  if (empty($errors)) { // If everything's OK.
        // Retrieve the user_id, psword, first_name and user_level for that
        // email/password combination
        $query = "SELECT member_id, passcode, user_name FROM members ";
        $query .= "WHERE user_name=?";
        $q = mysqli_stmt_init($dbcon);
        mysqli_stmt_prepare($q, $query);
                // bind $user_name to SQL Statement
        mysqli_stmt_bind_param($q, "s", $user_name);
        // execute query
        mysqli_stmt_execute($q);
        $result = mysqli_stmt_get_result($q);
        $row = mysqli_fetch_array($result, MYSQLI_NUM);
        if (mysqli_num_rows($result) == 1) {
                //if one database row (record) matches the input:-
                // Start the session, fetch the record and insert the
                // values in an array
                if (password_verify($password, $row[1])) {
                        session_start();
                        $_SESSION[ 'member_id' ] = $row[0];
```

```php
                    $_SESSION[ 'user_name' ] = $row[2] ;
                    header ( 'Location: forum.php' ) ;
            } else { // No password match was made.
                    $errors[] = 'User ID/Password entered does not match our records. ';
                    $errors[] = 'Perhaps you need to register, just click the Register ';
                    $errors[] = 'button on the header menu';
            }
        } else { // No e-mail match was made.
            $errors[] = 'User ID/Password entered does not match our records. ';
            $errors[] = 'Perhaps you need to register, just click the Register ';
            $errors[] = 'button on the header menu';
        }
    }
    if (!empty($errors)) {
            $errorstring = "Error! <br /> The following error(s) occurred:<br>";
            foreach ($errors as $msg) { // Print each error.
                    $errorstring .= " $msg<br>\n";
            }
            $errorstring .= "Please try again.<br>";
    }// End of if (!empty($errors)) IF.


}
catch(Exception $c) // We finally handle any problems here
    {
        // print "An Exception occurred. Message: " . $e->getMessage();
        print "The system is busy please try later";
        // $date = date('m.d.y h:i:s');
        // $errormessage = $e->getMessage();
        // $eMessage = $date . " | Exception Error | " , $errormessage . |\n";
        //    error_log($eMessage,3,ERROR_LOG);
        // e-mail support person to alert there is a problem
        //    error_log("Date/Time: $date - Exception Error, Check error log for
        //details", 1, noone@helpme.com, "Subject: Exception Error \nFrom:
        // Error Log <errorlog@helpme.com>" . "\r\n");
    }
catch(Error $e)
    {
        // print "An Error occurred. Message: " . $e->getMessage();
        print "The system is busy please try later";
        // $date = date('m.d.y h:i:s');
        // $errormessage = $e->getMessage();
        // $eMessage = $date . " | Error | " , $errormessage . |\n";
        // error_log($eMessage,3,ERROR_LOG);
        // e-mail support person to alert there is a problem
        //    error_log("Date/Time: $date - Error, Check error log for
        //details", 1, noone@helpme.com, "Subject: Error \nFrom:
        // Error Log <errorlog@helpme.com>" . "\r\n");
    }
}
?>
```

The validation is the same as in previous chapters. It displays error messages in the event of an unsuccessful login.

Logging Out

Logging out is an important security feature. Unless the user logs out (or closes their browser), the session is still active, and someone could access and change information. Listing 10-5c shows the code for the logout page.

Listing 10-5c. Creating the Logout File (logout.php)

```php
<?php
session_start();//access the current session.
// if no session variable exists then redirect the user
if (!isset($_SESSION['member_id'])) {
header("location:index.php");
exit();
//cancel the session and redirect the user:
}else{ //cancel the session
    $_SESSION = array(); // Destroy the variables
        $params = session_get_cookie_params();
        // Destroy the cookie
        setcookie(session_name(), ", time()-42000,
        $params["path"], $params["domain"],
        $params["secure"], $params["httponly"]);
if (session_status() == PHP_SESSION_ACTIVE) {
session_destroy(); } // Destroy the session itself
header("location:index.php");
        }
```

Once the user is logged out, they can access only the login or registration pages and the home page. The login page, described earlier, redirects registered users to the forums page, where they can choose which forum to view. The forum page is described next.

Creating a Gateway to a Choice of Quotes

The gateway page enables members to choose which category to view, as shown in Figure 10-6.

Figure 10-6. The forum.php page allows the user to choose which category of quote to view

Listing 10-6 gives the code for the gateway page.

The header block (case 4 of *header.php*) activates all buttons except Login and Register since the user is now logged in.

Listing 10-6. Creating a Gateway to the Two Categories (forum.php)

```php
<?php
// Start the session.
session_start() ;
//Redirect if not logged in.
if ( !isset( $_SESSION[ 'member_id' ] ) )
        { header("Location: login.php");
                exit(); }
$menu = 4;
?>
<!DOCTYPE html>
<html lang="cn">
<head>
        <title>Thank You Page</title>
        <meta charset="utf-8">
        <meta name="viewport" content="width=device-width,
                initial-scale=1, shrink-to-fit=no">
        <!-- Bootstrap CSS File -->
        <link rel="stylesheet"
                href="https://stackpath.bootstrapcdn.com/bootstrap/4.1.0/css/bootstrap.min.css"
                integrity="sha384-9gVQ4dYFwwWSjIDZnLEWnxCjeSWFphJ1wGPXr1jddIhOcgiu1
                Fw05qRGvFXOdJZ4"
                crossorigin="anonymous">
        <link rel="stylesheet" type="text/css" href="msgboard.css">
</head>
<body>
        <div class="container" style="margin-top:30px;border:
                2px black solid;">
        <!-- Header Section -->
        <header class="jumbotron text-center row" id="includeheader"
                style="margin-bottom:2px;
                background:linear-gradient(#0073e6,white); padding:10px;">
                <?php include('includes/header.php'); ?>
        </header>
        <!-- Body Section -->
        <div class="content mx-auto" id="contents">
        <div class="row mx-auto" style="padding-left: 0px; height: auto;">
        <div class="col-sm-12">
            <h4 class="text-center">Thanks for logging in.
            Choose a forum from the menu above.</h4>
        </div>
        </div>
        <footer class="jumbotron row mx-auto" id="includefooter"
                style="padding-bottom:1px; margin: 0px; padding-top:8px;
                background-color:white;">
```

```
            <div class="col-sm-12 text-center">
                <?php include('includes/footer.php'); ?>
            </div>
        </footer>
    </div>
    </div>
</body>
</html>
```

Before we create the two forum pages, we need to have some quotations to display in the forum pages. We will now create a form so that we can enter some quotations.

The Form for Posting Quotations

Figure 10-7 shows the posting form.

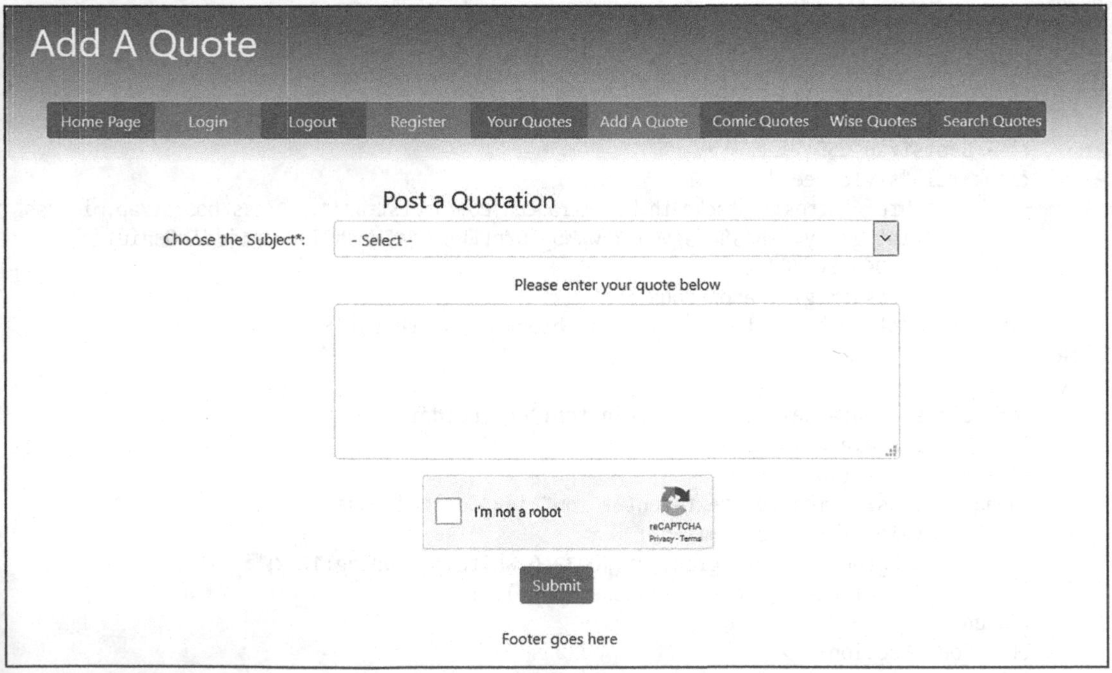

Figure 10-7. *The form for posting quotations*

You can use the word *Subject* or, if you want, you can replace it with *Category*. In this tutorial, they are synonymous. A pull-down menu is used for the subject for two reasons.

- We assumed that the message board owner wants to limit the number of subjects (categories) because the owner does not want members to create new subjects. Members will instead add new quotations to either the Comical Quotations subject or the Wise Quotations subject.

- The spelling needs to be consistent. A pull-down menu guarantees this. An owner can, of course, add new subjects (categories) to the pull-down menu.

Listing 10-7a gives the code for the posting page.

The included header block (case 8 of *header.php*) activates all buttons except Login, Logout, and Add a Quote.

Listing 10-7a. Creating the Form for Posting New Quotations (post.php)

```php
<?php
// Start the session.
session_start() ;
// Redirect if not logged in.
if ( !isset( $_SESSION[ 'member_id' ] ) )
    { header("Location: login.php");
exit(); }
$menu = 8;
if ($_SERVER['REQUEST_METHOD'] == 'POST') {
    //require("cap.php");
}
?>
<!DOCTYPE html>
<html lang="en">
<head>
    <title>Post A Quote Page</title>
    <meta charset="utf-8">
    <meta name="viewport" content="width=device-width, initial-scale=1, shrink-to-fit=no">
    <!-- Bootstrap CSS File -->
    <link rel="stylesheet"
            href="https://stackpath.bootstrapcdn.com/bootstrap/4.1.0/css/bootstrap.min.css"
            integrity=
"sha384-9gVQ4dYFwwWSjIDZnLEWnxCjeSWFphJiwGPXr1jddIhOegiu1FwO5qRGvFXOdJZ4"
    crossorigin="anonymous">
    <script src='https://www.google.com/recaptcha/api.js'></script>
    <link rel="stylesheet" type="text/css" href="msgboard.css">
</head>
<body>
    <div class="container" style="margin-top:30px;border: 2px black solid;">
    <!-- Header Section -->
    <header class="jumbotron text-center row" id="includeheader"
            style="margin-bottom:2px; background:linear-gradient(#0073e6,white); padding:10px;">
            <?php include('includes/header.php'); ?>
    </header>
    <!-- Body Section -->
    <div class="content mx-auto" id="contents">
    <div class="row mx-auto" style="padding-left: 0px; height: auto;">
    <div class="col-sm-10" style="padding-top: 20px;">
            <h4 class="text-center">Post a Quotation</h4>
    <!-- Display the form fields-->
    <form id="post_form" action="process_post.php" method="post" accept-charset="utf-8"   >
            <div class="form-group row">
                    <label for="question" class="col-sm-4 col-form-label text-right">
            Choose the Subject*:</label>
```

```
            <div class="col-sm-8">
                    <select id="subject" name="subject" class="form-control">
                    <option selected value="">- Select -</option>
                    <option value="Comic Quotes">Comic Quotes</option>
                    <option value="Wise Quotes">Wise Quotes</option>
                    </select>
            </div>
            </div>
    <div class="form-group row">
            <label for="" class="col-sm-4 col-form-label text-right"></label>
    <div class="col-sm-8 text-center">
                    <label for="message">Please enter your quote below</label>
                    <textarea class="form-control" id="message" name="message" rows="5"
                    cols="50"
                    value=
                            "<?php if (isset($_POST['message']))
                    echo htmlspecialchars($_POST['message'], ENT_QUOTES); ?>" >
            </textarea>
    </div>
    <div>
    <div class="form-group row">
    <label class="col-sm-4 col-form-label"></label>
    <div class="col-sm-8">
    <div class="g-recaptcha" style="margin-left: 90px;"
            data-sitekey="6LcrQ1wUAAAAAPxlrAkLuPdpY5qwS9rXF1j46fhq"></div>
    </div>
    </div>
    <div class="form-group row">
            <label for="" class="col-sm-3 col-form-label"></label>
    <div class="col-sm-8 text-center" style="padding-left: 40px;">
            <input id="submit" class="btn btn-primary" type="submit" name="submit"
             value="Submit">
    </div>
    </div>
</form>
</div>
<!--posting an entry into the database table automatically sends a message to the forum
moderator                                                                          #1
// Assign the subject-->
<!--<?php
    $subject = "Posting added to message board";
    $member = isset($_SESSION['user_name']) ? $_SESSION['user_name'] : "";
    $body = "Posting added by " . $member;
    mail("admin@myisp.co.uk", $subject, $body, "From:admin@myisp.co.uk\r\n");
    ?>-->
</div>
</div>
<footer class="jumbotron row mx-auto" id="includefooter"
    style="padding-bottom:1px; margin: 0px; padding-top:8px; background-color:white;">
    <div class="col-sm-12 text-center">
        <?php include('includes/footer.php'); ?>
    </div>
```

```
</footer>
</div>
</body>
</html>
```

Explanation of the Code

This section explains the code.

```
<!--posting an entry into the database table automaticlally sends a message to the forum
moderator                                                                              #1
// Assign the subject-->
<!--<?php
    $subject = "Posting added to message board";
    $member = isset($_SESSION['user_name']) ? $_SESSION['user_name'] : "";
    $body = "Posting added by " . $member;
    mail("admin@myisp.co.uk", $subject, $body, "From:admin@myisp.co.uk\r\n");
?>-->
```

Whenever a new quote is added to the forum, an e-mail is sent to an administrator. The administrator should then review the posting to ensure that it is appropriate. As noted before, the forum provider is responsible for the content of the forum. In the example, this e-mail section is commented out because this code will work only if the forum is loaded on a web server that provides PHP e-mail services.

The e-mail in this example is kept possible. The PHP function mail() has the following format: mail (to, subject, body, from).

The to and from must be e-mail addresses. The variables can be basic, like $subject is in this example, or it can be complex. In this listing, the username of the person posting the message is pulled from the session and then concatenated with some text to form the body of the e-mail. The items subject, to, and from create the header of the e-mail. The header is the top section of the e-mail; the body is the window below the header. The resulting e-mail will look like Table 10-4.

Table 10-4. *The Appearance of the E-mail*

From:	admin@myisp.co.uk
Date:	02 August 2018 17:26
To:	admin@myisp.co.uk
Subject:	Posting added to Quick Quotes message board

Posting added by lilythepink

Naturally, you must replace the dummy e-mail addresses with your own. Note that the two e-mail addresses are the same when sending an e-mail to yourself.

The database can, of course, be moderated by an administrator who is familiar with phpMyAdmin; however, it would be good to create a user-friendly administration facility for someone who is not familiar with phpMyAdmin. (Review the previous chapters, especially Chapter 3, for instructions on creating administration pages.) A user-friendly administration page allows the administrator to view a table of the latest posts. This table would have Delete and Edit links as described in Chapter 3. Optionally, an additional field could be added to the forum table to indicate which posts are approved. Then only approved quotes could be displayed. This would not allow any unapproved posts to be displayed.

■ **Note** E-mails will not be sent and received using your computer unless a PHP e-mail service is provided. When purchasing a host environment, make sure that PHP e-mail is included.

Processing the Postings

Listing 10-7b gives the code for *process_post.php*.

Listing 10-7b. Creating the File for Processing the Postings (process_post.php)

```php
<?php
// Start the session.
session_start() ;
// Redirect if not logged in.
if ( !isset( $_SESSION[ 'member_id' ] ) )
        { header("Location: login.php");
        exit(); }
//Connect to the database
require ( 'mysqli_connect.php' ) ;
// Has the form been submitted?
if ($_SERVER['REQUEST_METHOD'] == 'POST')
{
        // Check that the user has entered a subject and a message      #1
        $subject = filter_var( $_POST['subject'], FILTER_SANITIZE_STRING);
         if ( empty($subject ) ) { echo 'You forgot to select a subject.'; }

        $comment = filter_var( $_POST['message'], FILTER_SANITIZE_STRING);
        if ((!empty($comment)) && (strlen($comment) <= 480)) {
                // remove ability to create link in email
                $patterns = array("/http/", "/https/", "/\:/","/\/\//","/www./");
                $commenttrim = preg_replace($patterns," ", $comment);
        }else{ // if comment not valid display error page
                echo "You forgot to enter a message";
        }
        // If successful insert the post into the database table
        if( !empty($commenttrim) && !empty($subject) )
                {
                //Make the insert query                                  #2
                $query = "INSERT INTO forum (post_id, user_name, subject, message,
                post_date) ";
                $query .= "VALUES( ' ', ?, ?, ?, NOW() )";
                $q = mysqli_stmt_init($dbcon);
                mysqli_stmt_prepare($q, $query);
                // use prepared statement to ensure that only text is inserted
                // bind fields to SQL Statement
                $user_name = filter_var( $_SESSION['user_name'], FILTER_SANITIZE_STRING);
                mysqli_stmt_bind_param($q, 'sss', $user_name, $subject, $commenttrim);
                // execute query
                mysqli_stmt_execute($q);
```

```
                  if (mysqli_stmt_affected_rows($q) == 1) {
                          header ("Location: post_thanks.php");
                  }
           else
           {
                  echo "An Error has occurred in loading your posting";
           }
// Close the database connection
mysqli_close( $dbcon ) ;
}
  }
?>
```

Explanation of the Code

This section explains the code.

```
// Check that the user has entered a subject and a message                    #1
$subject = filter_var( $_POST['subject'], FILTER_SANITIZE_STRING);
if ( empty($subject ) ) { echo 'You forgot to select a subject.'; }

$comment = filter_var( $_POST['message'], FILTER_SANITIZE_STRING);
if ((!empty($comment)) && (strlen($comment) <= 480)) {
        // remove ability to create link in email
        $patterns = array("/http/", "/https/", "/\:/","/\/\//","/www./");
        $commenttrim = preg_replace($patterns," ", $comment);
```

The text area (as is all information coming from users) for messages is a magnet for malevolent people wanting to insert dangerous scripts. Therefore, special security filters must be built into the code. The message in the textarea (and subject) is cleaned by using the filter_var function with the FILTER_SANITIZE_STRING parameter. This makes the entry harmless. The use of a prepared statement also ensures that the string passed is handed as text and cannot cause harm.

You have met filter_var and FILTER_SANITIZE_STRING many times before. It will remove any unwanted characters, including apostrophes.

```
//Make the insert query                                                       #2
$query = "INSERT INTO forum (post_id, user_name, subject, message, post_date) ";
$query .= "VALUES( ' ', ?, ?, ?, NOW() )";
$q = mysqli_stmt_init($dbcon);
mysqli_stmt_prepare($q, $query);
// use prepared statement to ensure that only text is inserted
// bind fields to SQL Statement
$user_name = filter_var( $_SESSION['user_name'], FILTER_SANITIZE_STRING);
mysqli_stmt_bind_param($q, 'sss', $user_name, $subject, $commenttrim);
// execute query
mysqli_stmt_execute($q);
if (mysqli_stmt_affected_rows($q) == 1) {
        header ("Location: post_thanks.php");
```

The prepared insert statement uses the filtered session user_name, the previously filtered subject, and the previously filtered quote ($commenttrim). If for some reason the variables still contain harmful data, the prepared statement will use them as text and will not execute any code. Although the entries are now harmless from a security standpoint, they might still contain characters or information that is not appropriate for the message board. The administrator can correct the data or remove the posting.

Posting Some Quotations

Now that we have a form for inserting postings into the forum table, we will post the quotations shown in Table 10-5. You can also use phpMyAdmin to import the SQL file from the chapter download files. As each quotation is posted, you will be redirected to the forum page. However, you will not be able to view the quotations yet because we have not created the two pages for displaying them.

Table 10-5. *Post Some Quotations*

Log In As...	Subject (aka Forum)	Message
lilythepink	Wise Quotes	"Adversity causes some men to break: others to break records." William Arthur Ward
mechanic7	Comical Quotes	"I love deadlines. I like the whooshing sound they make as they fly by." Douglas Adams
lilythepink	Comical Quotes	"Golf is a good walk spoiled." Mark Twain
lilythepink	Comical Quotes	"Life is one darned thing after another." Mark Twain
giantstep12	Comical Quotes	"Give me golf clubs, fresh air and a beautiful partner and you can keep the golf clubs and fresh air" Jack Benny
mythking	Wise Quotes	"Nothing great was ever achieved without great enthusiasm." Ralph Waldo Emerson
mythking	Wise Quotes	"Wise sayings often fall on barren ground, but a kind word is never thrown away." Arthur Helps
mythking	Comical Quotes	"Many a small thing has been made large by the right kind of advertising." Mark Twain
mythking	Wise Quotes	"To do two things at once is to do neither." Publilius Syrus
giantstep12	Wise Quotes	"Anyone who has never made a mistake has never tried anything new." Albert Einstein
giantstep12	Comical Quotes	"Experience is simply the name we give our mistakes." Oscar Wilde
giantstep12	Comical Quotes	"If you want to recapture your youth, just cut off his allowance." Al Bernstein
mechanic7	Comical Quotes	"Technological progress has merely provided us with a more efficient means for going backwards." Aldous Huxley
lilythepink	Wise Quotes	"Real knowledge is to know the extent of one's ignorance." Confucius
mechanic7	Wise Quotes	"It is amazing what you can accomplish if you do not care who gets the credit." Harry S. Truman

■ **Remember**   The date and time of the postings will be added automatically.

When you have some quotations to display, they will appear on the home page (shown earlier in Figure 10-2).

The Comical Quotes Page

Figure 10-8 shows the comical quotes page.

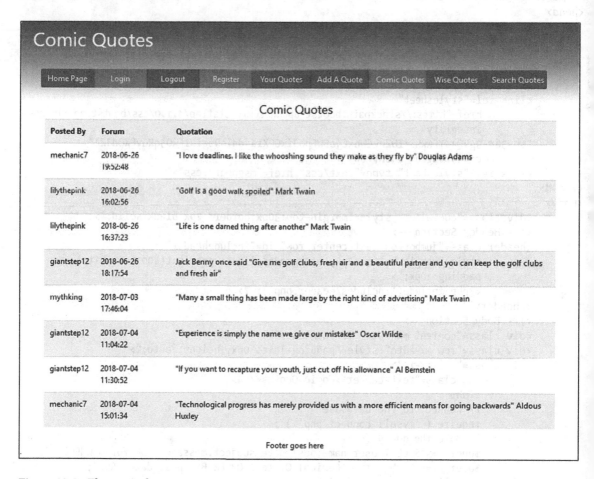

Posted By	Forum	Quotation
mechanic7	2018-06-26 19:52:48	"I love deadlines. I like the whooshing sound they make as they fly by" Douglas Adams
lilythepink	2018-06-26 16:02:56	"Golf is a good walk spoiled" Mark Twain
lilythepink	2018-06-26 16:37:23	"Life is one darned thing after another" Mark Twain
giantstep12	2018-06-26 18:17:54	Jack Benny once said "Give me golf clubs, fresh air and a beautiful partner and you can keep the golf clubs and fresh air"
mythking	2018-07-03 17:46:04	"Many a small thing has been made large by the right kind of advertising" Mark Twain
giantstep12	2018-07-04 11:04:22	"Experience is simply the name we give our mistakes" Oscar Wilde
giantstep12	2018-07-04 11:30:52	"If you want to recapture your youth, just cut off his allowance" Al Bernstein
mechanic7	2018-07-04 15:01:34	"Technological progress has merely provided us with a more efficient means for going backwards" Aldous Huxley

Figure 10-8. The comical quotes page

The code given in Listing 10-8 selects only the comical quotes from the database forum table.

Listing 10-8. Creating the Comical Quotes Page (forum_c.php)

```php
<?php // Start the session.
session_start() ;
// Redirect if not logged in.
if ( !isset( $_SESSION[ 'member_id' ] ) )
        { header("Location: login.php");
        exit(); }
$menu = 9;
?>
<!DOCTYPE html>
<html lang="en">
<head>
        <title>Message Board Home Page</title>
        <meta charset="utf-8">
        <meta name="viewport" content="width=device-width, initial-scale=1, shrink-to-
        fit=no">
        <!-- Bootstrap CSS File -->
        <link rel="stylesheet"
                href="https://stackpath.bootstrapcdn.com/bootstrap/4.1.0/css/bootstrap.min.css"
                integrity=
        "sha384-9gVQ4dYFwwWSjIDZnLEWnxCjeSWFphJiwGPXr1jddIhOegiu1FwO5qRGvFXOdJZ4"
                crossorigin="anonymous">
        <link rel="stylesheet" type="text/css" href="msgboard.css">
</head>
<body>
        <div class="container" style="margin-top:30px;border: 2px black solid;">
        <!-- Header Section -->
        <header class="jumbotron text-center row" id="includeheader"
                style="margin-bottom:2px; background:linear-gradient(#0073e6,white);
                padding:10px;">
                <?php include('includes/header.php'); ?>
        </header>
        <!-- Body Section -->
        <div class="content mx-auto" id="contents">
        <div class="row mx-auto" style="padding-left: 0px; height: auto;">
        <div class="col-sm-12">
                <h4 class="text-center">Comic Quotes</h4>
                <?php
                // Connect to the database
                require ( 'mysqli_connect.php' ) ;
                // Make the query                                                   #1
                $query = "SELECT user_name,post_date,subject,message FROM forum WHERE   ";
                $query .= "subject = 'Comical Quotes' ORDER BY 'post_date' ASC";
                $result = mysqli_query( $dbcon, $query ) ;
                if ( mysqli_num_rows( $result ) > 0 )
                {
                        ?>
                        <table class="table table-responsive table-striped col-sm-12"
                                style="background: white;color:black; padding-left: 20px;">
```

```
                <tr>
                        <th scope="col">Posted By</th>
                        <th scope="col">Forum</th>
                        <th scope="col">Quotation</th>
                </tr>
            <?php
            while ( $row = mysqli_fetch_array( $result, MYSQLI_ASSOC ))
            {
                    $user_name = htmlspecialchars($row['user_name'], ENT_QUOTES);
                    $post_date = htmlspecialchars($row['post_date'], ENT_QUOTES);
                    $message = htmlspecialchars($row['message'], ENT_QUOTES);
                    echo '<tr>
                            <td scope="row">' . $user_name . '</td>
                            <td scope="row">' . $post_date . '</td>
                            <td scope="row">' . $message . '</td>
                        </tr>';
                }
                echo '</table>' ;
            }
        else { echo 'There are currently no messages.' ; }
    mysqli_close( $dbcon ) ;
?>
</div>
</div>
<footer class="jumbotron row mx-auto" id="includefooter"
        style="padding-bottom:1px; margin: 0px; padding-top:8px; background-color:white;">
        <div class="col-sm-12 text-center">
                <?php include('includes/footer.php'); ?>
        </div>
</footer>
</div>
</div>
</body>
</html>
```

Explanation of the Code

Most of the code in Listing 10-8 will be familiar, and there are comments in the listing to remind you of important code lines.

We will now examine line #1:

```
// Make the query                                                              #1
$query = "SELECT user_name,post_date,subject,message FROM forum WHERE   ";
$query .= "subject = 'Comical Quotes' ORDER BY 'post_date' ASC";
```

The query selects only the comical quotes from the forum table. The quotes will be sorted in ascending order of posting—that is, oldest first.

The Header for the Comical Quotes Page

After viewing the comical quotes page, the user may also want to view the Wise Quotes page or insert their own quote. To enable the user to do this, the header block (case 9 of *header.php*), shown next, activates all buttons except Login, Register, and Comic Quotes. For the moment, several of these buttons will be inactive because we have not yet designed the relevant pages.

The buttons to be displayed are shown in the code snippet from *header.php* as follows:

```
case 9: //forum_c.php
        ?>
            <button type="button" style="width: 110px;"
                    class="btn btn-secondary bg-primary"
                    onclick="location.href =
                    'index.php?name=Quick Quotes'">
                    Home Page
            </button>

            <button type="button" style="width: 110px;" class=
                    btn btn-secondary bg-primary disabled"
                    onclick="location.href = "" >Login
            </button>

            <button type="button" style="width: 110px;"
                    class="btn btn-secondary bg-primary"
                    onclick="location.href =
                    'logout.php?name=Logout'">Logout
            </button>

            <button type="button" style="width: 110px;" class=
                    "btn btn-secondary bg-primary disabled"
                    onclick="location.href = "" >Register
            </button>

            <button type="button" style="width: 120px;"
                    class="btn btn-secondary bg-primary"
                    onclick="location.href =
                    'view_posts.php?name=Your Quotes'" >Your Quotes
            </button>

            <button type="button" style="width: 120px;"
                    class="btn btn-secondary bg-primary"
                    onclick="location.href = 'post.php?name=Add A Quote'">
                    Add A Quote
            </button>

            <button type="button" style="width: 120px;" class=
                    "btn btn-secondary bg-primary disabled"
                    onclick="location.href = "" >Comic Quotes
            </button>
```

```
      <button type="button" style="width: 120px;"
            class="btn btn-secondary bg-primary"
            onclick="location.href =
            'forum_w.php?name=Wise Quotes'">Wise Quotes
      </button>

      <button type="button" style="width: 120px;"
            class="btn btn-secondary bg-primary"
            onclick="location.href =
            'search.php?name=Search Quotes'" >Search Quotes
      </button>
   <?php
break;
```

The Wise Quotes Page

This page is almost the same as the Comical Quotes page except for the SQL query. Also, the Wise Quotes button is disabled, and the Comical Quotes button is enabled. Figure 10-9 shows the Wise Quotes page.

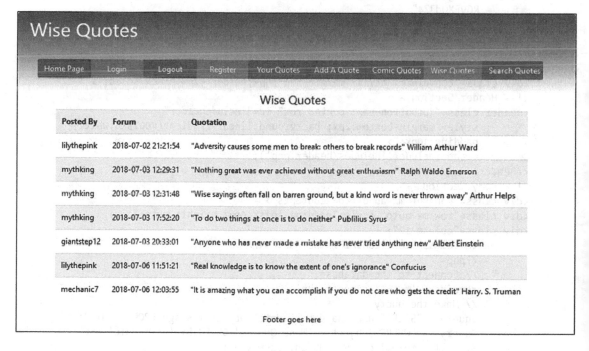

Figure 10-9. *A display of wise quotations*

The page displays only the wise quotes. Listing 10-9 gives the code for the Wise Quotes page.

Listing 10-9. Creating the Wise Quotes Page (forum_w.php)

```php
<?php // Start the session.
session_start() ;
// Redirect if not logged in.
if ( !isset( $_SESSION[ 'member_id' ] ) )
        { header("Location: login.php");
        exit(); }
$menu = 10;
?>
<!DOCTYPE html>
<html lang="en">
<head>
        <title>Message Board Home Page</title>
        <meta charset="utf-8">
        <meta name="viewport" content="width=device-width, initial-scale=1, shrink-to-fit=no">
        <!-- Bootstrap CSS File -->
        <link rel="stylesheet"
                href="https://stackpath.bootstrapcdn.com/bootstrap/4.1.0/css/bootstrap.min.css"
                integrity="sha384-9gVQ4dYFwwWSjIDZnLEWnxCjeSWFphJiwGPXr1jddIhOegiu1FwO5q
                RGvFXOdJZ4"
                crossorigin="anonymous">
        <link rel="stylesheet" type="text/css" href="msgboard.css">
</head>
<body>
        <div class="container" style="margin-top:30px;border: 2px black solid;">
        <!-- Header Section -->
        <header class="jumbotron text-center row" id="includeheader"
                style="margin-bottom:2px; background:linear-gradient(#0073e6,white);
                padding:10px;">
                <?php include('includes/header.php'); ?>
        </header>
        <!-- Body Section -->
        <div class="content mx-auto" id="contents">
        <div class="row mx-auto" style="padding-left: 0px; height: auto;">
        <div class="col-sm-12">
                <h4 class="text-center">Wise Quotes</h4>
                <?php
                // Connect to the database
                require ( 'mysqli_connect.php' ) ;
                // Make the query                                    #1
                $query = "SELECT user_name,post_date,subject,message FROM forum ";
                $query .= "WHERE subject = 'Wise Quotes' ORDER BY 'post_date' ASC";
                $result = mysqli_query( $dbcon, $query ) ;
                if ( mysqli_num_rows( $result ) > 0 )
                {
                        ?>
                        <table class="table table-responsive table-striped col-sm-12"
                                style="background: white;color:black; padding-left: 50px;">
                                <tr>
                                        <th scope="col">Posted By</th>
                                        <th scope="col">Forum</th>
```

```
                              <th scope="col">Quotation</th>
                    </tr>
          <?php
          while ( $row = mysqli_fetch_array( $result, MYSQLI_ASSOC ))
          {
                    $user_name = htmlspecialchars($row['user_name'], ENT_QUOTES);
                    $post_date = htmlspecialchars($row['post_date'], ENT_QUOTES);
                    $message = htmlspecialchars($row['message'], ENT_QUOTES);
                    echo '<tr>
                              <td scope="row">' . $user_name . '</td>
                              <td scope="row">' . $post_date . '</td>
                              <td scope="row">' . $message . '</td>
                    </tr>';
          }
     echo '</table>' ;
     }
     else { echo 'There are currently no messages.' ; }
     mysqli_close( $dbcon ) ;
?>
</div>
</div>
<footer class="jumbotron row mx-auto" id="includefooter"
     style="padding-bottom:1px; margin: 0px; padding-top:8px; background-color:white;">
     <div class="col-sm-12 text-center">
          <?php include('includes/footer.php'); ?>
     </div>
</footer>
</div>
</div>
</body>
</html>
```

Explanation of the Code

The code is almost identical to the listing for the Comical Quotes forum page, except for the items shown here:

```
// Make the query                                                                    #1
$query = "SELECT user_name,post_date,subject,message FROM forum ";
$query .= "WHERE subject = 'Wise Quotes' ORDER BY 'post_date' ASC";
```

The query selects only the records where the subject is "Wise Quotes." The quotes will be sorted in ascending order of posting—that is, oldest first.

As with the comical quotes page, a new header block (case 10 of *header.php*) will allow the user to redirect to the Comical Quotes page.

The Header for the Wise Quotes Page

The header block is identical to the header block for the Comical Quotes page except that the Wise Quotes button is deactivated, and the Comical Quotes button is activated. Note that the View your Posts and Search buttons will not work yet because the relevant pages have not been created.

```
case 10: //forum_w.php
        ?>
            <button type="button" style="width: 110px;" class="btn btn-secondary
            bg-primary"
                onclick="location.href = 'index.php?name=Quick Quotes'">
                Home Page
            </button>

            <button type="button" style="width: 110px;" class="btn btn-secondary
            bg-primary disabled"
                onclick="location.href = "" >Login
            </button>

            <button type="button" style="width: 110px;" class="btn btn-secondary
            bg-primary"
                onclick="location.href = 'logout.php?name=Logout'">Logout
            </button>

            <button type="button" style="width: 110px;" class="btn btn-secondary
            bg-primary disabled"
                onclick="location.href = "" >Register
            </button>

            <button type="button" style="width: 120px;" class="btn btn-secondary
            bg-primary"
                onclick="location.href = 'view_posts.php?name=Your Quotes'" >
                Your Quotes
            </button>

            <button type="button" style="width: 120px;" class="btn btn-secondary
            bg-primary"
                onclick="location.href = 'post.php?name=Add A Quotes'">
                Add A Quote
            </button>

            <button type="button" style="width: 120px;" class="btn btn-secondary
            bg-primary"
                onclick="location.href = 'forum_c.php?name=Comic Quotes'" >
                Comic Quotes
            </button>

            <button type="button" style="width: 120px;" class="btn btn-secondary
            bg-primary disabled"
                onclick="location.href = "">Wise Quotes
            </button>
```

```
            <button type="button" style="width: 120px;" class="btn btn-secondary
        bg-primary"
                    onclick="location.href = 'search.php?name=Search Quotes'" >
                Search Quotes
            </button>
        <?php
        break;
```

Adding Search Facilities

The most likely reasons for searching are as follows:

- Members may want to view a list of their own postings or postings by other contributors.

- Members might want to search the messages for particular words or phrases or quotes by a particular author.

Before we can implement these searches, we must create the pages that will display the search results. Figure 10-10 shows the display for viewing an individual member's postings.

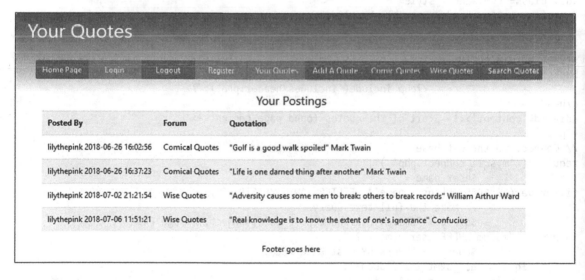

Figure 10-10. Displaying one member's postings

Listing 10-10 gives the code for the page displaying a member's posting.

Listing 10-10. Creating a Page to Display an Individual Member's Postings (view_posts.php)

```php
<?php
// Start the session.
session_start() ;
// Redirect if not logged in.
if ( !isset( $_SESSION[ 'member_id' ] ) )
```

```php
{ header("Location: login.php");
exit(); }
$menu = 7;
?>
<!DOCTYPE html>
<html lang="en">
<head>
        <title>View Postings Page</title>
        <meta charset="utf-8">
        <meta name="viewport" content=
"width=device-width, initial-scale=1, shrink-to-fit=no">
        <!-- Bootstrap CSS File -->
        <link rel="stylesheet"
                href="https://stackpath.bootstrapcdn.com/bootstrap/4.1.0/css/bootstrap.min.css"
                integrity="sha384-9gVQ4dYFwwWSjIDZnLEWnxCjeSWFphJiwGPXr1jddIhOegiu1FwO5q
                RGvFXOdJZ4"
                crossorigin="anonymous">
        <link rel="stylesheet" type="text/css" href="birds.css">
</head>
<body>
<div class="container" style=
"margin-top:30px;border: 2px black solid;">
<!-- Header Section -->
<header class="jumbotron text-center row" id="includeheader"
style="margin-bottom:2px;
background:linear-gradient(#0073e6,white); padding:10px;">
                        <?php include('includes/header.php'); ?>
</header>
<div id='content'><!--Start of the quotes found page content-->
<?php
// Connect to the database
require ( 'mysqli_connect.php' ) ;                                          //#1
                $user_name =
filter_var( $_SESSION['user_name'], FILTER_SANITIZE_STRING);
                // Make the full text query
                $query = "SELECT user_name,post_date,subject,message FROM ";
$query .= "forum WHERE user_name = ? ";
                $query .= "ORDER BY post_date ASC";
        $q = mysqli_stmt_init($dbcon);
        mysqli_stmt_prepare($q, $query);
        // bind $id to SQL Statement
                mysqli_stmt_bind_param($q, "s", $user_name);
        // execute query
        mysqli_stmt_execute($q);
        $result = mysqli_stmt_get_result($q);
                if (mysqli_num_rows($result) > 0) {
                        echo '<h4 class="text-center">Your Postings</h4>';
                        ?>
                        <table class=
"table table-responsive table-striped col-sm-12"
                                style="background: white;color:black;
padding-left: 40px;">
```

418

```
                          <tr>
                                  <th scope="col">Posted By</th>
                                  <th scope="col">Forum</th>
                                  <th scope="col">Quotation</th>
                          </tr>
                  <?php
                  while ( $row =
mysqli_fetch_array( $result, MYSQLI_ASSOC ))
                      {
                              $user_name =
htmlspecialchars($row['user_name'], ENT_QUOTES);
                              $post_date =
htmlspecialchars($row['post_date'], ENT_QUOTES);
                              $subject =
htmlspecialchars($row['subject'], ENT_QUOTES);
                              $message =
htmlspecialchars($row['message'], ENT_QUOTES);
                              echo '<tr>
                                  <td scope="row">' . $user_name . " " .
 $post_date . '</td>
                                  <td scope="row">' . $subject . '</td>
                                  <td scope="row">' . $message . '</td>
                          </tr>';
                      }
                  echo '</table>' ;
                  }
else { echo '<p class="text-center">
There are currently no messages.</p>' ; }
mysqli_close( $dbcon ) ;
?>
</div><!--End of the quotes found page content.-->
<footer class="jumbotron row mx-auto" id="includefooter"
style="padding-bottom:1px; margin: 0px; padding-top:8px;
background-color:white;">
<div class="col-sm-12 text-center">
                          <?php include('includes/footer.php'); ?>
                  </div>
</footer>
</div>
</body>
</html>
```

Explanation of the Code

You will have seen most of the code before, but the query needs some explanation.

```
require ( 'mysqli_connect.php' ) ;                                          //#1
              $user_name =
filter_var( $_SESSION['user_name'], FILTER_SANITIZE_STRING);
              // Make the full text query
```

```
               $query = "SELECT user_name,post_date,subject,message FROM ";
$query .= "forum WHERE user_name = ? ";
               $query .= "ORDER BY post_date ASC";
        $q = mysqli_stmt_init($dbcon);
        mysqli_stmt_prepare($q, $query);
        // bind $id to SQL Statement
               mysqli_stmt_bind_param($q, "s", $user_name);
        // execute query
        mysqli_stmt_execute($q);
```

The query selects the items to be displayed and specifies two conditions: show postings only for the username specified in the session ($user_name) and order the table row display in ascending order of date of posting.

The Header for *ViewPosts.php*

The header block will activate all buttons except Login, Register, and Your Quotes. The code is shown in the following snippet of code from *header.php*:

```
case 8: //post.php
          ?>
               <button type="button" style="width: 110px;" class="btn btn-secondary
               bg-primary"
                      onclick="location.href = 'index.php?name=Quick Quotes'">
                      Home Page
               </button>

               <button type="button" style="width: 110px;" class="btn btn-secondary
               bg-primary disabled"
                      onclick="location.href = "" >Login
               </button>

               <button type="button" style="width: 110px;" class="btn btn-secondary
               bg-primary"
                      onclick="location.href = 'logout.php?name=Logout'">
                      Logout
               </button>

               <button type="button" style="width: 110px;" class="btn btn-secondary
               bg-primary disabled"
                      onclick="location.href = "" >Register
               </button>

               <button type="button" style="width: 120px;" class="btn btn-secondary
               bg-primary"
                      onclick="location.href = 'view_posts.php?name=Your Quotes'" >
                      Your Quotes
               </button>
```

```
<button type="button" style="width: 120px;" class="btn btn-secondary
bg-primary disabled"
        onclick="location.href = "">Add A Quote
</button>

<button type="button" style="width: 120px;" class="btn btn-secondary
bg-primary"
        onclick="location.href = 'forum_c.php?name=Comic Quotes'" >
        Comic Quotes
</button>

<button type="button" style="width: 120px;" class="btn btn-secondary
bg-primary"
        onclick="location.href = 'forum_w.php?name=Wise Quotes'">
        Wise Quotes
</button>

<button type="button" style="width: 120px;" class="btn btn-secondary
bg-primary"
        onclick="location.href = 'search.php?name=Search Quotes'" >
        Search Quotes
</button>
<?php
break;
```

We will now enable a member's ability to do full-text searches.

Searching for Specific Words or Phrases

Members might want to see a table of quotes by Mark Twain or a list of quotes about golf; the members would therefore search for particular words or phrases. This will require a Search button in the header. As an alternative, a search field could be incorporated into the forum pages; however, to keep it simple, we will employ the easier method: using a button that links to a search form.

A full-text search will search though every message to find the word (or words). The column named messages must be indexed as FULL TEXT, as shown in the beginning of the chapter.

Full-text searches can be used on VARCHAR and TEXT columns. Full-text searches are case insensitive and will ignore the following:

- Partial words. If you want to search for *spoiled,* you have to search for the full word. Just searching for *spoil* won't return what you are looking for.

- Words containing less than four characters.

- Stop words. These are words that are extremely common, such as *the, a, an, as, by, his, her, with,* and *you.*

- A word or phrase that is included in more than 50 percent of the rows in the column being searched. The word or phrase in this case is treated as a stop word. This can usually be avoided by having four or more records in a table.

The Full Text Search Form

We will now create a form for searching specific words or phrases within messages (quotations).
Figure 10-11 shows the search form.

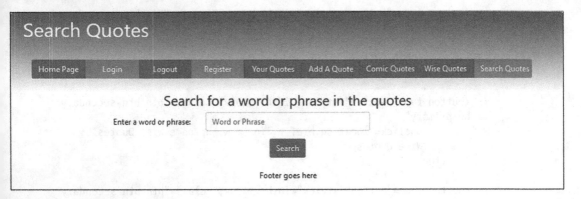

Figure 10-11. *The search form*

Listing 10-11 gives the code for the search form.

Listing 10-11. Creating the Search Form (search.php)

```php
<?php
// Start the session.
session_start() ;
// Redirect if not logged in.
if ( !isset( $_SESSION[ 'member_id' ] ) )
        { header("Location: login.php");
        exit(); }
$menu = 6;
?>
<!DOCTYPE html>
<html lang="en">
<head>
        <title>Search Page</title>
        <meta charset="utf-8">
        <meta name="viewport" content="width=device-width, initial-scale=1,
        shrink-to-fit=no">
        <!-- Bootstrap CSS File -->
        <link rel="stylesheet"
        href="https://stackpath.bootstrapcdn.com/bootstrap/4.1.0/css/bootstrap.min.css"
        integrity=
        "sha384-9gVQ4dYFwwWSjIDZnLEWnxCjeSWFphJiwGPXr1jddIhOegiu1FwO5qRGvFXOdJZ4"
        crossorigin="anonymous">
        <link rel="stylesheet" type="text/css" href="msgboard.css">
</head>
<body>
        <div class="container" style="margin-top:30px;border: 2px black solid;">
        <!-- Header Section -->
```

```
        <header class="jumbotron text-center row" id="includeheader"
                style="margin-bottom:2px; background:linear-gradient(#0073e6,white);
                padding:10px;">
                <?php include('includes/header.php'); ?>
        </header>
        <!-- Body Section -->
        <div class="content mx-auto" id="contents">
        <div class="row mx-auto" style="padding-left: 0px; height: auto;">
        <div class="col-sm-12">
                <h3 class="text-center">Search for a word or phrase in the quotes</h3>
                <form id="search" action="quotes_found.php" method="post">
                <div class="form-group row">
                <label for="target" class="col-sm-4 col-form-label text-right">Enter a word
                or phrase:</label>
                <div class="col-sm-4">
                        <input type="text" class="form-control" id="target" name="target"
                                placeholder="Word or Phrase" maxlength="60" size="40"
                                required
                                value=
                                        "<?php if (isset($_POST['target']))
                                echo htmlspecialchars($_POST['target'], ENT_QUOTES); ?>" >
                </div>
                 </div>
                <div class="form-group row">
                        <label for="" class="col-sm-2 col-form-label"></label>
                <div class="col-sm-8 text-center">
                        <input id="submit" class="btn btn-primary" type="submit"
                                name="submit" value="Search">
                </div>
        </div>
</form>
</div>
</div>
<footer class="jumbotron row mx-auto" id="includefooter"
        style="padding-bottom:1px; margin: 0px; padding-top:8px; background-color:white;">
        <div class="col-sm-12 text-center">
                <?php include('includes/footer.php'); ?>
  </div>
</footer>
</div>
</div>
</body>
</html>
```

The search form passes the search word (or words) to the page that displays the search results.

Displaying the Search Results

Figure 10-12 shows how the full-text search displays the results.

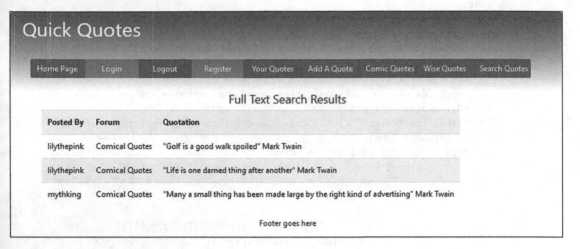

Figure 10-12. *Displaying the results of a full-text search for the words Mark Twain*

Note that the number of quotations by Mark Twain is less than 50 percent of all the quotations contained in our forum table. If the number of quotes by Mark Twain had been more than 50 percent of the quotations, no results would have been displayed. In our example database table, there are 23 quotes. Mark Twain is cited for three quotes; he is therefore cited for 13 percent of the total. Because this is less than 50 percent of the total, he will be found and displayed. If the table contained only six quotes, Mark Twain would be cited for 50 percent of the total, and therefore he would not be found. In other words, the group of words *Mark Twain* would be treated as if it was a stop word such as *his*, *her*, *with*, and *you*. If you know that a word or phrase exists in the database table, but a full-text search fails to find it, either you don't have enough quotes in the table or at least 50 percent of the quotes contain the search word or phrase. Listing 10-12a gives the code for the *quotes_found* page.

Listing 10-12a. Creating the Search Results Page (quotes_found.php)

```php
<?php
// Start the session.
session_start() ;
// Redirect if not logged in.
if ( !isset( $_SESSION[ 'member_id' ] ) )
        { header("Location: login.php");
        exit(); }
$menu = 4;
?>
<!DOCTYPE html>
<html lang="en">
<head>
```

```
        <title>Search Page</title>
        <meta charset="utf-8">
        <meta name="viewport" content="width=device-width, initial-scale=1,
        shrink-to-fit=no">
        <!-- Bootstrap CSS File -->
        <link rel="stylesheet"
                href="https://stackpath.bootstrapcdn.com/bootstrap/4.1.0/css/bootstrap.min.css"
                integrity=
"sha384-9gVQ4dYFwwWSjIDZnLEWnxCjeSWFphJiwGPXr1jddIhOegiu1FwO5qRGvFXOdJZ4"
                crossorigin="anonymous">
        <link rel="stylesheet" type="text/css" href="msgboard.css">
</head>
<body>
<div class="container" style="margin-top:30px;border: 2px black solid;">
<!-- Header Section -->
        <header class="jumbotron text-center row" id="includeheader"
                style="margin-bottom:2px; background:linear-gradient(#0073e6,white);
                padding:10px;">
                        <?php include('includes/header.php'); ?>
        </header>
<div id='content'><!--Start of the quotes found page content-->
<?php
        // Connect to the database
        require ( 'mysqli_connect.php' ) ;
        //if POST is set                                                    #1
        if($_SERVER['REQUEST_METHOD'] == 'POST' ) {
                $target = filter_var( $_POST['target'], FILTER_SANITIZE_STRING);
                // Make the full text query                                  #2
                $query = "SELECT user_name,post_date,subject,message FROM forum WHERE ";
                $query .= "MATCH (message) AGAINST ( ? ) ORDER BY post_date ASC";
                $q = mysqli_stmt_init($dbcon);
                mysqli_stmt_prepare($q, $query);
                // bind $id to SQL Statement
                mysqli_stmt_bind_param($q, "s", $target);
                // execute query
                mysqli_stmt_execute($q);
                $result = mysqli_stmt_get_result($q);
                if (mysqli_num_rows($result) > 0) {
                        echo '<h4 class="text-center">Full Text Search Results</h2>';
                        ?>
                        <table class="table table-responsive table-striped col-sm-12"
                                style="background: white;color:black; padding-left: 50px;">
                                <tr>
                                        <th scope="col">Posted By</th>
                                        <th scope="col">Forum</th>
                                        <th scope="col">Quotation</th>
                                </tr>
                        <?php
                        while ( $row = mysqli_fetch_array( $result, MYSQLI_ASSOC ))
                        {
                                $user_name = htmlspecialchars($row['user_name'], ENT_QUOTES);
```

425

```php
                              $subject = htmlspecialchars($row['subject'], ENT_QUOTES);
                              $message = htmlspecialchars($row['message'], ENT_QUOTES);
                              echo '<tr>
                                        <td scope="row">' . $user_name . '</td>
                                        <td scope="row">' . $subject . '</td>
                                        <td scope="row">' . $message . '</td>
                                   </tr>';
                        }
                        echo '</table>' ;
                  }
                  else { echo '<p class="text-center">There are currently no messages.</p>' ; }
        mysqli_close( $dbcon ) ;
                  }
?>
</div><!--End of the quotes found page content.-->
<footer class="jumbotron row mx-auto" id="includefooter"
        style="padding-bottom:1px; margin: 0px; padding-top:8px; background-color:white;">
        <div class="col-sm-12 text-center">
                  <?php include('includes/footer.php'); ?>
        </div>
</footer>
</div>
</body>
</html>
```

■ **Note**   If you run this file and you see the error message "Warning: mysqli_num_rows() expects parameter 1 to be mysqli_result, boolean given in…," you probably forgot to choose Full Text as the index for the message column the table.

Explanation of the Code

This section explains the code.

```php
//if POST is set                                                          #1
if($_SERVER['REQUEST_METHOD'] == 'POST' ) {
        $target = filter_var( $_POST['target'], FILTER_SANITIZE_STRING);
```

The search form sent the target word or phrase (such as *Mark Twain*) to this page, where it is assigned to the variable $target.

```php
// Make the full text query                                              #2
$query = "SELECT user_name,post_date,subject,message FROM forum WHERE ";
$query .= "MATCH (message) AGAINST ( ? ) ORDER BY post_date ASC";
$q = mysqli_stmt_init($dbcon);
mysqli_stmt_prepare($q, $query);
// bind $id to SQL Statement
mysqli_stmt_bind_param($q, "s", $target);
```

The full-text query searches the forum table for messages (quotations) that contain the words *Mark Twain* as stored in the variable $target, which is bound to the prepare statement. Note the brackets, the commas, and the double and single quote marks; they are important. The format for a full text search query is as follows:

```
SELECT list of items FROM some table WHERE MATCH (the column) AGAINST(the search words) ;
```

The keywords MATCH and AGAINST are the main differences between a standard SELECT query and a full-text search query.

The Header for the quotes_found Page

Listing 10-12b gives the code block for the header. This is also the same header used by forum.php.

Listing 10-12b. Creating the Header Block for the Quotes Found Page (header.php)

```
case 4: //forum.php //quotes_found.php
            ?>
                <button type="button" style="width: 110px;" class="btn btn-secondary
                bg-primary"
                    onclick="location.href = 'index.php?name=Quick Quotes'">
                    Home Page
                </button>

                <button type="button" style="width: 110px;" class="btn btn-secondary
                bg-primary disabled"
                    onclick="location.href = "" >Login
                </button>

                <button type="button" style="width: 110px;" class="btn btn-secondary
                bg-primary"
                    onclick="location.href = 'logout.php?name=Logout'">
Logout
                </button>

                <button type="button" style="width: 110px;" class="btn btn-secondary
                bg-primary disabled"
                    onclick="location.href = "" >Register
                </button>

                <button type="button" style="width: 120px;" class="btn btn-secondary
                bg-primary"
                    onclick="location.href = 'view_posts.php?name=Your Quotes'" >
                    Your Quotes
                </button>

                <button type="button" style="width: 120px;" class="btn btn-secondary
                bg-primary"
                    onclick="location.href = 'post.php?name=Add A Quote'">
                    Add A Quote
                </button>
```

```
                   <button type="button" style="width: 120px;" class="btn btn-secondary
                   bg-primary"
                          onclick="location.href = 'forum_c.php?name=Comic Quotes'" >
                          Comic Quotes
                   </button>

                   <button type="button" style="width: 120px;" class="btn btn-secondary
                   bg-primary"
                          onclick="location.href = 'forum_w.php?name=Wise Quotes'">
                          Wise Quotes
                   </button>

                   <button type="button" style="width: 120px;" class="btn btn-secondary
                   bg-primary"
                          onclick="location.href = 'search.php?name=Search Quotes'" >Search
                          Quotes
                   </button>
           <?php
           break;
```

Enhancing the Message Board

The message board in this chapter was greatly simplified for the benefit of readers who are not familiar with databases. By using the knowledge you gained from previous chapters, it is possible to add enhancements as follows:

- The pages for displaying the two categories of quotes could display paginated results. (Review Chapters 5, and 8 for a reminder of how to do this.)

- Members may want to change their passwords. (Review Chapter 3 for details.)

- Members may have forgotten their passwords; they can be sent a new password. This is covered in Chapter 11.

Converting the Message Board to a Forum

At the beginning of this chapter, we said that we would briefly describe a structure for converting the message board to a forum. A forum requires maximum normalization and atomicity. (See Chapter 9 to refresh your memory on the definition of those terms.) More tables are required, and several of these would be linked by queries containing the keyword JOIN.

A forum requires additional tables for threads and replies. The message board is moderated by the administrator as a result of an automatic e-mail containing the name of the poster and the date. When the quote was submitted, it is inserted immediately into the database table; a better solution is to create an additional column (approved) that must be set by the administrator to allow the quotes to be displayed to the members.

It would be helpful if the administrator had facilities to delete or edit a quote without using phpMyAdmin. The admin page could display a table of recent posts that contained links for editing and deleting, as described in Chapter 3.

The minimum number of tables required for a forum is four, as shown in Figure 10-13.

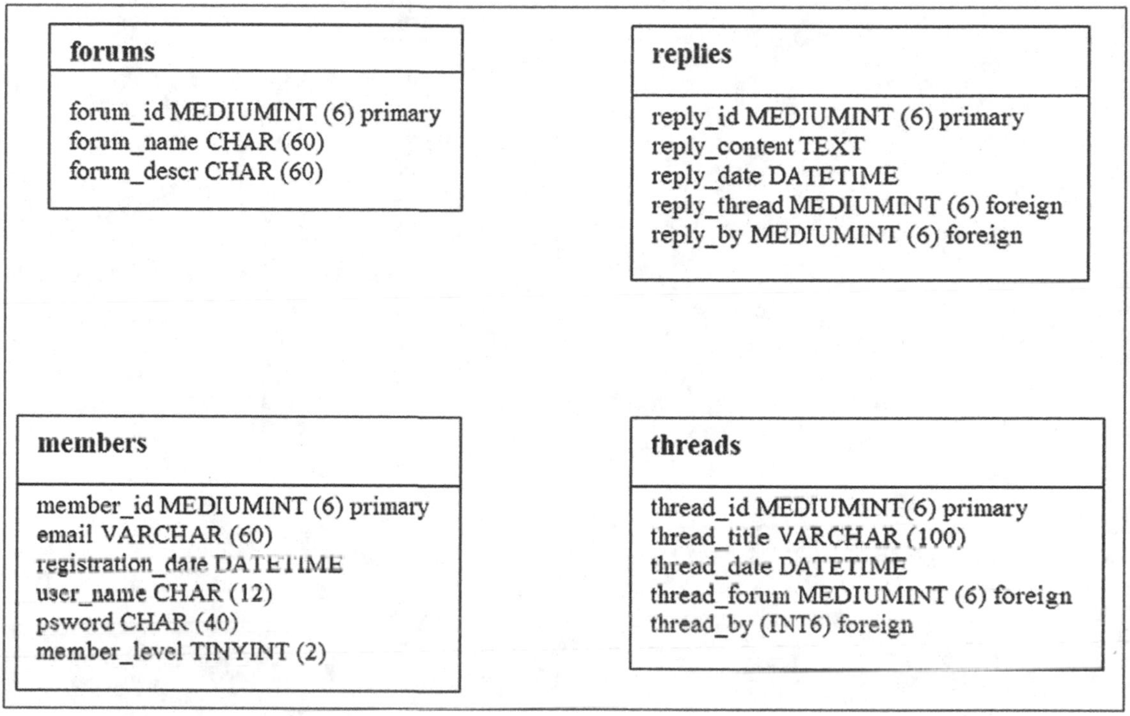

forums

forum_id MEDIUMINT (6) primary
forum_name CHAR (60)
forum_descr CHAR (60)

replies

reply_id MEDIUMINT (6) primary
reply_content TEXT
reply_date DATETIME
reply_thread MEDIUMINT (6) foreign
reply_by MEDIUMINT (6) foreign

members

member_id MEDIUMINT (6) primary
email VARCHAR (60)
registration_date DATETIME
user_name CHAR (12)
psword CHAR (40)
member_level TINYINT (2)

threads

thread_id MEDIUMINT(6) primary
thread_title VARCHAR (100)
thread_date DATETIME
thread_forum MEDIUMINT (6) foreign
thread_by (INT6) foreign

Figure 10-13. The tables for a very basic forum

Summary

In this chapter, we studied the plan and structure for a basic message board. We created a registration page and login form. We developed a gateway to two pages of quotes and then created those pages. We learned how to create a form for posting messages. We created two search forms: one enabled members to search for a list of their own postings, and another was designed to undertake full-text searches. Some enhancements to the basic message board were suggested, and finally a brief outline of a basic forum was provided. The next chapter describes a basic e-commerce website.

CHAPTER 11

■■■

E-commerce: A Brief Introduction

E-commerce websites accept payment in exchange for goods or services. A user orders from a range of goods or services displayed in the website's catalog pages. The details of the user's orders are stored in the website's database. Money passes from the user to the website owner. This is achieved by means of a payment system incorporated into the website. Finally, the ordered items are delivered to the user. Users can track the progress of their orders, update their account details, and, if necessary, contact a customer support department.

After completing this chapter, you will be able to

- Design a simple e-commerce site
- Create a website that interfaces with Paypal
- Create a website that includes a simple shopping cart
- Provide the user with the ability to recover a password

Two types of e-commerce sites would benefit from using a database: an online shop with an extensive range of goods or services, such as Amazon, and an online shop with a limited range of goods but with the intention of expanding the range. The brief outline for an e-commerce site in this chapter is based on the latter.

■ **Note** This chapter is a brief demonstration of the basic format for e-commerce websites. To make the basic principles as clear as possible and to save space, no alternative currencies are included. When adapting the websites for your territory, you would naturally change the content and currency to suit. As we have mentioned previously, when selling goods and services to multiple countries, you must make sure to follow the laws pertaining to online sales for each country.

This chapter describes two types of shopping cart, a PayPal cart and a custom cart. Each example is treated separately and includes its own database, tables, and files. The following are the two main sections of this chapter:

- Create a PayPal cart website
  - The PayPal cart home page
  - Administering the PayPal cart website
- Create a custom cart website
  - The custom cart home page
  - Administering the custom cart website
  - The checkout page

We will discuss a few of the important processes in this chapter. However, we will not cover every process required for an e-commerce site. This outline will provide you with a starting point for further study. This chapter contains very little code because the websites described combine most of the code already shown and explained in the previous chapters.

For instance:

- The registration page is like the registration page described in Chapter 6.
- Most of the administration facilities were described in Chapters 3 and 8.
- Chapter 9 described the use of multiple tables.
- The use of Bootstrap to create sites that display in any size device is shown throughout the book.

Login and logout pages were covered fully in several previous chapters. However, the login page in this chapter contains a link to enable users to retrieve a forgotten password; the code is provided for this feature.

■ **Note** This chapter is a brief introduction to an e-commerce website. Dealing fully with a practical example of an e-commerce website with its payment gateway, stock control system, order tracking, security measures, invoicing, and customer services would require a whole book. You will find a list of resources for designing and developing e-commerce websites in Appendix B.

We want to take the time to thank Roger St. Barbe for providing the images of colored etchings. His method of producing the etchings is fascinating; a précis of the process can be found on his website:

www.dolphin-gallery.co.uk

Although we state that each product is unique, Roger does produce a limited number of signed copies of each etching. For the sake of simplicity, in our example the Dove Gallery will stock only one copy. Adrian West owns the other paintings used in this chapter. The artist James Kessell (now deceased) was a double Royal Academy artist (London and Birmingham, United Kingdom).

■ **Note** The downloadable files for the PayPal shopping cart and custom shopping cart sections are included in separate subfolders. The *paypaldb.sql* and `customdb.sql` files are provided for installing the PayPal and custom databases and tables. The main folder can be downloaded from the Apress.com website.

Let's begin. The two most important topics for both shopping carts are security and careful planning.

Security Warning

Database-driven e-commerce websites can be extremely vulnerable; therefore, security is a primary concern. By heeding the following warnings, an e-commerce website could be reasonably secure.

- A developer should not attempt to launch an e-commerce website until they have achieved a high level of expertise with PHP, SQL, and the Maria/MySQL database.

- Complete knowledge of PHP *stored procedures* and *transactions* is essential for e-commerce.

- The developer must thoroughly understand the inherent security problems and risks that can occur.

- Developers must be aware of and fully comply with the data protection laws for their territory or country, especially with the laws governing online trading.

- The website should never store customers' bank and credit card details unless a costly and efficient security scheme is in place.

- It is safer to use a secure payment system such as PayPal, Stripe, or Authorize.net. Always choose the encoded versions of their shopping cart buttons. Use one of these payment systems to collect credit card and other sensitive information. Do not collect or store the information in your e-commerce databases.

- Use HTTPS pages, which are protected by Secure Sockets Layer (SSL).

Let's now examine a plan for creating an e-commerce website.

The Plan

As usual, the first step for designing a database means discussing the website owner's needs and then producing a plan to fulfill those requirements. After meeting with our client, we have determined the following requirements:

- The websites will sell original paintings and colored etchings.

- An administrator will be able to add or delete paintings and artists from the database tables by means of a user-friendly interface.

- A basic e-commerce database would use many tables, typically 12 or more, but for the first phase (what we will cover in this chapter) our site will use the following tables:

  - *user*: This table contains the administrator and registered users. The table will include the user's address, but for brevity it will not include an alternative delivery address.

  - *art*: This table contains a description of the paintings and will be used to display a catalog of the stock of paintings.

  - *artist*: This table contains the name of the artist. However, to save space, it will not contain the traditional brief description of the artist.

  - *Orders and order processing (custom cart only):* These tables will record and keep track of order details as demonstrated in the custom cart section.

■ **Note**   We have assumed that during the planning stage of the PayPal site, the owner decided that users should not be asked to register unless they would like to receive e-mailed updates, which will provide special offers or new acquisitions to the art gallery. Regarding the custom cart website, we have decided to incorporate up-front registration. An alternative approach would use registration at the checkout stage.

Creating the PayPal Cart Site

In this section, we will create an e-commerce site that uses PayPal to process all transactions. Let's begin by setting up the database, tables, and files.

Creating the PayPal Cart Database and Tables

Follow these steps:

1. In the *htdocs* folder within XAMPP or in the EasyPHP folder *eds_www*, create a new folder named *paypalcart*.

2. Download the paypalcart files for Chapter 11 from the book's page at Apress.com and unzip them in your new *paypalcart* folder.

3. Start XAMPP or EasyPHP, and in the address field of a browser enter `localhost/phpmyadmin/` to access phpMyAdmin.

4. Click the Databases tab and create a database named *paypaldb*. From the pull-down Collation list, choose utf8_general_ci and then click Create.

5. Click the Privileges tab and then scroll down and click Add new user.

6. Enter these details:

- *Username*: colossus
- *Password*: FstcOmput3r
- *Host*: localhost
- *Database name*: paypaldb

7. Click Go.

Viewing the Connection File

The code for the connection file is as follows:

```php
<?php
// Create a connection to the migrate database and to MySQL
// Set the encoding to utf-8
// Set the database access details as constants
Define ('DB_USER', 'colossus');
Define ('DB_PASSWORD', 'FstcOmput3r');
Define ('DB_HOST', 'localhost');
Define ('DB_NAME', 'paypaldb');
// Make the connection:
$dbcon = new mysqli(DB_HOST, DB_USER, DB_PASSWORD, DB_NAME);
// Set the encoding...optional but recommended
mysqli_set_charset($dbcon, 'utf8');
```

To test your connection file, enter this URL in the address field of a browser:

```
http://localhost/paypalcart/mysqli_connect.php
```

The displayed page should be completely empty.

Populating the PayPal Cart Tables

Use phpMyAdmin to import the tables and populate them.

1. In the left panel of phpMyAdmin, click the box next to the database paypaldb.

2. Do not enter anything on the next screen, but click the Import tab.

3. Click the Browse button and navigate to the *paypalcart* folder.

4. Import the *paypaldb.sql* dump file by clicking the Open button; the field will fill with the location of the file.

5. Ensure that the Character set in the pull-down menu is utf-8 and that the format is shown as SQL.

6. Click Go.

For your interest, Table 11-1 gives the column details for the PayPal cart art table. All the tables use the InnoDB storage engine.

Table 11-1. *The art Table Includes a Column for the PayPal Payment Code*

Column name	Type	Length/ Value	Default	Attributes	NULL	Index	A_I
art_id	INT	8	None	UNSIGNED	☐	PRIMARY	☑
thumb	VARCHAR	50	None		☐		☐
type	VARCHAR	50	None		☐		☐
price	DECIMAL	6,2	None	UNSIGNED	☐	INDEX	☐
medium	VARCHAR	50	None		☐		☐
artist	VARCHAR	50	None		☐		☐
mini-descr	VARCHAR	150	None		☐		☐
ppcode	Text	500	None		☐		☐

Note: Payment systems other than PayPal may require different values in the final column.

The first name and the middle name are set as NULL entries because some artists may rarely use those names such as Picasso. The Artists table is shown in Table 11-2.

Table 11-2. *The Artists Table*

Column name	Type	Length/ Value	Default	Attributes	NULL	Index	A_I
art_id	INT	8	None	UNSIGNED	☐	PRIMARY	☑
first_name	VARCHAR	30	None		☑		☐
middle_name	VARCHAR	30	None		☑		☐
last_name	VARCHAR	40	None		☐		☐

Table 11-3. *Details of How the artist Table Was Populated is shown in Table 11-4*

First name	Middle name	Last name
Adrian	W	West
Roger	St.	Barbe
James		Kessell

Table 11-4. *The Types and Attributes for a Minimal Users Table is shown in Table 11-5*

Column name	Type	Length/ Value	Default	Attributes	NULL	Index	A_I
user_id	MediumINT	8	None	UNSIGNED	☐	PRIMARY	☑
title	VARCHAR	12	None		☑		☐
first_name	VARCHAR	30	None		☐		☐
last_name	VARCHAR	40	None		☐		☐
email	VARCHAR	50	None		☐		☐
password	CHAR	60	None		☐		☐
registration_date	DATETIME				☐		☐
user_level	TINYINT	1	None	UNSIGNED	☐		☐
address1	VARCHAR	50	None		☐		☐
address2	VARCHAR	50	None		☑		☐
city	VARCHAR	50	None		☐		☐
state_country	VARCHAR	30	None		☐		☐
zcode_pcode	VARCHAR	10	None		☐		☐
phone	VARCHAR	15	None		☑		☐
secret	VARCHAR	30	None		☐		☐

A user_level column is included to enable the login page to differentiate between a registered user and an administrator. Users would have a default user_level of zero, and the administrator would be given a larger number that will direct them to an administration page. When any other user accesses the PayPal cart website, they do not need to log in to see the website's pages. A secret column has been included to provide additional information when the user forgets their password.

■ **Note** Here are the login details for the users; you will need Mr. Mike Rosoft's details to log in into the administration page and add new paintings.

Mr. Mike Rosoft, e-mail: miker@myisp.com, password: W111g@t3s, user_level: 1

Mrs. Rose Bush, e-mail: rbush@myisp.co.uk, password: R@db100ms, user_level: 0

To save space in the note, we have not included all the information that is contained in the *users.sql* file. The other details are used in this example PayPal cart website; therefore, they are not important.

The home page is discussed next.

The PayPal Cart Home Page

The home page and its code for the PayPal cart website are provided in the PayPal cart downloadable files. They are *index.php* and *transparent.css*.

Figure 11-1 shows the PayPal cart home page.

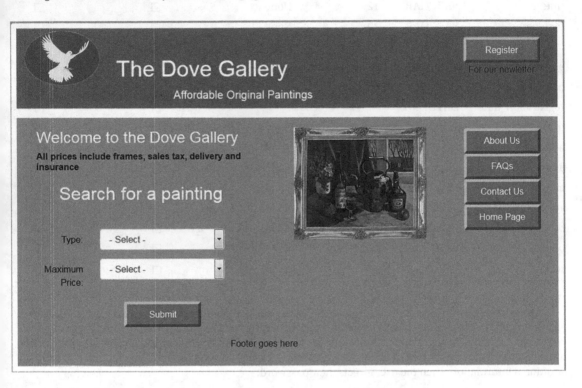

Figure 11-1. *The PayPal cart home page, which also acts as a search page*

Users do not have to log in or register to use the search facility that is built into the home page. The buyer's details for shipping the paintings will be provide by PayPal in an e-mail to the website's owner. The only person who must register and log in is the administrator to add or delete paintings. However, users can register if they want to receive a monthly newsletter. Listing 11-1 gives the code for the home page.

Listing 11-1. The PayPal Cart Home Page (index.php)

```php
<?php
$menu=7;
?>
<!DOCTYPE html>
<html lang="en">
<head>
  <title>PayPal Cart Index Page</title>
  <meta charset="utf-8">
  <meta name="viewport"
  content="width=device-width, initial-scale=1, shrink-to-fit=no">
```

```
<!-- Bootstrap CSS File -->
<link rel="stylesheet"
href=
"https://stackpath.bootstrapcdn.com/bootstrap/4.1.0/css/bootstrap.min.css"
  integrity=
"sha384-9gVQ4dYFwwWSjIDZnLEWnxCjeSWFphJiwGPXr1jddIhOegiu1FwO5qRGvFXOdJZ4"
  crossorigin="anonymous">
<link rel="stylesheet" type="text/css" href="transparent.css">
</head>
<body>
<div class="container" style="margin-top:10px">
<!-- Header Section -->
<header class="jumbotron text-center row mx-auto" id="includeheader">
<?php include('includes/header.php'); ?>
</header>
<!-- Body Section -->
<div class="content mx-auto" id="contents">
<div class="row mx-auto" style="padding-left: 20px; height: auto;">
<!-- Center Column Content Section -->
<div class="col-sm-6 text-center" style="padding:0px; margin-top: 5px;">
      <!--Start of found paintings content-->
      <form  action="found_paintings.php" method="post">
<div class="form-group row">
      <div class="col-sm-10 text-left"
            style="padding: 20px; padding-left: 30px;">
            <h3>Welcome to the Dove Gallery</h3>
            <h6 style="color: black;">
<b>All prices include frames, sales tax, delivery and insurance</b></h6>
            <h2 class="text-center">Search for a painting</h2>
      </div>
      <div class="col-sm-6">
</div>
</div>
      <div class="form-group row">
          <label for="type" class="col-sm-3 col-form-label text-right">
            Type:</label>
<div class="col-sm-6">
      <select id="type" name="type" class="form-control">
            <option selected value="">- Select -</option>
            <option value="still-life">Still Life</option>
            <option value="nature">Nature</option>
            <option value="abstract">Abstract</option>
</select>
</div>
</div>
      <div class="form-group row">
      <label for="price"
class="col-sm-3 col-form-label text-right">
Maximum Price:</label>
```

```
<div class="col-sm-6">
      <select id="price" name="price" class="form-control">
            <option selected value="">- Select -</option>
            <option value="40">&pound;40</option>
            <option value="80">&pound;80</option>
            <option value="800">&pound;800</option>
</select>
</div>
</div>
      <div class="form-group row">
            <label class="col-sm-3 col-form-label"></label>
      <div class="col-sm-6">
<input id="submit" class="btn btn-primary"
            type="submit" name="submit" value="Submit">
</div>
</div>
</form><!--End of the search content-->
</div>
<div class="col-sm-3 text-center"
style="padding:0px; margin-top: 5px;">
<img alt="Copper Kettle by James Kessell"
class="img-fluid float-left"
style="margin-top: 20px;"
src="images/k-copper-kettle-300.jpg">
</div>
<aside class="col-sm-3" id="includemenu">
            <?php include('includes/menu.php'); ?>
</aside>
</div>
<div class="form-group row">
<label class="col-sm-4"></label>
<div class="col-sm-8">
<footer class="jumbotron row" id="includefooter">
            <?php include('includes/footer.php'); ?>
</footer>
</div>
</div>
</div>
</div>
</body>
</html>
```

The HTML and Bootstrap format for this page and others demonstrated in this chapter are like what you have seen in other chapters. Therefore, we will not repeat the HTML code for each page. Also note that we are using one header file from previous chapters to handle all the pages.

Using the PayPal Cart Home Page to Search for Paintings

Figure 11-2 shows the result of searching for nature paintings that cost a maximum of £40.

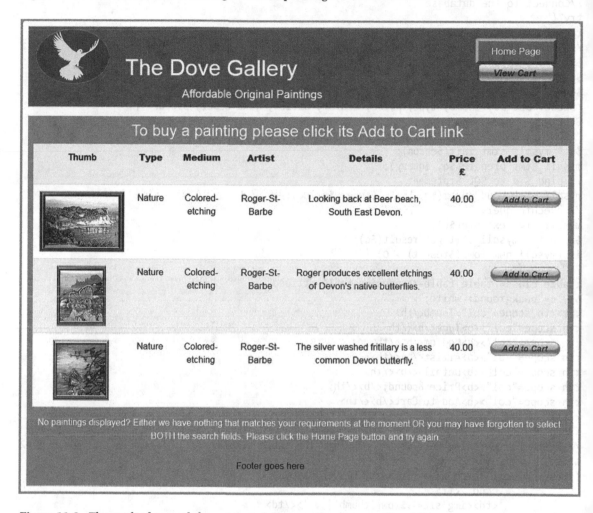

Figure 11-2. The result of a search for nature paintings costing no more than £40

■ **Note** The PayPal buttons will not be visible on the search results page unless you are connected to the Internet.

The HTML code for the *found_paintings.php* file can be downloaded and viewed from the Apress website. It is similar to code you have seen previously. Listing 11-2 shows the PHP code for displaying the found paintings.

Listing 11-2. Code to Show the Results of a Search (process_found_pics.php)

```php
<?php
//Connect to the database
try {
require ( 'mysqli_connect.php' ) ;
// Select the first three items from the art table                              #1
$type=$_SESSION['type'];
$price=$_SESSION['price'];
$query =
"SELECT art_id, thumb, type, price, medium, artist, mini_descr, ppcode ";
$query .=
"FROM art WHERE type= ? AND price <= ? ORDER BY price DESC LIMIT 3";
$q = mysqli_stmt_init($dbcon);
mysqli_stmt_prepare($q, $query);
// bind $id to SQL Statement
mysqli_stmt_bind_param($q, "si", $type, $price);
// execute query
mysqli_stmt_execute($q);
$result = mysqli_stmt_get_result($q);
if (mysqli_num_rows($result) > 0) {
?>
<table class="table table-responsive table-striped"
style="background: white;">
<tr><th scope="col">Thumb</th>
<th scope="col"><b>Type</b></th>
<th scope="col"><b>Medium</b></th>
<th scope="col"><b>Artist</b></th>
<th scope="col"><b>Details</b></th>
<th scope="col"><b>Price &pound;</b></th>
<th scope="col"><b>Add to Cart</b></th>
</tr>
<?php
// Fetch the matching records and populate the table display                     #2
while
($row = mysqli_fetch_array($result, MYSQLI_ASSOC)) {
          echo '<tr>
          <td><img src='.$row['thumb'] . '></td>
          <td>' . $row['type'] . '</td>
          <td>' . $row['medium'] . '</td>
          <td>' . $row['artist'] . '</td>
          <td>' . $row['mini_descr'] . '</td>
          <td>' . $row['price'] . '</td>
          <td>' . $row['ppcode'] . '</td>
          </tr>';
     }
?>
</table>
<?php
// Close the database connection.
     mysqli_close( $dbcon ) ;
}
```

```php
// Or notify the user that no matching paintings were found
else {
echo '<p>There are currently no items matching your search
criteria.</p>' ; }
}
catch(Exception $e)
{
        print "The system is busy, please try later";
        $error_string = date('mdYhis') . " | Found Pics | " .
$e->getMessage() . "\n";
        error_log($error_string,3,"/logs/exception_log.log");
        //error_log("Exception in Found Pics Program.
// Check log for details", 1, "noone@nowhere.com",
        //          "Subject: Found Pics Exception" . "\r\n");
        // You can turn off display of errors in php.ini
// display_errors = Off
        //print "An Exception occurred. Message: " .
// $e->getMessage();
}catch(Error $e)
{
        print "The system is busy, please come back later";
        $error_string = date('mdYhis') . " | Found Pics | " .
$e->getMessage() . "\n";
        error_log($error_string,3,"/logs/error_log.log");
        //error_log("Error in Found Pics Program.
//Check log for details", 1, "noone@nowhere.com",
        //       "Subject: Found Pics Error" . "\r\n");
        // You can turn off display of errors in php.ini
// display_errors = Off
        //print "An Error occurred. Message: " .
// $e->getMessage();
}
?>
```

Explanation of the Code

This section explains the code.

```php
// Select the first three items from the art table                          #1
$type=$_SESSION['type'];
$price=$_SESSION['price'];
$query =
"SELECT art_id, thumb, type, price, medium, artist, mini_descr, ppcode ";
$query .=
"FROM art WHERE type= ? AND price <= ? ORDER BY price DESC LIMIT 3";
```

For our demonstrations in this chapter, we have limited the display of the artwork to three that match the type and price the user has selected. We did this to reduce the code for this chapter. In a live environment, this code would need to be adjusted to include paging, as shown previously in this book.

```
// Fetch the matching records and populate the table display                    #2
while
($row = mysqli_fetch_array($result, MYSQLI_ASSOC)) {
            echo '<tr>
            <td><img src='.$row['thumb'] . '></td>
            <td>' . $row['type'] . '</td>
            <td>' . $row['medium'] . '</td>
            <td>' . $row['artist'] . '</td>
            <td>' . $row['mini_descr'] . '</td>
            <td>' . $row['price'] . '</td>
            <td>' . $row['ppcode'] . '</td>
            </tr>';
```

Within the table created, the PayPal code (ppcode) is displayed. This code will provide the user with the ability to add items to a PayPal cart, as discussed next.

Integrating with the PayPal Shopping Cart Buttons

PayPal is secure and familiar to millions throughout the world. The PayPal payment buttons are encoded so that the prices cannot be manipulated by rogue customers. When a product is paid for, PayPal will send the administrator an e-mail containing the following: the date and ID of the transaction, the amount paid, the e-mail address of the buyer, the buyer's delivery address, and a description of the purchased item.

The PayPal payment system will not be described in detail because this would need its own chapter (or two). A full description would probably become obsolete anyway because PayPal frequently updates the process. Instead of giving detailed instructions, we have provided this overview so that you know what to look for on the PayPal website. PayPal and other credit card verification resources provide plenty of instructions on their websites. Two helpful forums are listed in Appendix B. They will help you learn about configuring PayPal and will solve problems you might meet when integrating the cart buttons with your website.

To create a business account, access the PayPal website for your territory or country (e.g., www.paypal.com for the United States or www.paypal.co.uk for the United Kingdom). Registration is free and not difficult to set up. Then access your business account by clicking the Business tab and using search field to locate the code necessary for the buttons and logos.

Each product in an e-commerce catalog will require its unique code for the Add to Cart button; these can be fully configured using your account on the PayPal website. The code for each button can then be copied and pasted into the database's art table. In our example, this would be achieved by pasting the code into the PayPal text area of the administrator's page shown in Figure 11-4.

PayPal provides several credit/debit card logos. The logos inform users that payments can be made even if they do not have a PayPal account. Figure 11-3 shows two standard encoded PayPal buttons and a horizontal version of a credit/debit card logo.

The buttons in Figure 11-3 are not included with the downloadable files because they are generated by the PayPal code when the user is online.

Figure 11-3. The appearance of the buttons and credit/debit card logo

■ **Note**   Dummy codes for the PayPal buttons are used in this chapter's downloadable files. Your own PayPal buttons will be unique and will apply only to your own e-commerce website. PayPal will generate the code for you to copy and paste into the *admin_add_painting.php* file.

Dummy code has also been placed in the downloadable files for the Recaptcha verification. You will need to replace this code with your Recaptcha details.

The typical code for an Add to Cart button will be similar to the example in Listing 11-3a. PayPal could change this code, so make sure to copy the correct code from the PayPal website. For security, the ID value for each product is given here as XXXXXXX, but real-world buttons will have digits instead of *X*s.

Listing 11-3a.   Sample Code for a PayPal Add to Cart Button

```
<form target="paypal" action="https://www.paypal.com/cgi-bin/webscr" method="post">
<input name="cmd" value="_s-xclick" type="hidden">
<input name="hosted_button_id" value="XXXXXXX" type="hidden">
<p><input src=
"https://www.paypal.com/en_GB/i/btn/btn_cart_LG.gif" name="submit"
alt="PayPal - The safer, easier way to pay online."
Style="float: left;" border="0" type="image">
<img alt="" src="https://www.paypal.com/en_GB/i/scr/pixel.gif"
border="0" height="1" width="1"></p>
</form>
```

We are also placing a PayPal View Cart button in the header of the shop's found_paintings pages (located in *header.php*). The code for the View Cart button will be something like Listing 11-3b. As mentioned, the format of this code can be changed by PayPal. Always go to the PayPal website and download the newest format.

The e-mail address shown in bold type will be replaced by the website owner's (or the administrator's) e-mail address. When an order is checked out, PayPal will send the details in an e-mail to that address.

Listing 11-3b.   The Code for a PayPal View Cart Button

```
<form name="_xclick" target="paypal"
action="https://www.paypal.com/uk/cgi-bin/webscr" method="post">
<input type="hidden" name="cmd" value="_cart">
<input type="hidden" name="business" value="me@mybusiness.co.uk">
<input type="image" src="https://www.paypal.com/en_GB/i/btn/view_cart.gif" border="0"
name="submit"
alt="Make payments with PayPal - it's fast, free and secure!">
<input type="hidden" name="display" value="1">
</form>
```

■ **Caution**   When configuring a unique PayPal button for each product in your shop, the configuration must include the price, the currency, the name of the item being purchased, and the product identity number. Most important, ensure that you configure the PayPal buttons so that the buyer is prompted to enter a delivery address. The PayPal buttons will be automatically encoded.

Now let's look at some of the other pages of the website. The administrator will add paintings with the PayPal code using the Add a Painting page shown in Figure 11-4.

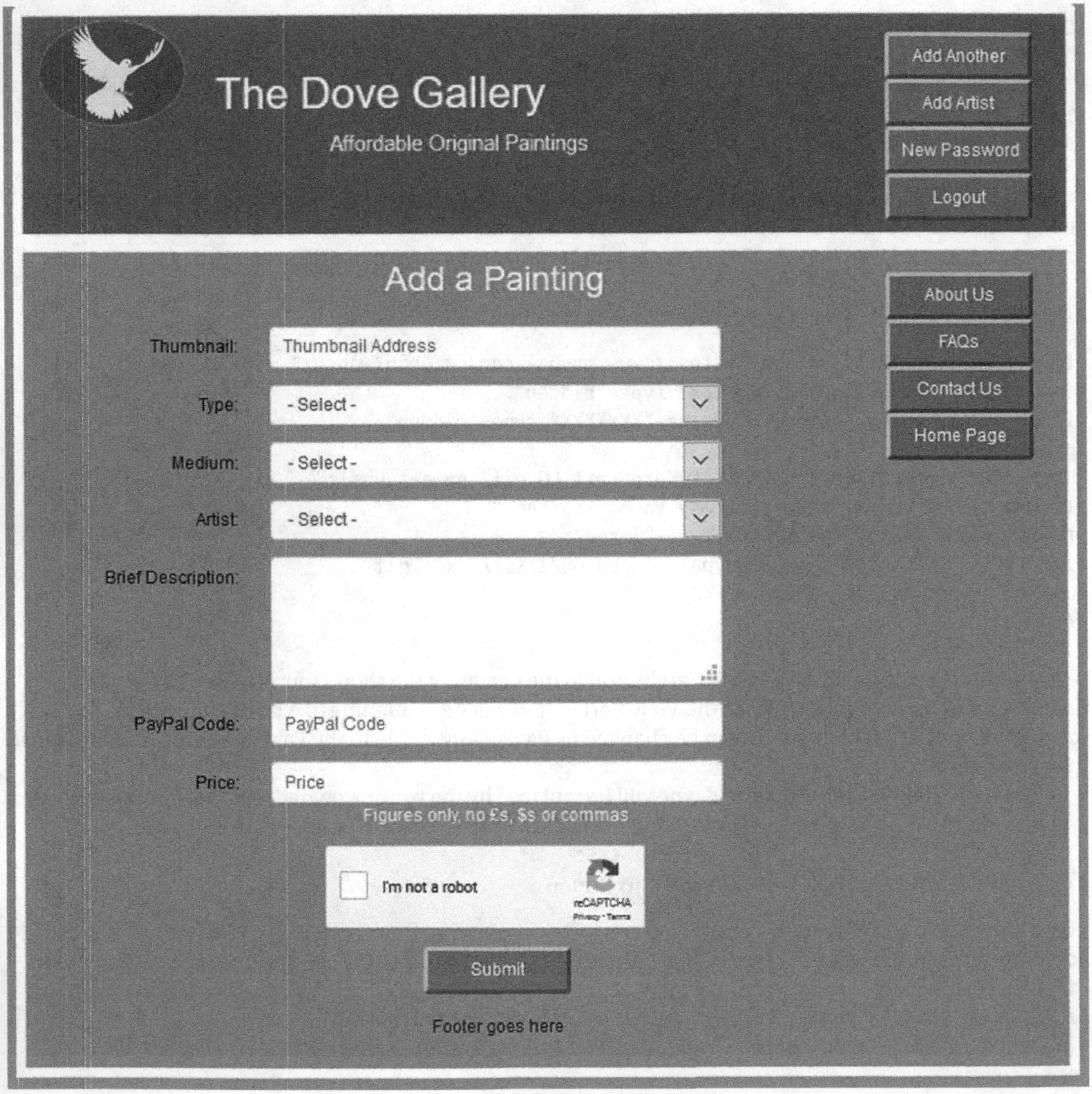

Figure 11-4. *The administrator's interface for adding paintings and the PayPal Add to Cart buttons*

The HTML code for the *admin_add_paintings.php* site is similar to other form code shown in this book. Therefore, it is not included here. However, you can download it from the Apress website and view it in your text editor. The form is submitted to the PHP file *admin_add_paintings.php*. Listing 11-4 provides this code.

Listing 11-4. Code for Adding Paintings (admin_add_painting.php)

```php
<?php
      $errors = array();
// Start an array to contain the error messages
// Check if a thumbnail url has been entered                              #1
      $thumbtrim = trim($_POST['thumb']);
            if ((!empty($thumbtrim)) &&
(filter_var($thumbtrim, FILTER_VALIDATE_URL))
                        && (strlen($thumbtrim) <= 50)) {
                  // no changes
            }
            else
            {
            $errors[] =
'Missing thumbnail url or wrong format. Max 50.';
            }
// Check for a type                                                       #2
      $typetrim = trim($_POST['type']);
      if ((!empty($typetrim)) &&
(preg_match('/[a-z\-\s\.]/i',$typetrim)) &&
                  (strlen($typetrim) <= 50)) {
      //Sanitize the trimmed type
      $typetrim = (filter_var($typetrim, FILTER_SANITIZE_STRING));
      }else{
$errors[] =
'Type missing or not alphabetic, -, period or space. Max 50.';
            }
// Has a price been entered?
$pricetrim = trim($_POST['price']);
if ((!empty($pricetrim)) && (strlen($pricetrim) <= 10)) {
      //Sanitize the trimmed price
            $pricetrim =
(filter_var($pricetrim, FILTER_SANITIZE_NUMBER_INT));
            $pricetrim = preg_replace('/\D+/', ", ($pricetrim));
      }else{
$errors[] =
'Price missing. Must be Numeric. Max ######.##.';
      }
// Has the medium been entered?
      $mediumtrim = trim($_POST['medium']);
      if ((!empty($mediumtrim)) &&
(preg_match('/[a-z\-\s\.]/i',$mediumtrim)) &&
                  (strlen($mediumtrim) <= 50)) {
      //Sanitize the trimmed medium
$mediumtrim = (filter_var($mediumtrim, FILTER_SANITIZE_STRING));
      }else{
$errors[] =
'Medium missing only alphabetic, -, period or space. Max 50.';
      }
      // Has the artist been entered?
      $artisttrim = trim($_POST['artist']);
```

```
        if ((!empty($artisttrim)) &&
(preg_match('/[a-z\-\s\.]/i',$artisttrim)) &&
                (strlen($artisttrim) <= 50)) {
            //Sanitize the trimmed artist
$artisttrim = (filter_var($artisttrim, FILTER_SANITIZE_STRING));
        }else{
$errors[] =
'Artist missing or not alphabetic, -, period or space. Max 50.';
        }
// Has a brief description been entered?
        $minitrim = trim($_POST['mini_descr']);
        if ((!empty($minitrim)) &&
(preg_match('/[a-z\-\s\.]/i',$minitrim)) &&
                (strlen($minitrim) <= 150)) {
        //Sanitize the trimmed artist
$minitrim = (filter_var($minitrim, FILTER_SANITIZE_STRING));
        }else{
        $errors[] =
'Description missing or not alphabetic, -, period or space. Max 50.';
        }
        // Has the PPcode been entered?
        $ppcodetrim = trim($_POST['ppcode']);
        if ((!empty($ppcodetrim)) &&
(strlen($ppcodetrim) <= 45)) {
        //Sanitize the trimmed ppcode
        $ppcodetrim =
(filter_var($minitrim, FILTER_SANITIZE_STRING));
}else{
            $errors[] =
'PayPal Code missing or not alphabetic, -, period or space. Max 50.';
        }
if (empty($errors)) { // If no errors were encountered
    // Register the painting in the database
try {
            require ('mysqli_connect.php');
// Connect to the database
            // Make the query:'
    $query = "INSERT INTO art" .
" (art_id, thumb, type, medium, artist, mini_descr, price, ppcode)";
        $query .= "VALUES ";
        $query .= "(' ', ?,?,?,?,?,?,?)";
        $q = mysqli_stmt_init($dbcon);
        mysqli_stmt_prepare($q, $query);
        // use prepared statement to ensure that only text is inserted
        // bind fields to SQL Statement
mysqli_stmt_bind_param($q, 'sssssss', $thumbtrim, $typetrim, $mediumtrim, $artisttrim,
$minitrim, $pricetrim, $ppcodetrim );
        // execute query
        mysqli_stmt_execute($q);
        if (mysqli_stmt_affected_rows($q) == 1) {
                echo '<h2 style="margin-left: 60px;">
```

```
The painting was successfully registered</h2><br>';
        } else { // If it was not registered
                // Error message:
                echo '<h2>System Error</h2>
                <p class="error">
The painting could not be added due to a system
 error. We apologize for any inconvenience.</p>';
                // Debugging message:
                //echo '<p>' . mysqli_error($dbcon) .
// '<br><br>Query: ' . $q . '</p>';
                } // End of if ($result)
                mysqli_close($dbcon); // Close the database connection.
}
catch(Exception $e)
{
                print "The system is busy, please try later";
                $error_string = date('mdYhis') .
" | Add Painting | " . $e-getMessage() . "\n";
                error_log($error_string,3,"/logs/exception_log.log");
                //error_log("Exception in Add Painting Program. " .
//" Check log for details", 1, "noone@nowhere.com",
//       "Subject: Add Painting Exception" . "\r\n");
                // You can turn off display of errors in php.ini
// display_errors = Off
                //print "An Exception occurred. Message: " .
//      $e->getMessage();
}
catch(Error $e)
{
                print "The system is busy, please come back later";
                $error_string = date('mdYhis') . " | Add Painting | " .
$e-getMessage() . "\n";
                error_log($error_string,3,"/logs/error_log.log");
                //error_log("Error in Add Painting Program. " .
//"Check log for details", 1, "noone@nowhere.com",
                //       "Subject: Add Painting Error" . "\r\n");
                // You can turn off display of errors in php.ini
// display_errors = Off
                //print "An Error occurred. Message: " .
// $e->getMessage();
}
} else { // Display the errors.
        echo '<h2>Error!</h2>
        <p class="error">The following error(s) occurred:<br>';
                foreach ($errors as $msg) { // Print each error.
                        echo " - $msg<br>\n";
                }
        echo '</p><h3>Please try again.</h3><p><br></p>';
}// End of if (empty($errors))
?>
```

Explanation of the Code

This section explains the code.

```
// Check if a thumbnail url has been entered                              #1
       $thumbtrim = trim($_POST['thumb']);
              if ((!empty($thumbtrim)) &&
(filter_var($thumbtrim, FILTER_VALIDATE_URL))
                          && (strlen($thumbtrim) <= 50)) {
                    // no changes
       }
       else
       {
       $errors[] =
'Missing thumbnail url or wrong format. Max 50.';
       }
```

The validation for thumb uses the filter_var property FILTER_VALIDATE_URL to ensure that the location of the artwork picture is formatted correctly.

```
// Check for a type                                                       #2
       $typetrim = trim($_POST['type']);
       if ((!empty($typetrim)) &&
(preg_match('/[a-z\-\s\.]/i',$typetrim)) &&
                    (strlen($typetrim) <= 50)) {
       //Sanitize the trimmed type
       $typetrim = (filter_var($typetrim, FILTER_SANITIZE_STRING));
              }else{
$errors[] =
'Type missing or not alphabetic, -, period or space. Max 50.';
              }
```

The validations for other values passed by the form include trimming of whitespace, checking the proper format using regular expressions, and sanitizing using filter_var. In this example, the regular expression allows alphabetic characters (a-z), dashes (-), spaces (s), and periods (.). We have previously discussed regular expressions. Additional information can be found in Appendix B.

Most of the coding to create the PayPal cart site is similar to code we have used in other chapters. Thus, we have not provided a lot of explanation. Some of the administration screens provided are the same as included within the custom cart example. We will look at these screens in the next section. Now let's create our own custom cart.

Creating a Custom Cart

Some e-commerce websites use their own custom shopping cart, and by this we mean a shopping cart designed by the website developer. Custom shopping carts are complex and require several interactive pages to replace the online PayPal system. The process is best described by a flowchart such as the one shown in Figure 11-5.

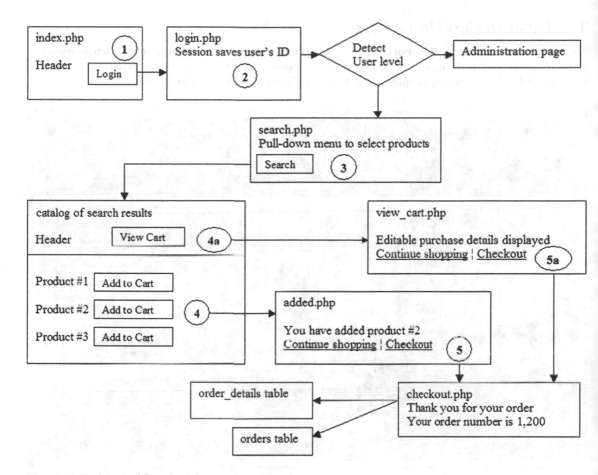

Figure 11-5. A typical flowchart for a custom shopping cart

The numbered circles indicate the steps taken by a user. After logging in (step 2), the user's ID is saved in a session that is accessible to all the subsequent pages. The user level is detected, and the user is redirected to a search page (step 3); our example has pull-down menus containing search criteria. The user selects the criteria and clicks the Search button. They are then redirected to a catalog of products that match the search criteria. If the user decides to buy a painting, they will click its Add to Cart button (step 4). This sends the product ID and the user ID to the cart; a message confirming the action is displayed (step 5). The display has a Continue shopping link and a link to the Checkout page. Clicking the Continue shopping link returns the user to the shopping page (step 4) where the user can add more products. If the user clicks the View cart button on the header menu, they will be shown a table displaying the products they have chosen and the cost. This table allows the user to change the quantities or remove an item from the cart. The user moves to the checkout to confirm the order, and then the order is processed. Let's look at how to create some of this functionality.

The Custom Cart Home Page

The custom cart home page does not include a search facility because the custom cart has a separate search page. We are requiring the user to log in to purchase any paintings. To encourage viewers to register, the home page displays tempting samples of the products. Figure 11-6 shows the home page.

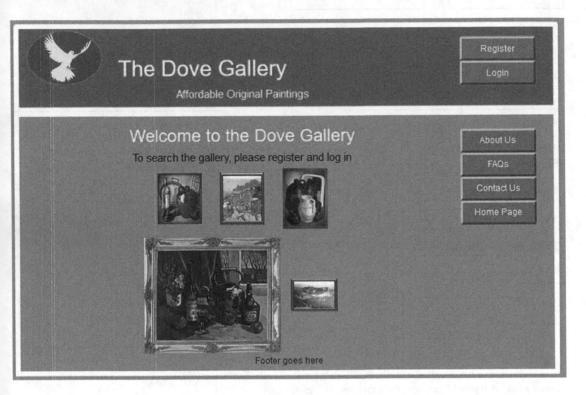

Figure 11-6. *The customcart home page*

The code for the home page and its CSS file are included in the downloadable files as *index.php* and *transparent.css*, respectively. Note the Register button and a Login button in the header. This provide a hint to the user that they must log in to purchase products. By displaying some of the products, users are encouraged to register.

Create the Custom Cart Database and Tables

The Custom Cart example uses its own database, tables, and code. To view the demonstration, follow these steps:

1. In the *htdocs* folder within XAMPP or in the *eds_www* folder in EasyPHP, create a new folder named *customcart*.

2. Download the customcart files for Chapter 11 from the book's page at Apress.com and unzip them in your new *customcart* folder.

3. Start Apache and MySQL in XAMPP or EasyPHP, and in the address field of a browser enter localhost/phpmyadmin/ to access phpMyAdmin.

4. Click the Databases tab and create a database named *customdb*. From the pull-down Collation list, choose utf8_general_ci and then click Create.

5. Click the Privileges tab and then scroll down and click Add new user.

6. Enter these details:

   - *Username*: turing

   - *Password*: En1gm3

   - *Host*: localhost

   - *Database name*: customdb

7. Click Go.

Under a new heading of View the Connection File, the code should be as follows:

```php
<?php
// Create a connection to the customdb database and to MySQL
// Set the encoding to utf-8
// Set the database access details as constants
DEFINE ('DB_USER', 'turing');
DEFINE ('DB_PASSWORD', 'En1gm3');
DEFINE ('DB_HOST', 'localhost');
DEFINE ('DB_NAME', 'customdb');
// Make the connection:
$dbcon = new mysqli(DB_HOST, DB_USER, DB_PASSWORD, DB_NAME);
// Set the encoding...optional but recommended
mysqli_set_charset($dbcon, 'utf8');
```

To test your connection file, enter this URL in the address field of a browser:

```
http://localhost/customcart/mysqli_connect.php
```

The page displayed should be completely empty.

Use phpMyAdmin to import the tables and populate them as follows:

1. In the left panel, click the box next to the database customdb.

2. Do not enter anything on the next screen, but click the Import tab.

3. Click the Browse button and navigate to the *customcart* folder.

4. Import the SQL dump files one by one by clicking them and then clicking the Open button; the field will fill with the URL of the dump file.

5. Ensure that the Character set in the pull-down menu is utf-8 and that the format is shown as SQL.

6. Click Go. Repeat steps 4 through 6 for each SQL dump file.

Exploring the Custom Shopping Cart

With Apache and MariaDB/MySQL running in XAMPP or EasyPHP, type **localhost/customcart/** in the address field of a browser and then follow these steps:

1. Log in as Rose Bush using the e-mail address rbush@myisp.co.uk and the password R@dbl00ms.

2. Select an item and price range and click the Submit button.

3. When the search results page appears, click one of the Add to Cart links.

4. Click the View cart menu button and then try changing the quantity from 1 to 2; then click the update cart button.

5. In the cart view, click the continue shopping link and add another painting to the cart and then click the View Cart button on the header menu. The total content of the cart will be displayed.

6. To remove a painting from the cart view, change its quantity to zero and click the update cart link.

For your information, the five customcart tables created by the SQL dump files and the file listings are shown next.

The minimal artists table has four columns, as shown in Table 11-5.

Table 11-5. *The artists Table*

Column name	Type	Length/ Value	Default	Attributes	NULL	Index	A_I
artist_id	INT	8	None	UNSIGNED	☐	PRIMARY	☑
first_name	VARCHAR	30	None		☐		☐
middle_name	VARCHAR	30	None		☐		☐
last_name	VARCHAR	30	None		☐		☐

The details of the paintings are stored in a table named *art* with seven columns, as shown in Table 11-6,

Table 11-6. *The art Table*

Column name	Type	Length/ Value	Default	Attributes	NULL	Index	A_I
art_id	INT	8	None	UNSIGNED	☐	PRIMARY	☑
thumb	VARCHAR	50	None		☐		☐
type	VARCHAR	30	None		☐		☐
medium	VARCHAR	50	None		☐		☐
artist	VARCHAR	50	None		☐		☐
mini_descr	VARCHAR	150	None		☐		☐
price	DECIMAL	6,2	None	UNSIGNED	☐	INDEX	☐

The column named *thumb* is for containing the URLs for thumbnail images of the paintings. The description column contains the name of the painting, its size, and some information about the picture such as whether an oil painting was painted on canvas or board. A real-world art table might also include a column for the URLs of enlarged versions of the paintings. Note that the downloadable table has no column for PayPal shopping cart button code.

The orders table is minimal having only four columns: the order ID, the user ID, the price, and the order date. This is shown in Table 11-7.

Table 11-7. *The orders Table*

Column name	Type	Length/ Value	Default	Attributes	NULL	Index	A_I
order_id	INT	8	None	UNSIGNED	☐	PRIMARY	☑
user_id	INT	8	None	UNSIGNED	☐	INDEX	☐
total_price	DECIMAL	7,2	None		☐		☐
order_date	DATETIME		None		☐	INDEX	☐
price	DECIMAL	6,2	None	UNSIGNED	☐	INDEX	☐

The orders table would need to be able to join to other tables.

A table named *order_contents* with five columns contains various IDs, the price, the quantity ordered, and the dispatch date, as shown in Table 11-8.

Table 11-8. *A Minimal Order Contents Table*

Column name	Type	Length/ Value	Default	Attributes	NULL	Index	A_I
content_id	INT	8	None	UNSIGNED	☐	PRIMARY	☑
order_id	INT	8	None	UNSIGNED	☐	INDEX	☐
art_id	INT	8	None	UNSIGNED	☐	INDEX	☐
price	DECIMAL	5,2	None	UNSIGNED	☐	INDEX	☐
quantity	INT	4	None	UNSIGNED	☐		☐
dispatch_date	DATETIME	60	None		☐		☐

This table joins to other tables. Normally there would be a column for quantity, and this is shown for completeness in Table 11-8, but if the paintings are originals (as in our example website), only one of each exists, in which case a quantity column would not be required. If the shop sold prints or ink cartridges, a quantity column would be essential. Columns for the dispatch address and special delivery instructions would also be included.

The simplistic order and order_contents tables are presented only to make the statement that similar tables would be part of an e-commerce website. In the real world, they would be joined to the other tables.

Finally, the users table for the custom cart website has 15 columns, as shown in Table 11-9.

Table 11-9. *The Types and Attributes for a Minimal Users Table*

Column name	Type	Length/ Value	Default	Attributes	NULL	Index	A_I
user_id	MEDIUMINT	8	None	UNSIGNED	☐	PRIMARY	☑
title	VARCHAR	12	None		☑		☐
first_name	VARCHAR	30	None		☐		☐
last_name	VARCHAR	40	None		☐		☐
email	VARCHAR	50	None		☐		☐
password	CHAR	60	None		☐		☐
registration_date	DATETIME		None		☐		☐
user_level	TINYINT	2	None	UNSIGNED	☐		☐
address1	VARCHAR	50	None		☐		☐
address2	VARCHAR	50	None		☐		☐
city	VARCHAR	50	None		☐		☐
state_country	VARCHAR	30	None		☐		☐
zcode_pcode	VARCHAR	10	None		☐		☐
phone	VARCHAR	15	None		☑		☐
secret	VARCHAR	30	None		☐		☐

A user_level column is included to enable the login page to differentiate between a registered user and an administrator. The users would have a user_level of 0, but the administrator has been given the number 1. We will soon see that the secret column will be used to help the user recover their password.

The downloadable file *users.sql* contains two registrations shown in Table 11-9. These user's details will be used when you explore the workings of the custom shopping cart later in the chapter.

■ **Note**   Here are the login details for the users:

Mr. Mike Rosoft, e-mail: miker@myisp.com, password: W111g@t3s, user_level: 51

Mrs. Rose Bush, e-mail: rbush@myisp.co.uk, password: R@db100ms, user_level: 0

To save space in the above note, we have not shown additional information that is contained in the table's *user.sql* file. We gave Mrs. Bush and Mr. Rosoft the same postal address because they are the same person. The other details are not accessed again in this example of a custom cart website; therefore, they are not important.

The Custom Cart Login Page

Figure 11-7 shows the *login.php* page.

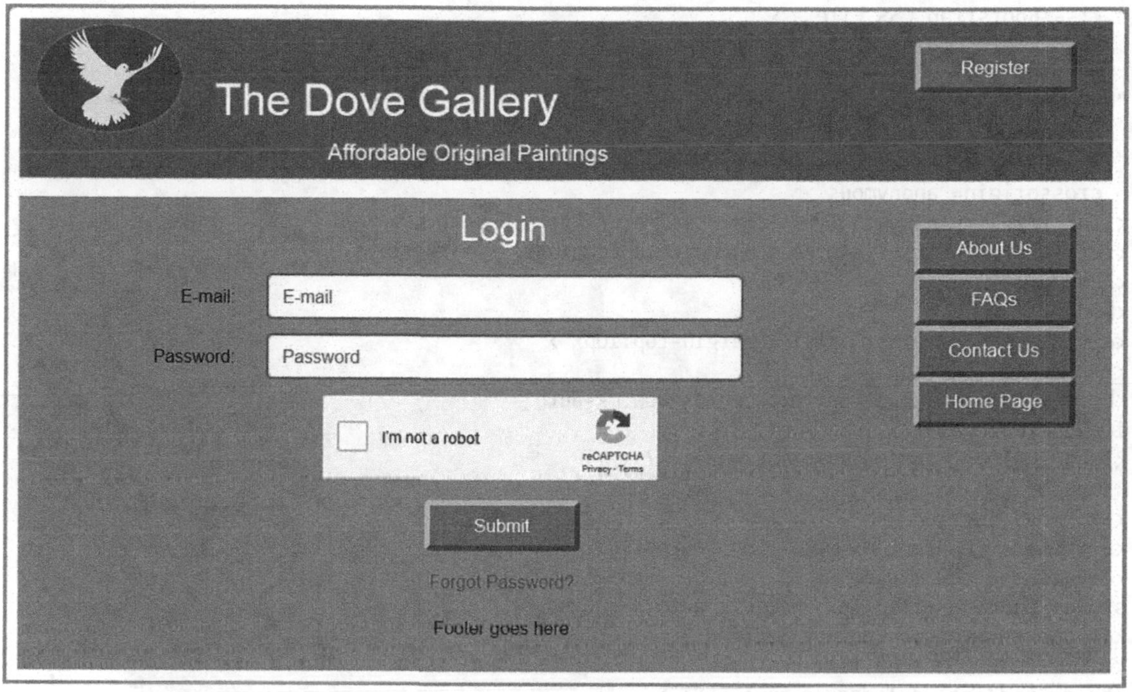

Figure 11-7. *The customcart and PayPal login page*

Note that the page has a Forgot Password? link. Let's look at the HTML code. The PHP code (*process_ login.php*) is the same as we have seen in previous chapters. You can view it from the files downloaded from the Apress site.

Listing 11-7 shows the code for the *login.php* page.

Listing 11-7. Creating the Login Page (login.php)

```php
<?php
$menu = 7;
if ($_SERVER['REQUEST_METHOD'] == 'POST') {
//require("cap.php");
}
?>
<!DOCTYPE html>
<html lang="en">
<head>
  <title>Template for an interactive web page</title>
  <meta charset="utf-8">
  <meta name="viewport"
content="width=device-width, initial-scale=1, shrink-to-fit=no">
```

```
  <!-- Bootstrap CSS File -->
  <link rel="stylesheet"
  href=
"https://stackpath.bootstrapcdn.com/bootstrap/4.1.0/css/bootstrap.min.css"
  integrity=
"sha384-9gVQ4dYFwwWSjIDZnLEWnxCjeSWFphJiwGPXr1jddIhOegiu1FwO5qRGvFXOdJZ4"
  crossorigin="anonymous">
<link rel="stylesheet" type="text/css" href="transparent.css">
<script src='https://www.google.com/recaptcha/api.js'></script>
</head>
<body>
<div class="container" style="margin-top:10px">
<!-- Header Section -->
<header class="jumbotron text-center row mx-auto"
id="includeheader">
<?php include('includes/header.php'); ?>
</header>
<!-- Body Section -->
<div class="content mx-auto" id="contents">
<div class="row mx-auto"
style="padding-left: 0px; height: auto;">
<!-- Center Column Content Section -->
<div class="col-sm-8 text-center"
style="padding:0px; margin-top: 5px;">
<!--Start of login content-->
<?php
// Display any error messages if present.
if ( isset( $errors ) && !empty( $errors ) )
{
        echo '<p id="err_msg">A problem occurred:<br>' ;
        foreach ( $errors as $msg ) { echo " - $msg<br>" ; }
                echo 'Please try again or ' .
'<a href="register-page.php">Register</a></p>' ;
}
?>
<!-- Display the login form fields -->
<form  action="process_login.php" method="post">
<div class="form-group row">
    <label class="col-sm-4 col-form-label"></label>
    <div class="col-sm-8">
<h2 style="margin-top: 10px;">Login</h2>
</div>
</div>
<div class="form-group row">
    <label for="email"
class="col-sm-4 col-form-label text-right">
E-mail:</label>
    <div class="col-sm-8">
      <input type="text" class="form-control" id="email"
name="email"
            placeholder="E-mail" maxlength="30" required
```

458

```
value=
            "<?php if (isset($_POST['email']))
            echo htmlspecialchars($_POST['email'], ENT_QUOTES); ?>" >
required >
    </div>
        </div>
<div class="form-group row">
    <label for="passcode"
class="col-sm-4 col-form-label text-right">
Password:</label>
<div class="col-sm-8">
        <input type="password" class="form-control"
id="passcode" name="passcode"
            placeholder="Password" minlength="8"
maxlength="12" required
value=
            "<?php if (isset($_POST['passcode']))
            echo htmlspecialchars($_POST['passcode'], ENT_QUOTES); ?>"
required >
</div>
</div>
<div class="form-group row">
<label class="col-sm-4 col-form-label"></label>
<div class="col-sm-8">
<div class="g-recaptcha" style="padding-left: 50px;"
data-sitekey="placeyourrecaptchasitekeyhere"></div>
</div>
</div>
<div class="form-group row">
<label class="col-sm-4 col-form-label"></label>
<div class="col-sm-8">
<input id="submit" class="btn btn-primary"
type="submit" name="submit" value="Submit">
</div>
</div>
<div class="form-group row">                                        <!--#1-->
        <label class="col-sm-4 col-form-label"></label>
        <div class="col-sm-8">
        <a href="forgot.php">Forgot Password?</a>
</div>
</div>
<div class="form-group row">
        <label class="col-sm-4 col-form-label"></label>
<div class="col-sm-8">
<footer class="jumbotron row" id="includefooter">
            <?php include('includes/footer.php'); ?>
</footer>
</div>
</div>
</form><!--End of the add a login content-->
</div>
```

```
<!-- Right-side Column Content Section -->
<aside class="col-sm-4" id="includemenu">
        <?php include('includes/menu.php'); ?>
        </aside>
</div>
</div>
</div>
</body>
</html>
```

Explanation of the Code

The login and logout files are available in the download files for this chapter. The code for the login page is the same as the book's previous login files except for the inclusion of the following statement:

```
<div class="form-group row">                                               <!--#1-->
        <label class="col-sm-4 col-form-label"></label>
        <div class="col-sm-8">
        <a href="forgot.php">Forgot Password?</a>
</div>
</div>
```

This is simply a link to the page named *forgot.php*. Listing 11-8 shows the code for *forgot.php*.

Retrieving a Forgotten Password

You may wonder why we left it so late before introducing a means of retrieving a forgotten password. Our reasoning was as follows:

- We decided that the more complex PHP code required would be best introduced in a later chapter when you have become more proficient in the use of PHP.

- Password retrieval was not necessary in the earlier tutorials because you were not interacting with real users who may have forgotten their passwords.

- We assumed that you would not attempt to migrate a database-driven website to an external host until you had at least reached Chapter 10.

- Password retrieval involves sending an e-mail to the user; this cannot be tested unless you either upload the website to a host or install an e-mail server on your computer.

If the user clicks the Forgot Password? link on the login page, they will see the screen shown in Figure 11-8.

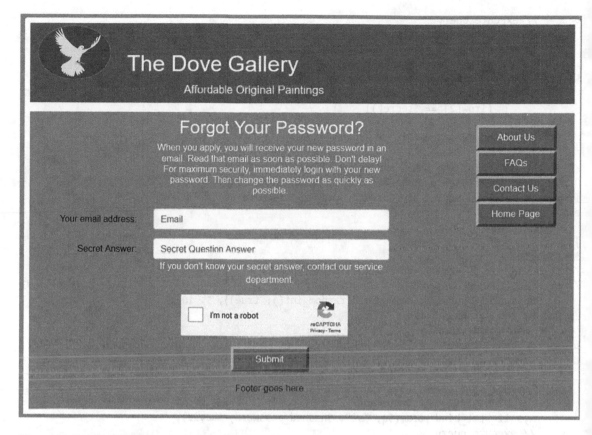

Figure 11-8. *The display for retrieving a forgotten password*

The HTML code for the *forgot.php* file is like other code shown earlier. Therefore, it is not included here. You can download it from the Apress website. However, let's look at the PHP code for the *process_forgot.php* page, shown in Listing 11-8.

Listing 11-8. Code for the Forgotten Password Page (process_forgot.php)

```php
<?php
try {
      require ('mysqli_connect.php');
      // Assign the value FALSE to the variable $buyid
      $buyid = FALSE;
// Validate the email address...
if (!empty($_POST['email'])) {
// Does that email address exist in the database?                              #1
      $query =
'SELECT user_id, user_level, secret FROM users WHERE email=?';
      $q = mysqli_stmt_init($dbcon);
      mysqli_stmt_prepare($q, $query);
      // bind $id to SQL Statement
      $email = htmlspecialchars($_POST['email'], ENT_QUOTES);
      mysqli_stmt_bind_param($q, "s", $email);
```

```php
    // execute query
    mysqli_stmt_execute($q);
    $result = mysqli_stmt_get_result($q);
    $row = mysqli_fetch_array($result, MYSQLI_NUM);
$secret = htmlspecialchars($_POST['secret'], ENT_QUOTES);
    if ((mysqli_num_rows($result) == 1) && ($row[1] == 0) &&                    //#2
        ($row[2] == $secret))
    {
        $buyid = $row[0];
    } else {
// If the buyid for the email address was not retrieved
    echo '<h6 style="padding-left:80px; padding-top: 20px;">
If your e-mail and secret are correct, you will receive an
e-mail</h6>';
    }
}
if ($buyid) {
// If buyid for the email address was retrieved,
// create a random password                                                    #3
    $password = substr ( md5(uniqid(random_int(), true)), 5, 10);
// Update the database table
    $hashed_password =
password_hash($password, PASSWORD_DEFAULT);
    $query = "UPDATE users SET password=? WHERE user_id=?";
    $q = mysqli_stmt_init($dbcon);
    mysqli_stmt_prepare($q, $query);
    // bind $id to SQL Statement
    mysqli_stmt_bind_param($q, "si", $hashed_password, $buyid);
    // execute query
    mysqli_stmt_execute($q);
    if (mysqli_stmt_affected_rows($q) == 1) {
// Send an email to the buyer                                                   #4
    $body = "Your password has been changed to '" . $password;
$body .= "'. Please login as soon as possible using the new password. ";
$body .= "Then change it immediately. otherwise, ";
$body .= "if a hacker has intercepted ";
$body .= "this email they will know your login details.";
    mail ($email, 'Your new password.', $body,
'From: admin@thedovegallery.co.uk');
// Echo a message and exit the code
echo '<h6 style="padding-left:80px; padding-top: 20px;">
Your password has been changed. ';
echo 'You will shortly receive the new temporary password ';
echo 'by email.</h6>';
    mysqli_close($dbcon);
    include ('includes/footer.php');
    exit(); // Stop the script.
} else { // If the query failed to run
    echo '<p class="error">Due to a system error, your password ';
  echo 'could not be changed. We apologize for any inconvenience. </p>';
}
}
```

```
mysqli_close($dbcon);
}
catch(Exception $e)
{
        print "The system is busy, please try later";
        $error_string = date('mdYhis') . " | Forgot Password | " .
$e-getMessage() . "\n";
        error_log($error_string,3,"/logs/exception_log.log");
        //error_log("Exception in Forgot Password Program.
// Check log for details", 1, "noone@nowhere.com",
        // "Subject: Forgot Password Exception" . "\r\n");
        // You can turn off display of errors in php.ini
// display_errors = Off
        //print "An Exception occurred. Message: " .
$e->getMessage();
}
catch(Error $e)
{
        print "The system is busy, please come back later";
        $error_string = date('mdYhis') . "| Forgot Password |".
$e-getMessage() . "\n";
        error_log($error_string,3,"/logs/error_log.log");
        //error_log("Error in Forgot Password Program.
// Check log for details", 1, "noone@nowhere.com",
        //      "Subject: Forgot Password Error" . "\r\n");
        // You can turn off display of errors in php.ini
// display_errors = Off
        //print "An Error occurred. Message:".
// $e->getMessage();
}
?>
```

Explanation of the Code

This section explains the code.

```
// Does that email address exist in the database?                          #1
     $query =
'SELECT user_id, user_level, secret FROM users WHERE email=?';
```

Verify that the e-mail is in the database. If it is not, an error message will display the following message: "If your e-mail and secret are correct, you will receive an e-mail."

This message does not tell the user that the e-mail does not exist because unauthorized users would then know that they need to keep attempting other e-mails until they discover a valid one.

```
if ((mysqli_num_rows($result) == 1) && ($row[1] == 0) &&        //#2
            ($row[2] == $secret))
      {
            $buyid = $row[0];
```

If the e-mail exists (a row was returned) and the user_level is 0 (not an administrator, to provide extra protection to the administration ID) and the secret message returned is correct, then set the $buyid to the user_id.

```
// create a random password                                                     #3
      $password = substr ( md5(uniqid(random_int(), true)), 5, 10);
// Update the database table
      $hashed_password =
password_hash($password, PASSWORD_DEFAULT);
      $query = "UPDATE users SET password=? WHERE user_id=?";
```

If the information is verified, create a random password, hash it, and save it to the record in the table.

```
// Send an email to the buyer                                                    #4
      $body = "Your password has been changed to '" . $password;
$body .= "'. Please login as soon as possible using the new password. ";
$body .= "Then change it immediately. otherwise, ";
$body .= "if a hacker has intercepted ";
$body .= "this email they will know your login details.";
      mail ($email, 'Your new password.', $body,
'From: admin@thedovegallery.co.uk');
```

Create an e-mail with the information, including the password, to log in. Remember, an e-mail server must exist on the system for e-mails to be sent.

■ **Note**   The code for logging out would be the same as in previous chapters.

The Custom Cart Search Page

The search page is similar to the home PayPal cart home page; it was renamed as *search.php*. Figure 11-9 show the search page.

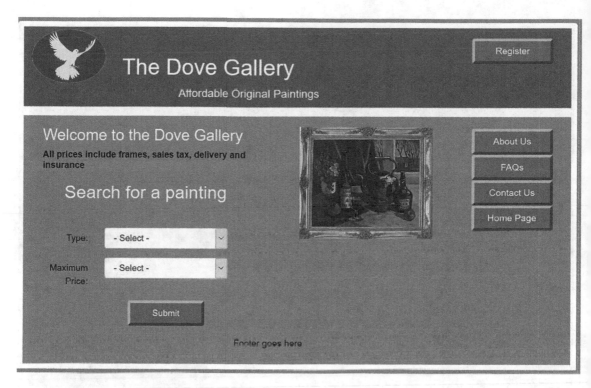

Figure 11-9. The customcart search page (users_search_page)

When the administrator logs in, they will be directed to an admin page, which is described next.

Adding Paintings to a Table for a Custom Shopping Cart

To add paintings to a database table intended for a custom shopping cart, the administration interface is almost the same as the one used for a PayPal cart, but the text area for the PayPal code is omitted. Figure 11-10 shows the new interface.

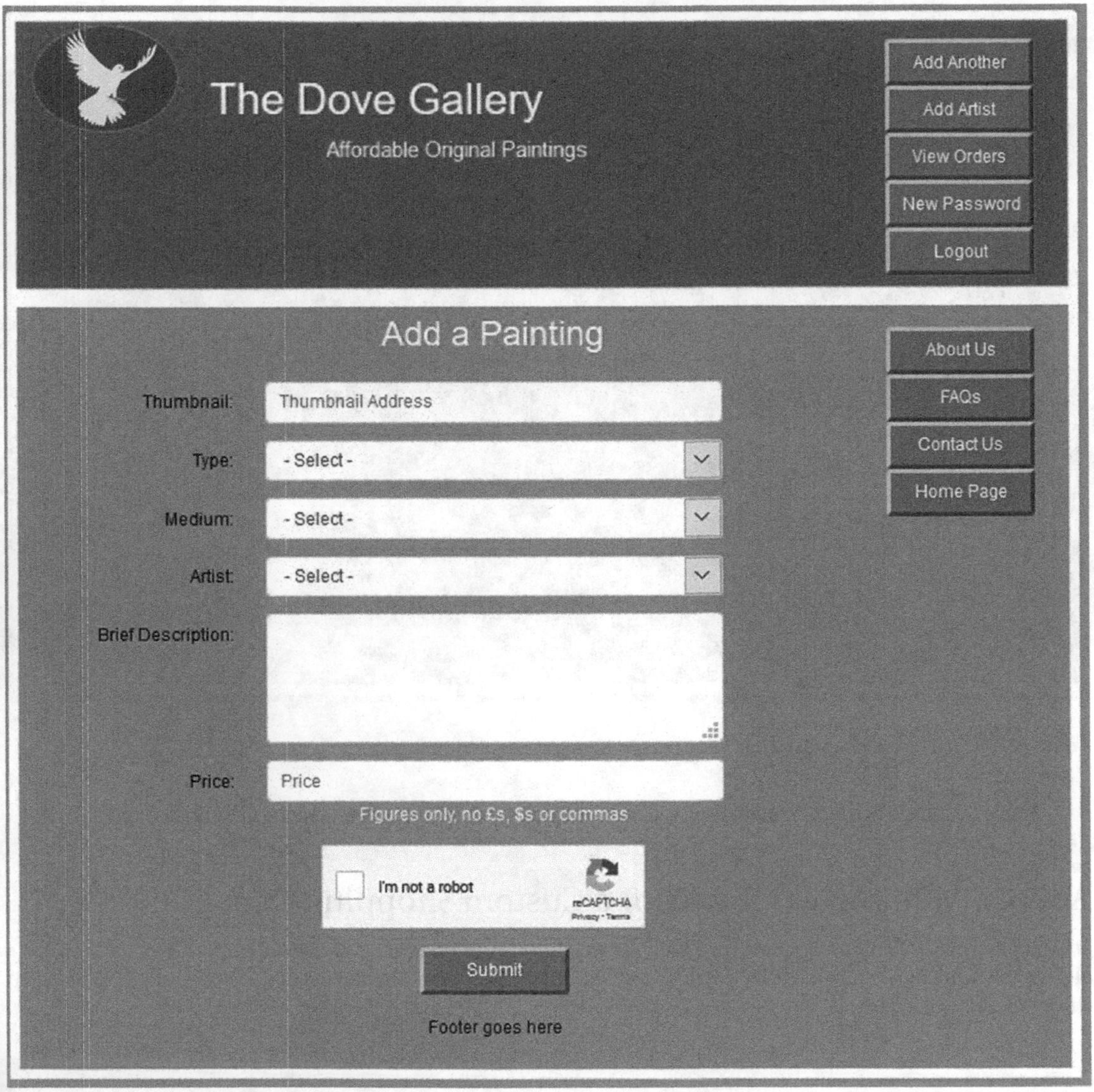

Figure 11-10. *The custom cart administration page (admin_page.php)*

Figure 11-11 shows the results of the search and the Add to Cart links.

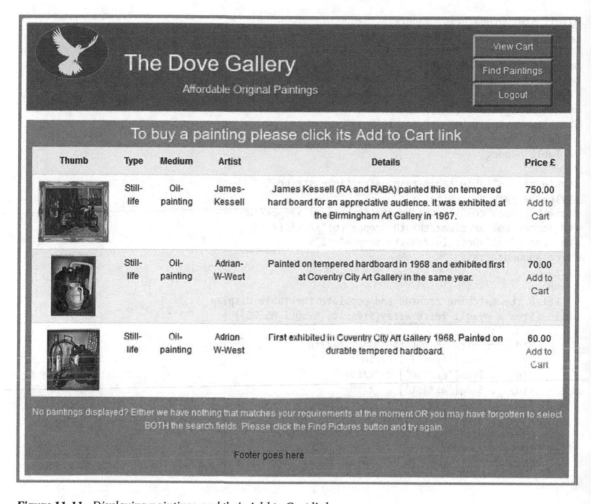

Figure 11-11. *Displaying paintings and their Add to Cart links*

Since the HTML code for the cart is similar to the cart shown in the PayPal cart, it is not shown here. However, you can view the *found_pics_cart.php* file from your downloaded files for details. The PHP code is shown in Listing 11-11.

Listing 11-11. Code for process_found_pics.php

```php
<?php
//Connect to the database
try {
require ( 'mysqli_connect.php' ) ;
// Select the first three items items from the art table
$type=$_SESSION['type'];
$price=$_SESSION['price'];
$query =
"SELECT art_id, thumb, type, price, medium, artist, mini_descr, ppcode";
$query .=
"FROM art WHERE type= ? AND price <= ? ORDER BY price DESC LIMIT 3";
$q = mysqli_stmt_init($dbcon);
```

```php
mysqli_stmt_prepare($q, $query);
// bind $id to SQL Statement
$type = htmlspecialchars($type, ENT_QUOTES);
$price = htmlspecialchars($_POST['price'], ENT_QUOTES);
mysqli_stmt_bind_param($q, "si", $type, $price);
// execute query
mysqli_stmt_execute($q);
$result = mysqli_stmt_get_result($q);
if (mysqli_num_rows($result) > 0) {
// Table header
?>
<table class="table table-responsive table-striped"
style="background: white;">
<tr><th scope="col">Thumb</th><th scope="col">Type</th>
<th scope="col">Medium</th><th scope="col">Artist</th>
<th scope="col">Details</th><th scope="col">
Price &pound;</th>
</tr>
<?php
// Fetch the matching records and populate the table display          #1
while ($row = mysqli_fetch_array($result, MYSQLI_ASSOC)) {
        echo '<tr>
        <td><img src='.$row['thumb'] . '></td>
        <td>' . $row['type'] . '</td>
        <td>' . $row['medium'] . '</td>
        <td>' . $row['artist'] . '</td>
        <td>' . $row['mini_descr'] . '</td>
        <td>' . $row['price'] .
        '<br><a href="added.php?id=' . $row['art_id'] .
'">Add to Cart</a></td>
        </tr>';
        }
?>
</table>
<?php
// Close the database connection.
  mysqli_close( $dbcon ) ;
}
// Or notify the user that no matching paintings were found
else {
echo '<p>There are currently no items matching your search '
echo 'criteria.</p>' ; }
}
catch(Exception $e)
{
        print "The system is busy, please try later";
        $error_string = date('mdYhis') . " | Found Pics | " .
$e->getMessage() . "\n";
        error_log($error_string,3,"/logs/exception_log.log");
        //error_log("Exception in Found Pics Program.
```

```
//Check log for details", 1, "noone@nowhere.com",
//      "Subject: Found Pics Exception" . "\r\n");
        // You can turn off display of errors in php.ini
//display_errors = Off
        //print "An Exception occurred. Message:".
//$e->getMessage();
}catch(Error $e)
{
        print "The system is busy, please come back later";
$error_string = date('mdYhis') . " | Found Pics | " .
$e->getMessage() . "\n";
        error_log($error_string,3,"/logs/error_log.log");
        //error_log("Error in Found Pics Program.
//Check log for details", 1, "noone@nowhere.com",
//      "Subject: Found Pics Error" . "\r\n");
        // You can turn off display of errors in php.ini
//display_errors = Off
        //print "An Error occurred. Message:".
//$e->getMessage();
}
?>
```

Explanation of the Code

This sections explains the code.

```
// Fetch the matching records and populate the table display          #1
while ($row = mysqli_fetch_array($result, MYSQLI_ASSOC)) {
        echo '<tr>
        <td><img src='.$row['thumb'] . '></td>
        <td>' . $row['type'] . '</td>
        <td>' . $row['medium'] . '</td>
        <td>' . $row['artist'] . '</td>
        <td>' . $row['mini_descr'] . '</td>
        <td>' . $row['price'] .
        '<br><a href="added.php?id=' . $row['art_id'] .
'">Add to Cart</a></td>
        </tr>';
```

The only difference between the custom cart code and the PayPal code is the link provided to the cart. In the custom cart code, the link is attached to the *added.php* program. In the PayPal program, it goes to the PayPal site. This custom cart link also passes the *art_id to added.php*.

When a painting has been added to the cart, the user is notified, as shown in Figure 11-12.

Figure 11-12. *Confirmation that a painting has been added to the shopping cart*

Note the two links below the confirmation message; the user can continue shopping to add more items to the cart. They can choose to view the cart contents by clicking View Cart link on the header menu. They could also use the second link to go straight to the checkout. Listing 11-12 gives the code for the confirmation page.

Listing 11-12. Creating the Confirmation Page (added.php)

```php
<?php
session_start();
if (!isset($_SESSION['user_id'])){
header('location:login.php');
exit();
}
$menu = 2;
?>
<!DOCTYPE html>
<html lang="en">
<head>
<title>Added to Cart</title>
<meta charset="utf-8">
<meta name="viewport"
content="width=device-width, initial-scale=1, shrink-to-fit=no">
<!-- Bootstrap CSS File -->
<link rel="stylesheet"
      href=
"https://stackpath.bootstrapcdn.com/bootstrap/4.1.0/css/bootstrap.min.css"
      integrity=
"sha384-9gVQ4dYFwwWSjIDZnLEWnxCjeSWFphJiwGPXr1jddIhOegiu1FwO5qRGvFXOdJZ4"
      crossorigin="anonymous">
<link rel="stylesheet" type="text/css" href="transparent.css">
</head>
<body>
<div class="container" style="margin-top:10px">
<!-- Header Section -->
<header class="jumbotron text-center row mx-auto"
id="includeheader">
<?php include('includes/header.php'); ?>
</header>
```

```
<!-- Body Section -->
<div class="content mx-auto" id="contents">
<div class="row mx-auto"
style="padding-left: 0px;margin-top: -17px; width: 90%; height: auto;">
<!-- Center Column Content Section -->
<div class="col-sm-12 text-center"
style="padding:0px; margin-top: 5px;">
<div id="content"><!--Start of added page-->
<p>
<?php
if ( isset( $_GET['id'] ) ) { $id = $_GET['id'] ; }
// Connect to the database
try {
require ( 'mysqli_connect.php' ) ;
// Get selected painting data from the  'art' table
            $query = "SELECT * FROM art ";
            $query .= "WHERE art_id = ? ";
            $q = mysqli_stmt_init($dbcon);
            mysqli_stmt_prepare($q, $query);
            // bind $id to SQL Statement
            mysqli_stmt_bind_param($q, "i", $id);
            // execute query
            mysqli_stmt_execute($q);
            $result = mysqli_stmt_get_result($q);
            $row = mysqli_fetch_array($result, MYSQLI_ASSOC);
            if (mysqli_num_rows($result) == 1) {
 // If the cart already contains one of those products              #1
            if ( isset( $_SESSION['cart'][$id] ) )
            {
    // Add another one of those paintings
    $_SESSION['cart'][$id]['quantity']++;
echo '<h3>Another one of those paintings has been added';
echo 'to your cart</h3>';
            }
            else
            {
   // Add a different painting                                      #2
            $_SESSION['cart'][$id]=
array ( 'quantity' => 1, 'price' => $row['price'] ) ;
     echo '<h3>A painting has been added to your cart</h3>';
            }
}
}
catch(Exception $e)
{
     print "The system is busy, please try later";
     $error_string = date('mdYhis') . " | Added  | " .
$e->getMessage() . "\n";
     error_log($error_string,3,"/logs/exception_log.log");
     //error_log("Exception in Added Program.
```

```php
// Check log for details", 1, "noone@nowhere.com",
      //     "Subject: Added Exception" . "\r\n");
      // You can turn off display of errors in php.ini
// display_errors = Off
      //print "An Exception occurred. Message: " .
//$e->getMessage();
}catch(Error $e)
{
      print "The system is busy, please come back later";
      $error_string = date('mdYhis') . " | Added | " .
$e->getMessage() . "\n";
      error_log($error_string,3,"/logs/error_log.log");
      //error_log("Error in Added Program.
//Check log for details", 1, "noone@nowhere.com",
      //     "Subject: Added Error" . "\r\n");
      // You can turn off display of errors in php.ini
//display_errors = Off
      //print "An Error occurred. Message: " . $e->getMessage();
}
// Close the database connection
mysqli_close($dbcon);
// Insert three links
echo '<p><a href="users_search_page.php">
Continue Shopping</a> |
<a href="checkout.php">Checkout</a></p>' ;
?>
<footer>
<?php include("includes/footer.php"); ?>
</footer>
</div>
</div><!--End of page content-->
</div>
</div>
</div>
</body>
</html>
```

Explanation of the Code

This section explains the code.

```php
// If the cart already contains one of those products          #1
            if ( isset( $_SESSION['cart'][$id] ) )
            {
      // Add another one of those paintings
      $_SESSION['cart'][$id]['quantity']++;
echo '<h3>Another one of those paintings has been added';
echo 'to your cart</h3>';
```

The details of the selected paintings are checked to determine which of two messages to display, either "A painting has been added" or "Another of those paintings has been added." The session variable cart contains a three-dimensional array with the indexes of id, quantity, and price. In layman's terms, the cart includes each order defined by the ID (what was purchased), quantity (how many), and the price (for each). The quantity value is increased (*{'quantity'}++*) by one if the user has already chosen to buy the painting (which is determined by the if statement).

```
// Add a different painting                                            #2
            $_SESSION['cart'][$id]=
array ( 'quantity' => 1, 'price' => $row['price'] ) ;
      echo '<h3>A painting has been added to your cart</h3>' ;
```

If the painting has not been selected before, a new array is created with the quantity set to 1 and the price sent from the value contained in the art table.

If the user chooses to view the cart, they will see the contents displayed, as shown in Figure 11-13.

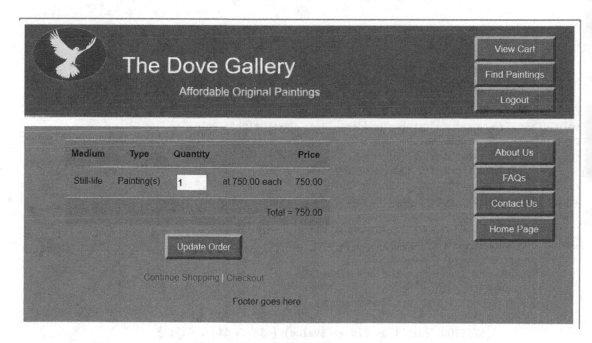

Figure 11-13. *The cart contains one still-life painting costing £750*

The quantity in the third column of the displayed table (seen in white) can be edited by the user. To remove a painting from the cart, the user will change the current figure to zero. After editing the quantity, the user must click the Update My Cart button to reveal the new subtotal (last column in the top row) and the revised total price.

User can click the Continue shopping link to select another painting. Let's assume that they select another oil painting costing £750; when viewing the cart, they will see the added painting and the new total cost, as shown in Figure 11-13.

The HTML code for *cart.php* can downloaded from the Apress website. The code is similar to the HTML code seen previously. Let's look at the PHP code that creates the interactive cart (Listing 11-13).

Listing 11-13. Code for the View Cart Page (process_cart.php)

```php
<?php
// If the user changes the quantity then Update the cart
    if(isset($_POST['qty'])) {
        foreach ( $_POST['qty'] as $art_id => $item_qty )          //1
        {
        // Ensure that the id and the quantity are integers
        // PHP would convert for us. But other languages would not
        $id = (int) $art_id;
        $qty = (int) $item_qty;
        // If the quantity is set to zero clear the session or
        // else store the changed quantity
        if ( $qty == 0 ) { unset ($_SESSION['cart'][$id]); }
        elseif ( $qty > 0 ) {
                $_SESSION['cart'][$id]['quantity'] = $qty; }
        }
        }
        // Set an initial variable for the total cost
        $total = 0;
        // Display the cart content
        if (!empty($_SESSION['cart']))
        {
?>
<div class="row mx-auto" style="padding-left: 0px; height: auto;">
<!-- Center Column Content Section -->
<div class="col-sm-4 text-center mx-auto"
        style="padding-left: 40px;"></div>
<div class="col-sm-10 text-center mx-auto"
        style="color: black; padding:20px; margin-top: 5px;">
<?php
        try {
        // Connect to the database.
        require ('mysqli_connect.php');
        // Get the items from the art table and
        //insert them into the cart
        $q = "SELECT * FROM art WHERE art_id IN (";
        foreach (                                                  //2
                $_SESSION['cart'] as $id => $value) { $q .= $id . ','; }
                $q = substr( $q, 0, -1 ) . ') ORDER BY art_id ASC';
                $result = mysqli_query ($dbcon, $q);
                // Create a form and a table
                echo '<form action="cart.php" method="post">';
                echo '<table class="table table-responsive table-striped"
                style=" color:black;">';
                echo '<tr><th scope="col">Medium</th><th scope="col">Type</th>';
                echo '<th scope="col">Quantity</th><th scope="col"></th>';
                echo '<th scope="col">Price</th></tr>';
                while ($row = mysqli_fetch_array ($result, MYSQLI_ASSOC))
                {
```

```
                    // Calculate the subtotals and the grand total                    #3
                    $subtotal = $_SESSION['cart'][$row['art_id']]['quantity'] *
                    $_SESSION['cart'][$row['art_id']]['price'];
                    $total += $subtotal;
                    // Display the table                                              #4
                    echo "<tr> <td>{$row['type']}</td><td>Painting(s)</td>
                    <td><input type=\"text\" size=\"3\"
              name=\"qty[{$row['art_id']}]\"
              value=\"{$_SESSION['cart'][$row['art_id']]['quantity']}\"></td>
                    <td>at {$row['price']} each </td>
                    <td style=\"text-align:right\">".
                    number_format ($subtotal, 2)."</td></tr>";
              }
        // Close the database connection
        mysqli_close($dbcon);
        // Display the total
        echo ' <tr><td colspan="5"
        style="text-align:right">Total = '.
        number_format($total,2).'</td></tr></table>';
        echo '<input id="submit" class="btn btn-primary"
        type="submit" name="submit" value="Update Order"></form>';
}
catch(Exception $e)
{
        print "The system is busy, please try later";
        $error_string = date('mdYhis') . " | Cart | " .
              $e-getMessage() . "\n";
        error_log($error_string,3,"/logs/exception_log.log");
        //error_log("Exception in Cart Program.
        //Check log for details", 1, "noone@nowhere.com",
        //    "Subject: Cart Exception" . "\r\n");
        // You can turn off display of errors in php.ini
        // display_errors = Off
        //print "An Exception occurred. Message: " .
        //$e->getMessage();
}
catch(Error $e)
{
        print "The system is busy, please come back later";
        $error_string = date('mdYhis') . " | Cart | " .
              $e-getMessage() . "\n";
        error_log($error_string,3,"/logs/error_log.log");
        //error_log("Error in Cart Program.
        //Check log for details", 1, "noone@nowhere.com",
        //    "Subject: Cart Error" . "\r\n");
        // You can turn off display of errors in php.ini
        //display_errors = Off
        //print "An Error occurred. Message:" .
        //$e->getMessage();
}
```

```
echo "</div>";
echo "</div>";
}
else
// Or display a message
{ echo
'<p style="padding: 60px;">Your cart is currently empty.</p>' ;
}
// Create some links
echo
'<p><a href="users_search_page.php">Continue Shopping</a>';
echo ' | <a href="checkout.php">Checkout</a>' ;
?>
```

Explanation of the Code

The comments within the listing explain the steps used to populate a cart. However, some items need a little more explanation as follows:

```
    foreach ( $_POST['qty'] as $art_id => $item_qty )                    //#1
```
The *view cart* process relies on sessions and some complex arrays. The function *foreach* is a special loop that works with arrays. In line **#1** the item $_POST['qty'] is an array containing the quantity of a product. The symbol => does not mean equal to or greater than, it is an array operator that associates the item *qty* with the $*art_id* of the product.
```
$q = "SELECT * FROM art WHERE art_id IN (";
foreach (                                                               //#2
$_SESSION['cart'] as $id => $value) { $q .= $id . ','; }
$q = substr( $q, 0, -1 ) . ') ORDER BY art_id ASC';
```

Values are added to a session array named *cart* shown here. The values include the $id, which is the $art_id and the price.

```
// Calculate the subtotals and the grand total                          #3
        $subtotal = $_SESSION['cart'][$row['art_id']]['quantity'] *
            $_SESSION['cart'][$row['art_id']]['price'];
        $total += $subtotal;    }
```

The quantity and price in each row of the cart are used to calculate the subtotal. Each row subtotal is then added to the total to produce the grand total due.

```
// Display the table                                                    #4
echo "<tr> <td>{$row['type']}</td><td>Painting(s)</td>
<td><input type=\"text\" size=\"3\"
name=\"qty[{$row['art_id']}]\" value=\"{$_SESSION['cart'][$row['art_id']]['quantity']}\"></td>
<td>at {$row['price']} each </td>
<td style=\"text-align:right\">".
number_format ($subtotal, 2)."</td></tr>";
```

The session arrays are used to insert values into the cells of the view cart table. Note that in the code that formats the table, the double quotes are escaped by using backslashes.

■ **Note** In a real-world website, to achieve the necessary standard of security, two techniques would be used: prepared statements and transactions. Transactions are beyond the scope of this book, but you can learn about them using the resources provided in Appendix B.

We will briefly mention the checkout page.

The Checkout Page

When the checkout link is clicked, four things happen.

- A "thank you" page appears, which also states the order number.
- The order details are posted to the order contents table.
- The order is entered in the order table.
- The shopping cart is emptied ready for the next purchases.

Figure 11-14 shows the "thank you" page.

Figure 11-14. The checkout "thank you" page

The checkout page generates the order number from the current date and time and the user's ID number. This information is sufficient for a help desk to look up the proper order if there are problems. The code for the checkout page is included in the downloadable files.

The Additional Administrative Tasks

The process of adding artists and paintings was described earlier in the chapter, but an administrator must perform several other tasks. Editing and deleting artists and paintings can be achieved by the techniques described in Chapter 3. Other tasks would usually be undertaken by an administration team; these duties would be order processing, shipping, stock control, financial control, and customer support. All these activities would be recorded in the appropriate database tables.

Summary

In this chapter, you learned about some of the many elements required for an e-commerce website. However, the need for brevity meant that we had to limit the number of elements. Because a practical e-commerce website needs an enormous number of files, the chapter's space was used to describe the main displays as seen by a user. The chapter was not a tutorial but a brief description of an e-commerce website followed by a demonstration of PayPal and a custom shopping cart.

The download code includes secured methods for accepting information from the user. The sites have also been designed for usage in any size device including smartphones.

We hope that you were able to appreciate the fact that e-commerce websites are complex and that the need for tight security is essential. We also hope that the chapter has inspired you to explore some of the e-commerce resources given in Appendix B.

CHAPTER 12

■ ■ ■

Take a Brief Look at Oracle MySQL 8

By now you may be wondering why we have not introduced Oracle's MySQL 8 database server. We first wanted to teach you techniques that work in any of the current levels of MariaDB and MySQL. For the most part, we have accomplished that task. Second, if you are happy with MariaDB or MySQL 5.7, you don't have to install MySQL 8. You could skip this chapter and everything we have shown you will work.

After completing this chapter, you will be able to

- Understand the features and tools available with Oracle's MySQL 8
- Install MySQL 8
- Use tools contained within MySQL Workbench
- Migrate a database to MySQL 8
- Create and modify databases in MySQL 8
- Create user IDs in MySQL 8

There are many strong features of MySQL 8, so let's look at the advantages of upgrading. You will see that version 8 has some great new features not available in the previous versions.

Advantages of Upgrading

The following improvements are in the free Community edition and the Enterprise edition:

- *MySQL document store*: You can use SQL-based and non-SQL-based databases older than SQL 8.
- *SQL user roles*: You can create administrative user IDs based on the traditional IT job roles.
- *An improved SQL Workbench*: There is no current version of phpMyAdmin that is compatible with MySQL 8. We will cover the features of MySQL Workbench in this chapter.
- *Improved security features*: Both editions use an improved openSSL protocol, meaning the open source Secure Sockets Layer (SSL) and Transport Layer Security (TLS) protocols, with default authentication. We will cover the default authentication in our examples in this chapter.

- *Password history*: You can maintain information about password history. Now it's possible to enable restrictions on the reuse of previous passwords.

- *Password hashing*: A new caching_sha2_password authentication is available. It implements SHA-256 password hashing and uses caching to address any latency issues. You will discover that PHP 7 does not currently support this new level of hashing.

- *Improved reliability*: Data Definition Language (DDL) statements have become crash safe. Metadata is now stored in a transactional data dictionary.

- *Improved InnoDB database engine*: The database engine has been improved.

- *Improved performance*: Performance is up to two times faster than MySQL 5.7.

- *New SQL commands*: There are NOWAIT and SKIP LOCKED alternatives when locking records and tables. SQL supports descending indexes with DESC in an index definition. It is no longer ignored. A grouping function can be used in GROUP BY queries that include a WITH ROLLUP modifier. ALTER TABLE supports better column renaming (RENAME COLUMN old_name TO new_name).

- *Updated SQL commands*: SELECT and UNION use the same syntax. NATURAL JOIN allows the use of the optional INNER keyword (NATURAL INNER JOIN). Right deep joins no longer require parentheses (JOIN ... JOIN ... ON ... ON). You can use parentheses around queries (SELECT ... UNION SELECT ...). Left-hand nesting of unions is now permitted in top-level statements. These changes follow the SQL standards.

- *Larger character set support by default*: Both editions include a lot more county character sets, such as Russia's. The default character set is utf8mb4 (`https://dev.mysql.com/doc/relnotes/mysql/8.0/en/news-8-0-0.html#mysqld-8-0-0-charset`).

- *GIS geography support*: Both editions include the Spatial Reference System (SRS).

- *New error logging*: Both editions use the MySQL component architecture.

- *JSON improvements*: There are new commands, new functions, improved sorting, and partial updates. You can use SQL commands to access JSON data. The data is returned as if it were a relational table.

The following improvements are available in the Enterprise edition only. It is not free, but there is a 30-day timeout version you can download for testing.

- *Backup and recovery*: Full, incremental, and partial backups. This includes point-in-time recovery. Backup compression is available.

- *High availability*: For integrated, native, and HA with the InnoDB cluster.

- *Encryption*: Key generation, digital signatures, and other features.

- *Authentication*: With other security systems including Microsoft Active Directory and PAM.

- *Firewall*: Protection against database attacks, including SQL injection.

- *Auditing*: Policy-based auditing.

- *Monitoring*: For managing the database infrastructure.

- *Cloud service*: Powered by Oracle Cloud. It supports SaaS, PaaS, and DBaaS applications.

For more details, visit https://dev.mysql.com/doc/relnotes/mysql/8.0/en/news-8-0-11.html.
As of the publication of this book, MySQL 8 is not integrated into XAMPP or easyPHP. The creators of these tools have chosen to support some of the original developers of MySQL and MariaDB. However, you will now discover that you can run two versions of MySQL (5.7 and 8.11) on your platform. Let's start by installing the Community Server version.

Installing MySQL 8 Community Server

Complete the following steps to install Oracle's MySQL 8 Community Server:

1. Go to https://dev.mysql.com/downloads/mysql/.

2. Scroll down to the Generally Available (GA) Releases area (see Figure 12-1).

Figure 12-1. *MySQL installer*

MySQL has a version for many of today's operating systems. If you are not using Windows, you can use the drop-down box shown at the top of Figure 12-1 to select the correct version. This demonstration will install the Windows version, but the procedures are similar for others.

3. Click the Go to Download Page button. The version we are selecting includes all the available tools for Windows.

4. Scroll down to the Generally Available (GA) Releases area (see Figure 12-2).

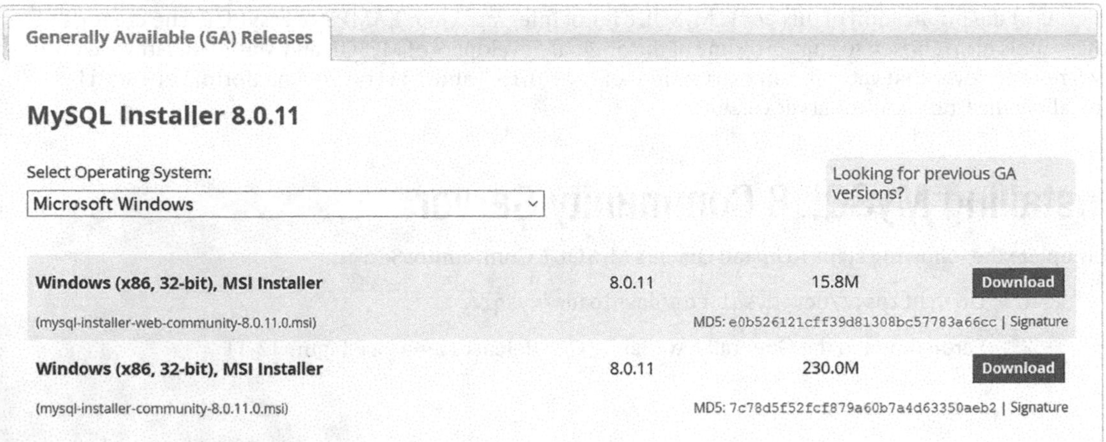

Generally Available (GA) Releases

MySQL Installer 8.0.11

Select Operating System:

Looking for previous GA versions?

Microsoft Windows

Windows (x86, 32-bit), MSI Installer	8.0.11	15.8M	Download
(mysql-installer-web-community-8.0.11.0.msi)		MD5: e0b526121cff39d81308bc57783a66cc | Signature	
Windows (x86, 32-bit), MSI Installer	8.0.11	230.0M	Download
(mysql-installer-community-8.0.11.0.msi)		MD5: 7c78d5f52fcf879a60b7a4d63350aeb2 | Signature	

Figure 12-2. *Selecting an installer*

The first selection (the web installer) keeps most of the software on the Internet until you select which items you want to install. It then downloads each as they are being installed. The second selection downloads all items at once. If you are connected to the Internet throughout the installation, use the first selection.

5. Click the install button (Download) next to the item you want to install.

6. The next screen suggests you sign in or create a free user ID for Oracle's latest updates and services. You can skip this by scrolling down to the bottom of the page and clicking the "No thanks, just start my download" link (see Figure 12-3).

Begin Your Download

mysql-installer-web-community-8.0.11.0.msi

Figure 12-3. *Starting the installer*

    7.   Click Save File.

The installer will be downloaded. Find its location and click it to begin the installation. See Figure 12-4.

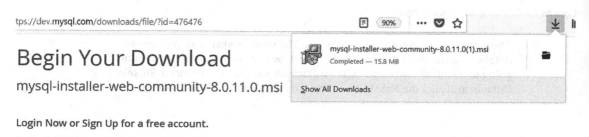

Figure 12-4. *Locating and starting the installer*

8. You may get a warning message that you have downloaded an executable file; if so, click OK. Windows will also ask if you want to allow the app to make changes to your system. Click Yes. The installer's license agreement will display. Check the "I accept" box and click Next. The screen shown in Figure 12-5 will appear.

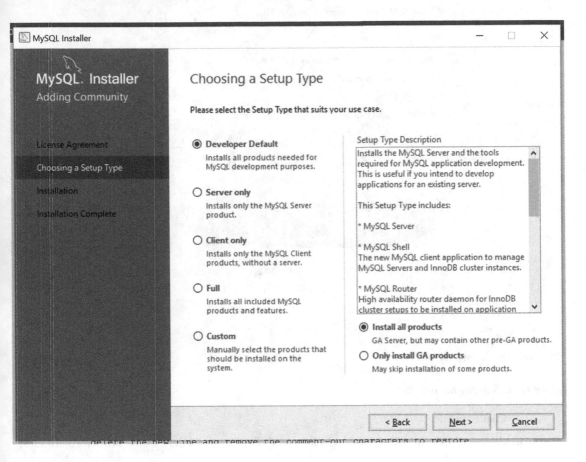

Figure 12-5. *Selecting a setup type*

9. There are five setup types you can select. The descriptions given are pretty detailed, so we won't describe them here. However, in this demo, we are not going to install all the products. We will install just the ones we need. So, select Custom and click the Next button. The screen in Figure 12-6 will appear.

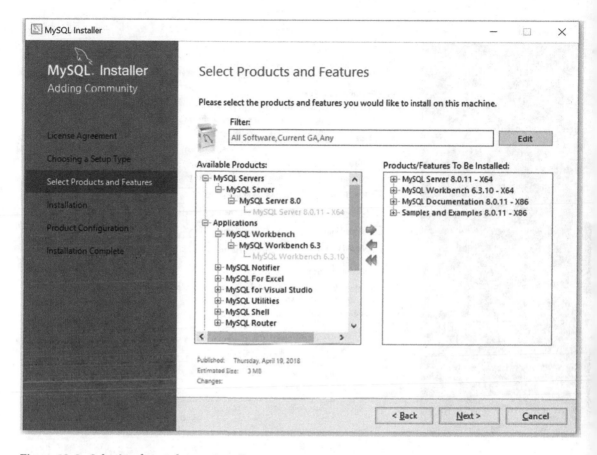

Figure 12-6. *Selecting the products to install*

10. For this demonstration, we want to install MySQL Server, MySQL Workbench, the documentation, and the examples. You will need to click the + sign next to each area (in some cases, several + signs) to find the product to install. Once you find the product, select it and click the green right arrow. The product should move to the right side of the screen. Once you see all the products required (see Figure 12-6) on the right side, click Next.

11. The products selected will be listed on the next screen. Verify that they are correct and then click the Execute button.

12. When all the products are installed, the button will change to a Next button. Click it.

13. The next screen will indicate that we need to do some product configurations for the server and the examples. Click Next.

14. The next screen will provide you with an opportunity to create databases that replicate. This is for large configurations where data can be spread out in many locations. We are testing only a small system, so we want the default (Standalone) selection. Click Next. The screen shown in Figure 12-7 will appear.

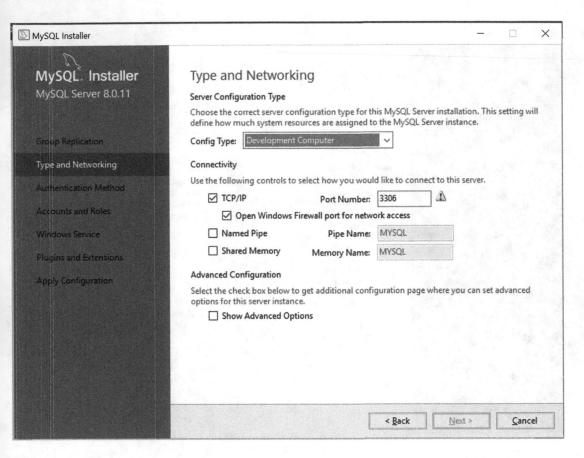

Figure 12-7. *Changing the port number*

15. The Config Type option should be set to Development Computer for our testing and development needs. However, it is important that the port number be changed from the default (3306) to another port (try 3307; the warning icon will tell you if there is a conflict). We can have both versions of MySQL running, if they use different ports. We currently have a conflict because MySQL 5.7 is using port 3306. Once you change the port, you can click Next. The screen in Figure 12-8 will appear.

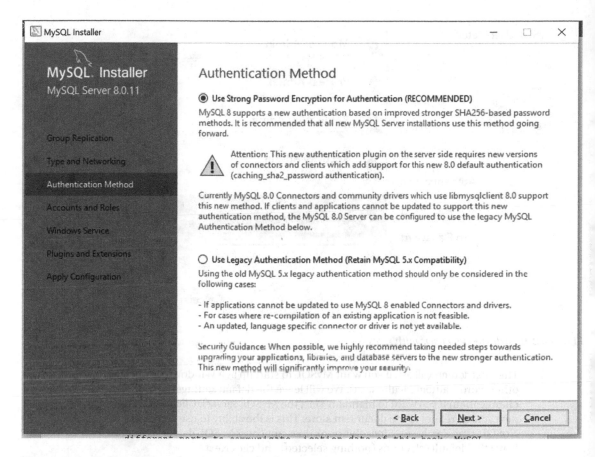

Figure 12-8. Changing the authentication method

16. Since PHP 7 currently does not work with the new Oracle Encryption technology, it is important that we select Use Legacy Authentication Method. Then click Next. You will then be requested to enter a root password. You must use this password every time you access MySQL 8 (this is a new feature). Make sure to enter a password that is secure that you will remember. Then click Next. You could, optionally, also create other user IDs and passwords based on roles (also a new feature) at this time (see Figure 12-9) or after the server has been installed. We will not install any special user IDs at this time.

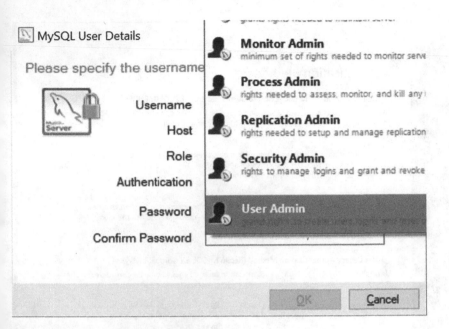

Figure 12-9. *Adding new users with roles*

17. The next screen will ask if you want MySQL to start up as a Windows service (in other words, automatically start). We will leave the default settings (or you can change them if you want to manually start the MySQL server). Click Next. The next screen relates to the document store. This is the ability to use and create NoSQL-type databases. Since this book does not cover NoSQL databases, we will leave the default selections (nothing selected) and click Next.

18. We will see the Apply Configuration screen. Click Execute, and the settings will be installed. Click Finish after the changes have occurred. It will now ask us about configurations of our sample data. Click the Next button. Enter your root password when requested. Click the Check button. This will verify that you can access the example database with the password provided. Click the Next button. The Apply Configuration screen will appear. Click Execute. This will apply the SQL scripts to install the sample data. Click Finish after completion. The Product Configuration screen will appear again. Click Next.

19. You should see an Installation Complete screen. Optionally the check box is selected to start MySQL Workbench. Since we are going to look at MySQL Workbench in the next section, you can keep it selected. Click Finish.

Congratulations! You have installed MySQL 8.0. Let's look at some of the features. First, we will explore MySQL Workbench.

Exploring the Features of MySQL Workbench

If you are like us, you love the features of phpMyAdmin, and you are resistant to discover another tool. However, MySQL Workbench has existed for a while. Many developers have used it for years to design databases with its visual flowchart tool (rather than code). Once the database is designed, SQL code can be generated to install the database and tables. It now also includes many more helpful tools. Workbench has been a separate product that you could install on your own. Now, as you have seen, we can install it as part of the MySQL server package. Let's take a look at some of its features.

If MySQL Workbench is not already running, you will find it under the MySQL folder. Click the icon to start it. The initial screen is actually pretty plain; it provides some basic information, including the version of MySQL you have installed and the port (3307) that MySQL is using for communication. The welcome screen is shown in Figure 12-10.

Figure 12-10. *The welcome screen for MySQL Workbench*

Let's start by clicking the diagram button, which is the second item below the shark database icon, this will display the model screen (Figure 12-11).

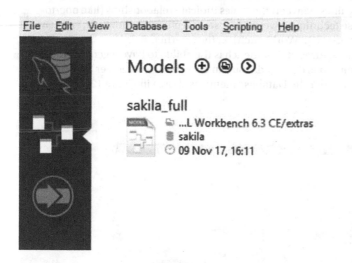

Figure 12-11. *The design models screen for MySQL Workbench*

In our example files we installed, the sakila_full model shows us a visual representation of a database with multiple tables. Click the name of the model on the right to see the details. The full model is shown in Figure 12-12.

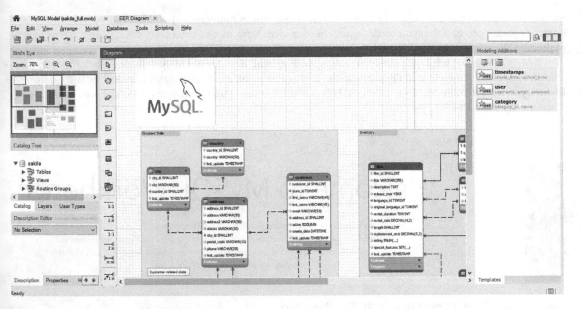

Figure 12-12. *The salika_full design model*

If you have read Chapter 9 or taken a database design class, this diagram should be familiar. This an entity-relationship (ER) diagram. These diagrams are used to create databases and tables that are in normal form. The format of the tables shown and the links between the tables indicate relationships (like one-to-many), attributes, and entities. Learning these techniques would take several chapters. However, you can find many useful videos (including some that use SQL Workbench) on the Internet.

As we mentioned earlier, one of the great features of Workbench is the ability to have it generate the SQL code (and install it) to create your database once it is designed. You can also "reverse engineer" a database back into design mode. This feature is located under the Database menu, as shown in Figure 12-13.

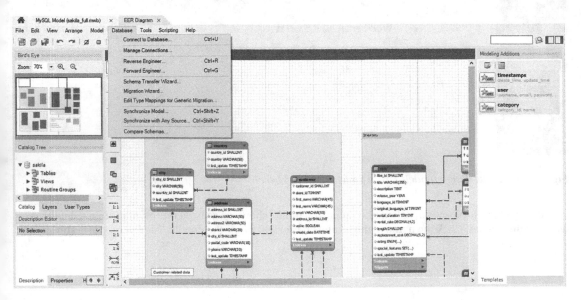

Figure 12-13. *Engineering a database*

If you click the MySQL Model tab at the top of the screen, you will see the existing schema of the sakila database (Figure 12-14).

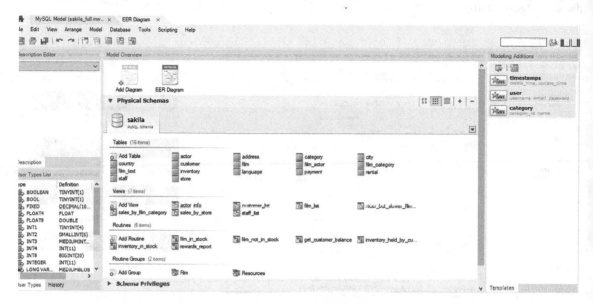

Figure 12-14. *The sakila database*

This is where we can create databases and tables in a similar way as with phpMyAdmin. We will come back to this location later. Close the data view by clicking the *X* icon on one of the tabs at the top of the screen. You should now be back to the welcome page (shown earlier in Figure 12-10). Locate the box containing the MySQL version and the port information (in the bottom-left corner of Figure 12-10). Click the box. The server dashboard will display (Figure 12-15).

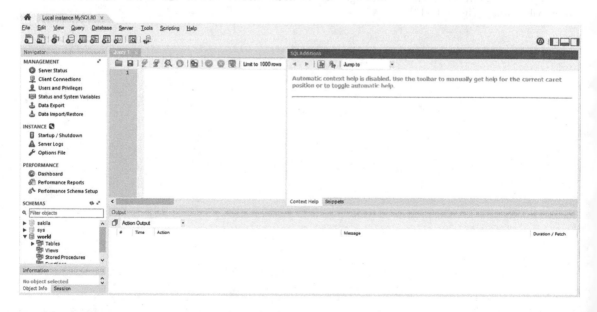

Figure 12-15. *The server dashboard*

The server dashboard provides the ability not only to monitor our databases but also to monitor the server itself. Click the server status selection at the top of the left-side menu. The server status screen will display (Figure 12-16).

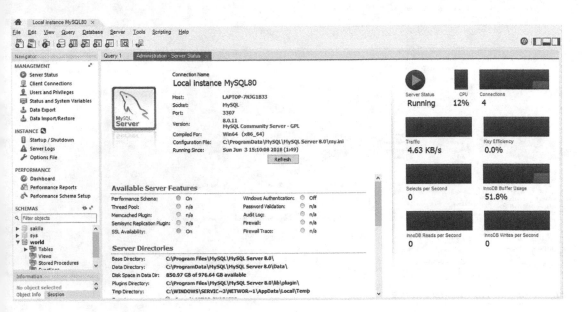

Figure 12-16. *The server status screen*

This screen provides a lot of great information about our server. In addition to the location of files, we can see what features are installed and turned on. We can refresh the server. Also, on the right side, we can see how well (efficient) our server is running. Click Client Connections on the left menu. The client status screen will display (Figure 12-17).

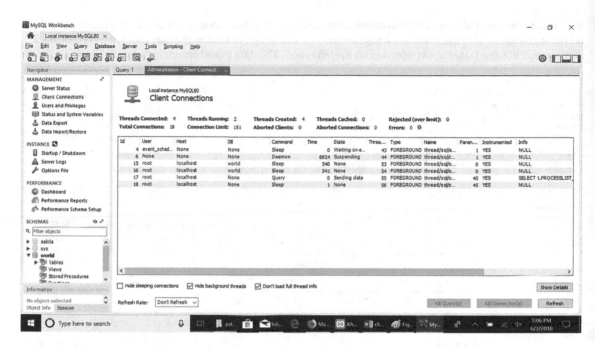

Figure 12-17. *The client status screen*

With this screen, we can monitor who is accessing our server (and databases). Click Users and Privileges on the left menu. The user and privileges screen is shown in Figure 12-18.

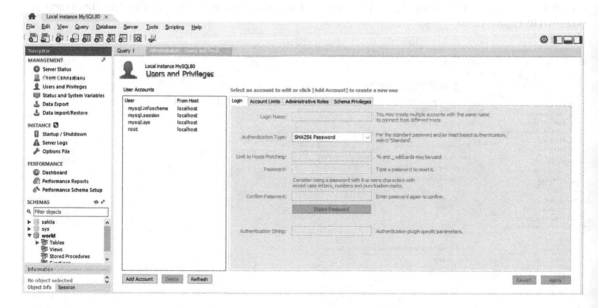

Figure 12-18. *The Users and Privileges screen*

This screen provides the ability to create additional user IDs that access and maintain the database and server. As mentioned in the installation instructions, we can assign IT roles to the user IDs. We will come back here soon. Click the Data Export selection on the left menu. The data export screen is shown in Figure 12-19.

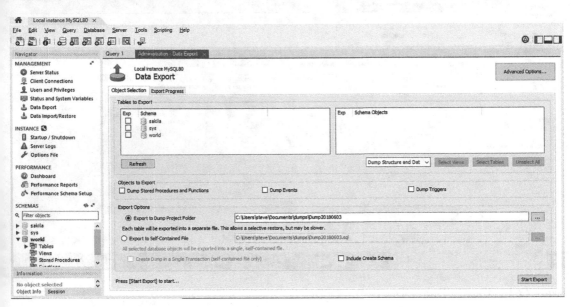

Figure 12-19. *The Data Export screen*

This is one of the locations where we can select data to export, select a location to export, and even schedule when we want to export data. Click the Data Import item on the left menu. The data import screen is shown in Figure 12-20.

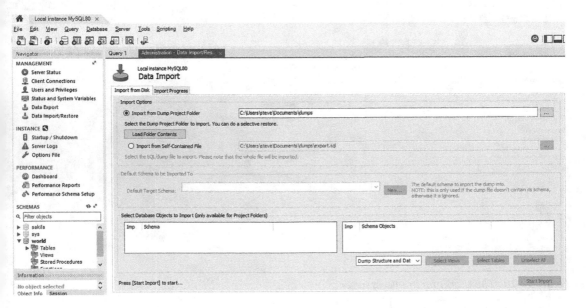

Figure 12-20. *The Data Import screen*

This is the screen we will use soon to import some of the databases we have created.

The server can also be started and stopped with the Startup/Shutdown selection on the left menu. Server logs can easily be viewed from the Server Logs link. Click Dashboard under Performance. The performance dashboard is shown in figure 12-21.

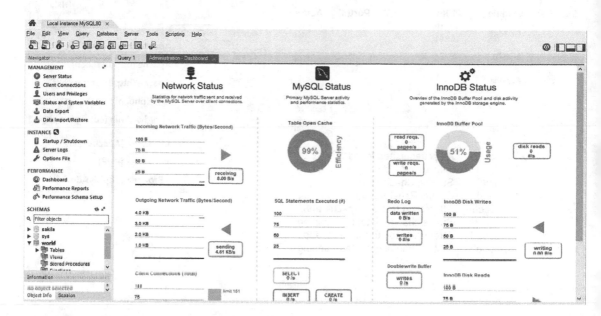

Figure 12-21. The Performance Dashboard screen

The MySQL Performance Dashboard provides a complete quick view of the performance of your server, the performance of MySQL, and the performance of the InnoDB database engine.

As you may have also noticed, you can also access the databases at the bottom left of the menu. Now that we have taken a quick view of Workbench, how can we use PHP 7 to access the MySQL 8 databases? We will discover this in the next section.

Connecting PHP 7 to the MySQL 8 Community Server

We must request that PHP communicate with our new version of MySQL. You will need to locate the *php. ini* configuration file. In XAMPP you can easily find the file by going into the Control Panel and clicking the config button to the right of the Apache server, as shown in Figure 12-22.

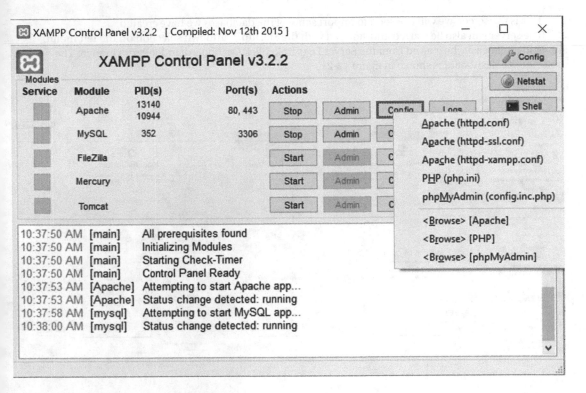

Figure 12-22. Finding the php.ini configuration file

Click the *php.ini* menu selection to open it. For easyPHP you will have to dig down into the development server folder to find the *php.ini* file. It should be in a location similar to the following link:

```
C:\Users\yourcomputername\EasyPHP-Devserver-17\EasyPHP-Devserver-17\eds-binaries\php\
php713vc14x86x170718155219
```

Of course, your version name and the build numbers will be different than shown. Once you find the file, open it with Notepad or another text editor.

Immediately save the current version of the config file with another name (and remember where you saved it) just in case you make a mistake and need to revert to the original settings. Now, find your search tool (under Edit in Notepad) and search for all locations of 3306 (or your default port number). If you are not sure of your MySQL port, you can see it displayed in the XAMPP Control Panel (Figure 12-22) or the EasyPHP Dashboard (under the Database Server information). For each location of the port (3306) in the *php.ini* file, replace it with your MySQL 8 server port number (3307). Then save the *php.ini* file.

Now use either XAMPP Control Panel or easyPHP Dashboard to turn Apache off and then on again. This will cause Apache to see your configuration changes.

■ **Note** After changing the *php.ini* configuration file, XAMPP and easyPHP will not be able to communicate or turn MySQL 8 on or off. Also, phpMyAdmin might not be able to communicate with MySQL 8. Ideally, the creators of these tools will provide upgrades that can eventually communicate with MySQL 8. We can establish communication with MySQL 8 without these tools, as covered next.

We now want to make sure that MySQL 8 is up and running. One quick way to do so is to test the port in your browser. Enter the following as the URL: **Localhost:3307**.

If MySQL is running, you will see a message similar to the following:

```
J���
8.0.11����
sI[R%9B�ÿÿÿ�ÿÃ���������█ }x+^{�mysql_native_password�!��ÿ„#08S01Got packets
out of order
```

Most of this does not tell us humans very much. However, you can see that MySQL 8.0.11 is up and running in this example. You would also see a similar message for MySQL 5.7 on port 3306. If you see a similar message, you are ready to test your communication between PHP 7 and MySQL 8. If you do not see this message, you can go into MySQL Workbench and turn MySQL 8 on as previously discussed.

To test our connection, let's create a simple test file, as shown here:

```php
<?php
// Create a connection to the WORLD UNDER MYSQL 8 database
// Set the encoding to utf-8
// Set the database access details as constants
Define ('DB_USER', 'root'); // or whatever userid you created
Define ('DB_PASSWORD', 'yourserverpassword');
// or whatever password you created
Define ('DB_HOST', 'localhost');
Define ('DB_NAME', 'world');
// Make the connection.
$dbcon = new mysqli(DB_HOST, DB_USER, DB_PASSWORD, DB_NAME);
// Set the encoding...optional but recommended
mysqli_set_charset($dbcon, 'utf8');
$query = "SELECT * FROM city";
$result = mysqli_query ($dbcon, $query); // Run the query.
if ($result) { // If it ran OK, display the records.
// Table header.
echo '<table class="table table-striped">
<tr><th scope="col">Name</th></tr>';
// Fetch and print all the records:
while ($row = mysqli_fetch_array($result, MYSQLI_ASSOC)) {
echo '<tr><td>' . $row['Name'] . '</td></tr>'; }
        echo '</table>'; // Close the table so that it is ready for displaying.
        mysqli_free_result ($result); // Free up the resources.
} else { // If it did not run OK.
// Error message:
echo '<p class="text-center">Nothing retrieved.';
// Debug message:
echo '<p>' . mysqli_error($dbcon) . '<br><br>Query: ' . $q . '</p>';
exit;
} // End of if ($result)
mysqli_close($dbcon); // Close the database connection.
?>
```

In the test file we created earlier, we are connecting to the world database (provided as an example under MySQL 8) and the city table to display city names. Place this code, or similar code, into one of the locations were you were previously executing your PHP files. Then type the URL location into your browser. If your connection was successful, you will see a list similar the output shown in Figure 12-23.

Name
Kabul
Qandahar
Herat
Mazar-e-Sharif
Amsterdam
Rotterdam
Haag
Utrecht
Eindhoven
Tilburg
Groningen
Breda
Apeldoorn
Nijmegen
Enschede
Haarlem
Almere
Arnhem

Figure 12-23. Testing our communication

Congratulations! PHP 7 is now communicating with MySQL 8. To switch back and forth between MySQL versions, just change the port values in the *php.ini* file as shown previously. Now we want to look at migrating our databases to MySQL 8.

Migrating to MySQL 8 Community Server

The good news is that your database migration from MySQL 5.7 to MySQL 8.11 will not be that difficult. All the coding we have shown you previously works in MySQL 8. Ideally, you have developed your code (as shown) with the InnoDB database engine (the default since MySQL 5.5) and with the UTF-8 configuration (also the default since MySQL 5.5). If you discover that your tables or databases are not using these defaults, you can modify your SQL code that you have dumped from your databases.

Let's step though the procedures to migrate a database from an earlier chapter.

1. Open phpMyAdmin. Well, we caught you on that one. Remember that we set the port to 3307? If we try to open phpMyAdmin, we will get error messages. Go back into *php.ini* and reset all occurrences of 3307 to 3306 and restart Apache and MySQL5/MariaDB. Now go into phpMyAdmin.

2. Select the simpleDB database (or any of the book's database examples).

3. Click the Export tab at the top.

4. Enter **simpleDB** for the template name (if it does not already exist in the drop-down box) and click Create. It should now be displayed in the drop-down box.

5. Click Go.

6. The code will open in your default text editor. Save the file as *simpleDB.sql*. View the contents of the file to make sure it does not indicate a different database engine (it should be InnoDB or none listed at all). If a different one is listed, you can remove the related code from the file. It will then load as InnoDB.

7. Open MySQL 8 Workbench under the MySQL folder on your computer.

8. Click the gray box containing the server level and port number to open the server navigator.

9. On the left menu, click the Import/Restore menu selection. The screen in Figure 12-24 will appear.

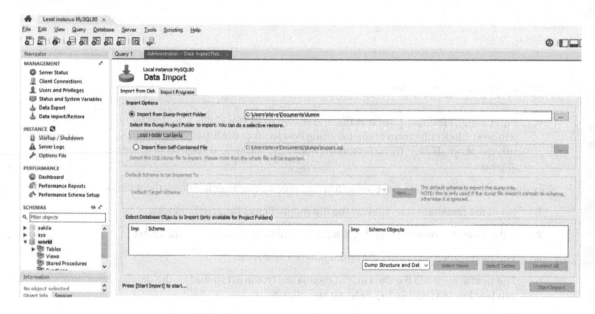

Figure 12-24. *Data Import page*

10. Select the Import from Self-Contained File radio button.

11. Click the three dots to the right to select and find the SQL file you just created. Click the New button next to the Default Schema drop-down box. Enter **simpleDB** (or the name of the database you are importing) and click OK. Now select the schema from the drop-down box. Click Start Import at the bottom right of the page. The SQL code will now run and import your database.

12. You may not notice the new database at the bottom left of the page. Hit the Reload button (two circular arrows) just above the box containing the database schemas. It should now appear.

13. Let's test our database. Go to the top menu and select Database. Then select Connect to Database. Enter your database name (**simpleDB**) in the Default Schema textbox. Click OK. The screen in Figure 12-25 will appear.

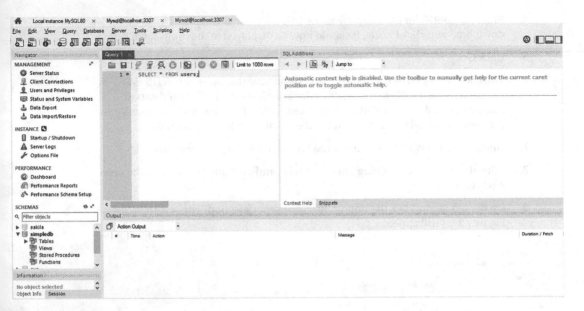

Figure 12-25. *Schema query window*

14. Enter a SQL command, such as the one shown in Figure 12-25, into the Query window. Click either one of the lightning bolt icons at the top of the window to run the script. If everything is working correctly, you should see a table of data appear.

Now that our table exists, let's have some fun and reverse engineer it. Follow these steps:

1. Go to the Database selection on the top menu. Select Reverse Engineer.

2. A parameter screen will appear. Keep all the default settings and click Next.

3. The next screen will verify the connections. Click Next.

4. The next screen will list the current databases. In the list should be the database you just loaded (simpledb). Select it and click Next.

5. The next screen will test the schema (database) to see whether it can be engineered. Click Next.

6. You will see a verification screen showing the database you are using. Click Execute.

7. A progress screen will appear. Click Next.

8. Finally, a screen telling you what was created will display. Click Finish. You should see a display similar to Figure 12-26.

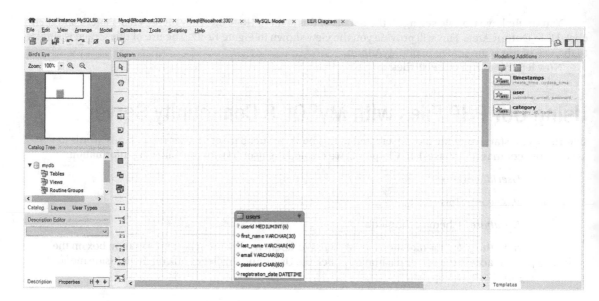

Figure 12-26. *The simpledb ER diagram window*

Congratulations, you just reverse engineered your database! Now you can make design changes and engineer it to produce an updated database.

You can also make changes in a similar way to phpMyAdmin. Close the ER diagram window by closing the tabs (click the *X*) at the top of the screen. This will return you to the schema query window (Figure 12-25). Find the table you want to adjust in the bottom-left schema (database) window. To the right of the table name you will see an information icon, a wrench icon, and a table icon. The information icon (when clicked) provides general information about the table. The table icon will display the data in the table. The wrench icon will allow us to make changes to the structure of the table. Click the wrench icon. The window in Figure 12-27 will appear.

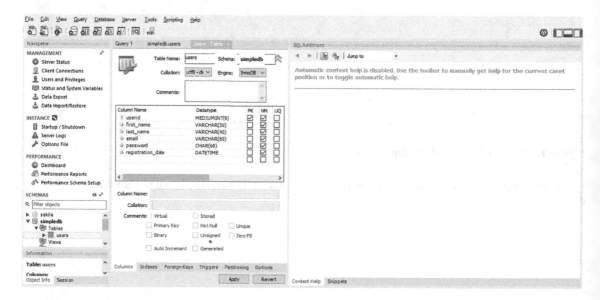

Figure 12-27. *The table structure screen*

You might have trouble seeing all the details of this screen. Go to the View menu, click Panels, and then click Hide Output Area. This will provide you the view shown in Figure 12-27. The use of this screen is similar to the use of the same screen in phpMyAdmin.

Now let's try to run our PHP files.

Using Our PHP Files with MySQL 8 Community Server

Before we can start using the files we created in this book, we need to set up user IDs and passwords to access our schemas (databases). In Chapter 2, we created the user ID with the following information:

- *Userid*: horatio

- *Password*: Hmsv1ct0ry

- *Database* (schema): simpledb

As shown in the previous directions, in MySQL Workbench, click the server information box on the welcome page to access the server dashboard. Click the Users and Privileges link on the left-side menu. The screen in Figure 12-28 will appear.

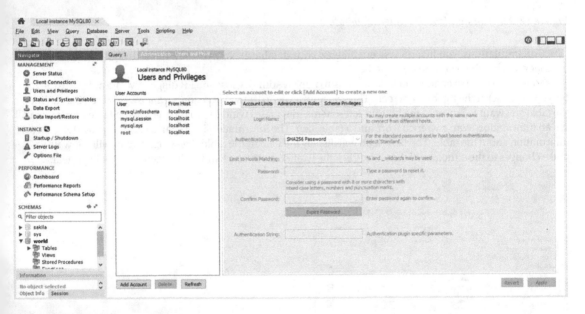

Figure 12-28. *The Users and Privileges screen*

Click the Add Account button at the lower left of the screen. The screen shown in Figure 12-29 will display.

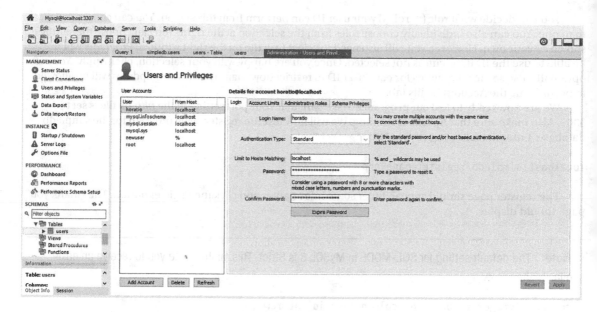

Figure 12-29. *New user account screen*

This screen is similar to the phpMyAdmin screen. Enter the information for the user. Notice that Authentication Type should be set to Standard. PHP 7 requires this setting. Once you have entered the required information, click Apply.

Now click the Administrative Roles tab. The screen in Figure 12-30 will display.

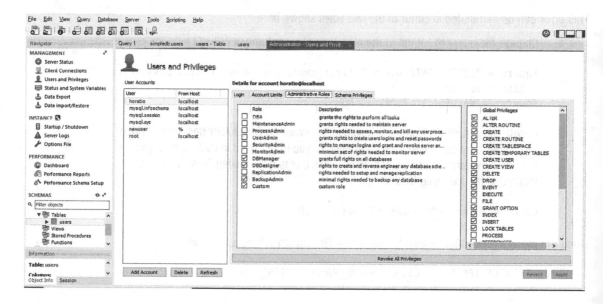

Figure 12-30. *Setting user roles*

You can decide what role (or roles) your user ID can perform from this screen. You can choose more than one. You can also individually choose roles from the selection at the right. You can choose the settings shown or your own. However, you will also need to select Execute on the right window. Programs will not be able to use the ID if Execute is not selected. Once you are happy with your selection, click Apply. You can optionally also set account limits for each user ID to restrict how many queries and updates will be allowed to occur using the Account Limits tab.

We are now ready to test our programs! Make sure that your port setting in the *php.ini* file is set to 3307. Also make sure that Apache is running. We will now test the register-page program for the simpledb database. Enter the following as your URL:

```
localhost/simpledb/register-page.php
```

The register page should appear. Enter some information and click the Register button. The "thank you" page should display.

■ **Note**   The default setting for SQL-MODE in MySQL 8 is Strict. This might cause you to receive an error similar to the following:

```
Incorrect integer value " for column 'userid' at row 1
```

A SQL INSERT statement, as shown next, can cause this problem when attempting to place a string into an integer location in a database:

```
$query = "INSERT INTO users ( userid, first_name, last_name, email, password, registration_date) ";
$query .="VALUES( ' ', ?, ?, ?, ?, NOW() )";
```

This error can be eliminated in either of the two ways shown here:

1. Change the query to not insert the auto-increment column. It will still auto-increment.

    ```
    $query = "INSERT INTO users ( first_name, last_name, email, password,
    registration_date) ";
    $query .="VALUES( ?, ?, ?, ?, NOW() )";
    ```

2. Locate the *my.ini* file. This file is saved in the *Program Data* folder under the C drive. The folder may be hidden from your view, so you might need to click View in your Windows Explorer window and then click the box to view hidden files. The file is located in the following location:

    ```
    C:/Program Data/My SQL/MYSQL Server 8.0
    ```

Open the file in a text editor. Search for *sql-mode*. The setting will be as follows:

```
sql-mode="STRICT_TRANS_TABLES,NO_ENGINE_SUBSTITUTION"
```

Now change the setting to sql-mode="". Save the file and restart MySQL 8 from within Workbench. Your registration should now work.

If you have other errors, you can review the migration documentation that can be accessed from the bottom icon on the left menu on the welcome page of MySQL Workbench. You can also enter your error messages in a search engine (Google) for suggestions on solutions.

You can go to the Client Connections screen (Figure 12-17) to view logging information for the accounts that you create.

Summary

This chapter provided you with a quick explanation of the advantages of using MySQL 8. You also discovered how to install the server and migrate your existing databases. In addition, you learned how to create a user ID that can be used by programs or the database administrator. You also learned about the features of MySQL Workbench.

APPENDIX A

■ ■ ■

Troubleshooting

As you worked through the chapters in this book, you probably encountered many error messages. This is normal. Even seasoned programmers see error messages as they develop new projects. If you can't immediately locate where a mistake was made, walk away and return later when your frustration has subsided. Sometimes leaving the problem for a day and returning to it fresh the next day can help you clear your mind and discover the problem.

■ **Tip** Make a copy of a faulty page and save it with a new name (or as a new version). This will allow you to experiment by changing the code on the copy rather than messing up the original code.

Humans can infer a meaning from poorly written or spoken grammar. For instance, despite the double negative, we know that "I ain't got no money" means the man is broke. When listening to a hesitant speaker, we mentally omit the "ums," "ers," and "you knows" from each sentence so that we can understand what the speaker means. Computers are unable to apply common sense to code containing mistakes or unnecessary characters. However, computers can provide helpful error messages, and they are usually right, *so read them carefully*.

Although error messages can be frustrating, they are an extremely valuable tool because we learn better and faster from our mistakes, and the error messages usually explain the mistakes in plain English. A small number of messages may seem cryptic, but familiarity will eventually help you to understand them.

■ **Tip** Don't try random changes to fix a problem; take time to think it through carefully. Then try one change at a time by commenting out and replacing the line(s) of code. If that change does not work, delete the new line and remove the comment-out characters to restore the original code. Comment out the sections where you think the error occurred, but be careful that your comment-outs do not cause a mismatch of curly brackets or other problems. Place the comment-outs around the code *between* a pair of existing curly brackets.

In this appendix, we have listed some of the most common problems, the error messages, and their solutions to help you be successful. If your problem is not in the list, try entering the error message into a search engine. There are many free sites and blogs that provide solutions to logical errors. Usually there is more than one possible solution provided. As stated already, before you try a suggested solution, save your original code in case the suggestion does not provide an answer to your problem.

Browser Quirks

In the event of a display fault, don't investigate the code until you have tried the page in a different browser. For example, if the page display is unsatisfactory in one browser but good in another, you will need to use a conditional style sheet for the browser that shows an unsatisfactory display. Alternatively, the latest version of a browser may require the addition of vendor-specific adjustments. Although most browsers now claim to be HTML5 and CSS3 compliant, there are usually exceptions that can cause you headaches.

Tables Not Displaying

When a table displays only the headings, it means that either the item being searched for does not exist in the database table or the search criteria does not match the data in the database table. Figure A-1 shows a typical case.

Figure A-1. A table may display only the headings

If you are sure that the data exists in the table being searched, then the problem is that the SQL SELECT query contains one or more incorrect items. A typical query would be as follows:

```
$q = "SELECT ref_number, location, thumb, price, type, mini_description, bedrooms, status
FROM houses WHERE location=? AND (price <= ?) AND type=? AND bedrooms=? ORDER BY ref_number
ASC ";
```

Make a hard copy of the query so that you can delete and restore items. Then look for items that have a corresponding item in the WHERE clause. Delete one matching pair at a time and test after each deletion.

If a populated table is then displayed, you know that the deleted item is the cause of the faulty display. You may find that the three pages involved in the process have differing entries. For instance, in the search page you may have the location items entered with hyphens such as South-Devon, Mid-Devon, and North-Devon, whereas in the administrator's add-a-house page you may have underscores such as South_Devon, Mid_Devon, and North_Devon.

A Style Change Has No Effect

This is particularly frustrating and is often due to a style in some file that is taking precedence over the style you are trying to change. The rogue style is probably lurking in one of the included files. To reduce the possibility of this error occurring, always strive to put the styles in the main external style sheet and avoid using inline styles.

If you are attempting to change a default Bootstrap style, usually you can create an ID for the control you want to style and then adjust the styling in a CSS file. There are also some already defined style changes available as classes within the Bootstrap code. Refer to the website (getbootstrap.com) or enter a search value in your browser that includes the control you want to adjust, such as *Bootstrap Button background color*.

Included Items Missing from the Display

Includes and Requires will appear only when you view the page using a browser. Check that XAMPP or easyPHP has been started and that Apache and MariaDB/MySQL are running. Also check that the included files are actually in the folder specified in the PHP code.

A Page Fails to Validate

If styling instructions appear in an included file, the W3C validator will display a failure message such as "Element style not allowed as child of element div." Remove the style instruction from included files and put the style in the main style sheet.

Bootstrap will cause validation errors, usually four identical errors referring to the use of XML. These errors take the following form:

```
Saw <?. Probable cause: Attempt to use an XML processing instruction in HTML.
(XML processing instructions are not supported in HTML.)
At line 18, column 4
```

You can safely ignore these errors as they do not affect the performance of a file in any way.

A PayPal Pull-Down Menu Does Not Work

Judging by the cries for help on the Internet, this is an occasionally frustrating problem. If using a pull-down menu results in a PayPal error message, you would normally check the code carefully to see whether you can spot the problem; this usually fails to produce a solution. If you upload the code to a forum for analysis, the forum normally confirms your own analysis, i.e., that the code is correct. At the time of writing, if you send an e-mail to PayPal, you will only receive a list of FAQs; rarely are the FAQs related to your problem.

To save time and frustration, don't fiddle with the PayPal code but simply log in to your PayPal account, set up a new pull-down menu, and copy the code; then replace the faulty code with the new code. When setting up the pull-down menu, omit the currency symbols such as £ because they will display as a square box or some other symbol. If you try to replace the currency symbols with an entity, the code will usually fail.

Access Denied

The error message looks something like this:

```
"Access denied for user 'root'@'localhost' <using password: YES>"
```

The YES means that the user entered a password. It does not mean that the user entered YES as the password. If the user failed to enter a password, you would see NO instead of YES.

The error message means that one or more of the items in your database connection file does not match the database details; it could be a misspelling in the connection file of any of the following items: user, password, host, or database name.

PHP Error Levels

The two main throwable levels are as follows:

- *Errors*: These errors halt the script, and the fault must be corrected. If your code is error-free, these are usually caused by external factors such as missing files or the computer is out of memory. These errors can be captured and handled by the program code, as we have seen in our examples. However, the proper reaction is to display a message and shut down the program.

- *Exceptions*: Exceptions may or may not be something that would need to shut down your program. For example, if the user attempts to divide by zero, you can capture the exception and ask the user not to do so. However, if a SQL statement causes an exception, something has not matched the column design of the database table. In this case, you would need to display a message and close down the program.

In the examples in this book, we have captured both separately. This would allow us to treat the responses differently if we so choose. In the examples we merely changed the information placed in the log file to indicate it was either an error or an exception. You can capture all errors and exceptions in one catch statement if you choose. You can even throw your own exceptions. For more information on exception and error handling, visit this page:

```
http://php.net/manual/en/language.exceptions.php
```

In a live environment, the displaying of error messages to the user must be turned off in the *php.ini* file in addition to handling the errors and exceptions with the try/catch blocks.

Call to an Undefined Function

You have called a function that you forgot to define, there is a spelling error in the function call, or you have defined a function in a file that you forgot to include. You may have called what you thought was a standard PHP function that does not actually exist.

Cannot Redeclare Function

You have created a function and declared it twice; remove one of the declarations. You can use include_once or require_once to ensure that any code inserted from external files will be included only once. This can reduce the chance of this problem occurring.

Undefined Index or Undefined Variable

Check the spelling of the index or variable, paying attention to the case of each letter. Check that the variable has been assigned a value. Perhaps you forgot to initiate the variable before you called it. A missing dollar sign at the beginning of a variable will also cause this error to appear.

Empty Variable Value

This error is caused by forgetting the initial dollar sign or misspelling a variable. Check the case of each letter in a variable.

Headers Already Sent

Perhaps you called a header function after you sent some HTML (or even a space) to the browser. The following piece of code will fail because the header statement is preceded by some HTML:

```
<html>
<?php
header("location:somefile.php");
?>
```

This statement will work:

```
<?php
header("location:somefile.php");
?>
<html>
```

If you put a space before the <?php, the error message will re-appear.

Blank Screen

This can be caused by the same fault that produces the "headers already sent" message.

If you are expecting a display produced by a looping array and nothing appears, you probably forgot that arrays start at zero, and you may have started your loop at 1.

Some incorrect HTML or PHP can produce a blank screen. The fault can also result from an error that has halted the script.

Unexpected End of File in Line xxx

This is a common PHP error, and it often refers to the last line in the file. It usually means you have a mismatched number of curly brackets or normal brackets. For instance, you may have 20 opening curly brackets but only 19 closing brackets. To find the missing bracket, try indenting the PHP code so that the brackets can be counted more easily. To find the error in a large file, print a hard copy of the code and then number all the left brackets with a red pen and all the right brackets with a green pen. The number of red brackets must equal the number of green brackets. You can also draw lines on the left margin of your paper from the opening brackets to the closing brackets. Often this error is caused by using a normal bracket instead of a curly bracket. Printing out your code can help you spot the difference.

In many code editor programs (such as Notepad++), you can click a bracket, and it will highlight the corresponding closing bracket (if there is one). This can help you count brackets. However, you still need to make sure the correct brackets correspond to each other.

Parse Error and Unexpected Characters

Almost all parse errors are caused by missing items in PHP statements. Opening curly brackets or normal brackets may not have matching closing brackets. Opening quotation marks may not have a closing quotation mark. If you forget to escape a quotation mark in a string, you will see a parse error. This section covers some typical parse error messages.

You will see something like "unexpected (/)" or "unexpected (,)." These are the easiest PHP parsing errors to spot because the PHP parser directs you to the line and column in the code where the error is located.

```
Parse error: expecting (,) or (;) in /somefile.php on line 10
```

Often this means you have forgotten to close the statement with a semicolon.

A missing normal bracket (}) or quote mark may also trigger this error.

If you see an error message like the following, you have omitted a closing semicolon, but this time it applies to the statement before line 10:

```
Parse error: unexpected T_echo, expecting (,) or (;) on /somefile.php on line 10
```

The incorrect nesting of quote marks can result in the "unexpected" type of error messages and a display that you did not expect.

The following code will produce a parse error:

```
$some_variable =  "table width="960px">";
```

The parser reads the first double quote and assumes that the double quote following the equal sign signals the end of the statement.

Use a pair of single quotes around 960px to prevent this, as follows:

```
$some_variable =  "table width='960px'>";
```

If you omit the final double quote, the parser will continue to read the code until it finds another double quote. This could be several lines down so that the error message refers to that line rather than the line where the error is located. If you can't find the error on the line stated in the error message, move back through the lines until you find the mistake.

Unexpected T_STRING

The usual causes are a missing semicolon, a missing quote, or a missing double quote. An example of a missing quote follows:

```
$somevariable = 'fname ;
```

It should have been as follows:

```
$somevariable = 'fname' ;
```

Unexpected T_ELSE

Often this error results from having an unnecessary semicolon after an if clause as follows:

```
if (some condition exists);
{
      $result = "that condition exists" ;
}
```

The error message can also appear if you have omitted one or more curly brackets or you have more than one else clause in block of code. If you have more than one else clause, change the earlier ones to elseif so that you have only one else clause in a block of code.

Wrong Equal Sign

Check your code to see where you have used the wrong equal sign. The rules for equal signs are as follows:

- A single equal sign (an assignment operator) is used to assign a value to a variable.

- If an item is to be checked if it is equal to another item, you must use a double equal sign (==). The case will be checked also. It must be the same for the items to be equal.

- If an item is to be absolutely identical (same uppercase and lowercase letters and same data type) to another item, you must use a triple equal sign (===). Remember that PHP will convert a "2" to a 2, if needed, to do a comparison. The following would be true because PHP will convert the string "2" to an integer 2 for you:

    ```
    $value = "2";
    if( $value == 2 )
    ```

The following would be false because you are checking that everything is exact:

```
if ( $value === 2 )
```

Failed to Open Stream

The server cannot find a file or an included file. Either the file being called is not in the correct folder or the file has a spelling error. Sometimes we can forget to give the correct path for the file. The error message can be the result of a statement like this:

```
<?php include("header.php") ?>;
```

Instead, the statement should have been as follows:

```
<?php include("includes/header.php") ?>;
```

Syntax Errors

SQL syntax errors produce an error message like this:

```
Error 1064 (42000): You have an error your SQL syntax
```

Fortunately, the message often gives a clue to the whereabouts and cause of the error. It will say something like this: "near * FROM members at line 6." This means that line 6 contains an asterisk, and near that asterisk you will find the error.

Warning: Division by Zero

Neither PHP nor mathematics allows division by zero. The message will indicate the location of the error so that you can correct it. Remember, this could be caused by a value that the user provided.

Display Is Not What Was Expected

Although many errors are the result of omitting characters, extraneous characters can display something you did not intend; for instance, the following code seems fine at first glance:

```
for ( $var = 0; $var =5; $var++ ) ;
{ echo "display something <br>";
}
```

The code was intended to loop through and display some variable five times. However, this does not happen. This is because there should not be a semicolon after the for statement. The unnecessary semicolon halts the loop.

Reference to a Primary Key Could Not Be Created

If you try to set a foreign key in one table that links to a primary key in another table, ensure that both keys have the same type and length. Otherwise, you will see an error message stating that the reference to the primary key could not be created.

Element <style> Not Allowed as Child of Element <div>

If this occurs when you use the W3C validator to check your code, it means that an included file contains an internal style using <style></style> tags. This included style will appear within the <body></body> section of the HTML document; style tags must appear within the <head></head> section. To remedy this, relocate the style in either the main style sheet or as a link in the <head></head> section of the HTML page.

Problem with Prepared Statement

If an error message refers to code in a prepared statement or to the line of bind parameters code, check that the number of question marks equals the number of bind parameters. Check that column names are used in the queries and that the bind parameter uses the variables containing the user's input, such as $fname, $ln, $e, and so on. Here is a correct example:

```
//If all the fields were filled out
$hp = password_hash($p, PASSWORD_DEFAULT);
// Register the user in the database...
$query = "INSERT INTO users (user_id, fname, lname, email, psword,";
$query .= "addr1, addr2, city, state_country, zcode_pcode, phone";
```

```
$query .= "registration_date) VALUES ";
$query .= "(' ', ?,?,?,?,?,?,?,?,?,?, NOW() )";
$q = mysqli_stmt_init($dbcon);
mysqli_stmt_prepare($q, $query);
// use prepared statement to ensure that only text is inserted
// bind the input from the form's fields to SQL Statement
mysqli_stmt_bind_param($q, 'ssssssssss', $fname, $ln, $e, $hp, $ad1, $ad2,
$cty, $cnty, $pcode, $ph);
// execute query
```

The INSERT statement contains 12 column names and 10 question marks. The user_id column name and the registration_date column name are both automatic, i.e., not typed in by the user. The 10 items typed in by the user are represented by 10 question marks and by 10 string symbols (s) in the bind parameters statement. The two automatic column names are represented by ' ' and NOW() in the query, but these must not appear in the bind parameters statement. Note that column names are used in the queries, but the bind parameter uses the variables containing the user's input (values), e.g., $fname, $ln, $c, and so on.

■ **Note**　You can also use PDO to create prepared statements. For more information, visit http://php.net/manual/en/book.pdo.php.

Logical Errors

Some of the most difficult errors to determine are logical errors. These are caused by a logic problem in your code. No error message will display. However, you will not get the results you are expecting. One common debugging method to find logical problems is to temporarily place echo statements throughout your code to discover where the program is flowing and what are the current values of key variables. Sometimes multiple messages as simple as "I am here" placed in your functions and other areas can help you determine what problem existed. Depending on what editor you have chosen to use, there may also be other debugger tools available.

The Internet Is Your Friend

It is worth repeating that if you get an error message you don't understand or you can't determine the problem, paste the message into a browser to discover how others have fixed the problem. There are also many free blogs that will allow you to paste your code that is causing problems. Remember to not paste any sensitive information (such as passwords) into these blogs! There are many programmers who respond to these blogs in an attempt to help you. The programming community does try to support each other. But do make sure to save your original code in case the suggestion did not work.

Summary

This chapter described some error messages, and appropriate solutions were suggested. No doubt you encountered many error messages as you worked through this book. In fact, you will always have to deal with error messages, unless you are superhuman. We recommend that if you recognize messages that are not mentioned in this chapter, make a note of them and record the solutions.

We have come to the end of this book, and you should now have an understanding of the basic principles for designing practical databases for websites. We hope you will regard this book as a starting point for further study of PHP, SQL, MariaDB, MySQL, and in particular security. This simplified approach to database design omitted such topics as object-oriented programming (OOP) and Ajax; none of them is essential, but they are alternatives to the techniques employed in this book. Appendix B will help you locate resources for further study. You can also learn more by combining techniques from the chapters in this book.

Remember, there is always more to learn as a programmer. A successful IT professional is always studying, practicing, and learning new techniques. You must stay current with today's standards and tools.

APPENDIX B

Resources

We have included this quick reference section to save you from having to search through the book for examples or an explanation of a certain piece of PHP/MySQL/MariaDB syntax. The PHP/MySQL/MariaDB references are in alphabetical order for rapid searching.

The quick references in this appendix refer only to the PHP and MySQL/MariaDB used in the book. PHP and MySQL/MariaDB can achieve much more; to extend your knowledge of PHP and MySQL/MariaDB beyond the examples in this book, refer to the resources at the end of this appendix.

This appendix covers five topics, as follows:

- PHP quick reference
- Bootstrap template
- MySQL and phpMyAdmin quick reference
- What next?
- Resources

PHP Quick Reference

This section is a quick reference to PHP.

Arrays

Arrays are variables that can store multiple values. The files in previous chapters used an array to store one or more error messages. The error array stored one type of element, i.e., error messages. Arrays can be created that can store records containing many different types of elements such as names, addresses, e-mail addresses, passwords, ages, registration dates, user levels, and phone numbers. The name of the array should relate to its contents, such as user_details, error_messages, or cereals.

In an array named *cereals*, the multiple values might be oats, barley, corn, and wheat. The array can be created using the following code:

```
$cereals = array[];
```

The values can be inserted as follows (note that the key for the first value is zero):

```
<?php
$cereals = array[];
$cereals[0] = "oats";
$cereals[1] = "barley";
```

```
$cereals[2] = "corn";
$cereals[3] = "wheat";
?>
```

The number inside the square brackets is known as the *key*. The first key in our example has a value of oats. The following code will display the content of the cereals array:

```
<html>
<head>
<title>The simple array page</title>
<meta charset=utf-8>
<style type="text/css">
.cntr {text-align:center; }
</style>
</head>
<body>
<h2 class="cntr">This is the Array Page</h2>
<p class="cntr">
<?php
$cereals = array();
$cereals[0] = "oats";
$cereals[1] = "barley";
$cereals[2] = "corn";
$cereals[3] = "wheat";
echo ("$cereals[0]" . "$cereals[1] " . "$cereals[2] " . $cereals[3]);
?>
</p>
</body>
</html>
```

This will display the following:

```
Oats barley corn wheat
```

Associative Arrays

Associative arrays allow you to use text instead of reference numbers for the key; this can provide more explicit code. Associative arrays use the array operator symbol (=>). (Note that this symbol does not mean equal to or greater than.) In the example given next, the => symbol indicates that the key Monday has the value of Clean car. The key is case sensitive, so *Monday* is not the same as *monday*. Let's look at an example with seven key/value pairs in an array that we will call *$events*.

■ **Caution** Pay particular attention to the punctuation and quotes. Especially remember not to add a comma after the final array value (Church in our example).

```
<html>
<head>
<title>The associative array page</title>
<meta charset="utf-8">
```

```
<style type="text/css">
h2 { margin-left:150px; }
p {margin-left:250px; text-align:left; }
</style>
</head>
<body>
        <h2 class="cntr">This is the associative array Page</h2>
        <?php
        $events = array(
                'Monday' => 'Clean car',
                'Tuesday' => 'Dental appointment',
                'Wednesday' => 'Shopping',
                'Thursday' => 'Gardening',
                'Friday' => 'Fishing',
                'Saturday' => 'Football match',
                'Sunday' => 'Church'
        );
        foreach($events as $day => $event) {
                echo "<p>$day: $event</p>\n";
        }
?>
</body>
</html>
```

The code produces the following display:

```
This is the associative array Page
Monday: Clean car
Tuesday: Dental appointment
Wednesday: Shopping
Thursday: Gardening
Friday: Fishing
Saturday: Football match
Sunday: Church
```

The downloadable files for this appendix include *simple_array.php* and *assoc_array.php*.

Comments

Comments prevent a piece of PHP code from displaying on the screen. They have three main uses.

- Reminding the programmer what a line of code achieves. Here's an example:

// The next script retrieves all the records from the users table.

- Disabling a piece code for troubleshooting.

- Disabling a session to check a page's styling and function.

PHP accepts three symbols to indicate a comment as follows:

```
//A single line comment
#A single line comment
/*A multiple line comment
```

```
    some text
    some text
    some text*/
```

Concatenation

Concatenating strings means joining them together by using a full stop; see $full_name, for example:

```php
<?php
$first_name = 'Annie';
$last_name = 'Versary';
$full_name = $first_name . ' ' . $last_name;
echo $full_name;
?>
```

The display is as follows:

```
Annie Versary
```

Constants

Items that never change are stored as *constants* using the function define(). The function takes two parameters: the name of the constant and its fixed value. Because we have no intention of changing our first name, we could define it as a constant as follows:

```php
<?php
define('MY_FNAME', 'Adrian');
echo = 'Hello ';
echo = MY_FNAME;
?>
```

The display is as follows:

```
Hello Adrian
```

Note that constants do not use a dollar sign because they are not variables. Constants are case insensitive. However, they are normally uppercase to easily detect within the code.

E-mailing with PHP

PHP provides an easy method for sending e-mails using the mail() function. The format is as follows:

```php
mail($to,$subject,$message,$headers);
```

You can confirm that your hosting company's e-mail server will respond to PHP instructions. Create a PHP file named *email.php*, or use the downloadable file, and insert your own e-mail address in place of the two dummy addresses.

```html
<!doctype html>
<html lang=en>
<head>
```

```
<title>Testing a simple email</title>
<meta charset=utf-8>
</head>
<body>
<?php
        mail("me@myisp.co.uk", "This is a subject", "This is the body of the email", ↵
        "From:me@myisp.co.uk\r\n");
?>
</body>
                        </html>
```

Upload the file *email.php* to your host provider and then access the file from a browser. You will see a blank page, but you should receive an e-mail via your usual e-mail client such as Windows Live Mail or a web mail client.

The more practical version of *multiple_email.php*, shown next, includes multiple recipients and uses variables instead of hard-coding. As a first test, we used an alternative e-mail address to replace recipient-1. The e-mail addresses of cooperative friends or colleagues were used for recipient-3 and recipient-4. The code shown next is provided in the downloadable files for the appendix:

```
<html>
<head>
<title>Testing an email for multiple recipients</title>
<meta charset="utf-8">
</head>
<body>
<?php
        $to = " me@myisp.co.uk, recipient-2@someisp.co.uk ";
        $subject = "My email test.";
        $message = "This is the body of the email";
        $headers = "From: me@myisp.co.uk\r\n";
        $headers .= "Reply-To: me@myisp.co.uk\r\n";
        $headers .= "CC: recipient-3@someisp.co.uk\r\n";
        $headers .= "BCC: recipient-4@someisp.com\r\n";
        mail($to,$subject,$message,$headers);
        if ( mail($to,$subject,$message,$headers) ) {                        //#1

         echo "The email has been sent!";}
        else { echo "The e-mail has failed!"; }
?>
</body>
</html>
```

The elements To:, CC:, and BCC: can consist of several recipients by using a comma-separated list, as shown in the line beginning with $to. To use the file with fewer recipients, simply delete the unwanted items. Save the file as *multiple_email.php*, upload the file to a host, and then access the file from a browser. You should receive the e-mail via your usual e-mail client such as Windows Live Mail or web mail.

Explanation of the Code

The top section of an e-mail is the header. The variable called *$headers* supplies the header with its content. The $headers variables are concatenated using a dot and an equal sign (.=) , and each one is moved down a line by the code (\r\n).

```
if ( mail($to,$subject,$message,$headers) ) {                              //#1
   echo "The email has been sent!";}
else { echo "The e-mail has failed!"; }
```

This block of code is optional and may be deleted; it will let you know whether the e-mail was sent or not, but it will not tell you whether it was received.

Functions

A function is a self-contained piece of reusable code that performs a task when called. PHP has more than 1,000 built-in functions. In this book, you have been using several built-in functions, such as array(), include(), require(), count(), and mysqli_connect().

You can create your own functions. A function name can contain letters, digits, and underscores but not hyphens; the name must not begin with a digit; and function names are not case sensitive. A function can be created by the web designer using the following format:

```
function function_name()
{ task to be performed; }

Example: function greeting()
         { echo "Hello user!" ; }
```

The function can be called from within a script as follows:

```
<?php
   greeting();
?>
```

This would display as "Hello user!"

include() vs. require()

Both functions pull a file into an HTML page or PHP script, with the difference being that if include() fails to retrieve the file, the script will display an error message and will continue to run; if require() encounters the same problem, it will stop the script. Use include() for including most files, but use require() for vital items such as accessing the database connection file. If the connection fails, it is pointless to continue running the script.

if, else, and elseif

A series of PHP conditional statements can take the following pattern:

if something is true
```
      Do this
```
elseif something else is true

> Do that

else

> Do something different from the previous two instructions.

You may use as many elseif statements as you like, but only one else is permitted, and it must be the last item in the list of conditionals.

When students look at the code for the registration page, they ask why several else clauses appear one after another when there should be only one. Some code that prompts the question is as follows:

```php
if (empty($errors)) { // If no problems occurred in the user's input
    //Determine whether the email address has already been registered for a user
    $q = "SELECT user_id FROM users WHERE email = '$e' ";
    $result=mysqli_query ($dbcon, $q) ;
    if (mysqli_num_rows($result) == 0){//The email address was not already registered ↵
    therefore register the user in the users table
        // Make the query
        $q = "INSERT INTO users (user_id, title, fname, lname, email, psword,
        registration_date,↵
        uname, class, addr1, addr2, city, county, pcode, phone, paid) VALUES (' ',
        '$title', ↵
        '$fn', '$ln', '$e', SHA1('$p'), NOW(), '$uname','$class', '$ad1', '$ad2',
        '$cty', ↵
        '$cnty', '$pcode', '$ph', '$pd')";
        ...
        $result = @mysqli_query ($dbcon, $q); // Run the query
        if ($result) { // If the query ran without a problem
            ...
            header ("location: register-thanks.php");
            ...
            exit();
        ...} else { // If the query failed to run
            // Error message
            ...
            echo '<h2>System Error</h2>
            <p class="error">
            You could not be registered due to a system error. We apologize for ↵
            the inconvenience.</p>';
            // Debugging message
            ...
            echo '<p>' . mysqli_error($dbcon) . '<br><br>Query: ' . $q . '</p>';
        } // End of if ($result)
            ...
            mysqli_close($dbcon); // Close the database connection.
            // Include the footer and stop the script
            ...
            include ('includes/footer.php');
            ...
            exit();
        ...
    }else{//The email address is already registered
        ...
```

```
                    echo '<p class="error">The email address is not acceptable because it
                    is ↵
                    already registered</p>';
          ...
          }
          ...
     }else{ // Display the errors
```

The Explanation

The ifs and elses are shown in bold type; there are three ifs and three elses. The three elses appear to be following each other, but in fact the ifs and elses are nested; they are each complete in themselves, as you will see from the formatted summary that follows:

```
if (empty($errors)) { //If no problems occur in the user's input, run the query
     if (mysqli_num_rows($result) == 0) { //The email address is not already registered, ↵
          so continue to run the query
               if ($result) { //If the query ran without a problem, continue to run the script
               }else{ //If the query fails to run, display an error message
     }else{ //The email address is already registered, display that information to the user
}else{ //If errors are detected, display the errors
```

Loops

A loop is a device that searches through an array or a file item by item; it functions by executing a block of code as long as a condition has not changed.

The while Loop

The while loop is used when the number of items that might be retrieved is unknown.

The following is the format for a while loop:

```
while (condition is true)
{
     do something
}
```

We used while loops in pages that retrieved the results of search queries. The code looped through the data in a database table and displayed records if they existed. This use of the while loop was as follows:

```
// Fetch and print all the records
while ($row = mysqli_fetch_array($result, MYSQLI_ASSOC)) {
     ...echo '<tr>…
}
```

While records were found, the rows were retrieved and displayed in a table.

The for Loop

The for loop and the foreach loop are used when the number of items is known. The for loop has the following format:

```
for (start value, last value, expression) {
        do something
}
```

The for loop used in the next example is restricted to a known number of iterations (i.e., 4):

```
<?php
for($x=0; $x<=3; $x++)
{
        echo "Iteration: $x<br>";
}
?>
```

The display would be as follows:

```
Iteration: 0
Iteration: 1
Iteration: 2
Iteration: 3
```

The foreach Loop

This is used with arrays with a known number of elements. If an array holds the three primary colors, you know there are three items; therefore, we use foreach. The foreach loop has the following format:

```
foreach ($array as $value)
{
        code to be executed
}
```

Here's an the example of an array holding the three primary colors:

```
<?php
$primaries = array("red","yellow","blue");
foreach ($primaries as $value) {
        echo "$value <br>";
}
?>
```

The display would be as follows:

```
red
yellow
blue
```

foreach was used in the next snippet of code for the registration pages in this book. Because the loop followed some code that detected a number of error messages (or no messages) in the $errors array, the number of messages is known to be either zero or a known amount.

```
} else { // Display the errors
    echo '<h2>Error!</h2>
    <p class="error">The following error(s) occurred:<br>';
    foreach ($errors as $msg) { // Display each error
        echo " - $msg<br>\n";
    }
        echo '</p><h3>Please try again.</h3><p><br></p>';
    }
```

The do while Loop

The do while loop executes the piece of code once, and then it will check the result. If the result is not equal to a predetermined amount, it will continue to loop until the result is equal to the predetermined amount. The do and the while are separated by the code that executes some task, as follows:

```
An initial variable;
do
{
        code to be executed;
}
while (condition is true);
```

Example:

```
<?php
$x=1;
do
 {
        echo "Number: $x <br>";
        $x = $x + 1;
}
while ($x<=3)
?>
```

The display would be as follows:

```
Number: 1
Number: 2
Number: 3
```

Numbers

Here are some examples of valid numbers for use in PHP scripts:

- *Valid integers*: 4 and -4

- *Valid floating-point numbers*: 4.0 or -4.0 or 40.44

- *Invalid numbers*: ¾ or 3a or 04.01.14

The mathematical operators for numbers are as follows: add (+), subtract (-), multiply (*), and divide (/).

Here's an example:

```php
<?php
  $price = 100;
  $sales_tax = 0.2;
  $total_price = $price + ($price * $sales_tax);
  echo $total_price;
?>
```

The total price displayed would be 120.

Prepared Statements

Prepared statements provide secure queries that prevent SQL injection attacks. If a prepared statement is not used, the entire query is sent to MySQL/MariaDB in a vulnerable form. Prepared statements split the query into two parts. First only the syntax is parsed and sent to MySQL (the statement). Then the values are specified in a separate piece of code (the bind). MySQL then assembles the two components. The following code demonstrates a prepared statement:

```
if (empty($errors)) { // If everything's OK.
// If no problems encountered, a register user in the database
//Determine whether the email address has already been registered
$query = "SELECT userid FROM users WHERE email = ? ";
$q = mysqli_stmt_init($dbcon);
mysqli_stmt_prepare($q, $query);
mysqli_stmt_bind_param($q,'s', $emailtrim);
mysqli_stmt_execute($q);
$result = mysqli_stmt_get_result($q);

if (mysqli_num_rows($result) == 0){//The email address has not been already
//registered, therefore register the user in the users table
        //-------------Valid Entries - Save to database -----
        //Start of the SUCCESSFUL SECTION. i.e. all the required fields
//were filled out
        $hashed_password = password_hash($password, PASSWORD_DEFAULT);
// Register the user in the database using an INSERT query
//Note that there are 15 elements in the query
        $query =
"INSERT INTO users (userid, title, first_name, last_name, email, password, class, ";
        $query .=
"address1, address2, city, state_country, zcode_pcode, phone, secret, registration_date) ";
//13 of the elements are provided by the user's entries and their values are //represented
by question marks. The two automatic items user_id and //Registration_date are represented
by ' ' and NOW ().
    $query .= "VALUES ";
        $query .= "(' ',?,?,?,?,?,?,?,?,?,?,?,?,?,NOW())";
$q = mysqli_stmt_init($dbcon);
mysqli_stmt_prepare($q, $query);
// use prepared statement to ensure that no dangerous code is inserted
// bind fields to SQL Statement
mysqli_stmt_bind_param($q, 'sssssssssssss',
$titletrim, $first_nametrim, $last_nametrim, $emailtrim, $hashed_password, $classtrim,
$address1trim,
```

```
$address2trim, $citytrim, $state_countrytrim, $zcode_pcodetrim, $phonetrim, $secrettrim);
// execute query
mysqli_stmt_execute($q);
if (mysqli_stmt_affected_rows($q) == 1) {
        header ("location: register-thanks.php?class=" . $classtrim);
} else {
      // echo 'Invalid query:' . $dbcon->error;
      $errorstring = "System is busy, please try later";
echo "<p class=' text-center col-sm-2' style='color:red'>$errorstring</p>";
        }
}else{//The email address is already registered
    $errorstring = 'The email address is already registered.';
echo "<p class=' text-center col-sm-2' style='color:red'>$errorstring</p>";
}
} else {//End of SUCCESSFUL SECTION
```

Sessions

The period of uninterrupted time that a user spends viewing a web site is called a *session*. By using a PHP built-in array named $_SESSION, a user's data can be stored in a session as they move from page to page. This is achieved by assigning the user's data to a session as follows:

```
if (isset($_POST['id'])
{
$id = $_POST['id'];
}
session_start()
$_SESSION['id'] = $id
do some action
```

The function session_start() must appear on every page where a session will be used. The function will then either start a session or access an existing session. The function must appear in the page code before anything is sent to the browser; it will not tolerate even a preceding space or empty line.

Logging In with a Session

We have used sessions in most chapters, and the login pages provide a typical example, as shown in the following snippet:

```
<?php
// Check if the login form on the login page has been submitted
if ($_SERVER['REQUEST_METHOD'] == 'POST') {
        require ('mysqli_connect.php'); //connect to database
        //Email validation code goes here and assign email alias as $e
        // Password validate code goes here and assign password alias as $p
        if ($e && $p){//if no problems were encountered
        // Fetch the user_id, first_name and user_level for that email/password combination:
        $hp = password_hash($p, PASSWORD_DEFAULT);
        $query = "SELECT user_id, fname, user_level FROM users WHERE (email=? AND psword=?)";
        $q = mysqli_stmt_init($dbcon);
```

```
mysqli_stmt_prepare($q, $query);
 // bind $id to SQL Statement
 mysqli_stmt_bind_param($q, "ss", $e, $hp);
 // execute query
 mysqli_stmt_execute($q);
$result = mysqli_stmt_get_result($q);
// Was there a record that matched the email/password combination
if (mysqli_num_rows($result) == 1) {//if a database record matched the user's input
// Fetch the record and set the session data
        session_start();                                                            #1
        $_SESSION = mysqli_fetch_array ($result, MYSQLI_ASSOC);
        $_SESSION['user_level'] = (int) $_SESSION['user_level']; // Ensure user level
        is an integer
        // Use a ternary operation to set the URL                                    #2
        $url = ($_SESSION['user_level'] === 1) ? 'admin-page.php' : 'members-page.php';
        header('Location: ' . $url); // Make the browser load either the members' or
        the admin page
        exit(); // Stop the script.
         mysqli_free_result($result);
        mysqli_close($dbcon);
    } else { // No match was made
    echo '<p class="error">The email address and password entered do not match our
    records.</p>'
}
} else { // If there was a system problem
    echo '<p class="error">Please try again.</p>';
}
    mysqli_close($dbcon);
} // End of submit conditional
?>
<!-- Display the form fields-->                                                      #3
<div id="loginfields">
<?php include ('login_page.inc.php'); ?>
</div>
```

Note that the session_start() function (line #1) is not preceded by anything that is sent to the browser. It is followed by code that takes the data from the found record and assigns the data to the session. A ternary operator (line #2) then uses the data stored in the session to make the browser load either the members page or the admin page. After the PHP code is processed, the code sends some information to the browser (line #3).

Logging Out

Sessions are located in the memory of the server for security, and closing the browser will end the session. However, if the user wants to log out and then browse the website's public pages, for security the user can log out, and the code in the logout page shown next will destroy the session:

```
<?php
session_start();//access the current session
// If no session id variable exists, redirect the user
if (!isset($_SESSION['user_id'])) {
```

```php
        header("location:index.php");
        exit();
}else{ //Destroy the session
        $_SESSION = array(); // Destroy the variables stored in the session
        session_destroy(); // Destroy the session itself
        setcookie (session_name(), '', time()-3600);
        setcookie('PHPSESSID', time()-3600,'/', 0, 0);//Destroy the cookie
        header("location:index.php");
        exit();
}
```

Ternary Operator

The ternary operator is a concise way of setting a conditional. The operator uses the symbols (?) and the colon (:). This example is taken from Chapter 3 of this book.

```php
// Use a ternary operation to set a page URL
$url = ($_SESSION['user_level'] === 1) ? 'admin-page.php' : 'members-page.php';
header('Location: ' . $url);
exit(); // Stop the script
```

The first part (enclosed in brackets) takes the user_level in the session array and asks if it is identical to 1. The three equal signs mean "identical to." The item after the question mark is stating that if the user_level is identical to 1, then assign *admin-page.php* to the variable named *$url*. The colon is the equivalent of else. Therefore, if user_level is not identical to 1, $url is set so that it directs the user to *members-page.php* (registered members have a user_level of 0). The variable $url therefore is set to a particular page, and the user is redirected to that page using the header() function.

```php
header('Location: ' . $url); // Make the browser load either the members' or the admin page
exit(); // Quit the script
```

The long-hand equivalent of the previous ternary statement is as follows:

```php
if ($_SESSION['user_level'] === 1) {
        header('location: admin-page.php');
        exit();
}else{
        header('location: members-page.php');
        exit();
}
```

Using Try/Catch

Here's how to use a try/catch block:

```php
<body>
<div id="container">
<header>
        Includes go here for header, nav, aside etc
        <div id="content"><!-- Start of the login page content. -->
        <?php
```

```
// This section processes submissions from the login form
// Check if the form has been submitted:
if ($_SERVER['REQUEST_METHOD'] == 'POST') {
//connect to database
try {
        require ('mysqli_connect.php');
        // Validate the email address
        if (!empty($_POST['email'])) {
                $e = mysqli_real_escape_string($dbcon, $_POST['email']);
        } else {
        $e = FALSE;
                echo '<p class="error">You forgot to enter your email address.
                </p>';
        }
        // Validate the password
        if (!empty($_POST['psword'])) {
                $p = mysqli_real_escape_string($dbcon, $_POST['psword']);
        } else {
            $p = FALSE;
                echo '<p class="error">You forgot to enter your password.</p>';
        }
        if ($e && $p){//if no problems
                // Retrieve the user_id, psword, first_name and user_level for that
                // email/password combination
        $q = "SELECT user_id, psword, fname, user_level FROM users WHERE email='$e'";
                $result = mysqli_query ($dbcon, $q);
        if($result == false) {
                throw new Exception(mysqli_error($dbcon)."\n$q");
        }
        // Run the query and assign it to the variable $result
        $result = mysqli_query ($dbcon, $q);
        // Count the number of rows that match the email/password combination
        //echo mysqli_num_rows($result);
        if (mysqli_num_rows($result) == 1) {
                //if one database row (record) matches the input:-
                // Start the session, fetch the record and insert the
                // values in an array
                $row = mysqli_fetch_array($result, MYSQLI_NUM);
                if (password_verify($p, $row[1])) {
                        session_start();
                        // Ensure that the user level is an integer.
                        $_SESSION['user_level'] = (int) $row[3];
                        // Use a ternary operation to set the URL
                        $url = ($_SESSION['user_level'] === 1) ? 'admin-page.php' :
                         'members-page.php';
                        header('Location: ' . $url);
                        // Make the browser load either the members or the admin page
                } else { // No password match was made.
                echo '<p class="error">Password/e-mail entered does not match our
                records.';
                        echo '<br>Perhaps you need to register, just click the Register ;
```

```
                        echo button on the header menu</p>';
                }
        } else { // No e-mail match was made.
                echo '<p class="error">Password/e-mail entered does not match our
                records.';
                echo '<br>Perhaps you need to register, just click the Register ';
                echo 'button on the header menu</p>';
        }
    } else { // If there was a problem.
            echo '<p class="error">Please try again.</p>';
    }
mysqli_free_result($result);
mysqli_close($dbcon);
}
catch(Exception $e)
{
print  "An Exception occurred. Message: " . $e->getMessage();
}
catch(Error $e)
{
print  "An Error occurred. Message: " . $e->getMessage();
}
} // no 'else' to allow user to enter values
?>
<!-- Display the form fields-->
<div>
        <?php require ('login_page.inc.php');  ?>
</div><br>
<footer>
        <?php include ('footer.php'); ?>
</footer>
</div>
</div>
</body>
</html>
```

The flow of a program will jump to the catch block whenever a problem occurs within a try block. In the previous example, the flow would jump to the catch block if the mysqli_connect file was missing or corrupt. It will also jump to the block if the SQL statements do not execute properly. These are examples of exceptions caused by the program. Thus, it will jump to the exception block. If errors occur, such as a system error, the code will jump to the error block. However, it will not jump to the block if the user inputs invalid information. This possibility is handed by the code within the program itself.

Validation and Sanitization Filters

The following script validates an e-mail address using the filter_var() function:

```
//If the email address is present trim it
    if (isset($_POST['email'])) {
            $etrim = trim($_POST['email']);
            //Validate the trimmed address
```

```
                $e = (filter_var($etrim, FILTER_VALIDATE_EMAIL));

        }else{
                $errors[] = 'Your email address is invalid or you forgot to enter your email
address.';
}
```

Malicious user input can be sanitized by means of the filter_var function. If a user inputs script into a registration form variable named $last_name, any HTML or JavaScript tags can be removed as follows:

```
$last_name ='<script>alert("some_alert ");</script>';
echo filter_var($last_name, FILTER_SANITIZE_STRING);
```

The <script></script> tags will be removed, leaving a harmless string.
Resources listing the filter_var functions are given later in this appendix.

Variables

Variables store values and can be accessed only on the page on which they are created. If you click a link to switch to another page, the next page knows nothing about that variable. However, there are ways of passing the variable's value to another page. Variables begin with a dollar sign, $. Following the dollar sign, the variable's name can be text (uppercase or lowercase), hyphens, or underscores. The name can include numbers but must not start with a number.

Here's an example: $first_name.

Variables are case sensitive; $Firstname is not the same as $firstname.

Variables: Predefined

You have used PHP predefined variables in most of the chapters . They allowed us to transfer data from a form to a handler or from one HTML page to another. Predefined variables always begin with a dollar sign and an underscore, as shown in the following four examples:

```
$_SERVER, $_POST['fname'] $_GET["fname"], $_SESSION['fname'],
```

In our tutorials, the predefined variable $_POST['fname'] was assigned to a shorter variable like this:

```
$fname = $_POST['fname'];
```

Variables: String

String variables are groups of characters enclosed in single or double quotes. Here's an example:

```
$my_pet = 'cat';    $animal = "dog";    $birthday = 'March 10th, 1952';
```

Bootstrap Template

Each HTML page in this textbook is formatted with Bootstrap. To keep the discussion of Bootstrap as simple as possible, the same basic template was used each time. This template is based on the use of 12 small columns.

```
<div class="container col-sm-12">
```

The content in the columns is defined by the use of rows.

```
<div class="row mx-auto">
```

Within each row, the columns can be divided as needed to lay out the display of information. In many examples, the rows were divided to provide the layout for labels and form input.

```
    <label for="user_name" class="col-sm-4 col-form-label">User Name*:</label>
      <div class="col-sm-8">
<input type="text" class="form-control" id="user_name" name="user_name">
  </div>
</div>
```

In the previous example, the row is divided into a four-column section to hold the label and an eight-column section to hold the text box.

H	H	H	H	H	H	H	H	H	H	H	H
L	L	L	L	I	I	I	I	I	I		
L	L	L	L	I	I	I	I	I	I		
F	F	F	F	F	F	F	F	F	F	F	

The previous table demonstrates the often-used layout for HTML pages in this textbook. The header (H) is defined with 12 columns that cover the width of the page. When a form is used, a label (L) is defined that covers four columns. The textbox (or other form input object) (I) is defined to cover six columns. The footer (F) is defined as the same width as the header, 12 columns.

If a third column is needed (the information column to the right), then the format is defined as follows:

H	H	H	H	H	H	H	H	H	H	H	H
L	L	L	L	I	I	I	I	I	I	X	X
L	L	L	L	I	I	I	I	I	I	X	X
F	F	F	F	F	F	F	F	F	F	F	F

The template includes the same size header (H) and footer (F). However, now the rows for the form have been expanded to the maximum of 12 columns. The label (L) is still four columns, and the input object (I) is still six columns. However, we now have added two columns for the information column (X).

Of course, there are exceptions and minor variations in the book; however, we have attempted to stay with one of these formats to keep things easier. One exception is the display of tables. When a table is displayed, depending on the amount of data it contains, it might be displayed with six, eight, or twelve columns.

For more information on Bootstrap, visit www.getbootstrap.com.

MySQL and phpMyAdmin Quick Reference

Here is how you connect to a database:

```
A typical connection file
// Create a connection to the database and to MySQL
// Set the encoding to utf-8
```

```
// Set the database access details as constants
define ('DB_USER', 'turing');
define ('DB_PASSWORD', 'COmput3rm3n');
define ('DB_HOST', 'localhost');
define ('DB_NAME', 'shopdb');
// Make the connection:
$dbcon = new mysqli(DB_HOST, DB_USER, DB_PASSWORD, DB_NAME);
// Set the encoding...optional but recommended
mysqli_set_charset($dbcon, 'utf8');
```

Always test the connection file before adding or populating tables. Create a test file named *test.php* as follows:

```
<!DOCTYPE html>
<html>
<head>
<title>test</title>
</head>
<body>
// Create a connection to the database and to MySQL
// Set the encoding to utf-8
// Set the database access details as constants
define ('DB_USER', 'turing');
define ('DB_PASSWORD', 'COmput3rm3n');
define ('DB_HOST', 'localhost');
define ('DB_NAME', 'shopdb');
// Make the connection:
$dbcon = new mysqli(DB_HOST, DB_USER, DB_PASSWORD, DB_NAME);
// Set the encoding...optional but recommended
mysqli_set_charset($dbcon, 'utf8');
</body>
</html>
```

date_time

When using phpMyAdmin to populate a table from scratch, the post_date or reg_date entry might automatically be the year zero BC with a time of 00.00. To solve this problem, edit the date/time column for each entry and click the icon to the right of the post_date or reg_date field. A pop-up date picker will enable you to add a date/time by moving the slide buttons in Figure B-1.

If you want to use the pop-up calendar while you are populating, enter everything else, but leave the date/time until last.

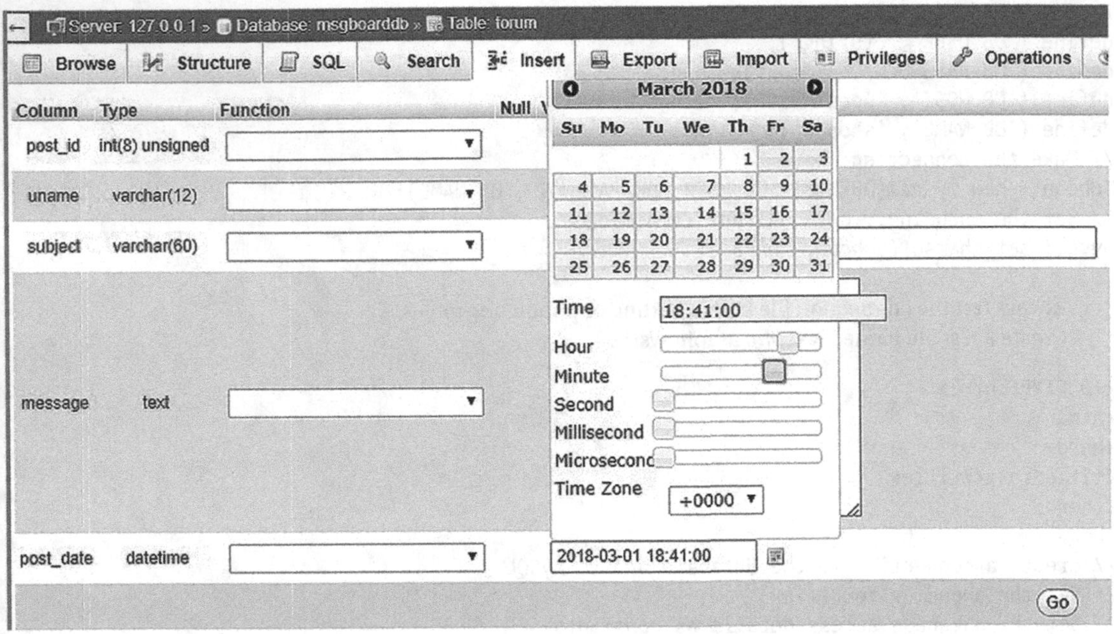

Figure B-1. *Database data input screen popup calendar*

INSERT

When using the INSERT query to insert data into a table, the query has two parts: the column names and the VALUES. This is shown in the following example:

```
$q = "INSERT INTO users (user_id, title, fname, lname, email, psword, registration_date) ↵
VALUES (' ', '$title', '$fn', '$ln', '$e', '$p', NOW())";
```

The number and order of the column names must exactly match the number and order of the values.

SELECT

The elements of a SELECT query must be in the following order:

```
SELECT (column or expression) AS (set an alias) FROM (table) WHERE (condition) ORDER BY (column)
```

AS and ORDER BY are optional and may be omitted. ORDER BY can be followed by the keyword ASC or DESC to specify how the selected items are to be ordered. The number of records selected can be specified by putting LIMIT and an integer at the end of the query.

UPDATE

Let's say Rose Bush has a user_id value of 15 and wants to alter her e-mail address. You can use the UPDATE query to change it as follows:

```
$q = "UPDATE users SET email ='rbush@mynewisp.co.uk' WHERE user_id = 15 LIMIT 1 ";
```

Storage Engines and phpMyAdmin

To view a list of quotations by Mark Twain, you would use a full-text search and enter the words *Mark Twain*. Early versions of MySQL insisted on using the MyISAM storage engine. Since MySQL version 5.6.4, the InnoDB storage engine allows full-text searches.

Changing the Storage Engine on an Existing Populated Table

The current storage engine used by mySQL/MariaDB is InnoDB. If you have older code and want to change an existing table's storage engine from MyISAM to InnoDB, this is quite easily accomplished in phpMyAdmin as long as you have not changed collations or decreased a column size. As a precaution, before changing the engine, always back up your table using the phpMyAdmin Export facility. After changing the engine, check that all is well with the website and then back up the table again. The steps are as follows:

1. In phpMyAdmin, click the name of your database in the left panel.

2. In the left panel, click the table you want to change.

3. Click the Operations tab.

4. Use the storage engine's pull-down menu to select the engine.

5. Click Go.

What Next?

We hope this book has inspired you to explore more advanced PHP techniques for developing databases. For increased reliability and integrity, you will need to learn about transactions.

Transactions ensure that items such as orders are truly completed before inserting them into the database table. Transactions allow the user to roll back to amend the order details or even cancel the order.

You might want to examine the merits of procedural PHP versus object-oriented PHP (OOP); both will produce the same outcome, but OOP can be advantageous for maintaining very large websites. This book used procedural PHP.

JavaScript, Ajax, and jQuery can add enhancements to a database-driven website; help on these topics is provided in the following resources. Use the resources to keep abreast of improvements and modifications in PHP and MYSQL. Most importantly, watch for any new developments for improving security. Because arrays and functions are central to PHP database design, try to learn more about them.

Now that you are familiar with the terminology used for MySQL/MariaDB databases and PHP, you will be able to benefit from the available books and online resources. The following resources will help you to move on from the basic techniques described in this book.

Resources

The following are resources that you may find helpful.

Books on PHP and MySQL for Databases

Before buying a book on PHP and MySQL/MariaDB, be sure to read the introduction on the book's web page (or online store). If possible, borrow a copy before committing to a purchase. You may find that the book is far too advanced, that it covers what you have already learned, or that it relies on frameworks that hide or complicate the basic code you want to learn. Also check for the latest edition of the book.

Here are some suggested reference books to help you advance your PHP skills:

PHP and MYSQL Web Development (fifth edition)
Authors: Luke Welling & Laura Thompson
ISBN-13: 978-1491978917
ISBN-10: 1491978910

PHP and MySQL for Dynamic Websites: Visual QuickPro Guide (5th Edition)
Authors: Larry Ullman (Author)
ISBN-13: 978-0134301846
ISBN-10: 0134301846

Learning PHP, MySQL & JavaScript: With jQuery
Author: Robin Nixon
ISBN-13: 978-1491978917
ISBN-10: 1491978910

Beginning PHP and MySQL (fifth edition)
Authors: Jason Gilmore and Frank M Kromann
ISBN-10: 1430260432
ISBN-13: 978-1430260431

Responsive Web Design with HTML5 and CSS3 (second edition)
Author: Ben Fain
ISBN-13: 978-1784398934
ISBN-10: 1784398934

PHP and MySQL Internet Resources

Here are some Internet resources:

- *www.htmlite.com/*: Great for practical PHP scripts and MySQL

- *http://larryullman.com/forums*: Larry Ullman's superb forum

- *www.phpbuilder.com*: Many PHP tutorials and a forum

- *www.w3schools.com/php/*: A good selection of PHP scripts

- *www.php.net*: The original PHP website

- *http://net.tutsplus.com/tutorials/php/getting-clean-with-php/*: Good examples of the use of filter_var for validating and sanitizing user input

E-commerce Resources

The previous book resources contain some information on e-commerce websites. The CD provided with *PHP and MYSQL Web Development* by Luke Welling and Laura Thompson has a good example of a custom shopping cart.

For resources dealing specifically with e-commerce, try *Effortless E-Commerce with PHP and MySQL* by Larry Ullman (New Riders, ISBN-13: 978-0-321-65622-3).

Online Tutorials

One online tutorial gives instructions using 20 videos averaging 15 minutes each. View this here:

`www.youtube.com/playlist?list=PL442E340A42191003`

Of course, you won't be able to create an e-commerce website by viewing videos; you also need a great deal of documentation so that you can study the code and adapt it. However, the videos give an excellent outline of the enormous amount of work that it requires to create a fully operational e-commerce website.

Resources for Creating a Forum

These are resources for creating a forum.

PayPal Forums

- For the United States: `https://www.paypal-community.com/t5/US-PayPal-Community/ct-p/US`

Third-Party Shopping Carts

Third-party shopping carts are available from the following resources:

- *Stripe* is a payment gateway for PHP-based websites. Charges are low for successful transactions, and it operates by means of a user's credit/debit card. The website development team will require a good knowledge of JavaScript because the gateway depends on JavaScript and jQuery. For more information, visit `https://stripe.com`. For the UK version, visit `https://stripe.com/gb`.

- *Authorize.net* is a U.S. and Canadian payment gateway that accepts credit/debit cards; it requires a setup fee of $99 and $20 monthly payments. You can find details at `www.authorize.net`.

Summary

This appendix provided an alphabetical list of the main PHP code required for creating interactive websites and databases. This was followed by a brief reference for MySQL/MariaDB and phpMyAdmin. The question "What next?" was posed, and some suggestions were offered. To help you to progress beyond the basic instruction given in this book, a list of resources was provided.

Index